Communication Law
in America

Communication Law in America

Second Edition

PAUL SIEGEL

With illustrations by
Katie Osowiecki

ROWMAN & LITTLEFIELD PUBLISHERS, INC.
Lanham • Boulder • New York • Toronto • Plymouth, UK

ROWMAN & LITTLEFIELD PUBLISHERS, INC.

Published in the United States of America
by Rowman & Littlefield Publishers, Inc.
A wholly owned subsidiary of The Rowman & Littlefield Publishing Group, Inc.
4501 Forbes Boulevard, Suite 200, Lanham, Maryland 20706
www.rowmanlittlefield.com

Estover Road, Plymouth PL6 7PY, United Kingdom

British Library Cataloguing in Publication Information Available

Library of Congress Cataloging-in-Publication Data

Siegel, Paul, 1954–
   Communication law in America / Paul Siegel.—2nd ed.
     p. cm.
   Includes bibliographical references and index.
   ISBN-13: 978-0-7425-5387-3 (pbk. : alk. paper)
   ISBN-10: 0-7425-5387-6 (pbk. : alk. paper)
   1. Mass media—Law and legislation—United States.   2. Press law—United States.
3. Freedom of speech—United States. I. Title.
KF2750.S53   2008
343.7309′9—dc22

                                             2007004165

Printed in the United States of America

♾ ™ The paper used in this publication meets the minimum requirements of American National
Standard for Information Sciences—Permanence of Paper for Printed Library Materials, ANSI/
NISO Z39.48-1992.

Brief Contents

Detailed Contents

For Franklyn S. Haiman

Professor Emeritus of Communication Studies
at Northwestern University

Frank, your enthusiasm for your subject matter was and is infectious. You have taught more than one generation that law is too important to be left only to lawyers. I am just one of thousands who owe you an immeasurable amount of gratitude.

Preface

Perhaps as you looked at this book's title page three words struck you as a bit out of place—"with illustrations by." Indeed, I suspect this is the first communication law book—the first law book?—ever to boast an in-house cartoonist. It seemed so natural a decision. The first edition of the text used the work of many fine editorial and popular "funny pages" cartoonists. While their work greatly enhanced the overall feel of that first edition, there was always the frustration for me of being a passive consumer, hoping that somewhere a cartoonist would have thought to take on as subject matter something related to communication law that I felt screamed out for satire. So, like the actor who really wants to direct, I thought it wise to find a single cartoonist to commission to create original work just for this book. I am thus grateful not only to our cartoonist, Katie Osowiecki, but also the two faculty members of the Hartford Art School—Bill Thomson and Mark Snyder—who sicced me on her.

Working with Katie was fascinating, not unlike the relationship between director and actor, but we also came to realize that the characters in cartoons are themselves actors who need to have motivation and an attitude toward their subject matter.

We also discovered that cartoon art needs to be updated and edited to fit new facts, just as does the overall narrative of a textbook. For example, we had to discard one of Katie's best cartoons—aimed at making fun of how the Bush administration apparently leaked to the press the fact that Valerie Plame, wife to Joseph Wilson (who famously undermined the main rationale for toppling Saddam Hussein by challenging the administration's assertion that Hussein tried to purchase materials for making nuclear weapons from the government of Niger), was a CIA operative. At first it appeared that former vice presidential chief of staff I. Lewis "Scooter" Libby was the first to leak Plame's identity to reporter-columnist Robert Novak. Since many commentators were suggesting that Libby's participation in the leak almost necessarily would implicate Vice President Cheney, and thus the Bush administration as a whole, I thought it defensible to run this cartoon in the section of chapter 7 where the Plame case is discussed:

But later developments suggested that the real leaker (at least the first leaker) was instead former deputy secretary of state Richard Armitage, who, unlike Libby, was (at

least initially) not presumed to have given the information to Novak out of any desire to retaliate against Joseph Wilson. Quite a soap opera, don't you think? In any event, at that juncture (which coincided with the deadline for adding new illustrations to the chapters themselves), we could no longer justify linking the leak to the Bush administration.

More recent evidence, which has emerged from Libby's trial (he was convicted in 2007 on charges of perjury and obstruction of justice related to the leak), has cast doubt on Armitage's claims that his own leaking was an innocent by-product of informal conversations he had with various reporters, that revealing Plame's identity was not a conscious goal. Evidence also now suggests that Vice President Cheney was directly involved in the decision to leak Plame's identity to the press. This evidence emerged a bit too late for us to change the formatting of chapter 7, but not too late to insert the cartoon under question in this preface. In future editions I may ask Katie to reimagine the above cartoon, perhaps depicting Libby or Cheney instead of Bush. Of course, by the time we are ready to produce the next edition, it may also be clearer than it is now whether the president himself had a direct role in the leak.

There are many other visual artifacts in this edition, beyond the cartoons. Many of these are artifacts from court cases themselves, obtained by me through numerous strokes of luck on eBay. Vintage book and magazine dealers Ethan DiStefano, Robert Simon, and Linda Tresham were especially helpful. Some artifacts were obtained only through the help of particular directly involved individuals, including Jeffrey Fister and Eileen Dugan of *West End Word*; attorney "RMJ" from Missouri; *Reader's Digest's* and *Conservative Digest's* Larry Abraham and Scott Stanley; Tracey McIntire from People for the Ethical Treatment of Animals; Roger Vann of the ACLU of Connecticut; Helen Harris of RP International; Daniel Shelton of Shelton Brothers Importers; Diana Palmentiero of Court TV; Michelle Sievers of ESPN; Glenn Gilbert of the *Lake County News Herald*; James McMullan; Hugo Zacchini (the "Human Cannonball"); James Earl Reid; Jeff Koons; Matthew Hunsberger; Tom Forsythe; Barbara Seelaus of Xerox; Johnnie Luevanos of Universal Studios; and humorists Tom Lehrer and George Carlin.

Concerning those visual artifacts from court cases, it should be admitted that some may cause discomfort. After all, the plaintiffs were upset enough by what they saw to hire a lawyer and sue. There are nude images in this book, including pictures of a very young Brooke Shields and an African-American athlete who clearly is supposed to be Muhammad Ali. There are headlines accusing individuals of some fairly outlandish behaviors. I offer my sincere apologies to readers who may be offended by any of the images reproduced here. It was and is my heartfelt belief that the adage about a picture being worth a thousand words rang true in each instance where I chose to reproduce rather than merely describe an artifact.

Additional individuals helped tremendously with research for this book, sometimes pointing me in the right direction, sometimes, I admit, doing my homework for me. Among these were Camille Broadway, Bill Buell, Jim Hemphill, Thomas E. Hemstock, Jr., Ella Holst, Bruce Lockard, Roger Mellen, Pat Petit, Lawrence Rosenfeld, Edward Samuels, Mike Sandusky, Stuart Sigman, Joshua Singer, Art Spitzer, Alex Tang, Lee Templeman, John Vivian, Kaitlin Walsh, and Lorelle Wilson.

Elissa Papirno, former long-time employee of the *Hartford Courant* (including a stint as its "Reader Representative") and former president of the Organization of News Ombudsmen, was kind enough to offer her global and sometimes line-by-line reactions to the page proofs.

Special thanks are due to Kris and Paul Oehlke, who spent the better part of a day at the Library of Congress for me, when they really should have been seeing the sites; Jeff Lofton, for doing his best under difficult conditions—namely, working with my highly nonphotogenic mug—to produce the "About the Author" photo; and Dan McNamara, who sat with me for hours to capture the movie stills reproduced in several parts of the book.

Thanks also to Ron Goldfarb, my lawyer/agent for the book's first edition, and Stephen Gillen, who performed the same roles for this edition. Mr. Gillen has also used the book in the classroom.

Shelley Levy, P.J. Moretti, and Teodora Rotaru helped calm my panic in the last few weeks prior to publication by working tirelessly in assisting with the preparation of the book's indexes.

Much gratitude is due also to my Rowman & Littlefield editors. Brenda Hadenfeldt and Bess Vanrenen showed support for the project from its earliest stages. The copy-editing process was made so much easier and yet more humbling by the talented contributions of Jehanne Schweitzer and especially Karen Schoen, who caught a handful of truly embarrassing errors on my part and who reminded me by example that standard legal citation formats are, to say the least, not my strong suit.

The first edition of *Communication Law in America* was dedicated to my father, Ernest Siegel, who passed away while the manuscript was in its nascent stages. My mother, Rita Siegel, is now also no longer with us, making me a member of the "Orphan's Club." In the normal course of events, this book would be dedicated to her. But both Mom and Dad were teachers and professors, and they would thus both understand and support my decision to dedicate this edition to my doctoral adviser, whom they met and for whom they had enormous respect.

■ ■ ■

For updates to this text, as well as full-color versions of many of
the illustrations from the text, see the author-maintained website,
at www.paulsiegelcommlaw.com.

Chapter 1

INTRODUCING THE AMERICAN LEGAL SYSTEM

Americans are fascinated with the law. Cop shows and lawyer shows have been popular prime-time television offerings for decades, with CBS's *CSI* and NBC's *Law and Order* franchises among the most popular recent examples of the genres. Real court cases, sometimes because they involve celebrities, and sometimes because the facts are bizarre or especially disturbing, receive intense media attention. And we love it. In the week following Michael Jackson's 2005 acquittal on child molestation charges, Fox News's rating rose 55 percent, MSNBC rose 80 percent, and CNN's popularity doubled.[1] For those who want to watch nonstop courtroom drama and discussions of the legal system, there is Court TV.

Why Are You Here?

That you are reading this book, of course, does not mean you are a cop show addict. More likely, you are enrolled in a college course such as Mass Media Law, Journalism Law, or Freedom of the Press. The course might even be required in your major and you may wonder why—especially if you envision your future in the fields of journalism, advertising, or public relations, rather than law.

One reason you should have a strong background in communication law is that legal questions arise every day in the workplace, and relatively few media organizations have in-house legal counsel to answer questions on a moment's notice. The course you are taking now will offer you the facts you need and the tools to research

---

1. "Cable News Channels See Ratings Soar After Jackson Verdict," *IMDB Online*, June 15, 2005, http://www.imdb.com/news/sb/2005-06-15 (accessed June 16, 2006).

new facts so that you can avoid or minimize legal liability. Media professionals should also be familiar with communication law because the history of journalism in the United States is inextricably intertwined with its legal history. Please recall this admonition if you find yourself rebelling at having to learn lots of court cases and judicial doctrines that seem at first blush to have very little to do with your own day-to-day functioning. Some of the case law discussed here involves radical political street-corner speakers, not modern-day journalists; the ways in which American courts have treated their legal claims have strong implications for how the media's rights are protected today.

Another reason for students in any major to learn about communication law is to develop a better understanding of their own society. We can learn a great deal about ourselves by seeing how others see us. Citizens of many other countries, including most of the more enlightened Western democracies around the world, consider the United States to be almost fetishistically attached to freedom of the press. Why is it, they wonder, that freedom of the press and freedom of speech almost inevitably win out in U.S. courts when they compete against other important interests? In the United States, for example, when a newsworthy trial is taking place, the general rule is to allow the media to report as much as possible to the public as quickly as possible. In Canada, it is taken for granted that the public will not be ill-served if it has to wait until the end of the trial to read all the gory details. So, which is more important, freedom of the press, or the right to a fair trial? There is no easy answer, but we will come to understand ourselves better as Americans if we become familiar with our own society's history of dealing with such conflicts.

Yet one more reason for becoming familiar with the precepts of communication law is that the U.S. political system works best if citizens participate actively in decision making. This does not necessarily constitute a call for you to run for office, but it does suggest that your vote and your ability to persuade others to your viewpoint through interpersonal communication are both more meaningful if you take the time to educate yourself about the important issues of the day. In other words, our representative democracy works to the extent that we all take responsibility for using our freedom of speech (and the corollary freedoms to listen and to learn) forcefully and frequently. In doing so, it surely helps to know the full gamut of our legal rights, as well as the limitations on those rights.

Sources of Communication Law

If you were to try to explain the U.S. system of law to a foreign friend, you would probably begin by pointing out that our federal government has three branches with complementary functions and that state and local governments also have a role to play. Communication law is really no different from any other kind of law in this regard. There are several different sources of law. The main ones are **constitutions**, statutes, **executive orders**, decisions by **administrative agencies**, and the **common law**. Let us take a look at each source.

Constitutions as Sources of Communication Law

One source of communication law is constitutions. Notice the use of the plural here. Every state has its own constitution. So although we start our discussion here with a summary of important features of the *federal* Constitution, we say more about state constitutions later.

The First Amendment.   To be sure, the section of the U.S. Constitution of most relevance to the act of communication is the First Amendment, which is part of the Bill of Rights. Here is the wording of that provision, which was adopted on December 15, 1791:

The First Amendment

Congress shall make no law respecting an establishment of religion, or prohibiting the free exercise thereof; or abridging the freedom of speech, or of the press; or the right of the people peaceably to assemble, and to petition the Government for a redress of grievances.

The first thing apparent from the text is that the amendment is not talking to *us*, but rather to our elected representatives. It does not tell us what we have or do not have a right to do. It is in the form of a list of admonitions to Congress, warning that *its* right to pass certain kinds of laws is restricted.

Although the First Amendment's reference to Congress has always been taken to refer to the entire federal government, individual states and localities were free to regulate the speech of their own citizens without running afoul of the First Amendment, at least until a U.S. Supreme Court ruling handed down more than 130 years after ratification of the Bill of Rights.[2] That decision is discussed in chapter 2.

The First Amendment's prohibitions apply even today only to *governmental* entities. When private individuals or companies prohibit us from engaging in some kinds of speech—perhaps our parents demand that we not talk about religious differences with them, or our employer (unless our employer *is* the government) asks that we not talk about politics with our coworkers—they are not in violation of the First Amendment.

Strange though it may seem, it is not always easy to discern whether an organization is part of the government or is purely private. Is your campus newspaper a pri-

---

2. *Gitlow v. New York*, 268 U.S. 652 (1925).

vate entity, like the *New York Times*? Or, to the extent that it receives government funding in the form of earmarked monies from mandatory student fees, is it an agent of the state? The answer to this question may determine if an outside group has a right to advertise in the paper.[3]

A few years ago, the U.S. Supreme Court was called upon to determine whether Amtrak had violated an artist's First Amendment rights when it refused him permission to rent a billboard in New York's Pennsylvania Station for the purpose of displaying one of his works.[4] The main issue the Court had to address was whether Amtrak qualified as a governmental agent, whether it was definitionally capable of violating anyone's First Amendment rights. The Court determined that even though the congressional act creating Amtrak explicitly set it up as a private corporation, the corporation's purpose was to provide a governmental function, and the directors would be ultimately accountable to the government. As such, Amtrak's behavior could possibly be a First Amendment violation.

More recently, the Supreme Court held that a nonprofit association regulating interscholastic sports in both public and private schools must be considered a governmental entity for the purposes of First Amendment challenges to its authority. The Court emphasized that the vast majority of the association's members were public schools and that the association's employees, although not technically government workers, nonetheless participated in the state's retirement system.[5]

Think again about the wording of the First Amendment. It contains five specific admonitions, five clauses. The first two—the **Establishment Clause** and the **Free Exercise Clause**—are often referred to together as the "religion clauses." The Establishment Clause is sometimes described as providing freedom *from* religious indoctrination and is frequently invoked in educational settings. This clause led the Supreme Court to forbid public school administrators from leading students in prayer,[6] or allowing organized prayer at graduation ceremonies[7] or even football games.[8] Similarly, laws requiring public schools to have students recognize a "moment of silence" at the beginning of the school day have generally been struck down,[9] but in 2001 the Supreme Court refused to interfere with a Virginia moment-of-silence law, which Chief Justice Rehnquist suggested had a valid nonreligious function—"to provide a moment for quiet reflection in the wake of high-profile instances of violence in our public schools."[10]

The Establishment Clause was the basis for not including units in "scientific crea-

---

3. *Mississippi Gay Alliance v. Goudelock*, 536 F. 2d 1073 (5th Cir. 1976).

4. *Lebron v. National Railroad Passenger Corporation*, 513 U.S. 374 (1995).

5. *Brentwood Academy v. Tennessee Secondary School Athletic Association*, 531 U.S. 288 (2001).

6. *School District v. Schempp*, 374 U.S. 203 (1963); *Engel v. Vitale*, 370 U.S. 421 (1962).

7. *Lee v. Weisman*, 505 U.S. 577 (1992).

8. *Santa Fe Independent School District v. Doe*, 530 U.S. 290 (2000).

9. *Wallace v. Jaffree*, 472 U.S. 38 (1985).

10. *Brown v. Gilmore*, 533 U.S. 1301, 1303 (2001).

tionism"[11] or "intelligent design"[12] in public school science classrooms. Although schools cannot force students to utter the Pledge of Allegiance,[13] the fact that the pledge includes the words "under God" is not itself a violation of the Establishment Clause.[14]

The Free Exercise Clause gives us the freedom *to* practice our religions to the extent that such practice does not interfere with a compelling governmental interest. For example, the Supreme Court exempted an Amish plaintiff from an otherwise generally applicable statute requiring school attendance until age seventeen[15] and a Seventh-Day Adventist from having to work on her Sabbath (Saturday) in order to retain her unemployment benefits.[16] More recent Supreme Court decisions have been stingier in their interpretation of the Free Exercise Clause, however; notably, in 1990 the Court accepted the firing of a plaintiff who had used peyote in a Native American religious ceremony.[17] That may not seem like a big deal, especially if you oppose illegal drug use, but Congress was concerned enough about the breadth of this decision that it attempted to overturn it by passing the Religious Freedom Restoration Act, which required that laws at any level of government that infringe on religious practice be supported by a very important, "compelling" interest. Continuing the conflict between branches of government, the Supreme Court partially struck down the act in a 1997 decision.[18]

One might think that the religion clauses have no relevance to the professional communicator, but such a conclusion would be both hasty and wrong. Although journalism law cases rarely invoke these parts of the First Amendment, one of the most important Supreme Court cases of the 1990s, which concerned the rights of newspaper editors, involved both of the religion clauses.[19] By a 5-4 vote, the Court ruled that the University of Virginia could not refuse to help fund a Christian students' group's cost of publishing its newspaper, called *Wide Awake*. There was tremendous difference of opinion among the justices concerning not only which part of the First Amendment should prevail but also whether the newspaper was religious enough to even trigger the Establishment Clause. So complex are the Court's recent religion-clause cases that the Virginia decision turned at least in part on the fact that

---

11. *Edwards v. Aguillard*, 482 U.S. 578 (1987).

12. *Kitzmiller v. Dover Area School District*, 400 F. Supp. 2d 707 (M.D. Pa. 2005).

13. *West Virginia State Board of Education v. Barnette*, 319 U.S. 624 (1943).

14. *Newdow v. United States Congress*, 328 F. 3d 466 (9th Cir. 2002). The Supreme Court heard the case, but failed to reach the constitutional issue. *Elk Grove Unified School District v. Newdow*, 542 U.S. 1 (2004).

15. *Wisconsin v. Yoder*, 406 U.S. 205 (1972).

16. *Sherbert v. Verner*, 374 U.S. 398 (1963).

17. *Employment Division, Department of Human Resources of Oregon v. Smith*, 494 U.S. 872 (1990).

18. *City of Boerne v. Flores*, 521 U.S. 507 (1997).

19. *Rosenberger v. University of Virginia*, 515 U.S. 819 (1995).

the monies went directly to the printer with whom the religious group had contracted, rather than directly to the group itself.

Let us skip ahead for a moment to the First Amendment's last clause, the one that gives us the right to "peacefully assemble" and to "petition the government for redress of grievances." Despite the comma between them, these two rights are usually thought of as part of the same whole. Traditionally the people's right to assemble has been seen as limited to gatherings with political purpose—that is, to express grievances, not to have a volleyball game. First Amendment decisions also often include reference to the "freedom of association," a related right not explicitly listed in the Constitution but which the Supreme Court has borrowed from labor law (a right to form unions) and interpreted over time as a First Amendment right applicable to both political[20] and nonpolitical[21] associations. Association is related to speech, the Court has told us, in that we often need to work together with others to most effectively make arguments in the public forum.[22] Freedom of association seems logically related to freedom of assembly as well. After all, an association can be thought of as "an assembly dispersed over time and space."[23]

As with the religion clauses, we might be tempted to conclude—again, wrongly—that the **Petition Clause** is of little relevance for journalists. But consider that in the early 1980s, Robert McDonald wrote a letter to President Reagan and to numerous other government officials asking that the pending appointment of David Smith as a U.S. attorney for North Carolina be rescinded. The letter accused Smith of violating the civil rights of many individuals while he was a state court judge, of "fraud," and of numerous "violations of professional ethics." When Smith learned of the letter, he sued McDonald for **defamation**, and Smith's novel defense—unsuccessful in this case—was that the Petition Clause should be read so as to give him absolute immunity from the lawsuit. After all, what purer example could we find of exercising one's Petition Clause rights than writing to one's president, imploring him to take a particular action?[24] More recently, a case from Colorado that reached the Supreme Court, although not actually argued on Petition Clause grounds, centered on an amendment to the state constitution that would surely have had the effect of limiting the ability of one group of Coloradans to petition their elected representatives for redress of grievances.[25] The Court struck down the amendment, which would have removed from the books any local civil rights statutes aimed at protecting the interests of lesbians and gay men, and would have prevented any new such laws from ever being passed. Only by passing another state constitutional amendment could gays achieve

---

20. *Clingman v. Beaver,* 544 U.S. 581 (2005); *McConnell v. FEC,* 540 U.S. 93 (2003).

21. *Boy Scouts of America v. Dale,* 530 U.S. 640 (2000).

22. *NAACP v. Alabama,* 357 U.S. 449 (1958).

23. C. Edwin Baker, "Scope of the First Amendment Freedom of Speech," 25 *UCLA Law Review* 964, 1032 (1978).

24. *McDonald v. Smith,* 472 U.S. 479 (1985).

25. *Romer v. Evans,* 517 U.S. 620 (1996).

protection against employment and housing discrimination. City council members and state representatives would be able to listen to gays' "petitions" but would not be able to act on them.

Petition Clause claims may become more frequent in future years because of a phenomenon called the **SLAPP suit**. The acronym stands for "strategic lawsuit against public participation," a kind of **libel** suit aimed at preventing citizen activists from speaking out against businesses and even against government officials. Many social critics argue that these suits are inconsistent with the spirit of the Petition Clause, in that they often result from citizens' comments at public hearings, the kind of forums that are specifically designed to have elected officials listen to grievances. In 2005, for example, the Delaware Supreme Court would not allow a city councilman to compel the unmasking of a critic who had posted anonymously to a weblog that the plaintiff had "character flaws" and suffered from paranoia and "mental deterioration."[26]

We will not spend much time here on the **Free Speech Clause** and the **Free Press Clause**, because they are the focus of almost this entire book. When courts are asked to determine whether a specific governmental action violates the First Amendment rights of media professionals, it is virtually always these two clauses that are at issue. One point does deserve special attention—that we are talking about two clauses rather than one. Does freedom of speech not include both oral and written communication? How can we explain this apparent redundancy in the Bill of Rights? Whatever may have been on the minds of our Founding Fathers, one school of thought today suggests that freedom of the *press* refers to the professional journalist.

Certainly members of the working press, with credentials, are able to go places and do things that other people cannot. Police will often permit only emergency personnel and reporters near the scenes of accidents. There is a separate section of desirable seats for members of the working press to watch the Supreme Court conduct **oral arguments**, whereas ordinary visitors must typically wait in line outdoors for many hours for one of the few seats available to the public. In most states, members of the working press are given some form of statutory immunity from having to testify about their news sources. The name we give to such statutes—**reporter shield laws**—is a clear indication that here too we have an example of freedom of the press meaning something different from and more than freedom of speech.

Former Supreme Court justice Potter Stewart thought it very appropriate that media professionals be given more First Amendment rights than the rest of us. He argued this position forcefully in an address at Yale Law School, later reprinted as a law review article. The title of the lecture and article consists of four words taken from the text of the First Amendment itself—*or of the press*. Stewart says that "the publishing business is, in short, the only organized private business that is given explicit constitutional protection."[27] Whether the working press should enjoy First Amendment

---

26. *John Doe #1 v. Cahill*, 884 A.2d 451 (Del. 2005).
27. Potter Stewart, "Or of the Press," 26 *Hastings Law Journal* 631, 633 (1975).

protections above and beyond those of ordinary citizens—and who should be considered a member of that "working press"—is a continuing focus of debate among legal scholars.[28] It is clear, however, that from time to time the Supreme Court has singled out the media for a special measure of freedom, as seen throughout this book.

Other Sources of Communication Law in the Federal Constitution.

The First Amendment is not the only part of the Bill of Rights of relevance to communication law. Consider the Fourth Amendment's protection against "unreasonable searches and seizures." This means that law enforcement officials generally may not detain us, frisk us, or rummage through our personal effects without first obtaining a **search warrant**. To get a search warrant, an officer must persuade a judge that there is probable cause to believe that important and clearly definable evidence will be uncovered by the search. Frequently, law enforcement officials, persuaded that the offices of a newspaper or television station are harboring evidence crucial to a criminal investigation, will search the premises of these media outlets. As we will see in chapter 9, the Supreme Court has said that the media have no special immunity from such searches,[29] and media outrage over that decision led Congress to pass a major piece of legislation that statutorily provides the press with protections that the Court refused to read into the Bill of Rights.[30] The Fourth Amendment is of relevance to communications professionals for yet another reason. As will be made clear in chapter 5, there have been times when media have cooperated so closely with law enforcement officials—accompanying them on raids, for example—that the reporters themselves may later be sued for violating the target's Fourth Amendment privacy rights. In 1999, the Supreme Court ruled that police may be in violation of the Fourth Amendment if they bring reporters along as they arrest a suspect or search his home.[31]

THINGS TO REMEMBER

The Five Clauses of the First Amendment

ESTABLISHMENT CLAUSE (Freedom *from* religious indoctrination)
FREE EXERCISE CLAUSE (Freedom *to* practice religion)
FREE SPEECH CLAUSE (Freedom of expression)
FREE PRESS CLAUSE (Freedom for the press as an institution)
PETITION CLAUSE (Freedom to complain to government officials)

---

28. See, for example, Mary Rose Papandrea, "Citizen Journalism and the Reporter's Privilege," 91 *Minnesota Law Review* 515 (2007).

29. *Zurcher v. Stanford Daily*, 436 U.S. 547 (1978).

30. The Privacy Protection Act of 1980.

31. *Wilson v. Layne*, 526 U.S. 603 (1999).

The Fifth and Fourteenth Amendments are also very relevant. The Fifth Amendment is probably best known for its protection against self-incrimination—thus the countless times we hear courtroom witnesses, real and fictional, "plead the Fifth." This amendment also tells the federal government—the Fourteenth Amendment has parallel wording applicable to the states—that it may not deprive persons of "life, liberty, or property without due process of law." It is this last provision that is most often of relevance to public communicators, because one aspect of **due process** that courts have demanded over the years is for laws and regulations to be worded precisely enough so that we know *how* to obey them. We expect that traffic regulations will spell out how many feet from a fire hydrant we must park our cars, rather than admonish us in vague terms "not to park too close." Similarly vague would be regulations prohibiting prisoners from mailing any correspondence that "unduly complains, magnifies grievances, or expresses inflammatory views or beliefs."[32] What is an "inflammatory" belief? When has one "magnified" a grievance rather than merely described it?

So important is a working knowledge of the Sixth Amendment for the professional communicator that this book devotes chapter 8 to the subject. The Sixth Amendment assures criminal suspects the right to a speedy and public trial by an impartial jury. There has likely always been a good deal of tension between First and Sixth Amendment guarantees—for example, what kinds of pretrial reportage might make it difficult to impanel an impartial jury? Once a trial has begun, may the trial judge impose restrictions on the press so that jurors do not learn in their living rooms things that would be inadmissible as evidence in the courtroom? The Supreme Court and lower courts have struggled with these kinds of questions for decades.

The Fourteenth Amendment, passed shortly after the end of the Civil War, is important to professional communicators for at least two reasons. First, that same due process language has been treated by the Supreme Court as a kind of funnel through which many provisions of the Bill of Rights—including freedom of speech and freedom of the press—have been applied to the states. This process is known as the **doctrine of incorporation**, and we say more about it in the next chapter. The Fourteenth Amendment also tells the states that they may not deny any person "the equal protection of its laws." This **Equal Protection Clause** has been the main grounds on which the media have successfully argued that statutes that single out media industries for special taxation or other obligations or that seem to discriminate among mass media should be invalidated by the courts.[33]

The Bill of Rights and later amendments are not the only federal constitutional provisions of relevance to the act of communication. Article I, Section 8 of the Constitution enumerates specific powers granted to Congress by the nation's founders. Here Congress is told that it may pass laws "to promote the progress of . . . useful arts, by

32. *Martinez v. Procunier*, 354 F. Supp. 1092 (N.D. Cal. 1973), *aff'd.*, 416 U.S. 396 (1974).
33. *Arkansas Writers' Project, Inc. v. Ragland*, 481 U.S. 221 (1987).

securing for limited times to authors . . . the exclusive right to their respective writing and discoveries." This section is the basis for U.S. **copyright** law, the main subject of chapter 6.

State Constitutions and Communication Law.

We must look not only to the federal Constitution but also to the various state constitutions as sources of communication law. Most state constitutional provisions concerning communication are coextensive with the First Amendment, granting no greater and no fewer rights than are given in the federal Constitution. Some states, however, have decided that their citizens will enjoy a larger measure of freedom of expression than will other Americans. Typically, the relevant sections of these state constitutions affirmatively give citizens the right to "freely speak, write, and publish." Notice that such wording is far more sweeping than the First Amendment, which tells Congress only that *it* may not abridge free speech. If citizens are told explicitly that they have a right to free speech, such a right would seem to prohibit even private individuals and corporations from abridging such a right. There need be no proof of "state action" to have an alleged infringement of freedom of speech taken seriously in a court of law.

The wording of state constitutional provisions often differs from that of the First Amendment in an opposite direction as well. Whereas the federal provision is worded quite absolutely—"Congress shall make *no* law" (emphasis added)—many state provisions put citizens on notice that they will be "responsible for any abuse" of their

---

THINGS TO REMEMBER

The U.S. Constitution and Communications Law: Beyond the First Amendment

FOURTH AMENDMENT
   Search of newsrooms
   Press has no constitutional right to avoid a legitimate search

FIFTH AMENDMENT
   Due process of law applied to federal government
   Void for vagueness doctrine

SIXTH AMENDMENT
   Right to a speedy, public, and fair trial
   Can conflict with press freedom

FOURTEENTH AMENDMENT
   Due process applied to the states
   Equal protection of laws

ARTICLE I, SECTION 8
   Authorizes copyright laws

freedom of speech. Then too, whereas the federal Constitution is silent with respect to the kinds of such abuses that might lead one individual to sue another, some state constitutions explicitly give citizens a right to sue for libel or invasion of privacy. Texans, for example, are assured in article I, section 13 of their constitution that the state's courts are open to them to press claims stemming from injuries done to their "lands, goods, person *or reputation*" (emphasis added).

By far the most frequently recurring question related to state constitutional free speech provisions has been whether one has a right to engage in political dialogue with and hand out leaflets to shoppers in privately owned malls. The U.S. Supreme Court has made clear that there is no federal constitutional right to speak out on issues of one's choosing when at a mall. Yet in that very same decision, the Court made equally clear that the states may conclude that their own constitutions grant such a right.[34] In the years since that decision, several states have addressed the same issue, with mixed results. Some states have found in their constitutions at least a limited right to engage in expressive activity on the grounds of privately owned shopping centers,[35] while others have instead concluded that their own constitutional provisions go no further than the protections granted in the First Amendment.[36]

Statutes as Sources of Communication Law

The U.S. Constitution takes up only a few dozen pages of text. By bulk, and probably also in terms of impact on our daily lives, we are far more affected by the laws passed every year by Congress, state legislatures, city councils, and numerous other local legislative bodies nationwide. States pass obscenity laws, Congress creates the **Freedom of Information Act**, and perhaps your municipality has a local ordinance governing the size and aesthetics of billboard advertising or other outdoor displays.[37] In each of these instances, the enactment of the law might not be the last word on any particular issue, because laws are often challenged in court by affected parties, who will claim that the laws violate state or federal constitutional provisions. This

---

34. *Pruneyard Shopping Center v. Robins,* 447 U.S. 74 (1980).

35. *Bock v. Westminster Mall,* 819 P.2d 55 (1991); *Batchelder v. Allied Stores International,* 445 N.E.2d 590 (Mass. 1983); *State v. Schmid,* 423 A.2d 615 (N.J. 1980); *State v. Cargill,* 851 P.2d 1141 (Or. 1993). *Alderwood Association v. Washington Environmental Council,* 635 P.2d 108 (Wash. 1981).

36. *Cologne v. Westfarms Association,* 469 A.2d 1201 (Conn. 1984); *State v. Lacey,* 465 N.W.2d 537 (Iowa 1991); *Woodland v. Michigan Citizens Lobby,* 378 N.W.2d 337 (Mich. 1985); *City of Billings v. Laedeke,* 805 P.2d 1348 (Mont. 1991); *SHAD Alliance v. Smith Haven Mall,* 488 N.E.2d 1211 (N.Y. 1985); *State v. Felmet,* 273 S.E.2d 708 (N.C. 1981); *Eastwood Mall v. Slanco,* 626 N.E.2d 59 (Ohio 1994); *Charleston Joint Venture v. McPherson,* 417 S.E.2d 544 (S.C. 1992); *Jacobs v. Major,* 407 N.W.2d 832 (Wis. 1987).

37. In 2007, for example, real estate tycoon Donald Trump reached an out-of-court settlement with the Palm Beach town council over fines imposed against him for violating a local zoning ordinance by displaying a too-large American flag on a too-high flagpole. Sally Apgar, "Trump Reaches Truce Over Flag at Huge Florida Home," *Chicago Tribune,* April 27, 2007, W15.

process of **judicial review** resulted, to cite just one example, in the striking down by the Supreme Court of the Communications Decency Act, through which Congress had attempted to prevent the posting of indecent messages likely to be seen by minors on the Internet.[38]

Even if litigants do not seek to have a law declared unconstitutional, they will sometimes feel the need to ask a court to clarify a law's meaning. We call this process **statutory construction.** One notable example is comedienne Carol Burnett's libel suit against the *National Enquirer*, which had published an article alleging that Burnett behaved very strangely, as if intoxicated, in a fancy restaurant. In that California libel law is slightly different for newspapers and for magazines, the court first needed to determine exactly what a newspaper *is* and how it differs from a magazine. Having done so, the court could then conclude that the *National Enquirer* is more of a magazine than a newspaper and could apply the appropriate state law.[39]

Sometimes the courts are thrust into the role of grammarians as they try to make sense of laws worded so poorly that if taken literally, cannot possibly be constitutional. This situation happened in *United States v. X-Citement Video, Inc.,*[40] a Supreme Court case stemming from the defendant's having sold to an undercover police officer some videotapes of then-underage porn star Traci Lords. The case involved the federal Protection of Children Against Sexual Exploitation Act, and the opinion includes a lengthy analysis by the Court of the placement of the word *knowingly* in a key sentence. A more recent example of statutory construction cast a panel of judges on the Second Circuit Court of Appeals as copyeditors, correcting Congress's having written a child pornography law so as to mandate a "fine or a prison term of up to ten years, *and* both" to the more logical "*or* both" construction.[41]

Executive Orders as Sources of Communication Law

As a general principle, the separation of powers that defines our form of government provides that Congress makes the laws, the president carries out the laws, and the judiciary interprets and determines the constitutionality of the laws. In reality, however, the president—and at other levels of government, governors and mayors—can also make law. The president does so by appointing officials to the various regulatory agencies, negotiating treaties and trade agreements, and issuing executive orders. In addition, the president has an enormous long-term effect on the law through the process of nominating persons for lifetime appointments as federal judges.

Professional journalists are keenly aware that the executive branch affects the overall atmosphere in which they conduct their jobs. Public access to governmental information is usually considered one facet of communication law. Indeed, this book

---

38. *Reno v. American Civil Liberties Union*, 521 U.S. 844 (1997).

39. *Burnett v. National Enquirer*, 144 Cal. App. 3d 991 (1983).

40. 513 U.S. 64 (1994).

41. *United States v. Pabon-Cruz*, 391 F.3d 86, 98 (2d Cir. 2004).

devotes a whole chapter to the issue. Such seemingly mundane matters as how often the president holds press conferences, how many employees are hired by each federal agency to expedite Freedom of Information Act requests, and what kind of guidance agency heads are given about how liberally or sparingly to exercise the power to "classify" government documents are thus all parts of communication law. Shortly after the 9/11 terrorist attacks, for example, then attorney general John Ashcroft distributed a memo to Freedom of Information Act staff throughout the federal bureaucracy advising them to be stingy about granting requests for possibly sensitive information.

Administrative Agencies and Communication Law

It was already mentioned that Article I of the U.S. Constitution enumerates the powers granted to Congress. These powers range broadly, from building roads to establishing procedures for immigration and naturalization, from printing money to maintaining the armed forces. Congress's power to regulate commerce among the states is also quite broad. The few hundred members of Congress could not possibly perform all of the many functions required of them without creating a sizable federal bureaucracy. So it is that Washington, D.C., is a veritable alphabet soup of hundreds of regulatory agencies and departments. Several of these agencies have responsibilities of direct relevance for the professional communicator.

Clearly the most important agency, especially if you plan a career in TV, radio, satellite communications, or cyberspace, is the **Federal Communications Commission (FCC)**. Chapter 12, where we examine those laws and regulations that apply exclusively to electronic media such as broadcasting and cable, also includes a detailed description of this agency's history and powers. Another agency whose rulings are relevant to communication law is the **Federal Trade Commission (FTC)**, one of whose powers is to set forth rules and mediate disputes to protect consumers from deceptive advertising. The **Food and Drug Administration (FDA)** also has a voice in the regulation of advertising for and labeling of—you guessed it—food and drugs. In the late 1990s, for example, tobacco companies became very concerned about the implications of a move toward allowing the FDA to classify cigarettes, because of their nicotine content, as "drug delivery systems." In 2000, however, the Supreme Court held that Congress never intended to give the FDA regulatory authority over cigarettes, including what if any kinds of advertising should be allowed for tobacco products.[42]

The Federal Election Commission (FEC) also has jurisdiction over issues of relevance to professional communicators, because federal legislation sets limits on certain kinds of candidate fund-raising and candidate expenditures. The vast majority of funds raised in national campaigns is used to buy advertising time on TV and radio,

---

42. *FDA v. Brown & Williamson Corp.*, 529 U.S. 120 (2000).

so the FEC's powers are of special relevance to media advertising salespersons and political-campaign consultants.

Although these federal agencies are likely the most important sources of communication law, media professionals will discover that dozens of other agencies also have some power over the way in which they conduct their business. To cite one example, in the mid-1980s the **Securities and Exchange Commission (SEC)** argued that it had the right to prevent anyone whose credentials as an investment adviser had been revoked by the commission (typically, because of criminal wrongdoing) from offering formal investment advice, even in a newsletter advice column. The Supreme Court determined that Congress never intended for the SEC to have this particular power.[43]

Common Law and the Law of Equity

Anyone who has watched police and lawyer programs on prime-time TV knows the scene well. An attorney is making a motion to the court, asking the judge to take a particular action. The opposing attorney objects. The judge appears thoughtful, glances in the direction of the first lawyer, and asks, "Can you cite any relevant **precedents?**"

The judge in this scenario is seeking guidance from common law, sometimes called judge-made law. Common law really means to argue based on tradition and custom,

---

THINGS TO REMEMBER

Communication Law: Beyond the U.S. Constitution

- State constitutions are a source of communication law:
  - Some states simply mimic the wording of the First Amendment.
  - Other states affirmatively enumerate citizens' communication rights.
  - Often, states give more rights than the First Amendment does.

- Statutes are a source of communication law:
  - Legislative bodies at all levels of government may pass laws or regulations.
  - Courts sometimes must decide if they are constitutional (judicial review).
  - Courts also may tell us what a law really means (statutory construction).

- Executive orders are sources of communication law:
  - The president often has "wiggle room" in the enforcement of laws.
  - Presidents also affect law through appointments, and through international negotiations.

Some of the many federal agencies that have an effect on communication law are the FCC, FTC, FDA, and FEC.

---

43. *Lowe v. SEC*, 472 U.S. 181 (1985).

ideally backed up with one or more prior court decisions on the same or a similar point. The U.S. legal system depends for its consistency upon a large body of common law, so that litigants can make some reasonable predictions about how courts will rule on specific issues today based on how they have ruled in the past.

Common law is not a uniquely American invention. Indeed, we imported the idea of lawmaking by precedent from English common law dating back many centuries before any British colonists set foot in the New World. Another less visible tradition that the United States borrowed from England is the right of litigants to seek a judicial remedy in **courts of equity** in situations where the common-law traditions cannot help. A detailed history of the relationship between the development of common law and the law of equity is beyond the scope of this book, in part because only four states—Arkansas, Delaware, Mississippi, and Tennessee—continue to maintain separate courts of equity. Still, it is important to realize that one impetus for the development of equity was a perceived dichotomy in English legal tradition between rights and remedies. Plaintiffs may have been able to establish to a court's satisfaction that they had been wronged, but no remedy existed in the law to make the plaintiff whole again.[44] The development of such remedies as **subpoenas** (compelling someone to appear before a court at a later date and to produce papers or otherwise give testimony in reply to specific judicial inquiries) and **injunctions** (ordering that a planned action not be taken, lest a litigant be irreparably wronged) was an outgrowth of the courts of equity. Whenever the phrase "common law" is used throughout the remainder of this text, reference will be made implicitly as well to the law of equity.

The common law should not be thought of as a judicial straitjacket, with no opportunity for evolution. The law does in fact change over time, in part because customs and traditions change. When faced with an arguably relevant precedent, a court always has several options available to it. The first option and the most likely one is to accept and follow the precedent. The Latin phrase **stare decisis**, or "let the decision stand," is often used as a catchphrase to refer to the practice of following precedent.

At the other extreme, a court may decide that the time has come to **overturn** a precedent, to admit forthrightly (at least sometimes it is done forthrightly) that the original decision was wrong. Occasionally a Supreme Court precedent in the field of communication law has been overturned. For example, the Supreme Court had held for many years that motion pictures were not deserving of constitutional protection. "The exhibition of moving pictures is a business, pure and simple, originated and conducted for profit like other spectacles," the Court said back in 1915, and "not to be regarded . . . as part of the press of the country, or as organs of public opinion" within the meaning of freedom of speech.[45] Not until the 1950s did the Supreme

---

44. Morton Gitelman, "The Separation of Law and Equity and the Arkansas Chancery Courts: Historical Anomalies and Political Realities," 17 *University of Arkansas at Little Rock Law Review* 215 (1995).

45. *Mutual Film Corp. v. Industrial Commission of Ohio*, 236 U.S. 230, 244 (1915).

Court explicitly overrule its earlier decision, finding that motion pictures had become "a significant medium for the communication of ideas."[46]

The Supreme Court also took several decades to change its mind about the place of advertising in the U.S. system of free expression. In a 1942 case, the Court held that advertising is completely outside the First Amendment's protection.[47] More than thirty years later, the Court changed its mind, holding for the first time that purely commercial advertising whose message is simply that person A offers to sell something to person B for a specified price is protected speech.[48] The development of the Court's commercial-speech doctrine is so important that it is a large part of the focus of chapter 10.

On rare occasions the Court has changed its mind without waiting for so many years to pass. Probably the best example is *West Virginia State Board of Education v. Barnette*, in which the Court ruled unconstitutional the practice of requiring that public school students recite the Pledge of Allegiance to the flag.[49] The Court had made a directly contrary ruling a mere three years earlier.[50]

Most of the time, courts follow precedents. Sometimes, especially after many years have passed since a precedent has been handed down, judges feel free to overturn the precedent, to change their minds. In between these two opposite actions are two other options for dealing with a precedent. Often, one or the other is employed en route to an eventual overturning.

The first of the two options is to **distinguish** the precedent, and the word means much the same in this context as it does in everyday conversation. When judges distinguish an earlier decision, they are really saying that the case is not a precedent worthy of following at all, *given the facts of the controversy now before them*. This last phrase is the key. The facts of the two cases are different. In communication law, the opportunities for building arguments in favor of distinguishing a precedent are many and varied. The earlier case might deal with a movie that has been found to meet the current definition of obscenity, whereas the case we are looking at today might involve a film that has some sexy scenes in it yet could not be considered so hard-core as to be obscene. The earlier decision might have been a libel case in which the plaintiff was a famous person, what the courts have come to call a **public figure**. If the case we are looking at today involves a libel plaintiff who is not at all famous, many features of libel law that were applied in the earlier case will be inapplicable. The earlier case might have involved political advertising on TV, whereas the current case involves political advertising in a newspaper. As it turns out, the law governing the same content in the two media is very different. The two situations again can thus be distinguished.

---

46. *Joseph Burstyn, Inc. v. Wilson*, 343 U.S. 495, 501 (1952).

47. *Valentine v. Chrestensen*, 316 U.S. 52 (1942).

48. *Virginia State Board of Pharmacy v. Virginia Citizens Consumer Council*, 425 U.S. 748 (1976).

49. 319 U.S. 624 (1943).

50. *Minersville School District v. Gobitis*, 310 U.S. 586 (1940).

The fourth and last option is to **modify** the earlier precedent. Knowing the dictionary definition of *modify* is not going to be much help here. In the law, to modify a precedent is to follow, in a very general way, the rule that seems to explain the earlier case but to at the same time show a recognition that something "out there, in the *real* world" has changed. Perhaps an example or two will clarify. In libel law, one of the things that plaintiffs must prove is that an utterance or publication was truly defamatory, that it damaged their reputation. Traditionally, we assumed that to accuse a woman of having had sexual relations before marriage would be defamatory. Suppose, however, that you live in a state where courts have held that societal customs and values have changed and that accusing an unmarried woman of not being chaste need not be defamatory. The general rule—libel demands a finding of defamation— still holds and we are still following it in principle, but the world has changed to the point where what used to be thought of as defamatory might no longer be considered so.

The Supreme Court's changing thinking about TV in courtrooms provides another example of modifying a precedent. In the 1960s, the Court overturned the swindling conviction of one of President Johnson's Texas friends because the TV cameras permitted at his trial created a zoo-like atmosphere.[51] Less than twenty years later, the Court upheld the **conspiracy** convictions of some Florida police officers who had argued unsuccessfully that TV at their trial was a violation of their constitutional rights.[52] How can we explain the two differing results, when the Court did not actually overturn the earlier case? Something "out there," in the real world, had changed. Television technology had grown more sophisticated and far less intrusive, to the point where the technology now could be introduced into the courtroom without disrupting the proceedings.

Having now reviewed the four options open to a court that is presented with a precedent for consideration, it should be emphasized that it is not always perfectly clear which option the court has exercised. Recall that we treated the question of whether films are protected by the First Amendment as an example of the Supreme Court's having overruled itself after a few decades had passed. That same constitutional history, however, could be seen as an example of modifying the earlier precedent. It could be argued that in the early days of motion pictures, films had no message to impart, no story to tell; they were merely toys. We flocked to the movie theaters because we were fascinated with the optical illusion itself. Perhaps, then, it would make no more sense to say that films are protected "expression" than to say that a telescope is protected expression. For the Court many years after that decision to recognize that motion pictures *now* were being used to tell stories, to delight but also to inspire and educate, would be more an example of modifying than of overruling. That which would have changed would not be the minds of the justices but the place of motion pictures in society.

51. *Estes v. Texas*, 381 U.S. 532 (1965).
52. *Chandler v. Florida*, 449 U.S. 560 (1981).

THINGS TO REMEMBER

Common Law Precedents

■ The common law, or "judge-made law," is the body of precedents that can inform a current controversy.
■ When presented with a precedent, a court may do one of four things:
  • Follow it (the principle of stare decisis)
  • Distinguish it
  • Modify it
  • Overturn it

Another reason it is not always clear which strategy a court has used is that there is a strong tendency in the law toward a kind of inertia against the outright overturning of precedents. As one commentator put it, "Most of what seems essentially false in judges' opinions" is "the repeated insistence that they are not changing the law at all when they obviously are."[53] It is worth noting too that in only slightly more than a handful of the two hundred or so times that the Supreme Court has overturned its prior rulings has it explicitly admitted that the earlier decision had been a mistake.[54]

An Overview of the American Judiciary

Now that we know what courts may do with common-law precedents, we need to develop an understanding of how the judiciary is structured in this country. In other words, what does it mean to "go to court"?

We should first realize that there is not one judicial system in the United States but rather a federal system, a system for each of the states, and one for the District of Columbia. There are thus fifty-two systems in all, without even counting the courts governing such places as Puerto Rico or the Virgin Islands. It is important to keep that in mind throughout this book, because we will often be able to offer only general-

53. M. Shapiro, "Incremental Decision Making," in *Courts, Law, and Judicial Processes*, ed. S. Sidney Ulmer (New York: Free Press, 1981), 316.

54. Philip P. Frickey, "Stare Decisis in Constitutional Cases: Reconsidering *National League of Cities*," 2 *Constitutional Commentary* 123, 128 n.21 (1985). Frickey found six examples of the Court's explicitly overturning one of its prior decisions. Since his article was published, two more cases can likely be added to the mix. In *Roper v. Simmons*, 543 U.S. 551 (2005), the Court held that the imposition of capital punishment on defendants whose crimes were committed as minors violates the Eighth Amendment, thus overturning a contrary decision from 1989. And in *Lawrence v. Texas*, 539 U.S. 558 (2003), the Court indicated that same-sex sexual conduct between consenting adults in private could not be criminalized, thus overturning a 1986 precedent.

izations rather than definitive answers about the status of a particular legal doctrine. The law varies from state to state and from one region of the federal judiciary to another.

While federal judges are appointed to life terms by the president, with the advice and consent of the Senate, the vast majority of state judges are elected. In states that elect their judges, a natural tension has long been recognized. On the one hand, if voters are to be called upon to elect their judiciaries, those voters should be fully informed about the candidates' backgrounds. But the practice of electioneering and the seeking of campaign contributions seem to some to be inconsistent with the cherished tradition of an impartial and independent judiciary. States deal with the tension in a variety of ways. Some use "retention elections," in which voters are asked only whether a judge should get to retain her seat (there are no alternative candidates offered on the ballot). Other states permit competing candidates but conduct nonpartisan elections in which candidates' party affiliations do not appear on ballots. Most state judges also enjoy far longer terms—as long as fifteen years in some jurisdictions—than their counterparts in the other branches of government. Then too, judicial candidates are often held to eligibility requirements—a law degree, or having been approved by an appointed judicial commission—equally unparalleled in the other branches.

Sometimes courts have had to adjudicate the constitutionality of rules governing the election of state judges. In 2002, the U.S. Supreme Court struck down a Minnesota law that prohibited judicial candidates there from making utterances that might even *appear* to commit them to a point of view on matters likely to come before their court. As Justice Scalia indicated in his majority opinion, "there is almost no legal or political issue that is unlikely to come before a judge."[55] And in 2005, a federal judge struck down the New York State system of selecting specific kinds of lower court judges by having a convention at which leaders of the major political parties would vote. The judge seemed to be saying, If you say you are going to have an election, have an election—let the *voters* have some direct say in who their party's judicial candidates will be.[56]

Concerning the wisdom of appointing or electing judges, the Capital Jury Project, a National Science Foundation–backed consortium of legal scholars, psychologists, and sociologists, released a study based on interviews with jurors in hundreds of capital murder trials.[57] The results pointed to an inability on the part of many jurors to understand the judges' instructions. Often state judges in such cases are loath to clarify boilerplate instructions, lest one wrong word result in an appealable error. Judges' reversal rates are often used against them in the next election. So the judges may simply instruct the jurors to reread the printed instructions, however confusing.

55. *Republican Party of Minnesota v. White*, 536 U.S. 765, 772 (2002).
56. *Torres v. New York State Board of Elections*, 411 F. Supp. 2d 212 (E.D.N.Y. 2005).
57. Stephen P. Garvey and Sheri Lynn Johnson, "Correcting Deadly Confusion: Responding to Jury Inquiries in Capital Cases," 85 *Cornell Law Review* 627 (2000).

A Three-Tiered Hierarchy

The structure of the judiciary itself need not be a source of complete bewilderment. Indeed, the hierarchy of courts in the states is almost without exception modeled after the federal system. There are three layers. At the bottom are the **trial courts**. In the federal system these are called **federal district courts**. The names of the trial courts vary greatly from state to state but are most frequently called **superior courts**.

Litigants who are unhappy with the trial court result have the option of bringing an appeal to the next layer of the judiciary. In the federal system, and in most states, these courts are called, intuitively enough, **appellate courts**. In the federal system these appellate courts govern a specific region of the country, called a **federal circuit**. There are thirteen such circuits. Eleven of them are given numbers. The **jurisdiction** of each of these appellate courts is as follows:

First: Maine, Massachusetts, New Hampshire, Rhode Island, Puerto Rico
Second: Connecticut, New York, Vermont
Third: Delaware, New Jersey, Pennsylvania (also the Virgin Islands)
Fourth: Maryland, North Carolina, South Carolina, Virginia, West Virginia
Fifth: Texas, Mississippi, Louisiana
Sixth: Kentucky, Michigan, Ohio, Tennessee
Seventh: Illinois, Indiana, Wisconsin
Eighth: Arkansas, Iowa, Minnesota, Missouri, Nebraska, North Dakota, South Dakota
Ninth: Alaska, Arizona, California, Hawaii, Idaho, Montana, Nevada, Oregon, Washington (also Guam and the Northern Mariana Islands)
Tenth: Colorado, Kansas, New Mexico, Oklahoma, Utah, Wyoming
Eleventh: Alabama, Florida, Georgia (also the Panama Canal Zone)

There is also an appellate court for the District of Columbia. That particular court has jurisdiction over most appeals from decisions of the FCC and other federal agencies. If you work in the electronic media or cable television industries, this court may thus be the most important one governing your professional life. The thirteenth federal appellate court is the one for the Federal Circuit, a special court created by Congress in 1982 to handle specialized appeals such as in patent and trademark cases.

Litigants who are not satisfied with an appellate ruling can sometimes take their grievance one step higher. The pinnacle of the judiciary in both the federal and state systems is also an appellate court, but it goes by a special name. We have already made reference many times in this chapter to the U.S. Supreme Court. The highest court in most states is also referred to as a supreme court, although there are some exceptions; New York's highest court, for example, is its Court of Appeals.

Although we often hear aggrieved parties vow that they will take their cases "all the way to the Supreme Court, if necessary," in fact this is romantic fancy because the justices of the Supreme Court have tremendous latitude about which of the thousands of appeals filed there will ever be heard. In recent years, the justices have chosen to hear far fewer cases than in the past, only eighty-two in its 2005-2006 term.[58] Many state supreme courts have similar discretion to determine which cases they will hear. As a result, litigants are often limited to having their grievances heard in two, rather than three, rungs of the judicial system.

The Scope of a Precedent

Thus far we have used the word *precedent* to refer to an earlier court decision that might lead a court today to rule similarly. Not all precedents are equal, however. A precedent in a state court in Wisconsin, for example, even if decided by that state's highest court, has no *binding* precedential value on a state judge in California. The California court might be persuaded by the logic of the Wisconsin court's arguments, but it is not required to follow the precedent. If a judge hears a case that raises issues that have never been raised before in his or her jurisdiction, the controversy is often referred to as one of **first impression**. If you have ever seen the film *Whose Life Is It Anyway?* you may recall the scene in which a trial judge comes to the hospital to decide whether Richard Dreyfuss's paraplegic character has a right to die. In this judge's jurisdiction, the issue was depicted as a case of first impression, although the judge was aware of precedents from other states.

You as a judge are bound by precedents only by higher courts in the same area, or jurisdiction, as your own. If you are a state trial court judge, you are bound by relevant decisions of the U.S. Supreme Court and by your state's supreme court, as well as by any appellate rulings from courts in the same appellate division (geographic region of the state) as your own. If you are a federal trial judge, you are bound by U.S. Supreme Court decisions, as well as by federal appellate decisions that come from the same circuit in which you find yourself. Until the U.S. Supreme Court gives guidance with a definitive ruling, there tend to be conflicting decisions among the circuits. We see frequent examples of this phenomenon throughout this book.

The U.S. Supreme Court is the ultimate arbiter of what the U.S. Constitution means. It must be emphasized, however, that the Court has no authority whatsoever to interpret state constitutions; that is the province of the individual state supreme courts. Perhaps the best example of this principle in practice in recent years is the question of whether state sodomy laws, laws that make certain consensual sexual practices illegal and which were often enforced disproportionately against homosexuals, are constitutional. The U.S. Supreme Court, in 1986, ruled 5-4 that the existence of such laws is not a violation of any federal constitutional principle.[59] Since that date,

---

58. Robert Barnes, "Justices Continue Trend of Hearing Fewer Cases," *Washington Post*, January 7, 2007, A4.

59. *Bowers v. Hardwick*, 478 U.S. 186 (1986).

however, numerous state appellate courts have ruled in consensual sodomy cases, and at least in three instances have found these laws in violation of their own state constitutions' privacy provisions.[60] Such decisions could not be appealed to the U.S. Supreme Court (which finally ruled in 2003—overturning the earlier 1986 decision—that the federal Constitution did, in fact, require the invalidating of remaining sodomy laws).[61]

The Current U.S. Supreme Court

Membership on the Supreme Court remained unchanged from 1994 until 2005, the second-most stable cast of characters in the Court's history. But in 2005 Justice Sandra Day O'Connor announced her intention to retire upon Senate confirmation of her replacement. A few months after O'Connor's announcement, Chief Justice William Rehnquist died in office and Judge John Roberts of the Court of Appeals for the D.C. Circuit, whose name President George W. Bush initially offered as a replacement for O'Connor, instead became the seventeenth chief justice. The Court began its 2005-2006 term with Justice O'Connor still seated, and Justice O'Connor remained on the Court until the Senate confirmed Judge Samuel Alito from the Third Circuit Court of Appeals as her replacement in early 2006. The chart on the facing page gives information on each justice, including the date of appointment and the name of the president who made the appointment. Note that seven of the nine justices were appointed by Republican presidents. U.S. Supreme Court justices are appointed, with the "advice and consent" of the Senate, to lifetime terms, as are all federal judges. The Senate confirmation process can be rather stormy, as evidenced in recent decades by the media spectacles surrounding Senate Judiciary Committee hearings on the candidacies of Judges Robert Bork (rejected) and Clarence Thomas (ultimately confirmed by a slim 52-48 vote in the full Senate).

Certainly volumes could be written about each justice's legal philosophy and more specifically, each justice's tendency to interpret the First Amendment either liberally or stingily. Such an undertaking will not be attempted here. Two necessarily oversimplified points will have to suffice for now. First, those jurists who enjoy well-deserved reputations as political conservatives may nonetheless believe in a rather broad interpretation of at least some First Amendment principles. Justice Antonin Scalia is probably the best example of this phenomenon on the current Court. Second, it is very misleading to label a justice as a First Amendment progressive or a First Amendment conservative without giving a bit of context. In the 1970s, for example, Justice John Paul Stevens wrote an opinion for the Court holding that a radio station had no First Amendment right to broadcast one of comedian George Carlin's "dirty words"

---

60. *Powell v. State*, 510 S.E.2d 18 (Ga. 1998); *Commonwealth v. Wasson*, 842 S.W.2d 487 (Ky. 1992); *State v. Morales*, 826 S.W.2d 201 (Tex. 1992).

61. *Lawrence v. Texas*, 539 U.S. 558 (2003).

The Justices

Name	Born	Appointment	Past Lives
John Roberts	01/27/55	2005 / G.W. Bush	Federal circuit court judge; associate counsel to the president; deputy solicitor general; private practice
Samuel Alito	04/01/50	2006 / G.W. Bush	Federal circuit court judge; U.S. attorney for New Jersey; deputy assistant attorney general; assistant to the solicitor general
Stephen Breyer	08/15/38	1994 / Clinton	Federal circuit court judge; law professor; chief counsel, U.S. Senate Judiciary Committee
Ruth Bader Ginsburg	03/15/33	1993 / Clinton	Federal circuit court judge; law professor; director, Women's Rights Project, ACLU
Anthony Kennedy	07/23/36	1988 / Reagan	Federal circuit court judge; law professor
Antonin Scalia	03/11/36	1986 / Reagan	Federal circuit court judge; assistant U.S. attorney general; law professor
David Souter	09/17/39	1990 / G.H.W. Bush	State supreme court justice; New Hampshire attorney general
John Paul Stevens	04/20/20	1975 / Ford	Federal circuit court judge; private practice
Clarence Thomas	06/23/46	1991 / G.H.W. Bush	Federal circuit court judge; director, civil rights, U.S. Department of Education; chairman, Equal Employment Opportunity Commission

From left to right: Standing: Stephen Breyer, Clarence Thomas, Ruth Bader Ginsburg, Samuel Alito. Seated: Anthony Kennedy, John Paul Stevens, Chief Justice John Roberts, Antonin Scalia, David Souter. Photo by Richard Strauss, Smithsonian Institution; Collection of the Supreme Court of the United States.

monologues. Although such an opinion would seem to qualify Justice Stevens for the conservative label, today he is viewed as perhaps the justice most supportive of First Amendment rights.

Going to Court—Civil or Criminal

Conflicts resulting in a trip to the courtroom are generally of two types, **civil** or **criminal**. The name of the proceeding is usually an indication of which category we have before us. Civil cases are given names of the form *A v. B* (e.g., *Smith v. Jones*), where person A is the **plaintiff** who is suing person B, the **defendant**. In criminal proceedings, the "plaintiff" becomes the government, which is said to **prosecute** the case against the defendant. Thus we may have names such as *United States v. Dennis*, *Georgia v. Stanley*, or *State v. Dalton*.

In civil disputes, the case begins with the plaintiff filing a **complaint** with the court, which enumerates the specific allegations of misconduct against the defendant. The defendant then has an opportunity to file a response to the complaint, referred to as the **answer**.

The process of **discovery** then takes place, and it can be both lengthy and costly.

The label makes sense because this step is when each side of the dispute discovers the nature of the other's case. Lawyers for one side will question the other's witnesses, and transcripts of such pretrial **depositions** are made and can be used later at trial to ensure that witnesses' stories remain consistent.

Typically a flurry of legal paper filings will then ensue. Some filings might seek to avoid a trial by having the court grant **summary judgment** to one side or the other (more frequently to the defense). Such an order would be appropriate if the judge believes that those facts on which both the plaintiff and defendant agree establish a scenario whereby one and only one legal answer is possible. Keep in mind that mass media defendants are often very unpopular with juries. As a result, motions for summary judgment are very important to professional communicators. Often, too, motions are made that are aimed at setting the ground rules, should a trial be necessary. In a sexual-abuse case involving juveniles, for example, will testimony from alleged victims be accepted on videotape? As we see in chapter 4, one of the most important pretrial issues to have settled in libel disputes is whether the plaintiff is a public figure or an ordinary private citizen. The answer to that one question often determines the ultimate winner and loser of the case.

If you have ever been called for jury duty, you may have noted that legal disputes are often settled at the last minute, even on the day a trial is scheduled to begin. Indeed, a very tiny percentage of court cases, civil or criminal, ever actually come to trial. Sometimes these pretrial settlements (in criminal law, they usually involve **plea bargaining** to a lesser charge) occur at the very last minute, after the careful questioning of potential jurors (called *voir dire*) has been completed and both sides see the jury that will actually hear the case.

Criminal cases involve some unique features with which communication professionals should have at least some familiarity. Typically the prosecution of the case begins with the arrest of the suspect. The **arraignment**, at which a judge formally reads to the suspect the charges against him or her and at which the suspect may make an initial **plea**, follows soon after. Should the defendant plead guilty, sentencing may take place immediately or soon after additional facts about any mitigating or aggravating circumstances surrounding the offense are brought to the judge's attention in the form of a presentencing report.

If the defendant pleads not guilty, there is usually at least one more major step in the process prior to a trial itself. In some settings this step is the **preliminary hearing**. In other jurisdictions, and in federal prosecutions, it is the seeking of an **indictment** by a **grand jury**. In either case, the purpose of this pretrial step is to ensure that the state does in fact have enough evidence against the defendant to justify "holding the defendant over," that the taxpayers' money will not be wasted by going to trial. Although grand juries and "real" juries (usually called **petit juries**) are typically drawn from the same jury pools (e.g., from voter registration lists), there are two important differences between the two. First, whereas petit jurors hear full-blown criminal trials, traditionally open to the press and public, the evidence presented to a grand jury by a district attorney is traditionally kept secret. Second, the burden of proof demanded by petit jurors is that the state establish its case "beyond a reasonable doubt," whereas grand jurors, to indict a suspect, need only find that there is **"probable cause"** to believe that the defendant is guilty.

Not all trials are jury trials, of course. The rules governing when litigants in a civil case have a right to a jury trial vary among jurisdictions. Sometimes it may be wise for one or the other party in a lawsuit to forgo that right. It is commonly believed, for example, that libel plaintiffs prefer jury trials, whereas media defendants in such trials prefer judge, or bench, trials. Juries are more likely to be swayed by the emotionalism and immediacy of seeing a wronged plaintiff, or so the reasoning goes, whereas they might not be swayed by the more abstract philosophies in support of freedom of the press—especially if the press got its facts wrong and hurt someone in their community.[62]

The Appeals Process

Whichever side wins at the trial level in a civil dispute, and if a criminal prosecution results in a conviction, an appeal may be the next step. There are many differences between trials and appellate hearings. Trials typically take much longer than appellate hearings. Only trials can have jurors and witnesses. Appellate hearings are much less populous affairs; typically one attorney for each side makes oral arguments in front of the court—which can be interrupted at any time by questions from the bench—for a half hour or so. The oral argument usually takes place weeks or months after lengthy position papers called **briefs** have been filed in court by each side. Some-

---

THINGS TO REMEMBER

The Basic Structure of the Legal System

- The federal judiciary has three levels—district courts, circuit courts of appeal, and the Supreme Court; most states mirror this system.
- The U.S. Supreme Court, as well as many other state supreme courts, is not required to accept any invitation to hear an appeal from lower courts.
- Lower court judges are legally *bound* to follow precedents only from higher courts in their own jurisdictions.
- Courts hear both civil cases (in which an individual plaintiff sues a defendant) and criminal prosecutions by the state.
- Prior to the convening of an actual trial, much discovery takes place, and there may also be motions to avoid a trial by seeking summary judgment.

---

62. Rodney A. Smolla, *Suing the Press: Libel, the Media, and Power* (New York: Oxford University Press, 1986), 194–195.

times parties beyond those immediately involved in the dispute file a brief. In a media law case, for example, organizations such as the American Society of Newspaper Editors or the National Association of Broadcasters may ask to have their thoughts on the controversy entertained by the court. The papers filed by such associations are called **amicus briefs,** "amicus" being Latin for "friend." Sometimes you may encounter the phrase **amicus curiae** ("friend of the court") to describe a group filing an amicus brief.

Although only trial courts have witnesses and jurors, in one sense it is the appellate courtroom that is more crowded. Trial courts generally are presided over by one judge, whereas at the appellate level a panel of judges is involved. In federal procedure, the appellate panels consist of three randomly assigned judges from that circuit. An **en banc** ruling by all the judges of a circuit (usually a dozen or more) may be sought as an intermediate level of appeal after an unsuccessful hearing in front of a three-judge panel and before petitioning the U.S. Supreme Court.

Another key difference between trial and appellate proceedings is the kind of issues

The speaker has apparently recently been promoted to an appellate court where, unlike at the trial level, there are no juries or witnesses for judges to scold (only lawyers).

addressed by the courts. Trial courts entertain questions of both fact and law, whereas appellate courts generally deal only with questions of law. One major exception to this general principle is the "**clearly erroneous rule**" of federal civil procedure. This rule permits a federal appellate court to look at the facts of the case independently if the court first determines that the trial judge made a clearly erroneous finding of fact. The rule is not often invoked. It is viewed as strong medicine, in part because leveling such an accusation against a lower court judge is rather insulting, and because invoking the rule is itself ultimately reviewable by a yet higher court.

Questions of fact ask, What happened? In a homicide case, for example, we would ask if this criminal suspect emptied a revolver into the deceased, and if the victim died from the wounds thus inflicted or from some other cause. Whether the answers to those and other facts demand a finding of first-degree or second-degree homicide, or involuntary manslaughter, however, is a **question of law**. In an obscenity prosecution, issues such as what kind of sexual acts are engaged in and with what frequency by the on-screen talent are questions of fact. Whether the film as a whole satisfies a statute's definition of obscenity and whether that definition in turn satisfies the requirements set forth by relevant Supreme Court rulings are questions of law.

This distinction can be very important to mass media defendants. Journalists frequently find that they are not very popular with most Americans and therefore with most American jurors. If an adverse trial court ruling stems in part from findings of law, the judgment is more easily appealable, and appellate judges have often shown themselves far more sympathetic to First Amendment arguments than were the jurors down below.

Decisions and Opinions

Because appellate courts have several judges hearing a dispute, the permutations of votes for one side or the other and the reasoning behind each such vote become more complicated than in a single-judge trial. A whole nomenclature has developed to describe such matters. Let us use the nine justices of the U.S. Supreme Court as the model in this discussion. We begin by emphasizing the rather intuitive distinction between a decision and an opinion. A **decision** tells us who wins the case, whereas an **opinion** tells us why. In the extreme, we might have a unanimous decision with nine separate opinions. Such a situation would tell us who prevailed, but would probably give lower courts little if any guidance as to what the decision really means or how to apply it to slightly different facts in the future.

First let us consider the **majority opinion**. (When you read actual Supreme Court cases, you will not find majority opinions referred to as such. Rather, you will typically find phrasing such as "Justice Green delivered the opinion for the Court, in which Justices Brown, White, Blue, and Orange joined.") U.S. Supreme Court majority opinions must command at least five votes, presuming that all nine members have participated in a case. For any number of reasons, however, fewer than nine may vote in any given case. Sometimes justices feel the need to **recuse** themselves—that is, to purposely decide not to participate in a case—for ethical reasons. Maybe one justice's daughter is a student at a university that is party to a case, or perhaps another owns stock in a corporation that is one of the litigants. If only seven justices participate in a case, four votes are all that are needed to produce a majority decision.

Majority opinions tend to have a certain structure. They will often begin by reciting the facts of the case, such as who did what to whom, who brought suit and why, and what the lower courts ruled. Typically at or near the very end of the opinion we will learn the Court's **holding**—what the case stands for, and what specific guidance the justices intend lower courts to take from their decision. The holdings of some landmark decisions are well known to most Americans, such as the *Gideon* holding that indigent criminal suspects must be provided with free legal counsel,[63] or the *Miranda* holding that information learned from suspects in police interrogations is inadmissible if the accused is not advised of certain of his or her constitutional rights prior to questioning.[64] Much of what appears in majority opinions between the recitation of the facts and the setting forth of the holding is called **dicta**. Some of the dicta may consist of reasoning in support of the Court's ultimate conclusion. Dicta often include predictable, almost formulaic repetitions of boilerplate paragraphs from previous cases. Virtually any case involving student newspapers, for example, no matter which side actually prevails, will include a famous dictum from the Vietnam War–era *Tinker* case to the effect that students do not "shed their constitutional rights to freedom of speech or expression at the schoolhouse gate."[65]

Dicta carry much less precedential value than the actual holding of a case, for at least two reasons. First, in our constitutional system of separation of powers, courts are empowered to decide immediate controversies set before them, not to create law in the abstract. Because dicta by their very nature often reach far beyond the immediate conflict being adjudicated, giving them too much weight would have the long-term effect of making the judiciary into a mini-legislature. Second, only the holding of a case tells the parties involved exactly why the one side has won, and only the holding is supposed to tell lower courts exactly what lesson to learn from the case at hand. Accordingly, judges do not have any immediate incentive to consider their dicta as carefully as they do their holdings, and the imprecision likely to result from this lack of incentive will ultimately be destructive. The two reasons for discounting dicta, then, concern issues of legitimacy and accuracy.[66]

A very special situation arises when the Supreme Court has only eight members sitting and produces a 4-4 tie vote. The lower court decision is affirmed, but that

---

63. *Gideon v. Wainwright*, 372 U.S. 335 (1963).

64. *Miranda v. Arizona*, 384 U.S. 436 (1966).

65. *Tinker v. Des Moines Independent Community School District*, 393 U.S. 503, 506 (1969).

66. Michael C. Dorf, "Dicta and Article III," 142 *University of Pennsylvania Law Review* 1997 (1994).

affirmance does not carry any binding precedential weight beyond the jurisdiction of the lower court; the Supreme Court's tie vote does not produce the "law of the land." Thus, if a case is appealed from the Wisconsin Supreme Court and results in such a 4-4 tie, the legal doctrine established by the lower court will be binding only in Wisconsin. In essence, the result is as if the case had never been heard by the U.S. Supreme Court. Typically, no opinion is written when a case produces a 4-4 tie.

From the vantage point of lower court judges looking to the U.S. Supreme Court for guidance, an especially troublesome result occurs when a clear majority decision is announced, but not enough justices can agree on the rationale behind the decision to produce a majority opinion. The opinion that commands the most votes—it might be three, it might be four—is referred to as a **plurality opinion**. The reasoning offered in such an opinion will not carry any precedential value, although it can offer some insights as to how the Court might react to slightly different situations in the future.

Assuming that a case does produce a clear majority opinion, some justices who voted with the winning side, and who even signed on to the majority opinion, may still feel the need to write a separate **concurring opinion** to indicate how their own views of the case may differ a bit from that espoused by the majority. Then too, a justice might "concur in the decision only," which means that the justice will vote with the majority but wants to emphasize that he or she wholly rejects the majority's reasoning. Concurring opinions are often written by the justice who provided the "swing vote" in a 5-4 decision. Justice Lewis Powell was famous for writing such opinions—Justice Kennedy seems to be his successor in this regard[67]—and we come across some of them in this book. As you may well imagine, the tone of such opinions frequently suggests that "I will go this far, *but no further.*"

The chance to write opinions is not restricted to those who vote on the winning side, of course. Those justices whose votes place them in the minority will produce at least one **dissenting opinion**. Sometimes the reasoning espoused by a dissenting justice today becomes the basis for a majority opinion tomorrow.

Two final categories of opinions you may encounter are the **per curiam opinion** and the **memorandum order**. *Per curiam* means "by the court," and a per curiam opinion is a majority opinion that is not signed by any particular justice. A memorandum order is a court decision that is not accompanied by an opinion; we learn who won but little, if anything, else.

Where to Find the Cases

There are at least two reasons you will want to learn how to find the full text of court opinions on your own, rather than depending entirely upon a book such as this one to summarize the leading cases. The first reason is that your instructor might

---

67. Miriam Cherry and Robert Rogers, "*Tiresias* and the Justices: Using Information Markets to Predict Supreme Court Decisions," 100 *Northwestern University Law Review* 1141, 1155 n.82 (2006).

THINGS TO REMEMBER

Appellate Procedures, Decisions and Opinions

- The losing party in a trial may bring an appeal to a higher court.
- Both parties will then file written briefs, followed by oral arguments before a panel of judges.
- Other parties may express their views through the use of amicus briefs.
- Losing parties in a federal appellate court can petition the entire court to hear the case again en banc, prior to contemplating a Supreme Court appeal.
- Generally appellate courts may only address questions of law, whereas trial courts look also at questions of fact.
- Decisions tell who wins a case; opinions tell why.
- The actual holding of a decision is its true precedential value; often the bulk of the text in an opinion consists of dicta, which have very limited precedential value.
- Depending on how many judges join an opinion, and which way they vote, the opinion may be referred to as majority, plurality, concurring, or dissenting.

require you to do some original research, rather than simply take exams on the material in this book. The second reason has a more long-term payoff. This book is already out of date. So rapid are changes in the law that any legal textbook, even assuming the speediest of production schedules, is several months out of date the moment it arrives at your bookstore. Your instructor will be able to provide updates pointing out, for example, court cases cited here that may have been overturned on appeal while we went to press. Your time with your instructor is limited, however, and it is thus a good idea to develop the ability to do your own updating as a media professional.

In the best of all possible worlds, you are taking this class at an institution that has a law school that permits students campus-wide to use the law library and that boasts convenient access to computer-assisted legal resources such as the Westlaw or LEXIS databases. Even if you do not have a law school on campus, your library probably maintains the kind of legal collection that will allow you to research court cases. If you are on a campus without such a collection, you might find it necessary to visit a neighboring campus or the library at your county courthouse.

Finding U.S. Supreme Court Cases.   Let us suppose you are listening to the radio one morning in the car on the way to school and you hear that the Supreme Court just handed down an important decision. (Decisions are usually released to the press at 10 a.m. eastern time.) Where are some of the different places you might be able to find it? If you have access to computer-assisted research, you will likely be able to find the full text of the opinion online within a few hours. In LEXIS, Supreme Court decisions are most conveniently found in the U.S. file within the GENFED

library. Numerous Internet websites also include Supreme Court and other court decisions. Several helpful websites for legal research are highlighted later in this chapter.

What if you do not have convenient online access? If the case is truly a landmark
decision, you may find very detailed excerpts of it published the next morning in
national newspapers such as the *New York Times* and the *Washington Post*. Within a
week or so, the full text will also be available in libraries around the country in a
publication called *United States Law Week* (abbreviated U.S.L.W. in citations). The
more traditional places to find the full text of U.S. Supreme Court opinions are in a
series called the *Supreme Court Reporter* (abbreviated S. Ct. in citations) and another
called *United States Reports* (abbreviated simply as U.S.). Yet another source owned by
many academic libraries is the *United States Supreme Court Reports, Lawyers' Edition*
(abbreviated L. Ed. or, for more recent cases, L. Ed. 2d), published by LEXIS.

Finding Other Court Decisions.   Federal district court opinions, when they
are published at all, appear most conveniently in a series from the St. Paul, Minnesota–based West Publishing called *Federal Supplement* (or F. Supp.). As of 1998, the
volume numbering system began anew (rather than climb higher than 999), and so
the most recent federal district cases are found in the *Federal Supplement, Second Series* (abbreviated F. Supp. 2d). Federal appellate decisions are found in another West
publication called the *Federal Reporter* (abbreviated simply as F.). In 1924, after publishing volume number 300, the *Federal Reporter* began numbering anew, and from
that date until 1993 cases were thus found in the *Federal Reporter, Second Series*
(F.2d). Volume 999 of the second series was published in 1993; thus the most recent
federal appellate decisions appear in the *Federal Reporter, Third Series* (F.3d). In 2001,
West Publishing created the *Federal Appendix* (Fed. Appx. or F. App'x) to make available otherwise unpublished circuit court of appeals decisions. Such opinions generally
may not be cited in legal documents as precedents, but lawyers and researchers still
like to have access to them. Since the *Federal Appendix* is such a new publication, we
have the added confusion that it is in its first series, though it is technically an appendix to the *Federal Reporter*'s third series.

Each state's judiciary publishes its own case reports. Thus we may see references,
for example, to the *Wisconsin Reporter* or the *New York Supplement*. Academic libraries at most colleges without law schools do not bother to subscribe to each and every
state's reporters. Rather, they tend to subscribe to yet another West series of publications. West's regional reporters conveniently break down the states into seven separate areas—the Atlantic (A.), the Pacific (P.), the Northeastern (N.E.), the
Northwestern (N.W.), the Southern (So.), the Southeastern (S.E.), and the Southwestern (S.W.). Two important caveats are in order. First, do not always look for logic,
geographic or otherwise, in the assignment of a state to a region. Illinois decisions are
found in the *Northeastern Reporter*, Michigan's in the *Northwestern Reporter*. Second,
because a case appears in one West regional reporter and not another is not at all
relevant to the precedential value of a case. In other words, do not confuse a federal

appellate decision's *circuit* (very important to know when determining the case's precedential scope) and a state decision's West Publishing region.

Here are the states that each of West's regional reporters covers:

Atlantic: Connecticut, Delaware, the District of Columbia, Maine, Maryland, New Hampshire, New Jersey, Pennsylvania, Rhode Island, Vermont

Northeastern: Illinois, Indiana, Massachusetts, New York, Ohio

Northwestern: Iowa, Michigan, Minnesota, Nebraska, North Dakota, South Dakota, Wisconsin

Pacific: Alaska, Arizona, California, Colorado, Hawaii, Idaho, Kansas, Montana, Nevada, New Mexico, Oklahoma, Oregon, Utah, Washington, Wyoming

Southeastern: Georgia, North Carolina, South Carolina, Virginia, West Virginia

Southern: Alabama, Florida, Louisiana, Mississippi

Southwestern: Arkansas, Kentucky, Missouri, Tennessee, Texas

Just as was the case with the reporting of federal appellate cases, when the volume number of a regional reporter gets very high, West will start numbering again in a new series. Some of the regional reporters are in their second series, some in their third.

Legal Citations.

If you have been glancing at the footnotes in this chapter, you have already been exposed to the way in which court decisions are cited. The general format is almost always the same. First we have the name of the case. Generically, the name is A v. B. At the trial level, this name means that A is the plaintiff and B the defendant. If this case has reached the appellate level, A would be the **appellant** (the unsuccessful litigant at the level below) and B would be the **respondent** (i.e., B won below).

The next part of the citation is the volume number, followed by the name of the reporter and the page number on which the text of the case begins. (Subsequent numbers indicate the pages on which specific material appears—for example, the page on which quoted text may be found.) Finally, in parentheses, is the date when the court decided the case. If the context would not otherwise already have indicated it, this date may be preceded by an abbreviation telling which court made the decision. With federal appellate decisions, this notation is typically the number of the federal circuit. With federal district decisions, it will be the name of the district court (every state has at least one federal district, and some may have an "eastern" and a "western" or a "northern" and a "southern" district). Because citations for the West regional reporters do not tell which state court issued a particular ruling—any of thirteen states' courts may have written a decision that ends up in the *Pacific Reporter*—we often find a reference to the specific court here too.

One additional complication needs mentioning. When a legal dispute has been through more than one layer of adjudication, we sometimes find it helpful to give its entire judicial "pedigree" in its citation. The most frequent additions to the citation thus indicate whether a lower court ruling has been affirmed (typically, abbreviated as *aff'd*) or reversed (*rev'd*) on appeal.

Let us look at an example:

Harper & Row v. Nation Enterprises,

557 F. Supp. 1067 (S.D.N.Y. 1983), *rev'd*, 723 F.2d 195 (2d Cir. 1983), *rev'd*, 471 U.S. 539 (1985).

This example is a full citation to a real court case that we discuss in chapter 6, when we talk about copyright. For now, what can we learn about the case's history from its citation?

The litigants are Harper & Row, a book publisher, and Nation Enterprises, the company that publishes the magazine the *Nation*.

The U.S. District Court for the Southern District of New York heard the case and issued its decision in 1983. The district court decision can be found beginning on page 1067 in volume 557 of the *Federal Supplement*. Whoever lost the case at this level (it turns out that Nation Enterprises lost) appealed to the Second Circuit Court of Appeals, whose decision can be found beginning on page 195 in volume 723 of the *Federal Reporter, Second Series*. We know further—from the first "rev'd" in the citation, even without reading the court's decision—that the appellate court reversed the lower court ruling. We know also that whoever lost the case in the Second Circuit (the prevailing party in the original trial) appealed the appellate decision to the Supreme Court, whose decision begins on page 539 in volume 471 of *United States Reports*. The second "rev'd" tells us that the Supreme Court made the appeal worthwhile, by reversing the appellate court, thus making the original winner the ultimate winner. There are times when the only citation available for an unpublished (or not yet published) court decision is one provided by a legal database such as Westlaw or LEXIS. These kinds of citations are very similar to more traditional ones, except that the year of the decision is given instead of a nonexistent volume number, and the database assigns its own number to the case in lieu of a page number. Thus, for example, a decision might be cited as 2006 U.S. Dist. LEXIS 25936, or 2006 U.S. App. LEXIS 9449, usually followed by an indication as to exactly which district court or which appellate court produced the decision.

Sometimes communication law cases that never get published in the official reporters discussed above do find their way into private publications such as the *Media Law Reporter* or the *United States Patents Quarterly*. In the pages of this book you will occasionally find citations to cases published in those outlets.

Some Additional Legal Research Tools

In these few pages, we cannot possibly cover everything you need to know about conducting legal research. Law students take full courses on the subject. Nonetheless, it is helpful to know how to find the text of laws themselves and how to find information about general principles of law even when you do not have a particular court case in mind.

You already know that you can obtain the full text of court cases from either official government publications or from West. The same is true of the texts of federal laws. Congress publishes an official version, called the *United States Code* (abbreviated U.S.C.). For several reasons, however, most researchers prefer to use privately published versions of the code—either West's *United States Code Annotated* (abbreviated U.S.C.A.). or LEXIS's *United States Code Service* (U.S.C.S.). These sources include not only the text of a law but also convenient references to other related statutes and court decisions that have interpreted the law or may have even struck down portions of it as unconstitutional. Each state publishes its own laws as well, and in each state at least one privately published annotated version of the law is also available.

Suppose you find yourself in a law library with a general research question in mind, rather than the name of a specific court case or citation to a particular statute. Although maneuvering through a legal collection can be quite daunting, there exist standard reference works in the law that are not really more difficult to use than ordinary encyclopedias. The *American Law Reports* (A.L.R.) series, for example, is a reference work consisting of appellate court cases that the editors believe have established important principles of law. The A.L.R. series is indexed topically and includes references to related court cases and to critical commentaries. *Corpus Juris Secundum*, published by West, is a helpful resource that boasts over a hundred volumes and a comprehensive index of legal subjects, including many of direct relevance to communication law. Another frequently consulted source is the second edition of *American Jurisprudence*, once published by Lawyers Cooperative Publishing, but since taken over by West. Several states have their own encyclopedias as well, such as *Massachusetts Jurisprudence* and *Illinois Law and Practice*.

Law review articles are also helpful research tools (even if judges sometimes report that they are little help in their own decision making because they are written more for theoreticians than for practitioners).[68] Virtually every major law school in this country and throughout the world publishes at least one scholarly journal, called a law review. Most law reviews, such as the *Harvard Law Review* or the *Yale Law Journal*, are designed to be of interest to a general legal audience. There are, however, a number of legal periodicals—some published by law schools, some by nonprofit

---

68. Adam Liptak, "When Rendering Decisions, Judges Are Finding Law Reviews Irrelevant," *New York Times*, March 19, 2007, A8.

associations—that specialize in communication law. Among them are *Communication Law and Policy*, *Communication and the Law*, the *Federal Communications Law Journal*, the *Journal of Freedom of Expression* (formerly the *Free Speech Yearbook*), *CommLaw Conspectus*, *Hastings Communications and Entertainment Law Journal*, the *Journal of Art and Entertainment Law*, *Loyola of Los Angeles Entertainment Law Review*, *Media Law and Policy*, *Michigan Telecommunications and Technology Law Review*, and *UCLA Entertainment Law Review*.

Just as the *Readers' Guide to Periodical Literature* is a handy guide to general circulation magazines, there are a few indexes to the major and even the more obscure law journals. By far the most often consulted such resource is the *Index to Legal Periodicals*. You can also search through law review articles online in LEXIS or in Westlaw.

The *Shepard's Citations* series can help you make sure that a case you have read is still "good law"—that it has not been overturned by a higher court. Your librarian or your instructor will be able to show you how to use this valuable reference. The online version of *Shepard's* is especially valuable, in that the user is forewarned that a given court case has received "negative references" and may have been overturned by later decisions.

Finally, there has been an explosion of freely available websites for legal research. Some are managed by individual colleges or universities, others by private companies and nonprofit organizations. Many such sites pop up every year, and so no listing of them can possibly be complete or up to date. One especially helpful website for students of communication law, maintained by Professor Dale Herbeck of Boston College, provides in one handy place the full text of dozens of landmark U.S. Supreme Court communication law decisions. The URL for the Herbeck website's compilation of court decisions is www.bc.edu/bc_org/avp/cas/comm/free_speech/decisions.html. You may also find some of the following sites helpful:

CourtTV (www.courttv.com). This cable network's website is a great source of background information, especially concerning high-profile cases.

FindLaw (www.findlaw.com). This company's site includes federal and state cases, law reviews, and information about law schools.

GPO Access (www.gpoaccess.gov). This site is maintained by the U.S. Government Printing Office and provides access to the U.S. Code, Public Laws, the Code of Federal Regulations, and the Federal Register, among other sources.

Internet Legal Research Guide (www.ilrg.com). This website is most useful as an index to other legal sites; it lists thousands of them worldwide.

Legal Information Institute (www.law.cornell.edu). This site, maintained by Cornell Law School, is a useful starting point for legal research.

Thomas (thomas.loc.gov). This website, maintained by the Library of Congress, is a great source of information on bills and legislative histories.

THINGS TO REMEMBER

Finding the Cases

- U. S. Supreme Court decisions can be found in many places:
  - *United States Reports* (abbreviated U.S.)
  - *Supreme Court Reporter* (S. Ct.)
  - *United States Law Week* (U.S.L.W.)
- Federal appellate decisions are most easily found in the *Federal Reporter* (F., F.2d, or F.3d).
- Federal district court decisions are found in the *Federal Supplement* (F. Supp. or F. Supp. 2d) or *Federal Appendix* (Fed. Appx. or F. App'x.).
- State decisions can be found in official state reporters or more frequently in academic libraries, in West Publishing's "regional reporters" (Atlantic, Pacific, Northeastern, Northwestern, Southern, Southeastern, and Southwestern).
- Legal citations are generally in the form of volume number, name of reporter, page number, court, and date decided, as in 878 S.W.2d 577 (Tex. 1994).
- The text of federal and state statutes follows a similar citation format.
- Law libraries also boast several topically organized encyclopedias and indexes that can help in doing research.
- Many websites can also be helpful to students of communication law.

Chapter Summary

What we call communication law actually comes from many sources, including the federal and state constitutions, statutes, actions by regulatory agencies, executive orders, and the common law.

With respect to the U.S. Constitution, the First Amendment—especially its Free Speech Clause and Free Press Clause—is of most importance to media professionals. Several other provisions of the Constitution have implications for the practice of journalism. Some state constitutions give individuals greater rights to free speech than does the First Amendment.

The common-law tradition of establishing and adjusting precedents is an important part of our jurisprudence. Courts may follow, modify, distinguish, or overturn an earlier case. Judges' decisions tell who wins a case; their opinions tell why they reached this result. Opinions may be majority, plurality, concurring, or dissenting. The federal judiciary, as well as most state systems, are in three layers, a trial level and two appellate levels. Trial courts deal with questions of law and fact, whereas appellate courts are generally restricted to matters of law.

Chapter 2

THE DEVELOPMENT OF FREEDOM OF SPEECH

Perhaps we should not be surprised by survey results reported in 2006 showing that far more Americans can name the Simpsons cartoon family or the judges on *American Idol* than can identify the protections offered by the First Amendment. And it gets worse:

- 21 percent thought that the First Amendment gives us a right to own pets.
- 20 percent thought it gives us a right to drive.
- 36 percent indicated that it gave women the right to vote (not actually done until 1920, in the Nineteenth Amendment).
- 55 percent reported that it gives us a right to a jury trial (this is actually in the Seventh Amendment).
- 38 percent believed that it is the source of the right against self-incrimination (this despite the ubiquity of the phrase "taking the *Fifth*").[1]

Certainly there is much misunderstanding about the First Amendment, and there are also many misconceptions about the historical development of freedom of speech in general. Americans often presume that freedom of speech began with our own colonial experience or was imported to the United States after having begun in England. In fact, an appreciation for freedom of expression can be traced to ancient Greece and to the Confucian era in China, indeed perhaps even to preliterate societies.[2] A lengthy discourse on freedom of speech through the ages is beyond the scope

---

1. McCormick Tribune Freedom Museum, "Characters from 'the Simpsons' More Well Known to Americans Than Their First Amendment Freedoms, Survey Finds," press release, March 1, 2006, http://www.freedommuseum.us/html/press.php.

2. Douglas Fraleigh and Joseph Tuman, *Freedom of Speech in the Marketplace of Ideas* (New York: St. Martin's Press, 1997), chapter 2.

of this book. Some familiarity with the concept as it was understood during the colonial period and the British experience that so influenced the Founding Fathers is, however, essential to understanding the various legal doctrines presented in subsequent chapters.

Speech as *the* American Freedom?

An often-repeated story tells of nineteenth-century statesman Daniel Webster who, when asked which of the many freedoms enjoyed by Americans is most important, unhesitatingly replied that it must be freedom of speech. If stripped of all other freedoms, his reasoning went, this freedom is the one he could use to win each of the others back. Along these lines, it is worth remembering also that when FDR delivered his famous "four freedoms" speech to Congress in 1941, the first of the "essential human freedoms" that he felt that all world citizens should be granted was freedom of speech.

Perhaps we should not carry this romance with free speech too far. The Founding Fathers have often had attributed to them the belief that freedom of speech was surely the most important of all the principles articulated in the Bill of Rights; after all, they did put it in the *First* Amendment. The facts get in the way of this assertion, however. What we now call the First Amendment was actually submitted as amendment number three in the Bill of Rights. The first two amendments—one dealing with apportionment of seats in the House of Representatives and the other prohibiting members of Congress from granting themselves a raise in salary that would take effect before the next election—failed to win approval.

Even if the "first-ness" of the First Amendment is a historic accident rather than a symbol of the founders' priorities, the wording of that constitutional provision seems to suggest that issues of freedom of speech and press were indeed very special to the document's drafters. The First Amendment is written as an absolute promise that Congress shall make *no* law abridging the freedoms enumerated within. Unlike the wording of many other nations' analogous guarantees and those in many state constitutions, there is no requirement that citizens behave "responsibly" to enjoy these rights. Think too of some of the other guarantees provided in the Bill of Rights. In the Fourth Amendment, for example, we learn that we are free only from "unreasonable" searches and seizures. The Fifth Amendment warns that our property, our liberty, and even our life can be taken away from us as long as the government follows an unarticulated set of rules that together constitute "due process." The Eighth Amendment does not, of course, protect us from any and all kinds of punishment, but only from the "cruel and unusual" ones; that same amendment also tells us that if we are suspected of a crime, we may be required to pay any amount of bail short of "excessive," should we wish to avoid staying in jail until our trial date.

A claimed reverence for freedom of speech does seem to be one of the most defining characteristics of our nation, even as compared with other Western-style democracies. (I say "claimed" reverence because Americans are also, paradoxically, notoriously disconnected from this freedom; the majority of citizens do not bother to vote, and far fewer get actively involved in the political process.) In the United States, for example, the existence of the Freedom of Information Act makes it more difficult for the government to withhold information from its citizens than is the case in Great Britain, which has its Official Secrets Act. For better or worse, the United States is very unusual in the degree to which it tolerates hate speech. Whereas some nations (such as India) have followed the American model of libel law that makes it very difficult for government officials to sue for defamation, both Canada and England have rejected it. The Canadian Supreme Court has embraced a theory, resoundingly rejected by the U.S. judiciary, of sexually oriented speech as a civil rights violation.

If participation in a system of freedom of expression is so much a part of what it means to be American, it behooves us to know something about the origins of that freedom. The discussion of that history is broken down into two time periods. The first covers the period from Europeans' arrival in the Americas up through World War I. Then the story is carried forward from that era—when the Supreme Court first began to give some guidance as to the meaning of the First Amendment—to the present.

Freedom of Speech from the Colonial Period through World War I

Ask any American ten-year-old why groups of British, Spanish, and other nationalities made the arduous journey across the Atlantic in the 1500s and beyond, and you will hear a tale of courageous and oppressed minorities seeking political and religious freedom. Certainly there is more than a kernel of truth to this assessment, although more mundane commercial interests also played a large part. Still, most of the individual groups of settlers were rather homogenous, especially in terms of their religious preferences. Thus, it is not surprising that many of these groups, once settled in what were to become the Americas, established communities every bit as inhospitable to those with differing views as were the regimes they fled.

The Puritans who settled the Massachusetts Bay Colony were not especially noted for tolerance of diverse views. Banishments, excommunication, public whippings, and mutilations were common punishments for speaking out against the faith or against the colony's government. Similarly harsh sanctions were often imposed in Connecticut and throughout New England. Governor Dale's code governing Virginia as of 1610, for example, established the death penalty for anyone who spoke out against the tenets of Christian faith. Even the most tolerant of the colonies seem rather intolerant by today's standards in that freedom of religious expression was generally granted only to professed Christians.

Concerning the early colonists' respect for the working press, consider that the very first newspaper in the New World, Benjamin Harris's *Publick Occurrences Both Foreign and Domestic*, was shut down in Massachusetts after its very first issue was printed. When James Franklin's *New England Courant* published an article critical of the colony's government, he was promptly jailed (during which time his younger brother Benjamin took over the paper).

To be fair, there is some evidence of increasing tolerance for dissenting views during the colonial period. Even as early as the 1600s, there was a trend toward treating those judged guilty of seditious libel (i.e., criticizing the government) more and more leniently. Punishments such as physical violence (ear cropping, breaking arms and legs, tongue boring, and whipping) and public humiliation (use of the pillory or the stocks, or simply forcing the accused to recant publicly and beg for forgiveness) gave way over time to sanctions such as fines or the required posting of a bond that would be forfeitable only in the event of further transgressions.[3]

Probably the most dramatic example of how strongly at least some of the colonists felt toward freedom of the press was the seditious libel prosecution in the 1730s of *New York Weekly Journal* publisher John Peter Zenger, who had been imprisoned for several months prior to his trial for publishing statements highly critical of the colony's governor, William Crosby. During this era, truth was not an accepted defense to the charge of sedition. Indeed, the logic of the day suggested that because the purpose of such laws was to avoid inflaming the passions of the people against the king and his governors, truthful criticisms would be all the more dangerous.

Andrew Hamilton, who made the closing arguments on behalf of Zenger, openly invited the jury to ignore the letter of the law and to find on behalf of Zenger precisely because he had not printed any substantial untruths. The jury did indeed acquit Zenger, to the delight of those assembled in the courtroom.

The founders would not have been able to muster the necessary votes to ensure the Constitution's adoption had they not assured their constituents that a Bill of Rights would be added. With respect to the First Amendment, there was considerable difference of opinion concerning whether the individual states should be enjoined from abridging citizens' freedom of expression or whether the proscription should apply only to the newly formed federal government. The latter view prevailed, and thus the amendment was phrased in terms of what *Congress* shall not do. Historians of the period point out also that it is not entirely clear what "freedom of speech" and "freedom of the press" meant to the drafters. Were citizens being promised freedom from any and all postpublication sanctions for communicative acts, or were they merely being assured that they would not be subject to **prior restraint**, to prepublica-

---

3. Larry D. Eldridge, *A Distant Heritage: The Growth of Free Speech in Early America* (New York: New York University Press, 1994).

tion censorship? A later section of this chapter explores the issue of prior restraint in more detail.

Despite the First Amendment's strong wording, it took a rather short amount of time for the new Congress to enact laws that abridged freedom of speech. France and England were at war, and fears ran high that the United States would be drawn into the war. Congress passed and President Adams signed the **Alien and Sedition Acts**. Collectively, these acts gave the government increased powers to detain and deport noncitizens and criminalized the dissemination of some kinds of criticisms of the government.

Persons convicted under the Sedition Act could be fined heavily and imprisoned for up to five years. There were over a dozen prosecutions under the law, several directed against editors of the leading opposition newspapers of the day. Two lessons can be culled from the Sedition Act. First, the act compels us to remember that the same founders who had voted for the Bill of Rights also convinced themselves of the need to stifle political speech. Second, the act was a strategic failure in that those jailed for violating it became folk heroes; moreover, the demise of the Federalists resulted in large part from popular animosity toward that party's support of the act.

The period between 1801 (when the Sedition Act expired) and 1917 (when Congress passed the **Espionage Act**, discussed below) is characterized by a lack of major developments in First Amendment jurisprudence (even though the Supreme Court

The Sedition Act of 1798

If any persons shall unlawfully combine or conspire together, with intent to oppose any measure or measures of the government of the United States, . . . and if any person or persons . . . shall counsel, advise or attempt to procure any insurrection, riot, unlawful assembly, or combination, . . . he or they shall be deemed guilty of a high misdemeanor. . . .

. . . If any person shall write, print, utter or publish, or shall cause or procure to be written, printed, uttered or published . . . any false, scandalous and malicious writing or writings against the government of the United States, or either house of the Congress . . . or the President . . . with intent to defame . . . or to bring them . . . into contempt or disrepute, or to excite against them . . . the hatred of the good people of the United States, or to stir up sedition within the United States . . . for opposing or resisting any law of the United States, or any act of the President of the United States, . . . then such person . . . shall be punished.

THINGS TO REMEMBER

The Colonial Experience Forward

- The early colonial experience included much political and religious intolerance.
- The Zenger jury concluded that true speech should not be punished.
- The founders chose not to apply the First Amendment to the individual states.
- For at least some of the founders, freedom of speech and freedom of the press probably only meant freedom from prior restraint.
- The fact that the First Amendment is *first* in the Bill of Rights is merely a coincidence.
- Despite the First Amendment, Congress quickly enacted the Sedition Act.

handed down dozens of decisions affecting the act of communication). Certainly there was much censorship in the Civil War era, especially directed against those speaking out against slavery.[4] And the latter portion of the nineteenth century required the courts to deal repeatedly with the issue of obscenity in response to congressional actions that, among other things, prohibited the use of the mails to send sexually oriented matter. By and large, at least with respect to definitive Supreme Court interpretations of the First Amendment, these "forgotten years"[5] were not a time of much doctrinal advance and also not the focus of much scholarship. Therefore, a discussion of the Court's First Amendment doctrine as it developed in the World War I era and beyond is appropriate.

Freedom of Speech Doctrine Emerges

In March 1993, a brutal triple murder was committed in Silver Spring, Maryland, a suburb of Washington, D.C. James Perry killed Mildred Horn, her eight-year-old quadriplegic son Trevor, and Trevor's nurse, Janice Saunders, by shooting Mildred Horn and Saunders through the eyes and by strangling the boy. Perry acted as a contract killer hired by Ms. Horn's ex-husband. After Perry was successfully prosecuted, the victims' families brought suit in federal court against the publisher of a book called *Hit Man*, which Perry apparently consulted in planning his crime.

A three-judge panel of the Court of Appeals for the Fourth Circuit held against the publisher in late 1997, finding that the book was little more than a blueprint for

---

4. Michael Kent Curtis, "The Curious History of Attempts to Suppress Antislavery Speech, Press, and Petition in 1835–37, 89 *Northwestern University Law Review* 785 (1996).

5. David M. Rabban, "The First Amendment in Its Forgotten Years," 90 *Yale Law Journal* 514 (1981).

homicide that inarguably aided and abetted Perry in the commission of his heinous offenses.[6]

Is such a ruling consistent with the First Amendment? What of a "copycat" terrorist who hones his or her craft by taking careful notes from detailed journalistic explanations as to how pipe bombs are constructed (after the Centennial Olympic Park bombing in Atlanta) or how fertilizer can be used as a powerfully destructive explosive (as in the Oklahoma City case)? Might victims' families be permitted to win damages from the likes of CNN? Consider also that many talented mystery writers include in their stories factual information that can similarly aid in the commission of future crimes.

The process of seeking answers to these questions is complicated and requires that we develop an understanding of the Supreme Court's doctrine concerning when speech that might incite others to commit crimes can itself be criminalized. This doctrine began to emerge in the World War I era and continued through the McCarthy period and beyond. It is not an exaggeration to say that the Court used the cases we discuss here to explain what the First Amendment means.

In the pages that follow you will learn much about antiwar activists, anarchists, and political dissidents of many persuasions. These early cases did not typically involve the mass media. Much of the doctrine that emerged from these cases, however, has laid the foundation for contemporary applications of the First Amendment in a wide variety of circumstances, from regulation of advertising to broadcast station licensing.

The Clear and Present Danger Test: *Schenck v. United States*

The United States had entered into the "war to end all wars," which would later be known as World War I. Almost without exception, even the freest of nations curtail the amount of liberty enjoyed by their citizens the moment war is declared. The United States in 1917 certainly manifested this tendency when Congress passed the Espionage Act (amended in 1918). Not surprisingly, the act forbade any attempt to cause insubordination among the military or in any way to obstruct the draft. It also criminalized any speech or writing deemed "disloyal, profane, scurrilous, or abusive" of "the form of government of the United States . . . or the flag." The penalty for violating the law could be as severe as twenty years' imprisonment.

Charles Schenck, the general secretary of the Socialist Party, was convicted under the Espionage Act for sending leaflets to young men who had been called and accepted for military service, imploring them to resist the draft and to recognize that draftees are little more than slaves. Writing for a unanimous Supreme Court, Justice Holmes upheld Schenck's conviction. The only acceptable justification for suppress-

---

6. *Rice v. Paladin Enterprises*, 128 F.3d 233 (4th Cir. 1997). The Supreme Court, in April 1998, refused to hear the appeal, thus setting the stage for a possible trial in the case. However, in May 1999, the parties entered into an out-of-court settlement involving a multimillion-dollar payment to the plaintiffs and the turning over to them of all the publisher's remaining copies of *Hit Man*.

ing political speech, Holmes concluded, is if the speaker's words "are used in such circumstances and are of such a nature as to create a clear and present danger that they will bring about the substantive evils that Congress has a right to prevent."[7] Holmes's opinion in *Schenck*—also remembered for having added to the lexicon the admonition that freedom of speech, although important, does not protect us from "falsely shouting fire in a theatre"—was the birth of the "clear and present danger" test for measuring the scope of First Amendment freedoms. It is interesting that although the test's first appearance is in the context of an opinion *upholding* a criminal conviction for engaging in dissident speech, in later years the test evolved to emphasize that the state's power to punish such speech is very limited. The Supreme Court has cited *Schenck*'s famous phrase dozens of times in adjudicating First Amendment issues ranging from leased-access channels on cable TV systems and FCC broadcast indecency standards to regulation of advertising and campaign-finance reform.

The Marketplace of Ideas: *Abrams v. United States*

A few months after *Schenck*, the Supreme Court upheld another Espionage Act conviction. In this instance, however, Justice Holmes (joined by Justice Brandeis) dissented and in so doing gave birth to a metaphor more influential than any other in the history of First Amendment jurisprudence. At issue again were antiwar leaflets, this time printed by Jacob Abrams and four other Russian nationals living in the United States and distributed by such means as dropping them out of an office building window. Writing for a seven-person majority, Justice Clarke found that the intent of the offending literature was "to persuade the persons to whom it was addressed to turn a deaf ear to patriotic appeals in behalf of the government of the United States, and to cease to render it assistance in the prosecution of the war."[8]

Justices Holmes and Brandeis expressed dismay for the defendants' being sentenced to twenty years in jail "for the publishing of two leaflets that [they] had as much right to publish as the government has to publish the Constitution of the United States now vainly invoked by them." For them, the defendants' intent was to express support for the Russian Revolution, not to hinder the U.S. war effort. The government's prosecution, the dissenters argued, did not seem aimed at the ends sought by the defendants, but rather at their political ideology itself. They argued that such government actions, designed to "sweep away all opposition," ignore the "theory of our Constitution" that "the best test of truth is the power of [a] thought to get itself accepted in the competition of the market."

The "marketplace of ideas" metaphor has served as a rationale for dozens of Supreme Court and hundreds of lower court decisions. As expressed by Justice Holmes, it seems to be an instrumental value, one whose good comes from its likelihood to

---

7. *Schenck v. United States*, 249 U.S. 47, 52 (1919).
8. *Abrams v. United States*, 250 U.S. 616, 620–621 (1919).

help the truth emerge. It can also be viewed as a good in and of itself. The FCC, for example, has claimed over the years to embrace the principle that a multitude of voices speaking over broadcast and cable channels is a desirable thing.

An intriguing variation on the marketplace of ideas metaphor is offered by Professor Robert Jensen of the University of Texas, who argues instead for a First Amendment philosophy built around the notion of a potluck dinner. Whereas marketplace theory presumes that ideas will compete and one will eventually win, the potluck metaphor presumes that there is more than enough truth to go around, that *the* truth will be found in combining the best features of many "dishes."[9]

Not Only Congress, but the States, Too: *Gitlow v. New York*

The First Amendment, it will be recalled, tells only the *federal* government (indeed, only Congress) that it may not abridge freedom of speech and freedom of the press. This decision was a conscious one on the part of the drafters, who considered and rejected an alternate phrasing that would have restricted the power of each individual state government as well. In 1925, 134 years after the formal adoption of the Bill of Rights, the Supreme Court somewhat unceremoniously held that the First Amendment bars the states, too, from abridging Americans' freedom of expression. Justice Sanford accomplished this change in one sentence: "For present purposes we may and do assume," he said, "that freedom of speech and of the press—which are protected by the First Amendment from abridgment by Congress—are among the fundamental personal rights and 'liberties' protected by the due process clause of the Fourteenth Amendment from impairment by the States."[10]

The context was the Supreme Court's decision to uphold Benjamin Gitlow's conviction, under New York's criminal anarchy statute, for having written a "Left Wing Manifesto" seeming to advocate the government's overthrow, by violent means if necessary. The majority opinion also posits a distinction between "abstract doctrine" or "academic discussion," which would presumably be protected by the First Amendment, and "language advocating, advising, or teaching the overthrow of organized government by unlawful means," which the New York law appropriately prohibited. The distinction was one that Justices Holmes and Brandeis found unacceptable, and they once again dissented. Gitlow was not trying to "induce an uprising against government at once"; at most he sought such action "at some indefinite time in the future." The dissenters thus emphasized that a "clear and present danger" must in fact be *present*.

The "More Speech" Prescription: *Whitney v. California*

Two years after the *Gitlow* decision made clear that the First Amendment applied not only to federal but also state infringements on free speech, another criminal syn-

---

9. Robert Jensen, "First Amendment Potluck," 3 *Communication Law and Policy* 563 (1998).
10. *Gitlow v. New York*, 268 U.S. 652, 666 (1925).

dicalism prosecution, this time from the other coast, was before the Supreme Court.[11] Anita Whitney, who coincidentally was the niece of former Supreme Court justice Stephen Field, had been an active member of the Communist Labor Party in California. The immediate impetus for her prosecution seems to have been her attendance at the party's organizing convention, where, although she herself argued for a more moderate stance, the gathered delegates voted their full allegiance to the goal of an international workers' revolution.

The Supreme Court unanimously upheld Whitney's conviction under the state law, largely because her attorneys did not timely raise the federal constitutional issue that might have led to her vindication: whether her participation at the party convention constituted a "clear and present danger" to the state. Thus, even Justice Brandeis's stirring words from the case were part of a concurring rather than dissenting opinion:

> No danger flowing from speech can be deemed clear and present, unless the incidence of the evil apprehended is so imminent that it may befall before there is opportunity for full discussion. If there be time to expose through discussion the falsehood and fallacies, to avert the evil by the processes of education, *the remedy to be applied is more speech, not enforced silence.*[12]

The emphasized phrase carries enormous implications for First Amendment jurisprudence. Rather than prohibit political, religious, or similar charitable groups from soliciting donations in airports, the "more speech, not enforced silence" prescription argues for the use of prominently placed signs and frequently made announcements to the effect that the solicitors are acting on their own behalf only, not with the approval of the airport's governing authority. Such additional speech might even caution the public to donate only to reputable organizations, to say "no" if in doubt. The *Whitney* rationale also seems to argue for permitting advertisers to use clever graphics and production techniques to make their print ads look almost like news articles and their infomercials resemble television interview programs, just as long as some additional speech explicitly alerting consumers that they are in fact advertisements is required. That same rationale suggests that attorneys who advertise that they will take cases on a contingency-fee basis—that clients "pay us nothing unless we win"—make clear somewhere in their ads the details of the promise. Does it apply only to the lawyers' own fees or also to reimbursement of out-of-pocket expenses such as court filing fees? In fact, courts and regulating agencies have used the *Whitney* rationale in all these kinds of situations and more.

---

11. *Whitney v. California*, 274 U.S. 357 (1927).
12. *Whitney*, 274 U.S. at 377 (Brandeis, J., concurring) (emphasis added). Justice Holmes joined in Justice Brandeis's opinion.

The Smith Act Cases

The cold war intensified in the late 1940s and throughout the 1950s. The atrocities that accompanied Joseph Stalin's reign began to come to light. Winston Churchill's famous "iron curtain" speech warned the free world that communism could be every bit as threatening as fascism. So it was that a statute passed by Congress in 1940 out of fear that radical right-wing politics could destroy the American way of life was now applied to the political left. The Alien Registration Act, popularly known as the **Smith Act**, criminalized advocacy of the government's overthrow as well as knowingly becoming part of a group whose members embraced such a goal. Eugene Dennis, the secretary-general of the American Communist Party, along with several other party officials, was prosecuted under the Smith Act. In upholding their convictions, Chief Justice Vinson wrote that the Smith Act was constitutional because it "is directed at advocacy, not discussion," that the clear and present danger test "cannot mean that before the Government may act, it must wait until the *putsch* is about to be executed, the plans have been laid and the signal is awaited." Rather, Vinson adopted the interpretation suggested by a lower court: "In each case [courts must decide] whether the gravity of the evil, discounted by its improbability, justifies such invasion of free speech as is necessary to avoid the danger."[13] There is always some competing interest to be balanced against free speech claims, Vinson was telling us, and one can hardly imagine a more serious counterweight than the fear that the government might be violently overthrown.

Whereas *Dennis* turned on the distinction between "advocacy" of revolution and mere "discussion" of revolution, six years later the Court shifted the line a bit, holding that advocacy of abstract doctrine would be permissible, but not advocacy of action. The occasion was the justices' reviewing the Smith Act convictions of fourteen leftists from California. The government's case against the accused consisted primarily of their having assumed leadership positions within the Communist Party and their having written some articles in the *Daily Worker*, the party's newspaper. This time, however, the Court overturned the convictions. Justice John Marshall Harlan's opinion criticized the lower court for having assumed that "advocacy, irrespective of its tendency to generate action, is punishable." Such an interpretation of the act is far too broad, Harlan concluded. Instead, the crucial distinction should be that "those to whom the advocacy is addressed must be urged to do something, now or in the future, rather than merely to believe in something."[14]

This doctrine was quite an advance over previous doctrine in terms of the amount of political speech it protected. The Court, however, had not yet completed its rewrit-

---

13. *Dennis v. United States*, 341 U.S. 494, 502, 509–510 (1951).
14. *Yates v. United States*, 354 U.S. 298, 320, 325 (1957).

ing of the "clear and present danger" test. That task would have to wait another dozen years.

The *Brandenburg* Test: Imminent Lawless Action

At a Ku Klux Klan rally on a farm in Hamilton County, Ohio, Klan leader Clarence Brandenburg told his handful of supporters that "we're not a revengent organization, but if our President, our Congress, our Supreme Court, continues to suppress the white, Caucasian race, it's possible that there might have to be some revengeance taken." Participants were also overheard to offer such prescriptions for society's ills as "bury the Niggers" and "send the Jews back to Israel." Brandenburg was convicted of violating Ohio's criminal syndicalism statute. The Supreme Court's unanimous decision overturning that conviction established the test that to this day still determines when political speech is protected by the First Amendment. The test, appearing in a short per curiam opinion, says that "the constitutional guarantees of free speech and free press do not permit a State to forbid or proscribe advocacy of the use of force or of law violation except where such advocacy is directed to inciting or producing imminent lawless action and is likely to incite or produce such action."[15]

Notice that the test has elements of both content and context. As to content, the Court emphasizes that only very specific kinds of advocacy may be prohibited. The "imminence" requirement is a forceful restatement of the earlier "clear and *present* danger" test. We know from later decisions that the Court takes the imminence requirement very seriously. In 1973, for example, a unanimous Court overturned a Vietnam War protester's incitement conviction in large part because he told his cohorts, in response to the police having set up barricades, that they would all "take the fucking street *later*." The Court's interpretation of this sentence was that "at best the statement could be taken as counsel for present moderation," and that "at worst it amounted to nothing more than advocacy of illegal action *at some indefinite future time*."[16]

The *Brandenburg* test's contextual elements are apparent from the demand that words must be *likely* to result in the speaker's desired lawbreaking. Speakers must be addressing an audience sufficiently sympathetic to their cause and sufficiently aroused to action that imminent illegality is, in fact, a likely outcome of their advocacy. This requirement leads us back to the *Hit Man* case introduced earlier in this chapter. The decision by the Fourth Circuit appellate panel is quite an anomaly, the first time a mass-distributed book has ever been held to constitute "incitement" under the *Brandenburg* test. More typically, courts find that mass media artifacts, whether print

---

15. *Brandenburg v. Ohio*, 395 U.S. 444, 447 (1969).
16. *Hess v. Indiana*, 414 U.S. 105, 108 (1973) (emphasis added).

media,[17] movies,[18] music,[19] or even video games,[20] are incapable of creating *imminent* lawless action.

That the publication of *Hit Man* may have led to actual homicides is disturbing, to be sure, but nowhere does the book suggest that readers target any specific individual. Not so some of the entries on the Nuremberg Files website, which disseminated names and addresses of doctors who perform abortions in the form of online "wanted" posters and expressed approval of those who carried out violent acts against such individuals. Such features of the site were "true threats," a closely divided Ninth Circuit Court of Appeals ruled, en banc.[21]

The USA Patriot Act

It is clear from our discussion of the evolution of First Amendment doctrine that the government often tries to abridge speech most when our national security is perceived to be in jeopardy. The Alien and Sedition Acts were passed to protect a nascent country, the Espionage Act when we were involved in "the war to end all wars," the Smith Act when the cold war with communism was in full swing. In each instance and others—such as President Lincoln's suspension of habeas corpus[22] during the Civil War, and the detention of Japanese Americans in internment camps during World War II—we have come to regret our excesses after the fact. If history is any guide, it is likely that we will look back upon our response to the 9/11 terrorist attacks as also being excessive in some ways.

Many of the issues with which historians will have to wrestle—whether detainees were inappropriately denied the protections accorded by the Geneva Conventions, how high up the chain of command fault for prisoner abuse lay[23]—although impor-

---

17. *Herceg v. Hustler Magazine*, 814 F.2d 1020 (5th Cir. 1987). But see *Braun v. Soldier of Fortune Magazine*, 968 F.2d 1110 (11th Cir. 1992), in which a magazine was held partially liable for a contract killing resulting from an advertiser who offered himself as a "gun for hire," a "professional mercenary" willing to consider "all jobs." Interestingly, the same magazine was let off the hook in an earlier case, where the offending advertiser more vaguely offered the services of a group of "ex-Marines" willing to engage in "high risk assignments." *Eimann v. Soldier of Fortune Magazine*, 880 F.2d 830 (5th Cir. 1989).

18. *Olivia N. v. National Broadcasting Co.*, 178 Cal. Rptr. 888 (Ct. App. 1981). The case involved a TV movie.

19. *Davidson v. Time Warner, Inc.*, 1997 U.S. Dist. LEXIS 21559, 25 Media L. Rep. (BNA) 1705 (S.D. Tex. 1997); *McCollum v. CBS, Inc.*, 249 Cal. Rptr. 187 (Ct. App. 1988).

20. *James v. Meow Media*, 300 F.3d 683 (6th Cir. 2002); *Wilson v. Midway Games*, 198 F. Supp. 2d 167 (D. Conn. 2002); *Sanders v. Acclaim Entertainment*, 188 F. Supp. 2d 1264 (D. Colo. 2002); *Watters v. TSR, Inc.*, 715 F. Supp. 819 (W.D. Ky. 1989).

21. *Planned Parenthood of the Columbia/Willamette, Inc. v. American Coalition of Life Activists*, 290 F.3d 1058 (9th Cir. 2002).

22. The phrase literally means "we have the body." It really amounts to a way of saying that we cannot imprison people arbitrarily.

23. See, e.g., *Rasul v. Rumsfeld*, 414 F. Supp. 2d 26 (D.D.C. 2006).

tant, are not directly relevant to *communication* law. The best-known legislative response to 9/11 was the almost immediate passage of the USA Patriot Act. At least two features of the law affect the act of communication. First, the law strengthens the government's hand when it denies a Freedom of Information Act (FOIA) request, whether from journalists or others, about matters arguably raising issues of national security. While a more complete explanation of the FOIA is postponed until chapter 7, suffice it to say for now that the government has successfully withheld details about who is being held in the prison at the U.S. naval base in Guantánamo Bay, Cuba, and the identity of their attorneys,[24] as well as details concerning how often the Department of Justice has used some of the new powers granted to it under the Patriot Act.[25]

One of those new powers granted to the FBI is the ability to issue "national security letters" (NSLs) without getting a judge's approval and without even presenting evidence that a targeted individual is suspected of a crime. The recipient of an NSL, generally a business or library listing the target as a patron, is subject to a **gag order** and may not discuss the FBI's demand with anyone. A Connecticut-based library association received an NSL about one of its patrons and tried to have the associated gag order lifted so that it could speak out publicly, including in front of a congressional committee, about the Patriot Act. A federal district court ruled in favor of the executive director of the library association,[26] but the injunction against the government's enforcement of the gag order was stayed by the Supreme Court for several months,[27] until the Second Circuit Court of Appeals determined that amendments to the act passed in 2006, explicitly giving librarians the right to appeal the use of national security letters, made the government's case moot.[28] In a press conference called to

ACLU attorney Ann Beeson together with Connecticut Library Connection plaintiff George Christian, who for many months was not permitted to tell anyone that he had received a national security letter from the FBI.

24. *Center for National Security Studies v. U.S. Department of Justice*, 331 F.3d 918 (D.C. Cir. 2003). But see *Associated Press v. U.S. Department of Defense*, 410 F. Supp. 2d 147 (S.D.N.Y. 2006).

25. *American Civil Liberties Union v. U.S. Department of Justice*, 321 F. Supp. 2d 24 (D.D.C. 2004); *American Civil Liberties Union v. U.S. Department of Justice*, 265 F. Supp. 2d 20 (D.D.C. 2003).

26. *Doe v. Gonzales*, 386 F. Supp. 2d 66 (D. Conn. 2005).

27. *Doe v. Gonzales*, 126 S. Ct. 1 (2005).

28. *Doe v. Gonzales*, 449 F. 3d 415 (2d Cir. 2006).

finally reveal their identities publicly, lead plaintiff George Christian, executive director of Connecticut's Library Connection, suggested that it was his and his cohorts' speech that had been rendered moot, that allowing him to speak only after Congress had acted was akin to "being allowed to call the fire department after the building has burned to the ground."[29]

There have also been rumblings about not only using the Patriot Act in the "war on terrorism" but adding state sedition laws and the federal Espionage Act to the arsenal as well. Those who argue for such prosecutions suggest that the First Amendment protections offered by, for example, *Brandenburg*'s "imminent lawless action" might not be applicable to the post-9/11 world. Brandenburg's speech was not uttered in wartime, after all.[30] Concerning the Espionage Act, Attorney General Alberto Gonzales has suggested using it to prosecute the *Washington Post* and the *New York Times* for publishing stories based on classified information about matters such as administration-sponsored secret prisons in eastern Europe (where "aggressive interrogation" techniques are presumably used) as well as warrantless surveillance of Americans' phone calls.[31]

Theories of First Amendment Adjudication

As we have seen, the Supreme Court's First Amendment jurisprudence began in earnest in the World War I era. The cases that produced this body of case law, culminating in the *Brandenburg* test, generally have involved criminal defendants whose words were uttered to incite presumably sympathetic listeners to engage in conduct that itself would likely be illegal. Such a scenario describes only one of many conflicts raising First Amendment issues. Most of the kinds of speech that define the scope of the chapters in this book—such as libel, invasion of privacy, covering the courts, and copyright and trademark infringements—do not involve speakers trying to incite others to take specific actions. It is no surprise, then, that there have been many different approaches to First Amendment litigation over the years. Indeed, neither the Supreme Court nor the many philosophers, political scientists, communication scholars, and law professors who have written lengthy essays on the topic have reached consensus as to what freedom of speech should include or when free speech claims should prevail over competing interests. In this section several of the competing theories of First Amendment adjudication are presented.

---

29. Lynn Tuohy, "Shushed No More," *Hartford Courant*, May 31, 2006, A1.

30. Adam Liptak, "Sedition: It Still Rolls off the Tongue," *New York Times*, May 7, 2006, sec. 4, 3.

31. Geoffrey Stone, "Scared of Scoops," *New York Times*, May 8, 2006, A21.

THINGS TO REMEMBER

Evolution of First Amendment Doctrine

- The Court's First Amendment doctrine emerged from cases involving incitement to illegal action.
- The following cases have involved the Espionage Act, the later Smith Act, or various state criminal syndicalism laws:
  - *Schenck v. United States*
    —Birth of the clear and present danger test
    —Falsely shouting fire in a crowded theater metaphor
  - *Abrams v. United States*
    —Marketplace of ideas
  - *Gitlow v. New York*
    —First Amendment now applies to the states, too
    —Holmes's dissent says that "every idea is an incitement"
  - *Whitney v. California*
    —Proper remedy to bad speech is more speech, not enforced silence
  - *Dennis v. United States*
    —"The gravity of the evil discounted by its improbability"
    —Actual advocacy versus "mere discussion"
  - *Yates v. United States*
    —Advocacy of action versus advocacy of abstract doctrine
  - *Brandenburg v. Ohio*
    —Advocacy of "imminent lawless action"
    —Must also be "likely to produce such action"
- There is also much litigation involving the Patriot Act, Congress's response to the 9/11 attacks.

Free Speech as the Absence of Prior Restraint?

Dating back at least to the sixteenth century, the preferred method of controlling the press in England had been to prevent offensive tracts from ever being published (rather than punishing the authors or the publishers after the fact). Either the Crown, the Church, or both controlled the printed word by licensing only a tiny group of publishing companies and requiring printers to post sizable monetary bonds that would be forfeited if their houses were ever to publish offensive materials.

The prevailing wisdom around the time of the American Revolution was that freedom of the press referred only to the absence of such prior restraints on the act of communication. The British jurist William Blackstone was a contemporary of the Founding Fathers, and James Madison, Thomas Jefferson, John Adams, and the others were quite familiar with Blackstone's *Commentaries on the Law of England*, published in 1769, which argued that the "liberty of speech . . . consists in laying no previous restraints upon publications, and not in freedom from censure for criminal matter when published."

As Steven Helle of the University of Illinois points out, one can argue both ends against the middle in a futile attempt to determine exactly what the founders themselves meant by "freedom of speech" and "freedom of the press." To be sure, Blackstone's definition of communication law was the prevailing one at the time. Did the framers adopt that definition as their own, or does their very act of crafting the First Amendment mean that they intended something more? Why enumerate protections for conduct already presumed to be protected? Then too, scholars have come down on both sides of the issue as to what should be made of Congress's having passed the Alien and Sedition Acts so soon after approving the First Amendment. Does the enactment of those oppressive laws count as evidence that the framers saw such after-the-fact punishments as consistent with the First Amendment, thus suggesting that the latter protected only against prior restraints? Then again, if the common wisdom was that the First Amendment protected only against prior restraints on communication, why the need for a law granting the government the "right" to prosecute seditious libel? Should not such a right be presumed?[32]

Whatever the framers may have meant by "freedom of the press," the more modern view, embraced by the U.S. Supreme Court at least since the 1930s, is that the First Amendment protects against more than prior restraints but that prior restraints are so especially odious that they carry with them "a heavy presumption against [their own] constitutional validity."[33] Writing in 1955, Thomas Emerson, a Yale law professor, offered the following rationales for treating prior restraints with a special measure of skepticism:[34]

- Whereas after-the-fact ("ex post facto") punishments are narrowly targeted at individual publications, prior restraints affect *all* publications.
- Even if a publisher is eventually punished for his or her writings, at least those writings will have entered the "marketplace of ideas"; prior restraints, on the other hand, deprive the citizenry of the ideas.
- Timing is sometimes very important to a publisher, but prior restraints place in the government's hands the power to decide not only if but also *when* a work will reach the public.
- As the adage "It is easier to beg forgiveness than request permission" suggests, the very existence of a mechanism for imposing prior restraints virtually ensures that censorship will be imposed, whereas the expense and inconvenience of forcing a publisher to face trial may make it less likely that after-the-fact punishments will be imposed.

---

32. Steven Helle, "Prior Restraint," in *Communication and the Law*, ed. W. Wat Hopkins (Northport, Ala.: Vision Press, 2000), 52–53.

33. *Bantam Books v. Sullivan*, 372 U.S. 58, 70 (1963).

34. Thomas Emerson, "The Doctrine of Prior Restraints," 70 *Law and Contemporary Problems* 648 (1955).

The Supreme Court's modern prior-restraint doctrine is usually traced to a 1931 decision, *Near v. Minnesota*. Jay Near, publisher of the controversial *Saturday Press*, was prosecuted as a "public nuisance" for publishing "malicious, scandalous, and defamatory articles" about the mayor of Minneapolis and other **public officials**, as well as the "Jewish race" in general. The case was one of prior restraint because the punishment meted out was an injunction that had the effect of closing down the newspaper. In holding the injunction unconstitutional, the Court allowed that freedom from prior restraints is not "absolutely unlimited," but it also made clear that such governmental censorship would be upheld "only in exceptional cases."[35]

Perhaps the most famous case of prior restraint ever to be decided by the Supreme Court involved the Pentagon Papers, classified government documents leaked to the *Washington Post* and the *New York Times* that showed some of the ways the government misled us about its participation in the Vietnam War.[36] After two conflicting federal appellate decisions were handed down, one enjoining the *New York Times* from publishing the papers, the other refusing to enjoin the *Post*, the Supreme Court granted expedited review and produced a somewhat confusing 6-3 decision rejecting the government's claim that publication of the papers posed a serious threat to the national security.

The majority's official pronouncement in the case was a surprisingly brief per curiam opinion, the thrust of which was that the government had not met the "heavy burden" of proof necessary to sustain a prior restraint on speech. The opinion does not, however, indicate exactly what the burden of proof should be or why in this case the government had failed to meet it.

Readers would have to muddle through nine separate opinions by the justices to make sense of the *Pentagon Papers* case. Two of the justices in the majority (Black and Douglas) espoused a rather absolutist view of the matter, suggesting that the government might never be able to justify a prior restraint on speech. Each of the other justices in the majority allowed that there might be circumstances in which prior restraints are permissible. Justice Stewart offered a description of the government's burden of proof that has since been cited dozens of times by lower courts. Prior restraints, Stewart suggested, should be permitted only when the state can demonstrate that publication will cause "direct, immediate, and irreparable damage."

In the late 1970s, the government had occasion to argue that such serious harm would result if the *Progressive* magazine were permitted to publish an article about the hydrogen bomb. The thesis of the article was that Americans were being lulled into a false sense of security about the unlikelihood of nuclear disaster. The article's author, whose training in the hard sciences was limited to a bachelor's degree, was able to piece together from readily available public documents a blueprint for constructing a working nuclear device. Federal district judge Robert Warren issued a re-

---

35. 283 U.S. 697, 716 (1931).
36. *New York Times Co. v. United States*, 403 U.S. 713 (1971).

straining order against the magazine.[37] Although he admitted that "cherished First Amendment rights" were at stake here, he feared that ruling for the magazine "could pave the way for thermonuclear annihilation for us all." The magazine appealed Judge Warren's ruling to the Seventh Circuit Court of Appeals in Chicago, which held oral arguments on the case in September 1979. The judges never had occasion to render their decision, however; while the case was pending, a handful of newspapers in other venues published essays highly similar to the one at issue in the case, and the government promptly dropped its case against the *Progressive,* which went to press with its hydrogen bomb piece in November, seven months later than it had planned.

In 1990 the Supreme Court refused to hear a prior-restraint controversy involving former Panamanian dictator Manuel Noriega, who had been seized by U.S. authorities and jailed in Miami on drug-trafficking charges. CNN had somehow obtained copies of tape-recorded conversations between Noriega and his attorneys. Noriega obtained an injunction prohibiting the cable network from airing the tapes and demanding that they be turned over to U.S. district court judge William Hoeveler for review.[38] The case was complicated by CNN's having disobeyed the judge's order. The network aired some tapes and withheld all the tapes from Hoeveler for ten days.

Although it is clear that the government takes on a heavy burden of proof when it imposes a prior restraint, it is not always clear what kinds of governmental actions count as prior restraints. For example, government employees may be required to sign documents promising never to reveal certain information they learn on the job, or they may be required to have any proposed publications cleared through their employers. The most celebrated cases involving such prepublication clearance agreements have involved employees of the Central Intelligence Agency. The courts have upheld the use of such agreements and have avoided the First Amendment issues involved by treating the disputes as straightforward "breach of contract" claims.[39] Also, as we see in chapter 11's discussion of obscenity law, the Supreme Court has upheld the government's confiscation of a convicted pornographer's entire inventory.[40] While this would seem to be a classic prior restraint akin to that suffered by Minnesota publisher Jay Near—publish a few offensive things and you will not be permitted to publish at all in the future—the Court held that it was not a restraint on speech. All the government had done was seize the defendant's property; it had not actually enjoined him from selling sexually oriented films and magazines in the future.

Finally, it is important to note that the Supreme Court, in a 1988 decision, made clear that the government's burden is greatly diminished when it imposes a prior re-

---

37. *United States v. Progressive,* 467 F. Supp. 990 (W.D. Wis. 1979).

38. *United States v. Noriega,* 752 F. Supp. 1045 (S.D. Fla. 1990).

39. *United States v. Snepp,* 444 U.S. 507 (1980); *Knopf v. Colby,* 509 F.2d 1362 (4th Cir. 1975); *United States v. Marchetti,* 466 F.2d 1309 (4th Cir. 1972).

40. *Alexander v. United States,* 509 U.S. 544 (1993).

straint on a newspaper published by public high school students. The case involved *Spectrum*, the student newspaper at Hazelwood East High School in a St. Louis, Missouri, suburb. When the school administration killed a couple of stories—one on student pregnancy, the other on coping with divorce—the student editor sued the school. In a 5-3 ruling, the Court held that public schools may exercise editorial control over student publications that "may fairly be characterized as part of the school curriculum, . . . so long as their actions are reasonably related to legitimate pedagogical concerns."[41] In 1999, a three-judge panel of the Sixth Circuit Court of Appeals caused quite a stir when it applied the *Hazelwood* reasoning to the university setting, upholding the actions of a Kentucky State University administrator who confiscated all copies of the school's yearbook for infractions such as failing to use the school's traditional official gold and green colors on the cover. In a later en banc ruling, however, the same court overturned itself, making clear that the *Hazelwood* decision's precedential value should be limited to the secondary school setting.[42]

First Amendment Absolutism

Recall the first five words of the First Amendment: "Congress shall make no law," it tells us, before enumerating the kinds of rights (including freedom of speech and freedom of the press) that the government may not abridge. The wording is absolute. It is not surprising, then, that some jurists and scholars have been known as First Amendment absolutists. Supreme Court Justice Hugo Black is probably most often associated with **absolutist theory**. When the founders drafted the First Amendment, Black said, "they knew what they were talking about." They consciously intended to prevent the government from telling its citizens "what they should believe or say or publish." That the First Amendment says "no law" is appropriate, he added, and "that is what I believe it means."[43]

First Amendment absolutism has obvious problems. There are numerous things one can do via speech that almost any reasonable person would agree should be illegal. Committing perjury is one example. So too is bribery, as is threatening to kill another human being. One way around this problem is to decide, somewhat artificially, that certain kinds of utterances simply will not count as *speech*. This strategy has been embraced by the Supreme Court, for example, with obscenity. Obscene messages have been declared outside the bounds of First Amendment protection. Period.

Another way to reconcile absolutism with practicality is to decide that the drafters of the Bill of Rights themselves had a relatively limited class of speech in mind when they used the phrase "freedom of speech." First Amendment theorist Alexander Meiklejohn is probably the best-known advocate of this approach. For Meiklejohn, "free-

---

41. *Hazelwood School District v. Kuhlmeier*, 484 U.S. 260, 271–273 (1988).

42. *Kincaid v. Gibson*, 191 F.3d 719 (6th Cir. 1999), *rev'd en banc*, 236 F.3d 342 (6th Cir. 2001).

43. Edmund Cahn, "Justice Black and First Amendment 'Absolutes': A Public Interview," 37 *New York University Law Review* 549, 554 (1962).

True First Amendment absolutism would seem to demand that the court accept the accused's ludicrous defense.

dom of speech" refers only to political speech, speech on the kinds of matters upon which the electorate may be called to vote.[44] (In later writings, Meiklejohn softened his stance somewhat to include within his definition of "the political" such matters as the arts, education, and the sciences.[45]) Meiklejohnian theory posits that political speech is absolutely protected by the First Amendment, whereas other lesser kinds of speech (advertising, for example) will find some protection in the Fifth Amendment. Engaging in such speech is seen as one of the liberties that the government may not take away without due process of law.

In recent years, Supreme Court Justice Anthony Kennedy has espoused a new kind of absolutism, what might be called "absolutism with exceptions." He argued that the First Amendment means what it says except for those categories of speech that the

---

44. Alexander Meiklejohn, *Free Speech and Its Relation to Self-Government* (New York: Harper & Row, 1948).

45. Alexander Meiklejohn, "The First Amendment Is an Absolute," 1961 *Supreme Court Review* 245, 255–257 (1961).

Court has long held fall outside the amendment's protection. Kennedy most clearly articulated his theory in a case that found the Court invalidating New York State's "Son of Sam" law, which prohibited criminals from making money by writing about their wrongdoing. Laws such as this one, Kennedy argued, amount to "raw censorship." For Kennedy, First Amendment adjudication should consist initially of asking whether the speech taken aim at by a particular law falls into the categorical exceptions to constitutional protection, such as knowing libel, obscenity, child pornography, and incitement to illegal action. If the speech does not fit into any of these categories, it enjoys absolute First Amendment protection.[46]

It is clear, then, that the "no" in "Congress shall make no law" is not to be taken literally. The legislative branch of government at all levels imposes a wide array of laws and regulations that may affect the act of communication. See the chart labeled "A Model of First Amendment Adjudication," which provides a necessarily simplified description of how the contemporary Supreme Court goes about determining if a specific law is constitutional. The model first reminds us that by definition, only the government can be guilty of violating the First Amendment. Assuming the government is involved, we next ask whether a given law is defective in some fairly generic ways, such as vagueness. The notion here is that if a law is unclear, even law-abiding citizens will not know how to obey it. For example, a Massachusetts-based beer importing firm sued Maine's Bureau of Liquor Enforcement for rejecting three beer-bottle labels as violative of the bureau's rule against "undignified or improper" illustrations. The plaintiff, Shelton Brothers of Belchertown, contended that the regulation was unconstitutionally vague. Other states that had rejected the same or similar labels from the same company had backed down after Shelton Brothers filed suit;[47] Maine eventually backed down as well.[48]

Next, courts consider whether the conduct a law or regulation seeks to abridge is primarily expressive—that is, whether it really triggers the First Amendment. That tax fraud or armed robbery may both involve speech does not make laws criminalizing such acts relevant to the First Amendment. Assuming that a law or regulation does implicate the First Amendment, courts will next consider whether the speech involved falls into categorical exceptions such as obscenity or deceptive advertising. If the answer is no, the final step is to apply whatever test or doctrine has been established by the courts to govern the kind of speech at issue. Commercial speech, for example, is generally governed by the *Central Hudson* test, presented in detail in chapter 10.

---

46. *Simon & Schuster, Inc. v. Members of the New York State Crime Victims Board*, 502 U.S. 105, 128 (Kennedy, J., concurring) (1991).

47. Jesse Leavenworth, "Santa's Butt Focus of Beer Case," *Hartford Courant*, December 5, 2006, D1.

48. William Dowd, "Beer Law at Home and Abroad," *Times Union* (Albany, N.Y.), January 18, 2007, D3.

This special holiday porter is made for winter - rich and warming, the way they like it at the North Pole. It was inspired by this famous line from a well-loved children's storybook:

"And Santa sat on his great butt, enjoying a hardy brew ..."

In case you find that amusing, the brewer hastens to point out that in England "butt" refers to a certain sized barrel customarily used for beer - a very large barrel, in fact, holding 108 Imperial gallons. Back in the day it was quite a normal thing for a brewery to put its beer up in a large butt for storage. Still snickering, eh? Get your mind out of the gutter, or Santa will be skipping your house entirely this year.

Peter Scholey
Brewer

Live Bottle
Conditioned Beer

GOVERNMENT WARNING: (1) ACCORDING TO THE SURGEON GENERAL, WOMEN SHOULD NOT DRINK ALCOHOLIC BEVERAGES DURING PREGNANCY BECAUSE OF THE RISK OF BIRTH DEFECTS. (2) CONSUMPTION OF ALCOHOLIC BEVERAGES IMPAIRS YOUR ABILITY TO DRIVE A CAR OR OPERATE MACHINERY, AND MAY CAUSE HEALTH PROBLEMS.

PRODUCT OF THE UNITED KINGDOM
Produced and Bottled by:
RIDGEWAY BREWING
Oxfordshire. RG8 0JW

IA - OR - VT - ME - CT
MA - DE - NY 5¢ REF
MI 10¢ REF
FL - OK+
CALIFORNIA
CASH REFUND

Santa's Butt
~ *Winter Porter* ~

50 cl e   1 pt. 9 FL. OZ. U.S.

Alc 6% Vol.

The State of Maine initially rejected this beer label's Santa illustration as "undignified" and "improper," a standard challenged by the importer as unconstitutionally vague.

Access Theory

Tulane University law student Donna Bird asked the *Times-Picayune* in New Orleans to publish an announcement of her "commitment ceremony" to Ms. Leslie Nehring, a pediatric critical-care nurse. The newspaper refused,[49] as have most but not all mainstream media outlets that have considered whether to open up their marriages and engagements pages to same-sex couples. This controversy has been repeated in numerous locales around the country in recent years, and it raises some interesting questions. Is accepting such announcements from gay males and lesbians more morally defensible than refusing them? Does it make good business sense? More directly relevant to the purview of this book, should Bird be able to force the paper to accept her announcement? (She did, in fact, seek the help of her local human relations commission, hoping it would find the newspaper to be in violation of local civil rights laws.)

Although the issue of gay commitment ceremony announcements is relatively new, the more general question as to whether the media may ever be forced to turn over column inches or broadcast airtime to outsiders has been debated for many decades. Best known among those who have argued for such compelled access is Professor Jerome Barron of the George Washington University Law School. In 1967, Barron

---

49. Susan Finch, "Lesbians Allege TP Bias in Commitment Policy," *Times-Picayune*, February 7, 1995, B1.

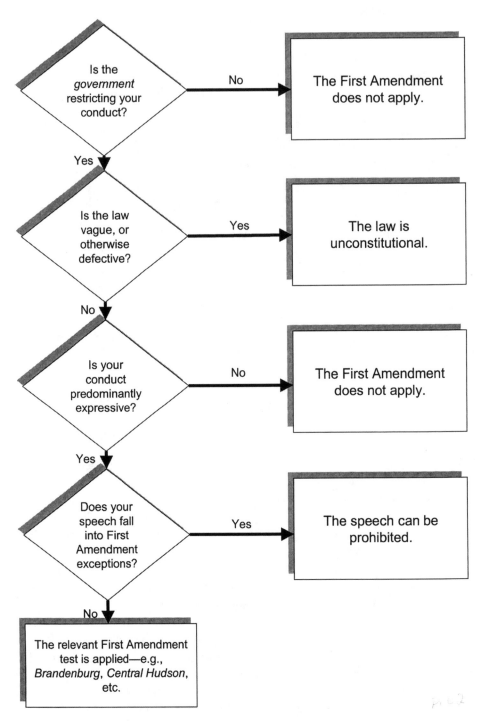

A Model of First Amendment Adjudication

published a seminal article in the *Harvard Law Review*[50] that he later expanded into a book.[51] Barron bemoaned the concentration of media ownership, which he described as an "economic revolution" placing "with fewer and fewer persons the power to decide whatever a larger and larger number shall see, hear, and read."

Access theorists have enjoyed only mixed success in the United States, depending on the specific medium involved. The print media are generally free from intrusions into their editorial discretion. Television and radio fare much differently. Section 315 of the Federal Communications Act, for example, provides a complicated array of rules and exceptions telling station managers that candidates for political office must be granted equal access to their airwaves. In the late 1990s and in the 2000 presidential campaign, several proposals for campaign-finance reform were predicated in part on the possibility of requiring broadcast stations to donate a certain number of hours of free airtime to candidates to alleviate the candidates' need to hustle for donor dollars. The cable television industry is also subject to some kinds of compelled access. In many locales, the city's contract with the cable franchise requires that a small number of stations be set aside for "community access," generally made available on a first-come, first-served basis to any community groups wishing to produce programming.

Although Barron was concerned primarily with the rights of the public to use the airwaves and the print media, another access issue is the relationship among reporters, editors, and publishers. Social critic A. J. Liebling reminds us that "freedom of the press is guaranteed only to those who own one," a lesson that media employees often learn the hard way. Former *New Republic* magazine editor Michael Kelly, for example, is generally presumed to have lost that job because he wrote one too many criticisms of Vice President Al Gore, a close friend of publisher Martin Peretz.[52] Or consider the plight of reporter Marsden Epworth, who was fired from the Torrington, Connecticut, *Register Citizen* for having mentioned, in an article generally touting the paper's new Sunday edition, that many subscribers were upset by distribution problems that found them "waiting in vain for their historic first edition." Publisher Geoffrey L. Moser let it be known that his staff was not permitted to "write anything that embarrasses the Journal Register Company."[53] In the absence of a clear employment contract to the contrary, reporters and editors, like most employees in the United States, serve at the pleasure of their bosses and can be fired at any time for any reason not otherwise in violation of the law. That their transgression may have been to communicate with the public is generally deemed irrelevant.

---

50. Jerome Barron, "Access to the Press: A New First Amendment Right," 80 *Harvard Law Review* 1641 (1967).

51. Jerome Barron, *Freedom of Press for Whom?: The Right of Access to Mass Media* (Bloomington: Indiana University Press, 1973).

52. Paul D. Colford, "Conservative Journals Are Yukking It Up," *Los Angeles Times*, February 5, 1998, 5.

53. "Darts and Laurels," *Columbia Journalism Review*, May 1994, 23.

Balancing Theories

The moment we reject absolutist positions, we are necessarily in the business of balancing of some kind. Courts engage in **ad hoc balancing** when they ask, "In this particular case, which is more important, freedom of speech or the competing interest?" One party's free speech claims will then be weighed against whatever interests form the opposing side's case. The competing interest might be to protect a plaintiff's reputation, as in libel cases. It could be to preserve the peace, as in incitement prosecutions. A state may have an antiobscenity law through which it seeks to preserve a certain moral climate. As Justice Harlan put it in a McCarthy-era case, First Amendment jurisprudence "always involves a balancing by the courts of the competing private and public interests at stake in the particular circumstances shown."[54]

In recent years, probably the best-known advocate of pure and simple balancing has been law and humanities professor Stanley Fish of Florida International University. In his provocatively titled 1994 book *There's No Such Thing as Free Speech, and It's a Good Thing, Too*, Fish seeks to debunk what he sees as unnecessarily fancy and somewhat intellectually dishonest theories of the First Amendment. Courts engage in balancing, he writes, and we should not be upset by this revelation. "When a court invalidates legislation because it infringes on protected speech," Fish says, "it is not because the speech in question is without consequences but because the consequences have been discounted in relation to a good that is judged to outweigh them."[55]

One thing about real-world First Amendment adjudication is missing from the ad hoc balancing model: courts cheat a bit in favor of the litigants raising First Amendment claims. So important is freedom of speech in the calculus of rights Americans enjoy that courts purposely tip the scales. Judges do not simply ask, "Which interest is more important in this particular case?" Rather, they ask, "Does the anti-free-speech litigant have a strong enough case to overcome the presumption in favor of free speech?"

This kind of inquiry is often referred to as **preferred-position balancing**. The Supreme Court has used the admittedly vague phrase "preferred position" to describe freedom of speech in over a dozen decisions since the 1940s. In a concurring opinion from a 1949 decision, Justice Frankfurter dismissed it as a "mischievous phrase" that "radiates a constitutional doctrine without avowing it . . . that any law touching communication is infected with presumptive invalidity."[56] Mischievous or not, the phrase does seem to mean something very much like what Frankfurter feared it had come to mean. When asked to determine the constitutionality of laws or regulations seeming to abridge a fundamental right such as freedom of speech (freedom of the press and freedom of religion are treated similarly), courts employ the highest level of scrutiny.

---

54. *Barenblatt v. United States*, 360 U.S. 109, 126 (1959).

55. Stanley Fish, *There's No Such Thing as Free Speech, and It's a Good Thing, Too* (New York: Oxford University Press, 1994), 106.

56. *Kovacs v. Cooper*, 336 U.S. 77, 89–90 (1949) (Frankfurter, J., concurring).

THINGS TO REMEMBER

Some Approaches to First Amendment Adjudication

- PRIOR-RESTRAINT DOCTRINE
  - In colonial times, freedom of the press likely meant only freedom from prepublication censorship.
  - Although the First Amendment also applies to after-the-fact punishments, prior restraints are still viewed by the Supreme Court as especially odious.

- ABSOLUTIST THEORY
  - The "no" in "Congress shall pass *no* law" is emphasized.
  - Alexander Meiklejohn said that only political speech is absolutely protected.
  - Justice Kennedy embraces "absolutism with exceptions."

- ACCESS THEORY
  - Freedom of the press should not be just for those who own one.
  - Courts have generally rejected it for print but accepted it somewhat for broadcast media.

- AD HOC BALANCING
  - Which is more important in this case, free speech or the competing interest?
  - Stanley Fish of Florida International University has revitalized interest in this approach.

- PREFERRED-POSITION BALANCING
  - This frequently used approach consists of balancing with a dishonest scale, assuming that free speech will win.

Using this "strict scrutiny," courts demand that the state have a "compelling interest" to infringe on the right to communicate. Preferred-position balancing is the theory of First Amendment adjudication most often employed by the modern Supreme Court (even though it does not use the phrase as often these days as in decades passed). This reality leads to a question that is as easy to articulate as it is difficult to answer: *why* is free speech so important that it occupies a preferred position?

The Value of Freedom of Expression

In the same concurring opinion from *Whitney v. California* that gave us the famous "more speech, not enforced silence" prescription, Justice Brandeis also provides us with an elegantly worded list of functions served by freedom of speech. "Those who won our independence," he wrote, believed that "freedom to think as you will and to speak as you think are means indispensable to the discovery and spread of political truth." He further contended that engaging in public discussion on the issues of the day is a "political duty" that should be recognized as a "fundamental principle of the American government." The opinion suggests too that law and order "cannot be secured merely through fear of punishment," that "it is hazardous to discourage thought, hope and imagination," because "fear breeds repression" and "repression breeds hate," the kind of hate that "menaces stable government."[57]

Freedom of speech, then, is important because it helps us find the truth; it is essential to our role as self-governors in a democracy, and it provides a kind of "safety valve" against possibly violent turmoil. Yale University law professor Thomas Emerson incorporated these three functions into his own theory of free speech and suggested also that free speech serves a more individual "self-fulfillment" function.[58]

The Truth-Seeking Function of Free Speech

Imagine for a moment that you are a member of a self-sustaining and very homogenous people—descendants of the *Gilligan's Island* crew, perhaps—who have been cut off from the outside world for many centuries. Such a society will tend to develop very strongly held, rather inflexible views of the world. For such a people, the phrase "we do it this way because . . . well, we have *always* done it this way" is not a laughable cliché but a matter-of-fact statement of allegiance to unquestioned wisdom.

Now suppose that one day, a ship from another land is seen approaching. Your people may very well convene something akin to a town meeting so that you can decide whether to welcome the visitors or hide all traces of your presence from them in the hope that they will go away. The former option would be a courageous one indeed, opening yourselves to interactions with strangers whose ways may be very different from your own.

Nineteenth-century philosopher John Stuart Mill did not depend on such an intercultural fantasy in setting forth his influential free speech theory, but the narrative does provide a convenient lens through which to examine his elegant defense of viewpoint diversity. Mill's famous 1859 essay, *On Liberty*, asks us to consider whether we would be open to a new idea or whether we would feel an urge to censor it. We cannot ignore the possibility that the new idea is more correct than our handed-down wisdom. For would-be censors "to refuse a hearing to an opinion because they are sure that it is false is to assume that their certainty is the same thing as absolute certainty."

Suppose, however, that we were magically able to view the "Gilligan Islanders" dilemma from an omniscient vantage point, and that the homogenous people's long-held truths were inarguably, unquestionably true. What benefit could possibly result from opening the door to the visitors' falsehoods? Mill answers that we will gain a "clearer perception and livelier impression" of our own truths, by their "collision with error"; failure to engage opposing views, Mill warns, will ensure that our own beliefs "will be held as a dead dogma, not a living truth, apt to give way before the slightest semblance of an argument. Truth thus held is but superstition."

---

57. 274 U.S. 357, 375 (1927) (Brandeis, J., concurring).
58. Thomas I. Emerson, *The System of Freedom of Expression* (New York: Random House, 1970).

In the real world, of course, we do not have the omniscience to know whose ideas are correct in advance of a full debate. Indeed, in most important clashes of ideas, the "truth" tends to be somewhere between the extremes. Yet we cannot often afford the luxury of waiting until all the facts are in. The modern world is characterized by the need to make decisions and take action on the basis of incomplete and often contradictory information. Professor Benjamin DuVal tells us that we derive our moral authority to make decisions and take actions by making, ironically enough, a "pact with the devil." The "devil" gives us permission to function, to act, only if we promise in return that we will not censor new ideas, that we will always keep ourselves open to the possibility that new facts will require that we alter our course of behavior.[59]

The Self-Governing Function of Free Speech

First Amendment scholar Alexander Meiklejohn's theory of freedom of expression emphasizes Americans' role as "self-governors." We vote on important matters of the day, or at least choose among candidates in large part on what they promise to do about those same issues. For Meiklejohn, just as the **Speech or Debate Clause** in Article I of the Constitution gives our elected federal representatives an absolute right to free speech in carrying out their duties, so too should the First Amendment be interpreted to give all Americans an absolute right to speak out about political issues.

In Meiklejohnian theory, political speech is the core of the system of free expression, protected absolutely by the First Amendment, whereas more private speech enjoys the far lesser degree of protection offered by the Fifth Amendment's Due Process Clause. When Oprah Winfrey uses her program to discuss the safety of federal meat-inspection programs, according to Meiklejohn, she and her guests enjoy absolute freedom from liability. If instead she devotes an hour to a movie star's personal bout with marital infidelity, the First Amendment might not be implicated at all.

Although the Supreme Court rejects Meiklejohn's argument that speech we do not need in our role as self-governors lacks First Amendment protection, it has on many occasions made clear that political speech is the most important kind. In 1995, for example, the Court overturned an Ohio law that required all printed campaign literature to include the name and address of the leaflet's author. The law's downfall was obvious early on, as the Court's opinion expressed amazement that the state had singled out "core political speech," "publications containing speech designed to influence the voters in an election," for regulation.[60] A few years earlier, the Court similarly invalidated a District of Columbia ordinance that prohibited the display within five hundred feet of any foreign embassy a sign bearing a message critical of that embassy's

---

59. Benjamin DuVal, "Free Communication of Ideas and the Quest for Truth: Toward a Teleological Approach to First Amendment Adjudication," 41 *George Washington Law Review* 161 (1972).

60. *McIntyre v. Ohio Elections Commission*, 514 U.S. 334, 345, 347 (1995).

government. The law had to be struck down, the Court held, in that it so obviously trampled on "classically protected" political speech.[61]

The Checking Function of Free Speech

In the United States the press is often referred to as the fourth estate, a way of emphasizing that we depend on a free press to keep us informed about the performance of the three branches of government—legislative, executive, and judicial. Much of what we think of as hard news involves the press looking over the shoulders of government bureaucrats and reporting about their successes and failures. The ABC News regular feature "Your Money," which looks at a specific government program and suggests to viewers whether they are getting a good return on their tax dollars, is a clear example of this watchdog function.

A 1977 article by Vincent Blasi argued that empowering the press to keep a watchful eye on the government is the main reason for valuing freedom of speech. He calls it the "checking function." Abuses by the government are "an especially serious evil," Blasi argued, more so than abuses by large corporations or other powerful agents. Government, after all, is unique in its "capacity to employ legitimized violence"—we give the police, not corporate CEOs, the right to use guns against us.[62] From Blasi's perspective, then, TV stations that showed us again and again the videotape of the Rodney King beating were engaged in the checking function. Reporting on whether Microsoft is engaged in monopolistic practices in restraint of trade is not part of the checking function unless the story's focus is the Department of Justice's decision to prosecute the company.

The Safety-Valve Function of Free Speech

If we suppress a viewpoint that we despise, does it go away? Or do its proponents go underground and does their discontent fester until it is all the more likely to be manifested in violence? The safety-valve function of free speech stems from the latter hypothesis. As Emerson explains, freedom of speech "promotes greater cohesion in a society because people are more ready to accept decisions that go against them if they have a part in the decision-making process." Unsuccessful advocates of change are less likely to foment violent revolution if they are at least allowed to advocate.[63]

More recently, Lee Bollinger, the president of Columbia University and former president of the University of Michigan, has argued that we benefit, for at least two reasons, from seeing the depth of dissatisfaction and dissent felt by those who feel driven to engage in extremist speech. First, some of their grievances may be real—

---

61. *Boos v. Barry*, 485 U.S. 312 (1988).

62. Vincent Blasi, "The Checking Value in First Amendment Theory," 2 *American Bar Foundation Research Journal* 521, 538 (1977).

63. Emerson, *The System of Freedom of Expression*, 7.

inadequate educational or employment opportunities, for example—and only by hearing them can we make public-policy decisions to address them. Second, it is "preferable to have these potentially disruptive individuals and groups operating in public rather than in private, where the unwanted weeds of frustration and revolt may grow more rapidly from inattention and where the falsehoods being propagated may less easily be exposed for their error." A system of freedom of expression thus acts as a "social thermometer for registering the presence of disease within the body politic and the best opportunity of administering a speedy cure."[64]

The Self-Fulfillment Function of Free Speech

Virtually anytime the media report on a survey about "things that frighten most Americans," being called on to deliver a speech in public ranks at or near the top. This finding obscures another reality about self-expression that may seem a contradiction yet is no less true: it feels good to express yourself.

Perhaps no event in recent times drives this point home more powerfully than the

One of the traditionally accepted values of freedom of speech is self-fulfillment, that expressing ourselves feels good. Might this cartoon also depict the "safety valve" function of free speech?

64. Lee Bollinger, *The Tolerant Society* (New York: Oxford University Press, 1986), 55.

May 2006 sentencing of 9/11 conspirator Zacarias Moussaoui to life imprisonment without parole. When Moussaoui loudly suggested to those in court that he had "won," Judge Brinkema cut him off, pointing out that he was being taken to a maximum-security facility where he will essentially be prevented from speaking publicly ever again. Instead of achieving the martyrdom he had sought, he would "die with a whimper," the judge intoned, quoting from poet T. S. Eliot.

C. Edwin Baker, who was a student of Emerson's at Yale, later went on to create his own freedom of speech theory, which emphasizes the self-fulfillment function of expression above all others. His theory leads to some intriguing propositions, such as defining advertising and other commercial speech as generally outside the protection of the First Amendment, in that speakers sending such messages are motivated by potential profits rather than by a desire for individual self-fulfillment. Baker argues further that even what we think of as political speech might be more appropriately viewed as highly personal expressions of self. Consider the plight of the war protestor at a rally, chanting "Stop this war now" or some similar slogan. Rarely do such speakers have any serious expectation that their singular act of political speech will affect the government's war policy or indeed even be heard by those in charge of prosecuting the war effort. Why do it then? The answer, in part, at least, is because engaging in such speech serves to define oneself to others, *as well as to oneself*, as a person in opposition.[65]

The Societal Self-Definition Function of Free Speech

These then are the traditionally accepted functions of freedom of speech: aiding the quest for truth, helping us in our role as self-governors, acting as a check on the government, serving as a "safety valve," and furthering individual self-fulfillment. Some writers have provided eloquent critiques of these functions and have found them deficient. In this section we look at two such writers, Lee Bollinger and Ruth McGaffey. Both Bollinger and McGaffey argue that the best way of explaining the uniquely American system of free expression is that the system itself serves to define what it means to be an American. This exploration will make more sense if we look at another similarity between the two theorists. Both authors derive much of their analysis from a 1970s incident involving the village of Skokie, Illinois. Frank Collin and his small group of neo-Nazis, after initially being denied a parade permit in Chicago, began to search for alternative local venues and settled on Skokie, a northwest suburb with a large Jewish population and an unusually large number of Holocaust survivors. The village responded by passing a series of laws designed to prevent Collin's proposed march, laws which were eventually found unconstitutional by a federal appellate court.[66]

---

65. C. Edwin Baker, *Human Liberty and Freedom of Speech* (New York: Oxford University Press, 1989), 53.

66. *Collin v. Smith*, 578 F.2d 1197 (7th Cir. 1978).

McGaffey attended the neo-Nazi group's demonstration, which eventually did take place in Chicago's Marquette Park and which attracted a large group of counterdemonstrators. McGaffey describes the screaming for blood on both sides. "This was not a football game, and the opposing yells were not those of friendly rivalry. The hatred was so thick you could feel it." The radio reported the next day that a body had been fished out of a lagoon in the park.

McGaffey's experience at the Marquette Park rally could not help but compel her to question Americans' assumptions about the value of free speech. Free speech's truth-seeking value notwithstanding, surely it should be possible to fashion laws that guarantee freedom of expression "without allowing every repulsive creep to tie up the police force of a huge city whenever he wants his ego inflated." As to the safety-valve function of free speech, McGaffey wonders whether "letting off that kind of steam prevents trouble or contributes to orderly change." Not surprisingly, she also finds herself unenthusiastic about the call to protect Collin's need for "self-fulfillment" through hate mongering. Yet McGaffey emerges from Chicago with a vital and new reason for protecting freedom of speech: We need to see that there are people "who will burn crosses or beat up Blacks or break windows in synagogues when their own little worlds are threatened." We need to permit such persons to engage in free speech, not for their benefit, but so that observers can "realize what a lousy bunch of people we are" and that "we must be a pretty strong country in order to have survived with so many lousy people."[67]

The argument may seem a bit circular: we should value free speech because it permits us to observe firsthand how tolerant of extremists we can be. Yet there is something about this "self-definition" rationale that seems to ring true, as Bollinger also finds. Bollinger calls his book outlining his own theory *The Tolerant Society* as if to emphasize that Americans enjoy seeing themselves as a tolerant people. He reminds us that the United States is virtually unique among free societies in its high degree of legal tolerance for ideas we hate. This tolerance does not mean we shy away from judgment: we do not, for example, equate the neo-Nazi movement with the civil rights movement. We feel strongly as a people, however, that we should use means *short of legal suppression* to express our disdain for race-baiters and other extremists. We can shun them. If they hold public office, we can demand their immediate resignation. But we should not fall into the trap of making their speech unlawful.[68]

Our system of freedom of expression serves to help us define ourselves as a people, and we take pride in this aspect of our collective self-concept. Bollinger finds some support for this proposition in portions of the federal appellate decision granting Frank Collin and his followers the right to march in Skokie. Consider this little zinger the court sent Collin's way: "It is, after all, in part the fact that our constitutional

---

67. Ruth McGaffey, "Freedom of Speech in Marquette Park: A Realistic Look at the Marketplace of Ideas," 17 *Free Speech Yearbook* 1, 8–9 (1978).

68. Bollinger, *The Tolerant Society*, 12–14.

THINGS TO REMEMBER

Functions of Free Speech

- THE TRUTH-SEEKING FUNCTION
  - John Stuart Mill emphasized the need to hear even false ideas to remind us why the true ideas are true.
  - Benjamin DuVal's "pact with the devil" allows us to make decisions only if we promise to remain open to new ideas.

- THE SELF-GOVERNING FUNCTION
  - Alexander Meiklejohn is most closely associated with the self-governing stance.
  - Political speech is an absolute First Amendment freedom.
  - Nonpolitical speech is a Fifth Amendment liberty.

- THE CHECKING FUNCTION
  - The free press is essential in a democracy as a fourth estate, the check on the other three branches of government.

- THE SAFETY VALVE FUNCTION
  - Political dissidents must be permitted to blow off steam.
  - Peaceful evolution helps avoid violent revolution.

- THE SELF-FULFILLMENT FUNCTION
  - Expressing ourselves feels good.
  - C. Edwin Baker's theory is based on this self-fulfillment function.

- THE SOCIETAL SELF-DEFINITION FUNCTION
  - Bollinger says that Americans like to think of themselves as a tolerant people.
  - McGaffey points to the need to see how "lousy" and intolerant we can be too.

system protects minorities unpopular at a particular time or place from governmental harassment and intimidation, that distinguishes life in this country from life under the Third Reich."[69] Implicit in the court's language is an admonition to all Americans: *celebrate*, do not lament, the high degree of tolerance for extremists demanded by the First Amendment.

Is Freedom of Expression Overrated?

All the First Amendment theories examined so far have in common an underlying assumption that free speech is a good thing. The theories differ only in terms of the answer they offer to the question of why it is a good thing. Many theorists, however, argue that freedom of expression is placed on too high a pedestal in the United States, that it is allowed to ride roughshod over more important rights and interests. In this

---

69. *Collin v. Smith*, 578 F.2d at 1201.

section we examine the thoughts of some Marxist, feminist, and critical race theorists who agree that freedom of speech as we typically understand it in this country is indeed overrated.

Karl Marx said that religion is "the opiate of the people." An emphasis on the afterlife, he suggested, is conveniently consistent with the need on the part of those in power to keep the masses contented with their small share of material resources in *this* life. Writing several generations later, a group of Marxists argued similarly that freedom of speech is an opiate, or at least a distraction. Chief among these writers was Herbert Marcuse, who pointed out that having the right to speak out against injustice is quite different from having any real power to change what he perceived as a fundamentally unjust system of allocating wealth.[70] For Marcuse and his followers, "free speech operates freely only because society realizes that free speech is devoid of any real power of change."[71]

One need not be a Marxist, of course, to level that same criticism against American journalism, especially TV news. That the main purpose of the news is not to inform but rather to entertain just enough so that viewers pay attention to the commercials is the thesis of Neil Postman's well-received book *Amusing Ourselves to Death*. Postman, who was a communications professor at New York University, described the "Now, this . . ." grammar of TV news. The phrase alerts us that the TV news item we have just seen "has no relevance to what one is about to see." It is the newscaster's way of saying "that you have thought long enough on the previous matter (approximately forty-five seconds), that you must not be morbidly preoccupied with it . . . and that you must now give your attention to another fragment of news or a commercial."[72]

Whereas Postman warns that the media discourage us from paying too close attention to the issues of the day, pioneering mass media theorists Paul Lazarsfeld and Robert Merton have argued that we may be guilty of paying such close attention to the information with which the media bombard us that we get lulled into political inactivity. We come to confuse *knowing* about social problems with *doing* something about them. They call this confusion the narcotizing dysfunction of media.[73]

To the extent that American media exist primarily to sell viewers' and readers' attentive eyeballs to advertisers, we expect to find a tendency to avoid airing any politi-

---

70. Herbert Marcuse, "Repressive Tolerance," in *A Critique of Pure Tolerance*, ed. Robert Paul Wolff, Barrington Moore, Jr., and Herbert Marcuse (Boston: Beacon Press, 1965), 81–123.

71. Joyce Flory, "Implications of Marcuse's Theory of Freedom for Freedom of Speech," in *Perspectives on Freedom of Speech*, ed. Thomas L. Tedford, John J. Makay, and David L. Jamison (Carbondale: Southern Illinois University Press, 1987), 77, 79.

72. Neil Postman, *Amusing Ourselves to Death: Public Discourse in the Age of Show Business* (New York: Penguin Books, 1985), 99–100.

73. Paul F. Lazarsfeld and Robert K. Merton, "Mass Communication, Popular Taste, and Organized Social Action," in *The Communication of Ideas*, ed. Lymon Bryson (New York: Harper, 1948), 95–118.

cal views that would disturb consumers too much, that make us tune out. Such a criticism is reminiscent of Dorothy Parker's famously stinging remark about an actress of her day whose performance "ran the gamut of emotions from 'A' to 'B.'" We rarely encounter truly radical political points of view in American media, many contemporary social critics argue. From this perspective, the spokespersons "from the left" and "from the right" that CNN used to so proudly pit against each other in its now defunct *Crossfire* program would be more accurately described as *a bit* left of center versus *a bit* right of center.

If the marketplace of ideas offers only a very limited spectrum of viewpoints, one possible result could be what sociologist Elisabeth Noelle-Neumann has described as the "spiral of silence." Consumers of news who themselves favor political views more on the fringes than one typically sees described in the media will become hesitant over time, afraid to share their views with others for fear of being branded a radical. The media will thus be less and less likely over time to be able to identify and feature responsible spokespersons for any but the most mainstream of perspectives.[74] It is perhaps worth noting that Noelle-Neumann was writing from anything but a Marxist perspective. Indeed, in her younger years she was apparently very active in the German Nazi Party.[75]

In recent years much scholarship has been written by feminists who, in the course of questioning the most basic assumptions of U.S. society, understandably have much to say about whether deference to First Amendment rights is always in women's best interest. These theorists say that the purpose of their scholarship is to ask "the woman question," sometimes phrased as, "What would the law be like if women had been considered by the drafters?"[76] Feminist theory has been applied to dozens of distinct areas of law, from bankruptcy to health care regulation.[77] Perhaps most relevant for the study of communication law are those feminists who have argued that we need to rethink our attitudes toward the use of pornographic images of women. By far the best-known writers in this area have been Andrea Dworkin[78] and Catherine MacKinnon.[79] We examine their antipornography arguments in chapter 11, which deals with obscenity and other sexually oriented speech.

---

74. Elisabeth Noelle-Neumann, *The Spiral of Silence* (Chicago: University of Chicago Press, 1984).

75. Christopher Simpson, "Elisabeth Noelle-Neumann's 'Spiral of Silence' and the Historical Context of Communication Theory," *Journal of Communication*, September 1996, 149–173.

76. Janet E. Ainsworth, "In a Different Register: The Pragmatics of Powerlessness in Police Interrogation," 103 *Yale Law Journal* 259, 262 (1993).

77. Lydia A. Clougherty, "Feminist Legal Methods and the First Amendment Defense to Sexual Harassment Liability," 75 *Nebraska Law Review* 1, 4 (1996).

78. Andrea Dworkin, *Pornography: Men Possessing Women* (New York: Plume, 1989); Andrea Dworkin, "Against the Male Flood: Censorship, Pornography, and Equality," 8 *Harvard Women's Law Journal* 1 (1985).

79. Catherine MacKinnon, *Only Words* (Cambridge, Mass.: Harvard University Press, 1993); Catherine MacKinnon, *Toward a Feminist Theory of the State* (Cambridge, Mass.: Harvard University Press, 1989); Catherine MacKinnon, *Feminism Unmodified* (Cambridge, Mass.: Harvard Uni-

---

THINGS TO REMEMBER

Some criticisms of the American style of free speech

- Some view free speech as an "opiate."
- The right to complain is not as important as the power to change things:
  - We confuse knowing about problems with doing something about them.
  - Political dialogue in the United States is merely a commodity to attract eyeballs to ads.
- The media cannot afford to offend us, so the marketplace of ideas is very narrow.
- Feminists and critical race theorists express concern:
  - We need to pay attention to the aggrieved person's narratives.
  - Free speech is not necessarily more important than equality.

Feminists are not the only representatives of historically oppressed groups to question what they perceive as the U.S. legal system's tendency to value free speech interests above concerns about inequality. Critical race theorists such as Mari Matsuda[80] and Richard Delgado[81] argue that the courts should not automatically assume that the First Amendment prohibits minority group members from bringing civil actions against persons who use racial epithets against them. These writers emphasize that whites and people of color live in two very different perceptual worlds. When confronted by the same stories of hate speech incidents, people of color react with alarm, hurt feelings, and a desire for redress, whereas most whites seek to dismiss such occurrences as "isolated pranks." The whole process of telling and listening to stories is crucial for critical race theorists, who argue in favor of a new "outsider jurisprudence" that will be more sympathetic to historically powerless groups.

Some Transcendent First Amendment Doctrines

The remainder of this book's chapters are organized around either message-content issues (libel, invasion of privacy, advertising) or issues unique to specific communications media (broadcast and cable, the Internet). Other important communication law issues transcend these categories. We deal here with four of them: the right to hear,

---

versity Press, 1987); Catharine MacKinnon, "Pornography, Civil Rights, and Speech," 20 *Harvard Civil Rights–Civil Liberties Law Review* 1 (1985).

80. Mari Matsuda, "Public Response to Racist Speech: Considering the Victim's Story," 87 *Michigan Law Review* 2320 (1989).

81. Richard Delgado, "Words That Wound: A Tort Action for Racial Insults, Epithets, and Name-Calling," 17 *Harvard Civil Rights–Civil Liberties Law Review* 133 (1982).

the right not to speak, the issue of symbolic conduct, and the kinds of content-neutral governmental policies often referred to as time, place, and manner regulations.

A Right to Hear (and Read)

The First Amendment tells us that Congress shall not abridge the freedom to speak. Over the years, the judiciary has come to recognize that freedom of speech would be incomplete were it not to entail also a right to hear (or read). The Supreme Court has emphasized in more than a dozen of its free speech cases that the First Amendment protects the act of communication and that this act involves not only senders of messages but receivers as well. As we see in later chapters focusing on obscenity and advertising, the right to hear is an integral part of the law governing those kinds of speech. Thus, for example, the Court has said that although selling or distributing obscene works can be criminalized, one may own and read in the privacy of one's own home virtually any sexually oriented materials that do not include lewd depictions of children.[82] And in the Court's 1976 decision first holding that purely commercial advertising is protected by the First Amendment, that protection was based primarily on the consumers' interest in obtaining comparative pricing information.[83]

The Court first made reference to a "right to hear" in the course of overturning a contempt of court judgment against the United Auto Workers president R. J. Thomas, who had delivered a speech, in defiance of a court order, to a group of Houston workers. Writing for a 5-4 majority, Justice Wiley Blount Rutledge found that both Thomas's right to speak and "the rights of the workers to hear what he had to say" were at issue.[84] The right to hear formed the basis of the Court's 1969 decision upholding the constitutionality of the **"fairness doctrine"** applied by the FCC to the broadcast media. That doctrine—which required that broadcast licensees not shy away from covering controversial issues and that such issues be covered in a balanced way—is no longer enforced. Nonetheless, the philosophy embraced by the Court at the time, that it is "the right of the viewers and listeners, not the right of the broadcasters, which is paramount," remains to this day one of the judiciary's most dramatic endorsements of a right to hear.[85]

The rights of PBS's viewers to hear carried the day in *FCC v. League of Women Voters of California*, which invalidated the portion of the Public Broadcasting Act of 1967 that prohibited PBS and NPR stations from editorializing on issues of the day. Editorializing, the Court held, can be an important means "of satisfying the public's interest in receiving a wide variety of ideas and views."[86] More recently, the Court invalidated a federal statute that prohibited virtually all government workers above a

82. *Stanley v. Georgia*, 394 U.S. 557 (1969).
83. *Virginia State Board of Pharmacy v. Virginia Citizens Consumer Council*, 425 U.S. 748 (1976).
84. *Thomas v. Collins*, 323 U.S. 516, 534 (1945).
85. *Red Lion Broadcasting v. FCC*, 395 U.S. 367, 390 (1969).
86. *FCC v. League of Women Voters of California*, 468 U.S. 364, 382 (1984).

certain salary scale to make any money "moonlighting" as writers or lecturers, even on matters wholly unrelated to their official job duties. The regulation, Justice Stevens found, imposed "a significant burden on the public's right to read and hear what the employees would otherwise have written and said."[87]

A Right *Not* to Speak

Anyone who has ever seen a real or fictional character on TV "take the Fifth" knows that the Bill of Rights boasts at least one protection against being forced to speak. The Fifth Amendment's provision is a very limited one, however, applying only to criminal suspects and others in danger of prosecution. The Supreme Court has also found a more generalized right not to speak in the First Amendment. In the beginnings of the modern civil rights movement, some southern states felt threatened by the emergence of groups such as the NAACP and employed a number of tactics to stifle their growth. One such tactic was compelling the groups to disclose their membership lists. In a 1957 decision, the Supreme Court blocked such forced disclosure, ruling in essence that such organizations have a right not to speak, at least when speaking would likely bring violent reprisals upon their supporters.[88]

In the 1988 presidential race, George Herbert Walker Bush criticized Michael Dukakis for vetoing legislation that would have required Massachusetts public school teachers to lead their students in a daily recitation of the Pledge of Allegiance. Dukakis defended his veto on the grounds that the law seemed inconsistent with a U.S. Supreme Court decision from the 1940s holding that public school students could not be forced to utter the pledge. Most interesting about the case for communication law is that the plaintiffs, a group of Jehovah's Witnesses, argued that the compelled speech was a violation of their right to practice their religion, a Free Exercise Clause issue. Justice Jackson's opinion for the Court, however, was based on the far broader "right not to speak" implicit in the Free Speech Clause. If the First Amendment allows us to speak our mind, surely it must also mean that the government may not compel us to "utter what is not in [our mind]," he wrote at the time.[89]

The right not to speak was emphasized even more forcefully in a later case involving another Jehovah's Witness, New Hampshire resident George Maynard, who strongly disagreed with the state motto ("Live Free or Die") and therefore covered up the words on his automobile license plate. In ruling for Maynard, the Supreme Court held explicitly that the First Amendment provides for "both the right to speak freely and the right to refrain from speaking at all."[90]

Note that the Jehovah's Witnesses in these two cases invoked the First Amendment as a shield from having to utter someone else's message: the Pledge of Allegiance in

---

87. *United States v. National Treasury Employees Union*, 513 U.S. 454, 470 (1995).
88. *NAACP v. Alabama*, 357 U.S. 449 (1958).
89. *West Virginia State Board of Education v. Barnette*, 319 U.S. 624, 634 (1943).
90. *Wooley v. Maynard*, 430 U.S. 705, 714 (1977).

one case, and the state's motto in the other. The right not to speak can also provide protection from being forced to express our own ideas. Although most of the witnesses who refused to testify in the 1950s before the House Committee on Un-American Activities invoked the Fifth Amendment right against self-incrimination, at least a few based their silence instead on the First Amendment right not to speak. Even though these litigants ultimately lost, the Supreme Court at least allowed that a First Amendment right of silence exists.[91]

In 2001 the Supreme Court had to determine under what circumstances political candidates might be forced to "speak" about controversial issues. Voters in Missouri amended their state constitution to require that future ballots include a reference in-

The Supreme Court held in 2001 that the State of Missouri may not insert the words "DECLINED TO PLEDGE TO SUPPORT TERM LIMITS" on ballots, lest candidates be forced to speak about the issue of term limits.

---

91. *Wilkinson v. United States,* 365 U.S. 399 (1961); *Barenblatt v. United States,* 360 U.S. 109 (1959).

dicating which candidates had "DECLINED TO PLEDGE TO SUPPORT TERM LIMITS." The Supreme Court overturned the provision as a violation of the First Amendment (among other federal constitutional provisions). Not only was Missouri guilty of compelling candidates to speak out on an issue they might otherwise choose to avoid, but the state was planning to punish candidates who did not take the preferred stance on that issue.[92]

Also in 2001, the Court struck down 1996 amendments to the Legal Services Corporation Act forbidding LSC-funded lawyers to bring suits with the purpose of altering welfare laws (though attorneys could bring actions on behalf of specific clients who had been denied benefits).[93] The prohibited categories of lawsuits were themselves instances of attorneys' speech, the Court majority concluded. The Court distinguished the case from its earlier decision in *Rust v. Sullivan*,[94] which forbade physicians who received federal family-planning funding to counsel patients about abortion. In *Rust* the government itself was "speaking" through its program. But when an LSC attorney sues the government, the administration in office already has the chance to speak (by contesting the lawsuit, both inside and outside the courtroom).

WHY MAN INVENTED FIRE.

The Supreme Court held that even the relatively few cattle ranchers who did not support government sponsorship of this message, and whose government assessments were used to pay for this and other ads, had no valid "right not to speak" claim.

The next year, the Supreme Court invalidated an ordinance of an Ohio town that required individuals who planned to do door-to-door canvassing within the community to first fill out a form with identifying information in order to obtain a permit. The rule violated the First Amendment right not to speak, Justice Stevens held for the majority, in that it would even prevent a resident from making "a spontaneous decision to go across the street and urge a neighbor to vote against the mayor . . . without first obtaining the mayor's permission."[95]

---

92. *Cook v. Gralike*, 531 U.S. 510 (2001).

93. *Legal Services Corporation v. Velazquez*, 531 U.S. 533 (2001).

94. 500 U.S. 173 (1991).

95. *Watchtower Bible and Tract Society of New York v. Village of Stratton*, 536 U.S. 150, 167 (2002).

Litigants have sometimes argued, with mixed results, that their First Amendment rights are violated when they are forced to support financially the speech of others whose views they find offensive. Teachers might be forced to join a union,[96] or lawyers a bar association;[97] their fees must be used for purposes directly germane to that membership, however, not for advocacy of political causes or candidates. Public universities, though, may use mandatory student activity fees to fund extracurricular student organizations—no matter how "offensive"—as long as funding is not a function of the groups' political viewpoint.[98]

There have also been a handful of Supreme Court cases involving government-mandated generic advertising campaigns touting the joys of eating fruit[99] or mushrooms[100] or beef. Whether farmers and ranchers can be forced to donate funds in support of such advertising campaigns seems to be a function of whether the Court frames the issue as one of a "right not to speak" or of "the government as speaker." The Court's most recent decision in this area, from 2005, involved the "Beef: It's what's for dinner" campaign, for which much of the funding came from a fee ($1 per head of cattle) assessed against ranchers by the U.S. Department of Agriculture. The unsuccessful plaintiffs argued that the government advertising "promote[d] beef as a generic product," thus "imped[ing] their efforts to promote the superiority of . . . American beef, grain-fed beef, or certified Angus or Hereford beef."[101] The Court's 6-3 decision treated the program as government speech, rather than as government-compelled private speech. As such, there was no First Amendment violation.

In 2006 the Supreme Court declined to review a federal appellate decision rejecting tobacco companies' argument that the State of California was violating their "right not to speak" by using funds from a cigarette surtax to produce and air television commercials highly critical of the industry.[102] Writing for a majority of the Ninth Circuit panel, Judge Betty Binns Fletcher described a "particularly striking" ad called "Rain":

> Children in a schoolyard are shown looking up while cigarettes rain down on them from the sky. A voiceover states "We have to sell cigarettes to your kids. We need half a million new smokers a year just to stay in business. So we advertise near schools, at candy counters. We lower our prices. We have to. It's nothing personal. You understand." At the conclusion, the narrator says, "The tobacco industry: how low will they go to make a profit?"[103]

---

96. *Abood v. Detroit Board of Education*, 431 U.S. 209 (1977).

97. *Keller v. State Bar of California*, 496 U.S. 1 (1990).

98. *Board of Regents of the University of Wisconsin v. Southworth*, 529 U.S. 217 (2000).

99. *Glickman v. Wileman Brothers and Elliott, Inc.*, 521 U.S. 457 (1997).

100. *United States v. United Foods*, 533 U.S. 405 (2001).

101. *Johanns v. Livestock Marketing Association*, 544 U.S. 550, 555–556 (2005).

102. *R.J. Reynolds Tobacco Company v. Shewry*, 423 F.3d 906, 912 (9th Cir. 2005), *cert. denied*, 546 U.S. 1176 (2006).

103. *Id.* at 912.

The court concluded that despite the use of the tobacco surtax to pay for the ads, the government was the speaker in them, not the tobacco companies. There was thus no violation of a posited First Amendment right not to speak.

Mass media litigants have benefited from a First Amendment right not to speak (or print). When the State of Florida tried to force the *Miami Herald* to publish a reply written by a candidate for office who had been criticized in the paper's editorial pages, the Supreme Court invalidated the statute that served as the state's basis for the request. The First Amendment prevents the government from compelling editors "to publish that which reason tells them should not be published," Chief Justice Burger wrote for the Court.[104]

Symbolic Conduct

The "speech" protected by the First Amendment need not involve spoken (or written) words. Human beings engage in many kinds of behaviors designed to send messages: marching, dancing, and sitting, as well as flag waving and flag burning. Over the years the courts have determined that, depending on the context, all these behaviors and more are within the First Amendment's protection. Justice Jackson, in the case invalidating West Virginia's requirement that public school students recite the Pledge of Allegiance, wrote that "symbolism is a primitive but effective way of communicating ideas, . . . a short cut from mind to mind."[105]

None of this is to suggest that all forms of symbolic conduct in all contexts will be granted First Amendment protection. This lesson was learned all too clearly by Vietnam War protestor David Paul O'Brien, who was found in violation of a federal law that forbade the knowing destruction of one's draft card. Upholding his conviction, the Supreme Court set forth a list of criteria still often used to determine when laws or regulations affecting symbolic conduct are compatible with the First Amendment. The *O'Brien* test demands that any such regulations "further an important and substantial government interest," that the state's interest be "unrelated to the suppression of free expression," and that "the incidental restriction on alleged First Amendment freedoms [be] no greater than is essential to the furtherance of that interest."[106] The federal statute under which O'Brien was prosecuted was deemed an expression of several legitimate state interests that were themselves unrelated to the defendant's message, such as ensuring the effective functioning of the Selective Service System.

A few years after *O'Brien*, the Supreme Court offered some further guidance as to the place of symbolic conduct within the system of freedom of expression. In response to the U.S. military's bombing of Cambodia and the killings at Kent State University, college student Harold Spence hung an upside down American flag with a peace sym-

---

104. *Miami Herald Publishing Co. v. Tornillo*, 418 U.S. 241, 256 (1974).
105. *West Virginia State Board of Education v. Barnette*, 319 U.S. 624, 632 (1943).
106. *United States v. O'Brien*, 391 U.S. 367, 376 (1968).

bol affixed to it from his Seattle, Washington, apartment window. The Supreme Court ruled that Spence's action was protected symbolic conduct, in that he had an "intent to convey a particularized message" and because "in the surrounding circumstances the likelihood was great that the message would be understood by those who viewed it."[107] The *Spence* test, which focuses on the speaker's communicational intent and on whether the message will indeed be perceived, is not incompatible with the *O'Brien* test. Indeed, the *Spence* Court indicated that the *O'Brien* test demanded the overturning of Spence's conviction. His prosecution (interestingly, for displaying a flag improperly rather than for "desecrating" the flag) resulted from the state's displeasure with his intended message and was thus not "unrelated to the suppression of free expression." Defendants charged with actually desecrating the flag have also escaped punishment under the *O'Brien* test.[108] Seven times in recent years—including once in 2005—the House of Representatives approved wording of a constitutional amendment that would outlaw flag desecration, thus undoing the effects of these rulings. Each time, the amendment was killed in the Senate (by just one vote in 2006).

The *O'Brien* test has been employed by the Court to adjudicate zoning regulations affecting "adult" movie theaters,[109] and even an outright ban of nightclubs featuring nude dancing.[110] States have more freedom to regulate otherwise protected First Amendment activity, the Court reasoned, if the regulations are unrelated to the expression itself, but rather are aimed at the "secondary effects" of the expression (such as increases in prostitution and other crime).

A fascinating kind of symbolic conduct that has been the source of controversy and litigation in recent years is the "self-help remedy" of destroying every copy of a newspaper one can find, if offended by an article within. Only a tiny handful of states have passed legislation to criminalize such action when the perpetrator buys the copies legitimately or when the paper is designed to be distributed free of charge. How can one "steal" something that is free, after all?[111] There has been at least one successful civil suit against such "mass trashers," but this involved a sheriff and his deputies, so there was "state action" involved, and the officials violated the First Amendment rights of the local newspaper.[112]

---

107. *Spence v. Washington*, 418 U.S. 405, 410–411 (1974).

108. *United States v. Eichman*, 496 U.S. 310 (1990); *Texas v. Johnson*, 491 U.S. 397 (1989).

109. *Young v. American Mini Theatres*, 427 U.S. 50 (1976).

110. *City of Erie v. Pap's A. M.*, 529 U.S. 277 (2000).

111. Clay Calvert, "All the News That's Fit to Steal: The First Amendment, a 'Free' Press & a Lagging Legislative Response," 25 *Loyola of Los Angeles Entertainment Law Review* 117 (2004-2005).

112. *Rossignol v. Voorhaar*, 316 F.3d 516 (4th Cir. 2003). Upon remand, the plaintiff newspaper won a summary judgment ruling against the sheriff and the deputies. 321 F. Supp. 2d 642 (D. Md. 2004).

"You Can't Do That *Here*!":
Time, Place, and Manner Restrictions

The *O'Brien* test, we have seen, asks us to consider whether a governmental regulation is aimed at the expressive components of conduct. We thus must recognize that a whole host of laws or regulations that may have the effect of stifling speech are not *designed* to keep any particular message from being heard. Suppose, for example, that you answer your door to a police officer advising you that your neighbors would appreciate it if you and your party guests make a bit less noise. The content of the message or messages being exchanged among your friends is not at issue in such a situation. The legal intervention stems instead from the *time* (late at night, perhaps, when neighbors are trying to sleep), *place* (a residential, as opposed to purely commercial, area of town), or *manner* (the decibel level itself) of the communication.

Although the Supreme Court has never ruled on a "noisy party complaint" case, it has upheld the notion that content-neutral limitations on a message's loudness or inappropriate choice of venue are permissible. In 1972, in his majority opinion upholding the conviction of a group of civil rights demonstrators for staging a potentially disruptive protest too close to a public school, Justice Marshall indicated why time, place, and manner restrictions were not only permissible but necessary. After all, "two parades cannot march on the same street simultaneously." Moreover, although "a silent vigil may not unduly interfere with a public library, making a speech in the reading room almost certainly would. . . . The crucial question is whether the manner of expression is basically incompatible with the normal activity of a particular place at a particular time."[113]

Over the years the Supreme Court has created a three-part test to determine the constitutionality of time, place, and manner restrictions on speech. First, the regulation must be content neutral. It must not be motivated by governmental displeasure at the specific message being sent. An ordinance forbidding the use of overly loud sound trucks, for example, passes this test in that it does not matter what is said, as long as it is not said at a deafening volume.[114] Similarly, a New York City regulation governing the loudness of amplified concerts in Central Park was upheld. After all, it did not prescribe one decibel level for rap music and another for the 1812 Overture.[115] And the regulatory scheme used by the City of Chicago was upheld because political activists, soccer players, and picnickers alike had to apply for a permit for any gathering of more than fifty people.[116] The city had been sued by a group wishing to demonstrate in favor of decriminalizing marijuana.

Second, the regulation must be narrowly tailored to further an important govern-

---

113. *Grayned v. City of Rockford, Illinois*, 408 U.S. 104, 115–116 (1972).
114. *Kovacs v. Cooper*, 336 U.S. 77 (1948).
115. *Ward v. Rock Against Racism*, 491 U.S. 781 (1989).
116. *Thomas v. Chicago Park District*, 534 U.S. 316 (2002).

ment interest. In 1939, the Supreme Court struck down as unconstitutional laws in a handful of cities that, in the interests of preventing littering, prohibited all distribution of printed literature on street corners. If these cities wanted to decrease littering, they should have more directly punished "those who actually throw papers on the streets," not persons engaged in otherwise protected First Amendment activity.[117] More recently, Richmond, Virginia's, practice of artificially privatizing streets immediately surrounding an inner-city public-housing complex and prohibiting entry to persons not having legitimate business to conduct within was upheld. The plan was narrowly tailored to further the government's interest in maintaining safety in an otherwise high-crime area.[118] The unanimity of the Supreme Court's decision may have been a function of the plaintiff's having been cited previously for destroying property in the housing complex.

Finally, a restriction on the time, place, and manner of communication must permit ample alternative means for speakers to transmit their messages. Thus, much to the dismay of a homeless persons' advocacy group organizing a political demonstration over several days in Lafayette Park (a small grassy area across the street from the White House), the Supreme Court upheld the constitutionality of a National Park Service regulation prohibiting sleeping overnight in the park. The regulation did not prevent the demonstrators from communicating the plight of the homeless, Justice White concluded. Indeed, as long as the participants were willing to take turns, they could collectively maintain a twenty-four hour presence in the park.[119] Or consider Justice Marshall's reasoning in a decision invalidating a New Jersey municipality's law against posting For Sale signs on residential lawns. The law, which was aimed at curbing the practice of panic selling stemming from racial fears, was admittedly not content neutral in that it proscribed one specific message. Marshall went out of his way to point out that the law also could not pass the "ample alternative means of communication" requirement in that the signs reach a specific audience—the casual buyer, not necessarily looking to buy a home and thus not in the habit of reading the classified pages or consulting real estate agents—not easily reached via any other medium.[120]

Public-Forum Analysis

As we have seen, the government may restrict or prohibit communication when the time, place, or manner is deemed inappropriate. There are also places where the government recognizes that communication is an especially appropriate activity. These are called "**public forums.**" The Court has recognized three kinds:

- *Quintessential Public Forums.* Public parks and street corners (so long as speakers do not impede the flow of vehicular or pedestrian traffic) have "by long tradition

---

117. *Schneider v. New Jersey*, 308 U.S. 147, 162 (1939).
118. *Virginia v. Hicks*, 539 U.S. 113 (2003).
119. *Clark v. Community for Creative Non-Violence*, 468 U.S. 288 (1984).
120. *Linmark Associates v. Township of Willingboro*, 431 U.S. 85, 93 (1977).

. . . been devoted to assembly and debate,"[121] and the government is thus compelled to protect the rights of speakers in these forums.

- *Limited Public Forums.* These include auditoriums and meeting rooms, which the government is not required to open up to outside use, but which once opened, must be administered in an evenhanded way, similar to the rules required for the quintessential public forums. Certainly this means that viewpoint-based discrimination is not permitted and all potential users must be treated equally. Thus, a school district in New York could not discriminate against a group of local Christians who wanted to use an elementary school's auditorium for an evening of prayer, singing, and reciting of Bible lessons. The school district had thought that the First Amendment's Establishment Clause forbade such use, but a 6-3 majority of the Court held otherwise.[122] And the District of Columbia was sued successfully by People for the Ethical Treatment of Animals (PETA) when PETA's application to participate in the city's "Party Animals" public sculpture forum with a "sad elephant" was rejected, although a "happy elephant" (one lacking the sad elephant's political stance against animal abuse) would have been accepted.[123] Public forums can also be "limited" in the sense of being open only to certain categories of speakers or even categories of discourse. For example, state university student fees might be used to pay for offices, mailboxes, photocopying, and the like only for student groups, not for outside community groups. A school board or city council meeting might be willing to hear from only those citizens who have something to say that is germane to the evening's agenda.

- *Nonpublic Forums.* This category refers to public property that is not by tradition or practice open as a speaking venue for all comers. The only constraint placed on the government in regulating the use of such property is that access to it should not be based on a potential speaker's viewpoint. An odd event associated with the 2006 State of the Union address provides a handy example. Perhaps you recall that two high-profile audience members were hastily escorted out of the Capitol—antiwar activist

Once the Washington, D.C., government opened up a public forum for "party animal" sculpture designs, it could not discriminate against the viewpoint espoused here by PETA. The blanket reads: "The CIRCUS is coming. See SHACKLES! BULL HOOKS! LONELINESS! All under the 'Big Top.'"

---

121. *Perry Education Association v. Perry Local Educators' Association*, 460 U.S. 37, 45 (1983).
122. *Good News Club v. Milford Central School*, 533 U.S. 98 (2001).
123. *PETA v. Gittens*, 360 F. Supp. 2d 28 (D.D.C. 2003).

THINGS TO REMEMBER

Some Additional First Amendment Doctrines

- The First Amendment includes a right to hear.
- It also includes a right not to speak.
- Free speech includes some kinds of symbolic conduct.
- The *O'Brien* test determines constitutionality of regulations aimed at symbolic conduct:
  - The regulation must further an important interest.
  - That interest must not be simply to stifle a specific message.
  - The regulation must be narrowly drawn.
- Time, place, and manner restrictions are not subject to strict scrutiny:
  - The regulations must be content neutral.
  - They must be narrowly tailored.
  - They must permit sufficient alternative means of communication.
- Government property has sometimes been held to be a public forum open to expressive activity.

Cindy Sheehan for wearing a T-shirt with the message "2245 Dead—How Many More?" and Beverly Young (the wife of a Florida Congressman), whose own T-shirt said "Support the Troops—Defending Our Freedom." Their expulsion was in furtherance of an old and possibly unconstitutionally vague rule against "demonstrating" in the Capitol building. Had there been litigation on the matter, however, the fact that both a pro– and an anti–Iraq War speaker were ejected would suggest that the police had not been guilty of viewpoint-based discrimination. (Sheehan, but not Young, was arrested along with being ejected, but the disorderly conduct charges were swiftly dropped.)

Regulating the *Business* of Communication

Not all legal interventions affecting communication industries should necessarily be considered communication law. If a local police chief, upset at the coverage given him by the town's "alternative" free weekly, effectively shuts down the paper by barging into the newsroom and confiscating the publisher's computer, we would have a clear (and clearly unconstitutional) example of "media law" at work. If that same publisher, however, is a divorced father who is tens of thousands of dollars behind in his child-support payments, the confiscation of that same computer through a judgment obtained by the Division of Family Services would not be at all relevant to the study of communication law.

Media industries are governed by much the same legal environment affecting other businesses. They must pay their workers at least the minimum wage. They must provide safe and nonharassing working conditions. They must contribute their legally mandated share of employees' Social Security payments.

In this final section of the chapter, three areas of the law that are applied to media industries just as to other industries are examined. When applied to the media, however, they have a special impact on the act of communication, either by determining who may speak or what may be said. The three topics to be addressed here are antitrust, taxation, and workplace laws.

Antitrust Laws

The Sherman Act of 1890 and the Clayton Act of 1914 give the Department of Justice license to bring both civil and criminal proceedings against businesses that function "in restraint of trade." Media outlets have often behaved in an anticompetitive manner, and sometimes this behavior has prompted the government to pursue them for antitrust violations. In 1951, the Supreme Court held that the Lorain Journal Company, a newspaper publisher in Ohio, was in violation of antitrust laws when it refused to accept advertising from businesses that had also advertised in competing local media.[124]

Several anticompetitive practices on the part of the publisher of the *Kansas City Star* attracted the government's attention a few years later. The company owned both the morning and afternoon daily papers (the *Kansas City Times* and the *Kansas City Star*, respectively), as well as the *Sunday Star*, a radio station, and a TV station. As in the earlier *Lorain Journal* case, here too the company's agents made clear to some local businesses that if they advertised in competing publications, their ads might not be welcome again in the company's papers. Also, advertisers wishing to patronize one of the company's newspapers were required to place ads in all three. Subscribers were similarly forced into a "take all three or get none" deal. Perhaps most troubling to the court was that the traditionally respected wall between the advertising and editorial functions of the newspaper had apparently come down in a distinctively anticompetitive manner. It seems that a major league baseball player was a partner in a local florist shop. He was told that if he failed to convince his partners to cease advertising the shop in a competing newspaper, coverage in the three newspapers of his baseball career would diminish or disappear.

Writing for a panel of three judges on the Eighth Circuit Court of Appeals, Judge Vogel thought it ironic that the newspaper publisher would try to shield itself from this Sherman Act prosecution by invoking the First Amendment. "Publishers of newspapers," he reminded the defendants, "must answer for their actions in the same manner as anyone else. . . . Freedom to print does not mean freedom to destroy."[125]

Newspapers have not been the only media industries to become antitrust defen-

---

124. *Lorain Journal Co. v. United States*, 342 U.S. 143 (1951).
125. *United States v. Kansas City Star Co.*, 240 F.2d 643, 666 (8th Cir. 1957).

dants over the years. The structure of the motion picture industry was shaped in large part by a 1948 Supreme Court decision holding that **block-booking** (whereby theater owners were forced by movie studios to exhibit their less desirable "B" movies along with the more popular films likely to produce a profit) was a violation of the Sherman Act.[126] Major Hollywood studios at the time also owned huge chains of theaters, an arrangement that produced its own host of anticompetitive practices. Independent theater owners naturally found it hard to get access to the best pictures, which the studios preferred to keep for their own screens. The government successfully pressured the studios to sell off their movie theaters in the late 1940s.

Perhaps the most dramatic litigation in recent years alleging anticompetitive practices on the part of a communications industry has been the Department of Justice's suit against Microsoft. The government alleged that Microsoft used its virtual monopoly in personal computer operating systems (Windows) to create an unfair advantage in marketing its own Internet browser (Internet Explorer). Microsoft argued that its browser is an integral part of its operating system and that to force it to remove Internet Explorer would be akin to forcing a cookie manufacturer to take the chocolate chips out of its cookies to protect the market share of companies that wished to sell consumers chocolate chips separately. At first it appeared that Microsoft would be broken up into at least two companies,[127] but a complicated series of motions and appeals followed, and the Bush administration's Justice Department dropped most of the demands made by the earlier Clinton administration. A settlement was approved by the D.C. Circuit Court of Appeals in 2004, which effectively ended the federal suit and companion suits by a handful of states and computer trade groups.[128] The settlement requires Microsoft to allow computer manufacturers more flexibility to include rival software companies' products on their desktop displays.

Antitrust laws can be triggered not only when a company engages in specific anticompetitive practices but also when one or a small group of companies simply grows so big that a monopoly or quasi monopoly results. Such monopolies can happen with media outlets just as they can among car manufacturers or soft drink producers. The federal government has often brought actions against media companies that have achieved too large a market share. For example, in the 1960s the Times Mirror Company, the owner of the *Los Angeles Times* and other newspapers, was forced to divest itself of newspapers it had recently purchased in neighboring San Bernardino County.[129] The government has also had to approve the many mergers that resulted from the Telecommunications Act of 1996, discussed in more detail in chapter 12.

---

126. *United States v. Paramount Pictures, Inc.*, 334 U.S. 131 (1948); see also *United States v. Loew's, Inc.*, 371 U.S. 38 (1962) (holding that movie studios' "block-booking" of films to TV stations violated antitrust laws).

127. *United States v. Microsoft Corp.*, 97 F. Supp. 2d 59 (D.D.C. 2000).

128. *Massachusetts v. Microsoft Corp.*, 373 F.3d 1199 (D.C. Cir. 2004).

129. *United States v. Times Mirror Co.*, 274 F. Supp. 606 (C.D. Cal. 1967), *aff'd*, 390 U.S. 712 (1968).

In 1970 Congress adopted the **Newspaper Preservation Act**, which permitted competing newspapers in the same town to function under a **joint operating agreement** (**JOA**) whereby the advertising, circulation, and printing portions of the two papers would be joined, but each paper would maintain separate editorial functions. These exceptions to the usual behaviors one would expect under existing antitrust law were to be permitted only if at least one of the two newspapers was otherwise in danger of failing. The act was thus the federal government's way of expressing the value of having more than one major newspaper in a community. In the late 1970s there were functioning JOAs in twenty-eight cities nationwide, but that number decreased by more than 50 percent by the end of the century, with most of the remaining agreements likely also to die out soon. Very few cities still have more than one newspaper, and even in those cities one paper is usually so clearly the marketplace leader that it has "little incentive . . . to agree to peaceful coexistence."[130]

Taxation

Although the press may be taxed in the same way as any industry,[131] taxes that discriminatorily target media outlets may be found unconstitutional. This principle was established clearly in a 1936 case from Louisiana, whose legislature had enacted a tax on the advertising revenues from newspapers with circulations of more than 20,000 subscribers. The tax seemed designed cleverly to burden, even silence, critics of Senator Huey Long, who was most vociferously challenged by editors of the state's largest newspapers. In his majority opinion striking down the law, Justice George Sutherland described the tax as "a deliberate and calculated device . . . to limit the circulation of information to which the public is entitled."[132]

Even in the absence of as colorful a figure as Huey Long, the Supreme Court reached a similar result in 1983, when it struck down a Minnesota tax on paper and ink that, by exempting the first $100,000 of use, effectively targeted the tax so narrowly that one newspaper paid almost two-thirds of it. Even if the legislature had no personal animus against the Minneapolis Star and Tribune Company, Justice O'Connor ruled, singling out only a few media companies for taxation presents too strong "a potential for abuse."[133]

The State of Arkansas was also held in violation of the First Amendment when it enacted a tax that at first blush would seem to be constitutional because it was aimed at "tangible personal property" generally. The constitutional infirmity was in the tax's application to some magazines but its exemption for locally published "religious,"

---

130. Paul Farhi, "The Death of the JOA," *American Journalism Review*, September 1999, 48–52.

131. *Arizona Publishing Co. v. O'Neil*, 304 U.S. 543 (1938); *City of Corona v. Corona Daily Independent*, 252 P.2d 56 (Cal. Ct. App. 1953).

132. *Grosjean v. American Press Co.*, 297 U.S. 233, 250 (1936).

133. *Minneapolis Star & Tribune Co. v. Minnesota Commissioner of Revenue*, 460 U.S. 575, 592 (1983).

"professional," and "trade and sports journals." Taxes may not discriminate on the basis of a publication's content, the Court ruled.[134] Similarly, Texas was not permitted to exempt only *religious* periodicals from a general sales tax. The Court's decision here rested upon the First Amendment's Establishment Clause.[135] The same constitutional provision was used in 1999 by the Pennsylvania Supreme Court to strike down a sales tax exemption for bibles and other religious publications.[136]

Taxes that apply to some but not all media industries do not necessarily violate the Constitution, however. In 1991, for example, the Supreme Court upheld an Arkansas sales tax levied against cable television companies but not magazines, newspapers, or even home satellite systems. Justice O'Connor's majority opinion indicated that "differential taxation of speakers, even members of the press, does not implicate the First Amendment unless the tax is directed at, or presents the danger of, suppressing particular ideas."[137] Whether a sales tax may constitutionally be applied to magazines while exempting newspapers is still an open question, however. Courts have come down on both sides of this issue.[138]

Workplace Law

Just as taxes that are applied to industry generally may be applied to media outlets, so must media industries obey relevant federal, state, and local labor laws in their relations with employees. Interesting questions often arise, however, when courts try to determine how to apply this body of law to professional communicators. In this section we look at two areas of labor law that have attracted much judicial attention: the Fair Labor Standards Act of 1938 (FLSA) and the National Labor Relations Act.

One of the key provisions of the FLSA is that employees not exempted from its scope must be paid overtime wages for work in excess of forty hours per week. Certain categories of professional employees are exempt from the act—thus the references to "exempt" and "nonexempt" employees in human resources offices nationwide—and courts have often been called on to determine when media employees should be considered exempt professionals. This body of case law often forces media litigants to make arguments contrary to their customary economic bargaining positions. Management must claim that the work of such employees is distinct and creative (and thus not qualifying for overtime pay), whereas workers counter that their output is routine and uninspired.[139]

---

134. *Arkansas Writers' Project, Inc. v. Ragland*, 481 U.S. 221 (1987).

135. *Texas Monthly, Inc. v. Bullock*, 489 U.S. 1 (1989).

136. *Haller v. Commonwealth*, 728 A.2d 351 (Pa. Super. Ct. 1999).

137. *Leathers v. Medlock*, 499 U.S. 439, 453 (1991).

138. *Southern Living v. Celauro*, 789 S.W.2d 251 (Tenn. 1990) (striking down the differential taxation of magazines and newspapers); *Hearst Corp. v. Iowa Department of Revenue & Finance*, 461 N.W.2d 295 (Iowa 1990) (upholding such differential treatment).

139. *Reich v. Newspapers of New England*, 44 F.3d 1060, 1075 n.12 (1st Cir. 1995); see also *Freeman v. National Broadcasting Co.*, 846 F. Supp. 1109, 1123 (S.D.N.Y. 1993).

Ever since the 1940s, the Secretary of Labor, who has initial responsibility for enforcement of the FLSA, has maintained that only a very small number of working journalists are "professionals" exempt from the act's overtime-pay provisions. Only
"editorial writers, columnists, critics, and 'top-flight' writers of analytical and interpre-
tative articles" should be considered exempt, the Department of Labor argues. Although
it is fair to say that the vast majority of reporters are valued for their "intelligence,
diligence, and accuracy," only these categories of employees are called on as their "primary duty" to produce work requiring "invention, imagination, or talent," work that
is "original and creative in character." The Department also emphasizes that reporters,
unlike other professionals such as doctors and lawyers, do not have to master a prescribed body of knowledge to function in their careers; they need not have journalism
degrees and often do not have college degrees at all. Courts have generally accepted the
Department of Labor's interpretation of the FLSA's applicability to the newsroom.[140]
The one exceptional case involved *Washington Post* writers who were considered professionals exempt from the FLSA's overtime-wages provisions. In that case, the court emphasized that *Washington Post* reporters are very highly paid national leaders in the field
of journalism, often called on to teach at universities, to write books, and to serve as
guests on talk shows and public affairs programs. Moreover, these reporters functioned
in a professionally collegial atmosphere that would be envied by their counterparts at
other papers. They were encouraged to generate their own story ideas and to decide
not only how to pursue stories but also when it might be wisest to "kill" a story.[141]

The National Labor Relations Act also has an impact on how media outlets are
regulated as businesses. The act provides most employees with the right to organize,
to form unions, to collectively bargain, and to engage in all these activities without
fear of retribution from their employers. But what happens if the employer is a newspaper and the alleged retribution takes the form of reassigning a reporter to new duties? Such was the case when Mitchell Stoddard, a columnist for the *Passaic Daily
News* in New Jersey, had been active in a union organizing drive and later learned
that his employer no longer planned to run his weekly column. The National Labor
Relations Board (NLRB) ordered the newspaper to restore the status quo, to continue
to run Stoddard's column. The newspaper appealed, arguing that the NLRB's chosen
remedy was a violation of its right to determine what will and will not run in its pages,
the "right not to speak" corollary First Amendment right discussed earlier in this
chapter. The D.C. Circuit Court of Appeals recognized that the NLRB's goals—to
ensure both that the company not be allowed to retaliate against Stoddard and that
"meaningful remedies for [future] victims of unlawful discrimination" be in place—

---

140. *Reich v. Newspapers of New England*, 44 F.3d 1060 (1st Cir. 1995); *Reich v. Gateway Press*,
13 F.3d 685 (3d Cir. 1994); *Freeman v. National Broadcasting Co.*, 846 F. Supp. 1109 (S.D.N.Y.
1993); *Dalheim v. KDFW-TV*, 706 F. Supp. 493 (N.D. Tex. 1988), *aff'd*, 918 F.2d 1220 (5th Cir.
1990).

141. *Sherwood v. Washington Post*, 677 F. Supp. 9 (D.D.C. 1988), *rev'd and remanded on other
grounds*, 871 F.2d 1144 (D.C. Cir. 1989).

THINGS TO REMEMBER

Regulating Media as a Business

- Federal antitrust laws have been used against
  - newspapers that refuse to accept advertising from businesses already advertising in competing media;
  - movie studios that demand theater owners to accept less-known "B" movies if they want to show the true blockbusters;
  - movie studios that own too many movie theaters; and
  - media companies that have grown so huge and command such a large market share that they threaten to stifle competition.
- The Newspaper Preservation Act sometimes permits otherwise competing newspapers to form Joint operating agreements to share noneditorial costs.
- The media may be subject to the same kinds of taxes as any other business, but taxes that single out the media, or that discriminate among media outlets, might be found unconstitutional.
- Taxes that exempt only *religious* media are especially likely to be found unconstitutional.
- Most media employees are considered "nonexempt" and thus eligible for certain benefits such as overtime pay.
- Journalists can generally be prevented by their employers from engaging in overt political activity.

were legitimate. Here, however, the NLRB went too far in that it injected itself "into the editorial decision-making process." The court remanded the case back to the NLRB, suggesting that an order "direct[ing] the Company to not discriminate against Stoddard on the basis of his union activity" might be a more appropriate remedy. On remand, the NLRB ordered the paper to restore Stoddard's "column-writing duties" but did not compel the paper to actually publish whatever columns he writes, just as long as that decision flows from considerations other than his union activities.[142]

The strained judicial compromise reached in this case underscores the more general proposition that deference to publishers' free press rights necessarily means that media company employees may have fewer free speech rights than workers in other industries.[143] Thus, for example, Washington's Fair Campaign Practices Act, which protects employees from retaliation for their off-the-job political activities, was held inapplicable to a newspaper reporter who had been dismissed by the Tacoma *Morning News Tribune* for having participated in a pro-choice abortion rally and for ignoring management's request that she refrain from any high-profile political activities. The

---

142. *Passaic Daily News v. NLRB*, 736 F.2d 1543 (D.C. Cir. 1984).

143. Louis Day, "The Journalist as Citizen Activist: The Ethical Limits of Free Speech," 4 *Communication Law and Policy* 1 (1999).

newspaper's need to protect its reputation for objectivity in reporting the news must prevail over the reporter's interests, the court held.[144]

Chapter Summary

Although freedom of speech can be traced back to the ancients, the American experience results primarily from the British common law. Early colonial experience was characterized by intolerance of dissent, and the Alien and Sedition Acts followed swiftly upon the formation of the new nation.

The Supreme Court had very little to say about the First Amendment's meaning until the World War I era, when, in a long series of cases continuing through the 1960s, the Court dealt with the issue of incitement to overthrowing the government or to other violent action. The current test for such speech is found in *Brandenburg v. Ohio*, a 1969 decision.

Over the years many competing First Amendment theories have been proposed, including absolutist theory, access theory, and various balancing approaches. Generally, the modern judiciary engages in preferred-position balancing.

Theorists have also identified many functions served by freedom of speech, including aiding in the search for the truth, enabling us to be better self-governors, acting as a check on government abuse, providing for individual fulfillment, serving as a societal safety valve, and simply helping us see ourselves as a tolerant people.

Other theorists, including Marxists, feminists, and critical race theorists, have questioned the place of freedom of speech in the hierarchy of values.

The First Amendment has been interpreted to include a right to hear, a right not to speak, and a right to engage in symbolic conduct.

Government restrictions on speech that are not aimed at the actual content of the message do not require as exacting scrutiny as purer forms of censorship.

---

144. *Nelson v. McClatchy Newspapers, Inc.*, 936 P.2d 1123 (Wash. 1997).

Chapter 3

DEFAMATION: COMMON-LAW ELEMENTS

Sometimes it seems as if Hollywood celebrities who are offended by their media coverage are as likely to sue for libel as they are to simply have their publicists try to set the record straight with a press release. In recent years Britney Spears has sued *US Weekly* magazine for publishing an article alleging that she and her husband had produced a sex tape,[1] Tom Cruise has sued on more than one occasion when the media have suggested he is gay,[2] Ashley Olsen has sued the *National Enquirer* for claiming she had been involved in a drug scandal,[3] and in England (where libel law is more friendly to plaintiffs than here in the United States), Elton John won an undisclosed settlement from the *London Times* for alleging that he acted a bit snooty at an AIDS fund-raiser, asking attendees to speak to him only if spoken to.[4]

Libel law is designed, of course, to protect a person's reputation from blemish. In Shakespeare's *Othello*, the treacherous Iago famously reminds us that an ordinary thief, one who "steals my purse . . . steals trash," but that a defamer, someone who "flinches from me my good name . . . makes me poor indeed." More routine though less poetic definitions of libel are readily available in standard legal publications. *Black's Law Dictionary* defines libel as "an intentional false communication . . . that injures another's reputation or good name." The *Restatement of Torts* reports that messages are libelous if they "tend so to harm the reputation of another as to lower him in the estimation of the community or to deter third persons from associating or dealing with him."

---

1. "Name Dropping," *Chicago Tribune*, March 19, 2006, C19.
2. "The Daily Dish," *Buffalo News*, January 17, 2003, C5.
3. Catherine Billey, "Ashley Olsen Strikes Back," *New York Times*, February 17, 2005, E2.
4. Richard Eldredge, "Sir Elton Wins Award for Libel, Helps Charity," *Atlanta Journal-Constitution*, February 17, 2006, 2G.

Britney Spears filed a $20 million lawsuit against *US Weekly* magazine for this article, which alleges that she and then-husband Kevin Federline had produced a home sex tape. The case was dismissed in late 2006.

Libel plaintiffs in recent years have included not only Hollywood figures but also such Washington politicos as Sidney Blumenthal[5] (former aide to President Clinton) and Gennifer Flowers[6] (who claimed to have had an ongoing affair with then-governor Clinton). Ordinary people also sue for libel, and as you will see in chapter 4, the law is more in their favor than it is for celebrities and public officials. But the

5. *Blumenthal v. Drudge*, 29 Media L. Rep. 1347 (D.D.C. 2001). Internet reporter Matt Drudge had alleged that Blumenthal was a wife beater.

6. *Flowers v. Carville*, 292 F. Supp. 2d 1225 (D. Nev. 2003), *aff'd*, 161 Fed. Appx. 697 (9th Cir. 2006). Carville, also a former Clinton aide, had accused Flowers of doctoring or otherwise selectively

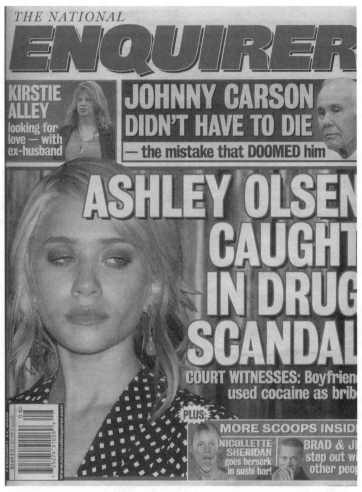

The cover story about Ashley Olsen prompted the former child star to sue for a reported $40 million.

cost of mounting a libel case can be steep, which may explain why so many plaintiffs are people whose names we already knew.

Media professionals are more likely to get into legal trouble over alleged libel than over any other issue this book addresses. The defendants' costs can be staggering. Jury awards in the millions of dollars are no longer especially newsworthy events. Even if the media defendant ultimately prevails, as typically happens at least on the appellate level, the legal fees involved and the enormous amount of time taken from writing

editing the audiotapes she used at her famous press conference during the 1992 presidential campaign.

new stories to defend old ones would alone constitute ample reason to avoid publishing defamatory materials.

For most of the country's history, that the press could be sued and even criminally prosecuted for libel—seventeen states still have **criminal libel** laws on the books, though they are rarely used—never seemed to raise any constitutional objections. The First Amendment, it will be recalled, tells *Congress* that it cannot abridge freedom of speech and of the press. Defamation had always been handled at the state level. Moreover, that the founders clearly knew of the existence of libel laws and mentioned not one word about them in the text of the Constitution seems to suggest that they saw no philosophic conflict between the system of freedom of expression they intended to create and the continuing use of laws against defamation. In this chapter, we examine the traditional common-law definition of libel as it has evolved in the states. In 1964, the U.S. Supreme Court intervened, ruling that the First Amendment does impose significant restrictions on libel law.[7] So dramatic have been the changes in libel since that seminal ruling that we devote chapter 4 to an examination of the Supreme Court's libel doctrine as it has developed in the past few decades.

Elements of a Libel Suit

Defamation can be defined as false statements of fact disseminated about a person that result in damage to that person's reputation. Traditionally, the law recognized separate actions for libel (written defamation) and **slander** (spoken defamation). In the several centuries after the invention of the printing press but before the discovery of radio, this separation was logical for at least two reasons. First, the unamplified spoken word could damage a person's reputation in the minds of only those who were physically present to hear the speech. Unless the speaker had access to a physical setting with extraordinary acoustics, the audience would probably be a few hundred people at most. In addition, the spoken word has a more ephemeral quality than the written word. The expression "here today, gone tomorrow" actually exaggerates the life of the spoken word, which is more accurately described as gone in the *moment* after it is uttered. The written word, by contrast, has a life that transcends space and time. Recipients of the message can show it to others, and they can discuss it and amplify its effects. Libel could reach a larger audience and do much more lasting harm than slander.

The advent of the electronic mass media muddied the waters to the point where today the distinction between libel and slander has all but disappeared in law. Even the least viewed programs on national network television, after all, reach an audience many times the size of the circulation figures for the country's most popular magazines and newspapers. Moreover, the widespread use of recording equipment ensures

---

7. *New York Times Co. v. Sullivan*, 376 U.S. 254 (1964).

that the spoken word now can have a shelf life as long as any written message. Although some states still make some parts of a libel suit easier to prove against a "libeler" than a "slanderer," such differences are few. Therefore, this book follows the lead of most courts and commentators by using the word *libel* to refer to both written and spoken defamatory utterances.

Generally speaking, libel plaintiffs must prove four elements in order to prevail.[8] They must establish defamation, of course, but also **publication**, **identification**, and **fault**. The discussion of the first three of these elements takes up the rest of this chapter. Because the Supreme Court's libel doctrine, which has been evolving since the 1960s, has focused almost entirely on the issue of fault, the discussion of that fourth element is necessarily rather lengthy and complex. Chapter 4 examines the Supreme Court's 1964 intervention into libel law as well as later cases that have fine-tuned and generally expanded the First Amendment protections provided in that case.

Defamation

Defamatory utterances are those that if believed, will make a listener think less highly of the persons described, avoid their company in social situations, or avoid seeking out their services in business relationships. The following discussion of this first element examines several key questions courts address as libel plaintiffs try to build their cases. First, we consider whether the defamatory meaning is explicit and obvious, or whether readers would need additional information to understand the insult. Then we focus on the audience, as we try to ascertain *in whose minds* the complainant has been damaged. Next, with respect to the message itself, we will see that courts have sometimes excused arguably libelous statements as "rhetorical hyperbole." The focus then shifts to the relationship between the defamation element and the kinds and amounts of damages successful plaintiffs may be awarded. Finally, we will examine how corporations, and even products, can be libeled.

Libel Per Se, Libel Per Quod, and Implied Libel.
Traditionally, the common law of libel has recognized two categories of defamatory statements. Although Supreme Court intervention into libel law has made the distinctions less important to litigants than was once the case, the categories still help to understand the overall concept of defamation. The first category of defamation is **libel per se**, allegations that would obviously, with no further embellishment by the speaker or special

---

8. Some writers include *falsity* as a fifth element. This book does not do so, reflecting the fact that the common law traditionally placed the burden of proof instead on the defendant to establish the truth of the defamatory statements. Moreover, in some states, even today, truth is not an absolute defense to a libel action. Although the Supreme Court has had some things to say about this issue, it has not gone so far as to wholly reverse the common-law tradition. This point will be expanded upon when we discuss the Court's ruling in *Philadelphia Newspapers, Inc. v. Hepps* in chapter 4.

knowledge on the part of the listener, damage the reputation of the persons described. Examples of defamation that have generally been recognized as libel per se include allegations of criminal wrongdoing, of gross incompetence in one's chosen career, of such serious moral failings as being a chronic liar, and of having a loathsome and contagious disease. To accuse a woman of sexual misconduct has also been viewed as libelous per se.[9] The second broad category of defamation is **libel per quod**. At one level, this category includes all libelous statements that do not fit into the traditional libel per se category. Another way of defining libel per quod is as a statement that seems innocent enough on its face but that when added to specific facts presumably already known by readers would be injurious to reputation. Suppose that a campus paper were to write that "Professor Jones was seen gardening in her backyard yesterday and appeared to be vigorous, energetic, and healthy." These would hardly seem to be defamatory statements, but what if Jones had recently filed for disability benefits? Knowledgeable readers might correctly surmise that the reporter had intended to suggest that Jones was engaged in fraud.

A concept often confused with libel per quod is **implied libel** (sometimes called **defamation by implication**). Libel per quod involves situations in which the plaintiff alleges that factual allegations were untrue. In the Professor Jones hypothetical in the above paragraph, the plaintiff would allege that it was actually someone else seen in her garden or that she was not "energetic" but rather was manifesting some very obvious difficulty bending down. By contrast, implied libel cases find plaintiffs admitting from the outset that the defendant's words are true. It is the implication of those admittedly true statements that burns, such plaintiffs allege. In a case from Iowa, for example, a sportswriter was accused in print of "rarely attending events on which he wrote columns." To the extent that words like "rarely" can be assigned a truth value, the claim was literally true, in that the plaintiff admitted that he attended fewer than one-fifth of the events about which he wrote. The implication of the admittedly true charge, the plaintiff alleged, was that it is customary for sportswriters to attend all or most events about which they write, or even that he was somehow unethical for writing about things of which he did not have direct knowledge.[10] Not all states or federal circuits are willing to adjudicate claims of implied libel. Some have held that only *explicit* falsehoods may be the subject of libel claims.

---

9. U.S. courts even in recent years have taken female libel plaintiffs' claims far more seriously when the defamatory statements concerned their sexual "virtue" rather than, say, their professional competence. Diane L. Borden, "Patterns of Harm: An Analysis of Gender and Defamation," 1 *Communication Law and Policy* 105, 133–134 (1997).

10. *Stevens v. Iowa Newspapers, Inc.*, 711 N.W.2d 732 (Iowa Ct. App. 2006), *aff'd*, 728 N.W. 2d 823 (Iowa 2007); see also *Nichols v. Moore*, 477 F.3d 396 (6th Cir. 2007) (accepting that Michigan recognizes actions for "defamation by implication," but finding that the brother of convicted Oklahoma City bomber Terry Nichols failed to establish such a claim against filmmaker Michael Moore's *Bowling for Columbine*).

THINGS TO REMEMBER

Libel Per Se, Libel Per Quod, and Implied Libel

Traditional libel per se categories include allegations of

- criminal activity;
  ("Jones is an embezzler"; "Smith is an organized crime lynchpin")
- professional incompetence;
  ("Siegel has left more sponges inside his patients than most households go through in a year.")
- serious character flaws;
  ("We would have loved to interview Chambers for this article, but he is such a chronic liar that it hardly seemed worth the effort.")
- having a "loathsome, contagious" disease; and
  ("Apparently the reason the star has not shown up on the set for the last two days is that he is dealing with his recent AIDS diagnosis.")
- lack of chastity attributed to an unmarried woman.
  ("Accounts of their wedding in the society pages that described the bride as 'blushing' and 'virginal' were, at best, half truths.")

Libel per quod involves

- defamatory allegations that do not fit these categories *or*
- defamation that can only be understood in conjunction with outside knowledge.

Implied libel refers to statements that

- are literally true *and*
- might be actionable because of their unspoken implications.

Who Has to Believe?   For a report to be found defamatory does not require that the vast majority of readers did in fact hold the libeled party in lower esteem after seeing the charges. A subject matter might be sufficiently esoteric that only a small percentage of readers will understand a statement's libelous meaning. No matter. Courts will gauge the negative effects of the libel on any right-minded individuals who together constitute a community of relevance to the plaintiff.[11]

Adjudication becomes quite complicated if a plaintiff's "community" is an identifiable group with values far different from those of the society at large. Would it be defamatory for the press to report that world-famous safecracker "Frankie the Fingers" has "lost his touch"? Certainly such an allegation, if believed, would make professional criminals less likely to seek out Frankie's services. The charge would also seem to fit into the traditional libel per se category of attributing "professional incompetence" to the person described. More generally, Professor Lyrissa Lidsky of the Uni-

---

11. See, e.g., *Ben-Oliel v. Press Publishing Co.*, 167 N.E. 432 (N.Y. 1929), in which only a newspaper's readers who were very knowledgeable about diverse Middle Eastern cultures would have understood why the article in question had defamatory elements.

Defendant Carroll O'Connor on the witness stand in *Perzigian v. O'Connor*, a libel case brought by the drug dealer indirectly involved with the suicide of O'Connor's son. © 1997 Court TV (O'Connor). Reprinted with permission.

versity of Florida points out that in some neighborhoods and in some social circles, being accused of having "cooperated with the police" might diminish one's reputation greatly.[12] The courts' general reply to these insights is that libel law is not concerned with how esteemed one is in the eyes of criminals, but rather with an utterance's effect on one's reputation among a community of listeners that is both substantial and respectable.

Sometimes a potential libel plaintiff's reputation in the mainstream community, long before publication of allegedly defamatory remarks, is so irredeemable that a few more insults could not hurt. Such **libel-proof plaintiffs**, as they are known in the law, are generally not able to prevail in defamation cases. This reasoning may have been what prompted the jury in the libel suit pressed by known drug dealer Harry Perzigian to find for the defendant, actor Carroll O'Connor, who had accused Perzigian of being a "partner in murder" after his son committed suicide while stoned.[13]

Another complication in adjudicating the defamation element of libel is that community standards are not static. To falsely assert that a person is black would surely not be considered defamatory today, but just as surely *was* considered defamatory in the first half of the twentieth century. Similarly, for a long time it was assumed that to falsely call someone homosexual was libelous, in part because the charge amounted to allegation of criminal wrongdoing. But the U.S. Supreme Court has told us that it is not a crime to have gay sex,[14] and courts adjudicating libel claims stemming from allegations of homosexuality have to deal with the more progressive social climate implied by that decision. In *Albright v. Morton*, for example, Madonna's former bodyguard and lover James Albright sued because his name was used in error in a caption to a photo in a Madonna biography that actually depicted another member of Madonna's entourage, an "outspoken homosexual" named José Guitierez.[15] The association of the incorrect caption with that photo, Albright claimed, falsely labeled him gay (even though the caption also explained that the person pictured was Madonna's "secret lover," with whom she had had a "stormy three-year relationship" during

12. Lyrissa Barnett Lidsky, "Defamation, Reputation and the Myth of Community," 71 *Washington Law Review* 1, 8 (1996).

13. Ann O'Neill and Joe Mozingo, "O'Connor Cleared of Defamation Suit," *Los Angeles Times*, July 26, 1997, A1.

14. *Lawrence v. Texas*, 539 U.S. 558 (2003).

15. 321 F. Supp. 2d 130 (D. Mass. 2004).

which time "they [had] planned to marry, and had even chosen names for their children"). Judge Nancy Gertner ruled for the defendants, holding that community standards had progressed to the point where a false attribution of homosexuality could no longer be considered libelous. A federal appellate court upheld the decision, but on the alternative grounds that the only readers who possibly would have inferred a defamatory meaning in the mislabeled photo were those who knew enough about Madonna's inner circle to know that the fellow pictured was gay (despite the very heterosexually focused attributions in the caption) but not enough to know that the person pictured was Guitierez rather than Albright.[16]

What Does It All Mean?   Sometimes language can be ambiguous, subject to multiple interpretations. The Supreme Court was asked if it was libelous for the

Madonna attends ex-lover Prince's concert with her secret lover and one-time bodyguard Jimmy Albright (left). Albright who bears an uncanny relationship to Carlos Leon, the father of Madonna's daughter, enjoyed a stormy three-year relationship with the star. They planned to marry, and had even chosen names for their children.

Plaintiff James Albright's libel suit failed because almost no one would infer that the person described in the photo's caption was gay, unless they already knew that the photo was actually of the gay Madonna entourage member José Guitierez. Such readers would also surely know that this was not a photo of Albright.

16. *Amrak Productions v. Morton*, 410 F.3d 69 (1st Cir. 2005).

THINGS TO REMEMBER

The Defamation Element and the Audience

- To be actionable, a libelous statement must be believed by a significant number of reasonable persons.
- That people who are themselves unsavory characters think less of you will not constitute your being libeled.
- Some libel plaintiffs are already held in such low esteem that they are deemed "libel-proof."
- Society's concept of what kinds of charges are libelous changes over time.

Greenbelt News Review in Maryland to suggest that local real estate developer Charles Bresler was in the process of "blackmailing" the city (a phrase used by several participants at Greenbelt City Council meetings). The developer had been engaged in negotiations with the city council to obtain certain zoning variances that would allow the construction of high-density housing on land owned by him. At the same time, the city was attempting to acquire another tract of his land for the construction of a new high school. Bresler made clear his intention to force the city to engage in extensive litigation concerning compensation for the school site should the zoning waivers he sought be denied.

Although the word "blackmail" could certainly refer to the criminal act of extortion, the Court held that the most natural interpretation of the paper's use of the word was more benign. "Even the most careless reader," Justice Stewart wrote for the majority, would recognize that the epithet was used only so as to suggest that "Bresler's negotiating position [was] extremely unreasonable."[17]

Colorful stuntman Evel Knievel discovered that the word *pimp* may be subject to the same kind of analysis Justice Stewart applied to "blackmail" in the *Bresler* case. Knievel sued for libel in reaction to a photo on one of ESPN's websites that showed him surrounded by his wife and an attractive young lady, with the caption "Evil Knievel proves that you're never too old to be a pimp." In dismissing his suit, the Ninth Circuit Court of Appeals concluded that no reasonable person could possibly believe that the word pimp was meant to accuse Knievel of criminal activity. The court cited a number of websites devoted to slang usage when it suggested that the word might actually have been intended as a compliment, suggesting that Knievel had achieved "mastery of a subject matter"—sex?—or was just plain "cool."[18]

Sometimes alleged libels are excused because they are most appropriately viewed as satires not to be taken literally. The Supreme Court of Texas dealt with such an

17. *Greenbelt Cooperative Publishing Association v. Bresler*, 398 U.S. 6, 14 (1970).
18. *Knievel v. ESPN*, 393 F.3d 1068, 1077 (9th Cir. 2005).

The original caption read: "Evel Knievel proves that you're never too old to be a pimp." The Ninth Circuit Court of Appeals held that the use of the word *pimp* in the context of over a dozen photos on an ESPN website with similarly irreverent captions could not be considered defamatory.

issue in dismissing a libel case against the *Texas Observer*, which had published a fictional article with some real names attached to it. Back in 1999, a thirteen-year-old in Ponder, Texas, was arrested because a term paper he had written described shooting a teacher and two classmates. Given the national attention focused on "zero-tolerance policies" adopted in response to the *real* school shootings at Columbine High School in Littleton, Colorado, and elsewhere, it is not surprising that such essays would result in some form of administrative intervention, but that the police detained the young man for several days seemed to many people a bit excessive, especially since the class assignment was to write a tale of horror.

A short while later, the *Observer* published an article that on its surface purported to be a factual account of the arrest of a six-year-old student for her book report on Maurice Sendak's classic children's book *Where the Wild Things Are*. The name of the student was fictional, but not those of some of the adults—among them plaintiff and local district attorney Bruce Isaacks—depicted in varying degrees of panic.

Do they make handcuffs this small? Be afraid of this little girl.

The over-the-top nature of this photo and caption, as well as numerous other textual cues, led the Texas Supreme Court to conclude that a *Texas Observer* article was not defamatory.

Reasonable people could not take this article seriously, the court held, because there were numerous clues to the piece's satiric intent, such as a photo of the young miscreant "holding a stuffed animal, captioned 'Do they make handcuffs this small? Be afraid of this little girl.'" Other clues pointed out by the court included the article's reference to the fictitious religious group called Godfearing Opponents of Freedom ("GOOF"), as well as nonsensical quotes attributed to admittedly real public figures (such as the local judge who was quoted as saying that "panic and overreaction" are appropriate responses to student misbehavior.[19]

When Readers Fail to Read.   It is unreasonable to expect that regular readers of newspapers—a dying breed altogether, by many accounts—will pore over every single word in any given day's edition. Instead, we often skim headlines. We might read the first few paragraphs of a story but choose not to follow it to the **jump** (where it continues on another page). Or we might glance at and draw conclusions from photos in the paper without reading fully their explanatory captions.

Imagine reading the following headline and excerpts from the opening sentences of a 1970 *Seattle Post-Intelligencer* article:

The High Cost of a Divorce

Five years ago, Barbara Evans hired a lawyer to represent her in a divorce action. . . .
Today the lawyer owns the home, worth between $55,000 and $65,000, which Mrs. Evans received as part of the 1966 divorce settlement. . . .

How would you interpret these words? Might you presume that the attorney had swindled or at least grossly overcharged Evans? The federal appellate court thought so and expressed concern that readers would not learn until toward the very end of the article that Evans had been charged only $3,000 by her attorney and that she lost her house because of a complicated set of events involving second, third, and even fourth mortgages set in motion by the failure of her ex-husband to meet the financial obligations placed on him by the divorce court. The attorney had done no wrong, but one would have to read the article's additional fifty or so paragraphs and flip pages three times before realizing how misleading the opening had been. Granting summary judgment to the newspaper, as the lower court had done, was deemed inappropriate by the appellate court. "What a newspaper regards as newsworthy usually makes its appearance in the headline and lead paragraphs," the court wrote. "This is what is intended to compel the reader's attention."[20]

---

19. *New Times, Inc. v. Isaacks*, 146 S.W.3d 144 (Tex. 2004).
20. *McNair v. The Hearst Corp.*, 494 F.2d 1309, 1311 (9th Cir. 1974).

A similar result was reached in Brian "Kato" Kaelin's lawsuit against the publisher of the *National Examiner* tabloid. The week after O. J. Simpson was acquitted in the homicides of Nicole Brown Simpson and Ron Goldman, the paper ran a large headline proclaiming that the "COPS THINK KATO DID IT!" In overturning a lower court decision granting summary judgment to the defendant publishers, the Court of Appeals for the Ninth Circuit emphasized that readers would not learn until turning to the article itself, on page 17, that at worst Kaelin might be suspected of not telling all that he knows and thus of having derailed the prosecution's case. He was not a suspect in the homicides themselves. The amount of effort readers would need to expend to learn the true meaning of the headline was extraordinary, the court said, because the tabloid's layout is different and the headline "is unlike a conventional headline that immediately precedes a newspaper story."[21]

The *National Examiner* could be held liable for this headline alone, even though the article itself did not suggest that the "it" Kato Kaelin may have done was to commit homicide.

Sometimes a provocative headline combined with an otherwise unexceptional photograph may be defamatory, especially if added disclaimers are ineffective. This is what happened when the cover of *Boston* magazine's May 2003 issue boasted that readers would find inside an article headlined "The Mating Habits of the Suburban High School Teenager," with a "superhead" above, in an only slightly smaller font, adding: "They hook up online. They hook up in real life. With prom season looming, meet your kids—they might know more about sex than you do." The thrust of the

---

21. *Kaelin v. Globe Communications Corp.*, 162 F.3d 1036 (9th Cir. 1998).

article, according to the First Circuit Court of Appeals, was that "teenagers in the greater Boston area have become more sexually promiscuous over the span of the last decade, . . . that high school has replaced college as the time for sexual experimentation, . . . [and] that, among teenagers, oral sex is the new second base and sex is the new kissing, that no strings 'hooking up' and Internet porn and online cybersex have often replaced dating," and that "today's eastern Massachusetts teens are both sexually advanced and sexually daring." Most of the first two pages of the article consisted of a photograph of five teens taken at a local prom, in which Ms. Stacy Stanton's face was most prominent. The photo's caption, which alerted readers that "the individuals pictured are unrelated to the people or events described in this story," was in such a small font that Ms. Stanton's libel suit would have to go to trial, the appellate court held.[22]

A federal appellate court held that together, the headline and photo suggested that the teens depicted (including the plaintiff) were themselves highly promiscuous. A disclaiming caption was deemed far too small and too oddly placed to dissuade readers from such an erroneous conclusion. The disclaimer appears between the article text and the writer's byline.

---

22. *Stanton v. Metro Corp.*, 438 F.3d 119 (1st Cir. 2006).

THINGS TO REMEMBER

Defamation and Meaning

- Highly inflammatory remarks that fall into the category of rhetorical hyperbole are generally not actionable as libel.
- A misleading newspaper headline can be libelous even if nothing in the article itself is libelous.
- A clarifying or disclaiming statement that does not appear until very late in an article might not save a publisher from liability for earlier sections of the article.
- Liability for a libelous photo might not be eliminated by a disclaiming caption that is not prominent enough to be seen along with the photo.

Defaming People, Corporations, and Products. Most of the libel cases used as examples so far have involved individual plaintiffs. Another commonality among the plaintiffs is that they were living when they brought suit. Libel suits cannot be brought on behalf of deceased individuals; the logic is that when you are dead, you really do not care very much about what others think of you. Libel suits commenced by a living plaintiff who dies while the litigation is pending, however, can be pursued by the deceased's heirs or estate. Then too, libelous statements are sometimes painted with such a broad brush that they affect the reputations of persons closely associated with the individual specifically mentioned in an article. For example, if you suggest in an obituary that a particular individual was a member in good standing of an international network of swingers and spouse swappers, the deceased's widow might choose to sue you for having thus libeled *her* by implication.

Individuals are not the only potential libel plaintiffs. Corporations often sue for libel, as do nonprofit associations and labor unions. To falsely claim that an organization has engaged in fraudulent or deceptive practices can be, as one would expect, just as libelous as to make the same charges against an individual. The Church of Scientology, for example, has often sued for libel and under related causes of action.[23]

Corporations may also sue for libel if a story falsely alleges that the company is on the brink of financial disaster. Such a story prompted a legal dispute that reached the Supreme Court in 1985. A credit-reporting agency, in a newsletter with limited circulation, mistakenly reported that a construction company in Vermont had filed for bankruptcy. It seems that a teenager hired as a "stringer" for Dun & Bradstreet misinterpreted a document showing that a former employee of Greenmoss Builders had filed for *personal* bankruptcy.[24]

---

23. *Church of Scientology v. Behar*, 238 F.3d 168 (2d Cir. 2001); *Church of Scientology v. Daniels*, 992 F.2d 1329 (4th Cir. 1993); *Church of Scientology v. Flynn*, 744 F.2d 694 (9th Cir. 1984); *Church of Scientology v. Foley*, 640 F.2d 1335 (D.C. Cir. 1981); *Church of Scientology v. Adams*, 584 F.2d 893 (9th Cir. 1978).

24. *Dun & Bradstreet v. Greenmoss Builders*, 472 U.S. 749 (1985).

Sometimes corporations will sue because of negative comments made about their products or services themselves. In such situations, where there is not even a hint in the allegedly libelous report that the company itself has engaged in dishonesty, only that the product is an inferior one, the cause of action is called **trade libel**, or **product disparagement**. It is important to understand the difference between defaming the company and disparaging one of its products. If, through overreliance on misinformed sources or through other shoddy reporting, you publish an article alleging that a certain model of automobile is unsafe, you might open yourself up to a trade libel suit. If the same article alleges that the car's manufacturers likely knew that the car was a road hazard, but rushed to bring it to market anyway, the company would also be able to sue for ordinary libel.

A phenomenon that has received considerable media attention is the enactment in several states of "veggie libel" laws. These statutes, passed in the 1990s by more than a dozen states, permit producers of perishable food products to sue anyone who makes false statements about their products that result in a loss of revenue. The impetus for the laws was industry frustration at an unsuccessful lawsuit against the producers of the CBS program *60 Minutes*, which in 1989 broadcast a story warning viewers that the residue from a pesticide called Alar could make apples carcinogenic.[25] The story had been based largely on studies done with laboratory animals; no epidemiological reports were available regarding the effect on humans. The federal courts found that this limitation in the available scientific data was insufficient for any reasonable jury to find that *60 Minutes'* conclusions were false. In 1997, a cattle feed operator in Amarillo, Texas, used that state's veggie libel law to bring an ultimately unsuccessful suit against Oprah Winfrey, claiming that her TV talk show's discussion of mad cow disease resulted in plummeting beef sales and a personal loss of millions of dollars. The "veggie libel" aspect of the law was removed from jury consideration, because the trial judge determined that the Texas statute was applicable only to "perishable food products," not to cattle.[26] These kinds of statutes have already received a fair amount of critical commentary in legal academic circles, and the consensus seems to be that most of them will, if challenged, be struck down as unconstitutional infringements on freedom of speech.[27]

How Much Does It Hurt?
When people bring civil suits against each other, the end result they seek is usually the awarding of money damages. How much money plaintiffs are awarded is, at least in part, a function of the ways in which and how

---

25. *Auvil v. CBS 60 Minutes*, 800 F. Supp. 928 (E.D. Wash. 1992), *aff'd*, 67 F.3d 816 (9th Cir. 1995).

26. *Texas Beef Group v. Winfrey*, 11 F. Supp. 2d 858 (N.D. Tex. 1998), *aff'd*, 212 F.3d 597 (5th Cir. 2000).

27. See, e.g., David J. Bederman, Scott M. Christensen, and Scott Dean Quesenberry, "Of Banana Bills and Veggie Hate Crimes: The Constitutionality of Agricultural Disparagement Statutes," 34 *Harvard Journal on Legislation* 135 (1997).

THINGS TO REMEMBER

Defamation and the Plaintiff

- Libel actions generally cannot be brought on behalf of deceased individuals.
- Corporations can sue for libelous remarks suggesting that their officers or employees have engaged in fraudulent or other reprehensible activities.
- Corporations can sue for *trade libel* or *product disparagement* when the offensive criticisms concern the product line itself, rather than its manufacturers.
- In the 1990s more than a dozen states passed "veggie libel" laws, which specifically targeted speech suggesting that perishable food products are unsafe.

badly they were hurt. As a result, in libel law the matter of damages is almost inextricable from the element of defamation.

Generally speaking, the law recognizes two broad categories of damages—compensatory and punitive. **Punitive damages** are designed to punish the defendants for outrageous behavior, as well as to make an example of them that may deter others. Juries may not reach the issue of punitive damages unless some form of **compensatory damages** are also granted. The logic here is straightforward enough: no matter how egregious the press's behavior, they should not be punished unless they did some harm by that behavior. As we see in the next chapter, the U.S. Supreme Court's intervention into the law of libel in recent decades has put additional limits on the kinds of situations that permit the awarding of punitive damages.[28]

Compensatory damages fall into three subcategories. **Presumed damages** are much what the name implies. Common-law practice is for juries to grant presumed damages without demanding that plaintiffs demonstrate how, specifically, they were harmed. In libel law, presumed damages tended to be sought in cases involving the libel per se category of defamation discussed earlier. Libel per se plaintiffs did not have to prove how or why the words written about them damaged their reputation, in that some categories of accusations, if believed, could be presumed to lower one's standing in a community.

The other two subcategories of compensatory damages have names that may seem counterintuitive. **Actual damages** can be distinguished from presumed damages in that the plaintiff must at least make some showing of harm. But the harm can be a rather intangible one. Defamation actions are quite different in this way from, say, medical malpractice suits. In the latter kind of case, we expect to see the crutches, the neck braces, the prognoses of expert witnesses. To win actual damages, the Supreme Court has said, libel plaintiffs need only show that they have suffered "impairment of reputation and standing in the community, personal humiliation, [or] mental anguish and suffering."

---

28. *Gertz v. Robert Welch, Inc.*, 418 U.S. 323, 348 (1974).

Actual damages, then, do not require that plaintiffs demonstrate anything in the way of measurable, tangible harm. If a plaintiff *is* able to pinpoint actual dollar amounts of loss resulting from libel, such as from being terminated because an employer believed the lies or being thrown out by a landlord, we move into the realm of what are called **special damages**. References to special damages are most frequently seen in trade libel cases where a company tries to establish the specific amount of market share forfeited as a result of remarks disparaging of its products.

Publication

The word *publication* is an unfortunate one as applied to libel law. It is misleading in two ways. First, it seems to suggest, erroneously, that only the mass media can possibly libel anyone, because we tend to think of "publishing" as something only media industries do (maybe only print media). Second, it suggests that defamatory comments must reach a mass audience before they can be actionable.

In libel law, however, *publication* has a very narrow and special meaning. It means that the speaker or writer has shared the allegedly defamatory comments about another person with at least one third party. (Of course, because the defamation element requires that many people actually believe the untruths, we assume here that the one person you tell in turn spreads the word to others.) If you complain directly to your teacher that you think he is having an affair with a classmate, that would be one-to-one communication, with no publication; if you share this same conjecture with your teacher's spouse, or the dean, the element of publication will have been established.

Legal doctrines that have evolved over centuries usually pick up a few exceptions along the way, and so it is with the concept of publication. There are times when person A saying something nasty to person B *about* person B can be sufficient to establish publication. Such is the case if the defamation is offered in a context where it is all but unavoidable that the recipient will himself have to share it with at least one third party. Such instances are collectively referred to in libel law as **self-publication**. For example, writing an insulting letter to a blind person could consti-

---

THINGS TO REMEMBER

Damages

- Punitive Damages
  Designed to punish the defamer and to deter others
- Compensatory Damages
  - *Presumed:* no proof of harm needed
  - *Actual:* some proof of harm needed, but it does not need to be very tangible
  - *Special:* highly specific and measurable proof of harm required

tute publication, because the person will likely have to seek out a sighted individual to read the letter aloud. The same would be true of a letter written to and about a preliterate child. A more recent phenomenon is for courts to hold that an employer's letter of termination to an employee can be sufficient to find publication, because the fired employee will feel compelled to share the reasons for termination during interviews with potential future employers.[29]

It is important that we not confuse the elements of defamation and publication. Whereas publication requires that only one third party hear or read the libelous remarks, defamation requires that the remarks were capable of lowering the defamed person's status with an undefined but fairly sizable number of potential recipients of the message.

The element of publication becomes more complicated and also becomes of special relevance to media professionals when we recognize that the **republication** of a libel can be just as actionable as the original act of libel. Your printing or broadcasting that "Smith said Jones is a child molester" can create as much liability for you as had been created for Smith. You would similarly be in trouble if you reported, however matter-of-factly, that "there is a rumor floating about that Jones is a child molester."

There are exceptions to this general rule against republication. In some jurisdictions newspapers that publish stories from reputable wire services will escape liability.[30] This wire services defense, dating from the 1930s,[31] is actually a special instance of a more general rule that if the media outlet had legitimate cause to believe in the reliability of the original source, the dissemination of that source's words should not be actionable. "The rationale behind the defense," a Michigan court recently wrote, "is that no local news organization could assume the burden of verifying every news item reported to it by established news-gathering agencies and continue to satisfy the demands of modern society for up-to-the-minute global information."[32]

Not everyone involved in the process of spreading a defamatory message to a larger audience is necessarily liable for damages. There is a long-standing exception for bookstores and similar enterprises. We do not expect bookstore and magazine rack managers to be personally responsible for every word and every picture in their entire inventory. Similarly, if person A spreads a libelous remark about person B in a phone conversation with person C, we do not hold the telephone company liable. Internet service providers (ISPs) are given similar protection from liability for nasty things their subscribers might say to and about each other (see chapter 13 for a more complete explanation).

---

29. Markita D. Cooper, "Between a Rock and a Hard Case: Time for a New Doctrine of Compelled Self-Publication," 72 *Notre Dame Law Review* 373 (1997).

30. *Gay v. Williams*, 486 F. Supp. 12 (Alaska 1979).

31. *Layne v. Tribune Co.*, 146 So. 234 (Fla. 1933).

32. *Howe v. Detroit Free Press*, 555 N.W.2d 738, 741 (Mich. Ct. App. 1996).

The doctrine of republication dictates that even the completely factual reporting that "there *is* an unsubstantiated rumor floating about . . ." can be actionable, just as much as a firsthand defamation.

Another way for the media to avoid liability after having republished a libelous statement is to invoke the **neutral-reportage** defense. This defense, which is accepted in only a few jurisdictions, permits the press to report in a fair and unbiased manner newsworthy allegations made by any prominent and responsible speaker about public officials or well-known public personalities. Neutral reportage was first recognized by the U.S. Court of Appeals for the Second Circuit in 1977, in a case where the *New York Times* and the National Audubon Society defended themselves against a libel suit from a small group of scientists whose opposition to a ban on the pesticide DDT led an Audubon official to accuse them of being "paid to lie." The *Times* reprinted the charge in a story it did on the controversy surrounding pesticides. In ruling for the media organizations, Judge Kaufman argued that the public would be the ultimate loser if the press were not permitted to report that "a responsible, prominent organization had made such serious charges against a public figure."[33]

Another privilege, sometimes called **fair report**, can protect the media from a libel judgment when the defamatory statements republished were first made in an official government proceeding or document. The privilege seems logically consistent with

---

33. *Edwards v. National Audubon Society*, 556 F.2d 113, 129 (2d Cir. 1977).

the Speech or Debate Clause (Article I, Section 6 of the U.S. Constitution), as well as similar provisions in many state constitutions, which gives legislators **absolute privilege** to say whatever they please when conducting their official duties. If our representatives cannot be prosecuted or sued for any utterance they make in their official capacities, should not the news media that tell us about those utterances also be protected?

Constitutional provisions such as the Speech or Debate Clause are often said to be sources of absolute privilege. But the word *absolute* may be misleading, in that courts will ask how closely tied to a legislator's official functions the circumstances surrounding a libelous utterance were. Certainly the legislator will enjoy absolute immunity for utterances made during the course of floor debate or during committee hearings. Senator William Proxmire of Wisconsin, however, learned the hard way that the privilege does not extend absolutely to all utterances on political issues. Proxmire was in the habit of publicizing from time to time what he liked to call his "Golden Fleece Awards." His goal was to shed light on government expenditures that seem especially wasteful. Proxmire gave one of his awards to federal agencies that had funded the primate aggression research conducted by Dr. Ronald Hutchinson of the Kalamazoo State Mental Hospital. The *Congressional Record* reveals Proxmire's having charged that Hutchinson's "transparently worthless" research "should make the taxpayers as well as his monkeys grind their teeth."[34]

When Hutchinson's libel suit against Proxmire reached the Supreme Court, the majority held that the means used by the senator to publicize his Golden Fleece Award—issuing press releases, sending a newsletter to a mailing list of approximately 100,000, and appearing on at least one television interview program—were not closely enough tied to his speech making in the Senate chamber itself to warrant absolute immunity.

The fair-report privilege applies to the proceedings of any legislative body, from Congress to the local school board, that is empowered to make public policy. The privilege protects accurate reports of statements made by those who convene such meetings and any member of the public who is authorized to speak to them. It also covers defamatory statements that originate in citizen petitions or similar documents that are recognized and "received" by legislative bodies.

The privilege is a qualified one. It can be overcome by a finding that the media's report of a proceeding was not "fair and accurate." Even if the report of official governmental proceedings is accurate, if a news story goes beyond those facts to offer commentary on the credibility of the participants, the privilege may still fail. A 2000 decision from the Minnesota Supreme Court, for example, concerned a newspaper article correctly reporting that a private citizen attending a city council meeting alleged that a local police officer sold illegal drugs. Summary judgment awarded to the

---

34. *Hutchinson v. Proxmire*, 443 U.S. 111, 116 (1979).

newspaper was overturned by the state supreme court because the newspaper also reported on a follow-up interview with the police chief and reminded readers that the citizen who had first made the accusation was a frequent contributor to the paper's editorial pages.[35]

Accurate reports of defamatory utterances or documents from the executive branch of government are also often covered by the qualified privilege. Certainly reports of presidential, gubernatorial, and mayoral press conferences and press releases are protected. In some jurisdictions, even far less public documents from the executive branch may be covered. A California appellate court, for example, exonerated a San Francisco newspaper for articles it had written about alleged financial improprieties in the Center for Pre-Hospital Research and Training at the University of California at San Francisco. The center had been created to provide support for nonphysicians such as EMTs and firefighters, whose roles often require that they be proficient in performing some kinds of emergency medical procedures. The articles, which accused the center of having created secret checking accounts for improper expenditures and having billed some clients for services never rendered, were deemed to be within the scope of the fair-report privilege because they were based on a confidential report created by the state auditor.[36]

Be careful about quoting the cop on the beat, however. It is one thing to report on some kind of official police document, quite another to base a story on informal statements. As a general rule, reporters hoping for the fair-report privilege's protection should be more cautious the lower the rank of the source for the reprinted libel and the less formal the communication in which the libel originated.

That the fair-report privilege is also applicable to judicial proceedings is especially important to the press since virtually every comment made about a defendant in open court beyond name, address, and age is likely to be defamatory in some way. Fortunately for the media, the privilege applies to any statements or official documents issued by any of the participants, including witnesses, jurors, the judge, and the litigating parties themselves. Moreover, the privilege has often been held to apply to judicial documents that are never read in open court. Consider, for example, a very colorful libel case from Pennsylvania prompted by HarperCollins's publication of a book called *Masters of Deception: The Gang That Ruled Cyberspace*. The book tells of nefarious activities engaged in by a group of college-age computer hackers, one of which was to break into private computer systems to obtain and then fraudulently use others' long-distance calling-card codes. Here is how the book described the group's having rationalized the crime:

> It seemed victimless to them. They needed the numbers to fund calls to further their education. Who was being hurt? Not the person whose calling card number got used,

35. *Moreno v. Crookston Times Printing Co.*, 610 N.W.2d 321 (Minn. 2000).
36. *Braun v. Chronicle Publishing Company*, 52 Cal. App. 4th 1036 (1997).

because that person would dispute the bill and never have to pay. Not the phone company, because the filched phone calls emanated from a reservoir of limitless capacity. It was like riding the rails. The trains were running anyway, and a hobo wouldn't displace any cargo in the boxcar.[37]

These comments were among many that the plaintiffs thought defamatory. The court held, however, that these statements, to the extent they were accurate, were protected by the fair-report privilege because they had been obtained from such official documents as a presentencing report written on one of the hackers and a letter from the assistant district attorney to the judge.

Whether the fair-report privilege extends to republication of documents from foreign countries is an issue that has produced contradictory results in different jurisdictions. The Fourth Circuit Court of Appeals was the first to rule on the question, in *Lee v. Dong-A Ilbo*.[38] That case involved several Korean-American newspapers and a television station that had published or broadcast stories, based on documents from the South Korean government, alleging that a South Korean citizen living in the United States was viewed by South Korea as an enemy North Korean agent. The court held that the fair-report privilege did not apply to documents from foreign governments. Similarly, in 2005, a federal district court in Washington, D.C., held that republication of a document from a Russian investigative service was not protected by the fair-report privilege, though the defendant won on other grounds.[39] But a federal district court in Pennsylvania (part of the Third Circuit) protected the *Boston Globe* and other media from a defamation suit stemming from reports that Howard Friedman, a U.S. citizen, would be denied future entry into Israel. The report was based on a press release issued by three ministers of the Israeli government, which claimed that Friedman had been "associated with planning illegal activities in Israel."[40]

The press may also forfeit its rights to the privilege if its story, in independently defamatory ways, goes beyond the official proceedings or proclamations from which it draws facts. If the government document upon which you base your story says that Jones "has troubles at home" and you report that "Jones is a spouse abuser," the privilege will not apply to you. The privilege also is restricted to situations in which you make obvious to your readers the source of your facts. You must make a clear attribution in your story, and ideally in your headline as well. Although there are many times when the media may use anonymous sources, the use of such sources would seem to logically preclude a media defendant's invoking the fair-report privilege.

The old journalistic admonition to "get it *right*" is of special import here, since the fair-report privilege is forfeited if your story is not an accurate report of an otherwise

---

37. *Wilson v. Slatalla*, 970 F. Supp. 405, 410 (E.D. Pa. 1997).
38. 849 F.2d 876 (4th Cir. 1988).
39. *Oao Alfa Bank v. Center for Public Integrity*, 387 F. Supp. 2d 20 (D.D.C. 2005).
40. *Friedman v. Israel Labour Party*, 957 F. Supp. 701 (E.D. Pa. 1997).

protected government proceeding or document. The Supreme Court of Ohio allowed a libel suit to go forward against a newspaper for having reported that "Amherst attorney James Young is facing a contempt of court citation." As it turns out, there was an Amherst attorney named James Young, and an attorney named James Young had in fact been held in contempt of court a few days prior to the story's run. But the attorney who had been found in contempt was a James H. Young, and *his* usual place of business was Cleveland.[41] Making the right criticisms of the wrong person can not only defeat the chance to fall back on the fair-report privilege but can also serve to establish for the plaintiff the third element of a libel case—identification.

Identification

The third element of libel in the common law is identification. While one might think intuitively that this element would be rather straightforward, in fact it carries its own complications. Three such complications are explored here: the relationship between naming and identifying, the special problems posed by fictional writing, and problems that emerge when libel is attributed to only some members of identifiable groups of various sizes.

Naming and Identifying.

The case of the Cleveland (not Amherst!) attorney just mentioned serves as a powerful reminder that libel suits are often prompted by an omitted middle initial, a misspelling, or some other misidentification. Misidentify one person and you may succeed in defaming another. Generally, reporters are wise to identify with a vengeance whenever anything potentially defamatory is being associated with a named individual. Such identification means using a person's full name

---

THINGS TO REMEMBER

The Publication Element

- Only one additional person needs to hear the libel.
- Republication of a libel can be just as actionable as the original publication.
- Wire services, common carriers, and bookstores are generally excluded from republication liability.
- Some jurisdictions also offer the neutral-reportage defense, protecting the press broadly against liability as long as they report in a fair and unbiased way the fact of person A's having criticized person B.
- A fair-report privilege is also recognized concerning republication of libel initially made in an official meeting or publication.

---

41. *Young v. The Morning Journal*, 669 N.E.2d 1136 (Ohio 1996).

(with middle initial where appropriate), age, and full address, and perhaps even occupation.

As you begin to read full texts of court opinions, either on the job or as a requirement of this course, the phrase you will most frequently encounter when judges make reference to the element of identification is that the allegedly libelous statements must be "of or concerning" the plaintiff. It is important to recognize that the element of identification can be proved even if you never once use the plaintiff's name in your story. In one case, for example, a Philadelphia police captain serving on the city's sex crimes squad implied that a young woman, described only as a "Bryn Mawr student," may have filed a false report alleging she had been carjacked, robbed, and raped. The woman sued not only the police captain but also the local media that had broadcast his allegations. In denying the defendants' motion for summary judgment, which was based in large part on the plaintiff's never having been named, the court reminded us that naming and identifying are two different things. There were simply too many details about the young woman in the story—that she reported being raped on a particular day after attending a party at the University of Pennsylvania, that she was a

You might not need to include this much detail to avoid a misidentification, but at least provide some characteristics beyond the suspect's name.

student at a well-known and relatively small college, that she drove a Nissan, and so on—to deny the likelihood that she would be identifiable.[42]

Identification in Fiction.   The whole notion of applying libel law to works of fiction is troubling. After all, for a journalist to admit that she has knowingly published falsehoods would be an odd thing indeed, an admission likely to help a libel plaintiff prevail. But novelists purposely write falsehoods. As a result, when libel suits are brought against fiction writers, the cases tend to focus almost exclusively on the element of identification.[43]

One of the most often cited libel cases involving fiction will likely provoke the reaction "only in California, and only in the 1970s."[44] Writer Gwen Davis Mitchell became a member of one of Dr. Paul Bindrim's "nude marathon" psychotherapy groups. Because Mitchell had already published a best-selling book, Bindrim was suspicious enough to insist that she would be welcome as a client like any other, but not if she intended to write about the experience. He had her sign a contract to that effect, but shortly thereafter she signed another contract—this one with Doubleday for a six-figure advance on a novel about the nude encounter group movement. The book, called *Touching*, depicted "Dr. Simon Herford" as a psychotherapist who conducted nude encounter groups. One of the scenes Bindrim felt most defamed him was a discussion, during a group session, between Herford and a minister who lamented that his wife was not amenable to coming to the encounter group. Although Bindrim's own recordings of the sessions showed that such a scene took place, the novel's version has Herford using highly vulgar language to insist that the minister exercise more authority over his wife ("You better grab her by the cunt and drag her here!").

The defendants argued unsuccessfully that Herford could not be viewed by reasonable jurors as a Bindrim surrogate. The court found the differences between the real and fictional therapists too few and too inconsequential. Herford was a psychiatrist, Bindrim a psychologist; Herford had long white hair and sideburns, Bindrim was clean shaven with short hair. Because a comparison of the book with Bindrim's tape recordings of the real sessions persuaded the court that the novel was based almost entirely on Mitchell's participation in the encounter group, the case was permitted to go forward for a jury to decide if Bindrim could establish all the elements of libel.

The *Bindrim* case serves as an example of a fascinating paradox that emerges when libel suits flow from fiction. The more disparate the actual events and those depicted in a fictional work, the less likely will a protagonist be identified in the readers' minds as anything but a fictional character. Yet it is that very distortion in fiction that might be the basis for the claim that the book or film at issue is defamatory. In other words,

---

42. *Weinstein v. Bullick*, 827 F. Supp. 1193 (E.D. Pa. 1993) *aff'd*, 77 F.3d 465 (3d Cir. 1996).

43. Matthew Savare, "Falsity, Fault, and Fiction: A New Standard for Defamation in Fiction," 12 *UCLA Entertainment Law Review* 129, 138 (2004).

44. *Bindrim v. Mitchell*, 92 Cal. App. 3d 61 (1979).

that a scene does indeed depart from reality can serve as an argument for either the plaintiff or the defendant.

In *Geisler v. Petrocelli*, the Court of Appeals for the Second Circuit ruled that Melanie Geisler's libel suit against the author and publisher of the novel *Match Set* could go forward.[45] The book tells the tale, as the court put it, of "the odyssey of a female transsexual athlete through the allegedly corrupt and corrupting world of the women's professional tennis circuit." The book's main character is described in a way that the court found very similar to Geisler's appearance. Moreover, the author, who had made the plaintiff's acquaintance when the two of them had worked at a small publishing house, named the character—you guessed it!—Melanie Geisler.

"At least change the name, stupid!" seems to also be the lesson of the Illinois Supreme Court's decision in *Bryson v. News America Publications, Inc.*, in which a purportedly fictional short story about high school classmates appearing in *Seventeen* magazine accused a character—by the name of Bryson!—of being a "slut."[46] Ah, but every lesson seems to have an exception. Some courts have refused to assume that a libel plaintiff has been "identified" by a character name in a fictional work even when the surnames are identical, at least if the names are very common ones.[47]

The Numbers Game.

Sometimes, libel plaintiffs cannot prove that they have been identified in a defamatory utterance *as an individual* and assert instead that they have been libeled by dint of their membership in a particular group. Predicting whether such plaintiffs will prevail sometimes may seem more art than science,[48] but some general principles can be culled from the case law.

First is the general principle that membership in a very large group will not give one standing to sue for libel as a result of the group's having been defamed. No individual attorney or group of attorneys would be able to win damages by suing any of the authors or publishers of the various "dead lawyer joke" compilations we find in most larger bookstores. Senator Jones could not win a suit against a radio talk show host for making the bald assertion that "all politicians are crooks." Do these examples sound outlandish and fantastic? Consider that in 1980 one court was called upon to rule that no individual of Polish descent could by law have been defamed by the Polish jokes in a popular film,[49] and another ruled that no individual Muslim can claim to have been defamed by a film (*Death of a Princess*) alleged to have insulted hundreds of millions of the faithful worldwide.[50] Or consider two more recent controversies, both from New York. A suit involving the CBS program *60 Minutes* was halted when

---

45. 616 F.2d 636 (2d Cir. 1980).

46. 672 N.E.2d 1207 (Ill. 1996).

47. *Allen v. Gordon*, 86 A.D.2d 514 (N.Y. App. Div. 1982).

48. Jeffrey S. Bromme, "Group Defamation: Five Guiding Factors," 64 *Texas Law Review* 591 (1985).

49. *Mikolinski v. Burt Reynolds Production Co.*, 409 N.E.2d 1324 (Mass. App. Ct. 1980).

50. *Talal v. Fanning*, 506 F. Supp. 186 (N.D. Cal. 1980).

the court held that a broadcast story's general admonishment about dealing with Nigerian businessmen could not be viewed as defamatory of any individual member of the class.[51] In another case, the Second Circuit Court of Appeals refused to find actionable identification even when an administrator of New York City's Javits Convention Center publicly opined that "over 65% of [the center's thousand-plus union personnel] were either convicted felons or associated with organized crime."[52] It is hard to avoid believing that the court in this latter case really felt the official had engaged in rhetorical hyperbole—how else to explain the precision of the statistic applied to such huge numbers?

As a general rule, then, the larger the group, the more difficult it is for an individual plaintiff to prove identification. Similarly, the smaller the number of people in the group alleged to have a defamatory trait, the more difficult it will be for individuals within the group to prevail. Defamatory statements alleging that "one" or "a few" members of a group manifest a particularly loathsome quality will be less likely to lead to liability than statements claiming that "all" or "the vast majority of" a group's members can be so characterized. In some states, including New York, courts have fashioned what is called an **"intensity of suspicion"** test that seems as elegant a summary as one will find of the conjunction of the two principles just mentioned.[53] The larger the group, the less likely that any individual member of it will have been singled out for suspicion. Similarly, if the size of the group is held constant, more suspicion is aroused about any particular member to the extent that a large percentage of the group is alleged to have a negative characteristic.

What happens if one unnamed member of a relatively small group is defamed? Such was the case when all twenty-one members of the Bellingham, Massachusetts, police force took umbrage at a column in the weekly *Woonsocket Call and Evening Reporter* that closed with the query, "Is it true that a Bellingham cop locked himself and a female companion in the back of a cruiser in a town sandpit and had to radio for help?" The federal district court that first heard the case dismissed it, finding that there was no actionable identification. "If you say 11 out of 12 people are corrupt, or if you said 20 out of 21 police officers or maybe even 12 out of 21 are corrupt, or even one out of six is corrupt," the lower court judge admitted, "you would have a different situation." The appellate court affirmed the lower court's ruling, reasoning that "here we deal with a defamatory statement aimed at only one unidentified member of a group of 21. By no stretch of imagination can it be thought to suggest that the conduct of the one is typical of all. Noting the individual's membership in the group does not suggest a common determinant of character so much as simply a practical reference point."[54]

---

51. *Anyanwu v. CBS*, 887 F. Supp. 690 (S.D.N.Y. 1995).
52. *Abramson v. Pataki*, 278 F.3d 93 (2d Cir. 2002).
53. *Brady v. Ottaway Newspaper*, 445 N.Y.S.2d 786, 793–795 (N.Y. App. Div. 1981).
54. *Arcand v. Evening Call Publishing Co.*, 567 F.2d 1163 (1st Cir. 1977).

If the lesson of the case involving the Bellingham, Massachusetts, police is that the media can rest easy should they libel only one out of twenty-one, a more recent decision from North Carolina will give an added measure of comfort, in that the odds improved to one out of nine. It seems that the owner of a commercial building ran a deli and a florist shop and rented out space to several other small businesses. When a group of medical technicians was planning to go for lunch at the deli, one of their colleagues discouraged them from doing so, asserting that "someone over there" (of the nine persons employed at the deli) has AIDS. Rumors about the unnamed deli employee with AIDS were eventually covered in local print and broadcast media. When the various workers sued for libel, their claim was denied on the grounds of a failure to establish identification.[55]

The arithmetic does not always work in the media's favor, however. Consider the case of the retired U.S. Bureau of Prisons officer against the producers of the 1960s ABC series *The Untouchables*.[56] A two-part episode of the series told the predominantly true story of gangster Al Capone's transfer in 1934 from a prison in Georgia to the infamous Alcatraz prison in the middle of San Francisco Bay. The producers, however, added fictional scenes depicting one of the two guards assigned to Capone taking a bribe from the gangster, apparently as a down payment on expected help with a planned escape. When the other guard demands to be cut in on the deal, he is instead gunned down by Capone's cohorts. The plaintiff was one of the two guards who really had been assigned to Capone's railway car (out of fifteen or sixteen guards altogether who were involved in some way with the transfer). In this case, which could just as easily have been included in the earlier discussion of defamation through fiction, the court first determined that the relevant ratio was one in two, not one in sixteen. Having made this preliminary decision, the court had no difficulty determining that the case could go forward to a jury.

Our discussion of "the numbers game" in libel law would not be complete without at least brief mention of the issue of hate speech codes. Such regulations, adopted by many colleges, seem at first blush to have much in common with libel law, in that they typically prohibit speech that expresses very negative things about a person associated with or attributable to that person's race, religion, gender, or sexual orientation. These are really not libel provisions, however, for a number of reasons. First, such regulations are not designed to protect victims' reputations, but rather their feelings. Indeed, an insulting epithet generally will not trigger the rules unless the comment is made directly to a specific individual. Comments made *about* that individual, in front of others, would not be covered. (Hate speech codes are not libel laws.) Second, for such codes to have any chance of being found constitutional, they must be restricted to situations in which a violent breach of the peace is likely to occur. Al-

---

55. *Chapman v. Byrd*, 475 S.E.2d 734 (N.C. Ct. App. 1996).
56. *American Broadcasting–Paramount Theatres, Inc. v. Simpson*, 126 S.E.2d 873 (Ga. Ct. App. 1962).

though libel law may be thought of in a grand, historical way as an evolution away from violence such as dueling, contemporary libel plaintiffs need not establish the likelihood of violence as an element of their suits. Finally, whereas libel has been a respected area of tort law for centuries, with every state in the union boasting a libel statute, a complex mosaic of case law, or both, those few court decisions involving campus hate speech codes have uniformly struck down the rules as violations of the First Amendment.[57]

Fault

Suppose that you are the owner of a duplex, occupying one unit and leasing the other, in a relatively temperate climate such as in North Carolina. You go away on a vacation in October, and during your absence, your hometown experiences a freak ice storm. Your tenant's child slips and falls on the ice in front of your property. Does it seem fair that you can be sued in such a circumstance? You were not home and were thus unable to clear the sidewalk, and you had no reason to make arrangements for anyone else to do it for you. Yet in some jurisdictions in the United States, you could indeed be held liable for the child's injuries under the doctrine of **strict liability**, the notion that a person who causes injury to another should make retribution, even if no negligence is involved. A few generations ago, this doctrine was embraced throughout the country, and it has by no means disappeared from U.S. law. In some instances, such as product liability, the tendency over time has been to embrace strict liability rather than demand that the plaintiffs prove an article was manufactured neg-

---

THINGS TO REMEMBER

The Identification Element of Libel

- It is possible to be identified for the purposes of a libel case without having been explicitly named.
- Even purportedly fictional accounts, such as movies and novels, can lead to libel suits if an unsympathetically drawn character can be shown to be identifiable as a living real person.
- No single individual member will succeed as a libel plaintiff if a huge category of persons (such as lawyers, politicians, or Jews) is defamed.
- When dealing with smaller groups, the rules are a bit murkier, with some courts having depended on an "intensity of suspicion" test suggesting that plaintiffs become more likely to prevail when the number in the whole group is small and the number alleged to have a particularly unsavory characteristic is a high proportion of that larger group.

---

57. *UWM Post, Inc. v. Board of Regents of the University of Wisconsin*, 774 F. Supp. 1163 (E.D. Wis. 1991); *Doe v. University of Michigan*, 721 F. Supp. 852 (E.D. Mich. 1989).

ligently.[58] Other contemporary examples include workers' compensation laws as well as doctrines holding employers responsible for their employees' actions, even without a showing of corporate negligence. For example, in 2005 the Supreme Court let stand a $1 million judgment against Royal Caribbean stemming from the off-ship misconduct of one of its employees, without any finding of fault on the company's part.[59]

Now imagine for a moment a world in which the doctrine of strict liability were applied to defamation. Hurt someone's reputation by something you print or broadcast, and you must pay, even if your error is an innocent one. Misidentify a criminal suspect by using the wrong middle initial, and no amount of apologizing will get you off the hook.

In fact, libel law operated this way in many jurisdictions prior to the Supreme Court's landmark decision in 1964, *New York Times Co. v. Sullivan*.[60] Although there are many ways of describing the significance of the case, one way is to say the Court constitutionalized the fault element of libel. An examination of *Sullivan* and its progeny is the subject of chapter 4. Before that, however, we examine some of the arguments available to libel defendants even before the Supreme Court made this whole area of the law more "speaker-friendly."

Some Common-Law and Statutory Defenses to Libel

You have already been exposed to at least some defenses available to communicators who are sued for libel. To argue that the plaintiff has failed to establish one or more of the elements of libel is, after all, a defense. Defendants, as seen in the discussion of the identification element, might argue that the seemingly libelous remarks were not "of or concerning" the plaintiff. Then, too, the fair-report and neutral-reportage privileges are often used to suggest that although *re*publication may have taken place, the libel suit should not be permitted to go forward. Several other libel defenses are available to litigants, some unique to this particular tort, others more globally available to defendants in any kind of civil case.

One of the surest ways to defeat a libel suit is to point out that the plaintiff failed to honor the applicable **statute of limitations**. To avoid clogging the courts with "stale" claims—witnesses die, memories fade, evidence is lost—virtually all civil and criminal actions must be brought within a statutorily prescribed time limit. Statutes of limitations for libel vary from state to state, typically extending for one or two years after

---

58. Robert J. Samuelson, "Streamlining Product Liability Suits," *Los Angeles Times*, June 24, 1994, B7.

59. *Doe v. Celebrity Cruises*, 394 F.3d 891 (11th Cir. 2004), *cert. denied*, 2005 U.S. LEXIS 8179 (2005).

60. 376 U.S. 254 (1964).

publication. A few states recognize a three-year limitation. In most jurisdictions, the clock starts running the moment the defamation is published, not when the potential plaintiff learns about the publication. In this context, "published" refers to when the material was made generally available. In the case of broadcast stations, this time is easy to figure out. The first broadcast is the date of publication. Things are a bit more complex with printed materials. We cannot always go by the copyright date or the cover date. Books that reach the bookstores late in the year often list the following year on the copyright page. Similarly, magazines are often postdated by several weeks so that they appear "fresher" on newsstands and in subscribers' homes.

The truth defense, demonstrating that allegedly defamatory statements are true, is a very powerful defense in defamation cases. It may seem puzzling to describe truth as merely a *defense* in libel law, as if suggesting that the communicator is presumed guilty, that the article is presumed false. Should not the burden be on the plaintiff to *prove* that the story is false?

The courts have not yet provided a uniform answer to this question. Traditionally, in common law, a libel *was* presumed false. If that tradition seems quirky and unfair by today's standards, try thinking about it another way. In common law, Americans' reputations were presumed unsullied and pure until proven otherwise. For an added sense of perspective, consider that the Alien and Sedition Acts discussed in chapter 2, although viewed as reprehensible in retrospect, at the time could be seen as a step forward for freedom of the press in that they, unlike libel law at the time, at least permitted truth to be used as a defense.[61] In any event, because the Supreme Court has held in recent years that the First Amendment places some limitations on the common-law tradition of requiring the defendant to prove truth, we will have much more to say about this issue in the next chapter. For now, suffice it to say that in those situations where the plaintiff must prove falsity to prevail, it will not do to point out one or a handful of inconsequential errors extraneous to the libel alleged. If my story alleges that you have been prosecuted for embezzling $30,000 from one employer and $400,000 from another, you will not have proved falsity by showing that my figures are ever so slightly off, or that I spelled one of the employers' names wrong. You must prove that the gist or the "sting" of the article is false.

Consent is a rarely encountered but still respected libel defense. Should you interview a subject who, knowing full well the nature of the allegations you intend to print, expressly gives you permission to go ahead, the subject will not be able to prevail in a libel suit against you stemming from those allegations. Courts sometimes infer consent from the plaintiff's conduct. For example, if it can be shown that a plaintiff herself has told others of the yet-unpublished defamatory statements against her, some courts might hold that a defamation suit cannot stand. If the supposed libel had the power to damage her reputation, the reasoning goes, she would have kept them to

---

61. Norman L. Rosenberg, *Protecting the Best Men: An Interpretive History of the Law of Libel* (Chapel Hill: University of North Carolina Press, 1986), 86–87.

In this admittedly surreal scenario, the *Tribune*'s error would not open it up to damages for libel, because the gist or "sting" of what it said about the attorney's client was true.

herself. In one case involving the relationship between an employer and an employee rather than a reporter and source, a state appellate court held that there can be no defamation in an employee's personnel file if the only additional pairs of eyes to have seen the alleged libel belonged to persons shown the file by the employee himself.[62]

In our earlier discussion of the element of defamation, we encountered cases where the defendant successfully argued that the alleged libel could not possibly have hurt the plaintiff's reputation because the statements were "mere hyperbole" and not to be taken literally. Hyperbole is really a special instance of the more general common-law defense called **fair comment**, which posits that to be defamatory, an utterance must make a specific factual claim. Opinions, if offered without any personal animus toward the person being judged (thus the "fair" in fair comment), cannot be the cause of a libel action. The fair-comment privilege can be abused and thus disallowed if your opinion is presented in such a way as to suggest that you have certain facts at your disposal that you are choosing not to share with your readers and that these important but undisclosed facts form the basis for your negative assessment of a potential plaintiff. This approach might be called the "if you only knew what I know" posture. If, however, you either forthrightly reveal the facts that led you to your opinions or have cause to believe that those facts are already known to your readers (for example, if this one article concerns an incident so much in the news that only a hermit could have missed earlier accounts), the privilege will generally be respected.

Here too the Supreme Court (and some lower courts trying to make sense of relevant Supreme Court decisions) has made some moves toward constitutionalizing this

---

62. *Pressley v. Continental Can Co.*, 250 S.E.2d 676 (N.C. Ct. App. 1979).

common-law defense. Thus we discuss the fact-versus-opinion distinction again in chapter 4, this time from a First Amendment perspective.

Chapter Summary

Libel law has been around for many centuries, and exists to enable persons who feel their reputations have been sullied to recover damages from anyone who has spread untruths about them.

A plaintiff must generally establish four elements to prevail: that a specific allegation is in fact likely to damage his or her reputation, that the defamation was published (seen by at least one third party), that the plaintiff was identified in some way, and that the publisher manifested some degree of fault. Traditionally, falsity did not have to be proved; it was assumed, with truth being a common-law defense.

Phrases amounting to mere rhetorical hyperbole are not actionable. Republication of libels from other sources can be as actionable as the publication of the original statements. Exceptions are often made for the fair reporting of libelous statements made in official proceedings.

Not only individuals, but also corporations, can sue for libel. If a company's product rather than its officers has been maligned, the proper cause of action is product disparagement, rather than libel itself.

Identification can exist even if the plaintiff has not been explicitly named in the offensive publication and can result from the publication of a fictional work. A plaintiff's chances of prevailing in the case of a defamation aimed at a group of which he or she is part diminishes as the group grows larger and the proportion of its members alleged to possess the defamatory quality grows smaller.

Plaintiffs can receive compensatory damages to make them whole. Sometimes such damages are presumed; or they might be actual damages, requiring at least some proof of harm. Special damages demand the most specific and tangible proof of harm. In some jurisdictions punitive damages are also permitted.

Even before the Supreme Court constitutionalized libel—the subject of the next chapter—several defenses were available to defamation suits. Defendants might be able to show that their publication was substantially true. It might be alleged that a plaintiff consented, explicitly or implicitly, to the publication. The defense called fair comment, which argues that the publication consisted of nothing more than opinion, rather than assertions of fact, might be invoked. In addition, defendants can always show that plaintiffs failed to establish one or more of the tort's elements, or that the suit was not filed timely (i.e., that the statute of limitations expired).

Chapter 4

DEFAMATION: FIRST AMENDMENT LIMITATIONS

Acandidate for sheriff in Cameron County, Texas, sued a local paper for reporting that he had suggested in a debate that "No Anglo can be sheriff of Cameron County." In fact he had never used the word *Anglo,* but he had said that "you have to be bi-cultural to understand what is going on in our neighborhoods." The Supreme Court of Texas ruled in 2005 that the newspaper accounts were accurate, that politicians properly don't have much control over what portions of a campaign appearance will be deemed most newsworthy by the press.[1]

A police officer in Woodcliff Lake, New Jersey, sued a local resident who had accused him of perjury concerning a series of parking tickets. The resident's charge was apparently based on discrepancies he noted between what the officer had told him in person about the tickets and the story the officer offered in court at a later date. The resident even had a tape recording of the original conversation to back up his claim. The Supreme Court of New Jersey, noting that the crime of perjury involves more than making discrepant statements (a perjurer must intend to lie, and indeed intend to mislead an official fact finder such as a jury by his lies), nonetheless found for the local resident.[2]

What these two cases have in common is the presumption made by each court that the libel plaintiffs, because they are public officials, should have a very heavy burden of proof. This presumption is the legacy of *New York Times Co. v. Sullivan,* the U.S. Supreme Court's landmark libel ruling from 1964.[3]

To fully grasp the significance of the case, we have to remind ourselves a bit about the times in which it was decided. The 1960s were, after all, the decade in which Con-

---

1. *Freedom Newspapers of Texas v. Cantu,* 168 S.W.3d 847 (Tex. 2005).
2. *DeAngelis v. Hill,* 847 A.2d 1261 (N.J. 2004).
3. 376 U.S. 254 (1964).

gress began the arduous task of dismantling our nation's long legacy of *institutional* racial discrimination. The Civil Rights Act, the Voting Rights Act, the Fair Housing Act, all aimed at making "whites only" signs relics of the past, were crucial pieces of legislation that emerged from this era.

Recall too that the 1960s were before CNN, before TV news organizations could switch instantly to "live satellite feeds" from locations all over the globe, even before all the major networks had expanded to thirty minutes of nightly news. Most Americans received three or four TV stations total. It is perhaps no surprise, then, that we were so dependent on newspapers of record, such as the *New York Times,* to stay abreast of the civil rights struggle being waged in the South.

Introducing *New York Times Co. v. Sullivan*

It was against this backdrop that the Supreme Court found a vehicle by which to impose constitutional limitations on the tort of defamation: a jury award for libel in the amount of $500,000 to L. B. Sullivan, a city commissioner in Montgomery, Alabama, whose duties included oversight of the local police department. Sullivan's suit was prompted by the *New York Times* publication in March 1960 of a full-page paid political advertisement placed by a group of civil rights leaders calling themselves "the Committee to Defend Martin Luther King and the Struggle for Freedom in the South."

There were several inaccuracies in the advertisement, among them the following:

- The students sang "The Star-Spangled Banner," not "My Country, 'Tis of Thee."
- Police did not "ring" the campus (although they were deployed there in large numbers).
- Students were expelled not for leading this particular state capitol demonstration but for demanding service at a lunch counter in the county courthouse.
- The follow-up student protest against the expulsions involved most (but not all) of the student body and consisted of a one-day "strike," not a mass refusal to register.
- The student dining hall was never padlocked.
- The local police disputed the allegation that King had been "assaulted."
- Martin Luther King, Jr., had been arrested only four times, not seven.
- Sullivan had not been police commissioner at the time of three of these arrests; nor did he have anything to do with the perjury indictment against King.

Perhaps you found some of these errors substantive ones and others so innocuous as to be a waste of the Court's time. Would Sullivan's reputation have been damaged by the factual errors in the advertisement? The Court's review of the trial record suggests that Sullivan did not do a very good job of showing how he was harmed. He produced only one relevant witness on the point, a former employer who indicated

Heed Their Rising Voices

From the *New York Times,* March 29, 1960.

As the whole world knows by now thousands of Southern Negro students are engaged in widespread non-violent demonstrations in positive affirmation of the right to live in human dignity as guaranteed by the U.S. Constitution and the Bill of Rights. In their efforts to uphold these guarantees, they are being met by an unprecedented wave of terror by those who would deny and negate the document which the whole world looks upon as setting the pattern for modern freedom.

In Montgomery, Alabama, after students sang "My Country, 'Tis of Thee" on the State Capitol steps, their leaders were expelled from school, and truckloads of police armed with shotguns and tear-gas ringed the Alabama State College campus. When the entire student body protested to state authorities by refusing to register, their dining hall was padlocked in an attempt to starve them into submission.

Small wonder that the Southern violators of the Constitution fear this new, non-violent brand of freedom fighter. Small wonder that they are determined to destroy the one man who, more than any other, symbolizes the new spirit now sweeping the South—the Reverend Dr. Martin Luther King, Jr.

Again and again the Southern violators have answered Dr. King's peaceful protests with intimidation and violence. They have bombed his home, almost killing his wife and child. They have assaulted his person. They have arrested him seven times—for "speeding," "loitering," and similar "offenses." And now they have charged him with "perjury"—a felony under which they could imprison him for ten years.

We urge you to join hands with our fellow Americans in the South by supporting, with your dollars, this combined appeal for all three needs—the defense of Martin Luther King, the support of the embattled students, and the struggle for the right to vote.

that the allegations made in the advertisement were serious ones and that he would be hesitant to hire anyone who was guilty of those allegations. This same witness, however, testified that he did not believe in the truth of the allegations, an admission that certainly helped the defendant more than the plaintiff. Add to the equation that Sullivan's name is not mentioned once in the advertisement, and you may think that the Court could have overturned the Alabama jury's damages award of $500,000 without producing a memorable landmark decision. Might the Supreme Court have decided that the plaintiff had not met his burden of proving the libel elements of defamation or of identification thus avoiding any constitutional issues?

The Court could not simply rule that the Alabama courts did a bad job of applying that state's own law of defamation. There would then be no *federal* constitutional issue involved. The Supreme Court, if it wanted to reverse the damages award, would have to say something about the relationship of the First Amendment to the law of defamation. Still, it is fair to say that the Court went much further than it had to if overturning the lower court decision was its only goal.

The Birth of the Actual-Malice Rule

The U.S. Supreme Court unanimously overturned the libel judgment against the New York Times Company on the grounds that the plaintiff had not established that the newspaper's level of fault was sufficient to justify liability. Writing for the Court, Justice Brennan set forth the central holding of the case: when a public official sues for damages because of an allegedly defamatory falsehood concerning his or her **official conduct**, the First Amendment demands that the plaintiff prove, with **convincing clarity**, that the statement was made with **actual malice**—that is, with knowledge that it was false or with reckless disregard as to whether it was true or false.[4] Several of these phrases require explication. Because later court cases have attempted to clarify the definitions of "public official," "official conduct," and even "actual malice" itself, those terms are discussed further when we begin to look at *Sullivan*'s progeny.

The term *convincing clarity* is a general legal term of art that tells us what the plaintiff's level of proof must be. You are likely already familiar with one or both of the other two levels of proof that together govern the vast majority of court proceedings in the United States—proof "beyond a reasonable doubt" and proof "by a preponderance of the evidence."

The government, when it prosecutes a criminal defendant, must establish its case beyond a reasonable doubt. How much doubt is "reasonable" doubt? There really is no one right answer to this question. Beyond *any* doubt would mean that you are 100 percent sure of the defendant's guilt. Does "beyond a reasonable doubt" mean 99 percent sure? Or 95 percent sure? Judges' instructions to jurors tend not to provide such mathematical equivalents. It is fair to say, however, that if your own internal mental rule translates into a probability of guilt much lower than 90 percent, a good criminal defense lawyer will do anything possible to keep you off the jury.

Plaintiffs in most civil suits—the kinds dealt with on TV by Judge Judy—must

---

4. *New York Times Co. v. Sullivan*, 376 U.S. 254 (1964). Justices Black, Douglas, and Goldberg wrote or joined concurring opinions in which they argued for a more absolute rule than that espoused by Brennan. The concurrences interpreted the First Amendment as providing absolute immunity for any and all statements made about public officials' official conduct or even (in Justice Black's words) "about public affairs" generally.

establish proof by a "preponderance of the evidence" to prevail. This level of proof has an intuitive, mathematical feel to it. Preponderance means "more than not," or any probability greater than 50 percent.

What, then, is "convincing clarity"? You have probably already guessed correctly that it is defined as a standard somewhere in between "preponderance of the evidence" and "beyond a reasonable doubt." Sometimes it is defined as a level of evidentiary proof so clear as to leave no *substantial* doubt in your mind to the contrary. Although "substantial" doubt is clearly more than "reasonable" doubt, how much more is anyone's guess.

The Court Applies the Actual-Malice Standard to the *Sullivan* Facts

In finding that the *New York Times* did not manifest the high level of fault demanded by the actual-malice standard, the Court emphasized two factors. First, the newspaper staff genuinely believed at the time of publication that the charges made in the advertisement were "substantially true." Second, the Court found that the most stinging charges did not refer to Sullivan, even obliquely.

Sullivan's attorneys successfully established at trial that had the *Times* staff responsible for accepting the advertisement taken the time to fact-check—simply by using the paper's own previous editions—they would have identified many of the falsities in the ad. The failure to check facts, however, was not sufficient evidence of actual malice, the Court held, in part because many of the signatories to the advertisement were very well-respected civil rights leaders.

THINGS TO REMEMBER

Conceptualizing the *New York Times Co. v. Sullivan* Holding

- *New York Times Co. v. Sullivan* established the "actual malice" rule, which can be expressed as

$$PO\ (OC) \rightarrow AM\ (CC).$$

Translation: When *public officials* sue because of criticism about their *official conduct*, they must prove *actual malice* with *convincing clarity*.

- "Actual malice" is defined as publishing a knowing falsehood, or publishing with "reckless disregard of truth or falsity."
- "Convincing clarity" is a level of proof somewhere between that required for a criminal prosecution ("beyond a reasonable doubt") and that required for an ordinary civil suit ("by a preponderance of the evidence").

New York Times Co. v. Sullivan is remembered as a landmark decision not only because of the establishment of the actual-malice rule but also because much of Justice Brennan's language in other parts of the opinion has proved so very influential over the years. The next few sections describe the further significance of the *Sullivan* ruling beyond the holding itself.

The Relationship between Libel and Sedition Laws

The Alien and Sedition Acts, discussed in chapter 2, prescribed jail terms of up to five years for "false, scandalous and malicious" statements made against the president, members of Congress, or the government itself. Libel suits brought by public officials angered by criticisms of their official conduct, Justice Brennan said in *Sullivan*, are uncomfortably reminiscent of such sedition prosecutions. The imposition of sanctions against those who criticize the government is "inconsistent with the First Amendment," he said. The spirit of the First Amendment is "a profound national commitment to the principle that debate on public issues should be uninhibited, robust, and wide-open, and that [such debate] may well include vehement, caustic, and sometimes unpleasantly sharp attacks on government and public officials."

That *Sullivan* was a civil libel case rather than a criminal prosecution was immaterial from the Court's perspective. "What a State may not constitutionally bring about by means of a criminal statute," Brennan admonished the Alabama's public officials, "is likewise beyond the reach of its civil law of libel." To hold otherwise would open up "the possibility that a good-faith critic of government will be penalized for his criticism, [a] proposition [that] strikes at the very center of the constitutionally protected area of free expression."

Two Famous Metaphors: "Breathing Space" and the "Chilling Effect"

The actual-malice test does not permit recovery of damages anytime defamatory falsehoods appear. Indeed, the test provides a high degree of protection for errors, as long as the publishers are neither liars nor wholly irresponsible. In *Sullivan*, Justice Brennan developed two metaphors to help explain why it is so important to permit citizen-critics such a high degree of latitude.

The first metaphor—"breathing space"—describes the latitude that must be provided to journalists commenting on public affairs. As Justice Brennan put it in *Sullivan*, "Erroneous statement is inevitable in free debate," and "it must be protected if the freedoms of expression are to have the breathing space that they need to survive."

The second metaphor—a "chilling effect"—is the opposite side of the coin. It represents journalistic timidity and the effect of making the avoidance of publishing any falsity one's most important governing principle. "There can be little doubt," Brennan warned, that reporters not given a bit of leeway will feel this chilling effect, and that "public debate and advocacy will be constrained."

Some Unanswered Questions from *Sullivan*

New York Times Co. v. Sullivan is certainly the most important U.S. libel decision to date. Indeed, much of contemporary libel doctrine can be seen as a fine-tuning or an elaboration of issues raised in the 1964 landmark opinion. For that reason, the majority of this chapter is devoted to examining a number of questions left unanswered in *Sullivan* but that have since received some additional explication from the Court.

Who Is a "Public Official"?

The actual-malice rule applies only when libel plaintiffs are public officials. But who among those on the government payroll are public officials? Must they be elected, or can they be appointed? Is anyone who draws a public paycheck, from a state university president down to each of the school's department secretaries and janitors, to be included? The *Sullivan* Court decided not to decide. The 1964 decision was not the occasion "to determine how far down into the lower ranks of government employees the 'public official' designation would extend for purposes of this rule, or otherwise to specify categories of persons who would or would not be included," Justice Brennan said.

The truth is that there is no national consensus about who is and who is not considered a public official for purposes of the actual-malice rule. Still, the Supreme Court gave some guidance in a 1966 case that came about because a columnist (Rosenblatt) for the *Laconia Evening Citizen* in New Hampshire, in the course of praising the new supervisor of the Belknap County Recreation Area, seemed to imply—the

---

THINGS TO REMEMBER

New York Times Co. v. Sullivan: Beyond the Holding

- The First Amendment is "a profound national commitment to the principle that debate on public issues should be uninhibited, robust, and wide-open."
- Allowing public officials to sue for libel too easily is inconsistent with this commitment and uncomfortably reminiscent of sedition prosecutions.
- The press must be granted a certain amount of wiggle room, called "breathing space," to make innocent errors.
- Without such breathing space the press will experience the "chilling effect" of self-censorship, and we will all be deprived of valuable *true* speech.

relevant section began, "What happened to all the money *last* year? And every other year?"[5]—that the former supervisor (Baer) was a poor financial manager at best, an embezzler at worst. Reversing the jury's damage award imposed against the columnist, the Supreme Court sent the case back to the lower court to determine if the former recreation supervisor should be considered a public official and therefore if he should have had to prove actual malice. (That Baer was a *former* supervisor was not deemed relevant, because the allegedly libelous remarks were made about his tenure as supervisor. Later cases make clear that *candidates* for public office can also be considered public officials for the purposes of applying the actual malice test.)

In the course of remanding the case, the Court reminded us that the earlier *New York Times Co. v. Sullivan* decision requires that Americans enjoy freedom to criticize "those responsible for government operations." This concern dictates a broad definition of "public official," Justice Brennan said. The phrase must apply "at the very least to those among the hierarchy of government employees who have, or appear to the public to have, substantial responsibility for or control over the conduct of governmental affairs. . . . The employee's position must be one which would invite public scrutiny and discussion of the person holding it, entirely apart from the scrutiny and discussion occasioned by the particular charges in controversy."

This definition posits two related but distinguishable criteria. The first criterion is that the government employee must occupy a responsible enough position to have an effect on policies, to have "responsibility" or "control." Thus, while the case law is mixed as to whether public school teachers or even principals are public officials, there is little doubt that a school superintendent would have to prove actual malice.

The second criterion is perhaps best understood by conjuring up an image of two neighbors gossiping (about weighty public affairs, of course!) at the backyard fence. Public officials are those who occupy positions with responsibilities of sufficient concern that we are likely to gossip about them long before anyone publishes an allegedly libelous article about them, and certainly long before they ever bring suit for libel.

These criteria seem clear enough, but that does not mean that courts around the country have always been in agreement about how to apply them.[6] A 2005 decision from California, for example, laments contradictory case law in the state concerning whether a deputy public defender should be considered a public official.[7] Some jurisdictions seem to apply the actual-malice rule only to elected public officials. In 2004, for example, a federal district court in Massachusetts would not consider an assistant state's attorney (who is appointed, not elected) a public official.[8] Similarly, a Connecticut court in 2005 refused to find a recreation supervisor a public official, in part

---

5. *Rosenblatt v. Baer*, 383 U.S. 75, 78 (1966).

6. *Danny R. Veilleux*, "Who Is a Public Official for Purposes of Defamation Action?" 444 A.L.R. 5th 193 (2006).

7. *Ghafur v. Bernstein*, 32 Cal. Rptr. 3d 626, 631 (Ct. App. 2005).

8. *Mandel v. Boston Phoenix*, 322 F. Supp. 2d 39 (D. Mass. 2004).

because this was not an elected post.[9] Recall that the Supreme Court in *Rosenblatt v. Baer* itself did not assume that former recreation supervisor Baer was a public official—it sent the question back to the trial court for its consideration.

What Is "Official Conduct"?

The paid advertisement that formed the basis of L. B. Sullivan's libel suit against the *New York Times* made specific allegations about police conduct in Montgomery, Alabama. To the extent that the commissioner in charge of the police force there was thus being criticized, such allegations surely concerned his "official conduct." Beyond that, we learn nothing from the Supreme Court's 1964 decision to help future litigants determine the difference between criticisms of official conduct and more personal attacks that would presumably not trigger the actual-malice rule.

In a pair of later decisions, however, the Court does provide some guidance. The first of these, decided just shortly after *New York Times Co. v. Sullivan*, involved New Orleans–area district attorney Jim Garrison (the same Garrison played by Kevin Costner in Oliver Stone's film *JFK*), who was the defendant in a criminal libel prosecution stemming from a press conference during which he criticized several local criminal court judges.[10] Their huge backlog of cases, he alleged, could be attributed to their "inefficiency, laziness, and excessive vacations," and the difficulty in prosecuting local vice cases was a direct result of their failure to reimburse the expenses incurred by undercover police officers. The *Garrison* decision overturning the criminal libel conviction is remembered today for two reasons. First, the Court used the occasion to apply the actual-malice rule to criminal libel cases. In so doing, the Court recognized, but did not answer, the larger question of whether criminal libel statutes could ever be constitutionally applied against those who criticize public officials. Second, and more important for our present purposes, is how the Court handled the state's argu-

---

THINGS TO REMEMBER

Who Is a Public Official?

- Not all public employees are public officials for purposes of the *Sullivan* rule.
- Public officials are persons who
  - have substantial responsibility over the conduct of governmental affairs and
  - occupy positions that invite public scrutiny.
- Despite the rule, it is not always easy to figure out which government employees are to be considered public officials.

---

9. *McIntyre v. Piscottano*, 2005 Conn. Super LEXIS 1526 (2005).
10. *Garrison v. Louisiana*, 379 U.S. 64 (1964).

ment that the actual-malice rule should be inapplicable, in that Garrison's criticisms—especially the charge of "laziness"—dealt not only with the judges' official conduct but also with their overall personalities. "Any criticism of the manner in which a public official performs his duties will tend to affect his private, as well as his public, reputation," Justice Brennan wrote for the Court. "Few personal attributes are more germane to fitness for office than dishonesty, malfeasance, or improper motivation, even though these characteristics may also affect the official's private character."

Seven years later the Court gave a bit more guidance as to what constitutes "official conduct" for purposes of applying the actual-malice doctrine. The *Monitor Patriot*, a Concord, New Hampshire, newspaper, referred to U.S. senatorial candidate Alphonse Roy as a "former small-time bootlegger," that is, as someone who had profited from the illegal sale of hard liquor during the Prohibition era. In overturning the jury's $20,000 damages award to Roy, Justice Stewart concluded that "a charge of criminal conduct, no matter how remote in time or place, can never be irrelevant to an official's or a candidate's fitness for office."[11]

Who Else Should Be Required to Prove Actual Malice?

One of the Supreme Court's chief rationales for constitutionalizing the libel tort is our national commitment to the principle "that debate on public issues should be uninhibited, robust, and wide-open."[12] Public issues, of course, do not always involve public officials. They might involve captains of industry and scientists, and both celebrities and obscure persons caught up in a controversial matter. The Supreme Court showed its recognition of this fact when, in ruling simultaneously on two cases in 1967, it extended the actual-malice rule to allegedly libelous statements made about "public figures." The two cases—*Curtis Publishing Co. v. Butts* and *Associated Press v. Walker*—share the same citation,[13] but have very different facts and produced opposite outcomes. The first case came about because the *Saturday Evening Post* had ac-

---

THINGS TO REMEMBER

What Is "Official Conduct?"

- Some attributions of personal characteristics (such as laziness) have clear implications for the performance of one's official conduct.
- Any allegation of criminal behavior, no matter how long ago, is relevant to one's official conduct.

---

11. *Monitor Patriot Co. v. Roy*, 401 U.S. 265, 266, 277 (1971).
12. *New York Times Co. v. Sullivan*, 376 U.S. 254, 270 (1964).
13. 388 U.S. 130 (1967).

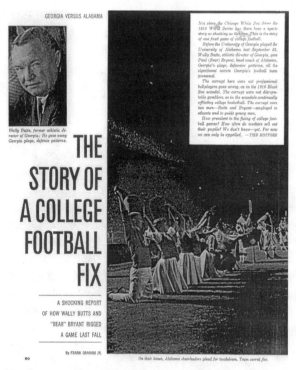

GEORGIA VERSUS ALABAMA

Wally Butts, former athletic director of Georgia: He gave away Georgia plays, defense patterns.

THE STORY OF A COLLEGE FOOTBALL FIX

A SHOCKING REPORT
OF HOW WALLY BUTTS AND
"BEAR" BRYANT RIGGED
A GAME LAST FALL

By FRANK GRAHAM JR.

On their knees, Alabama cheerleaders plead for touchdown. Team scored five.

The Supreme Court ruled that elements of this article—which accused a college athletic director of fixing a football game—were actionable, in part because the news value was not so "hot" as to justify failing to check sources further.

cused Wally Butts, then–athletic director of the University of Georgia, of fixing a football game between that school and the University of Alabama. Butts could not be considered a public official, because the athletic program at Georgia was administered by a corporation funded wholly by the private sector.

The article, "The Story of a College Football Fix," quotes an Atlanta businessman who claims that his phone's wires got crossed with those of Butts, thus allowing him to listen in on the Georgia coach's conversation with his counterpart at Alabama, during which he revealed what sounded like the kinds of team secrets that can determine game outcomes. At trial, however, it came out that the overheard phone conversation had been greatly misunderstood by the eavesdropper, that the substance of the two coach's banter did not involve any kind of inside facts or "trade secrets" about game plans. By a 5-4 vote, the Supreme Court upheld the lower court's award of almost a half million dollars to Butts, concluding that the magazine had engaged in reprehensibly shoddy journalism, failing to take even "elementary precautions." Their main source had a criminal background, yet his story was accepted without independent support. In addition, the magazine should have made at least some attempt "to find out whether Alabama had adjusted its plans after the alleged divulgence of information." When the Court added to the equation the fact that the *Post* writer assigned to the story knew very little about football, the majority concluded that the magazine's conduct represented "an extreme departure from the standards of investigation and reporting ordinarily adhered to by responsible publishers."

The companion case resulted from a reporter's eyewitness dispatch to the Associated Press (AP) wire service describing a riot at the University of Mississippi in response to the use of the National Guard to help smooth James Meredith's enrollment there in the autumn of 1962. Meredith, of course, was the university's first black student. The account said that former major general Edwin Walker—who had a long and distinguished military career but who was a private citizen at both the time of the riot and the time of the publication by the AP—had "taken command of the violent crowd and had personally led a charge against federal marshals." It also described Walker as encouraging rioters to use violence and giving them technical advice on combating the effects of tear gas. At his libel trial against the Associated Press, Walker testified that he was on the university campus and did talk to a group of students, but that his message to them was to exercise self-restraint and to remain peaceful. The jury awarded him $500,000 in compensatory damages; the trial judge reversed the jury's additional award of $300,000 in punitive damages.

The Supreme Court unanimously overturned the award to Walker. The Court emphasized that the story of the events on the University of Mississippi campus, unlike the one about coach Butts, was "news which required immediate dissemination." Also unlike the situation in the companion case, in this case the AP's news source was a correspondent who "gave every indication of being trustworthy and competent," especially to staffers "familiar with General Walker's prior publicized statements on the underlying controversy."

These companion cases are remembered today for two important issues related to the actual-malice standard. First and most important, the Court used the cases as a vehicle to make clear that the *Sullivan* rule would apply not only to public officials but to public figures as well. Second, the Court also began to offer judges guidance in determining whether a journalist is guilty of actual malice. Specifically, the Court will be a bit more forgiving of journalistic errors if the news being disseminated to the public is "hard" news about important political events, if it is "hot" news that must be gotten out quickly, and perhaps too if the specific media outlet's tight deadline precludes careful verification of every single last fact.

If the *Butts* and *Walker* cases together serve to emphasize that the identity of the plaintiff will go a long way toward determining who will prevail in a libel suit, the Court injected some confusion into the issue a few years later. In 1971, the Court was unable to produce a majority opinion in a case resulting from a Philadelphia-area radio station's having referred to a local businessman as a "smut merchant," but a plurality opinion signed by three of the justices argued for extending the "actual mal-

THINGS TO REMEMBER

Application of the Actual-Malice Rule to Public Figures

Within three years of the *Sullivan* case, the Court decided to demand that not only public officials but also public figures prove actual malice to establish a libel claim.

ice" protection to any publication focusing on a topic of public interest, regardless of the identity of the plaintiff.[14] Three years later, in the landmark *Gertz v. Robert Welch, Inc.* decision discussed at more length later in this chapter, a clear majority of the Court rejected the *Rosenbloom* plurality's logic and reaffirmed that it is primarily whether the plaintiff is a public official or public figure that will determine whether the actual-malice standard applies.[15]

What Are the Actual-Malice Rule's Implications for the Truth Defense?

In the common-law tort of libel, it will be recalled from chapter 3, one of the most powerful defenses was to establish that the gist or "sting" of the defamatory remarks was substantially true. Recall too that when we call truth a *defense*, we emphasize that the plaintiff need not prove falsity as an element of libel. In common law, defamatory statements are presumed to be false. The alternative—because arguments require presumptions and burdens of proof—is that we presume the plaintiff really is a scoundrel or a liar or a spouse beater.

How does the *New York Times Co. v. Sullivan* actual-malice rule affect the place of truth and falsity in libel law? Plaintiffs who are able to prove actual malice by the first of the two options provided in the Supreme Court's definition—that the defendant published a "knowing falsehood"—will obviously have laid to rest any ambiguity about the truth or falsity of the defamation. It seems also that the second route, proving actual malice as the dissemination of libel with "reckless disregard" as to truth or falsity, carries with it at least a strong implication that the publication's allegations must have been false. Why sue someone for recklessly publishing the *truth*, for getting it *right* (even if by accident or sheer luck)?

To prove actual malice, then, is to prove falsity, but what of plaintiffs who do not have to prove actual malice? These plaintiffs are neither public officials nor public figures. Public officials who sue because of defamations that have nothing to do with

14. *Rosenbloom v. Metromedia, Inc.*, 403 U.S. 29 (1971).
15. 418 U.S. 323 (1974).

their official conduct are also under consideration. Do they have the burden of proving falsity, or does the common-law rule prevail?

The Supreme Court gave at least a partial answer to this question in 1986, when it decided *Philadelphia Newspapers, Inc. v. Hepps*.[16] At issue were articles in the *Philadelphia Inquirer* linking local businessman Maurice Hepps to organized crime and alleging that his company exercised a measure of control over the State Liquor Control Board. The Pennsylvania Supreme Court, overturning a lower court finding for the newspaper, held that the jury should have been explicitly instructed that Hepps did not have the burden of proving falsity. By a 5-4 vote, the U.S. Supreme Court reversed the state high court. Writing for the majority, Justice O'Connor admitted that an ironclad rule requiring all libel plaintiffs to prove falsity would be imperfect in that there will be times when defamatory statements, while untrue, cannot be proven untrue. Yet always placing the burden of showing truth on the defendants, she argued, would stifle too much speech. She emerged with a compromise position, holding that "the common-law presumption that defamatory speech is false cannot stand *when a plaintiff seeks damages against a media defendant for speech of public concern*" (emphasis added).

The holding in *Hepps* provides a clue to a larger truth about the Supreme Court's post–*New York Times Co. v. Sullivan* defamation jurisprudence generally. That body of case law can be understood and organized far more easily if three important questions are kept in mind:

- Who is the plaintiff (a public official or public figure, or a private individual)?
- Who is the defendant (media or nonmedia)?
- What was the libel about (an issue of public importance or a private matter)?

The Court has in essence set up a two-by-two-by-two matrix, creating eight possible combinations of situations. More often than not, the answer to a question about the constitutional dimension of libel law is "it depends," and what it depends on is how these three questions are answered. If the question is "Who has the burden of proof regarding truth or falsity," the answer seems to be that in at least five of the eight situations, the burden is shouldered by the plaintiff. Why five of eight? In all four situations in which the answer to the first question is that the plaintiff is a public person (assuming for public officials that their official conduct is at issue), that plaintiff has the burden of proving falsity. In at least one set of circumstances, even purely private plaintiffs must prove falsity: when the defendant is the media *and* the offending publication is about a matter of public interest. With respect to the remaining three boxes—private plaintiffs suing nonmedia entities (regardless of the subject matter of the defamation) and private plaintiffs suing the media over a publication on a topic not of public concern—the First Amendment as interpreted by the Supreme

16. 475 U.S. 767 (1986).

Court offers no guidance as to who shoulders the burden of proof regarding truth or falsity.

Is the Presence of Actual Malice a Legal or a Factual Question?

In chapter 1, the distinction between questions of fact and questions of law was introduced. That distinction becomes crucial in the Supreme Court's libel jurisprudence; it becomes a big money issue in that the vast majority of libel suits are lost by the media at the trial level, but a majority of those are overturned in favor of the defendants at the appellate level. Libel defendants are therefore hungry to find plausible and fruitful grounds for appeal.

Given that so much of the constitutionalized tort of libel focuses on the level of fault manifested by defendants, whether a trial court finding of actual malice is a question of fact (generally not appealable) or a question of law (appealable) was a crucial question left unanswered in *New York Times Co. v. Sullivan*. Twenty years later, the Court did provide an answer, one that lawyer and author Floyd Abrams hailed as a reaffirmation of "one of the most important pillars on which *Sullivan* stands: the constitutional requirement of independent appellate review to assure that juries and trial courts do not overcome or circumvent the First Amendment."[17]

The facts in *Bose Corp. v. Consumers Union*[18] will likely seem not nearly as exciting as the lofty language often used to describe the legal doctrine the case created. The case resulted from what Justice Stevens described in his majority opinion as "an unusual metaphor in a critical review of an unusual loudspeaker system." The speaker system was Bose's 901 model, and the review was published in the May 1970 issue of *Consumer Reports*. The reviewers, after offering some positive comments about the speaker system, cautioned that listeners "could pinpoint the location of various instruments much more easily with a standard speaker than with the Bose system." With this system, the reviewers added, "individual instruments . . . seemed to grow to gigantic proportions and tended to wander about the room." Prospective buyers,

---

THINGS TO REMEMBER

The First Amendment and the Truth Defense

- Proving actual malice includes the proof of falsity.
- Those who do not have to prove actual malice will still have to prove falsity if they sue a media defendant about a story on a topic of public concern.

---

17. Floyd Abrams, "The Supreme Court Turns a New Page in Libel," 70 *American Bar Association Journal* 89 (1984).

18. 466 U.S. 485 (1984).

in the reviewers' opinion, might not be very happy with the system "after the novelty [wears] off."

The trial court ruled that Bose would be considered a public figure for the purposes of this product disparagement suit because of the unusual nature of the speaker system and the aggressive advertising by the company to promote it. Thus, actual malice was the required level of fault, and the court was satisfied that this level of fault had been demonstrated at trial. Where the magazine's panel of listeners reported that sound from the speakers seemed to "wander about the room," the court took it to mean "all over the room," not simply (as the evaluators *said* at trial that they meant) "along the wall," *between* the two speakers. The court concluded that the difference between what the evaluators meant and what they actually wrote was substantial enough to constitute actual malice.

If you find this discussion a bit silly, you are not alone. In his dissenting opinion, Justice Rehnquist disparagingly referred to this whole Bose speakers controversy as "The Case of the Wandering Instruments," and suggested that it would be much more at home in *The Adventures of Sherlock Holmes* than in the Court's official proceedings.

In any event, the trial court assessed damages against the magazine publisher and the federal appellate court reversed, finding that the editors were guilty at most "of using imprecise language in the article—perhaps resulting from an attempt to produce a readable article for its mass audience." The question in front of the Supreme Court, then, was whether the appellate court had overstepped its bounds by assessing anew and independently the question of whether the magazine manifested actual malice. Is actual malice a question of law or of fact?

Intuitively, one might suppose that actual malice can be either a question of fact or a question of law. A jury that finds that the defendant published a "knowing falsehood"—in other words, that he lied—would seem to be making an inference of fact. Trying to guess what was going on in another person's mind at some relevant time in the past is difficult; it is more art than science, but it is an issue of fact. Either he knew or he did not know that he was publishing a falsehood.

Conversely, the intuitive approach would also suggest that if the jury depends instead upon the alternative definition of actual malice, that the defendant published with "reckless disregard as to truth or falsity," it will have settled a question of law rather than of fact. How far must a publisher deviate from accepted journalistic practices before we are ready to say that she has crossed over the line between mere negligence and actual malice? This kind of judgment is precisely what is normally thought of as a question of law.

As it turns out, only Justice White's dissenting opinion embraced this perspective. Dissenting Justices Rehnquist and O'Connor went further, arguing that the question of actual malice is at its core a factual question in all circumstances.

The majority opinion does not really answer the question, but it does provide a rule to guide lower courts in the future. Writing for the majority, Justice Stevens emphasized that independent appellate review has been held by the Court to be required by the First Amendment in many contexts, from commercial speech to obscenity. Here similarly, the Court concluded that "the question whether the evidence in the record in a defamation case is of the convincing clarity required to strip the utterance of First Amendment protection is not merely a question for the trier of fact." Taking on the responsibility of determining the issue of fault for itself, the majority found that testimony offered by Consumer Union's chief engineer may have manifested a "capacity for rationalization," but not a degree of culpability approaching actual malice. As if in response to Justice Rehnquist's expressed disdain for the banality of the dispute before it, the majority further concluded that "the difference between hearing violin sounds move around the room and hearing them wander back and forth fits easily within the breathing space that gives life to the First Amendment."

The majority did not ever explicitly tell us that actual malice is a legal as opposed to a factual question, and this failure to settle the question forthrightly has been much criticized. Still, the Court concluded that the strong First Amendment interests involved outweigh the interests reflected in the "clearly erroneous rule," which was discussed briefly in chapter 1.[19] That rule tells federal appellate judges that they should defer to the lower court on matters of fact and that this deference should be especially strong when assessments of witness credibility are at issue. After all, only the trial participants see and hear firsthand the demeanor of witnesses, and they are thus in a far better position to determine veracity than are appellate judges reading trial transcripts months or years later. The "clearly erroneous" rule, Justice Stevens held for the majority, "does not prescribe the standard of review to be applied in reviewing a determination of actual malice in a case governed by *New York Times Co. v. Sullivan*." Rather, "appellate judges in such a case must exercise independent judgment and determine whether the record establishes actual malice with convincing clarity."

THINGS TO REMEMBER

Appealing Actual Malice

- A trial court finding that a libel defendant has manifested actual malice with convincing clarity is an appealable finding.
- This rule has significant financial implications for media libel defendants, who tend to lose most libel cases at the trial level but often win on appeal.

---

19. The "clearly erroneous" rule is found in Rule 52 (a) of the Federal Rules of Civil Procedure.

Can Editorial Pressure to Produce Sensational Stories Constitute Partial Evidence of Actual Malice?

In the spring of 1985, media outlets nationwide were using their editorial pages to express dismay and even a bit of panic over a decision issued by the Court of Appeals for the D.C. Circuit. Mobil Oil president William Tavoulareas had sued the *Washington Post* for suggesting, in an article published in November 1979, that he had improperly used his influence to help set up his son Peter as a partner in a huge shipping business that had multimillion-dollar contracts with Mobil. The majority of the three-judge appellate panel hearing the case in 1985 made much of the fact that *Post* editor Bob Woodward put his staff under great pressure to produce, in his words, the kind of "holy shit story" for which he himself became famous during Watergate. Might not reporters who are under the gun to write such "high-impact investigative stories of wrongdoing" be likely to see an international scandal where others would see only a father trying to help out his son? The appellate panel concluded that Woodward's colorful phrase "is relevant to the inquiry of whether a newspaper's employees acted in reckless disregard of whether a statement is false or not."[20]

The *Post*'s appeal to the full appellate court produced a very different result. The en banc court overturned the panel, holding that "managerial pressure to produce [hard-hitting investigative] stories cannot, as a matter of law, constitute evidence of actual malice" and adding that investigative reports serve "one of the highest functions of the press in our society."

The Supreme Court never heard the *Tavoulareas* case, and the media celebration of the en banc decision may have been both overly jubilant and premature. In the years since *Tavoulareas*, the notion that juries cannot use as evidence of actual malice the fact that reporters felt obliged to write hard-hitting investigative pieces has not spread beyond the D.C. Circuit. Even before *Tavoulareas*, Chief Justice Warren's concurring opinion from the case discussed earlier involving University of Georgia football coach Wally Butts had suggested one reason the plaintiff there correctly prevailed: the *Saturday Evening Post* staff had been under enormous pressure to increase circulation and advertising revenues through stories that Warren described as "sophisticated muckraking," those that are designed to "provoke people," to "make them mad."[21] That this language was later cited with approval by an opinion signed by eight members of the Court would seem to suggest further that the relevant language from the en banc decision in *Tavoulareas* stands virtually alone.[22]

Moreover, in 1988, the Sixth Circuit Court of Appeals, although superficially expressing agreement with the D.C. Circuit's reasoning in *Tavoulareas*, ultimately rejected what had so comforted the press about the earlier decision by adding that libel

---

20. *Tavoulareas v. Piro*, 759 F.2d 90 (D.C. Cir. 1985), *rev'd en banc*, 817 F.2d 762 (D.C. Cir. 1987).

21. *Curtis Publishing Co. v. Butts*, 388 U.S. 130, 169 (1967) (Warren, C.J., concurring).

22. *St. Amant v. Thompson*, 390 U.S. 727, 732 n.3 (1968).

juries should not be required to "blind [themselves] to evidence of editorial pressure for sensationalistic stories."[23] This was admittedly dicta that the Supreme Court never cited while upholding the Sixth Circuit's decision.

What Other Journalistic Behaviors Might Constitute Actual Malice?

The Supreme Court's decision in the *Harte-Hanks* case from the Sixth Circuit (mentioned above) is worthy of study for reasons that go beyond the implicit rejection of the *Tavoulareas* logic. The case was an important and disturbing one from the perspective of many commentators, who emphasized that this was the first time the Court permitted a finding of actual malice largely on the basis of what the press did *not* do or say, rather than on what it actually published. Whether or not one accepts the validity of the media's assessment, the Court used the case as a vehicle to give further guidance as to what kinds of newsroom practices might constitute actual malice. A brief review of the facts gives a better understanding of how the Court did this.

Harte-Hanks stemmed from accusations that Daniel Connaughton, a candidate for municipal judge, had offered financial rewards of various kinds to two women who had testified at a grand jury investigating the incumbent judge's staff for, ironically enough, bribery. A jury awarded Connaughton $200,000 in damages, but the trial judge reversed that award, finding that the plaintiff had not proved actual malice. The appellate court, although not conducting as thoroughly independent a review of the actual-malice question as the Supreme Court would have preferred, concluded that there was actual malice and reinstated the jury award. The Supreme Court affirmed this judgment and in so doing identified a number of factors that led it to conclude that the newspaper had acted with actual malice. Among these factors was the newspaper's reliance on a highly questionable source while failing to interview easily identifiable persons likely to present evidence at odds with the paper's eventual

---

THINGS TO REMEMBER

Investigative Journalism and the First Amendment

- The Court of Appeals for the D.C. Circuit has held that juries may not consider as evidence of actual malice the fact that reporters may have been under pressure to produce hard-hitting investigative pieces.
- The Sixth Circuit seems to have rejected this approach, and it is not yet clear how the Supreme Court would rule on the issue.

---

23. *Connaughton v. Harte-Hanks Communications, Inc.*, 842 F.2d 825, 834 (6th Cir. 1988), *aff'd*, 491 U.S. 657 (1989).

accusations. In addition, the paper failed to listen to a tape recording it knew to exist of the conversation in which Connaughton allegedly offered tangible rewards to the grand jury witnesses. These factors and others led the Court to conclude that the paper had made a "deliberate decision not to acquire knowledge" of important facts. It was this "purposeful avoidance of the truth" that Justice Stevens's majority opinion said compelled the Court to find actual malice.

Additional guidance concerning the kinds of behaviors juries trying to assess communicators' level of fault might consider comes from a Louisiana case involving a televised political speech, but in which the speaker rather than the media was the defendant.[24] Phil St. Amant, a candidate for sheriff in Baton Rouge, strongly hinted in his speech that his opponent, deputy sheriff Herman Thompson, was guilty of accepting bribes from the president of the local Teamsters union. Although the result of the case was to overturn a modest libel judgment against St. Amant on the ground that he had no reason to doubt the veracity of his source, Justice White's majority opinion also provided the following list of transgressions that might constitute actual malice:

- A story is fabricated by the defendant, is the product of his imagination, or is based wholly on an unverified anonymous telephone call.
- The publisher's allegations are so inherently improbable that only a reckless man would have put them in circulation.
- There are obvious reasons to doubt the veracity of the informant or the accuracy of the informant's reports.

In 1991, the Supreme Court was called on to determine whether a reporter's attribution to an interviewed source of direct quotes that were never actually uttered could be evidence of actual malice. *Masson v. New Yorker Magazine, Inc.*[25] arose out of an article written by Janet Malcolm about Dr. Jeffrey Masson that appeared in two consecutive issues of the magazine in 1983. Both litigants agreed that the articles, which told the story of how Masson lost his position as the director of the Sigmund Freud Archives as a result of his outspoken criticism of Freudian psychoanalysis, were based largely on forty hours of tape-recorded interviews. The picture Malcolm painted of Masson was hardly flattering. As one reviewer put it, Masson was depicted as "a grandiose egoist—mean-spirited, self-serving, full of braggadocio, impossibly arrogant and, in the end, a destructive fool."[26]

The federal trial court granted summary judgment to Malcolm and the magazine, finding that the six alleged misattributions had not altered the "substantive content" of Masson's actual remarks, or were at least "rational interpretations" of some of

---

24. *St. Amant v. Thompson*, 390 U.S. 727 (1968).
25. 501 U.S. 496 (1991).
26. Robert Coles, "Freudianism and Its Malcontents," *Boston Globe*, May 27, 1984, 58.

Masson's more ambiguous comments. The Supreme Court reversed with respect to five of the six quotes and in so doing, fashioned a slightly different rule from that embraced by the lower courts. Summary judgment based on allegedly defamatory misquotes should be permitted, Justice Kennedy wrote for the majority, as long as the printed account does not represent "a material change in the meaning conveyed" by the actual utterance.[27]

Is There Such a Thing as a Defamatory *Opinion*?

In chapter 3, mention was made of the common-law libel defense known as fair comment, which reminds us that defamation plaintiffs must be able to prove that the damaging utterances made about them contained specific *factual* allegations. Pure opinions, at least theoretically, would not be actionable. The Supreme Court—and lower courts attempting to apply relevant Supreme Court doctrine—has in recent years applied a First Amendment analysis to the fact-versus-opinion distinction.

The somewhat confusing story of the Court's "protected opinion" doctrine began with an off-the-cuff bit of dicta in a 1974 decision. *Gertz v. Robert Welch, Inc.* involved a conservative magazine publisher who accused a civil rights attorney of being part of a Communist conspiracy to discredit law enforcement officials. The majority opinion included the following words: "We begin with the common ground. Under the First Amendment there is no such thing as a false idea. However pernicious an opinion may seem, we depend for its correction not on the conscience of judges and juries but on the competition of other ideas."[28]

At least two questions arise from this passage. The first, to which the Court would not provide any answer until sixteen years later, was whether it meant by its dramatic tone to create absolute immunity from liability for any utterance that could plausibly be called an opinion. Many lower courts took the Court to mean precisely that. The

---

THINGS TO REMEMBER

Nailing Down the Actual Malice Concept

- Juries might find actual malice if the media
  - depend on a single, anonymous phone call as their source;
  - publish without checking a charge that seems very likely, on its face, to be false; or
  - show no skepticism toward a source who is almost certainly lying.
- Juries may not find actual malice in the inaccuracy of exact quotes attributed to a source unless the meaning of the source's words has been materially changed.

---

27. *Masson*, 501 U.S. at 517.
28. 418 U.S. 323, 339–340 (1974).

second question was whatever special measure of First Amendment protection against libel suits would be granted to opinions, how would one *distinguish* facts from opinions? In the years following *Gertz*, several lower courts offered their own thoughts regarding this second question. One of the most influential suggestions was provided by the Court of Appeals for the D.C. Circuit, in *Ollman v. Evans*.[29]

Columnists Rowland Evans and Robert Novak had written an editorial opposing the impending appointment of Bertell Ollman, a well-known professor of political science, to a department chair position at the University of Maryland. Ollman, who blamed the university's ultimate decision not to hire him on the fallout from the editorial, was depicted not only as a Marxist, but also as someone who believed in using the classroom to proselytize in support of Marxist ideology. It was another assertion that gave the appellate court the most difficulty. Was it an assertion of fact or of opinion when Evans and Novak quoted an unnamed colleague of Ollman's—described as a "political scientist in a major eastern university whose scholarship and reputation as a liberal is well known"—for the proposition that Ollman "has no status within the profession, but is a pure and simple activist"?

The *Ollman* court was a very divided one. The eleven judges produced seven separate opinions and a 6-5 vote concluding that the "no status" allegation as well as all the other remarks that offended Ollman were protected opinion. In his plurality opinion, Judge Kenneth Starr (later of Whitewater and "Monicagate" fame) lamented that "the Supreme Court provided little guidance in *Gertz* itself as to the manner in which the distinction between fact and opinion is to be discerned." Such a distinction, he added, "is by no means as easy a question as might appear at first blush." He suggested that courts trying to distinguish facts from opinions should pose these questions:

- What is the common usage or meaning of the words?

  Generally there will be a definiteness about facts that are missing from opinions. "He is a convicted felon" is thus much less likely to be deemed protected opinion than "He is a fascist." Accusing a journalist of "sloppy and irresponsible reporting" would surely not be actionable, but to accuse the same journalist of "making up fictitious sources whenever it suited her" might be.
- How verifiable is the statement?

  Is the statement objectively capable of proof or disproof? Although there might be some overlap between this inquiry and the one above, verifiability raises important constitutional issues. "Insofar as a statement is unverifiable, the First Amendment is endangered when attempts are made to prove the statement true or false."
- What is the immediate context in which the words appear?

  Look at the paragraphs before and after the allegedly libelous remark. Perhaps look at the entire article or column for guidance. Recall *Greenbelt Cooperative Pub-*

---

29. 750 F.2d 970 (D.C. Cir. 1984) (en banc).

lishing Association v. Bresler,[30] discussed in chapter 3. In that case, the plaintiff was referred to as a "blackmailer" in a local newspaper, but the immediate context of the article made clear that the commentator meant only that Bresler, a real estate developer, had driven a hard bargain with the city council, not that he was guilty of extortion.

- What is the larger social context in which the words appear?

    Consider, for example, the mind-set with which readers approach the various sections of a newspaper. In an editorial column, readers are conditioned to expect opinions rather than hard facts. Other courts have said the same of editorial cartoons, sports sections, and restaurant reviews.

Although the *Ollman* test became quite influential, Judge Starr was the first to admit that any such calculus designed to help judges work through the immeasurably complicated issue of the meaning of words was bound to be imperfect. In 1990, the Supreme Court weighed in again on the fact-versus-opinion distinction in *Milkovich v. Lorain Journal Co.*[31] There is a great degree of ambiguity in the case. One commentator has suggested that lower courts have been so confused by the decision that they have gone in at least eight different directions in trying to apply it.[32] Still, it is fair to say that as a result of *Milkovich*, many libel suits that previously would have been dismissed in response to defendants' motions for summary judgment have instead gone to trial.

The *Milkovich* case stemmed from a lawsuit against the Ohio High School Athletic Association, which had conducted an investigation into an altercation that took place at a high school wrestling match and resulted in some injuries. Maple Heights High School wrestling coach Michael Milkovich testified at that judicial proceeding, which resulted in the lifting of sanctions against the Maple Heights wrestling team that had been imposed by the association. A local newspaper article commenting on the proceedings seemed to accuse Milkovich of perjury.

Writing for a 7-2 majority, Chief Justice Rehnquist expressed concern that lower courts had made too much of the dicta from *Gertz* that "there is no such thing as a false idea." That passage was never intended "to create a wholesale defamation exemption for anything that might be labeled 'opinion,'" Rehnquist added. A contrary reading would "ignore the fact that expressions of 'opinion' may often imply an assertion of objective fact." Rehnquist further chided the defendants for proposing that "a number of factors developed by the lower courts (in what we hold was a mistaken reliance on the *Gertz* dictum) be considered" in distinguishing facts from opinions. Clearly Rehnquist had in mind here such formulas as the *Ollman* four-part test. Such

---

30. 398 U.S. 6 (1970).

31. 497 U.S. 1 (1990).

32. Kathryn Dix Sowle, "A Matter of Opinion: Milkovich Four Years Later," 3 *William and Mary Bill of Rights Journal* 467 (1994).

tests are unneeded, Rehnquist explained, because "the 'breathing space' which 'free-doms of expression require in order to survive' is adequately secured by existing constitutional doctrine without the creation of an artificial dichotomy between 'opinion' and fact."[33]

Perhaps there is a bit of irony in the fact that the *Milkovich* majority, even while criticizing lower courts for trying to fashion rules to distinguish facts from opinions, itself needed to determine if the charges leveled against the wrestling coach carried factual elements—in other words, needed to separate fact from opinion. Many commentators have thus suggested that the Court "simply jettisoned the terminology rather than the essence of the fact-opinion distinction."[34] In any event, Rehnquist had little difficulty concluding that the newspaper article did raise very specific factual allegations about Milkovich that should be considered by a jury rather than subject to summary judgment for the defendant. "The dispositive question in the present case," he wrote, is "whether or not a reasonable factfinder could conclude that the statements . . . imply an assertion that petitioner Milkovich perjured himself in a judicial proceeding. We think this question must be answered in the affirmative."[35]

Although Chief Justice Rehnquist rejected the defense's argument that the First Amendment always "mandates an inquiry into whether a statement is 'opinion' or 'fact,'" he went out of his way to remind us that in many situations, existing Supreme Court precedents already serve to protect statements of opinion. Certainly in any case where actual malice is the required level of fault, a finding of false fact is necessarily a part of the plaintiff's burden. So too, after the *Hepps* case discussed earlier, plaintiffs suing media defendants over matters of public concern have the burden of proving that *false* allegations of fact have been made. *Milkovich*'s effects would thus chiefly be felt by defendants, especially nonmedia defendants, whose utterances are not deemed to touch on matters of public concern.

A 1997 decision from the Court of Appeals for the First Circuit involved such a defendant. Levinsky's is a small chain of Portland, Maine, retail clothing stores that was feeling a great deal of competition from the Wal-Mart stores that had recently opened in the area. It embarked on a playful radio advertising campaign with "David versus Goliath" elements aimed at preserving its market share. (The copy for one such ad read, "Levinsky's has a great selection and the lowest prices in Maine on Levi's jeans, Dockers, and denim shirts. Wal-Mart doesn't carry Levi's—but we did get a good buy on a toaster."). A reporter for *BIZ*, a Portland business magazine decided to do a story about the "store wars"; a couple of criticisms aimed at Levinsky's made to the reporter in an interview with a Wal-Mart official formed the basis for the

---

33. *Milkovich*, 497 U.S. at 18–19 (citations omitted).

34. Martin F. Hansen, "Fact, Opinion, and Consensus: The Verifiability of Allegedly Defamatory Speech," 62 *George Washington Law Review* 43, 45 (1993); see also Jerry J. Phillips, "Opinion and Defamation: The Camel in the Tent," 57 *Tennessee Law Review* 647, 675 (1990); Nat Stern, "Defamation, Epistemology, and the Erosion (but Not Destruction) of the Opinion Privilege," 57 *Tennessee Law Review* 595, 614 (1990).

35. *Milkovich*, 497 U.S. at 21.

Maple Beat the Law with the "Big Lie"

(from the *News-Herald,* January 8, 1975)

Yesterday in the Franklin County Common Pleas Court, Judge Paul Martin over-turned an Ohio High School Athletic Association decision to suspend the Maple Heights wrestling team from this year's state tournament. . . .

But there is something much more important involved here than whether Maple was denied due process by the OHSAA, the basis of the temporary in-junction.

When a person takes on a job in a school, whether it be as a teacher, coach, administrator or even maintenance worker, it is well to remember that his pri-mary job is that of educator.

There is scarcely a person concerned with school who doesn't leave his mark in some way on the young people who pass his way—many are the lessons taken away from school by students which weren't learned from a lesson plan or out of a book. They come from personal experiences with and observations of their superiors and peers, from watching actions and reactions.

Such a lesson was learned (or relearned) yesterday by the student body of Maple Heights High School, and by anyone who attended the Maple-Mentor wrestling meet of last Feb. 8. . . . A lesson which, sadly, in view of the events of the past year, is well they learned early. It is simply this: If you get in a jam, lie your way out.

If you're successful enough, and powerful enough, and can sound sincere enough, you stand an excellent chance of making the lie stand up, regardless of what really happened.

The teachers responsible were mainly head Maple wrestling coach, Mike Mil-kovich, and former superintendent of schools H. Donald Scott.

Last winter they were faced with a difficult situation. Milkovich's ranting from the side of the mat and egging the crowd on against the meet official and the opposing team . . . resulted in . . . a brawl. . . .

Naturally, . . . the two men were called on the carpet to account for the inci-dent. But they declined to walk into the hearing and face up to their responsibili-ties. . . . Instead they chose to come to the hearing and misrepresent the things that happened to the OHSAA Board of Control. . . .

I was among the 2,000-plus witnesses of the meet at which the trouble broke out, and I also attended the hearing before the OHSAA, so I was in a unique position of being the only non-involved party to observe both the meet itself and the Milkovich-Scott version presented to the board. Any resemblance be-tween the two occurrences is purely coincidental.

Anyone who attended the meet, whether he be from Maple Heights, Mentor, or impartial observer, knows in his heart that Milkovich and Scott lied at the hearing after each having given his solemn oath to tell the truth.

But they got away with it. Is that the kind of lesson we want our young people learning from their high school administrators and coaches? I think not.

resulting lawsuit.[36] The Wal-Mart spokesperson alleged first that one of the Levinsky outlets was "trashy" and that customers who call the local outlet are "sometimes put on hold for 20 minutes, or the phone is never picked up at all." Although the court determined that the "trashy" remark is sufficiently vague so as not to carry any clear factual allegations, the "20 minutes" remark was not deemed to be protected opinion. The statement uses a "specific time frame," one that is not so implausible as to constitute rhetorical hyperbole. Indeed, the assertion could be "verified or rebutted by objective evidence of how Levinsky's staff handled telephone calls."

Suppose that the Wal-Mart spokesperson had not referred to a specific time frame? What if he instead said something like, "You can be kept on hold *forever* when you try to reach those folks by phone"? Clearly such an utterance would be protected as rhetorical hyperbole, as a form of opinion so outlandish as to never be taken literally. Should not the second half of the actual "20 minutes" utterance—the suggestion that the phone might "never be picked up at all"—thus go a long way toward protecting the entire assertion? The court rejected this argument, finding that the second portion of the statement might be taken quite literally to mean that, at least on some occasions, workers "did not bother to answer the telephone."

In the end, the case was remanded to the district court, in part to determine if the statements at issue concerned speech on a matter of public concern (in which case the $600,000 in damages that had been awarded could not stand without a finding of actual malice).

THINGS TO REMEMBER

Facts and Opinions

- In an offhand comment from *Gertz v. Robert Welch, Inc.* (1974), the Supreme Court implied that libel suits could never succeed against pure statements of opinion.
- Several lower courts then tried to find ways of distinguishing facts from opinions. One of the more influential tests emerged in the appellate decision in *Ollman v. Evans*, which said that courts should look at the following:

  - The everyday meanings of the words in question
  - Whether the words are verifiable
  - The immediate context
  - The larger social context

- In 1990 (*Milkovich v. Lorain Journal Company*), the Supreme Court tried to put the matter in perspective by emphasizing that libel defendants cannot escape liability simply by prefacing their defamatory utterances with "I think that . . ."
- Courts still struggle with the distinction between facts and opinions.

---

36. *Levinsky's v. Wal-Mart*, 127 F.3d 122 (1st Cir. 1997).

Can Libel Plaintiffs Use the Tort of Intentional Infliction of Emotional Distress as a Way of Avoiding the Actual-Malice Requirement?

In the early 1980s, the makers of Campari liqueur embarked on a clever ad campaign designed to capitalize on what might otherwise be considered a shortcoming of the product. The drink, which has been described as "distinct," "bittersweet," and "strictly an acquired taste," often does not appeal to persons tasting it for the first time.[37] Madison Avenue's solution was to produce slick print ads featuring a celebrity talking about his or her "first time." On the surface, personalities such as actor Tony Roberts would be talking about their first time tasting Campari, but there would always be a naughty double entendre suggesting that the spokesperson's first sexual experience was the real subject under discussion.

Someone at *Hustler* magazine determined that a parody of the Campari campaign, using Reverend Jerry Falwell as the celebrity spokesperson, would be a handy vehicle for expressing the publication's distaste for the well-known leader of the Christian right. The parody, which appeared on the inside front cover of the magazine's November 1983 issue, boasted Falwell's photo alongside the caption, "Jerry Falwell talks about his first time." The "ad" was presented as the transcript of a fictitious interview with its subject. Unlike the Campari ads, here the double entendre was more than a hint. Indeed, the text made clear that Falwell's first time sampling the liqueur was also his first time having sex, with his mother, as it turns out, in an outhouse.

Mr. Falwell was not amused, and he instructed his attorneys to sue the magazine and publisher Larry Flynt. They employed three legal theories in their quest for damages: libel, invasion of privacy, and a third tort called intentional infliction of emotional distress. Invasion of privacy is the subject of the next chapter and need not be of concern here, save to say that the State of Virginia, where Falwell brought his suit, did not recognize the category of privacy invasion for which he sought recovery. The jury ruled against Falwell on his libel claim, finding unsurprisingly that no one could possibly take the text of the ad parody seriously and that his reputation was therefore not damaged.

It is the playing out of the third claim that makes the case an important one beyond the mere fact of the litigants' celebrity. The jury provided Falwell with a fairly sizable damages award on his emotional distress claim, and this award was in front of the U.S. Supreme Court on appeal.[38] Would Falwell be permitted to keep the award even though the jury held that there was no libel here?

A little history of the emotional distress tort will help us answer that question. Emotional distress is a relative newcomer to the American scene, having been recog-

---

37. Rodney A. Smolla, *Jerry Falwell v. Larry Flynt: The First Amendment on Trial* (Chicago and Urbana: University of Illinois Press, 1988), 21.

38. *Hustler Magazine v. Falwell*, 485 U.S. 46 (1988).

Jerry Falwell talks about his first time.*

FALWELL: My first time was in an outhouse outside Lynchburg, Virginia.

INTERVIEWER: Wasn't it a little cramped?

FALWELL: Not after I kicked the goat out.

INTERVIEWER: I see. You must tell me all about it.

FALWELL: I never *really* expected to make it with Mom, but then after she showed all the other guys in town such a good time, I figured, "What the hell!"

INTERVIEWER: But your mom? Isn't that a bit odd?

FALWELL: I don't think so. Looks don't mean that much to me in a woman.

INTERVIEWER: Go on.

FALWELL: Well, we were drunk off our God-fearing asses on Campari, ginger ale and soda—that's called a Fire and Brimstone—at the time. And Mom looked better than a Baptist whore with a $100 donation.

INTERVIEWER: Campari in the crapper with Mom . . . how interesting. Well, how was it?

FALWELL: The Campari was great, but Mom passed out before I could come.

INTERVIEWER: Did you ever try it again?

FALWELL: Sure . . .

lots of times. But not in the outhouse. Between Mom and the shit, the flies were too much to bear.

INTERVIEWER: We meant the Campari.

FALWELL: Oh, yeah. I always get sloshed before I go out to the pulpit. You don't think I could lay down all that bullshit *sober*, do you?

© 1983—Imported by Campari U.S.A., New York, NY 48°proof Spirit Aperitif (Liqueur)

Campari, like all liquor, was made to mix you up. It's a light, 48-proof, refreshing spirit, just mild enough to make you drink too much before you know you're schnockered. For your first time, mix it with orange juice. Or maybe some white wine. Then you won't remember anything the next morning. **Campari. The mixable that smarts.**

CAMPARI® You'll never forget your first time.

*AD PARODY—NOT TO BE TAKEN SERIOUSLY

The Supreme Court held that this ad parody was protected speech.

nized only sporadically in the past hundred years or so. As its name implies, the tort is supposed to provide a remedy for persons whose feelings have been hurt by the malicious, intentional acts of others. That the tort sometimes goes by the name "outrage" serves to remind us that the conduct of the perpetrator—typically an overly zealous bill collector or a prankster with a perverse sense of humor—has to be truly outlandish. Sometimes the offensive behavior is much more *conduct* than *communication*. If you shoot my treasured family pet in my presence and in the presence of my young child, you will certainly have caused us both enormous emotional distress. Falsely telling someone that a loved one has died is also an example of this tort.

The *Falwell* case did not present the typical emotional distress set of facts, and indeed the plaintiff's attorneys added the claim almost as an afterthought. Yet it seemed a sensible legal strategy. In Virginia, and in many jurisdictions, the tort has four elements:

- The wrongdoer's conduct is intentional or reckless.
- The conduct is so "outrageous" as to offend generally accepted standards of decency.
- The conduct is in fact the cause of the plaintiff's emotional distress.
- The emotional distress thus caused is severe.

It is probably not surprising that Falwell's attorneys were able to persuade the jury that the four elements had been satisfied. In one deposition, Flynt candidly admitted that he had set out to "get" Falwell, to "assassinate" his reputation. Further, how many acts that could be attributed to a man would be more "outrageous," more beyond any reasonable standards of decency, than that he had sex with his mother in a stinking, fly-infested toilet? Would not seeing oneself, and one's mother, so depicted, cause severe emotional distress, even if we know "intellectually" that no one would actually believe that the outlandish allegation is true? As Chief Justice Rehnquist allowed in his opinion for a unanimous Supreme Court, the *Hustler* ad parody was obviously offensive to Falwell, "and doubtless gross and repugnant in the eyes of most others."

Nonetheless, the Court ruled against Falwell. "There is no doubt," Rehnquist allowed, that the *Hustler* ad parody was "at best a distant cousin" of the kinds of political cartoons and commentaries, caustic though they often have been, that have enriched civil discourse since the nation's birth. "Public discourse would probably suffer little or no harm" if it were possible to outlaw the *Hustler* ad without also abridging valuable political speech, but simply calling the ad "outrageous" does not help to create a workable standard.

The Court thus held that public figures and public officials may not recover damages for intentional infliction of emotional distress resulting from publications concerning them unless they are first able to demonstrate actual malice. In other words, if your libel suit fails, so too must your cause of action for emotional distress. The damages award was reversed.

May Libel Plaintiffs Ask Reporters about Their "State of Mind" When They Went to Press?

Certain catchphrases are born in Washington and are well known to political news junkies. From Justice Clarence Thomas's confirmation hearings came the reference to "high-tech lynching." The one-liner best remembered from the Iran-Contra hearings is probably the protestation of Oliver North's attorney that he was not just a "potted plant." Then there was Tennessee senator Howard Baker's famous recurring question from the Watergate hearings: "What did the President know, and when did he know it?"

Baker's question reminds us that an agent's state of mind is often more important than his or her actual conduct. The *Sullivan* actual-malice test is an example of just such an instance. That a media outlet published a false and defamatory remark does not alone make the publisher liable for damages; we need to know more. To paraphrase Baker, the actual-malice inquiry seeks to answer the question, "What did the reporters and editors know (regarding the truth or falsity of that which they were about to publish), and when did they know it?"

Libel plaintiff Anthony Herbert thought it only fair that he be able to ask reporters these questions directly as he was preparing his case against the producers of CBS's *60 Minutes* program. By a 6-3 vote, the Supreme Court agreed. A retired army officer, Herbert had served extended duty in Vietnam. He came to public attention when he accused superiors of covering up various wartime atrocities. *60 Minutes* did a piece about the accusations, suggesting that they were invented by Herbert as a way of rationalizing his having been disciplined by the army, including having been relieved of his command.

In pretrial discovery, *60 Minutes* producer Barry Lando refused to answer questions aimed at gauging his state of mind during the preparation of the story. How, for example, did he evaluate the credibility of his sources for the story when they gave

THINGS TO REMEMBER

Intentional Infliction of Emotional Distress

■ Sometimes called the tort of outrage, emotional distress suits are designed to protect plaintiffs from hurt feelings rather than damaged reputations.
■ If an emotional-distress suit is prompted by a publication about the plaintiff, he or she can prevail only by first proving actual malice.

Herbert v. Lando (1979) stands for the principle that libel plaintiffs do have the right to ask defendants what they were thinking when they published the statements at issue.

him conflicting accounts of events? Answers to inquiries such as this one would be crucial to Herbert's case in that he clearly would need to prove actual malice.

To agree with Lando's assertion that the First Amendment protects him from having to answer such questions, Justice White wrote for the Court majority, "would constitute a substantial interference with the ability of a defamation plaintiff to establish the ingredients of malice as required by *New York Times*." Plaintiffs must be able to delve "into the thoughts, opinions, and conclusions of the publisher."[39]

The defendants also argued that the inquiries being made of them would lay bare the substance and tone of internal communications among *60 Minutes* staffers, and that such conversations and exchanges of memoranda would necessarily become less candid in the long run. White was unimpressed with this argument, finding instead that the very structure of the actual-malice test would almost always foster, rather

---

39. *Herbert v. Lando*, 441 U.S. 153, 170 (1979).

than inhibit, media introspection. Under *New York Times Co. v. Sullivan*, only reck-lessly published errors are sources of potential liability; thus, given exposure to liabil-ity when there is knowing or reckless error, "there is even *more* reason to resort to prepublication precautions, such as a frank interchange of fact and opinion. Accord-ingly, we find it difficult to believe that error-avoiding procedures will be terminated or stifled simply because there is liability for culpable error and because the editorial process will itself be examined."

May the Press Print Things Learned in the Pretrial Discovery Process?

Pretrial discovery, including the compelled disclosure of documents and of de-posed testimony, can be a harrowing process. In 1984 the Supreme Court was asked whether a media outlet being sued for libel could use the information it was learning about the plaintiff through the discovery process in follow-up articles about the con-troversy that occasioned the lawsuit. Perhaps not surprisingly, the Court's answer was no. *Seattle Times Co. v. Rhinehart* resulted from a series of articles in the 1970s that focused critical attention on a local religious group called the Aquarian Foundation, of which Keith Rhinehart was spiritual leader.[40] As part of the pretrial discovery, the newspaper sought disclosure of the foundation's financial records, including the names and addresses of the group's donors. Rhinehart argued that such compelled disclosure would violate the donors' privacy and their First Amendment rights (of association and of religion) and that it might subject them to violent reprisals. In addition, Rhinehart sought a protective order prohibiting the newspaper from dis-seminating any information learned from the entire pretrial discovery process.

Writing for a unanimous Court, Justice Powell distinguished between the com-pelled disclosure of the information sought by the newspaper in its role as a libel defendant, and the newspaper's desire to share any such information with the public. "As in all civil litigation," he wrote, "petitioners gained the information they wish to disseminate only by virtue of the trial court's discovery processes. . . . A litigant has

---

THINGS TO REMEMBER	

Access to Reporters' Notes

- Proving actual malice requires plaintiffs to probe the minds of reporters and editors.
- Plaintiffs will therefore be permitted, in pretrial discovery, to examine and question defendants about their notes and their outtakes (footage they shot but chose not to air).

---

40. 467 U.S. 20 (1984).

THINGS TO REMEMBER

The Discovery Process

- The pretrial discovery process enables media libel defendants to learn many things about plaintiffs that they would not otherwise have a constitutional right to learn.
- Therefore, there is no First Amendment violation in enjoining the media from publishing information learned only through the discovery process.

no First Amendment right of access to information made available only for purposes of trying his suit." The Court held, however, that the newspaper could publish any information it obtained from sources apart from the discovery process.

What Is the Plaintiff's Burden of Proof in Combating a Defendant's Motion to Dismiss?

Journalists these days are about as unpopular with the masses as are public officials. Jury libel judgments in the millions are not the novelties that they used to be. As a result, the media are eager to resolve libel litigation at the pretrial stage to avoid actually going to trial. The Supreme Court provided much comfort to the press when it ruled in 1986 that libel plaintiffs who would in the normal course of events have to prove actual malice *with convincing clarity* at trial must meet that same burden of proof when arguing that they should have a right to go to trial—that is, when they are combating a defendant's motion for summary judgment.[41]

Columnist Jack Anderson, in a series of articles appearing in his *Investigator* magazine, described the director of Liberty Lobby (a "citizens' lobby") as "an American Hitler": a neo-Nazi, an anti-Semite, a racist, and a fascist. The director sued for libel, alleging that there were over two dozen factually inaccurate and defamatory statements in the articles. The defendant, Anderson, filed a motion for summary judgment, and the crucial issue posed by the case was whether the plaintiff, to defeat the defendant's motion, would have to persuade the judge of his ability to establish actual malice with convincing clarity to a jury's satisfaction or if he need only demonstrate actual malice by a preponderance of the evidence (i.e., that it was simply *more likely than not* that Anderson's magazine had published with actual malice). By a 6-3 vote, with Justice White writing for the majority, the Supreme Court decided that the higher burden of proof is the appropriate one, in that the judge's role at this stage of the litigation is to mirror a hypothetical jury's decision making.

Technically, the *Liberty Lobby* doctrine applies only to libel cases decided in federal

---

41. *Anderson v. Liberty Lobby, Inc.*, 477 U.S. 242 (1986).

THINGS TO REMEMBER

Motions to Dismiss a Libel Claim

- The same "convincing clarity" burden of proof that applies to actual-malice trials also dictates the level of proof that a libel plaintiff must demonstrate to defeat a defendant's motion to dismiss.
- This ruling is important from the media's perspective because it is very expensive to go to trial, even if one is destined to ultimately prevail.

courts. Still, the vast majority of the states embrace the doctrine as well. Only two states—Alaska[42] and Texas—have explicitly rejected the rule. The Texas Supreme Court, in 2000, reaffirmed its belief that summary judgment in libel cases brought against a media defendant is appropriate only where the defendant successfully refutes one of the elements of libel.[43]

May Libel Plaintiffs Shop Around for a Favorable Jurisdiction?

When Montgomery, Alabama, police commissioner L. B. Sullivan sued the *New York Times* for libel, he did so in Alabama, rather than in New York. It would be a very foolish plaintiff's attorney who advised him to do otherwise. A New York jury would have almost certainly refused to award damages to Mr. Sullivan.

Are the jurisdictions where a libel plaintiff may file suit limited to his and the defendant's states of residency? The Supreme Court, by a unanimous vote in 1984, gave plaintiffs many more choices. Indeed, they can bring suit anywhere that the libelous statements were circulated.

Kathy Keeton, a resident of New York State, wished to sue *Hustler* magazine, which was officially incorporated in Ohio and had its main offices in California. So naturally she brought suit in . . . New Hampshire. There was a method to the madness: New Hampshire was the only state whose statute of limitations—a full six years—had not run out. Further, although New Hampshire was by no means the state where the magazine had the most subscribers, between 10,000 and 15,000 copies of *Hustler* were regularly distributed there. The Supreme Court held that the district court had improperly dismissed the suit. "The tort of libel," Justice Rehnquist wrote, "is generally held to occur wherever the offending material is circulated. . . . The reputation of the libel victim may suffer harm even in a State in which he has hitherto been anonymous." Rehnquist made clear too that a libel plaintiff's right to "forum shop" is not limited to a search for states with the longest statutes of limitation. Keeton's decision

---

42. *Moffatt v. Brown*, 751 P.2d 939, 943 (Alaska 1988).
43. *Huckabee v. Time Warner Entertainment Co.*, 19 S.W.3d 413 (Tex. 2000).

to sue in New Hampshire "is no different from the litigation strategy of countless plaintiffs who seek a forum with favorable substantive or procedural rules or sympathetic local populations."[44]

May a Newspaper Be Forced to Publish a Reply Submitted by a *Potential* Libel Plaintiff?

Pat Tornillo was a candidate for the Florida House of Representatives. After the *Miami Herald* published two editorials opposing his candidacy, Tornillo invoked a Florida statute that provided that candidates who are "assailed regarding [their] personal character or official record by any newspaper" have a right "to demand that the newspaper print, free of cost to the candidate, any reply the candidate may make to the newspaper's charges." The newspaper refused Tornillo's request and sought a judicial determination of the statute's constitutionality.

Professor Jerome Barron of the George Washington University Law School, one of the nation's leading access theorists, argued in front of the Supreme Court that the spirit of the First Amendment is furthered rather than inhibited by such **right-of-reply statutes**. A unanimous Court, with Chief Justice Burger writing, rejected the argument. "The Florida statute," he wrote, "exacts a penalty on the basis of the content of a newspaper." Worse yet, publishers not willing to incur the costs of printing what they would prefer not to print "might well conclude that the safe course is to avoid controversy."[45]

It is important to keep separate in our minds the category of right-of-reply statutes invalidated here by the Court and another category of laws called **retraction statutes**. The latter kind of law does not *demand* that the media publish anything. Rather, it gives the press a measure of protection from a later libel suit if it *chooses* first to publish a retraction (i.e., its own admission that the defamatory statements it had disseminated were in error). A majority of the states have such laws on the books. Typically they limit the kinds of damages that libel plaintiffs may collect if the offending media

---

THINGS TO REMEMBER

Forum Shopping

- Libel plaintiffs may bring their suits in any state where the allegedly defamatory statements were generally circulated.
- Plaintiffs will often use this latitude to "forum shop," to choose a jurisdiction where the law, the judges, or the jury pools are especially likely to be sympathetic to their cases.

---

44. *Keeton v. Hustler Magazine, Inc.*, 465 U.S. 770, 777, 779 (1984).
45. *Miami Herald Publishing Co. v. Tornillo*, 418 U.S. 241, 256–257 (1974).

THINGS TO REMEMBER

Right-of-Reply Statutes

- The print media cannot be forced by statute to publish a reply from an aggrieved party:
  - Publishing such coerced replies costs valuable space and money.
  - To avoid such costs, editors might timidly avoid offending *anyone*.
- Right-of-reply statutes should not be confused with retraction statutes, which provide media with a form of relief in libel suits if they first publish a requested retraction.

---

outlet publishes a retraction. Some states even demand that potential libel plaintiffs first request a retraction before they may bring a full-blown libel suit. And in North Dakota, the law provides that as long as the original libel is corrected in a later issue or the requestor fails to demonstrate the falsity of the defamatory remark, the defendant will enjoy immunity from any damages (except special damages).

Wholly apart from its relationship to libel reform efforts, the *Tornillo* case is important because it emphasizes that our nation's regulatory philosophy varies tremendously depending on the specific communication medium involved. This particular case involved a newspaper, and the print media traditionally enjoy the largest measure of First Amendment freedom. Broadcast media enjoy far less freedom. Indeed, in a case decided by the Court several years earlier (but never once cited by Burger's *Tornillo* opinion, a fact that itself has certainly not escaped critical commentary), the Court had affirmed the constitutionality of federal legislation applying to broadcast media the same kind of right-of-reply rule at issue here. More is said about *Red Lion Broadcasting Co. v. FCC*[46] in chapter 12, which focuses on the electronic media.

Gertz v. Robert Welch, Inc.: The Supreme Court's Other Landmark Libel Decision

Lower court judges were beseeching the Supreme Court for a bit of clarity regarding when the actual-malice test applies. Why? Because in 1971, the Court produced anything *but* clarity when, in *Rosenbloom v. Metromedia, Inc.*, its members penned five separate opinions, not one of which commanded more than three votes.[47] Looking back at those opinions, Justice Powell wrote for the *Gertz* majority that they "not only reveal disagreement about the appropriate result in that case, they also reflect divergent traditions of thought about the general problem of reconciling the law of defa-

---

46. 395 U.S. 367 (1969).
47. 403 U.S. 29 (1971).

mation with the First Amendment."[48] The upshot was that Justice Brennan's plurality opinion in *Rosenbloom*, which rejected the rule from *New York Times Co. v. Sullivan* that the identity of the plaintiff would determine if actual malice need be proved in favor of letting the public interest in the subject matter of the alleged libel determine the required proof of fault, was treated by many lower courts as if it were majority doctrine. The confusion ended in 1974, when the Court reaffirmed the actual-malice rule originally articulated in *New York Times Co. v. Sullivan*.

Here, briefly, are the facts of the case. Chicago-based civil rights attorney Elmer Gertz was hired by the family of a young man who had been killed by the police. The officer at fault had already been convicted of second-degree murder; Gertz was to handle the family's civil litigation against him. Robert Welch's magazine, *American Opinion*, a publication of the John Birch Society, published an article alleging that testimony against the cop was perjured and that Gertz was part of a Communist conspiracy to discredit law enforcement officials. The article called Gertz a Leninist and "Communist fronter," and a former leader of the "Marxist League for Industrial Democracy."

When Gertz sued for defamation, he was awarded $50,000 in damages by the jury. But the trial judge threw out the award. By the time the case first reached the appellate level, the Supreme Court's *Rosenbloom* decision had been handed down. Thus, the appellate court also rejected the jury award, out of concern that the jury might not have understood that the constitutional privilege from *New York Times Co. v. Sullivan* should now apply to *any* article about a public issue.

In a 5–4 ruling, the *Gertz* Court held that the civil rights attorney was a private figure who should not have to prove actual malice. The Court thus reversed the lower court's directed verdict for the defendant. The Court opted for a new trial rather than simply reinstating the jury award because the jury apparently was instructed that it could find for a private plaintiff even in the absence of any level of fault on the part of the publisher. The Court soundly rejected this logic in *Gertz*. Let us look at the several principles that *Gertz v. Robert Welch, Inc.* added to the law of libel.

A Reaffirmation of the "Who Is the Plaintiff" Question

Earlier in this chapter it was suggested that much of the Supreme Court's libel doctrine can be organized around three questions: Who is the plaintiff? Who is the defendant? Does the alleged libel concern a matter of public interest? In *Rosenbloom*, the Court flirted with discarding the question of the plaintiff's identity, letting the subject matter of the defamatory remarks determine the appropriate level of fault instead. As Justice Brennan's plurality opinion in *Rosenbloom* put it, "If a matter is a subject of public or general interest, it cannot suddenly become less so merely because a private individual is involved."[49]

---

48. *Gertz v. Robert Welch, Inc.* 418 U.S. 323, 333 (1974).
49. *Rosenbloom v. Metromedia, Inc.*, 403 U.S. 29, 43 (1971) (Brennan, J., plurality).

The *Gertz* majority opinion rejects the *Rosenbloom* plurality position and emphasizes the continued wisdom of looking toward the identity of the plaintiff as the proper gauge of the level of fault required to recover for libel. Focusing on the kind of libel plaintiff, Justice Powell wrote, is the best means of establishing the proper balance "between the needs of the press and the individual's claim to compensation for wrongful injury."[50]

It is appropriate to focus on whether the plaintiff is a public or a private individual, Powell explained, for two reasons. First, public plaintiffs do not need to sue to be vindicated in that they can engage in "self-help" remedies instead. If they call a press conference to combat charges made against them, people will come. Powell's second reason for treating public plaintiffs differently is that they usually have *chosen* to be media personalities. People who seek public office, or fame, "run the risk of closer public scrutiny."

Two Kinds of Public Figures

In the *Butts* and *Walker* cases decided together in 1967, the Supreme Court extended the *Sullivan* actual-malice rule to public figures. The *Gertz* decision clarifies

I HAVEN'T CHOSEN MY CAUSE YET, BUT I INTEND TO USE IT TO FULFILL MY LIFELONG AMBITION OF BECOMING A LIMITED PURPOSE PUBLIC FIGURE

and extends those holdings by pointing out that there are actually two kinds of public figures. "For the most part those who attain this status," Justice Powell wrote, "have assumed roles of especial prominence in the affairs of society." These people are household names, the truly famous. Criticize them, and they will have to prove actual malice to recover damages from you, regardless of the specific subject matter of the defamatory remarks. Since *Gertz*, these plaintiffs are often referred to as "general" or "all-purpose" public figures to distinguish them from the second category.

The second group, "limited" or "limited-purpose" public figures, might not be truly famous, but they have "thrust themselves to the forefront of particular public controversies in order to influence the resolution of the issues involved," thus inviting both "attention" and "comment."

---

50. *Gertz*, 418 U.S. at 343.

When these personalities become libel plaintiffs, the First Amendment demands that they prove actual malice only if the defamatory remarks concern the specific political issue in which they have become involved. An automobile company middle manager who gives speeches around the country on driving safety will have to prove actual malice if you accuse her of having a string of traffic violations on her record, but not if you point out she has had an abortion. The reverse would be true of a pro-life activist. Accuse her of having had an abortion and the actual malice rule will be triggered, but allegations about driving while intoxicated will be considered a more private libel.

The States Retain (Almost) Complete Control over the Fault Element in Private Libel Suits

Public officials always have to prove actual malice when they sue for libel, as do general public figures. Limited public figures will at least sometimes have to prove actual malice. What, though, does the First Amendment say about the degree of fault that a truly private plaintiff—or a limited public figure who is maligned in an area of life wholly unrelated to his or her political activism—must prove? Very little, Justice Powell told us. Consider Powell's assessment of the truly private libel plaintiff's plight: "He has not accepted public office or assumed an influential role in ordering society. . . . He has relinquished no part of his interest in the protection of his own good name, and consequently he has a more compelling call on the courts for redress of injury inflicted by defamatory falsehood." The Court majority therefore interpreted the First Amendment to give the individual states enormous latitude should they wish to tip the scales in favor of private parties' reputational interests. As long as states do not permit recovery under a strict liability standard (one requiring no finding of fault at all), they will be on sound constitutional footing. The majority of states require that private plaintiffs prove that defamatory remarks were made with negligence. About a dozen states demand a somewhat higher demonstration of fault, which they call "gross negligence." In some jurisdictions—New York among them[51]—which of these two standards applies to private plaintiffs is a function of whether the article triggering the libel suit is deemed to be on a matter of public or private interest. A small handful of states demand that all libel plaintiffs, public or private, prove actual malice.

If You Want Punitive or Presumed Damages, You Must Prove Actual Malice

"The common law of defamation," Justice Powell's majority opinion reminds us,

is an oddity of tort law, for it allows recovery of purportedly compensatory damages without evidence of actual loss. Under the traditional rules pertaining to actions for

---

51. *Huggins v. Moore*, 726 N.E.2d 456 (N.Y. 1999).

libel, the existence of injury is presumed from the fact of publication. Juries may award substantial sums as compensation for supposed damage to reputation without any proof that such harm actually occurred.[52]

The awarding of presumed and punitive damages must be kept in check, Powell argued, because it can inhibit the vigorous exercise of First Amendment freedoms, and because it invites juries to punish those who hold unpopular political opinions. The *Gertz* majority opinion will thus limit the damages available to libel plaintiffs who do not prove actual malice to an award designed to compensate for "actual injury." Powell did not try to provide a single definition for actual injury, but he made clear that it is not limited to "out-of-pocket loss" (the kinds of damages described in chapter 3 as "special damages"). States may feel free to include within actual injury such harms as "impairment of reputation and standing in the community, personal humiliation, and mental anguish and suffering"; moreover, there "need be no evidence which assigns an actual dollar value to the injury."

The "if you want punitive or presumed damages, you must prove actual malice" rule articulated in *Gertz* was limited in a later decision to those situations in which the allegedly libelous remark is on a matter of public interest. (Again the two-by-two-by-two matrix is in play.) The case, *Dun & Bradstreet, Inc. v. Greenmoss Builders*,[53] involved an erroneous report to the effect that a local business was in bankruptcy, which appeared in a financial newsletter with limited circulation. Although the Court voted 5-4 and failed to produce a majority opinion, five of the justices determined that the false report concerned a matter of private rather than public interest and distinguished the *Gertz* rule concerning punitive or presumed damages. The original judgment from the trial court, consisting of $50,000 in compensatory damages and $300,000 in punitive damages (the latter amount may have stemmed from the jury's shock at Dun & Bradstreet's having depended on the unchecked and unedited report from a seventeen-year-old high school student it had hired as a "stringer"), would be permitted to stand. Interestingly, the Vermont Supreme Court had also distinguished the *Gertz* rule and had itself reinstated the original damages award, but it did so on the grounds that *Gertz*'s rule about punitive damages should apply only to media defendants, whereas this particular financial newsletter's circulation was too small to qualify as a mass medium. The Supreme Court's finding that the state supreme court was right but for the wrong reasons is largely a result of a lack of precision in the *Gertz* decision itself. At several places in the 1974 decision, reference is made to "publishing" and "broadcasting" of defamations, but the Court majority never indicated clearly whether it intended the decision to be restricted to suits involving media defendants. One thing is clear, though: the *Gertz* majority nowhere indicated that its decision should be limited to defamatory statements concerning matters of public

52. *Gertz*, 418 U.S. at 349.
53. 472 U.S. 749 (1985).

THINGS TO REMEMBER

Gertz v. Robert Welch, Inc. (1974)

- *Gertz v. Welch* reinforces the importance of the plaintiff's identity (public figure or public official, or private citizen) as the main determinant of whether actual malice must be proved.
- The case gives two public policy reasons for treating public plaintiffs differently:
  - They generally chose the limelight.
  - They often have access to the media to refute any damaging remarks.
- The case establishes that there are two kinds of public figures:
  - All-purpose or general public figures, who always must prove actual malice
  - Limited public figures, who must prove actual malice only if the libelous remarks concerned the controversy they sought out
- The case emphasizes that with respect to private plaintiffs, individual states are free to determine what level of fault such plaintiffs must show (mere negligence, actual malice, or something in between).
- It says that all plaintiffs must prove harm to win damages (diluting the libel per se category from common law).
- It holds that plaintiffs who wish to receive punitive damages must prove actual malice (in a later case, the Court limited this rule to situations involving libel on a matter of public interest).

interest. To the extent that the *Dun & Bradstreet* plurality opinion suggests otherwise, it is revisionist history, and the opinion has been soundly criticized on that account.

All Libel Plaintiffs Must Prove Harm to Receive Damages (the End of Libel Per Se?)

In the chapter 3 review of the elements of the common law of libel, the distinction between libel *per se* (utterances that are obviously defamatory) and libel *per quod* (statements whose defamatory nature is not apparent unless the audience has additional facts at its disposal) was introduced. Traditionally, in libel per se situations the plaintiff did not need to prove damages; it was assumed that a person falsely accused of being a criminal or an incompetent had been damaged.

Certainly the *Gertz* majority opinion does express concern that the ready availability of presumed damages (the kind of award that most logically fits libel per se situations) gives juries too much freedom to stifle debate on important issues of the day. The Supreme Court fashioned a two-part remedy. First it established the rule, from which it retreated a bit in the later *Dun & Bradstreet* decision, requiring plaintiffs seeking presumed damages to prove actual malice. Second, it required plaintiffs who were not otherwise required to prove actual malice to show some kind of actual harm. Only the second rule is relevant to the libel per se category, and it surely represents a partial repudiation of the category. Under the first rule, however, presumed damages are still permitted, and proving actual malice is really quite irrelevant to whether or not the plaintiff has been harmed. Thus the majority opinion does not sound the death knell for the distinction between libel per se and libel per quod.

A fascinating feature of *Gertz*, however, is that Justice White's dissenting opinion makes clear that he assumed the Court *had* in fact gotten rid of presumed damages and thus the whole category of libel per se. "The impact of today's decision on the traditional law of libel is immediately obvious and indisputable," he wrote. "No longer will the plaintiff be able to rest his case with proof of a libel defamatory on its face or proof of a slander historically actionable per se." For whatever combination of reasons, Justice White's interpretation of what the *Gertz* majority had done has been accepted by many courts and commentators. Section 569 of the *Restatement of Torts*, for example, assumes that *Gertz v. Robert Welch, Inc.* discredited traditional notions of libel per se.

A Final Word on Avoiding Libel Suits

An individual sees a description of herself in the media that she finds false and defamatory. She steams about it for a time and then retains an attorney and files suit against the offending publisher. That may be the way we presume libel suits happen, but it omits a crucial step. A large majority of potential libel plaintiffs pay a visit to the media outlet that defamed them before they even seek out legal advice. How the editors there treat the aggrieved individual often determines whether a libel suit ever gets filed.[54] At least three characteristics of the mass media tend to result in the potential plaintiff's being so dissatisfied with the encounter that the person becomes a real-life plaintiff:[55]

- *Future Orientation.* News organizations tend to be focused on what is going into the paper tomorrow, and do not always have mechanisms in place to deal with controversies from previous editions. Individuals who complain about yesterday's news (rather than offering a tip about what might be tomorrow's news) thus tend to be shunted from department to department and put on hold indefinitely.
- *Nay-Saying Habit.* Editors become very accustomed to saying no, especially to turning down reader-generated story ideas that more often than not amount to "vanity press" about family members. They develop a siege mentality and then apply it inappropriately to very legitimate requests for retractions or some other kind of vindication from persons who have been harmed by the media's errors.

---

54. Randall Bezanson, Gilbert Cranberg, and John Soloski, *Libel Law and the Press: Myth and Reality* (New York: Free Press, 1987); Edward A. Adams, "Does Alternative Dispute Resolution Work with Libel Suits? Iowa Program Hopes to Find Out," *National Law Journal*, March 21, 1988, 4.

55. Gilbert Cranberg, "The Libel Alternative," *Columbia Journalism Review*, January 1986.

- *Reluctance to Admit Mistakes.* Because journalists' work is by its very nature open to public scrutiny, reporters and editors can be especially defensive about their errors. This defensiveness, applied to an aggrieved individual seeking redress, often results in escalation, a shouting match likely to drive the complainant to an attorney's office.

Professor Gilbert Cranberg suggests that media outlets will increase the chances of persuading unhappy parties not to sue by adopting the following policies:

- Sensitize writers to the power they wield over people's lives.
- Emphasize the importance of handling complaints in a humane manner.
- Consider the use of an ombudsman to serve as an independent readers' advocate.
- Fire anyone who tries to hide a serious complaint.

Of course, the single best way to avoid libel suits is to breathe life into what has become cliché, the journalistic credo admonishing reporters and editors to "get it right." Still, factual error is unavoidable, and the most highly reputable newspapers usually have more than a few errors in every single issue. That libel juries nowadays so frequently emerge from their deliberations with a decision awarding huge amounts of damages to plaintiffs means that professional communicators should know more than a bit about the law of defamation.

Chapter Summary

The landmark 1964 libel case, *New York Times Co. v. Sullivan*, establishes that public officials who sue for libel because of criticisms relevant to their official conduct must prove actual malice—that is, that the defendant either knew the accusations were false or at least published with "reckless disregard of truth or falsity"—with "convincing clarity." The Supreme Court emphasized that making it too easy for governmental officials to recover damages for libel is too hauntingly reminiscent of criminal prosecutions for sedition. Journalists must be given enough "breathing room" to make honest errors, the Court said, or they will experience the "chilling effect" of self-censorship.

Later cases have fine-tuned and extended the actual-malice rule in many ways. "Public officials" include those who have policymaking authority and whose positions invite public scrutiny. Criticisms of "official conduct" include any accusations of criminal wrongdoing, as well as attributions of certain kinds of personal characteristics that have clear implications for public life. Not only public officials but also "public figures" must prove actual malice. So too must anybody who wants punitive damages (if the alleged libel touches on a matter of public importance).

Even private plaintiffs, if suing the media over a matter of public importance, must prove falsity as an element of their cases. Independent appellate review is required on the question of actual malice. Statements of pure opinions, ones that do not carry explicit or implicit factual allegations, cannot be the impetus for a libel suit.

Plaintiffs who must prove actual malice may have access to reporters' notes and outtakes as part of the pretrial discovery process.

"Convincing clarity" is the burden of proof on plaintiffs seeking to defeat a motion to dismiss.

Libel plaintiffs may bring suit in any state where the allegedly libelous remarks were in general circulation.

All libel plaintiffs must prove some degree of harm to win damages. Individual states are given a great degree of leeway to determine what level of proof of fault is required of private plaintiffs.

Chapter 5

INVASIONS OF PRIVACY

P*rivacy* has so many meanings in the law that we have to begin this chapter with an unavoidably lengthy description of the meanings that are beyond the scope of this book. We often use the word *privacy* to talk about the delicate relationship between individual autonomy and the need for governmental regulation. Such matters are the province of the constitutional law of privacy. Perhaps because the word *privacy* does not appear anywhere in the U.S. Constitution, the evolution of the Supreme Court's privacy doctrine is long and complicated, one of the most intriguing tales in the modern history of constitutional law. First recognized explicitly in 1965,[1] the constitutional right to privacy has been seen as one of many liberties protected by the Fourteenth Amendment—which tells government it may not take away our "life, liberty or property without due process of law"—ever since the landmark abortion ruling, *Roe v. Wade.*[2] Motorcyclists who want to ride without a helmet,[3] terminally ill patients who wish to "die with dignity,"[4] and even in one case a teacher claiming a right to have a sexual relationship with a former student[5] have all based their arguments on the constitutional right to privacy.

The Fourth Amendment's protection against unreasonable searches and seizures is often invoked as a backdrop to legal discussions about privacy. Anyone who watches cop shows on TV knows that criminal trials are often preceded by exclusionary hearings, where it is argued that certain evidence should never be seen by the jury, because the manner in which the police obtained it violated the defendant's Fourth Amendment privacy rights. Of course, one does not have to be a criminal to have Fourth Amendment privacy claims. This constitutional provision was at the heart of the de-

---

1. *Griswold v. Connecticut*, 381 U.S. 479 (1965).
2. 410 U.S. 113, 153 (1973).
3. *Easyriders Freedom F.I.G.H.T. v. Hannigan*, 92 F.3d 1486 (9th Cir. 1996).
4. *Vacco v. Quill*, 521 U.S. 793 (1997).
5. *Flaskamp v. Dearborn Public Schools*, 385 F.3d 935 (6th Cir. 2004).

bate surrounding the Justice Department's warrantless telephone monitoring in the wake of the 9/11 attacks.[6]

Beyond the Constitution itself, but still part of the delicate relationship between individual and state, sometimes the government passes laws that are designed to protect personal information about individuals. For example, the federal Fair Credit Reporting Act gives us the right to review our credit histories and to require that the credit rating bureaus include our side of the story concerning any items we contest. The Stored Communications Act may have been violated by phone companies that, as was revealed in 2006, apparently provided the National Security Agency with millions of records of subscribers' phone calls—not what we said on the phone, but whom we called.[7]

Another federal statute, the Family Educational Rights and Privacy Act, was the focus of a 2002 Supreme Court decision addressing the practice of having students exchange test papers after their completion and use the teacher's feedback to grade each other's papers. Did such a practice violate the act, which forbids schools to release students' educational records without parental consent? The Court ruled that the act was not designed to cover such practices as "peer grading," which teachers might deem an important part of the educational process.[8]

In the field of communication law, privacy refers to issues quite different from the kinds of controversies so far presented. Instead of concerning ourselves with ways in which government might infringe on our personal autonomy, students of the law of privacy in communication focus on the relationship between the media and the people from whom they seek information and about whom they write. We now begin our more formal exploration of this body of law with a discussion of two seminal publications, seventy years apart.

THINGS TO REMEMBER

Privacy Beyond Communication Law

As it is usually conceived, the scope of privacy affecting communication law does not focus on

- Fourth Amendment "search and seizure" cases;
- privacy as a fundamental liberty protected by the Fourteenth Amendment; or
- specific statutes governing control of personal information.

---

6. Bill Nichols and John Diamond, "Controversy Shadows Hayden Confirmation: Phone-Records Revelation Looms Over Hearings," *USA Today*, May 12, 2006, 10A.

7. "Lawyers Debate the Legality of Domestic Spying," *Morning Edition*, National Public Radio, May 18, 2006.

8. *Owasso Independent School District v. Falvo*, 534 U.S. 426 (2002).

A Tale of Two Law Review Articles

There is a great degree of concern in this country about the use of technology—surveillance cameras, software that can monitor the strokes we make on a computer keyboard, sophisticated databases that create elaborate profiles of our purchasing habits, and so on—to invade our privacy. Such concerns are not new, of course. Indeed, it is not much of an exaggeration to say that when two prominent lawyers wrote about their similar concerns over a hundred years ago,[9] they laid the foundation for modern U.S. privacy law. Compared with the centuries-old body of libel law, then, privacy is a relative newcomer to the American legal scene, even if it does predate the microchip. Boston attorneys Samuel Warren and Louis Brandeis—the latter of whom would later achieve lasting fame as a U.S. Supreme Court justice—expressed their concern that such "recent inventions" as *instantaneous photographs* . . . have invaded the sacred precincts of private and domestic life." The italicized phrase does not refer to digital cameras or Polaroids but to photographic technology having advanced to the point where subjects did not have to remain motionless for twenty minutes to have their images captured on film. At the time, this advance seemed a huge encroachment on personal privacy. In the early days of photography, subjects may have always appeared stiff and ghostlike, but at least the potential for being photographed in a "candid" moment had not yet arrived.

Warren and Brandeis recognized that technological advances were not the only cause of privacy invasion. Indeed, citizens' privacy was most threatened by the combination of the "prurient taste" of the masses and the willingness on the part of the working press to satisfy that taste by filling "column after column . . . with idle gossip," by "overstepping in every direction the obvious bounds of propriety and of decency." (Contemporary social critics say much the same thing about cable networks' filling their twenty-four-hour "news hole" with salacious details of one after another homicide.) To combat these journalistic excesses, Warren and Brandeis concluded, nothing less than the creation of a new legal cause of action aimed at protecting the right to privacy, the "right to be let alone," would do.

Whereas Warren and Brandeis's essay was *pre*scriptive, telling readers what the law *should* do, a second law review article written seventy years later served as a *de*scriptive model of how the American law of privacy had developed in the first half of the twentieth century. William Prosser, then the dean of the University of California, Berkeley's law school, reviewed thousands of court cases and concluded that privacy law had really become four separate torts.[10] **Appropriation** occurs when our name or "likeness" (i.e., face, voice, or anything so closely associated with us so as to transmit

9. Samuel Warren and Louis Brandeis, "The Right to Privacy," 4 *Harvard Law Review* 193 (1890).

10. William Prosser, "Privacy," 48 *California Law Review* 383 (1960).

our identity) is used without permission for commercial purposes. The aggrieved party's interest in such conflicts seems to be more a proprietary one—"How dare you make money by exploiting me?"—rather than the more psychological harm to one's feelings that we normally associate with privacy invasions. As such, this category of cases really is more closely aligned to the issue of copyright (the subject of chapter 6) than to any intuitive notion of privacy. **Intrusion** refers to an invasion of one's personal space. The use of telephoto lenses or hidden microphones, or the incessant shadowing and stalking of a subject, might be deemed actionable intrusions. Such excesses, whether committed by media employees or others, would seem to have much in common with ordinary trespass. **False-light** invasions of privacy, as we see later, closely resemble libel actions, with the key distinction being that the statements made about the unwilling subject need not be technically defamatory. The final tort is the one that Warren and Brandeis themselves seem to have had in mind. It has come to be called the "public disclosure of true but embarrassing facts," or more succinctly, **public disclosure**. This category expresses the proposition that there are some kinds of highly personal but true information that no one has a right to publicize about us.

A caveat is in order before we examine these four torts in more depth. We must remember that privacy law varies tremendously from state to state. Only about half the states recognize all four torts identified by Prosser in 1960. Which states recognize which torts is not a static set of facts; state supreme courts continue to decide either to embrace or to reject one or more of the Prosserian torts. For example, Colorado explicitly rejected the false-light tort in a 2002 decision.[11] In short, if you have a very specific question about the privacy implications of a story you are preparing, you will need to know which of the torts is recognized in your own jurisdiction.

Appropriation

Appropriation, sometimes called *misappropriation*, consists of the unauthorized use of a person's name or "likeness"—voice, picture, and the like—for commercial purposes. This tort was the first of the four to develop in U.S. law following the publication of the famous Warren and Brandeis law review article. The first state to officially recognize the tort was New York, which did so by statute in 1903 in response to a ruling from that state's highest court the year before permitting the unauthorized use of a child's photo to advertise a milling company's flour.[12] The first state court to recognize a common-law right (i.e., prior to passage of any explicit statutes) to sue for misappropriation was Georgia.[13] By 1939, so many states had embraced a right of

---

11. *Denver Publishing Co. v. Bueno*, 54 P.3d 893 (Colo. 2002).
12. *Roberson v. Rochester Folding Box Co.*, 64 N.E. 442 (N.Y. 1902).
13. *Pavesich v. New England Life Insurance Co.*, 50 S.E. 68 (Ga. 1905).

THINGS TO REMEMBER

The Development of Privacy Law in the United States

- Compared with libel, the law of privacy is a newcomer to American law.
- It can be traced back to the 1890 publication of a *Harvard Law Review* article by Samuel Warren and Louis Brandeis.
- Most states now recognize at least one of the four distinct privacy actions identified by William Prosser in 1960:
  - Appropriation of one's name or likeness for commercial gain
  - Intrusion into another person's personal space
  - False-light invasions (similar to libel)
  - Public disclosure of true but embarrassing facts
- All four of these actions are part of the tort law of privacy, which should not be confused with the constitutional right to privacy.
- Apart from the Prosser torts, specific laws and regulations are often created that are designed to further our privacy rights.

privacy against unauthorized appropriations that the tort was included in the American Law Institute's treatise called the *Restatement of Torts*.[14]

Two Actions or One?

Appropriation is actually a hybrid tort. There are two different kinds of grievances involved. The first is the feeling of shame, humiliation, or even damaged reputation associated with having our name or photo disseminated widely in ways over which we have no control. The harm is likely most severe when our name is associated with a cause or a product with which we wholly disapprove, as in a strict vegetarian seeming to endorse a fast-food hamburger chain. The second is simply lost income. If you steal my name or photo to sell your product, you will have enriched yourself unfairly at my expense. If anyone deserves to make money off my name, it is me. Sometimes this claim is referred to separately in the law as the **right to publicity**, and it applies primarily to celebrities. At least thirty-five states have explicitly embraced the right to publicity.[15]

In some situations, plaintiffs are able to argue plausibly both that the commercial value of their name has been stolen and that the nature of the theft is one that personally embarrasses them. This was comedian Johnny Carson's dual claim when he sued the manufacturer of a line of portable toilets called—you probably guessed

---

14. Irwin R. Kramer, "The Birth of Privacy Law: A Century since Warren and Brandeis," 39 *Catholic University Law Review* 703, 718 (1990).

15. Edwin McPherson, "Gonna Wash That Right of Publicity Right Out of My Hair," 4 *John Marshall Review of Intellectual Property Law* 349, 351 n.22 (2005).

The Sixth Circuit Court of Appeals ruled in favor of comedian Johnny Carson in his misappropriation claim against a portable toilet manufacturer, in part because Carson demonstrated his awareness of the commercial value of his name, as evidenced by, among other products cited by the court, the Johnny Carson line of apparel.

it—"Here's Johnny!"[16] The defendant-entrepreneur in this case continued the wordplay by labeling his product "the world's foremost commodian." Carson was not amused, arguing that it went beyond embarrassing to "odious" to be associated with such a product. Although the court determined that the applicable right to privacy did not protect celebrities' hurt feelings in such commercial situations, it ruled for Carson on the more tangible publicity claim. Carson had shown over the years his awareness that he could profit from the commercial exploitation of his own celebrity status, such as through his marketing of a sportswear line bearing his name.

What Is a Likeness?

In a sense, the *Carson* case staked out new ground, in that the product did not usurp the comedian's name, but rather a phrase that had come to be closely associated with that name (and with Ed McMahon's slow, rising-pitched delivery). Indeed, the appellate majority emphasized, there would have been no violation of Carson's right of publicity had the defendant called his product the "John William Carson Portable Toilet," which would have been a more literal taking of Carson's name but would not have amounted to a taking of his identity as a celebrity.

Anything likely to make readers conjure up in their minds a particular individual can constitute that person's "name or likeness" for the purpose of misappropriation actions. Conversely, not every use of a celebrity's name will be associated closely enough with the marketability of the person's identity to be the focus of an appropriation lawsuit. For example, there was a somewhat famous "T. J. Hooker" long before the TV series of that name ever showed up on the air. An artist well known for his carvings of ducks and other fowl, Hooker sued the producers of the TV series. The court rejected his claim, however, finding that the television producers surely had not

16. *Carson v. Here's Johnny Portable Toilets, Inc.*, 698 F.2d 831 (6th Cir. 1983).

chosen the name for their series "in order to avail themselves of his reputation as an extraordinary woodcarver."[17]

What else may be treated as a "likeness"? Certainly an identifiable photo of an individual can be a likeness, as we saw in the early New York case against the flour milling company. A sketch or drawing can also be actionable, as the publishers of *Playgirl* magazine discovered when their February 1978 issue included a drawing of a nude black male seated in the corner of a boxing ring.[18] "Even a cursory inspection of the picture," a federal district court in New York concluded, "strongly suggests that the facial characteristics of the black male portrayed are those of Muhammad Ali. The cheekbones, broad nose and wide-set brown eyes, together with the distinctive smile and close-cropped black hair are recognizable as the features of the plaintiff, one of the most widely known athletes of our time." The court also took note of the ad's use of the phrase "The Greatest," long associated with Ali.

Both the striking physical resemblance to Muhammad Ali and the use of the phrase "The Greatest" in the copy were enough to persuade a federal court that this was a misappropriation of the boxer's image.

Even a fictional character can constitute a likeness. Groucho Marx's estate, for example, sued the producers of the Broadway musical *A Day in Hollywood, A Night in the Ukraine*, the second act of which playfully inserted the Marx Brothers characters into a Chekhovian plot. The defendants eventually prevailed on the grounds that the right of publicity could not, in the state of California, be passed on to Marx's heirs. More important for our purposes is the fact that the federal district court made clear that the right of publicity is broad enough to protect the fictional characters audiences worldwide know as "the Marx Brothers," characters which "hav[e] no relation to [the] real personalities" of Julius (Groucho), Leo (Chico), or Adolf (Harpo) Marx.[19]

An infringement can be found even when the actors are less than human. Samsung Corporation created a series of humorous TV ads that pictured the company's 1980s

---

17. *Hooker v. Columbia Pictures*, 551 F. Supp. 1060, 1062 (N.D. Ill. 1982).

18. *Ali v. Playgirl*, 447 F. Supp. 723 (S.D.N.Y. 1978).

19. *Groucho Marx Productions v. Day and Night Co.*, 523 F. Supp. 485 (S.D.N.Y. 1981), *overturned on other grounds*, 689 F.2d 317 (2d Cir. 1982); see also *Chaplin v. Amador*, 93 Cal. App. 358, 360 (1928).

A federal district court held that the right of publicity can cover even fictional "likenesses" such as the Marx Brothers, used without authorization in this Broadway show. Although the decision was overturned on other grounds, this finding remains intact.

models of audio and video products in whimsical futuristic scenes, as if to suggest that such equipment would still be working many years hence. One ad featured a robot wearing a wig, gown, and jewelry reminiscent of Vanna White, posed next to a game board like that featured in *Wheel of Fortune*. The caption read, "Longest-running game show. 2012 A.D." White sued. The federal appellate court recognized that this case could not be handled as a "name or likeness" dispute. A "likeness" must truly resemble the original, and no sane viewer would think that the robot in the ad really *was* Vanna White. Accordingly, the court expanded the right of publicity (in California, at least) to cover celebrities' "identities."[20] The 2-1 decision—Judge Alex Kozinski wrote a stinging dissent—has been greatly criticized as overly broad, giving Hollywood celebrities virtual veto power over any satiric representations of them in commercial messages.[21]

In another case, actors George Wendt and John Ratzenberger—best known for their long-running portrayals of Norm and Cliff, respectively—sued the creators of the *Cheers*-like bars one used to see at airports, which boasted three-dimensional animatronic figures (called "Bob" and "Hank") designed to look very much like Norm and Cliff. Interestingly, the actors could not prevail on this ground alone, because one of the defendant companies owned the copyright to *Cheers* and to all the fictional personages who patronized it. The plaintiffs did prevail, however, over defendants' motion for summary judgment. "While it is true that [Wendt's and Ratzenberger's] fame arose in large part through their participation in *Cheers*," the court reasoned, "an actor or actress does not lose the right to control the commercial exploitation of his or her likeness by portraying a fictional character."[22]

20. *White v. Samsung Electronics America, Inc.*, 971 F.2d 1395 (9th Cir. 1992), *reh'g denied*, 989 F.2d 1512 (1993).

21. See, e.g., Patricia B. Frank, "*White v. Samsung Electronics America, Inc.*: The Right of Publicity Spins Its Wheels," 55 *Ohio State Law Journal* 1115 (1994).

22. *Wendt v. Host International, Inc.*, 125 F.3d 806 (9th Cir. 1997), *reh'g denied*, 197 F.3d 1284 (9th Cir. 1999).

The Ninth Circuit Court of Appeals ruled that this Samsung ad was an actionable misappropriation of Vanna White's likeness.

Look-Alikes and Sound-Alikes

The law of privacy has developed to cover situations in which defendants have not misappropriated an *actual* image of a celebrity, but rather have done their best to create an *ersatz* image of that celebrity, often using the services of persons who make their living as celebrity imposters. We usually refer to these as the "look-alike" and "sound-alike" cases. In one such case, Jackie Onassis won a judgment against Christian Dior for employing the services of Jackie O. look-alike Barbara Reynolds in a slick magazine ad campaign appearing in publications such as *Esquire, Harper's Bazaar,* the *New Yorker,* and the *New York Times Magazine.* The New York statute governing the case addressed only situations in which a plaintiff's "name, portrait or picture" is used without consent for a commercial purpose. The court, however, in ruling for Onassis, concluded that the use of look-alikes could not be permitted as a means of skirting the intent of the law, asserting that "the commercial hitchhiker seeking to travel on the fame of another will have to learn to pay the fare."[23]

Film director Woody Allen was a plaintiff in a similar case, which was prompted

---

23. *Onassis v. Christian Dior-New York, Inc.*, 472 N.Y.S.2d 254, 261 (N.Y. Sup. Ct. 1984).

The portion of a head behind Gene Shalit (the fellow in the center with the pronounced mustache) is not Jackie Onassis but impersonator Barbara Reynolds. So striking is the resemblance that readers would incorrectly assume Ms. Onassis had participated in the ad campaign.

by print ads for National Video that used celebrity look-alike Phil Boroff.[24] That readers would think of Allen was ensured not only by Boroff's physical resemblance to Allen but also by the *Annie Hall* and *Bananas* videotapes shown on the store counter. Judge Constance Baker Motley allowed that celebrity look-alikes such as Boroff enjoy their own rights to publicity, a right to sell *their* likeness to anyone perceiving a commercial value in it. Thus Judge Motley had to address "the almost metaphysical question of when one person's face, presented in a certain context, becomes, as a matter of law, the face of another." She granted summary judgment to Allen, but on the grounds that the advertisement was a violation of the federal Lanham Act prohibiting unfair business practices such as the untruthful suggestion that a product has received a particular endorsement. Resolving the dispute in this manner freed Motley from having to rule definitively on Allen's publicity claim. The judge did give some indication, however, that the situation here might be distinguishable from the Barbara Reynolds photograph in the Onassis case. In that earlier case, Motley concluded, readers were led to no other possible conclusion than that Onassis herself had chosen to appear in the ad campaign. Boroff's depiction of Allen, on the other hand, might be seen as merely *evocative* of the latter's persona or image, since the two men did not look identical. Another Phil Boroff photo used in an ad for the Men's World clothing stores, this time with Boroff holding a clarinet—further evocative of Woody Allen for readers who know that the actor/director frequently plays the instrument in a New York tavern—led to further litigation a few years later. Again, the court ruled for Allen, on Lanham Act grounds, having been unimpressed with the fact that the ad included a "small lightface type" disclaimer to the effect that the person depicted was a celebrity look-alike.[25]

Celebrities have also brought suit complaining about advertisements that mimic their distinctive speaking or singing voices. Early cases involving celebrities such as actor Bert Lahr, singer Nancy Sinatra, and the 1960s rock group The Fifth Dimension were unsuccessful.[26] In each of these cases, the courts ruled that the plaintiffs had no cause of action, that the right of appropriation (in the relevant jurisdictions) was not designed or intended to cover such sound-alike situations. The legal climate seems to be changing, however, largely as a result of Bette Midler's suit against Ford Motor Company and its advertising agency for hiring one of her former backup singers to imitate the "Divine Miss M's" rendition of the old Beach Boys tune "Do You Want To Dance?" in a Mercury Sable commercial.[27] The appellate panel ruling in favor of Midler distinguished the facts before it from those in the earlier Nancy Sinatra case by emphasizing that Sinatra's claim was much more closely tied to her association in

---

24. *Allen v. National Video, Inc.*, 610 F. Supp. 612 (S.D.N.Y. 1985).

25. *Allen v. Men's World Outlet*, 679 F. Supp. 360 (S.D.N.Y. 1988).

26. *Sinatra v. Goodyear Tire and Rubber Company*, 435 F.2d 711 (9th Cir. 1970), *cert. denied*, 402 U.S. 906 (1971); *Davis v. TWA*, 297 F. Supp. 1145 (C.D. Cal. 1969); *Lahr v. Adell Chemical Company*, 195 F. Supp. 702 (D. Mass. 1961), *aff'd*, 300 F.2d 256 (1st Cir. 1962).

27. *Midler v. Ford Motor Co.*, 849 F.2d 460 (9th Cir. 1988).

Even though the fellow depicted here was not deemed a dead ringer for Woody Allen, there were enough cues in the ad to suggest falsely that the famous movie director had endorsed the National Video chain.

the public mind with a particular song to which she did not own the rights ("These Boots Were Made for Walking"), whereas Midler claimed that her distinctive singing voice had been misappropriated. The *Midler* court saw its ruling as a relatively narrow one, having demanded that the plaintiff establish both that the imitation was deliberate and that the plaintiff's vocal style was distinctive and well known.

Some Folks Who Can't Sue: The "Political Figures" Exception

The movie *Contact*, the faith-versus-science parable in which Jodie Foster spends her professional life listening for extraterrestrials and then goes traipsing off to meet them, boasts guest appearances, "as themselves," by several CNN journalists and President Clinton. While the CNN reporters contracted to appear on film, Clinton appeared against his will. Footage of actual speeches were cleverly spliced into the film's narrative. White House counsel Charles Ruff fired off a letter to *Contact* director Robert Zemeckis, complaining of the "improper" use of Clinton's public statements. The White House made clear that it had no intention to sue the filmmaker;

indeed, the pattern of relevant precedents suggests that Clinton could not have prevailed.

One such precedent involved *Smothers Brothers Comedy Hour* regular Pat Paulsen, who announced on air in 1967 that he was definitely *not* running for president, all the while conducting a fully orchestrated yet wholly tongue-in-cheek campaign under the auspices of the "Straight Talking American Government" ticket (yes, that's right—the "STAG Party"). Comic candidate Paulsen sued the distributors of a poster that bore a blowup of a photo of him with a banner reading "1968" draped across his chest "in the manner, if not with the style, of a beauty pageant contestant." Paulsen asked a state court in New York to prevent any further distribution of the poster, which he claimed was a violation of, among other things, his statutory right to privacy. The court refused on the grounds that Paulsen had entered the political arena, "where the sensibilities of the participants must bow to the superior public interest in completely unfettered and unabridged free discussion of whatever persuasion, merit or style."[28] More recently, the producers of Rush Limbaugh's radio program were unable to shut down a competing liberal-bent radio talk show

President Clinton would almost certainly have failed had he tried to sue the producers of the feature film *Contact* for its unauthorized use of videotape excerpts from a number of his political speeches.

that called itself *After the Rush*.[29] Although the court determined that enough factual questions remained unresolved to require a trial on the merits, it did grant summary judgment to the defendants on the narrow question as to whether the use of this name constituted a misappropriation of Limbaugh's celebrity identity.

That political figures will almost certainly lose their misappropriations suits does not always deter them from trying to silence those who use their name or likeness without permission. In late 1997, for example, New York City's mayor, Rudy Giuliani, ordered the local transit authority to remove ads that had been placed on the sides of buses by the publishers of *New York* magazine. The ad campaign's theme took advantage of the mayor's reputation for self-aggrandizement, with a caption that read "*New York* magazine—possibly the only good thing in New York Rudy hasn't taken credit for." The magazine sued the Metropolitan Transit Authority and obtained an injunction precluding the agency from refusing the ads.[30] Three years later, the mayor's

28. *Paulsen v. Personality Posters, Inc.*, 299 N.Y.S. 2d 501, 503 (N.Y. Sup. Ct. 1968).
29. *Pam Media, Inc. v. American Research Corp.*, 889 F. Supp. 1403 (D. Colo. 1995).
30. *New York Magazine v. Metropolitan Transportation Authority*, 136 F.3d 123 (2d Cir. 1998).

image was used without his permission in a much-criticized public-education campaign conducted by People for the Ethical Treatment of Animals (PETA). A takeoff on the dairy industry's famous "Got Milk?" campaign, PETA's ad used a milk-mustached Giuliani to make a serious point about a posited correlation between dairy-product intake and prostate cancer. News reports indicated that Giuliani considered suing, but a sheepish PETA promptly withdrew the campaign and apologized to the mayor for making light of his own cancer diagnosis. As tasteless as this particular use of the mayor's likeness may have been, it is highly unlikely that a lawsuit for misappropriation would have succeeded.

Folks Who Cannot Be Sued?
The Newsworthiness (and Other) Defenses

The Pat Paulsen and Rush Limbaugh cases are examples of the "politicians can't sue for misappropriation" rule as well as the more general rule that what might otherwise seem an actionable misappropriation of a celebrity's name or likeness can be deemed protected speech if it entails some kind of political commentary. Courts have sometimes gone a bit further, creating what has come to be known as the "newspaper exception" to misappropriation torts. Newspapers and other news media are often permitted to create printed works and other artifacts, the marketing of which would likely be actionable if engaged in by any other entity. San Francisco 49ers quarterback Joe Montana found out about this exception when he unsuccessfully attempted to enjoin the *San Jose Mercury News* from selling posters bearing an artist's drawing of him that had previously appeared in a special section of the newspaper celebrating

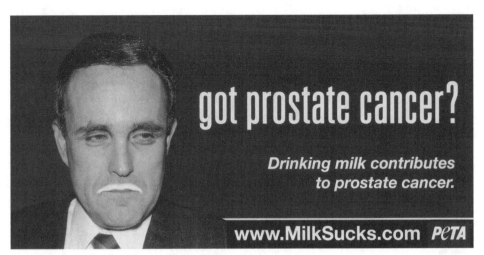

Had Mayor Giuliani chosen to sue PETA for this admittedly tasteless ad parody, his suit would surely have been dismissed. © 2000 People for the Ethical Treatment of Animals. Reprinted with permission.

the team's record of four Super Bowl championships in ten years.[31] The court ruled that just as the publisher surely had the right to print the drawing shortly after the 1990 Super Bowl, so too must he have the right to republish it a few weeks later still.

The pattern of judicial results involving the highly litigious Elvis Presley estate is also instructive. Elvis Presley Enterprises has aggressively litigated against those it perceives to be infringing on the King's name and likeness, the offenses having ranged from the unauthorized marketing of posters to the naming of a bistro "The Velvet Elvis." In general, whenever the presiding court has applied the laws of a state that itself recognizes a right of publicity descendible to one's heirs or estate, those seeking to present the unauthorized exploitation of Presley's work (usually the estate itself) have prevailed.[32] A striking counterexample is found in a legal conflict surrounding Elvis's famous Madison Square Garden concerts in 1972. RCA had an exclusive contract with him to market recordings of those events, but this contract was deemed unenforceable against *Current Audio* magazine, which planned to use as its cover a playable LP recording of excerpts from the press conference given by Presley on the evening of one of the New York performances. Whatever might be the scope of Presley's right of publicity, the court concluded, it "has no application to the use of a picture or name in connection with the dissemination of news or public interest presentations, notwithstanding that such activities are also carried on for a profit."[33]

Even though the model here had nothing to do with the awful narrative, New York's highest court held that the magazine could not be held liable for damages, because the general topic of date rape is highly newsworthy.

---

31. *Montana v. San Jose Mercury News*, 34 Cal. App. 4th 790 (1995).

32. *Elvis Presley Enterprises v. Elvisly Yours, Inc.*, 936 F.2d 889 (6th Cir. 1991); *Elvis Presley Enterprises v. Capece*, 950 F. Supp. 783 (S.D. Tex. 1996); *Estate of Presley v. Russen*, 513 F. Supp. 1339 (D.N.J. 1981); *Factors Etc., Inc. v. Creative Card Company*, 444 F. Supp. 279 (S.D.N.Y. 1977). Compare those cases with *Factors Etc., Inc. v. Pro Arts, Inc.*, 652 F.2d 278 (2d Cir. 1981) (applying Tennessee law and finding no inheritable right of publicity).

33. *Current Audio, Inc. v. RCA*, 337 N.Y.S.2d 949, 954 (N.Y. Sup. Ct. 1972).

New York allows a very broad newsworthiness defense, as is apparent from a case involving a professional model who had consented to having her photos used in *YM* magazine but was shocked at the specific nature of the use. Three photos of the plaintiff illustrated the magazine's "Love Crisis" column, which featured a letter ostensibly written by a fourteen-year-old reader who had "gotten trashed and had sex with three guys." New York's Court of Appeals (the state's highest court) held the state privacy law inapplicable to such a clearly newsworthy use, noting that the column confronted important issues such as underage drinking and date rape.[34] In many other jurisdictions the use of the photos might have been actionable as a false-light invasion of privacy, but New York recognizes only misappropriation.

What might otherwise be an actionable misappropriation of a celebrity's name and likeness may escape liability if it entails a degree of parody. Thus, for example, when the Major League Baseball Players Association sued the distributor of a line of baseball cards that made satiric comments about the players depicted rather than reporting the usual statistics, the Ninth Circuit Court of Appeals found that the cards "provide social commentary on public figures," and are no less protected by the First Amendment just because they do so with humor and caricature.[35]

The line between news and advertising is sometimes a fine one, a lesson learned by Dustin Hoffman when he sued the publishers of *Los Angeles* magazine for imposing his face from a poster publicizing his starring role in *Tootsie* on a professional model's body in a photo spread that included similarly superimposed contemporary designer garments on fifteen other movie stars as well. The photo spread was accompanied by a playful article called "The Ultimate Fashion Show: Grand Illusions," which made clear that Hoffman had been re-outfitted in a "butter-colored silk gown by Richard Tyler"—rather than the red sequined dress from the original movie poster—and shoes by Ralph Lauren. Although the designers whose products were featured in the article no doubt were happy with the free publicity—the magazine sought and received no payment from them—this was not the kind of *commercial* exploitation envisioned under California law, the court found. Rather, it was journalism, "a combination of fashion photography, humor, and visual and verbal editorial comment on classic films and famous actors."[36]

Similarly, an activist group supporting President Bush's proposal to privatize Social Security (and thus critical of AARP's opposition to the proposal) was permitted to use a photo of a gay male couple kissing without the couple's authorization, because the point the group intended to make—that AARP could not be trusted, because it opposed the Iraq War and supported gay marriage—was clearly political.[37]

In Florida the misappropriation doctrine is applied very narrowly, only to unau-

34. *Messenger v. Gruner + Jahr Printing and Publishing*, 727 N.E.2d 549 (N.Y. 2000).

35. *Cardtoons v. Major League Baseball Players Association*, 95 F.3d 959 (10th Cir. 1996).

36. *Hoffman v. Capital Cities/ABC, Inc.*, 255 F.3d 1180, 1185 (9th Cir. 2001).

37. *Raymen v. United States Seniors Association*, 409 F. Supp. 2d 15 (D.D.C. 2006).

The distributor of Cardtoons demonstrates it was possible to make fun of Barry Bonds long before the steroid scandal.

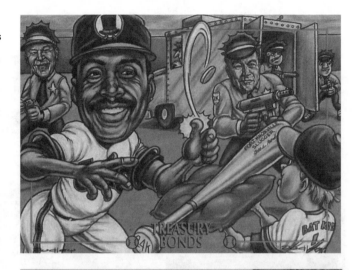

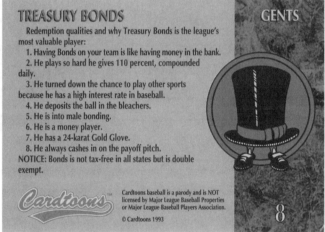

thorized uses of a plaintiff's name or likeness in advertising. Thus, for example, the movie *The Perfect Storm* could not be subject to a misappropriation suit brought by a surviving child of Captain Billy Tyne (played in the movie by George Clooney), because a movie was not deemed a commercial use.[38] The ruling was a narrow one, with the court making clear that it did not intend to foreclose the plaintiff's possible additional claims under the false-light category of privacy.

Although the newsworthiness defense can be a powerful one, a misappropriation is not necessarily forgiven just because the defendant can argue that he is trying to make a (newsworthy?) political point. Thus, for example, a disgruntled former faculty

---

38. *Tyne v. Time Warner*, 901 So. 2d 802 (Fla. 2005).

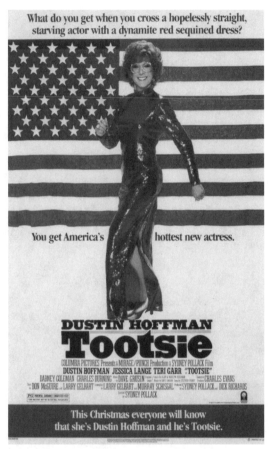

This photo from a *Los Angeles* magazine spread (left) was not deemed a *commercial* use of Dustin Hoffman's image. Even though the image was purposely similar to the image used in the original movie poster for *Tootsie*, and even though readers might be persuaded to buy the Richard Tyler gown shown in the magazine, this was deemed journalism, not commercialism.

member from the University of Evansville was enjoined from using e-mail accounts and website addresses that seemed to have been created by, or seemed to be associated with, various university administrators he intended to criticize. The professor was free to express his views (presuming they were not libelous), but he could not do so in a way that misappropriated the university's good name.[39]

Another limitation of the newsworthiness defense flows from the very strange set of facts that produced the U.S. Supreme Court's only decision to date in a misappro-

---

39. *Felsher v. University of Evansville*, 755 N.E.2d 589 (Ind. 2001). The court also held that only individuals can have privacy interests, not the university itself; accordingly, the decision was based on state unfair-competition and trademark laws, rather than on the misappropriation tort itself.

priation case. That *Zacchini v. Scripps-Howard Broadcasting Co.*[40] is typically referred to in the literature as "the human cannonball case" gives some indication of the unusual dispute involved. Circus performer Hugo Zacchini was in the habit of allowing himself to be shot out of a cannon into a net some two hundred feet away. In late summer of 1972, he was slated to perform his act, which takes approximately fifteen seconds from start to finish, at the Geauga County Fair in Burton, Ohio. A local TV reporter, without Zacchini's permission, filmed the act and broadcast it on the 11 p.m. news. By a 5-4 vote, the Supreme Court determined that the First Amendment would not protect the news media here from an otherwise legitimate suit for misappropriation. "Wherever the line in particular situations is to be drawn between media reports that are protected and those that are not," Justice White wrote for the majority, "we are quite sure that the First and Fourteenth Amendments do not immunize the media when they broadcast a performer's entire act without his consent. The Constitution no more prevents a State from requiring [the TV station] to compensate [Zacchini] for broadcasting his act on television than it would privilege [the TV station] to film and broadcast a copyrighted dramatic work without liability to the copyright owner." Although the *Zacchini* case has been greatly criticized—when an entire "act" lasts only fifteen seconds, after all, how can one do a TV story about it *without* "appropriating" the whole thing?—the general rule espoused is in most circumstances quite sensible. That the middle-aged version of the Rolling Stones continue to

Pictured is "Hugo Zacchini, the younger son of Edmond," often billed as The Human Cannonball. His suit against an Ohio TV station resulted in what is still the Supreme Court's only "right of publicity" decision. Reprinted with permission.

---

40. 433 U.S. 562 (1977).

enjoy successful concert tours certainly gives the media license to report on the performances as news events, but no TV station would think it could get away with
broadcasting its videotaped version of an entire concert as a "documentary special"
without paying Mick and the boys big bucks. In any event, precisely because the factual situation in *Zacchini* was so unusual, it has been virtually ignored over the years,
except when courts have felt the need to distinguish it from the conflict being adjudicated at the time.

The *Booth* Rule

Courts have also recognized a more specialized news media defense that protects
promotional materials. Sometimes known as the *Booth* rule after a case involving the
actress Shirley Booth (who played the title character on TV's *Hazel*), this doctrine
tells media outlets that they are free to use materials they have already published in
future advertisements for the same magazine or newspaper. Your local TV news no
doubt does this all the time in slick spots containing short sound bites from previous
stories, trumpeting its ability to get the news "first" and "best." In Booth's case, *Holiday* magazine, which had run an authorized photo of the actress vacationing in Jamaica in one issue, the next year reprinted that photo in a full-page ad for the
magazine. The court held that such media self-promotion is protected speech that
cannot be the subject of misappropriation suits.[41]

In some jurisdictions the *Booth* rule has been broadened to permit a media outlet
to use previously published materials not only for self-promotion within its own
pages but also in advertisements placed in other media. Former New York Jets quarterback Joe Namath, for example, was unsuccessful in his suit against *Sports Illustrated*
for using a photo of him that had previously appeared in that magazine in a later
advertising campaign to drum up subscriptions that ran in *Cosmopolitan* using the
heading "The Man You Love Loves Joe Namath").[42]

Also, *New York* magazine was permitted, in a 1970s television ad, to refer to its special
issue looking back at 1949 as "the year we entered modern times." The special issue included an article by feminist Betty Friedan that described her earlier life as a housewife and
included a family photo, the further dissemination of which offended Friedan's ex-
husband, Carl. A federal district court concluded that, in New York at least, under the *Booth*
rule, since the magazine itself had every right to publish the photo, even without Mr. Friedan's permission (as a result of Ms. Friedan's status as a highly newsworthy figure), any
advertisement touting the magazine article enjoys the same privilege as the article itself.[43]

---

41. *Booth v. Curtis Publishing*, 182 N.E.2d 812 (N.Y. 1962).
42. *Namath v. Sports Illustrated*, 363 N.Y.S.2d 276 (N.Y. Sup. Ct. 1975), *aff'd*, 371 N.Y.S. 2d 10
(N.Y. App. Div. 1975), *aff'd*, 352 N.E.2d 584 (1976).
43. *Friedan v. Friedan*, 414 F. Supp. 77 (S.D.N.Y. 1976).

Shirley Booth and chapeau, from a recent issue of Holiday

YOU'RE UP TO YOUR EARS IN OPULENCE

Holiday wades right in at Jamaica's Round Hill colony for a close-up look at how the other half of one per cent lives it up. The company is entertaining; the mood is delightfully intimate. Slim Aaron's perceptive camera captures these elusive spirits in mid-flight.

This is rich, it's Holiday, it's wonderful. With Holiday's highly personal point of view —expressed in a creative blend of words and pictures—the exotic names, places and pleasures become familiar, and the familiar becomes freshly exciting.

It's exhilarating to Holiday readers—some 875,000 high-income families who are just naturally goers, doers, buyers, trend starters. Holiday whets their appetites for more of the good things in life, puts them in an expansive Holiday mood.

What a provocative selling opportunity for advertisers!

There's a rewarding new world for you in HOLIDAY

New York's highest court held that *Holiday* magazine needed no further permission from actress Shirley Booth to run this advertisement, a look back at an article from the year earlier that had featured a photo of Ms. Booth.

Consent as a Defense

Permission is an additional, if obvious, defense worthy of at least passing mention. Misappropriation is, after all, the *unauthorized* use of another's name or likeness for commercial benefit. Authorized uses typically come in the form of licensing contracts, such as those entered into by just about all the celebrity endorsers we see in advertising campaigns. Even in the case of noncelebrity models, wise photographers will insist on a signature on a release form explicitly authorizing use of the individual's likeness. Whether such permission will be for a single specified use or will allow the photographer to reuse the image in unlimited future media and perhaps even to alter the image can be subjects of negotiation. When dealing with models who are minors, a parent or legal guardian must sign such a release. Just how much power parents have to give such permission on behalf of their children was the source of litigation involving Brooke Shields, whose mother signed away their rights to photos taken of Brooke by noted artist Garry Gross and destined initially for a Playboy Press book called *Sugar and Spice*, but which were used in many magazines internationally. The courts even-

The man you love loves Joe Namath.

Of course he loves you best. But he also loves sports. So why fight it? This Christmas, give him what any sports lover is sure to want—a year of Sports Illustrated.

Does he like pro football, basketball, baseball, hockey? Tennis, golf, sailing, scuba-diving? Sports Illustrated covers them all, with yards of great color pictures and some of the most vivid writing anywhere.

So you can be sure—this is one gift that will fit him perfectly, no matter what size or age he is. And it's one gift that won't be put away and forgotten soon after Christmas. Every week... season after season...52 times next year...he'll be opening up a new surprise package from you. You save $2 on every subscription after the first

one. So it pays to give Sports Illustrated to all the sports lovers in your life.

Just fill in and mail the attached order card—it's the easiest shopping trip you'll make this Christmas season.

As soon as we get your order, we'll send you handsome gift announcements to sign and put under the tree. And if you act soon, we'll be able to start your gift subscriptions right at the holidays with our spectacular year-end Double Issue.

Think about it—is there any other gift that gives a man so much good healthy pleasure... for so long...for so little money?

Mail the attached card right now. He'll love Sports Illustrated—and love you for it.

SPORTS ILLUSTRATED FOR CHRISTMAS

Following the *Booth* rule, New York's Court of Appeals held that Jets quarterback Joe Namath had no legal recourse against *Sports Illustrated* for using a photo of him previously used as news for a more commercial purpose—drumming up subscriptions from *Cosmopolitan* readers.

tually held that the permission was binding; interestingly, because of a quirk of New York law, the result might have been different had Ms. Shields been deemed a child "performer" rather than merely a "model."[44]

How explicit permission must be is a question that has resulted in contradictory decisions. Consider first a rather bizarre case involving a former news anchor from the Youngstown, Ohio, market, Catherine Bosley. While vacationing with her husband in Florida, Bosley participated in a wet T-shirt contest. Imagine her embarrassment when video of her fully nude performance appeared in numerous online and other outlets, including a video in the "Dream Girls" series. The defendant pointed out that signs had been placed prominently in the bar's dressing rooms, exits, and the stage itself:

NOTICE: The event you have entered is being filmed by a video production company. By entering the "stage" beyond this sign, you are hereby consenting and agreeing to

44. *Shields v. Gross*, 58 N.Y.2d 338, 345–346 (1983).

your picture and image being used for any reproduction of any type and sale without any further compensation.

The contest's emcee also announced from the stage that the event was being filmed. Moreover, many of the photos of Bosley at issue in the litigation were hardly candid— she was looking directly at the camera, thus implicitly offering her consent to be photographed. Nonetheless, the court held, explicit consent was needed—if not in writing then at least orally—to negate Bosley's misappropriation claim.[45]

Compare the *Bosley* case with an Alabama Supreme Court decision involving Sam and Joseph Schifano, who often attended dog races at a local park and on one occasion were photographed while sitting in "the Winner's Circle," a special section of the park that could be reserved upon payment of additional fees.[46] That photo later was used by the Greene County Greyhound Park in a brochure touting the advantages of the Winner's Circle. The plaintiff's suit alleging (among other things) misappropriation was unsuccessful. The unanimous court opinion emphasized that the plaintiffs had given implicit permission because a clear announcement had been made within the park about the photo to be taken and the camera was mounted on a tripod in clear view and only a few feet away from the plaintiffs, neither of whom objected or moved.

Ms. Shields was not happy having this photo continue to be exploited after she reached majority, but the authorization granted by her mother was deemed binding.

How can we reconcile the *Bosley* and *Schifano* cases, apart from the fact that they deal with laws in two different states (Florida and Alabama)? Perhaps one distinguishing feature is that once the Florida promoters learned that they had been blessed with a celebrity's image, they touted that fact aggressively in their marketing of the nude footage. By contrast, the Schifanos are not celebrities, and their names were never even mentioned in the brochure for the park.

Intrusion

Unique among the four privacy torts, intrusion concerns news *gathering* rather than news *reporting*. If, for example, shoving a microphone into a subject's face can ever

---

45. *Bosley v. WildwetT.Com*, 310 F. Supp. 2d 914 (N.D. Ohio 2004).
46. *Schifano v. Greene County Greyhound Park, Inc.*, 624 So. 2d 178 (Ala. 1993).

THINGS TO REMEMBER

Appropriation

- There are two distinct grievances:
  - Purely financial ("How dare you profit from my good name?")
  - Personal dignity ("You could not pay me enough to be associated with that particular product!")
- A "likeness" for purposes of appropriation suits is anything that conjures up in readers' minds the image of the plaintiff.
- Even fictional characters can have recognizable "likenesses."
- A new category of appropriation suits has emerged in recent years, protecting against look-alike and sound-alike "takings."
- Politicians who sue over appropriations of their likenesses almost always lose, usually because courts conclude that the resulting "speech" is a form of political commentary.
- An otherwise actionable appropriation can be saved if it is part of a legitimate news story.
- Some courts have created a "newspaper exception" to the tort, permitting the media to sell posters or similar items that would almost certainly be considered commercial misappropriations if marketed by nonmedia companies.

be an actionable intrusion, it will be so even if no news story ever results. The *Restatement (Second) of Torts* says that we can be held liable for intrusion if we "intentionally intrude, physically or otherwise, upon the solitude or seclusion of another or his private affairs or concerns," and if that intrusion "would be highly offensive to a reasonable person."[47] Depending on the jurisdiction—about four-fifths of the states recognize the tort—actionable intrusions may consist of the use of telephoto lenses or hidden recording equipment, incessant surveillance, or the failure to identify oneself as a reporter.

Precisely because the actionable harm in intrusion cases occurs via the news-*gathering* process, the First Amendment offers the press only very limited, if any, protection. As one writer put it, "To deny holding the tabloid media liable for an intrusive invasion of privacy is similar to holding a local television news crew immune from tort liability for its van intentionally running over someone on its way to cover a big story."[48]

Reasonable Expectation of Privacy

Intrusion cases are very much bound by context, and courts often ask whether the plaintiff had a reasonable expectation of privacy in the situation that gave rise to the

---

47. *Restatement (Second) of Torts* § 652B (1977).

48. Eduardo W. Gonzalez, "'Get That Camera out Of My Face!' An Examination of the Viability of Suing 'Tabloid Television' for Invasion of Privacy," 51 *University of Miami Law Review* 935, 952 (1997).

complaint. This is a concept borrowed from the Fourth Amendment constitutional right to privacy against unreasonable searches and seizures. In the constitutional realm, for example, we have more of an expectation of privacy in our homes[49] than while walking on the street,[50] more of an expectation of privacy in the actual content of our phone conversations[51] than in the fact that we called a specific number (in large part because monthly phone bills have almost always documented the numbers we call).[52]

In constitutional cases, the person complaining of a privacy invasion is typically a criminal defendant. By contrast, in media privacy cases the person whose privacy was purportedly invaded tends to be the civil plaintiff. In one of the more frequently cited media intrusion cases, a federal appellate court upheld a judgment against a pair of *Life* magazine reporters who, acting pursuant to an agreement with the Los Angeles district attorney's office, pretended to be potential patients and entered the premises of a disabled veteran who apparently was practicing medicine without a license. The magazine's liability was based not so much on the reporters' lack of candor with the plaintiff as on their having used a hidden camera and audio-recording device. "One who invites another to his home or office takes a risk that the visitor may not be what he seems," the court allowed, "and that the visitor may repeat all he hears and observes when he leaves. But he does not and should not be required to take the risk that what is heard and seen will be transmitted by photograph or recording, or in our modern world, in full living color and hi-fi to the public at large or to any segment of it that the visitor may select."[53] In other words, it is not reasonable to expect that reporters will tell us the truth, even in gaining access to our place of business, but it is reasonable to expect they will not record us surreptitiously while deceiving us about their identity.

Despite the quoted words from the *Dietemann* case offered above, more recent decisions citing it as a precedent case often emphasize the fact that the reporters lied about their identities as the more important violation of the plaintiff's reasonable privacy expectation. For example, an American Airlines flight attendant interviewed outside her doorway by an ABC news producer the day after her service as part of the crew on O. J. Simpson's flight from Los Angeles to Chicago (the night Nicole Brown Simpson and Ron Goldman were found murdered) was unsuccessful in her intrusion suit against the network, even though she was unaware she was being taped. The federal appellate court distinguished these facts from those of the *Dietemann* case described earlier, in that here no one "had gained entrance into another's home by subterfuge."[54]

---

49. *Weeks v. United States*, 232 U.S. 383 (1914).
50. *Terry v. Ohio*, 392 U.S. 1 (1968).
51. *Katz v. United States*, 389 U.S. 347 (1967).
52. *Smith v. Maryland*, 442 U.S. 735 (1979).
53. *Dietemann v. Time, Inc.*, 449 F.2d 245, 249 (9th Cir. 1971).
54. *DeTeresa v. ABC*, 121 F.3d 460, 466 (9th Cir. 1997).

The original caption read: "Dietemann, arrested by investigator Grant Leake, holds a pair of turtles which he studies 'because they are vegetarians, and so are a good many of my patients.'" The actions of the *Life* magazine reporters would have been actionable, the *Dietemann* case held, even if this article had never appeared in print.

While it is generally true that we must expect less privacy when we are out and about than when we are in the sanctity of our homes, even in public we might enjoy some privacy against photographers hounding us. The leading case here, though many years ago, concerned Jacqueline Onassis and children Caroline and John, Jr. Her nemesis for years had been freelance photographer Ronald Galella, who trailed Onassis everywhere, hiding in bushes and behind coatracks in restaurants and even intruding into her children's schools. The remedy applied by the court was an injunction against further harassment by Galella; it did not prohibit him from photographing the family, although it required that he stand as far as one hundred yards away from his subjects.[55] An appellate court later affirmed the order, but reduced the distance for most situations to twenty-five feet. Although the legal controversy ultimately turned on the question of whether Galella was guilty of violating New York's criminal

---

55. *Galella v. Onassis*, 353 F. Supp. 196 (S.D.N.Y. 1972), *aff'd*, 487 F.2d 986 (2d Cir. 1973).

harassment statute, Judge Cooper made clear that the photographer's conduct also constituted "tortious invasion of privacy."

Recall that the *Restatement*'s definition of intrusion depends in part on "offensiveness." In particular contexts, especially offensive intrusions may violate our expectations of privacy. Consider a California Supreme Court decision involving automobile accident victim Ruth Shulman, whose conversations with an attending nurse while she was rescued from her car and while being transported to a local hospital in a rescue helicopter were filmed without her consent.[56] Writing for the majority, Judge Werdegar admitted that there normally would be no reasonable expectation of privacy against the media's coverage of an accident scene. Anyone who watches local TV news regularly knows that such stories are commonplace. But here the media's intrusion on Ms. Shulman's privacy could be actionable, in part because the attending nurse herself was induced by the media representatives to wear a microphone, a practice the court found a "highly offensive" way "to intercept what would otherwise be private conversations with an injured patient," taking advantage of Shulman's "vulnerability and confusion."

In Fourth Amendment cases, there is no reasonable expectation of privacy in—and thus the police need not obtain a warrant to seize—materials that are not hidden, that are in plain sight.[57] Analogously, in the tort law governing privacy and the media, courts have held that there is no intrusion when the media photograph or record, from a public place, what disinterested passersby could just as easily have seen or heard for themselves. In *Mark v. Seattle Times*, a KING-TV cameraman had set up his equipment against the window of a locked pharmacy—it is not clear from the court record whether the camera itself was on public or private property—to record the actions of pharmacist Albert Mark, who had recently been indicted for Medicaid fraud.[58] The Washington Supreme Court determined that the cameraman's conduct was not actionable, because he merely made a record of "a public sight which anyone would be free to see." An Ohio court reached a similar result when a Cleveland TV station filmed, in the county sheriff's department building, a drug felony suspect being transported from his interrogation to the booking room. "Liability for intrusion does not exist," the court held, if the media "merely observe, film, or record a person in a public place, such as a courthouse or a police station."[59] Another reporter, this time in Arkansas, was not held liable for making and later broadcasting audio recordings of a DWI suspect; the court emphasized that the suspect was behaving in a loud and abusive manner that could readily have been overheard by anyone in the area.[60]

---

56. *Shulman v. Group W Productions, Inc.*, 955 P.2d 469 (Cal. 1998).

57. *Coolidge v. New Hampshire*, 403 U.S. 443 (1971).

58. 635 P.2d 1081 (Wash. 1981).

59. *Haynik v. Zimlich*, 508 N.E.2d 195, 200 (Ohio Com. Pleas 1986).

60. *Holman v. Central Arkansas Broadcasting Co.*, 610 F.2d 542 (8th Cir. 1979).

Everyday experience would suggest that conversations might be wholly private or wholly public but that most are somewhere in between. The California Supreme Court considered in 1999 whether semiprivate conversations—in this case between two participants in a busy room of office cubicles, where the talking likely could be overheard by at least a small number of nearby coworkers—could enjoy enough expectation of privacy to be protected by the intrusion tort. ABC had sent reporter Stacy Lescht to become a temporary employee of the Psychic Marketing Group (PMG), a company marketing the services of telephone psychics. Lescht used a concealed camera (in her hat) and microphone (in her bra) to produce footage that was eventually aired on *Primetime Live*. Included in the surreptitious taping were conversations between Lescht and PMG employee Mark Sanders, who sued the TV network for intrusion. A unanimous state supreme court concluded that a conversation otherwise protected against concealed taping does not lose that protection when a small number of others might have overheard the conversation on their own. The expectation of privacy need not be absolute or complete; there can be "an expectation of limited privacy." The court added, in a passage designed to emphasize the narrowness of its holding but which will surely demand clarification in later cases, that "investigative journalists [do not] necessarily commit a tort by secretly recording events and conversations in offices, stores or other workplaces," and that "whether a reasonable expectation of privacy is violated by such recording depends on the exact nature of the conduct and all the surrounding circumstances."[61]

If the *Sanders* court is reminding us that context is everything when determining whether a conversation is private, an earlier decision from New York says much the same about the question of whether a place is public or private. CBS's New York affiliate, Channel 2, sent a camera crew to a Manhattan restaurant that had been cited for health-code violations. As a state court described the scene, the station's employees "burst into" the restaurant with lights and cameras running, and in the ensuing chaos, some patrons left without paying their checks, while others "hid their faces behind napkins or table cloths." The restaurant was awarded damages for CBS's trespass. That the restaurant is a public accommodation is irrelevant, the court held, because the camera crew was not there to partake of what was being offered to the public—that is, food and drink.[62]

The plain-sight exception to intrusion is apparently not limited to mass media defendants. Consider an odd case involving feuding neighbors in Illinois, one of whom affixed a surveillance camera to his own home that recorded activities in his neighbor's driveway and garage twenty-four hours a day. The neighbor sued, but a state appellate court pointed out that any attentive passerby, and certainly a roofer or tree trimmer, would have had access to the same spaces monitored by the camera.[63]

---

61. *Sanders v. ABC, Inc.*, 978 P.2d 67, 69 (Cal. 1999).
62. *Le Mistral, Inc., v. CBS, Inc.*, 402 N.Y.S.2d 815 (App. Div. 1978).
63. *Schiller v. Mitchell*, 828 N.E.2d 323 (Ill. App. Ct. 2005).

"Ride-Along" Intrusions

One of the more popular genres of television fare in recent years has been "reality programs" that show live footage of police officers stopping, questioning, searching, and arresting suspects, or of emergency fire and medical teams responding to calls for assistance. Sometimes the events take place in public places, such as on city streets. At other times, law enforcement or other emergency workers may be called into private residences. In a unanimous 1999 decision, the Supreme Court held that law enforcement agencies may be found in violation of the Fourth Amendment for inviting media to observe their activities conducted in a private residence.[64] Dominic Wilson was wanted by federal authorities for violating his probation on previous charges of robbery, theft, and assault with intent to rob. U.S. Marshals obtained a warrant authorizing a predawn storming of Wilson's home in Rockville, Maryland, and invited the *Washington Post* along. As it happens, the police had the address wrong and wound up pointing several guns not at the suspect but at his father. Chief Justice Rehnquist's opinion for the Court makes clear that police may invite to events such as the execution of search and arrest warrants only nonparticipants who have a direct stake in the event, such as crime victims who can identify their stolen property. The individual law enforcement agents executing the warrant were immune from liability, the Court held, largely because the relevant case law had been contradictory, thus not giving them sufficient notice as to their constitutional obligations. Because the Wilsons sued only the U.S. Marshals and not the *Washington Post*, lower court decisions must be examined to see what liability the media may have when they participate in such ride-alongs.

In a relatively early case of this type, the widow of a heart attack victim sued NBC and its Los Angeles affiliate, KNBC, after they had accompanied the paramedics called to treat the victim. A segment of the resulting video appeared on the *NBC Nightly News* as well as in an on-air advertisement for a future "mini-documentary" about the paramedics, despite the fact that the family never consented to either the taping or the physical intrusion into their home by the media. A state appellate court found that the plaintiff had stated a sufficient claim for invasion of privacy to defeat the defendant's motion for summary judgment. In doing so, the court admitted that the performance of emergency medical personnel is a very newsworthy subject matter but emphasized that newsworthiness is wholly irrelevant to the intrusion tort.[65]

In another California case, this time involving CBS's *Street Stories* program, a victim of domestic violence consented to a film crew's having accompanied the county Mobile Crisis Intervention Team onto her property. Accordingly, the court held that she could not proceed with her intrusion claim against the media company. However, because her consent was based on the crew's false representation to her that the video

---

64. *Wilson v. Layne*, 526 U.S. 603 (1999).
65. *Miller v. National Broadcasting Co.*, 232 Cal. Rptr. 668 (Ct. App. 1986).

would be used only for internal training purposes, rather than national broadcast, the court permitted her to pursue her fraud claim.[66]

Also unsuccessful in her intrusion suit was an Oregon resident who sought damages against KATU-TV of Portland. The station's crew had accompanied local police officers in their execution of a search warrant at the home of the plaintiff, who did not consent to the filming. Even though the crew might very well be guilty of trespass, the court reminded us that the tort of intrusion requires that the alleged invasion on a complainant's privacy be "highly offensive." The appellate court here refused to overturn the jury's finding that this particular trespass was not sufficiently offensive to constitute tortious intrusion.[67]

CBS's *Street Stories* program was also the subject of a New York case in which the camera crew was invited by the Secret Service to observe as their agents executed a search warrant at the home of a man suspected of credit card fraud. Despite the objections of the suspect's wife and child, the camera crew followed the Secret Service's clear instructions to continue filming, especially while the agents interviewed the wife about articles found during the search. None of the footage was ever broadcast by CBS. The federal district court concluded that CBS had become so closely intertwined with the Secret Service's functioning as to be considered a "state's agent" that could be sued for violating citizens' *constitutional* right to privacy.[68] Similarly, in another case, the Court of Appeals for the Ninth Circuit declared that CNN could be sued not only for trespass but also for violating a Montana plaintiff's civil rights. The network had accompanied U.S. Fish and Wildlife agents, who suspected Paul Berger of poisoning endangered species, on a search of Berger's ranch. The court was especially concerned by the fact that CNN entered into an elaborate agreement with the government agency, under which the network was granted permission to film as long as it promised not to air the footage until a jury was impaneled or a plea bargain struck.[69]

In contrast to those cases, a police search of a St. Louis, Missouri, home, one of whose residents was suspected of keeping illegal weapons, produced a federal appellate ruling relieving the media of any constitutional liability. The court emphasized that the crew from local station, KSDK, although *invited* by the police to accompany

66. *Baugh v. CBS, Inc.*, 828 F. Supp. 745 (N.D. Cal. 1993).

67. *Magenis v. Fisher Broadcasting, Inc.*, 798 P.2d 1106 (Or. Ct. App. 1990). This case predates by nine years the Supreme Court's ruling in *Wilson v. Layne*, discussed earlier. It is anyone's guess what might happen today if another Oregon resident chose to sue not only the TV station but also the local police.

68. *Ayeni v. CBS, Inc.*, 848 F. Supp. 362 (E.D.N.Y. 1994), *aff'd sub nom*, *Ayeni v. Mottola*, 35 F.3d 680 (2d Cir. 1994), *cert. denied*, 514 U.S. 1062 (1995). The change in the case's name at the appellate level reflects CBS's having been removed as a defendant because the network reached an out-of-court settlement with the plaintiff.

69. *Berger v. Hanlon*, 129 F.3d 505, 515 (9th Cir. 1997). Technically, the Supreme Court, in *Wilson v. Layne*, affirmed this decision as well, although no separate discussion of the case's facts are presented.

them as they executed a search warrant, were not in any way *directed* by the officials to enter or not to enter, to film or not to film.[70] The federal court declined to rule directly on the plaintiff's additional tort claims against the TV station, suggesting that those claims be brought instead into state court.

In short, the more the media's presence and on-site conduct are controlled directly by the police, the more likely that presence can lead to media liability. An exception to this generalization may by found in cases in which the search warrant explicitly authorizes videotaping or similar recording of evidence.[71]

Intrusions and Fraud

In the *Dietemann* case, it will be recalled, the *Life* magazine reporters were held liable not because they engaged in deception to obtain their story (by pretending to be in need of medical attention) but because of the surreptitious use of recording equipment. Does this mean that the media are always free to lie with impunity to obtain access to a residence or business? Does a newsworthy end justify a deceptive means?

As several courts have pointed out, deception is a necessary component of some kinds of reportage, from the restaurant critic who dons a disguise to avoid VIP treatment to the use of paired "testers" to uncover discriminatory housing and employment practices. In a 1995 decision, Judge Richard Posner of the Seventh Circuit Court of Appeals concluded that reporters cannot be held liable for trespass as long as their deceptions do not grant them access to truly private areas and they do not reveal "intimate details" of their subjects' lives.[72]

A few years later, a damage award of over $300,000 was assessed against producers of the ABC television newsmagazine *Primetime Live*, after their reporters' fraudulently obtained employment as Food Lion meat wrappers to research a story on unsafe meat preparation and marketing practices. On appeal, only a nominal award of two dollars for "breach of loyalty" (taking wages from an employer while engaged in practices designed to hurt the interests of that employer) was permitted to stand. The Fourth Circuit Court of Appeals threw out the huge punitive damages award, which had been based on the reporters' fraudulent misrepresentation of their employment and educational backgrounds, finding that the real harm suffered by Food Lion was a function not of those false statements but of the broadcast story resulting from the undercover operation. The court held further that if Food Lion wanted to be compensated for the harm caused to its reputation, it would have to sue for libel (and to prove that ABC published with actual malice).[73]

Perhaps you are familiar with the "To Catch a Predator" series on *Dateline NBC*,

---

70. *Parker v. Boyer*, 93 F.3d 445 (8th Cir. 1996).
71. *Prahl v. Brosamle*, 295 N.W.2d 768 (Wis. Ct. App. 1980).
72. *Desnick v. American Broadcasting Company*, 44 F.3d 1345 (7th Cir. 1995).
73. *Food Lion, v. Capital Cities Cable/ABC*, 194 F.3d 505 (4th Cir. 1999).

in which the show's producers, along with a concerned citizens' group called Perverted Justice, set up sting operations in private homes where adult Internet chat room participants arrive with what appears to be an intention to have sex with a minor. The sting's targets are greeted not by a Lolita but by NBC's Chris Hansen, whose physical demeanor, vocal tone, and word choice clearly lead many targets to infer, at least initially, that Hansen is a cop (or perhaps the youngster's father).[74] Certainly the sting's targets are unappealing characters, and many have already been incarcerated for charges flowing from the Internet chats captured by Perverted Justice. It will be interesting to see, however, if any of the men caught in the sting, especially those who are acquitted of criminal charges, commence invasion-of-privacy suits against NBC. A court asked to adjudicate such a claim would necessarily examine the relationship between the TV network and the cooperating law enforcement agencies, and expert sociolinguistic testimony might very well suggest that Hansen, while not impersonating a police officer in the criminal sense (he does not flash a badge or wear a uniform), was engaged in "copspeak."

A Note about Wiretapping

As we have already seen, one cannot discuss the privacy tort called intrusion without also talking about such related torts as trespass and fraud. It is also important to realize that certain kinds of news-gathering practices, whether or not they technically meet the definition of the intrusion tort in your state, might open you up to criminal prosecution. Chief among these are the use of mechanical devices to monitor or record conversations (whether in person or telephonic) or to read another person's e-mail or similar computer communications. Both federal and state statutes can govern these behaviors.

The law generally recognizes a difference between **third-party monitoring** (wherein person A records a conversation between persons B and C) and **participant monitoring** (person A records her own conversation with person B). An example of the former category became a mini-scandal in 1997 when a Florida couple, using a police scanner, intercepted House Speaker Newt Gingrich's private cellular phone conversations and made recordings of them available to the news media.

Gingrich was under investigation by the House ethics committee for questionable fund-raising practices surrounding a college course he offered by teleconference. The intercepted conversations seemed to contradict Gingrich's promise to the committee not to contest its decision to reprimand him. Although the *New York Times* and other media likely were not in violation of the law for publishing excerpts of the conversations, the Florida couple pled guilty to violating the Electronic Communications Privacy Act (ECPA) of 1986. In 1999, a federal appellate court determined that a civil

---

74. Douglas McCollam, "The Shame Game: 'To Catch a Predator' Is Propping Up NBC's *Dateline*, but at What Cost?" *Columbia Journalism Review*, January/February 2007, 28, 30.

suit against the Democratic congressman who had received the tapes from the couple and made them available to the media could go forward.[75]

The ECPA criminalizes third-party monitoring (the act refers to "interception") of oral messages as well as those sent by e-mail,[76] satellite, and cellular phones. A U.S. attorney in New York used the statute to prosecute the Fort Lee, New Jersey–based Breaking News Network (BNN) for intercepting beeper messages sent by the police and other emergency crews, as well as by the mayor's office. BNN, whose clients included the Associated Press wire service as well as several New York newspapers and TV stations, was known for providing useful leads for fast-breaking crime stories. The company and three of its executives pled guilty, and BNN was fined $35,000.[77]

The act was also at issue in a 1990 case involving the syndicated TV program *Inside Edition*, which had surreptitiously videotaped a New York physician then under investigation by the New York State Department of Health, Office of Professional Medical Conduct for his highly unusual and allegedly fraudulent manner of treating overweight patients. The doctor obtained a ten-day temporary restraining order against the TV producers, prohibiting them from broadcasting the footage obtained in a manner likely prohibited by the act. An appellate court overturned the order, however, finding that even if the TV staff was guilty of violating the act, that issue is wholly separable from the First Amendment right to share whatever information they had obtained with their viewers.[78]

Other laws against participant and third-party monitoring are generally less strict than the ECPA. Most media representatives would agree that tape-recording other people's comments without their permission is ethically questionable at best. If you decide that you have a compelling need to engage in such behavior, you certainly will want to know if your jurisdiction criminalizes participant monitoring. Under federal law there is no criminal liability for surreptitious participant taping. Your local phone company, however, acting under directions from the FCC, likely has a policy prohibiting you from taping conversations unless all parties consent.

The majority of states use the same rules as the federal model, permitting recording of phone conversations as long as at least one party is aware of the taping. About ten states, however, require that all parties consent to the taping of phone conversations. One such state is Maryland. Thus, when Linda Tripp taped Monica Lewinsky's tales of White House sexual escapades without the latter's knowledge, she probably violated the law (although the prosecutor dropped his case in May 2000 because so much of it was built around testimony for which Tripp had already been granted immunity

---

75. *Boehner v. McDermott*, 191 F.3d 463 (D.C. Cir. 1999).

76. It should be kept in mind, however, that in the workplace your employer, not you, owns the e-mail system; thus it is not illegal under current law for businesses to monitor and store transmissions sent to and by their employees.

77. Adam Lisberg, "They Start Spreading the News," *Record* (Bergen County), January 13, 2003, A1.

78. *In re King World Productions*, 898 F.2d 56 (6th Cir. 1990).

by special prosecutor Kenneth Starr). A similar statute in Florida was upheld by that state's supreme court against a First Amendment challenge brought by a Miami TV station and newspaper. "The ancient art of investigative reporting was successfully practiced long before the invention of electronic devices," the court wrote, adding that "hidden mechanical contrivances" have not become, even in the modern age, "indispensable tools of investigative reporting."[79] Rest assured, too, that the producers of the *Dateline NBC* "To Catch a Predator" series, when they set up sting operations to capture on tape Internet predators who believe they are traveling to meet an underage potential sex partner, do so only in states that permit participant monitoring.

At least one court has held, even in the face of a state statute seeming to prohibit participant taping, that any party who does not manifest an objective expectation of privacy in the conversation—for example, by lowering his or her voice, closing doors, or otherwise demonstrating that it is a "private" conversation—forfeits the right to recover damages. At issue in that case was the surreptitious audio and video recording of conversations with the manager of a fish market by the producers of ABC's *Primetime Live*, which was investigating allegations of unsanitary conditions in the industry.[80]

Can wiretapping laws make reporters liable for broadcasting or publishing illegally taped conversations even if the media had no role in the taping? A radio station in Wyoming Valley, Pennsylvania, broadcast excerpts of cellular telephone conversations between a local high school teacher and the head of the teachers' union negotiating team. In the conversation, the union official expressed anger at the school board for leaking too many details of the negotiations to the local newspaper rather than sitting down with the union in good faith. In what we can presume was a bit of rhetorical hyperbole, the union official planned to "blow off the front porches" of some of the board members' homes. An unknown individual intercepted and taped the conversation and then left the tape in the mailbox of the president of the local taxpayers' association, who in turn gave it to a local radio talk show host. After the tapes were broadcast, the teacher and the union representative sued the radio talk show host under federal and state wiretapping laws.

By a 6-3 vote, the U.S. Supreme Court held that the relevant federal statutes (the Omnibus Crime Control and Safe Street Act, as amended by the Electronic Communications Privacy Act) cannot constitutionally be applied to someone who was not involved in the recording of the conversation—at least not when the topic of the resulting broadcast is of clear public interest.[81] (Careful readers will recall that the public interest value of a story was an important feature in libel law as well. The issue will surface again when we talk about false-light invasions of privacy.) Writing for the majority, Justice Stevens called to mind the famous Pentagon Papers case (see chapter

---

79. *Shevin v. Sunbeam Television Corp.*, 351 So. 2d 723, 727 (Fla. 1977).
80. *Russell v. American Broadcasting Co., Inc.*, 1995 U.S. Dist. LEXIS 7528 (N.D. Ill. 1995).
81. *Bartnicki v. Vopper*, 532 U.S. 514 (2001).

THINGS TO REMEMBER

Intrusion

- Unique among the four privacy torts, intrusion does not require that anything be published. Therefore, the First Amendment is not a very helpful defense.
- There is generally no intrusion if the media capture images of scenes that any passerby could have seen (unless the media otherwise act egregiously).
- The Supreme Court has ruled that law enforcement officials might be in violation of suspects' constitutional privacy rights when they invite the media on "ride-along" observations; some courts have held that the media themselves may be sued for both tortious claims and for civil rights violations when they participate in the execution of a search warrant.
- That employees of news organizations sometimes lie to their subjects to gain access to property and obtain information is usually not sufficient to create an actionable intrusion claim.
- Reporters who surreptitiously record phone conversations with subjects not only run the risk of civil suit; they may be in violation of federal and state criminal statutes as well.

2), in which the Court upheld "the right of the press to publish information of great public concern obtained from documents stolen by a third party."

False Light

The next of the four privacy torts identified by Prosser has much in common with libel. False-light plaintiffs, like libel plaintiffs, sue because falsehoods have been spread about them. There is one very important difference between false light and libel, however. Plaintiffs in false-light privacy suits need not prove that the falsities told about them are actually defamatory, only that they are offensive. In actuality, the vast majority of false-light plaintiffs sue because of defamatory statements about them. In such cases, the false-light claim seems to be a fallback option in controversies that should be litigated as libel actions. Indeed, when these plaintiffs prevail, it is usually on the defamation claim; moreover, false light's reputation as a "backdoor" libel vehicle has led many states to reject the tort altogether.

Two Tales of Survivors: The Supreme Court and False Light

That the inaccuracies alleged in false-light claims need not be defamatory is apparent from the facts surrounding the leading Supreme Court false-light decision; the falsity at issue might even be described as laudatory, as painting the plaintiffs in an inappropriately heroic light. *Time, Inc. v. Hill* began in 1952, when James Hill and his

ACTUAL EVENT, as reported in newspaper, took place in isolated house about 10 miles from Philadelphia. There three convicts from

Lewisburg penitentiary held family of James Hill as prisoners while they hid from manhunt. All three convicts were later captured.

TRUE CRIME INSPIRES TENSE PLAY

The ordeal of a family trapped by convicts gives Broadway a new thriller, 'The Desperate Hours'

Three years ago Americans all over the country read about the desperate ordeal of the James Hill family, who were held prisoners in their home outside Philadelphia by three escaped convicts. Later they read about it in Joseph Hayes's novel, *The Desperate Hours*, inspired by the family's experience. Now they can see the story re-enacted in Hayes's Broadway play based on the book, and next year will see it in his movie, which has

been filmed but is being held up until the play has a chance to pay off.

The play, directed by Robert Montgomery and expertly acted, is a heart-stopping account of how a family rose to heroism in a crisis. LIFE photographed the play during its Philadelphia tryout, transported some of the actors to the actual house where the Hills were besieged. On the next page scenes from the play are re-enacted on the site of the crime.

Life magazine's article used the "news hook" of the opening of a new Broadway play to remind readers about the real-life incident upon which the drama was loosely based.

family were held hostage in their own Philadelphia-area home by three escaped convicts. A novel called *The Desperate Hours*, loosely based on the Hill family's ordeal, came out soon after. The novel was turned into a Broadway play starring Robert Montgomery. The February 1955 *Life* magazine article that became the subject of the lawsuit also reported on the then-upcoming movie version. The magazine article caused his family anguish, Hill alleged, not only because it exposed them anew to national attention for an episode of their lives that they would have preferred to put behind them but also because the article was fundamentally false. *Life* readers were led to the incorrect belief that the play was a completely factual retelling of the Hill family's experiences. As awful as the real ordeal was, Hill claimed, the *Life* account made it appear far worse. The magazine took the cast of the play, then performing in Philadelphia, to the original site of the crime. (The Hill family had since moved to Connecticut.) There they reenacted scenes from the play, captured by *Life* photographers. One such photo, labeled "Brutish Convict," pictured Hill's son being "roughed up"; a picture captioned "Daring Daughter" showed Hill's daughter biting the hand of a convict to make him drop a gun; a third photo depicted Hill himself throwing the convict's gun through a door in a "Brave Try" to rescue his family.

None of the incidents depicted in the photos ever really happened. Indeed, in an interview with the press shortly after the convicts were captured in 1952, Hill emphasized that they "had treated the family courteously, had not molested them, and had not been at all violent." Hill could not sue for libel, of course. Where is the defamation in being depicted as being a bit more heroic in an adverse situation than you really were?

BRUTISH CONVICT (George Matthews) roughs up the young son, Ralphie (Malcolm Brodrick), who shows his spunk by talking up to the criminals. The hand of another convict holds a revolver (foreground) to terrorize family

BRAVE TRY to save family fails when father (Karl Malden) has to toss out gun because son is held as hostage.

DARING DAUGHTER (Patricia Peardon) bites hand of youngest convict (George Grizzard), makes him drop gun.

Additional photos from *Time, Inc. v. Hill* that were cited by the Supreme Court as evidence that the article did imply that the Hill family's ordeal was worse than it really had been. (Nonetheless, the magazine was vindicated by dint of the newsworthiness of its subject matter.)

In overturning a lower court's award of $30,000 in compensatory damages to Hill, the Supreme Court unanimously held that false-light privacy actions involving news-worthy events cannot stand in the absence of a finding of actual malice—that is, that the defendant knew the story was false or published with reckless disregard as to its truth or falsity. By constitutionalizing the tort in this way, the Court demonstrated its concern that false-light plaintiffs not be able to circumvent too easily the First Amendment protections granted the press three years earlier in the landmark *New York Times Co. v. Sullivan* libel decision.[82]

The Supreme Court made a second false-light ruling in 1974. The case involved a Cleveland *Plain Dealer* article about the death of Melvin Cantrell, who perished along with forty-three other people when the Silver Bridge across the Ohio River at Point Pleasant, West Virginia, collapsed. A follow-up story published about eight months after the accident emphasized the "abject poverty" in which Cantrell's widow and children lived. At one point, the article says that Mrs. Cantrell "will talk neither about what happened nor about how they are doing" and that she "wears the same mask of non-expression she wore at the funeral."[83]

So, where was the falsity here? It seems that Mrs. Cantrell was not at home when the reporter and photographer came by to pursue their story. In other words, all references to what she looked like or to what she would or would not agree to talk about were, depending on one's perspective about such matters, either examples of poetic license or just plain lies. The Supreme Court thus had no difficulty ruling, in an 8-1 vote, that the original jury award of compensatory damages was a proper one.

False Light and Distortion

When text or photos appear out of context or in ways that omit key information, false-light claims sometimes result. Let us look at two early cases from California that both stemmed from publication of the same photograph. The opposite rulings in the cases are a function of the photo's being used appropriately by one publication but in a distortive manner by the other.

John Gill and his wife were photographed without their knowledge while they were "seated in an affectionate pose" at a candy and ice-cream stand in the Los Angeles Farmers' Market. In one of the two cases, the Gills sued *Harper's Bazaar* magazine, which used their photo to illustrate a whimsical article titled "And So the World Goes Round, " described by Justice Spence of the California Supreme Court as "a short commentary reaffirming the poet's conviction that the world could not revolve with-out love."[84] With respect to this use of the photo, the magazine publishers prevailed. The photo was not used in a context that would offend persons of reasonable sensibility.

---

82. *Time, Inc. v. Hill*, 385 U.S. 374 (1967).
83. *Cantrell v. Forest City Publishing Co.*, 419 U.S. 245, 248 (1974).
84. *Gill v. Hearst Publishing Co.*, 253 P.2d 441, 442 (Cal. 1953).

This photo was the common feature of the two *Gill* cases.

The very same photo also showed up in the *Ladies' Home Journal*, but this time it was part of an article whose theme was that only some kinds of love—those based on an enduring affection, rather than simply physical attraction—are desirable and praiseworthy. Associated with the Gills' photo was a caption reading, "Publicized as glamorous, desirable, 'love at first sight' is a bad risk." The article refers to this kind of love as "wrong," as "founded upon 100 percent sex attraction," and as likely to lead to divorce. The Gills claimed that the article cast them, a "happily married" couple of "high moral reputation," in a hurtfully false light. The California Supreme Court agreed, finding that this use of the photo was "seriously humiliating and disturbing" in that it calls to mind "the intimate and private relationship between the opposite sexes and marriage."[85]

In another classic case, the publishers of the *Saturday Evening Post* erred when they used a 1947 photo depicting a young girl who was lying in the street after having been almost run over by a car. The photo, which had previously run in a Birmingham, Alabama, newspaper, was used in an article about pedestrian carelessness, "They Ask

85. *Gill v. Curtis Publishing Co.*, 239 P.2d 630 (Cal. 1952).

to Be Killed," and was accompanied by the text "Safety education in schools has reduced child accidents measurably, but *unpredictable darting through traffic* still takes a sobering toll."[86] The magazine's use of the photo, even though some twenty months after the accident, was not the problem, the court explained. Instead, liability stemmed from the article's false implication that the young victim was responsible for her own duress.

Another example of distortion involved misuse of video footage by the ABC affiliate in Washington, D.C., WJLA-TV. Plaintiff Linda Duncan was one of several persons shown standing on a crowded downtown Washington street while the news anchor made reference to "the 20 million Americans who have herpes."[87] Although the damages awarded Duncan were minimal—$750 of the $2.1 million she had sought—the case does suggest an important rule for TV journalists. If the spoken text of your story deals with potentially embarrassing subjects, make sure that none of the people you might use in your "establishing shots" are recognizable. If need be, use footage of feet, not faces.

Context is clearly important in false-light cases. Use of the Gill photo was actionable when the context was distortive (almost to the point of being defamatory), but

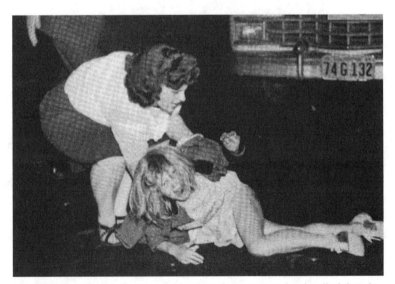

The *Saturday Evening Post* used this photo in a context that implied that the young girl, rather than the driver, was responsible for her having almost been run over.

---

86. *Leverton v. Curtis Publishing*, 192 F.2d 974 (3d Cir. 1951).

87. *Duncan v. WJLA-TV*, 10 Media L. Rep. (BNA) 1395 (D.D.C. 1984), *reh'g denied*, 1984 U.S. Dist. LEXIS 21273.

not so when used innocently. The news anchor's script was the distortive context in the WJLA-TV case. In a case involving *Baywatch* heartthrob José Solano, distortion was found not so much in a photo as in the way the photo was touted. The January 1999 issue of *Playgirl* magazine boasted a cover photo of a bare-chested Solano. In the upper left-hand corner of the cover were the words "TV Guys," accompanied by the headline "Primetime's Sexy Young Stars Exposed." The cover also promised "12 Sizzling Centerfolds Ready to Score with You." And in the cover's lower right-hand corner were the words "Baywatch's Best Body, José Solano."

Think about it: "Exposed." "Centerfold." "Best Body." Perhaps it was no surprise that Solano's false-light suit alleged that a reasonable reader of the cover would infer that a nude layout of the star could be found in that issue's pages. In fact, Solano's only appearance within the magazine was a tame quarter-page head-and-shoulders photo "showing him fully dressed in a tee shirt and sweater, alongside a brief profile of the actor." The court determined that Solano should have his day in court (that the lower court erred in granting summary judgment to *Playgirl*), because "a jury

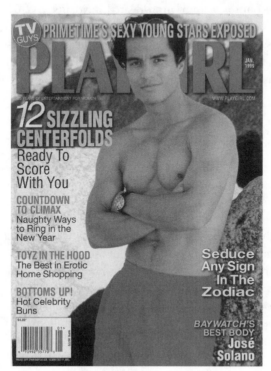

Mr. Solano alleged that this cover of *Playgirl* magazine strongly hinted that readers would find a nude layout of him inside.

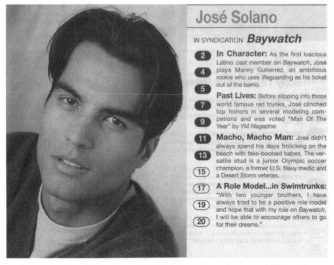

José Solano

IN SYNDICATION **Baywatch**

(2) **In Character:** As the first luscious Latino cast member on *Baywatch*, José (4) plays Manny Gutierrez, an ambitious rookie who uses lifeguarding as his ticket (5) out of the barrio.

(7) **Past Lives:** Before slipping into those world famous red trunks, José clinched top honors in several modeling com- (9) petions and was voted "Man Of The Year" by *YM Magazine*.

(11) **Macho, Macho Man:** José didn't always spend his days frolicking on the beach with fake-boobed babes. The ver- (13) satile stud is a junior Olympic soccer champion, a former U.S. Navy medic and (15) a Desert Storm veteran.

(17) **A Role Model...in Swimtrunks:** "With two younger brothers, I have (19) always tried to be a positive role model and hope that with my role on *Baywatch*, (20) I will be able to encourage others to go for their dreams."

In the context of *Solano v. Playgirl*, the magazine would have been on stronger legal footing if Mr. Solano's photo here were nude.

reasonably could conclude that the *Playgirl* cover conveyed the message that Solano was not the wholesome person he claimed to be, that he was willing to—or was 'washed up' and had to—sell himself naked to a women's sex magazine."[88]

Whether a given context is distortive is an audience-focused inquiry, of course; put another way, distortion is in the eye of the beholder. Thus, for example, a plaintiff who is the aunt and godfather to a mobster's young son could not establish false light when the mobster's autobiography included a photo of her holding young Joey at his christening. Yes, the court allowed, many of the book's other photos were of mob-related incidents. Indeed, on the very same page as the photo at issue here was another picture, this one of a Cadillac being hauled out of a Chicago sanitary canal, with a caption indicating that a decomposed body had been found in the trunk. But no reasonable reader would believe that the plaintiff's photo on this page reveals anything more than her family relationship to the book's author.[89]

False Light and Fictionalization

Another group of false-light cases result from the deliberate use of falsehood for the purpose of creating fictional accounts. TV docudramas, movies whose plots are based on real events but that take liberties with events, and historical novels have been the typical works to prompt such lawsuits.

Supermarket tabloids have a reputation for creating wholly fictional works more for the entertainment than for the edification of their readers. It is not surprising that they have frequently been defendants in libel and invasion of privacy suits. A particularly hilarious case involved the publishers of the *Sun*, which ran a completely fictitious story about one "Audrey Wiles," described as having quit her paper route—at the age of 101!—because an extramarital affair with a millionaire client on her route had left her pregnant. Since the story was a complete fabrication about a nonexistent subject—there was no Audrey Wiles—one would think that the article would have

---

88. *Solano v. Playgirl*, 292 F.3d 1078 (9th Cir. 2002).
89. *Raveling v. HarperCollins*, 33 Media L. Rep. (BNA) 1417 (7th Cir. 2005).

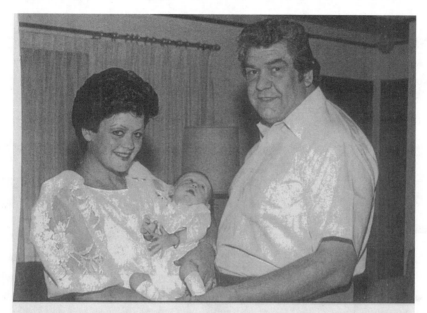

My son Joey's christening in 1983 was one of the proudest moments of my life. Here, my sister-in-law, Gail Barone, cradles him in her arms while Joey's godfather, Sal Bastone, beams into

The woman holding the child—correctly identified as the mobster-author's sister-in-law—could not maintain a false-light invasion of privacy suit, because reasonable readers would understand that one can be related to the mob without being a mobster.

resulted in nothing more than a few chuckles. The newspaper, however, made the mistake of illustrating the story with photographs of the very real Nellie Mitchell, who was herself just a few years shy of the century mark and who was well known in Baxter County, Arkansas, as the operator of a local newsstand who did indeed deliver papers. The newspaper apparently obtained the photos from its own files, having been one of many media outlets that had done a factual account of Mitchell's longevity and industriousness some ten years earlier. Although Mitchell's libel claim against the newspaper was rejected by the jury, she prevailed in her false-light privacy suit. Refusing to overturn the jury's finding, the court emphasized that readers who looked only at the cover page of the newspaper would not necessarily realize that the story to be found inside was complete fiction. Moreover, the court held, the newspaper could not avoid liability by dint of the implausibility of the facts asserted in the story.[90]

---

90. *People's Bank and Trust Company of Mountain Home v. Globe International*, 978 F.2d 1065 (8th. Cir. 1992).

THINGS TO REMEMBER

False Light

- The false-light tort is similar to libel, except that the remarks that cast the plaintiff in a false light need not be defamatory; they can simply be embarrassing (and false).
- In 1967, the Supreme Court ruled that false-light plaintiffs who sue over stories on a matter of public interest must prove actual malice, just as if they had sued for libel.
- Falsity often results from the distortive use of photos or from purposive fictionalization (as in docudramas).

Privacy in Only One of Four Torts?

The first three torts discussed in this chapter add very little to the body of law that existed before the famous Warren and Brandeis article encouraged the judiciary to respect privacy as an independent tort claim. We have already seen how closely intertwined the intrusion tort is to ordinary trespass. Whereas we traditionally think of trespasses as unauthorized presence on another's property, intrusions are more akin to stalking in that they intrude on a personal bubble of privacy that travels with the possessor.

The misappropriation tort also adds very little to the law not already present in statutory and common-law copyright protections. Copyright is discussed in the next chapter. For now, suffice it to say that copyright is designed to protect an artist or writer's finished product (a book, a play, choreographic notations, etc.). At first blush, it would thus seem that the misappropriation tort is conceptually distinct from copyright, in that the former protects us from the unauthorized use of our "name or likeness," of our identity. We do not usually think of our name or our identity as finished products, as things we have created. Consider, though, that the most typical misappropriation cases involve celebrity plaintiffs who have worked hard to instill a commercial value to their name or likeness. What they seek to protect with this kind of misappropriation suit is thus every bit as much a "product" of the celebrity's sweat equity as is the artist's painting or the author's monograph.

Chapter 6 also discusses trademark law. For purposes of the present discussion, we need only know that **trademarks** are designed to protect consumers from confusion, to ensure that the products they purchase are indeed what they believe them to be, manufactured by the company they believe to be the producer. Recall, however, that misappropriation plaintiffs often argue that consumers will be confused, that they will mistakenly believe that a celebrity has lent his or her name to a product. Again, the tort adds little to the law that was not there before.

False-light invasion-of-privacy suits have frequently been maligned as attempted end runs around the constitutional protections accorded to libel defendants. As one commentator points out, "courts waste judicial resources untangling genuine claims of defamation from duplicative false light claims."[91] The Supreme Court, of course, expressed its own skepticism about false light when, in *Time, Inc. v. Hill*, it applied the *New York Times Co. v. Sullivan* "actual malice" rule to false-light suits whenever the revelation prompting the suit is a newsworthy one.[92]

Less a Legal Than an Ethical Issue?

Public disclosure, then, is the only one of the four torts that truly adds anything new to the law. The remainder of this chapter is devoted to an explication of that tort. While it is important for communications professionals to understand the nature of the tort, it should be admitted at the outset that plaintiffs rarely win these suits. Writing in the early 1980s, Professor Diane Zimmerman reported that her exhaustive search of the literature uncovered only eighteen successful public-disclosure suits since the tort's birth in the beginning of the twentieth century. Several of these suits were reports of defendants' unsuccessful motions for summary judgment; such defendants may have ultimately prevailed at a trial unreported in the literature.[93] A few years later, a detailed statistical analysis of libel and privacy suits revealed that mass media defendants ultimately won public-disclosure suits more than 97 percent of the time.[94] Successful public-disclosure suits have likely become even less frequent in that both surveys reported data that predate an important Supreme Court decision, *Florida Star v. B. J. F.*, which is discussed later in this chapter.

As we review the structure and history of the public-disclosure tort, you may want to consider the ethical, not just the legal, questions posed by the case law. If we ask only if we *may* publish truths that will embarrass the subject of our disclosures, the answer is almost always yes. The more interesting question is almost always going to be, *should* we publish?

As I was preparing this edition of the textbook, I experienced my own ethical dilemma concerning privacy invasions. There was a California court case in 2001 stemming from a *Sports Illustrated* exposé of high school sports coaches with police records as pedophiles.[95] This cover story included a photo of a Little League baseball team, and the article made it clear that the coach had molested five of the eight players pictured. From a purely pedagogic perspective, this would have been a wonderful

---

91. Susan Hallender, "A Call for the End of the False Light Invasion of Privacy Action as It Relates to Docudramas," 15 *Seton Hall Journal of Sports and Entertainment Law* 275 (2005).

92. *Time, Inc. v. Hill*, 385 U.S. 374 (1967).

93. Diane L. Zimmerman, "Requiem for a Heavyweight: A Farewell to Warren and Brandeis's Privacy Tort," 68 *Cornell Law Review* 291, 293 n.5 (1983).

94. Randall Bezanson, Gilbert Cranberg, and John Soloski, *Libel Law and the Press: Myth and Reality* (New York: The Free Press, 1987), 116.

95. *M. G. v. Time Warner*, 107 Cal. Rptr. 2d 504 (Ct. App. 2001).

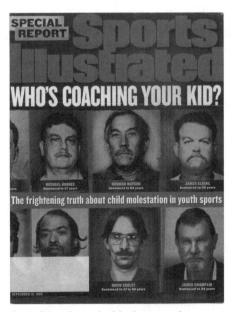

One of the photos inside the magazine—part of this cover story—depicts the Little League team where one of these coaches worked. Do you agree with our decision not to reprint that photo here?

photo to reprint in this chapter, indeed to begin the chapter. After all, the case is a perfect springboard to talk about the difference between false-light and public-disclosure privacy claims, as well as the relationship between privacy and libel. The five students who had been molested would have a "public disclosure" suit against the magazine because their outrage was caused by the *true* revelation of their victimhood. For the remaining Little Leaguers in the photo, the cause of action would instead be "false light," in that the photo *falsely* implied that they too had been victims. For none of the pictured youngsters would there be a viable defamation claim, since to be thought of (even falsely) as a crime victim is not libel; it does not diminish one's reputation.

Yes, it would have been a great photo to reprint here, and despite the fact that the California court told the plaintiffs their suit against Time Warner could go forward, my own educational use of the photo here would be protected both from invasion of privacy and copyright-infringement claims (for the latter, see the discussion of fair use in chapter 6). But for obvious reasons, I could not bring myself to do it. The incidents of sexual abuse discussed in the magazine article were only a few years old, and the victims (and their teammates) are now young adults, no doubt trying to move on from this terrible memory. I suppose the argument could be made that the damage has already been done. Many more thousands of people have already seen the photo in *Sports Illustrated* than would ever see it in this textbook, and that same photo was used in a later HBO special, which was likely seen by over a million people. Yet there was that gnawing feeling that I should not be adding to the plaintiffs' grief or making the readers of this textbook even symbolic accomplices in the prolonging of that discomfort.

Public Disclosure

In April 1992, tennis star Arthur Ashe held a news conference to reveal that he had AIDS. The immediate impetus for Ashe's decision to go public with information that had previously been known only to his wife and a small number of close friends was the fact that *USA Today*'s editors had heard rumors of his illness and had confronted him about those rumors. Suppose Ashe had not decided to preempt the paper's scoop, that he instead implored the media to keep his secret, a request that surely would not have been uniformly honored. Suppose further that he had brought a public-disclosure suit against any and all media outlets that chose to reveal this highly intimate information. Such a suit, as will soon become apparent, would almost certainly have failed.

Although the public-disclosure tort is not recognized in all American jurisdictions, those that do recognize it generally agree on its elements. A plaintiff must prove that

- the defendant publicly disclosed information about the plaintiff;
- the information was private (i.e., previously unknown to others);
- the disclosure would be highly offensive to a reasonable person; and
- the information is not newsworthy.

Let us examine each element in turn.

Publicly Disclosing Information

Unlike in defamation law, where all that is required is for one third party to hear the libelous statement, here the private facts must be made available to a wide audience to be actionable. "Wide" does not necessarily mean millions, however, and the mass media are not the only potential defendants in such cases. Employers who reveal intimate details of an employee's life to her coworkers, for example, have sometimes been found liable for damages under this tort. For example, a former town marshal in Winthrop, Washington, was permitted to sue the town for revealing that the reason for his termination was his epilepsy.[96] Or consider the case of *Boyles v. Kerr*, in which a teenager and several of his friends set up a hidden video camera to tape him having sex with his girlfriend.[97] Her suit against the amateur videographers succeeded, even though they had apparently shown the tape to fewer than a dozen others.

Information That Was Previously *Private*

One cannot be held accountable for violating another's privacy if what is revealed was already widely known or readily available to all who wished to see. An often-cited case for this point is *Neff v. Time, Inc.*, in which a particularly enthusiastic Pittsburgh Steelers fan was upset enough about a *Sports Illustrated* photo narrative about him to bring suit against the magazine's publisher.[98] Neff and several other fans were, in the court's words, "jumping up and down in full view of the fans in the stadium" and

---

96. *White v. Town of Winthrop*, 116 P.3d 1034 (Wash. Ct. App. 2005).
97. 806 S.W.2d 255 (Tex. Ct. App. 1991).
98. 406 F. Supp. 858 (W.D. Pa. 1976).

Plaintiff Neff could not recover for invasion of privacy resulting from publication of this photo, because his conduct was recorded in a highly public place, which means that his wild expression and undone trouser fly were not truly private.

"waving Steeler banners and drinking beer." They also seemed to be "slightly inebriated," "screaming and howling" and "hamming it up" for the photographer. Neff apparently did not realize that his trouser fly was completely open—not to the point "of being revealing," but enough for the court to charge the magazine's editors, who selected for publication that one particular photo from among thousands available to them, with "utmost bad taste." Neff could not recover damages, the court concluded, because he "was photographed in a public place for a newsworthy article."

More recently, the Tenth Circuit Court of Appeals held that there could be no invasion of privacy in even the unauthorized taking and publishing of an open-casket photo at the funeral of a young man who was killed in Iraq. The deceased was the first member of the Oklahoma National Guard to be killed in action since the Korean War; as such his funeral was deemed a highly newsworthy event, with over 1,200 in attendance, including the state's governor. The photo was published in *Harper's Magazine* and in the French magazine *Le Monde 2*, even though the deceased parent's had given clear instructions to the funeral director that the press were not to take pictures of the open casket.[99]

Another unsuccessful privacy plaintiff was Oliver Sipple, who achieved a degree of fame in the autumn of 1975, when President Ford was visiting San Francisco. Sipple foiled Sara Jane Moore's attempt to shoot Ford by grabbing her arm and deflecting the shot. As one can imagine, the national news media were abuzz with the

99. *Showler v. Harper's Magazine Foundation*, 2007 U.S. App. LEXIS 7025 (10th Cir. 2007).

story. When newspapers in San Francisco and elsewhere reported that Sipple happened to be gay—the first time most of his family learned of his sexual orientation—he took umbrage and sued. His invasion-of-privacy claims failed, at least in part because what was revealed about him was not deemed sufficiently *private* to meet the tort's demands.[100] He was well known within the gay community, the court pointed out, having participated in numerous gay pride parades and even having developed a friendship with openly gay San Francisco Board of Supervisors member Harvey Milk.[101]

Sipple's sexual orientation was known to many people, even if not to his family. Other court decisions have emphasized the other side of the coin, that a plaintiff's having revealed his secrets to a select group of close ones will not alone defeat an invasion-of-privacy suit. Consider the case of *Multimedia WMAZ, Inc. v. Kubach.*[102] A Georgia television station invited Kubach, who had AIDS, to discuss his disease on a live call-in show, promising him that his face would be sufficiently disguised through computer digitization so as to be unrecognizable. For at least the first seven seconds of the broadcast, however, the digitization was faulty and Kubach was easily identifiable to the entire Macon, Georgia, audience. When Kubach brought suit against the station, the station argued that the information revealed about him was not truly private, because he had shared the fact of his illness with family members, friends, medical personnel, and members of his AIDS support group, likely as many as sixty people in all. The court rejected this argument, emphasizing that even such a relatively large number of confidants pales in comparison to "the entire television viewing public."

Some courts have had a slightly different take on the requirement that the facts revealed be *private*. Instead of focusing on how readily available the information was prior to the offensive disclosure, these courts concentrate on the nature of the information itself. For example, Minnesota gubernatorial candidate Jon Grunseth, whose high-level lobbying position frequently brought him to Washington, D.C., sued a Marriott hotel there for releasing to Minnesota newspapers a copy of a receipt that helped the media corroborate an allegation of a longtime affair he had apparently conducted with a Washington-area woman. Although the ruling against him was ultimately based on his having failed to file suit before the statute of limitations had run out, the court volunteered that his invasion-of-privacy suit could not have succeeded anyway. The receipt at issue did not contain "private facts," the court pointed out. "The only facts the hotel receipt can be said to show," Judge Kessler wrote, "are that Plaintiff arrived at the J. W. Marriott on July 12, 1989, departed on July 13, 1989, made three long distance and four local calls (with no indication of to whom), placed

---

100. The court also emphasized the newsworthiness of Sipple's sexual orientation, especially in that President Ford apparently had not made any effort to express his gratitude toward the man. Whether the president was thus manifesting some kind of antihomosexual bias was deemed by the court an important question worth pursuing.

101. *Sipple v. Chronicle Publishing Co.*, 201 Cal. Rptr. 665 (Ct. App. 1984).

102. 443 S.E.2d 491 (Ga. Ct. App. 1994).

Invasion-of-privacy suits brought by Oliver Sipple, shown here foiling President Ford's would-be assassin (indicated by the black arrow), were unsuccessful because his status as a homosexual was not deemed truly private. Note that the woman most clearly depicted in the foreground is not the would-be assassin. © 1975, AP Photo/*San Francisco Examiner*, Gordon Stone. Reprinted with permission.

a modestly priced order with room service, ordered a movie, and made a purchase from the refreshment center."[103]

Highly Offensive Revelations

The public-disclosure tort also requires that the private information revealed be of a kind that would be found highly offensive by reasonable people. Consider the text of a *Time* magazine article from March 13, 1939, which resulted in one of the most often-cited invasion-of-privacy suits:

STARVING GLUTTON

One night last week pretty Mrs. Dorothy Barber of Kansas City grabbed a candy bar, packed up some clothes, and walked to General Hospital. "I want to stay here," she said between bites. "I want to eat all the time. I can finish a normal meal and be back in the kitchen in ten minutes, eating again."

103. *Grunseth v. Marriott Corp.*, 872 F. Supp. 1069, 1075–1076 (D.D.C. 1995), *aff'd*, 79 F.3d 169 (D.C. Cir. 1996).

Dr. R. K. Simpson immediately packed her off to a ward, ordered a big meal from the hospital kitchen while he questioned Mrs. Barber. He found that although she had eaten enough in the past year to feed a family of ten, she had lost 25 pounds. After a preliminary examination Dr. Simpson thought that Mrs. Barber's pancreas might be functioning abnormally, that it might be burning up too much sugar in her blood and somehow causing an excessive flow of digestive juices, which sharpened her appetite.

While he made painstaking laboratory tests and discussed the advisability of a rare operation, Mrs. Barber lay in bed and ate.[104]

Accompanying the brief article was a photo of Mrs. Dorothy Barber in bed in a long-sleeved hospital gown, a close-up picture showing only her face, head, and arms, with the bedclothes over her chest. The caption read, "Insatiable Eater Barber— She Eats for Ten." The Missouri Supreme Court, while allowing the need to educate the public about even unusual medical conditions, noted that medical textbooks typically preserve the anonymity of the afflicted persons depicted within. "If there is any right of privacy at all, it should include the right to obtain medical treatment at home or in a hospital for an individual personal condition (at least if it is not contagious or dangerous to others) without personal publicity."

In another early and often-cited case, an Alabama newspaper ran on its front page an embarrassing photo of Flora Bell Graham, who, while attending the Cullman County Fair, accompanied her children to the "Fun House." As she was leaving the building, her dress was blown up by air jets and "her body was exposed from the waist down, with the exception of that portion covered by her panties." It was at that moment that the paper's photographer snapped the shot, unbeknownst to Graham. In ruling for the plaintiff, the court engaged in what we would likely today think of as a bit of rhetorical excess. "Not only was this photograph embarrassing to one of normal sensibilities," Justice Harwood wrote for the Alabama Supreme Court, "we think it could properly be classified as obscene, in that obscene means 'offensive to

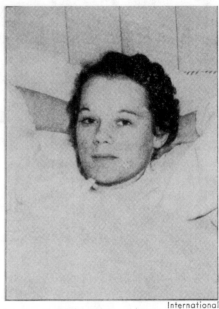

International

Insatiable-Eater Barber
She eats for ten.

Although Mrs. Barber's successful suit against *Time* magazine was based on the public-disclosure tort, it certainly had strong "intrusion" elements, in that we usually think of our hospital room as a very private place.

---

104. *Barber v. Time, Inc.*, 159 S.W.2d 291, 292 (Mo. 1942).

modesty or decency' or expressing to the mind or view something which delicacy, purity, or decency forbid to be expressed."[105]

Another case frequently cited in support of the principle that unconscionable intrusions into individuals' privacy should be restrained concerned Frederick Wiseman's documentary *Titicut Follies*.[106] The film depicted conditions in the Massachusetts Correctional Institution at Bridgewater, which housed "insane persons charged with crime, and defective delinquents." As a result of the suit, for many years showings of the film were restricted to audiences of mental health and similar

The documentary *Titicut Follies* was subject to a restrictive order for many years, in deference to the privacy interests of the mental patients.

professionals. Only in recent years, largely owing to most of the patients having passed away, has the film been made available for general release. Although the restrictions were apparently based on fear that the film would subject the inmates to intense humiliation, several commentators suggested that the real impetus behind the suit was government officials' fear that the unconscionable conditions at Bridgewater would be exposed to public view.

Graham and *Barber* are rather old cases, and the *Titicut Follies* case is open to conflicting interpretations. They may be more historic anomalies than anything else— given the influence on women's fashion of such stars as Madonna and Britney Spears, can we really imagine a contemporary court referring to a photo like the one of Graham as "obscene"? Nowadays, even when publication of private information is deemed "offensive," courts rarely impose liability, a fact due in large part to the impact of the tort's final element—a lack of newsworthiness.

Newsworthiness: Has the Defense Swallowed the Tort?

Newsworthiness is often referred to somewhat inaccurately as a defense to public-disclosure suits. But this statement misplaces the burden of proof. In actuality, the burden is on the plaintiff to demonstrate that the offensive revelations of private information are *not* newsworthy, are *not* of public concern. In any event, it is clear that

105. *Daily Times Democrat v. Graham*, 162 So. 2d 474, 477 (Ala. 1964).
106. *Commonwealth of Massachusetts v. Wiseman*, 249 N.E.2d 610 (Mass. 1969), *cert. denied*, 398 U.S. 960 (1970).

courts have made it very difficult indeed for plaintiffs to establish that revelations of embarrassing truths about them lack newsworthiness.

One of the leading cases on this point concerned young William Sidis, who might be described as the "Doogie Howser" of his day, although his field of endeavor was mathematics rather than medicine. At the age of eleven, Sidis lectured to distinguished mathematicians on the subject of four-dimensional bodies. When he was sixteen, he graduated from Harvard College, amid considerable public attention. Then Sidis dropped out of public sight for many years and became something of a recluse, at least until the *New Yorker* found him.

The magazine often included within its pages a feature called "Where Are They Now?" which, as its name implies, sought to bring readers up-to-date on the once famous. The article's subtitle, "April Fool," neatly encapsulates what the Second Circuit Court of Appeals saw as the piece's condescending and abusive tone toward Mr. Sidis. The magazine focused on the "bizarre ways" in which Sidis's genius was manifested, such as his penchant for collecting streetcar transfers.

Although the court concluded that the essay was "merciless in its dissection of intimate details of its subject's personal life," Sidis's privacy claim was rejected. There are times, Judge Swan wrote, when "the public interest in obtaining information becomes dominant over the individual's desire for privacy."[107] This was surely such a case, the court concluded, in that the *New Yorker* piece had at least the potential for answering a very important question: whether Sidis had lived up to his earlier promise. The answer to that question cannot help but have implications for public policy. After all, how better to determine if society's treatment of child prodigies is for the good than to examine the lives of such persons when they are no longer children?

Just to give a sense of how felicitous courts have been to claims of newsworthiness in recent years, consider Carl DeGregorio's unsuccessful invasion of privacy suit against CBS. The plaintiff, a construction worker, was upset at the station's having included in a story on "Romance in New York" video footage of him walking hand in hand with an unmarried female coworker. The court surmised that "the perceived novelty of these two hard hats walking in romantic linkage apparently triggered the camera crew's interest." Ever the gentleman, DeGregorio pleaded with the CBS crew to not run the footage. "It would not look good," he pleaded, because he was married and the young woman was herself engaged to be married. His plea was not heeded, thus his suit for invasion of privacy. In dismissing the claims against the TV network, the court interpreted "newsworthiness" as broad enough to include "an exploration of prevailing attitudes towards [romance]."[108]

Does newsworthiness wear off over time? Do persons whose fame has faded have

---

107. *Sidis v. F-R Publications*, 113 F.2d 806 (2d Cir. 1940). Interestingly, the author of the *New Yorker* essay retained a bit of privacy himself. The interviewer was noted humorist James Thurber, writing under the pseudonym Jared Manley.

108. *DeGregorio v. CBS, Inc.*, 473 N.Y.S.2d 922 (Sup. Ct. 1984).

a right to live in relative anonymity? Although the *Sidis* case seems to stand for the principle "once newsworthy, always newsworthy," courts have sometimes been deferential to plaintiffs trying to turn over a new leaf and start anew, to forget and have their neighbors not learn of embarrassing features of their past.

A leading case had been *Briscoe v. Reader's Digest Association*, which involved the magazine's story about the crime of truck hijacking, a small part of which reminded readers of Briscoe's conviction years before for this offense.[109] The California Supreme Court ruled for Briscoe, emphasizing that he had "abandoned his life of shame and become entirely rehabilitated and has thereafter at all times lived an exemplary, virtuous and honorable life," that he had "assumed a place in respectable society and made many friends who were not aware of the incident in his earlier life." But *Briscoe* was expressly overruled by the California Supreme Court in 2005, in a case holding that the media can never be liable for publishing true but embarrassing revelations about a plaintiff's long-ago criminal activity, at least if the media obtain their facts from official documents. At issue was an episode of the Discovery Channel's documentary series *The Prosecutors*, which aired in 2001 and recalled the facts of a hired-gun homicide from thirteen years earlier, for which plaintiff Steven Gates was charged as a coconspirator.[110] The court held that relevant U.S. Supreme Court privacy decisions had undermined the logic underpinning the much earlier *Briscoe* decision. California has not been alone in its rejection of liability for accurate reporting, based on government records, of a plaintiff's long-ago embarrassments.[111]

Professor Diane Zimmerman reports that *Briscoe* and cases like it are indeed historic artifacts, and she is pleased by this turn of events. "It is difficult to imagine how the passage of time could constitute a serious consideration in determining newsworthiness," she argues. "Such a standard would make the exploration of modern history a hazardous enterprise."[112]

The media have little to fear from public-disclosure suits these days, Zimmerman argues, because, more often than not, courts asked to adjudicate the issue of newsworthiness have come to embrace a model that she calls "leave it to the press." The familiar and enduring masthead of the *New York Times* boasts that readers will find within "all the news that's fit to print." Courts that are called on to adjudicate the media's newsworthiness defense in public-disclosure suits seem to take these words to heart, ruling in perhaps circular fashion that if a subject matter has appeared in the news media, it must be news—that is, it must be news*worthy*. Zimmerman sees this view as only appropriate. The press "has a better mechanism for testing newsworthiness than do the courts;" she argues, in that media outlets' economic survival "depends upon their ability to provide a product that the public will buy."

109. 483 P.2d 34 (1971).

110. *Gates v. Discovery Communications*, 101 P.3d 552 (Cal. 2004).

111. See, for example, *Uranga v. Federated Publications, Inc.*, 67 P.3d 29 (Idaho 2003) (unearthing of a public record from over forty years ago not a violation of privacy).

112. Zimmerman, "Requiem for a Heavyweight," *supra* note 93.

There are at least two more reasons why public-disclosure cases have become all but unwinnable. The first requires us to recognize that the law has not always treated the elements of the tort as independent; rather, they sometimes are allowed to flow together. Thus, a court's adjudication of the newsworthiness issue often leads it to make conclusions about other elements, such as whether revelations were truly private or whether they were highly offensive.

It is hard to imagine a category of revelation both more private and more highly offensive than allegations of childhood sexual abuse. In a case decided in the early 1990s by a federal district court in Pennsylvania, the offensiveness of the revelations was further compounded by the fact that the mother and daughter who had accused the father were promised falsely by the media that their names would not be used and that their silhouetted picture would be unrecognizable. Their invasion-of-privacy suit was unsuccessful because the court found that the story was highly newsworthy, especially given that the accused was a former police chief. For a court to rule in favor of the media in such a case is hardly remarkable. What is puzzling, however, is that the court allowed the newsworthiness of the information to compel the conclusions that the revelations were neither private information nor highly offensive ("except in the abstract," the court allowed).[113]

A second reason that it might be time to bury the public-disclosure tort is that the Supreme Court has weighed in on the issue of the tort's constitutionality. Although the Court has stopped short of immunizing the press for reports of the truth, it has come mighty close to doing just that.

The Supreme Court and the Public-Disclosure Tort

No suit for public disclosure has ever withstood U.S. Supreme Court scrutiny. Although there only have been two such cases, a careful reading of them provides further support for the principle that the public-disclosure tort has been virtually removed from the law.

Both cases involved press reports of rape that included the victim's name. In *Cox Broadcasting Corp. v. Cohn*, WSB-TV in Georgia reported the name of the victim of a vicious gang rape and homicide, information its reporter had obtained from the official indictment provided to him by the clerk of the court.[114] The deceased's father then brought a privacy suit against the owner of the broadcast station.

The Court declined in *Cox Broadcasting* to rule on the central question—"whether truthful publications may *ever* be subjected to civil or criminal liability consistently with the First Amendment" (emphasis added)—instead emphasizing the specific facts of the case to produce a narrow holding. Cohn may not prevail, the Court held, but

---

113. *Morgan by and through Chambon v. Celender,* 780 F. Supp. 307, 310 (W.D. Pa. 1992).
114. 420 U.S. 469 (1975).

THINGS TO REMEMBER

Public Disclosure

- Public disclosure is the only one of the four privacy torts that really added anything new to the law.
- The tort consists of four elements:
  - Information is published.
  - That information was previously private.
  - The revelation offends public sensibilities.
  - The revelation is not newsworthy.
- In recent years, the "newsworthiness defense" seems to have swallowed the tort.
- It is virtually impossible for public-disclosure plaintiffs to prevail against the media.

only because the broadcaster obtained the private information from a governmental source.

Florida Star v. B. J. F. also involved the reporting of a rape victim's name, but there were two important differences between the facts here and in the earlier *Cox Broadcasting* case.[115] First, the rape victim was still alive (and her rapist still at large). Indeed, as a result of the publication from which the suit flowed, the rapist phoned the victim's mother, threatening to attack her again. Second, although here too the media obtained the victim's name from a governmental source, the reporter clearly was on notice from the outset that the information was given to him by mistake. To be sure, BJF's name was included in the sheriff department's incident report, but prominently displayed in the same courtroom where that paper was distributed to reporters was a sign reminding the media that Florida law prohibited publication of the names of sex-crime victims.

Here, as in *Cox Broadcasting*, the Court makes clear that it does not intend to close the door on the possibility that a future public-disclosure plaintiff might prevail against the press for its reporting of admittedly true information. "Our cases have carefully eschewed reaching [the] ultimate question" of whether "truthful publication may [ever] be punished consistent with the First Amendment," the majority further cautioned. The Court came rather close to reaching that ultimate question, however. Whereas it could simply have followed *Cox Broadcasting* to rest its holding on the basis that the *Florida Star* reporter had obtained the victim's name from a governmental source, it chose not to do so. The earlier case was different, the Court tells us, in that a trial was under way in that case, thus tipping the First Amendment scales in favor of the public's right to observe the judicial process. Here, there was only a police report; a trial had not begun, a suspect had not yet even been identified. The Court held instead that the *Florida Star*'s story could not be sanctioned because the victim's

---

115. 491 U.S. 524 (1989).

name was "lawfully obtained." Although the Court later suggests that even truthful, lawfully obtained information might be the impetus for a successful public-disclosure suit, it emphasizes even here that the state would need to be furthering a "narrowly tailored" interest of "the highest order." If helping to protect the life of a rape victim whose assailant has not yet been apprehended does not constitute such a compelling state's interest, one wonders if anything possibly could.

Chapter Summary

The law of privacy is a relative newcomer to the United States, owing much of its birth to an 1890 law review article. Generally, states now recognize at least some of four distinct privacy torts: appropriation, intrusion, false light, and public disclosure.

Appropriation means the exploiting of another person's name or likeness for commercial gain. Suits can be prompted by the use of models chosen to look like or sound like a celebrity. Uses that can plausibly be considered political speech rarely result in liability. Further, the media have virtual carte blanche to exploit commercially images that they have previously used in a legitimate news context.

The intrusion tort does not necessarily involve publication at all. The offense occurs at the news-gathering stage, as in stalking a news subject or otherwise intruding relentlessly into his or her personal space. News media have been put on alert by a number of recent decisions that if they cooperate too closely with law enforcement officials in the live coverage of the execution of search warrants or police raids, they might be sued along with the government for violation of the subject's civil rights.

False-light actions are similar to libel claims except that the publication need only be embarrassing; it need not be defamatory. When suing over revelations of matters of public concern, false-light plaintiffs must prove actual malice.

Appropriation is very similar to copyright and trademark infringements. Intrusion is an offshoot of trespass law. False-light suits are often thought of as attempts to circumvent the constitutional protections offered to libel defendants. In that sense, public disclosure, which makes actionable the reporting of true but embarrassing, previously private, non-newsworthy facts, is the only one of the four torts that adds much to the law. Since at least the early 1990s, in large part because the courts embrace the newsworthiness defense so wholeheartedly, public-disclosure plaintiffs almost never prevail against the media.

Chapter 6

COPYRIGHT AND TRADEMARK

A n old folk song in the labor movement asks, "Which side are you on?" From this vantage point, the subject matter of the current chapter is unique. Professional communicators—journalists, film producers, novelists, musicians, or more likely, their production companies or similar agents—are just as likely to be plaintiffs as defendants in copyright-infringement suits (and to a lesser extent, in trademark litigation as well). Authors are sued by other authors,[1] musicians by other musicians,[2] and film producers by playwrights[3] or novelists[4] who claim the basis for today's blockbuster was really their lesser known but equally worthy work.

Consider also how conflicted most universities feel about their own role in this area of law. On the one hand, institutions of higher learning will embrace the rights of their faculty who write books and other creative works that qualify for copyright protection. University libraries, however, also argue strenuously for the right to make

---

1. See, e.g., *SunTrust Bank v. Houghton Mifflin*, 268 F.3d 1257 (11th Cir. 2001) (holding that *The Wind Done Gone*, while similar to *Gone With the Wind* in many respects, was a parody and thus not a copyright violation); *Brown v. Perdue*, 76 U.S.P.Q.2d (BNA) 1012 (S.D.N.Y. 2005) (dismissing suit by author of *Daughter of God* against author of *The Da Vinci Code*).

2. See, e.g., *Jorgensen v. Sony Music Entertainment*, 167 Fed. Appx. 427 (2d Cir. 2005) (dismissing suit claiming that "My Heart Will Go On" of *Titanic* fame was a rip-off of the much lesser-known song "Long Lost Lover").

3. *Hudson v. Imagine Entertainment Corp.*, 2004 U.S. Dist. LEXIS 11508 (E.D.N.Y. 2004), *aff'd*, 128 Fed. Appx. 178 (2d Cir. 2005) (holding that the film *Life* was not an infringement of the script to the play *No Harm, No Foul*).

4. *Beal v. Paramount Pictures*, 20 F.3d 454 (11th Cir. 1994) (holding that the Eddie Murphy movie *Coming to America* was not a copyright infringement on the novel *The Arab Heart*). Steven Spielberg's film *Amistad* was also the subject of a lawsuit by novelist Barbara Chase-Riboud, ultimately dropped by the plaintiff.

photocopies for scholarly use of book chapters or journal articles without seeking the permission of or feeling the need to reimburse those authors.[5]

Article I, Section 8 of the Constitution tells Congress that it may create laws to protect "for limited times to authors and inventors the exclusive right to their respective writings and discoveries." The body of law designed to protect inventors is patent law. Most patents remain in force for seventeen years, although patents issued after 1995 last for twenty years. To be sure, there are occasional patent disputes surrounding communication technologies. For example, in 2005 we learned that our TiVo digital recording systems were not a violation of a similar unit patented by a company called Pause Technology.[6] But since patent law can cover just about any technology—including the proverbial "better mousetrap"—it is generally beyond the scope of this book.

The two other areas of law that stem from the Article I, Section 8 excerpt cited in the previous paragraph are copyright and trademark. Copyright protects a creative work itself, such as a book, movie, play, photograph, or song. Trademark is designed to protect the slogans, logos, and trade names used by companies to identify their products to avoid consumer confusion. If you think you are buying a pair of Nike sneakers, you would be very upset if your purchase was not in fact manufactured by that particular company. Although the two bodies of law protect different things, the philosophy behind them is remarkably similar. Both copyright and trademark are designed to protect the interests of the public itself, although the immediate beneficiary may be an individual artist or corporation. In the case of copyright, protection of the financial interests of authors and other creative artists exists to encourage them to produce so that we all can enjoy the fruits of their labors. Trademark also creates a financial incentive for businesses to create worthwhile goods and services. Such companies want the public to have pleasant mental associations with their brand names and logos. Again, a body of law designed in the end to benefit the public at large does its work by giving financial incentives to others who will then create things we will want to consume.

There was no copyright infringement in the use of the Three Stooges' film in the background in this scene from *The Long Kiss Goodnight,* because the copyright to the Stooges' film had already expired.

---

5. Kenneth D. Crews, *Copyright, Fair Use, and the Challenge for Universities* (Chicago: University of Chicago Press, 1993).

6. *Pause Technology v. TiVo,* 419 F.3d 1326 (Fed. Cir. 2005).

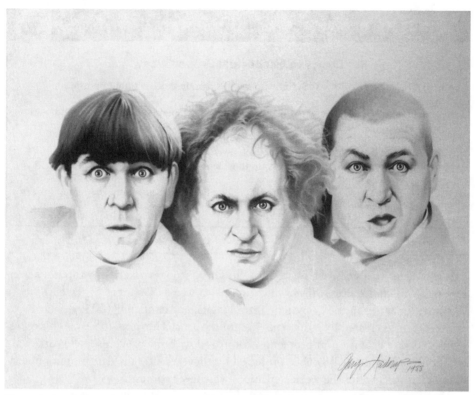

The artist here was liable for damages because he had taken the Three Stooges' trademarked image; their likeness does not expire in the same way that copyrights on their movies do.

One key difference between the two bodies of law is that copyright protection lasts for a fixed period of time, whereas trademark protection can continue as long as a company is in the business of marketing the products identified by a particular trademark (and as long it renews the trademark every ten years). The distinction was crucial in a court decision from 2000 involving the Three Stooges. The company that owns the rights to market the Three Stooges sued the producers of *The Long Kiss Goodnight*, a popular film that used, without permission, a thirty-second segment of the Three Stooges' film *Disorder in the Court* as the background for one scene. The court ruled for the defendant because the copyright on the Three Stooges' film had long since expired. The court opinion indicates, however, that a different case would have been presented—one involving trademark rather than copyright—had the defendant instead been in the business of selling T-shirts with pictures of Moe, Larry, and Curly on them.[7] Indeed, the very next year the California Supreme Court upheld

---

7. *Comedy III Productions, Inc. v. New Line Cinema*, 200 F.3d 593, 596 (9th Cir. 2000).

THINGS TO REMEMBER

Basics of Intellectual Property Law

- Article I, Section 8 of the U.S. Constitution gives Congress the right to protect intellectual property.
- The three main branches of intellectual property law are patent, trademark, and copyright:
  - Patent protects functional devices and is beyond the scope of this book.
  - Copyright protects creative works such as writing, music, and art.
  - Trademark protects trade names, slogans, logos, and other images used to identify a company's goods.
- Copyrights for new works last for the life of the author, plus seventy years; trademarks can last as long as they are used in commerce.

damages against an artist who had used the Three Stooges' likeness without authorization for his charcoal drawings, which were also sold as T-shirts.[8]

Under the terms of the Copyright Term Extension Act of 1998 (CTEA), new copyrights for works created by individuals last for the artist's life plus 70 years. This represents a 20-year extension in protection compared with the previous law. Works with corporate authorship will now be protected for 95 years after the date of first publication, or 120 years after the work's creation, whichever comes first.

The new copyright act provided a measure of retroactivity in that works already created and otherwise due to enter the public domain will also enjoy a twenty-year extension in protection. This latter provision seemed to some constitutionally suspect. After all, Article I, Section 8 tells Congress that it may enact copyright laws "to promote" the creation of artistic and literary works. Retroactive extensions of a copyright's term promote nothing, the argument goes, because the affected works are already in existence. How can I encourage you to do something you have already done? Also, it was argued that Congress's practice of extending the duration of copyright again and again, to the point of preventing any relatively recent works from entering the public domain, was at odds with Article I, Section 8's admonition that the monopolies granted by **intellectual property** law should be "for *limited* times" (emphasis added). But the Supreme Court upheld the law, reminding us that the CTEA's extension of copyright's duration was only one of many, that the term of copyright protection had been extended several times since the first copyright law was passed in 1790 (providing for a maximum of only twenty-eight years' protection). The most recent extension made sense for several reasons, Justice Ginsburg's majority opinion concluded. The CTEA brought American copyright law in closer harmony with European law, as articulated in the Berne Convention for the Protection of Literary and Artistic

---

8. *Comedy III Productions, Inc. v. Saderup*, 21 P.3d 797 (Cal. 2001).

Works, which the United States joined in 1989. Further, extending copyright's duration made sense because Americans live longer than we used to and we have children later in life than we used to. "Life plus fifty years" provides less of a legacy for our children if we die when they are fifty rather than when they are seventy-five.[9]

The Law of Copyright

Let us suppose that twenty years from now, you have achieved a level of fame in your chosen field that makes yours a household name as much as the best-known and admired movie stars, sports figures, or political leaders. Imagine further that a former boyfriend or girlfriend, out of spite or greed, decides to write a "kiss and tell" book in which you will feature prominently and that this author intends to reprint several love letters from you still in his or her possession. You bring suit, seeking an injunction against the use of your letters in the book, as well as the return of the original letters to you. The chances are that your first wish will be honored but not your second, because the love letters, the actual papers with your handwriting on them, are the physical property of your ex-flame. You gave them freely, and a gift is a gift. The words you used to express your feelings at the time may still belong to you, however, and only you can decide if and when they will ever be published. That is the essence of the law of intellectual property, of which copyright is part. We use the word "property" to describe it, even though what is possessed is somewhat ethereal or intangible.

The first copyright law in the United States was adopted in 1790. Copyright law was significantly revised in 1909 and again in 1976. Most of the discussion in this chapter is based on the 1976 law, although it too has been revised in some ways since then, not only to extend the duration of copyright protection but also to make allowances for new technologies.

Copyright's Scope

U.S. copyright law protects "original works of authorship, fixed in any tangible medium of expression." The statute enumerates many general categories of creative works, including literary works; musical works (both the musical notes and the lyrics, if any); dramatic works (i.e., plays, including musicals); pantomimes and choreographic works; pictorial, graphic, and sculptural works; motion pictures and other audiovisual works; sound recordings; and architectural works.

A few clarifying points are in order. First, do not get carried away by the word *literary* in the first category. Yes, works of great literature are protected here, but so too is the letter a college student writes to her parents asking for more money. This book you are reading is copyrighted, and so too are the sample examination questions

---

9. *Eldred v. Ashcroft*, 537 U.S. 186 (2003).

in the instructor's manual. In other words, *words* is the key. The first category protects creative works that are made up of words.

As with literary works, we should not assume that "pictorial," "graphic," and "sculptural" works will always be the kinds of high-art creations collected by museums. Copyright also covers such useful art as clothing design. In a suit involving competing dress designers, for example, the Court of Appeals for the Second Circuit accepted as copyrightable a design consisting of "a geometric arrangement of color blocks banded in heavy lines" used on women's pullover tops.[10]

With respect to musical works, it is important to note that copyright protection can apply to the composition itself (as expressed typically in sheet music) and also to a particular performance of the composition (as set down in a "tangible" medium such as a CD). A particular arrangement of a well-known melody can itself be copyrightable and indeed quite valuable, as is the case, for example, with Nelson Riddle's arrangements of many of the tunes made popular by Frank Sinatra.

What does it mean to say that a work must be "fixed" in some kind of "tangible medium of expression" to be copyrightable? Consider the "pantomimes and choreographic works" category as an example. If you dance up a storm at a party, no matter how much you impress the other guests and how many of them try to mimic your steps, your creation is not yet copyrightable. The reason is not just because it was live and spontaneous. Your dazzling artistry will not be copyrightable even if you can repeat it step by step, move by move, on command. If, however, you commit to writing something resembling choreographic notation for your dance steps—and you need not be very professional about it—you will have a potentially copyrightable work. The requirement that a work be set down in some fixed medium applies to all the categories.

To be copyrightable, a work must also be "original." Being original does not mean that it must be the expression of an earth-shattering, paradigm-shifting revelation. The law is not nearly so strict. Even when dozens of photojournalists cover the same event, each of the individual photos they produce is copyrightable, even though most of us would have a hard time telling one from the other. In one case, a copyright was issued for a rectangular-shaped rock with the words of a poem—itself in the public domain—inscribed on it;[11] in another, a court was not ready to find that even an arrangement of percussive sounds lasting just one measure lacked sufficient creativity to merit copyright.[12]

What is original in your work might be simply the way you have organized others' materials. Newspapers' sports pages frequently include very detailed information about the records of two baseball pitchers about to face each other in an important game. The statistics that are included in such a feature—overall win-loss record, more

---

10. *North Coast Industries v. Jason Maxwell, Inc.*, 972 F.2d 1031 (2d Cir. 1992).

11. *Kay Berry, Inc. v. Taylor Gifts*, 421 F.3d 199 (3d Cir. 2005).

12. *Vargas v. Pfizer, Inc.*, 418 F. Supp. 2d 369 (S.D.N.Y. 2005).

focused win-loss record against this particular opponent, and so on—are themselves not copyrightable because they are readily available facts.[13] The writer's choice of which statistics to present and how to present them, however, may enjoy copyright protection.[14] This kind of work is referred to by the U.S. Copyright Office as a **compilation**, which the Copyright Act defines as "a work formed by the collection and assembly of preexisting materials or of data that are selected, coordinated, or arranged in such a way that the resulting work as a whole constitutes an original work of authorship."

Not every collection of preexisting materials will be copyrightable, however. The organizer-author must demonstrate at least a modicum of creativity. The Supreme Court said as much in 1991 when it held that the names and phone numbers in an ordinary telephone directory (white pages) are not protected by copyright. A small publishing company in Kansas decided to create a multi-area white pages that would encompass about a dozen local phone company dialing areas. This way, users would avoid the hassle of having to consult multiple directories and the expense of having to make large numbers of directory assistance calls. One of the telephone companies in the area, however, refused to sell the publisher the rights to use its directory's listings as a basis for the larger book. When the publishing company decided to use the data anyway, without permission, a lawsuit resulted. The Court held that the telephone company's own listings were not legitimately copyrightable in the first place. All that the company did was to "take the data provided by its subscribers and list it alphabetically by surname." The resulting book was "a garden-variety white pages directory, devoid of even the slightest trace of creativity."[15]

Collective works are special kinds of compilations in which the individual components are themselves original works of authorship eligible for copyright (and, indeed, that may have been granted copyright protection previously). A collection of previously published short stories or poems is a good example. The collection itself becomes copyrightable, although the editor of the compilation will not then take over ownership of the copyrights already accruing to the individual contributors to the volume. Note, too, that the editor must obtain permission to reprint each of the works still covered by copyright.

What about movie adaptations of novels or stage plays? These works fit into the category of **derivative works**, which build on preexisting works by recasting, transforming, or adapting them. A colorized version of a previously black-and-white movie is such a derivative work, as can be a movie or TV program that has been made accessible to the deaf or the blind through the addition of closed captioning or descriptive video services. Creators of the derivative work are granted copyrights only for those creative elements that they added to the original, however. The people who

---

13. *National Basketball Association v. Motorola*, 105 F.3d 841 (2d Cir. 1997).

14. *Kregos v. Associated Press*, 3 F.3d 656 (2d Cir. 1993).

15. *Feist Publications, Inc. v. Rural Telephone Service Co.*, 499 U.S. 340, 362 (1991).

add closed captioning to a TV program, for example, do not by this action earn a copyright to the program itself, only to the captioned version of it.

Things That Cannot Be Copyrighted

Not everything that can be set down into some fixed medium of communication is copyrightable. The *Feist* case discussed in the previous section—the one involving the competing telephone directories—serves as a reminder that mere facts cannot be copyrighted.

Consistent with the Copyright Act's insistence that the law is designed to protect works that are already created (rather than in the nascent planning stages), mere ideas are not copyrightable, even if they seem to be fairly well-developed ideas. This was a lesson learned by Hwesu Murray, a former NBC employee who claimed that the idea for *The Cosby Show* was stolen from him.[16] In 1980, four years before Dr. Cliff Huxtable and family took America's viewing audience by storm, Murray wrote a memo to his superiors suggesting that Cosby be enticed to star in a sitcom—he suggested it might be called "Father's Day"—whose main character would be portrayed as "a devoted family man" rather than "a buffoon, a supermasculine menial, or a phantom." The show would fuse comedy and serious subjects, much as did the old *Dick Van Dyke Show*, but "with a Black perspective." Whatever NBC may have appropriated from Murray's memo, the court found, was not copyrightable. Rather, it was the mere combination of two ideas that had been percolating among network executives for some time: the traditional situation comedy, but with blacks cast in nonstereotypical roles. That Cosby himself had expressed a desire to star in a family situation comedy as long ago as the 1960s (when he was starring in *I Spy*) certainly did not help Murray's claim to originality. It would be different had Murray submitted a script for a

---

THINGS TO REMEMBER

Copyright's Scope

- Even the most mundane "literary works" are protected by copyright.
- Computer software is treated as a literary work.
- A work must be set down in some fixed medium before it becomes eligible for protection.
- At least a modicum of creativity in the work is also required.
- Mere facts are not copyrightable.
- A creative compilation of facts, however, may sometimes be copyrightable.
- A collection of others' previously copyrighted works may itself be copyrightable.
- "Derivative" adaptations of earlier works can be copyrightable.

---

16. *Murray v. National Broadcasting Co.*, 844 F.2d 988 (2d Cir. 1988).

pilot episode and had NBC "borrowed" too freely from it. But the mere idea for even a "new" and "revolutionary" TV series was not protectable.

Also not copyrightable are works that the case law often refers to as "trivial," which is simply another way of emphasizing that originality is one requirement for copyright. The Copyright Office has set forth four categories of such trivial materials.[17]

The first category consists of words and short phrases such as names, titles, and slogans. In a 2005 case, the First Circuit Court of Appeals rejected a songwriter's claim that the song title and lyric "You're the One for Me," merited protection. The phrase is "common" to the point of being "trite," the court said.[18] Had the court ruled otherwise, could not Neil Sedaka sue Led Zeppelin for use of the song title "Stairway to Heaven"?

A federal appellate court held that neither the glass-in-glass method used by artist Richard Satava to produce his piece (on the left) nor the idea of encasing a depiction of a jellyfish in the glass was copyrightable. Fellow artist Christopher Lowry, creator of the work on the right, thus escaped liability.

The second category of trivial, uncopyrightable works consists of formulas or methods of instruction. Thus, for example, the folks who created Golden Tee, the popular golf video game, could not prevail against a competitor that used very similar language in its own in-game instructions for operating the "track ball" mechanism common to both.[19] In another case, Richard Satava, a sculptor well known for his glass-in-glass "jellyfish" designs, was unsuccessful in his copyright-infringement suit against a competing artist whose work was highly similar. To hold otherwise would make this method of sculpting—a "centuries-old art form"—subject to copyright protection, something the court was not ready to do.[20] In this case neither the glass-in-glass *method* nor the *idea* of depicting a jellyfish was deemed copyrightable.

The third category of trivial works, the "blank forms" category, includes time cards, graph paper, scorecards, and address books, which are all designed for recording information but do not themselves convey any information.[21] The fourth and final category consists of works that are entirely dependent on information that is common property. Included here are standard calendars, height and weight charts, tape mea-

---

17. 37 C.F.R. § 202.1 (2006).
18. *Johnson v. Gordon*, 409 F.3d 12 (1st Cir. 2005).
19. *Incredible Technologies, Inc. v. Virtual Technologies, Inc.*, 400 F.3d 1007 (7th Cir. 2005).
20. *Satava v. Lowry*, 323 F.3d 805 (9th Cir. 2003).
21. See, e.g., *Tastefully Simple, Inc. v. Two Sisters Gourmet*, 134 Fed. Appx. 1 (6th Cir. 2005).

sures, and rulers. Obviously, if the author does add some originality to the commonplace, as we see in the decorative calendars sold by numerous companies, copyright can accrue to the unique design features involved.

How Can You Protect Your Copyright?

It was a classic *Seinfeld* episode. The "Soup Nazi," the owner-manager of a small carryout restaurant serving only soup, had a maddeningly authoritarian nature. He demanded that his customers follow a highly scripted routine for ordering their lunch, lest they be banished from the premises ("Out! OUT! No soup for YOU!"). It seems that Jerry Seinfeld's pal Elaine incurred the Soup Nazi's wrath but managed to get back at him when she discovered that an armoire once belonging to the proprietor had dozens of his handwritten recipes in its drawers. "Why, I can copy these and deliver them to every restaurant in town. I can publish them!" she exclaims. In the episode's closing sequence, we learn that the Soup Nazi saw the handwriting on the wall and was going out of business.

Would copyright law really have permitted Elaine to copy and publish the recipes? The earlier example of the love letters and the kiss-and-tell book should give you the answer. Elaine may own the paper on which the recipes are written, but she does not own the recipes themselves. Would the Soup Nazi have had to take some affirmative steps, however, to establish his copyright? The shortest correct answer to that question is—yes and no. At least since 1989, American law accepts that a copyright is born the moment a creative work—and this would include original recipes for different kinds of soup—is written down. Despite the ubiquity of copyright notices on everything from books to CD liner notes, the copyright holder is not legally required to take any affirmative steps to "earn" a copyright.

It would be foolish, however, *not* to register a copyrightable work to which the writer attributes significant value. Should you ever need to bring suit against another person who has infringed on your copyright, registration of your work enables you to obtain money damages and sometimes attorneys' fees as well. Prominent notice of such registration also puts potential infringers on notice that this work is, in fact, protected.

Registration is very easy. One need only pay a modest fee to the federal Copyright Office, fill out the appropriate form depending on the specific medium involved, and place a copyright notice on existing copies of the work. You will also be asked to provide the office with two copies of the work to be copyrighted.[22]

Copyright notices generally consist of three elements:

- The internationally accepted symbol © (for sound recordings), or the word "copyright" or its abbreviation "copr."

---

22. More information can be obtained from the Public Information Office, Library of Congress, Copyright Office, 101 Independence Avenue, S.E., Washington, DC 20559-6000.

- The date of the copyright (typically the date of publication).
- The name of the copyright holder.

The Copyright Office gives detailed suggestions concerning where to place a copyright notice.[23] For books, the following places are appropriate for the copyright notice: the title page or the page immediately following it, either side of the front cover or of the back cover, or the first (or last) page of the main text. Any of those places are also fine for a periodical, which might instead feature the copyright notice as part of its masthead. For computer disks and other works that require the use of some kind of machine to read, it is acceptable to have the copyright notice appear to the user the moment he or she logs on, or indeed to have the notice visible as long as the program is running. Also acceptable is the use of some kind of gummed label on the disk itself. Motion picture copyright notices generally appear with or near the title or credits, and either at the beginning or the very end of the film. Three-dimensional works of art, such as sculpture, become a bit tricky. The regulations suggest that artists affix copyright notices in some appropriate manner (such as cementing) either to the work itself or to its base or mounting.

Who Owns the Copyright?

Usually the answer to the question of who owns a copyright is rather straightforward. The creator of a work—the author or artist—is the natural owner of a copyright to his or her work. Authors and artists do not always work alone, however. They may have collaborators, such as a lyricist joining forces with a composer, or a small group of writers who coauthor a book. In such cases, in the absence of a contract to the contrary, the creators will jointly and equally own a copyright.

Who owns the copyright to a motion picture? In the United States, even though film critics are fond of using the French word *auteur* (as in "writer" or "creator") when speaking of a film's director, typically the film studio insists that it be granted the copyright to the finished work before it will risk millions of dollars and take on a project. Most other countries recognize what is called *le droit moral* (the "moral rights") of artists, which protects film directors' reputational interests in the integrity of their work even if they have signed away their financial rights to the studios. In those countries, directors have a great deal to say about whether or how their work can be altered, such as in the colorization of black-and-white films, the editing of films for television, and the creation of interactive CD-ROM versions of the movie narrative. The United States generally does not recognize such rights. Thus, for example, a former producer of some of Woody Allen's films was deemed to have the right to edit them for TV and airplane viewing, even over Allen's objections.[24]

---

23. Copyright Office and Procedures, General Provisions, Methods of Affixation and the Positions of Copyright Notice on Various Types of Works, 37 C.F.R. § 201.20 (2006).

24. *Moses Productions v. Sweetland Films*, 819 N.Y.S. 2d 211 (Sup. Ct. 2006).

The clash between the U.S. copyright system and *le droit moral* was at issue when media mogul Ted Turner purchased the MGM Studios film library and made clear his intention to colorize many of the collection's older black-and-white films. Directors and other artists cried foul and unsuccessfully lobbied Congress to bring U.S. law in line with the international standard. When Turner contracted with a French television station to air a colorized version of John Huston's *The Asphalt Jungle*, the director obtained an injunction—in France, based on French law—that prevented the distribution of the colorized film in that country.

Another complication affecting the ownership of copyrights is the **work-for-hire doctrine**. The general principle is quite straightforward. If your job description includes creating works that are copyrightable—such as drafting speeches for your company's president or writing and editing the company newsletter—your employer rather than you will be the owner of the copyright.

The issue becomes a bit more complex when the artist or author is a contractor rather than an employee. In this context, a contractor can be anyone from a freelance reporter to an advertising agency hired to create a marketing brochure to a photographer asked to take appetizing photos of a restaurant's main dishes for its website. The Supreme Court provided some guidance for situations such as these in a rather poignant 1989 decision, *Community for Creative Non-Violence v. Reid*.[25] The Community for Creative Non-Violence (CCNV), an organization dedicated to advocacy on behalf of the homeless, approached sculptor James Earl Reid to create a Nativity scene featuring, in lieu of the traditional Holy Family, an infant and two adult African-American figures huddled for warmth on a steam grate. Reid donated his services but was to be reimbursed for materials. Neither he nor CCNV founder Mitch Snyder apparently ever discussed the issue of copyright. After the completed statue had been on display for a few weeks in the winter of 1985-1986, it was sent to Reid for some needed repairs. A few months later, CCNV's request for the statue's return was denied, and both Reid and Snyder, in that order, filed competing certificates of registration for the sculpture with the Copyright Office.

In holding that Reid should not be considered an employee of CCNV, the unanimous Court concluded that many factors should go into such determinations, including the hiring party's right to control the manner and means by which the product is accomplished, the nature of the skill required to complete the project, and the extent of the hired party's discretion over when and how long to work. Using these criteria, the Court concluded that Reid should be considered an independent contractor rather than an employee.

Bringing a Copyright-Infringement Suit

The word *copyright* seems to say it all. It grants the owner the right to "copy" the protected work. Copyright infringement is thus the unauthorized copying of that

---

25. 490 U.S. 730 (1989).

AND STILL THERE IS NO ROOM AT THE INN

The Supreme Court held that the creation of this work was not covered by the work-for-hire doctrine, in part because the sculptor used his own artistic vision to settle upon key design elements. *Third World America: A Contemporary Nativity.* © 1985 James Earl Reid, sculptor.

THINGS TO REMEMBER

Recognition of Copyrights

- Things that are generally not copyrightable include the following:
  - Mere ideas
  - Methods of instruction
  - "Trivial works" such as names, titles, slogans, and blank forms
- Copyright attaches to a work the moment it is set down.
- Registering a work is necessary, however, to win damages against an infringer.
- The Copyright Office provides detailed instructions for posting a copyright notice on or near the work.
- The artistic creator is the "natural" owner of the copyright, but often the "work for hire" doctrine dictates that the person or group footing the bill is the true owner.

protected work. It can refer to obviously illegal actions such as marketing bootleg copies of movies or musical recordings. The creation of adaptations of protected works (e.g., making a movie of a popular novel) without permission is similarly forbidden. So too is the "public performance" of a work without permission. This part of the Copyright Act means that it is technically a violation of the law for a family restaurant, if it fails to pay licensing fees to the appropriate music clearinghouse, to have its staff sing "Happy Birthday" to its patrons on that special day.

In the real world, most copyright conflicts do not result in litigation. More typically, a letter is drafted by the potential plaintiff to the suspected infringer demanding that the infringement stop. If the case does go to court, typical remedies are an injunction, as well as damages that can include both the plaintiff's lost income and the income illegally obtained by the infringer. These are not necessarily the same thing. If, without your permission, I create a movie based on your book, I might create more income for you than you had been enjoying on your own, because viewing my film might encourage viewers to "read more about it." You may nonetheless be entitled to receive my profits as part of your damages award. Alternatively, there are statutorily prescribed damage awards that plaintiffs may fall back on. As of 2006, these awards range from $650 to $30,000, with some exceptions. For example, judges have the discretion, in the case of defendants who can prove that they innocently infringed on a copyright ("I obtained permission from the person listed on the copyright notice. How was I to know that he did not really own the work?"), to reduce the minimum award to $200. At the other end, in the event of especially egregious violations, such as the kind of willful taking involved when the copyright holder explicitly rejects your request for rights to reprint a protected work, but you do it anyway, the maximum statutorily prescribed award can be as high as $150,000. The extreme case of systematic marketing of bootlegged works can be a criminal offense, punishable by a hefty fine and some jail time.

Copyright owners who choose to bring suit must prove three elements: originality, access, and substantial similarity.

Originality.

Originality.   A copyright-infringement plaintiff must first establish that the material alleged to have been stolen was original enough to have been legitimately copyrightable in the first place. This lesson was driven home by the Supreme Court in *Feist Publications, Inc. v. Rural Telephone Service Co.*, a case mentioned in the earlier discussion of compilations.[26] In that case, a phone company sued a publisher for copying its subscriber listings in the course of compiling its own phone directory designed to cover a wider territory. The key issue in front of the Court was whether the alphabetical listings in the Rural Telephone Service Company's book should ever have been granted a copyright. Writing for the majority, Justice O'Connor concluded that

---

26. 499 U.S. 340 (1991).

the phone company's listing of its subscribers' names, addresses, and telephone numbers was not sufficiently original to be copyrightable.

We already know that works must be "creative" if they are to be copyrightable. The originality element of a copyright-infringement suit might therefore be thought of as a reality check—was the plaintiff's work *really* creative or original enough? Or was the copyright given to the artist in error?

Access.   The element of access in copyright-infringement suits is somewhat analogous to proving that a criminal defendant had the opportunity to commit the crime. One cannot steal what one never knew existed. It is not often possible to prove access in the sense of producing a witness to testify that the defendant became aware of the plaintiff's original work at a certain place and time. Often, access is demonstrated more inferentially. Thus, when former Beatle George Harrison was sued because his song "My Sweet Lord" seemed to be an unauthorized copying of the earlier hit song "He's So Fine," the plaintiff pointed to how popular the Chiffons hit had been in its day (it was at the top of the Billboard charts for five weeks).[27]

It is a truism of life in Hollywood that once you "make it," your personal staff had better include someone on the payroll whose job it is to open your mail so that you can never be accused of having had access to an unsolicited work—such as a song or a screenplay—that some future plaintiff may send you. Although there is some truth to the truism, the lesson of a court case involving the Jim Carrey film *The Truman Show* might be that the fears are exaggerated.[28] Writer Craig Mowry was not able to establish that anyone connected to the movie had seen the script for his own unpublished screenplay (*The Crew*), which he claimed was the basis for *The Truman Show*. Yes, he had sent dozens of copies of the screenplay to well-placed Hollywood directors, producers, and writers, some of whom testified that they in turn had shared it with others. Finding some humor in Mowry's singling out a pair of high-powered real estate agents with Hollywood connections as recipients of his script, a federal judge replied that if this is what the plaintiff meant when he said he had disseminated the script to people in the entertainment industry, then "Mowry's definition of 'entertainment industry' seems to include everyone in Los Angeles who may 'know' people in the industry (including, perhaps, all the unemployed actors and actresses who wait tables or park cars while waiting for their break)."

Substantial Similarity.   Except in those instances in which a defendant has clearly marketed bootleg or otherwise unauthorized copies of an original work, it is necessary for a plaintiff to demonstrate that the fruit of the infringer's labors are so

---

27. *Bright Tunes Music v. Harrisongs Music*, 420 F. Supp. 177 (1976).

28. *Mowry v. Viacom International*, 75 U.S.P.Q.2d (BNA) (S.D.N.Y. 2005); see also *Bea v. Home Box Office*, 47 U.S.P.Q.2d (BNA) 1766 (E.D. Va. 1998); *Jason v. Fonda*, 526 F. Supp. 774 (C.D. Cal. 1981).

similar to his or her own copyrighted work as to constitute the theft of intellectual property. Courts typically employ a form of the familiar "reasonable person" test: are the two works being compared so similar as to suggest to a reasonable person that one was copied from the other? Sometimes the test is augmented by a more exacting comparison of specific features—for example, the plot, the melody, the setting—of the plaintiff's and defendant's works. In the case against George Harrison mentioned above, the court found it helpful to reprint short snippets from the sheet music to "He's So Fine" and "My Sweet Lord" in its decision.

In another case that turned on the issue of similarity, federal district court judge Gerhard Gesell had no difficulty determining that the publishers of the then-fledgling *Conservative Digest* had copied the cover design from the far more established *Reader's Digest*.[29] He thus issued an injunction against further infringement and awarded nominal damages. The cover design was protected both by copyright law (as an artistic work in its own right) and by trademark law (as a way of letting consumers know that this was indeed the popular magazine with which they are familiar). Judge Gesell analyzed design features such as composition (the placement of the table of contents, magazine name, date, and cover price), fonts, and the use of boldface type.

Let us look at how one court dealt with the issue of substantial similarity between two films. All these years after the film's release, the motion picture industry still ranks *Jaws* among the top-grossing films of all time. It is no surprise, then, that Universal Studios was and is very protective of the copyright to the film. Universal brought suit against a company that was planning to market a film called *Great White*. The federal district court judge, who issued an injunction against the distribution of the latter film, was dumbstruck by the numerous similarities between the works. Indeed, several full pages of the court's opinion are taken up with descriptions of those similarities. That the creators of *Great White* originally planned to call their work *The Last Jaws* and that a main character in the film was named Peter Benton (author Peter Benchley wrote the novel upon which *Jaws* was based) suggested that they wished for their work "to be as closely connected with [the original] *Jaws* as possible."[30] The textbox on page 248 presents some of the main similarities between the two films identified by the court.

In an often-cited case from the Second Circuit, substantial similarity between photographer Art Rogers's photo of a couple cradling their eight German shepherd puppies and artist Jeff Koons's sculpture based on that photo was seen not only by using the "reasonable person" test but also because of the odd facts of the case.[31] The trial record makes clear that Koons purchased a note card depicting the Rogers photo and was sufficiently impressed that he instructed an Italian studio to fashion a wood

29. *Reader's Digest Association v. Conservative Digest, Inc.*, 642 F. Supp. 144, 145 (D.D.C. 1986), *aff'd*, 821 F.2d 800 (D.C. Cir. 1987).

30. *Universal City Studios v. Film Ventures International*, 543 F. Supp. 1134 (C.D. Cal. 1982).

31. *Rogers v. Koons*, 960 F.2d 301 (2d Cir. 1992).

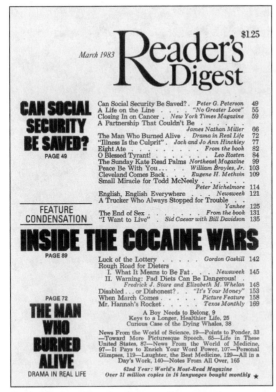

Clearly the overall "feel" of these two covers is similar, but what words would you use to describe the specific design elements that have been copied?

sculpture faithful to the photo. There were several exchanges back and forth between Koons and the studio artisans in which he reminded them again and again that this or that feature (the size of the young woman's nose, the variety of hues in the dog's fur, etc.) needed to be "as per the photograph."

There are at least two circumstances in which a court will permit a great deal of similarity between works without finding infringement. The first situation arises when a central idea common to both works (recall that ideas may not be copyrighted) can only be expressed in a very small number of ways. This is referred to in copyright law as the doctrine of **idea-expression merger.** In one frequently cited case, the First Circuit Court of Appeals concluded that the English words available to describe highly similar fragrances—for example, eucalyptus, cranberry, gardenia, mulberry, peach, raspberry jubilee, French vanilla, cinnamon rolls—will necessarily themselves also be similar or even identical. The court admitted that the message about a candle's scent conveyed by "cinnamon rolls" might equally well be conveyed by "cinnamon sticks" or "cinnamon toast" or just plain "cinnamon." But the merger doctrine does not demand that there be only *one* way of conveying an idea, it demands that the

Substantial Similarity between Two Films

(from *Universal City Studios v. Film Ventures International*, 543 F. Supp. 1134 (C.D. Cal. 1982))

Jaws	*Great White*
• The opening scene includes many underwater shots of a swimmer, repeated bass tones to indicate the approach of the shark and to build tension, and the swimmer's becoming the first victim of the shark.	• The opening scene includes many underwater shots of a windsurfer, repeated musical bass tones to indicate the approach of the shark and to build tension, and the windsurfer's becoming the first victim of the shark.
• There is a boat scene in which, to the sound of bass tones, the shark approaches the boat, bumps it, and causes a boy to fall into the water. The boy is rescued before the shark attacks.	• There is a boat scene in which, to the sound of bass tones, the shark approaches the boat, bumps it, and causes a girl to fall into the water. The girl is rescued before the shark attacks.
• A bathing cap, which looks like the head of a shark, floats through the water.	• A broken surfboard, which looks like the fin of a shark, floats through the water.
• The local mayor plays down the news of the shark in the interest of local tourism.	• A gubernatorial candidate plays down the news of the shark in the interest of local tourism.
• After the police chief's child has gone into a state of shock because of the shark, the politician apologizes to the father in the hospital and as an act of contrition signs a contract hiring the salty skipper to hunt the shark.	• After the shark expert's child is injured by the shark, the politician apologizes to the father in the hospital and as an act of contrition personally hunts for the shark.
• The action revolves primarily around a salty English-accented skipper, a shark expert, and the local police chief who go out in a boat to hunt the shark.	• The action revolves primarily around a salty English-accented skipper and a local shark expert who go out in a boat to hunt the shark.
• In the finale, the skipper is eaten by the shark, and then the police chief kills the shark by exploding a canister of compressed air which the shark has swallowed.	• In the finale, the skipper is eaten by the shark, and then the shark expert kills the shark by detonating dynamite which the shark has swallowed.

The court in *Rogers v. Koons* determined that the similarity between the photo at left and the sculpture depicted at right would be apparent to any reasonable juror.

available means of expressing that idea be highly limited. Thus, one scented-candle manufacturer could not sue another for stealing its product labels.[32] More recently we see that the manufacturer of software designed to prompt trained emergency medical teams, step by step, through their performance of CPR could not prevail over the manufacturer of a defibrillator device called the "AED Plus." Not surprisingly, the case concerned both patent and copyright claims. The copyright claim centered around the exact words used by the two devices to teach or remind users how to perform CPR. One simply cannot own the right to such phrases as "stay calm," "give two breaths," and "if no pulse, continue" in this context, the court held. The "idea" of reminding people—in the moment when a life is at stake—how to perform CPR is inseparable from the expression of that idea. There are not too many word choices that would be appropriate.[33]

The second situation typically (though not always) arises in the context of litigation involving motion pictures and is governed by the *scènes-à-faire* **doctrine**. The doctrine posits that when directors choose a particular locale for their story, they commit themselves to including a number of highly predictable filmic moments. Thus, for example, the author of a series of children's books about a park filled with dinosaurs was unsuccessful in his suit alleging that *Jurassic Park* was an infringement of his copyright. That both the plaintiff's and defendant's works took place in a "dinosaur park" meant that such features as electrified fences, automated tours, dinosaur nurseries, and uniformed workers were virtually unavoidable.[34] Similarly, the produc-

---

32. *Yankee Candle Co. v. Bridgewater Candle Co.*, 259 F.3d 24 (1st Cir. 2001).

33. *Hutchins v. Zoll Medical Corporation*, 430 F. Supp. 2d 24 (D. Mass. 2006).

34. *Williams v. Crichton*, 84 F.2d 581 (2d Cir. 1996).

Judge Phyllis Kravitch wrote several pages describing similarities and differences between the photo of the *Bird Girl* statue on the book cover and on the movie poster. Do you agree with her that the latter boasts enough dissimilarities to avoid copyright infringement?

ers and screenwriters of the movie *Fort Apache, the Bronx* successfully defended against a lawsuit by the author of a book called *Fort Apache*. The two works were inarguably similar in theme. Both took place in the New York City Police Department's Forty-First Precinct in the South Bronx. The plaintiff pointed to several deeper similarities between the two works, including the use of third- or fourth-generation Irish policemen from Queens as central characters, as well as such dramatic elements as cockfights, drunks, stripped cars, prostitutes, rats, and unsuccessful foot chases of fleeing criminals. Such components of the two works, the court ruled, could not constitute copyright infringement, because they "would appear in any realistic work about the work of policemen in the South Bronx."[35]

---

35. *Walker v. Time Life Films*, 784 F.2d 44, 50 (2d Cir. 1986).

It should be noted that the *scènes-à-faire* doctrine is not limited to motion pictures. The *Incredible Technologies* case discussed earlier in this chapter—the one involving the video game Golden Tee—invoked the doctrine as well. There are only so many ways to teach a video game user how to use a tracking ball, the court held. And in a case involving the eerie statue known as the *Bird Girl* featured on the cover of the book *Midnight in the Garden of Good and Evil* and later in both the film and in posters promoting the film, a federal appellate court held that the overall notion of using eerie photography to evoke the mood of a cemetery is a classic example of unprotectable *scènes à faire*. The dispute arose because photographer Jack Leigh, who had been commissioned by Random House to create images appropriate for the original book cover, believed that the use by Warner Bros. of the same cemetery and the same *Bird Girl* image as he had used for the book was a copyright violation. Likely not, the court held, in that the aspects of the Leigh photo that were legitimately copyrightable—the selection of lighting, shading, timing, angle, and film—were not taken, even if the book cover and the film posters are highly similar.[36]

Defending against a Copyright-Infringement Suit: The Fair-Use Doctrine

As we have seen, plaintiffs in copyright-infringement suits must prove three elements: originality, access, and substantial similarity. Thus, we already know some of the arguments that defendants in such suits are likely to make—that is, "the plaintiff has failed to establish one or more elements, and here is why." Technically, because the burden of proof in establishing these elements is on the plaintiff, defendants' counterarguments do not constitute legal "defenses." A defense in this context is better thought of as an admission of copying, with an explanation. By far the most important defense in copyright-infringement suits is the one that invokes the **fair-use**

THINGS TO REMEMBER

Proving Copyright Infringement

- Copyright-infringement plaintiffs may be awarded both their own lost profits and any profits illegally accrued by the defendant.
- The Copyright Act itself also provides specific dollar amounts of damages.
- Especially egregious infringements may also constitute a criminal offense.
- The main elements of an infringement suit are originality, access, and substantial similarity.
- The idea-expression merger and *scènes-à-faire* doctrines may excuse works that would otherwise be considered substantially similar to the plaintiff's work.

---

36. *Leigh v. Warner Brothers*, 210 F.3d 1210 (11th Cir. 2000).

doctrine, which is codified as section 107 of the Copyright Act. The basic philosophy underlying fair use is that there are some instances of copying that must be protected, either because they provide some societal good or at least because they do not do a great deal of harm to the copyright holders. Many commentators have suggested that if the Copyright Act did not provide this kind of defense, courts would have had to create it as a kind of First Amendment counterweight in favor of speech. Indeed, one of the themes to be developed in chapter 13—the Internet chapter—is that new technologies are making it more difficult to enjoy our right to fair use of copyrighted materials and that courts may very well intervene to rebalance the scales.

Section 107 is structured as a list of four questions that courts must ask as they try to determine if a particular taking that would otherwise be seen as an actionable copyright infringement should be excused as a fair use. The first question focuses on the actions of the alleged infringer: what is the nature of the use to which the defendant has put this copyrighted work? Some kinds of uses—such as for nonprofit educational purposes or to make critical commentary on or satirize the original work—are especially deserving of protection. The second question shifts the court's focus to the nature of the original copyrighted work. Here, too, the thrust of this question is that certain kinds of works are more protected than others. The third question asks how much of the work was taken, reflecting Congress's belief that writers should almost always be able to quote small sections of others' work without seeking permission. Finally, courts must ask what often turns out to be the most important inquiry of all: what is the likely financial effect of this unauthorized taking on the potential value of the original copyright?

The four questions are somewhat interdependent. Thus, for example, some kinds of uses (the first question) may permit a larger amount of taking from the original work (the third question) than would otherwise be the case.

Setting the Stage: Three Supreme Court Decisions.
Although we examine many examples of case law in the explication of the fair-use questions to follow, three specific Supreme Court decisions are referred to over and over again. Therefore, a short description of the facts and rulings for each of the decisions is in order.

Home Videotapers Are Not Criminals: The *Sony* Case.
If you assume that you have the right to use a VCR at home to record broadcast TV programs, even though the on-air copyright notice for such programs typically advises viewers that "unauthorized copying" is strictly prohibited, you are correct. (It is not clear if that right will be extended to the use of digital technologies—DVRs, TiVo—to make home recordings.)[37] What you may not realize is how very close you came to losing this right in 1984, when the Supreme Court produced a 5-4 decision in favor of the home ta-

---

37. *Newmark v. Turner Broadcasting Network*, 226 F. Supp. 2d 1215 (C.D. Cal. 2002).

The Fair-Use Doctrine

(from section 107 of the Copyright Act)

[T]he fair use of a copyrighted work . . . for purposes such as criticism, comment, news reporting, teaching (including multiple copies for classroom use), scholarship, or research, is not an infringement of copyright. In determining whether the use made of a work in any particular case is a fair use the factors to be considered shall include—

(1) the purpose and character of the use, including whether such use is of a commercial nature or is for nonprofit educational purposes;
(2) the nature of the copyrighted work;
(3) the amount and substantiality of the portion used in relation to the copyrighted work as a whole; and
(4) the effect of the use upon the potential market for or value of the copyrighted work.

The fact that a work is unpublished shall not itself bar a finding of fair use if such finding is made upon consideration of all the above factors.

---

pers.[38] In more recent years, scholars who have pored over the papers of the late justice Thurgood Marshall have discovered that the case was almost decided the other way.[39]

The *"Betamax"* case—a charmingly anachronistic nickname, given the victory of the VHS format over Sony's Beta format for VCRs, and now the supremacy of DVDs over the VHS technology—was filed because TV and movie production studios were afraid that large-scale home taping of their programs would greatly diminish the value of their copyrights. If you tape a daytime soap opera for viewing when you return home from work (a practice called **time shifting**), you may be tempted to "fast forward" through the commercials. Copyright owners worry about this because the fewer the number of people known to view the commercials, the less advertisers will be willing to pay the TV networks for airtime, and thus the less TV networks will be willing to pay the program producers. Then too, you might like this specific episode of your favorite soap opera so much that you keep the tape to watch again and again. This practice, intuitively enough called **library building**, will have obvious implica-

---

38. *Sony Corporation of America v. Universal City Studios,* 464 U.S. 417 (1984).

39. Paul Goldstein, *Copyright's Highway: The Law and Lore of Copyright from Gutenberg to the Celestial Jukebox* (New York: Hill and Wang, 1994), 149.

tions for the market value of a TV series in that reruns will have an even smaller audience than they otherwise would have.

Naming millions of VCR purchasers as defendants would have been more than a bit unwieldy, of course, so the plaintiffs instead went after Sony Corporation, one of the major manufacturers of home taping equipment, as well as a small sample of retail outlets known to sell VCRs. Sony's advertising agency was also named as a defendant because it was alleged that the marketing campaign for Betamax machines encouraged purchasers to tape copyrighted programs from broadcast stations. Universal City Studios and Disney, the main plaintiffs, sought an injunction against the sale of video recorders or, barring that, some form of mandatory royalties on the sale of each machine (and perhaps on the sale of blank videotapes as well). The Supreme Court denied the injunction. The majority's reasoning, which we examine in more detail when we return to an explication of section 107, was based largely on the first and fourth fair-use inquiries—that is, the nature of the infringer's use of the copyrighted material and this use's effect on the value of the copyright.

Newsworthiness and Copyright Infringement: President Ford's Memoirs. The underlying facts in *Harper & Row, Publishers, Inc. v. Nation Enterprises* could have been part of a mystery novel.[40] Victor Navasky, editor of the *Nation* magazine, received a mysterious stranger one evening in March 1979, a stranger who had in his or her possession a copy of former president Gerald Ford's memoirs, scheduled to be published in the next few weeks by Harper & Row (jointly with the *Reader's Digest*) under the title *A Time to Heal*. Harper & Row had also contracted with *Time* magazine to publish excerpts from the book, timed to increase book sales. The mysterious stranger made clear that Navasky could look at the manuscript but could not keep it or make photocopies from it. Over the next twenty-four to seventy-two hours, Navasky took detailed notes from the Ford memoirs, including several hundred words of direct quotes. Believing that some of the revelations in the memoirs were so newsworthy that they should be brought to the public without delay, the *Nation* scooped the other publishers by including in its April 3, 1979, issue an article of about 2,250 words based on President Ford's manuscript.

Not surprisingly, the copyright owners of *A Time to Heal* sued the *Nation*, which defended itself in part by arguing that the specific words taken from Ford constituted a kind of contemporary history and were thus uncopyrightable facts. The Court rejected this argument as well as several arguments the defendant made based on the fair-use doctrine. The majority ruling, as we shall see, says much about the Court's current interpretation of this most frequently raised defense to copyright infringement.

A Pretty (Hairy) Decision: Roy Orbison and 2 Live Crew. The rap group 2 Live Crew took Roy Orbison's 1960s hit "Oh, Pretty Woman" and, depending on one's

---

40. 471 U.S. 539 (1985).

point of view, either created a work of biting social commentary on the song and on the hypocritical culture from which it sprang or simply ripped off the original for their own enrichment. The Orbison song tells the tale of a lonely man who, while walking the street late at night, encounters a woman who seems much too beautiful to consider spending time with him. "Don't walk on by," he pleads with her. "Don't make me cry." Just as he is about to leave for another lonely night at home, he finds he has guessed wrong and that the pretty woman is indeed walking his way.

The Luther Campbell version recorded by 2 Live Crew has a quite different theme. Their "pretty woman" is likened to Cousin It of *Addams Family* fame, transmogrified into a "bald-headed," "hairy," and "two-timing" creature. This latter description carries with it a silver lining of sorts, as the lead vocalist expresses relief that there is a good chance "the baby ain't mine."

Fundamentally, *Campbell v. Acuff-Rose Music, Inc.* is about the relationship between the fair-use doctrine and the long-accepted notion that comedians who use satire or parody should be allowed to point their audience's attention at various other cultural artifacts without having to obtain permission from those who own the copyright to such works.[41] Yet there has always been tremendous disagreement among courts as to the proper scope of the parodist's license. Should it cover any work that borrows from the original and that also happens to be funny, or must the comedy stem from a statement about the original work? Moreover, is the parodist's protection from copyright-infringement suits something separate from and greater than the fair-use doctrine, or should the defendant's satiric intent simply be one of the bits of data used in answering the four questions? The Supreme Court ruled unanimously in favor of 2 Live Crew, although it embraced the narrower definition of parody and made clear that defenses based on comedic intent will be handled as part of traditional fair-use analysis.

Fair-Use Inquiry #1: The Purpose and Character of the Use. Section 107 of the Copyright Act tells us that nonprofit educational uses of another's work are likely to be protected, as are unauthorized reproductions for the purposes of "criticism, comment, news reporting, teaching (including multiple copies for classroom use), scholarship, or research."

As the discussion of the 2 Live Crew case indicates, one kind of "criticism" or "comment" often at issue in copyright-infringement litigation is parody. In that 1994 decision, Justice Souter's unanimous opinion makes clear that the Court's definition of parody is narrow.

Those comedic works most likely to be protected by fair-use analysis are the ones that comment on the original work. Writers who borrow from earlier works only to make their own job easier will likely not enjoy any special degree of protection. As Souter put it, if the new work "has no critical bearing on the substance or style of the

---

41. 510 U.S. 569 (1994).

original composition," if the only reason the defendant borrowed from the original was "to get attention" or "to avoid the drudgery" of creating something truly new, the fairness of the use "diminishes accordingly, if it does not vanish."

Why do such parodists borrow other's melodies? Probably for two reasons. First, there is a higher probability that listeners will remember the lyrics if they already know the melody. Doesn't this reason, however, fit into the category of using the original work to "get attention," as Justice Souter put it? Second, it is plainly easier to write lyrics alone, which is another way of saying, again borrowing from Souter, that one "avoids the drudgery" of writing an accompanying melody.

Most parodists, and perhaps especially most parody songwriters, will not enjoy automatic protection under *Campbell*'s holding, because most comic songwriters borrow a melody for reasons other than making fun of the song itself. Let us take the example of the popular songwriting and performing troupe called the Capitol Steps, a Washington-based group whose founding members are all current or former congressional staffers. When they inquired musically, "Wouldn't It Be Hillary?" they were not making fun of Lerner and Lowe's "Wouldn't It Be Lovely?" but rather the Democrats' electoral prospects for 2008. In "It Don't Mean a Thing If Your State's Not a Swing," their target is not Duke Ellington but our electoral system's encouraging presidential candidates to focus all their resources on the few states whose outcomes are up for grabs. "The Bimbo Collection" is aimed squarely at Bill Clinton's sexual exploits, not the pining of Kermit the Frog (of "Rainbow Connection" fame) for Miss Piggy. Similarly, "Here's to You, Reverend Robertson" is a pointed barb at the head of the Christian Broadcasting Network and has nothing to do with Mrs. Robinson of Simon and Garfunkel and *The Graduate* fame.

Certainly some musical parodists do in fact make fun of the songs whose melodies (and sometimes, lyrics) they borrow. Ray Stevens's tune, "I Need Your Help, Barry Manilow," is a respectful but also cutting critique of both Manilow and his fan base. "Into the Words," one of the cuts from the *Forbidden Broadway, Vol. 2* CD, is a highly sophisticated send-up of both the musical *Into the Woods* and Stephen Sondheim's work in general. Even some of the Capitol Steps' work would fit clearly into the category of protected parody, such as their condemnation of the jingoism they see in Lee Greenwood's "God Bless the USA" (which had been used as George Herbert Walker Bush's campaign song), expressed in their own "God Bless My Chevrolet."

The producers of the long-running NBC program *Saturday Night Live* successfully defended against a copyright-infringement suit stemming from a skit depicting the city fathers of the biblical town of Sodom devising a public relations campaign for their town reminiscent of the one that New York had recently embarked on. The skit's finale had the participants singing "I Love Sodom" to the tune of "I Love New York," the centerpiece of the New York campaign. The court got the joke and recognized that it was at the expense, at least in part, of the earlier tune's creators. Thus the *SNL* team had achieved a pure parody.[42] In another musical example, disc jockey Rick Dees

---

42. *Elsmere Music, Inc. v. National Broadcasting Co.*, 623 F.2d 252 (2d Cir. 1980).

was sued, unsuccessfully, for having written and performed "When Sonny Sniffs Glue," which the courts understood to be a send-up of both the 1950s jazzy standard "When Sunny Gets Blue" and Johnny Mathis's distinctive version of the earlier tune.[43]

Post-*Campbell* courts have sometimes been pretty strict in their application of the decision, unwilling to allow comic uses of copyrighted works that fail to target the works taken. One often-cited case involved a book highly critical of the original O. J. Simpson murder trial.[44] The book, called *The Cat Not in the Hat: A Parody by Dr. Juice*, borrowed heavily for its verse structure from such Dr. Seuss classics as *The Cat in the Hat* and *One Fish, Two Fish, Red Fish, Blue Fish*.[45] The purported parody was not protected, the Ninth Circuit Court of Appeals tells us, because it does not make fun of Dr. Seuss; it merely uses Dr. Seuss to make fun of something wholly unrelated.

On the other hand, both before and after *Campbell*, parodies that inarguably make fun of a plaintiff's work usually have prevailed. Consider a few examples of visual parodies. The magazine *Vanity Fair* made quite a splash when it featured a nude and very pregnant Demi Moore on its August 1991 cover. Judge Newman of the Second Circuit Court of Appeals commented that photographer Annie Leibovitz posed Moore "in profile, with her right hand and arm covering her breasts and her left hand supporting her distended stomach—a well-known pose evocative of Botticelli's Birth of Venus." When Paramount Pictures, as part of its publicity campaign for the Leslie Nielsen film *Naked Gun 33 1/3: The Final Insult*, superimposed Nielsen's face on a torso chosen to closely resemble Moore's—the composite photo's caption was "Due This March"—Leibovitz sued. She did not prevail against Paramount Pictures, however, because the studio's promotional photo was at least partially a comment on her own work. If the message of the *Vanity Fair* photo was, as Leibovitz allowed, one woman's "self-confidence or feeling of pride in being beautiful and pregnant," Paramount's "ridiculous image of a smirking, foolish-looking pregnant man" was clearly designed to offer a differing view of the subject matter.[46]

Sometimes, unlike in the Leibovitz case, the photographer in a visual parody case is the defendant. Tom Forsythe created a series of seventy-eight photographs depicting Barbie dolls in various comical settings all related to food preparation. This "Food Chain Barbie" series was deemed a protected parody of "the objectification of women" that Barbie dolls both exemplify and encourage.[47]

Parody is really just a subset of a larger category of potential fair uses of copyrighted material: the excerpting from another's work to comment on it or to criticize it. Thus, a drama critic does not need to obtain permission to quote from a play's

43. *Fisher v. Dees*, 794 F.2d 432 (9th Cir. 1986).

44. *Dr. Seuss Enterprises v. Penguin Books*, 109 F.3d 1394 (9th Cir. 1997).

45. Page 3 of *The Cat Not in the Hat* begins, "One Knife? Two Knife? Red Knife. Dead Wife."

46. *Leibovitz v. Paramount Pictures Corp.*, 137 F.3d 109 (2d Cir. 1998).

47. *Mattell, Inc. v. Walking Mountain Productions*, 353 F.3d 792 (9th Cir. 2003).

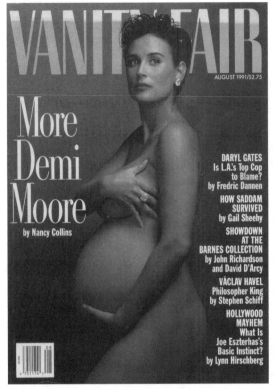 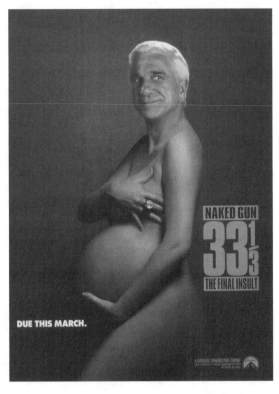

Photographer Annie Leibovitz was unsuccessful in her lawsuit against the producers of the Leslie Nielsen film, who clearly intended to conjure up in readers' minds an image of the earlier Demi Moore photograph.

dialogue. A film critic can show excerpts from a copyrighted film in the course of doing a movie review for the TV news. Jon Stewart's *The Daily Show* did not need to obtain the permission of New York–based cable-access program host Sandra Kane—known for her partial or complete nudity while performing on camera—to use a six-second clip from her show to comment on how community-access cable is too frequently more like "public *excess*."[48]

Author Gerald Celente did not need to obtain permission to reproduce in his book *Trends 2000* virtually all of a pro-nuclear-power advertisement paid for by a group called the U.S. Council for Energy Awareness and run in *National Geographic* magazine. Why was no permission needed? Because his purpose in reprinting the ad was to criticize what he saw as the ludicrous notion of suggesting that a farmer would grow so enamored of its neighboring nuclear power plant. His critique refers to Elsie as "the glowing cow" and accuses the nuclear industry's advertising campaign of "dis-

48. *Kane v. Comedy Partners*, 68 U.S.P.Q.2d (BNA) 1748 (S.D.N.Y. 2003), *aff'd*, 98 Fed. Appx. 73 (2d Cir. 2004).

These images are among the scores included in Tom Forsythe's "Food Chain Barbie" series, which was the target of an unsuccessful copyright-infringement suit by Mattel.

tracting us from absorbing what we already knew"—namely, that nuclear waste is very dangerous.[49]

In an especially ironic example of criticism as a protected use, Reverend Jerry Falwell and the Moral Majority were permitted to send copies of the famous Campari parody ad, the same one that upset Falwell enough to prompt him to sue *Hustler* magazine for libel (see the discussion of the case in chapter 4), to his supporters as part of a direct-mail solicitation. Although the court concluded that the mailing had commercial elements in that it was designed to raise money to defray Falwell's legal expenses, the unauthorized copying of the offensive ad was done primarily "to rebut

The small print of this ad from a 1993 issue of *National Geographic*, as the court in *Baraban v. Time Warner, Inc.* summarizes it, "describes the harmonious relationship between the Ihlenfeldt family and the nuclear power plant 'a mile up the road' and extols the virtues of nuclear power." Author Gerald Celente was protected by the fair-use defense because his purpose in reproducing the ad in his book was to criticize it.

---

49. *Baraban v. Time Warner, Inc.*, 2000 U.S. Dist. LEXIS 4447 (S.D.N.Y. 2000).

the personal attack upon Falwell and make a political comment about pornography."[50]

In the *Sony* case, the "nature of the use" issue was not related to parody or criticism. Nor was it a case focusing on a particular use of a specific copyrighted work. Rather, the Sony case concerned a technology's potential for performing a whole host of "uses." One reason the Court refused to stop the manufacturing and marketing of VCRs was that the machines could be used in many ways that do not violate the Copyright Act. Some broadcast programs, such as very old movies, are no longer protected by copyright. Other programs are "born in the public domain," such as C-SPAN's live coverage of congressional floor debates. In addition, some copyright holders would not be at all upset to learn that consumers were time shifting their programs for later viewing. For example, Fred Rogers, the host of *Mister Rogers' Neighborhood* on PBS, testified at trial that he encouraged parents to tape his program and then view it at a more convenient time, with their children. The Court also determined that the use of VCRs to do nothing more than time shift (rather than to make multiple copies of tapes and sell them to others, or even to build a permanent home library) is a nonprofit use consistent with the Copyright Act.

Defendants who can demonstrate that their use of another's copyrighted materials was for a nonprofit educational purpose are given considerable deference in fair-use analysis. The Copyright Act does not itself provide clear guidance as to how to balance the interests of copyright holders with those of teachers wishing to present examples in their classes or to distribute varied readings to their students. The House of Representatives created a report called the *Agreement on Guidelines for Classroom Copying in Not-for-Profit Educational Institutions* (usually referred to more succinctly as the *Classroom Guidelines*) around the time of the 1976 act's adoption. Although this report is not formally part of the statute itself, courts have sometimes employed the *Classroom Guidelines* in fair-use analyses. The guidelines are built around three main issues: **brevity**, **spontaneity**, and **cumulative effect**.

The brevity requirement permits teachers to make a single copy of a book chapter or an article for their own scholarly use or to prepare to teach a class about the work. Making multiple copies to distribute to students, however, triggers overall length limits (e.g., 250 words for a poem, 2,500 words for an article, no more than 10 percent of the total length of a book) that are quite rigid. Spontaneity means that a teacher is more likely to be permitted to make multiple copies if there is not enough time to contact the copyright holder for permission. The cumulative effect requirement limits teachers to copying no more than two works by the same author, no more than three from the same anthology, and no more than nine works total for classroom distribution during any single semester.

The guidelines make certain explicit prohibitions above and beyond the matters of brevity, spontaneity, and cumulative effect. Perhaps most important is that at no time

---

50. *Hustler Magazine, Inc. v. Moral Majority, Inc.*, 796 F.2d 1148, 1152 (9th Cir. 1986).

should copying be used as a substitute for anthologies, compilations, or collective works. Nor should copying be used for works designed to be "consumable," such as workbooks, exercises, and standardized tests. All copying must be a result of the individual teacher's inspiration rather than directed by any higher administrative authority. Finally, students may not be charged any fees beyond the actual cost of the copying.

Separately created guidelines govern the use by teachers of homemade videotapes from broadcast programs. The general rule here is that educators may retain and use any such videos only for forty-five days, after which the videos must be erased or destroyed. These guidelines are also not officially part of the Copyright Act, although Congress has endorsed them and placed them in the *Congressional Record*.

Sometimes the most hotly contested issue in a copyright-infringement dispute is whether the use should be considered nonprofit or commercial. This question was central to two important lower federal court cases governing professors' use of commercial photocopying shops to create customized textbooks for their students. In both cases, courts emphasized that the copy outlets made a profit and that this profit was enhanced by their failure to pay royalties to the copyright holders of the individual works being compiled. The first case involved the Kinko's chain, whose outlets are found in cities and college towns nationwide. From the students' perspective, such "Professor's Publishing" anthologies may have been for educational use, but the court found that they were a primarily commercial enterprise.[51] The second case involved a more local but equally commercial copying enterprise in Ann Arbor, Michigan, run by a self-taught legal scholar who persuaded himself, to his detriment, that the earlier Kinko's decision was an aberration. The Court of Appeals for the Sixth Circuit, ruling en banc, used much the same reasoning as did the district court in the Kinko's case, allowing that the students' use of the copied materials may have been an educational one but that the plaintiffs were complaining about the for-profit intermediary, the copy shop. The court majority explicitly refused to decide whether there would have been copyright infringement if the professors or students themselves had made the desired copies rather than contract with the photocopy shop.[52]

In the Supreme Court case concerning President Ford's memoirs, discussed earlier, the *Nation* magazine argued that its unauthorized use of purloined excerpts from the unpublished Harper & Row book should be protected as news reporting. The Court majority, however, emphasized that the magazine's motivation was commercial, that it intended to "scoop" the copyright holders. Moreover, the opinion rejects the newsworthiness defense outright, finding that "the public's interest in learning this news as fast as possible" does not necessarily outweigh the author's right to control the timing and circumstances of his work's publication. "The promise of copyright would

---

51. *Basic Books, Inc., v. Kinko's Graphics Corp.*, 758 F. Supp. 1522 (S.D.N.Y. 1991).
52. *Princeton University Press v. Michigan Document Services*, 99 F.3d 1381 (6th Cir. 1996).

be an empty one," Justice O'Connor wrote, "if it could be avoided merely by dubbing the infringement a fair use 'news report' of the book."[53]

Uses of copyrighted works that are "incidental" or "fortuitous" have often been protected as fair uses. The UCLA law professor Melville Nimmer uses the example of a motion picture in which an actor is seen reading a magazine, its cover clearly visible. The magazine would not be able to sue the film's producers for copyright infringement.[54] A case from New York City is instructive. WABC-TV televised the annual San Gennaro Festival from the Little Italy section of Manhattan, which included footage of a band playing a song called "Dove sta Zaza," by the Italian composer Giuseppe Cioffi. The owners of the copyright to the song sued the station, but the court ruled that the news crew had no advance knowledge that this particular song was to be played, that they had come to cover a bona fide news event, and that their use of the excerpts from the song was "incidental to the overall informative purpose of the newscast."[55]

Although this area of the law is quite unsettled, it is fair to say that defendants who specifically seek out particular copyrighted works will not be as readily protected by the fair-use doctrine as was WABC-TV. In 1997, for example, HBO and BET unsuccessfully sought summary judgment against a plaintiff whose artistic poster was used as part of the set in an episode of the sitcom *Roc*. The court emphasized that the producers purposely chose to use this specific piece of art for the same reason the artist created it: to be decorative.[56] A different result was reached by the same federal appellate court, however, in a case involving the motion picture *Seven*, about a deranged photographer, a serial killer who does his deeds in the manner of the seven deadly sins. At one point in the film, detectives search the photographer's apartment and encounter on the wall a light box with a number of transparencies attached to it. Jorge Antonio Sandoval claimed that the transparencies were images of several of his own black-and-white photos, and New Line Cinema did not contest this allegation. The court ruled for the movie producers nonetheless, emphasizing that the images were seen on-screen for such a short time and in such an obscured way as to make them almost unidentifiable as Sandoval's creations. Technically this was not a fair-use finding at all. Rather, the court found that the images as used in the film were no longer "substantially similar" to the originals.[57]

In another dispute that never went to trial, sculptor Frederick E. Hart settled out of court with the producers of the Warner Bros. film *The Devil's Advocate*, starring Keanu Reeves and Al Pacino. In the film, Pacino's Lucifer is a high-powered attorney who has followed young Reeves's career as an attorney from a distance for reasons

---

53. *Harper & Row, Publishers, Inc. v. Nation Enterprises*, 471 U.S. 539, 556–557 (1985).

54. Melville B. Nimmer and David Nimmer, *Nimmer on Copyright* (New York: Matthew Bender, 1997), § 13.05(D)3.

55. *Italian Book Corp. v. ABC*, 458 F. Supp. 65, 68 (S.D.N.Y. 1978).

56. *Ringgold v. Black Entertainment Television*, 126 F.3d 70, 79 (2d Cir. 1997).

57. *Sandoval v. New Line Cinema*, 147 F.3d 215 (2d. Cir. 1998).

Although the images on the light box (upper left of image) were legitimately copyrighted by artist Jorge Antonio Sandoval, the producers of the movie *Seven* were permitted this short and incidental use without permission or license.

that become apparent only in the final scene. In that scene, Pacino's office wall is dominated by a large sculpture, one that Hart thought a little too reminiscent of his own famous *Ex Nihilo* (*Out of Nothing*). In this climactic scene, the wall comes to life, its component characters engaging in a wide variety of sexual acts. Had the suit gone to trial, Warner Bros. might have argued that its use of the Hart sculpture was only incidental to the film narrative. If you have seen the film, you know that this argument would likely have failed. The final scene emphasizes the sculpture, employing

---

THINGS TO REMEMBER

The Nature of the Use

- Parody, a comedic work that makes fun of an earlier copyrighted work, may be protected as a fair use.
- Parody is a special case of the more general category of comment on the original work.
- Nonprofit and educational uses receive an extra weighting in fair-use analysis.
- It is not always easy to determine if a use is commercial or educational (or both).
- The *Classroom Guidelines* accompanying the Copyright Act provide highly specific and rather strict rules for educators.
- Unauthorized uses that are so incidental or unintended as to be "fortuitous" will generally be excused.

Sculptor Frederick Hart's suit against Warner Bros. for the unauthorized use of his sculpture *Ex Nihilo* in this scene from *The Devil's Advocate* was settled out of court.

it as a kind of Greek chorus commenting on the Faustian offer Pacino extends to Reeves.

Fair-Use Inquiry #2: The Nature of the Work.

Recall that the outcome of the *Harper & Row* case discussed above was based in part on the fact that President Ford's memoirs had not yet been published. The majority reasoned that because one of the rights that the Copyright Act explicitly protects is authors' choice of if, when, and how their work will come to press, unauthorized takings of not-yet-published works are especially troublesome.

A small handful of lower court cases following on the heels of the Ford memoirs case applied the same strictness against defendants who planned to quote from works that likely would never be published by their original authors. Thus, biographer Ian Hamilton, contracted to write a book about the reclusive literary figure J. D. Salinger, was not permitted to quote from any of the personal letters written by Salinger that had found their way into various university archives. The court quoted from Justice O'Connor's *Harper & Row* opinion for the proposition that "under ordinary circumstances, the author's right to control the first public appearance of his undisseminated expression will outweigh a claim of fair use."[58] Similarly, a biography of Church of Scientology founder L. Ron Hubbard was found in violation of the Copyright Act because of the unauthorized inclusion of Hubbard's unpublished correspondence.[59]

A biography of the late African-American writer Richard Wright was permitted to go forward, notwithstanding his heir's protestations at the biographer's unauthorized

58. *Salinger v. Random House*, 811 F.2d 90, 95 (2d Cir. 1987).
59. *New Era Publications International v. Henry Holt & Co.*, 873 F.2d 576 (2d Cir. 1989).

use of some of Wright's unpublished letters. Even here, however, the court's fair-use analysis counted against the defendant with respect to the unpublished nature of the original work. The court distinguished this case from the one involving Salinger on the relatively narrow grounds that here the writer paraphrased loosely more than he quoted directly and depended on the letters more for (uncopyrightable) facts than for protected expression.[60] Largely out of concern that lower courts were misinterpreting the *Harper & Row* decision to suggest that defendants should almost never prevail if they disseminate others' unpublished works, Congress amended the Copyright Act in 1992, inserting in Section 107 this admonition: "The fact that a work is unpublished shall not itself bar a finding of fair use." Still, it is a fair bet that the unpublished status of a protected work will more often than not count against defendants who plan to publish the writings without authorization.

Note also that a not-yet-published work is distinguished in copyright law from a work that is out of print. With respect to the latter, the *Classroom Guidelines* suggest an extra measure of leeway in copying. After all, consumers would likely not be able to buy even a single copy of the book, much less multiple copies for classroom distribution.

Another way that courts handle the "nature of the work" inquiry is to determine whether the original work was laden with facts and statistics or was highly expressive and artistic. At the extreme, the taking of purely factual material is necessarily a fair use, in that such material is not itself copyrightable in the first place. Such was the lesson of *Feist*, the case involving the competing telephone directories, discussed earlier. An interesting case from the 1970s concerned a company that proposed to create a specialized index that would list all persons ever named in *New York Times* articles. The company used the newspaper's own indices to cull the information they required. The novel question posed by the case was, in the court's words, "whether or not millions of names scattered over more than one hundred volumes and integrated with a great mass of other data" constitutes a copyrightable compilation (and whether employing such data to create a new index can be a fair use). That the newspaper's own indexes were "rather in the nature of a collection of facts than in the nature of a creative or imaginative work" meant that the defendants had "greater license to use portions of the *Times Index* under the fair-use doctrine than they would have if a creative work had been involved," the court added. The newspaper was not granted the injunction it sought against the defendant's new index.[61]

A special method of adjudicating the "nature of the work" issue arises when the work is truly unique and when its dissemination is of clear public interest. The long and complicated history of litigation and legislation surrounding the famous Zapruder film of President Kennedy's assassination is the most often cited example. Dallas dressmaker Abraham Zapruder just happened to be making a home movie of the

---

60. *Wright v. Warner Books*, 953 F.2d 731 (2d Cir. 1991).
61. *New York Times Co. v. Roxbury Data Interface, Inc.*, 434 F. Supp. 217 (D.N.J. 1977).

JFK motorcade at the precise time the fatal shots were fired. His eight-millimeter film is surely one of the most important pieces of archival footage of the twentieth century. The publisher of *Life* magazine purchased the rights to the film from Zapruder for $150,000. A book critical of the government's investigation of the assassination called *Six Seconds in Dallas* appeared in 1967. The author of the book, who did not have access to the Zapruder film itself, instead used line sketches, each one copied from a different frame from the film, as reprinted earlier in *Life* magazine. The magazine publisher's resulting infringement suit was dismissed, because the public interest "in having the fullest information available on the murder of President Kennedy" necessitated that this particular film be made available to writers wishing to comment on this defining historical event.[62] Time, Inc. sold the rights to the film back to the Zapruder family for the token sum of one dollar in 1975. In 1992, Congress passed the JFK Assassination Records Collection Act, and in 1997, a special review board created by that act declared the Zapruder film an official record that the government would thus be entitled to confiscate.[63] The board told the Zapruders to make whatever arrangements were necessary to transfer ownership to the government by August 1998. A year of negotiations resulted in payment of $16 million to the Zapruders. During those negotiations, the family arranged to have an Illinois company market a digitally enhanced copy of their original film. Thus *Image of an Assassination*, a forty-five minute documentary incorporating a new version of the twenty-six second film, became available in video stores.

Fair-Use Inquiry #3: The Amount Taken.   It has already been mentioned that the four fair-use inquiries are interdependent, that the answer to one may affect the court's adjudication of others as well. This fact is very clear in the way that

---

THINGS TO REMEMBER

The Nature of the Work

- Not-yet-published works are especially deserving of protection to preserve the author's right to determine how, when, and if such works will be published.
- Works that are out of print are given a bit less protection from unauthorized copying than are other works.
- The courts also give fact-laden works less protection than more artistic works.
- If the dissemination of a work is judged to be of strong public interest, or if it is the only way of bringing important information to the public (the Zapruder film of the JFK assassination being the best-known example), such a determination will also be factored into the fair-use inquiry.

---

62. *Time, Inc. v. Bernard Geis Associates*, 293 F. Supp. 130 (S.D.N.Y. 1968).
63. 62 Fed. Reg. 27,008 (May 16, 1997).

judges deal with the third inquiry, the "how much was taken?" issue. How much you are allowed to take depends on both the nature of the original work and the nature of your use.

If copyrighted works vary along a continuum from the factually heavy to the more artistically creative, it is no surprise that defendants are permitted greater latitude in taking from the former than the latter kinds of works. Call to mind again the *Feist* case involving the rural telephone books. The defendant in that case took virtually the entire book compiled by the plaintiff, minus a few pages of introduction and a certain percentage of alphabetical listings that were discarded because they did not fit into the geographic scope of the new book. The Court permitted this taking, however, on the grounds that the material that was taken was purely factual.

Clearly, the length of the original work is important to consider as well. Indeed, in section 107 of the Copyright Act, the precise wording of the third question asks courts to consider "the amount and substantiality of the portion used in relation to the copyrighted work as a whole." This is Congress's way of saying that taking fifty words from a hundred-word poem is less likely to be considered a fair use than is taking five hundred words from a full-length novel.

In the *Sony* case, the Court refused to enjoin the production or marketing of VCRs even though they are often are used to make copies of an entire work. That case was unusual, however, because, in a sense, the machines themselves were the defendants. The basis of the decision was that VCRs can be used in ways that are not violations of the Copyright Act. At most, the manufacturers of the units might have been guilty of **contributory infringement**, rather than **direct infringement**, on anyone's copyright.

The *Harper & Row* case posed an intriguing problem for the Court. If the question in section 107 was to be viewed as a purely quantitative issue, the *Nation* magazine surely should have won. After all, it quoted only a few hundred words from a soon-to-be-published full-length book. The Court's explanation for its ruling against the magazine is relevant to the "how much did you take?" inquiry in at least two ways. First, Justice O'Connor makes clear that this part of the fair-use analysis has not only quantitative but also qualitative dimensions. Quoting from an earlier decision, she chided the defendant that "no plagiarist can excuse the wrong by showing how much . . . he did not pirate."[64] What the *Nation* took from President Ford's memoirs was the heart of the book, she emphasized. The magazine editor's testimony made clear that he purposely chose the book's most powerful passages, the ones that would convey the "absolute certainty with which [Ford] expressed himself."

A second important feature of the *Harper & Row* decision is that O'Connor's fair-use analysis seems to deviate from the instructions, such as they are, in the Copyright Act itself. Whereas section 107 tells courts to adjudicate the third fair-use inquiry by

---

64. 471 U.S. 539, 565 (1985) (quoting *Sheldon v. Metro-Goldwyn Pictures Corp.*, 81 F.2d 49, 56 (2d Cir. 1936), *cert. denied*, 298 U.S. 669 (1936)).

comparing what was stolen to the length of "the copyrighted work as a whole," O'Connor also considered the length of the resulting *Nation* magazine story. At one point she reports that 13 percent of the magazine article consisted of quotes from President Ford himself. Thus, the vast majority of the *Nation* essay was at least original enough not to have been lifted verbatim from someone else. Even here, though, her analysis becomes more qualitative than quantitative, as she concludes that the article "is structured around the quoted excerpts," that they "serve as its dramatic focal points," that they play a "key role in the infringing work."

The general topic of how parodies are treated within fair-use analysis has already been introduced. With respect to the third inquiry, the general rule, not surprisingly, is that a parody is permitted to "take" more from the original than might other kinds of works. Parodists may, minimally, take whatever is necessary to "conjure up the original" in the minds of the listeners. Clearly this standard is not very precise. It is fair to say, however, based on the "Oh, Pretty Woman" and "When Sonny Sniffs Glue" cases discussed earlier, that musical parodists may with impunity use the complete melody of the original if the new lyrics are indeed a critical commentary on the earlier work, rather than a more general comedic statement about society or a commentary aimed at some specific entity other than the original.

Fair-Use Inquiry #4: The Effect of the Taking on the Copyright's Value.

Copyright law is at its heart a way of protecting a property interest. It is therefore not surprising that this fourth inquiry, in which courts are to determine how much the value of the original work's copyright has been damaged, is crucial. Indeed, Justice O'Connor's opinion in the *Harper & Row* case makes clear that this fourth and last inquiry "is undoubtedly the single most important element of fair use." In that case, the Court was presented with an unusually clear and measurable example of harm. After the *Nation* went to press, *Time* magazine canceled its contract

---

THINGS TO REMEMBER

The Amount Taken

- How much defendants are allowed to "take" is often a function both of the nature of their use and the nature of the original work.
- Although section 107 of the Copyright Act directs courts to consider "the amount and substantiality of the portion used in relation to the copyrighted work as a whole," courts often add to the equation the ratio of unoriginal to original words in the defendant's creation.
- There is also a qualitative dimension to the test, in that defendants are likely to be held liable for taking the "heart" of a work, no matter how few words are actually taken.
- Parodists are permitted to take, minimally, whatever is necessary to "conjure up the original" in the minds of readers.

with Harper & Row (which had been for the exclusive right to print excerpts from the book) and refused to pay the remaining money due the book publisher.

In the *Sony* case, the Court had to deal with the VCR manufacturers' argument that their machines actually enhanced the value of the plaintiffs' copyrights. After all, the reasoning went, many people use video recorders primarily as video players and depend on professionally prerecorded movies for their in-home video entertainment. Were there no VCRs, the whole home-video market never would have developed, and the video-rental and sales industry represented a tremendous new stream of revenue for Universal City and other movie studios. Although the Court ultimately ruled for the VCR manufacturers on other grounds (the machines' potential for noninfringing uses), Justice O'Connor made it clear that this argument by the defendants must be rejected. Successful plaintiffs in an infringement suit are entitled not only to any revenues they may have lost but also to profits the defendants have illegitimately earned. The fourth fair-use inquiry, then, allows plaintiffs to say to defendants, "How dare you make money off of my copyright, without my permission, even if your doing so makes money for me as well!"

The fourth fair-use inquiry concerns the copyright holders' financial interests not only in the work already created and marketed but also in any future derivative works they may choose to market in the future. That is one of the key reasons the Court was not able to settle every issue before it in the case involving 2 Live Crew and had to remand the case to a lower court. What if Acuff-Rose, which owned the copyright to Roy Orbison's "Oh, Pretty Woman," had decided to license a rap music version of the song itself? Would the 2 Live Crew parody supplant the market for such a work, thus diminishing its value? The Court correctly expressed its skepticism at such a scenario, realizing that a straightforward rap version of a song and a parody of a song that happens to be sung in a rap idiom probably would appeal to different markets. Then too, one reason parodies are given special deference within fair-use analysis is that parody is precisely the kind of derivative work that artists and authors are least likely to market. Very few writers choose to make fun of their own work.

Parody's potential for dampening the market for the original might be a function of the satire's bite. Ray Stevens, for example, wrote a parody of Barry Manilow's music ("I Need Your Help, Barry Manilow") that makes fun of the megastar and his fans ("No one knows how to suffer quite like you"). If listeners were to be swayed by Stevens's musical "argument" that Manilow is an overly sentimental songwriter whose devotees have a maudlin, masochistic streak, the value of the latter's copyrights would surely be diminished. This diminution, however is not the kind the law is designed to protect.

Indeed, a "taking" of a copyrighted work, assuming it would not otherwise be actionable, cannot become so simply because the defendant's use of the work results in decreased sales of the original creator's works. Perhaps the leading example of this phenomenon is a 1977 decision involving the *Miami Herald* and *TV Guide*. The newspaper had decided to expand its coverage of television by offering a free weekly TV

The copy in this ad argued that the *Herald*'s TV magazine was better than *TV Guide* and described several specific reasons, such as more listings. The court ruled that even if the running of this ad led to reduced sales for *TV Guide*, that loss was due to the arguments rather than the unauthorized use of the magazine's cover and thus was not actionable.

magazine. It launched the new supplement with an advertising campaign in the newspaper itself, the thrust of which was to suggest that here was quite a bargain compared with subscribing to *TV Guide* because consumers received a thick multifaceted newspaper plus a viewing guide. The ads included a pictorial comparison of the covers of the two magazines. In response to the resulting copyright-infringement suit brought by the *TV Guide*'s publishers, the court allowed that the ads "may have had the effect of drawing customers away," but concluded that any such result would stem from the logic of the *Herald*'s arguments to consumers, not from the use of the *TV Guide* covers.[65]

When diminution of the original copyright's value flows from the taking itself, the defendant is almost certain to lose both the fourth fair-use inquiry and the litigation. This is apparent in a number of cases involving book publishers seeking to capitalize on the popularity of a motion picture or television series. In one case, a company marketed a book called *Welcome to Twin Peaks: A Complete Guide to Who's Who and What's What*, aimed at the somewhat cultish devotees of the highly stylized TV show. Obviously such a book is unlikely to dampen the market for the program itself—the reruns, the home videos, and so forth—but that was not the point, the court held. The crucial issue was that the producers of the TV program had already licensed some books related to the show and might have wanted to license more.[66] Similarly, the publishers of *The Seinfeld Aptitude Test* trivia book—in homage to the TV show, they organized the questions into five categories of increasing difficulty, from "Wuss" to "Master of Your Domain"—were held to be in violation of the Copyright Act. It mattered not, the court held, that the *Seinfeld* producers had thus far chosen not to exploit the derivative market themselves. That is an economic choice that copyright law must respect.[67] A similar result was reached in a 1998 suit by Paramount Pictures against a company marketing *The Joy of Trek*, a book designed to "explain the Star Trek phenomenon to the non-Trekker, particularly someone who finds him or herself involved in a relationship with a Trekker."[68]

Finally, it is worth noting a 2006 decision involving a company called Clean Flicks, which was in the business of editing sex and gore from commercial movies. The company took so seriously this fourth fair-use factor that it required all of its customers to buy an original unedited version of the requested movie title in addition to the edited version it provided. The major movie studios would not be losing money through this enterprise, Clean Flicks argued. After all, any customers seeking out a sanitized version of a major movie clearly "would not have themselves purchased the [unedited] versions because of the objectionable content." Thus, if anything, Clean

---

65. *Triangle Publications, Inc. v. Knight-Ridder Newspapers, Inc.*, 626 F.2d 1171 (5th Cir. 1980).

66. *Twin Peaks Productions, Inc. v. Publications International, Ltd.*, 996 F.2d 1366 (2d Cir. 1993).

67. *Castle Rock Entertainment v. Carol Publishing Group*, 150 F.3d 132 (2d Cir. 1998).

68. *Paramount Pictures Corp. v. Carol Publishing Group*, 25 F. Supp. 2d 372 (S.D.N.Y. 1998), *aff'd*, 181 F.3d 83 (2d Cir. 1999).

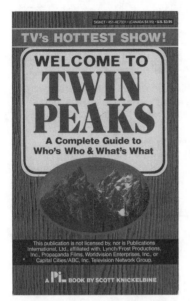 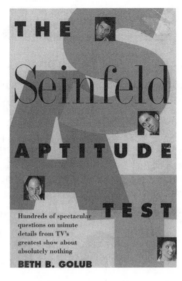 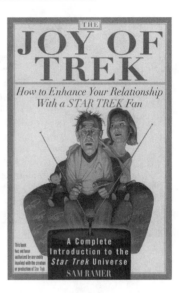

Imitation may be the sincerest form of flattery, but in these cases, it was also actionable, as publishers of these books were held to have infringed on the copyrights owned by the producers of the respective television programs.

Flicks' and similar companies' business models resulted in more, not less, money flowing to the major studios. Perhaps true, but irrelevant, Judge Richard Matsch held. Copyright law dictates that the major studios have the right to decide for themselves whether or not to enter the "sanitized" movie market.[69]

The Law of Trademarks

Imagine you are taking a long car trip, alone. You have been on the road for over ten hours, and your body is telling you to start seeking lodging for the night. You pass a number of motels with names that suggest a bit of local color but nothing about the cleanliness or overall quality of the property. Indeed, a few of them look a bit scuzzy. Then your eyes catch sight of a familiar name and logo—it really does not matter for present purposes whether it is Holiday Inn or Ramada or any of their well-known competitors—and you pull into the driveway, confident that you will enjoy a comfortable stay. If this narrative rings true for you, you already have a good intuitive feel for trademark law. Trademarks exist to give consumers a sense of predictability and thus to help businesses earn a deserved brand loyalty.

---

69. *Clean Flicks of Colorado v. Soderbergh*, 433 F. Supp. 2d 1236 (D. Colo. 2006).

THINGS TO REMEMBER

The Effect of the Taking on the Copyright's Value

- Most courts treat this last fair-use inquiry as the most important of the four.
- Infringers will be held liable even for profits they have earned from marketing works to new markets the original copyright owner may never have intended to reach or profit from.
- Even if an infringement can be shown to have increased the monies flowing to the copyright holder, defendants will still be held liable for the amount of their own profits.
- Diminution of the original copyright's value is actionable only if the taking itself (rather than, say, criticism hurled within the new work at the original work) is the cause of the diminished value.

Kinds of Marks

In the Unites States, trademarks are protected by the Lanham Act of 1946. The act defines trademarks as any word, name, symbol, or device that a company may use to distinguish its products or services from its competition. Marks can be familiar brand names. They can also be slogans, such as American Express's admonition, "Don't Leave Home Without It." Distinctive shapes can also be marks, the best-known example probably being the shape of Coca-Cola bottles. Even a color can be protected under trademark law.[70]

The word *trademark* is used somewhat generically here. Technically, trademarks apply to a company's products, whereas a company that offers primarily a service (such as the hotel chains in the example above) seek protection instead for its **service marks**. The law also recognizes an interest in protecting **collective marks**, which serve the needs of associations of businesses. The Chamber of Commerce, the National Restaurant Association, and the National Association of Broadcasters all represent many companies with overlapping interests and all are eligible to register their own marks. You have probably also seen **certification marks**, which do not refer to a product in its entirety but rather to a feature of that product. Probably the best known is that provided by Underwriters Laboratories ("UL approved") to appliance manufacturers. The promise of "REAL" cheese on a frozen pizza is another example. Certification marks can also be used to indicate a product's origins, as in Idaho potatoes or New Zealand wool. Finally, the Lanham Act provides for protection of the overall packaging through which a product or service is marketed.[71] This protection is called **trade dress**.

---

70. *Qualitex Company v. Jacobson Products*, 514 U.S. 159 (1995); *In re Owens-Corning Fiberglass Corp.*, 774 F.2d 1116, 1128 (Fed. Cir. 1985).

71. *Wal-Mart v. Samara Brothers*, 529 U.S. 205 (2000); *Two Pesos, Inc. v. Taco Cabana, Inc.*, 505 U.S. 763 (1992).

What Makes a Mark Protectable?

In copyright law, a creation is protected from the moment it is set down in some kind of finished form. Trademark law is quite different in this respect. You might create a terribly clever slogan or an eye-catching logo. Neither is protectable under trademark law until you actually establish a track record of using it in commerce, or at least what the U.S. Patent and Trademark Office calls a "bona fide intention" to use your mark within the next six months.

Just as not every conceivable "creation" is copyrightable, not every possible mark is protectable by trademark law. The law of copyright demands a measure of originality. Trademark law requires **distinctiveness**, which means that the mark does something more than simply describe the product or service. You cannot register the exclusive right to market "lead" pencils because being made of lead is part of the definition of any pencil. But even purely descriptive terms can sometimes become distinctive and thus protectable, over time. A **descriptive mark** is protected if a company can demonstrate that it has been marketing its wares under a specific name for so long and with such success that the public has developed a mental association between the name and the product. The Steak and Brew restaurant chain, for example, has chosen a name for itself that describes its menu offerings fairly well, yet the name is now a protected service mark because of a demonstrable history of public acceptance. American Airlines is another example. The name at first blush seems to designate any airline company that happens to be based in the United States, or even somewhere in the Western Hemisphere, yet most people clearly associate the name with a specific company. When a word or phrase that would otherwise be considered merely descriptive becomes distinctive in this way, it has acquired a **secondary meaning**, sometimes referred to instead as **acquired distinctiveness**. Company owners' surnames generally must acquire distinctiveness before they can be protected. Names such as "Perdue" chickens and "Kingsford" charcoal are generally protected only to the extent that the companies can demonstrate that the public strongly associates the names with a specific product line.[72]

One currently unsettled area of the law is the extent to which "800" telephone numbers or Internet domain names employing words that would otherwise be purely descriptive may nonetheless enjoy a degree of protection as the public comes to associate the number or the name with a particular company.[73] Can only one company that sells flowers, for example, make a point of telling customers that its phone number is easy to remember because it spells out "F-L-O-W-E-R-S"?

It is generally preferable from the marketer's perspective if a mark can be distinc-

---

72. *The Kingsford Products Co. v. Stephen T. Kingsford*, 931 F.2d 63 (10th Cir. 1991).

73. *Dranoff-Perlstein Associates v. Sklar*, 967 F.2d 852 (3d Cir. 1992); *Dial-A-Mattress Franchise Corp. v. Page*, 880 F.2d 675 (2d Cir. 1989); *CD Solutions, Inc. v. Tooker*, 15 F. Supp. 2d 986 (D. Or. 1998); W. Scott Petty, "Can a 'Generic' Domain Name Infringe a Registered Mark?" *Intellectual Property Today*, August 1998, 39

tive from the time of its creation. Trademark law refers to such marks as "inherently distinctive," and they are sometimes called "strong" marks. Generally a mark can be inherently distinctive in three ways. The first way is if the mark is fanciful, if it has no life apart from its association with the product it seeks to market. Such marks are not found in any dictionary but are created out of thin air, often with the help of a high-powered advertising agency. The name "Prell" applied to a shampoo is a fanciful name. So too are marks such as "Xerox" copying machines and "Clorox" bleach. A mark can also be inherently distinctive if it is arbitrary. Arbitrary marks do have established dictionary meanings, but the specific product or service is not inherently related to that dictionary meaning. "Boston" as applied to contact lens supplies is one such example; others are "Apple" computers and "Camel" cigarettes. Finally, a mark can be inherently distinctive if it is suggestive, that is, if it suggests, without explicitly describing, a product or service's qualities or features. "Head and Shoulders" shampoo is such a mark, and a rather clever one, aimed at suggesting that this product will help you prevent dandruff flakes on your clothing (the "shoulders" part). If the product were instead called "Anti-Dandruff Shampoo," the mark would be merely descriptive and thus unprotected.

Likelihood of Confusion

Generally plaintiffs can establish that their trademarks have been infringed in two ways. The first way is to show that the public is likely to be confused by the defendant's use of a highly similar mark, that it will presume incorrectly that the products or services are the plaintiff's or at least that the plaintiff authorized use of the mark. This is called the "**likelihood of confusion**" standard. Historically it has been limited both by geography and product line. A trademark infringement is less likely to be found if the alleged infringer is marketing goods or services in a geographic region

---

THINGS TO REMEMBER

The Basics of Trademark Law

- The Lanham Act protects trademarks, service marks, collective marks, certification marks, and trade dress. The word *trademark* is often used to refer to any of these categories of emblems.
- A trademark is any word, logo, slogan, or similar device used to call to mind a specific manufacturer's goods or services.
- The law protects only distinctive marks, those that do something more than simply describe the product or service.
- Marks can be distinctive from their birth (as in the case of fanciful, arbitrary, and suggestive marks), or they may be descriptive terms that have become distinctive over time through the acquisition of a secondary meaning.

far removed from where the plaintiff conducts business. Although this limitation is not as important with respect to large companies that market their goods nationally or internationally, it still comes into play when litigants are relatively local concerns. Thus, for example, the famous Sardi's restaurant in New York City was unable to enjoin the owner of a small neighborhood pub in California from using a highly similar name.[74]

Also, the law traditionally protected companies' trademarks only from those who sought to market product lines highly similar to their own. Often referred to as **product proximity**, this general rule says that trademark infringement is more likely to be found if the two products at issue are similar enough to compete plausibly with each other. To cite one early example, the manufacturer of "V-8" vitamin supplements was successfully sued by the manufacturer of the famous vegetable juice of the same name.[75]

Dilution

The second way a company might infringe on a competing company's trademark is through dilution. The distinction between dilution and the more traditional likelihood-of-confusion standard in trademark law is not always easily discernible and can seem confusingly circular. This confusion emerges because the accepted definition of dilution, as articulated first only in state statutes but as of 1996 in the federal Lanham Act as well, does not require that the plaintiff's and defendant's product lines be at all similar. Dilution statutes have been supported on the grounds that any unauthorized use of another's trademarks can diminish the value of those trademarks through a process sometimes called **blurring**. In the trademark-infringement literature, a hypothetical example of "Buick aspirin tablets" is often used. If the public began to believe mistakenly that General Motors had begun to sell analgesics, there would be a traditional likelihood-of-confusion suit. But what if the market were simultaneously flooded with a host of other "Buick" products, from toothbrushes to hammers? Infringement still might exist, but based on the alternative theory—blurring—that consumers would no longer think only of cars when they encounter the trademark "Buick."[76]

Thus, even though dilution claims do not technically require a finding of likely confusion, a plaintiff's chances of success tend to be better the greater the similarity between the plaintiff's and the defendant's product lines. Thus, for example, the company that then owned the rights to the LEXIS computer database was not able to

---

74. *Sardi's Restaurant Corp. v. Sardie*, 755 F.2d 719 (9th Cir. 1985); cf. *Good Earth Corp. v. M. D. Horton and Associates*, 1998 U.S. App. LEXIS 12572 (9th Cir. 1998).

75. *Standard Brands, Inc. v. Smidler*, 151 F.2d 34 (2d Cir. 1945).

76. Eric Prager, "The Federal Trademark Dilution Act of 1995: Substantial Likelihood of Confusion," 7 *Fordham Intellectual Property, Media & Entertainment Law Journal* 121, 123 n.8 (1996).

enjoin the car manufacturer from using the Lexus mark. The court emphasized that not only were the two companies in very different enterprises but also the plaintiff's service mark, very well known to attorneys and similar professionals, was not at all familiar to the lay public.[77]

One category of dilution claim is more clearly distinct from ordinary trademark-infringement cases: "**tarnishment**" claims against uses that tend to disparage the plaintiff's trademarks. Consider, for example, the Coca-Cola Company's suit against the distributors of a popular counterculture poster depicting an "exact blown-up reproduction of plaintiff's familiar 'Coca-Cola' trademark and distinctive format except for the substitution of the script letters 'ine' for '-Cola,' so that the poster reads 'Enjoy Cocaine.'" In the course of granting the plaintiff the requested injunction, the court emphasized that in the highly competitive soft drink industry, "even the slightest negative connotation concerning a particular beverage" may have a significant effect on market share.[78]

Trademark Parody

A tarnishment claim will generally not succeed, however, if the defendant can demonstrate that the unauthorized use of the plaintiff's trademark was for the purpose of parody or some other related kind of political commentary. Thus, L.L. Bean, Inc. was not able to enjoin publication of a spoof called "L.L. Beam's Back-To-School-Sex-Catalog,"[79] and the "San Diego Chicken" sports mascot was permitted to make fun of PBS's "Barney" the dinosaur by having a stand-in for the purple creature perform an athletically demanding dance sequence.[80]

In the summer of 2000, MasterCard International sued presidential candidate Ralph Nader for copyright and trademark infringement. The candidate was running a thirty-second TV ad (duplicated on his website) that borrowed the credit card company's successful "priceless" tagline to argue for the pricelessness of "the truth," which the ad argued would emerge only if Nader were permitted to participate in the presidential debates. A federal district court in New York produced an unpublished decision for Nader, finding that the credit card company had failed to establish how it was being harmed.[81]

In 2003, in a highly watched case, federal district court judge Denny Chin dismissed a trademark claim brought in New York by Fox News and its commentator Bill O'Reilly alleging that left-of-center author and media personality Al Franken had infringed on their rights by using the phrase "Fair and Balanced" on the cover of a book clearly designed to make fun of both Fox in general and O'Reilly in particular.

77. *Mead Data Central v. Toyota Motor Sales*, 875 F.2d 1026 (2d. Cir. 1989).
78. *Coca-Cola Co. v. Gemini Rising*, 346 F. Supp. 1183 (E.D.N.Y. 1972).
79. *L.L. Bean, Inc. v. Drake Publishers, Inc.*, 811 F.2d 26 (1st Cir. 1987).
80. *Lyons Partnership v. Giannoulas*, 179 F.3d 384 (5th Cir. 1999).
81. Valerie Sieminski, "First Amendment Priceless," *National Journal*, October 2, 2000, B12.

Chin concluded that it is highly unlikely that purchasers of books of political commentary are so unsophisticated as to believe, based on the appearance of the trademarked phrase, that Fox had somehow sponsored the Franken book.[82]

Use It or Lose It: The Fear of "Going Generic"

A company whose marketing of a protected product or service ceases for two years will generally be presumed to have abandoned the related trademark. In that case, the trademark will become part of the public domain, and any competitor can use it in commerce. Often, corporations place advertisements in the *Columbia Journalism Review* and similar trade magazines in an effort to remind opinion leaders of the companies' continued interest in their trademark, because abandonment can also be inferred from a marketer's failure to police others' inappropriate use of its trademarks. Thus, it is not at all unusual for a reporter who publishes an article that carelessly misuses a trademark somewhere in the text—for example, uses "Xerox" as a noun or a verb

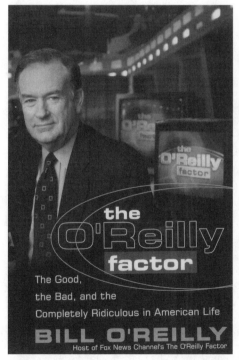 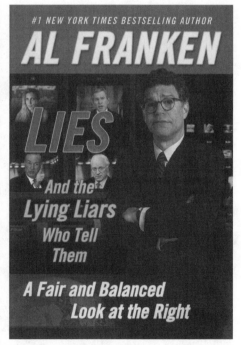

A federal district court felt it was an "easy case" in deciding that Al Franken was parodying rather than infringing upon whatever rights Bill O'Reilly might have in the phrase "Fair and Balanced."

---

82. *Fox News Network v. Penguin Group*, 2003 U.S. Dist. LEXIS 18693 (S.D.N.Y. 2003).

instead of as an adjective describing one particular company's photocopying machines—to receive a letter from one of the offended corporation's officers or attorneys. Although such letters sometimes read like threats of litigation, in fact corporations almost never sue reporters about these careless lapses. Indeed, the more important reason for sending the letter is that the company's file copy of it and other similar correspondence may become an important part of the company's proof, if it ever needs such proof, that it has not abandoned its trademarks.

Sometimes a company will lose the protection of a trademark through no fault of its own. This loss occurs if the trademark becomes "generic," that is, if the word itself becomes so well accepted by the public that the mental association with a particular company dissipates. There is a certain irony to all of this, of course. The most successfully marketed trademarks are perhaps the most likely to become generic over time. Regardless of how and why this reality of language evolution happens, the logic behind ending trademark protection is straightforward enough. If the public perceives that a certain word denotes a whole category of products rather than a particular

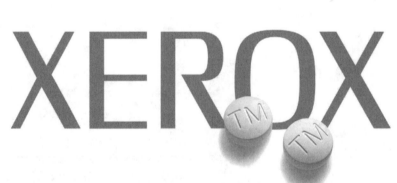

Firms such as Xerox invest literally billions of dollars in the value of their trademarks and thus use many strategies, including the periodic placement of ads such as this one, to protect those marks. Note that the slogan "There's a new way to look at it" is one that Xerox has used in a wide variety of ads; it has no direct relevance to the issue of protecting one's trademark from becoming generic. The Xerox folks ask us to remind readers that trademark is a nation-by-nation legal issue; for example, "aspirin" may no longer enjoy trademark protection in the United States but still enjoys protection in some other markets. Reprinted courtesy of Xerox Corporation.

THINGS TO REMEMBER

Protecting One's Trademark

- Trademarks are infringed upon when the likelihood of confusion is introduced as to whose products or services a customer is actually buying.
- Even actions that do not necessarily create confusion may still result in liability if they diminish a trademark's distinctiveness by diluting it.
- Courts generally recognize two varieties of trademark dilution: blurring and tarnishment.
- Unauthorized uses that might otherwise be considered tarnishing dilutions may be protected nonetheless as trademark parodies.
- A trademark may lose its protectability if, over time, consumers come to perceive the mark as a generic word describing the entire product category. Words such as cellophane, aspirin, and escalator, all once trademarks of specific companies, have gone this route.

company's goods, continuing to protect the trademark would result in the originator's monopoly not only in the use of the word but also in the ability to market that category of products. It may surprise you to learn some of the names for products currently on the market that once were the exclusive trademarks of a specific company.

Aspirin is one example;[83] other examples include escalators,[84] yo-yos,[85] thermoses,[86] "the pill" (as applied to contraceptive pills),[87] cola (not "Coca-Cola," just "cola"),[88] and cellophane.[89] It is no wonder that companies spend so much energy and resources protecting their valuable trademarks. Who among us, after all, has not misused such brand names as Xerox, Post-it, or Google?

Chapter Summary

Copyright law is designed to protect the rights of authors and artists and to encourage them to create. It covers everything from music to literary works, from architectural drawings to computer software. A work must be set down in some fixed medium and must manifest some degree of creativity to be eligible for protection. Mere facts are not copyrightable, although a creative compilation of facts may sometimes be copy-

---

83. *Bayer Co. v. United Drug Co.*, 272 F. 505 (N.Y. 1921).
84. *Haughton Elevator Co. v. Seeberger*, 85 U.S.P.Q. (BNA) 80 (1950).
85. *Donald F. Duncan, Inc. v. Royal Tops Mfg.*, 343 F.2d 655 (7th Cir. 1965).
86. *King-Seeley Thermos Co. v. Aladdin Industries*, 321 F.2d 577 (2d Cir. 1963).
87. *In re G.D. Searle & Co.*, 360 F.2d 650 (1966).
88. *Coca-Cola Co. v. Snow Crest Beverages*, 162 F.2d 280 (1st Cir. 1947).
89. *DuPont Cellophane Co. v. Waxed Products Co.*, 85 F.2d 75 (2d Cir. 1936).

rightable. In some instances, the natural owner of a copyright will be an employer, rather than the actual creative artist.

Copyright-infringement suits must establish originality (the plaintiff's work was legitimately copyrightable in the first place), access (the defendant was aware of the plaintiff's work), and substantial similarity (the defendant's work actually does constitute an infringement on the plaintiff's work).

The most important defense to a lawsuit is the fair-use doctrine, which asks courts to make four inquiries, examining the nature of the use (whether for purely commercial or for educational or other productive purposes); the nature of the work (whether already published or not; whether factual or artistic); how much was taken; and the likely effect on the potential value of the original copyright.

Trademark law's province is commerce, and it is designed to avoid consumer confusion in the marketplace. The word *trademark* is often used as shorthand to refer to trademarks, service marks, collective marks, certification marks, and trade dress, all of which are protected by the Lanham Act.

The law protects only distinctive marks, those that do something more than simply describe the product or service. Marks can be distinctive from their birth (as in the case of fanciful, arbitrary, or suggestive marks), or they may be otherwise merely descriptive terms that have become distinctive over time through the acquisition of a secondary meaning.

Typically, trademark-infringement lawsuits seek to establish that consumers are likely to be confused by the defendant's conduct as to the true source of goods or services. Infringement suits based on dilution do not require such proof, especially in the case of tarnishment claims. But even a use that may tarnish the public image of a trademark may be protected speech if it serves as a parody on the original.

Trademark holders' biggest fear is that their marks will be so successful that they become generic, that is, the public starts associating them with the entire industry's offerings rather than just that of one company. For example, "aspirin," "escalator," and "yo-yo" are now generic terms, although at one time they were protected trademarks.

Chapter 7

ACCESS TO INFORMATION

D espite the adage that "ignorance is bliss," it is probably a more accurate description of human nature to say that we hate being kept in the dark, or "out of the loop" as they say in Washington. Indeed, historians tell us that it is not the bumbling Watergate burglary that resulted in Richard Nixon's downfall but the cover-up that followed. Similarly, it was not the sex in the Oval Office itself that was the immediate source of Bill Clinton's impeachment but the failure to admit it and especially that omnipresent video clip in which he claimed "I did not have sex with that woman . . . Monica Lewinsky."

More recently, George W. Bush's administration suffered an embarrassing blow when *USA Today* revealed that the U.S. Department of Education had retained the services of a major public relations firm to help promote the president's "No Child Left Behind" initiatives, which provide for increased testing and student choice.[1] The PR firm in turn paid media personalities to speak highly of the president's plan (while not revealing the fact that they had been paid, of course). Syndicated columnist and radio talk show host Armstrong Williams admitted that he had been paid $240,000 for his kind words. Along the same lines, we learned from the *New York Times* that the Bush administration spent over $200 million to produce video news releases sent to TV stations nationwide.[2] Although the government agencies involved never instructed the station news directors to conceal the origin of the tapes, many did so, perhaps more out of laziness or embarrassment than chicanery. Again, to the extent there was public outrage over these incidents, the concern was not that the government was spending money to convince the American public of a particular point of view, but that the public did not know the government was the source of the news stories and the commentators' kind words.

---

1. Greg Toppo, "White House Paid Journalist to Promote Law," *USA Today*, January 7, 2005, 1A.

2. Anne. E. Kornblut, "Administration Is Warned about Its Publicity Videos," *New York Times*, February 19, 2005, A11.

The Bush administration suffered much embarrassment when its secret payments to commentators such as Armstrong Williams were revealed.

Another scandal illustrative of Americans' distaste for having secrets kept from us was playing out in my new home state of Connecticut as this book was going to press. William J. Sullivan, the state's chief justice, retired in early 2006 and apparently wanted to do all he could to ensure that Justice Peter Zarella, the governor's favored candidate to replace him, would be able to receive confirmation effortlessly. But Sullivan was not content to sing Zarella's praises publicly; he also purposely delayed the release of a court opinion he feared would prove controversial for his successor. That opinion, written in February 2005 but not officially released until May 2006, concerned the state's Freedom of Information Act and found Zarella voting with the majority in a 4-3 decision holding that certain judicial records were not subject to disclosure under the state law.[3] The decision itself was fairly routine, although the strategic delay in its release was anything but. When news of the artificial delay was revealed—by the acting chief justice—Zarella promptly removed his name from nomination. After much haggling, Sullivan agreed to testify about the scandal in front of the legislature's judiciary committee and the Judicial Review Council. The latter body made official findings chastising the former chief justice and imposing a fifteen-day suspension from his new status in semiretirement as a "senior justice."[4] So here we have a situation in which a fairly routine court decision dealing with access to government information alters the course of state government, because the delay of the decision's release was itself a denial of the public's access to government information. Clearly, residents of Connecticut get mighty upset at being kept in the dark.

---

3. *Clerk of the Superior Court v. Freedom of Information Commission*, 895 A.2d 743 (Conn. 2006).
4. Lynn Tuohy, "Court Saga Left Bruises, Balm," *Hartford Courant*, March 17, 2007, A1.

A First Amendment Right to Know?

The First Amendment's guarantees of freedom of speech and freedom of the press, the U.S. Supreme Court has said on a number of occasions, at least imply a corollary right to hear, to listen, to read. A group of concerned students successfully challenged a Long Island, New York, school board's decision to remove books from high school and junior high school libraries. Announcing the decision of the Court in *Board of Education v. Pico* (there was no majority opinion), Justice Brennan remarked that the justices have frequently held, "in a variety of contexts," that the First Amendment protects not only the right to speak but also "the right to receive information and ideas."[5] Within the realm of sexually oriented speech (see chapter 11), although states are free to pass antiobscenity laws that comport with certain federal guidelines, no state may make criminal the mere act of *reading* obscene materials.[6] In the 1960s, when the postmaster general sought to prevent the use of the mails for sending "Communist propaganda" to any persons who did not explicitly request it, the Court ruled that he had overstepped his bounds by placing such a requirement on readers. "It would be a barren marketplace of ideas that had only sellers and no buyers," Justice Brennan wrote.[7] In another case, although choosing to defer to the attorney general's refusal of an entry visa to a well-known Marxist scholar who wished to offer a series of lectures at American universities, the Court went out of its way to say that whatever First Amendment interests were involved here were those of the potential audience members.[8]

These cases all have something in common: the pairing of a willing speaker and an equally willing listener. Whatever First Amendment right to hear might exist, it cannot compel others to speak. Reporters assigned to cover a local crime story understand that the victim's relatives and friends have no obligation to answer their questions. A press credential is not a subpoena.

Suppose, however, that you are a reporter assigned to cover not one particular crime but overall violent crime statistics in your community. Do you have a First Amendment right to compel your government—local, state, or federal—to release to you the information you seek? It may surprise you to learn that the answer is no. Justice Stewart, in a famous lecture at Yale Law School, explained that "there is no constitutional right to have access to particular government information," that "the Constitution itself is neither a Freedom of Information Act nor an Official Secrets Act."[9]

In that same speech, Justice Stewart allowed that "Congress may provide a resolu-

---

5. 457 U.S. 853, 867 (1982).
6. *Stanley v. Georgia*, 394 U.S. 557 (1969).
7. *Lamont v. Postmaster General*, 381 U.S. 301, 308 (1965).
8. *Kleindienst v. Mandel*, 408 U.S. 753 (1972).
9. Potter Stewart, "Or of the Press," 26 *Hastings Law Journal* 631, 636 (1975).

tion," if it wishes. As it turns out, Congress and the individual state legislatures have stepped in to provide a measure of statutory support for the news-gathering process. Much of this chapter is devoted to a discussion of legislation designed to promote openness, especially the federal Freedom of Information Act. After considering some additional federal legislation (the Government in the Sunshine Act and the Federal Advisory Committee Act), we examine the general pattern of state laws designed to mirror and sometimes go beyond the federal legislation. Finally, we consider ways in which media outlets themselves sometimes stand in the way of the "public's right to know."

A small caveat is in order first: it has become increasingly difficult to distinguish between news gathering and news reporting. Some media activities seem to fit into both categories simultaneously. Among these are the televising of live and unedited events. The bizarre slow-motion "chase" involving O. J. Simpson's white Bronco is probably the most vividly recalled example. The technological ability of the electronic media to cover events live both around the corner and halfway around the world cannot help but have significant implications for the traditionally accepted distinctions between news gathering and news reporting.

News Gathering: The Constitutional Framework

"I don't have to tell you that it gets mighty hot in Philadelphia in July!" So said columnist and author George Will to the Senate Committee on Rules and Administration back in 1985. Will was testifying—unsuccessfully, as it turned out—against a bill that was about to open Senate floor debates to regular gavel-to-gavel TV coverage (thus also indirectly creating what is now known as the C-SPAN 2 cable network). Will feared that bringing TV cameras into the Senate, which the founders designed as the more deliberative body of Congress, would greatly diminish the quality of debate. It is very clear that the Founding Fathers would not support this degree of openness, Will argued. After all, when the Continental Congress was convened in Philadelphia in the summer of 1787 for the purpose of writing the Constitution, the doors and windows were bolted shut.

There is a great deal of evidence from the records of those debates in Philadelphia and the contemporaneous writings of Thomas Jefferson, James Madison, and others suggesting that Will was right. The founders did not presume that the right to report news includes a constitutional right to gather news. That would not necessarily prevent the more modern Supreme Court, of course, from interpreting the First Amendment more expansively. As we see in chapter 8, the Court has fashioned a fairly extensive First Amendment right to attend court proceedings and to write about what transpires in the courtroom. Yet the Court has refused to create a more expansive First Amendment right to gather news from the government.

No Special Access Rights for the Press: A Tale of Three Prisons

It was in 1972 that the Court came closest to suggesting that the First Amendment, properly interpreted, includes at least a qualified right to gather news. In *Branzburg v. Hayes*, the Court ruled that a reporter for the Louisville *Courier-Journal* did not have a First Amendment right to disobey a subpoena to testify in front of a grand jury concerning stories he had written about local trafficking in illegal drugs. Even though the decision ultimately went against the reporter, Justice White allowed that "freedom of the press could be eviscerated" if there were no First Amendment protection for seeking out the news.[10] Whatever solace the press may have taken from those words began to seem misplaced two years later, when the Court handed down two cases on the same day that both rejected reporters' claims that their First Amendment right to gather news had been abridged. The first, *Pell v. Procunier*, concerned a California Department of Corrections regulation providing that reporters would have access to prisons and might be able to interview inmates chosen by the prison staff but that reporters could not themselves select any particular inmates for interviews.[11] Prison officials argued that the policy was necessary to prevent certain prisoners from becoming "celebrities" who were able to influence other prisoners to emulate their own noncooperative conduct. Writing for the Court's majority, Justice Stewart upheld the prison regulation. The Constitution, he concluded, does not "require government to accord the press special access to information not shared by members of the public generally. . . . The right to speak and publish does not carry with it the unrestrained right to gather information."

The second case, *Saxbe v. Washington Post Co.*, involved a Federal Bureau of Prisons regulation virtually identical to the California rule against requesting a specific prisoner to interview.[12] Writing for the same 5-4 majority, Justice Stewart emphasized that there were ample alternative means by which reporters could gather information about the correctional systems without enjoying carte blanche to interview anyone they chose. They could carry on correspondence with inmates. They could tour the prisons, even the most secure sections of the facilities, and interact with any inmates they happened to encounter. And, of course, they could always interview *former* prisoners.

Four years later, the Court dealt with yet another prison-access case.[13] KQED sought radio and television access to a particular portion of the Alameda County Jail (in the San Francisco Bay area) that had been the site of an inmate suicide as well as a number of alleged beatings and rapes. The litigation that ensued produced a fragmented Court decision, with two justices not participating and the remaining seven unable to agree on a majority opinion. Taken together, the plurality opinion (written

---

10. *Branzburg v. Hayes*, 408 U.S. 665, 681 (1972).

11. 417 U.S. 817 (1974).

12. 417 U.S. 843 (1974).

13. *Houchins v. KQED, Inc.*, 438 U.S. 1 (1978).

by Chief Justice Burger and joined by Justices Rehnquist and White) and Justice Stewart's separate concurrence nonetheless make clear that the Court was again unwilling to put much stock in the notion of a First Amendment right to gather news. The plurality opinion allows that there is a strong public benefit to be derived from access to information about jail conditions but asserts that there is "no basis for reading into the Constitution a right of the public or the media to enter these institutions, with camera equipment, and take moving and still pictures of inmates for broadcast purposes." The First Amendment does not mean that the media are guaranteed "a right of access to all sources of information within government control."

Justice Stewart's separate concurring opinion provided the needed fourth vote in this case. He agreed that KQED personnel were legitimately denied access to specific sections of jail, precisely because the public was denied the same access. In those portions of the jail where the public had been granted access, however, Stewart insisted that broadcast media representatives must be permitted to bring in their electronic equipment.

Access to Other Places

The Supreme Court's decisions in these three prison cases are very consistent with more general principles governing the relationship between the press and government authorities empowered to control the security of specific spaces. Thus, even though both the press and the public are generally free to traverse public streets and parks, anyone who disobeys a police officer's legitimate order to disperse in an emergency (such as the site of an automobile accident) may be prosecuted for crimes such as obstructing the law, resisting arrest, or trespassing.[14] More typically, media personnel with appropriate identification are permitted to cross police barricades, although in most jurisdictions this practice is entirely at the discretion of the officers on the scene.

In the case of spaces that might be *owned* by the public but generally not *open* to the public (such as military bases or power-generating plants), trespassers are even more likely to be arrested.[15] Also, elaborate procedures exist for determining how and when reporters will be permitted access by the military to international war zones. There have been ongoing tensions between the media and Pentagon officials about this issue for many years, resulting in cycles of openness and secrecy. It is commonly believed that reporting from Vietnam led to diminished public support for the war. A wary Pentagon thus succeeded for the most part in keeping the press away from the war zone in the early 1980s when the United States invaded Grenada. Media outrage spurred Congress to appoint an independent commission, which recommended that a small number of media organizations be allowed to serve as stand-ins for the

14. *State v. Lashinsky*, 404 A.2d 1121 (N.J. 1979); *City of Oak Creek v. Ah King*, 436 N.W.2d 285 (Wis. 1989).

15. *Greer v. Spock*, 424 U.S. 828 (1976).

press as a whole in a system of "pooled" reporting. This "pooled" reporting system was used in the 1991 Persian Gulf War, but the press complained about the "video game" aspect of the war, with Pentagon briefings consisting largely of replays of successful "smart bomb" target hits. How many of the bombs were *not* so smart, the press wondered. A 1991 lawsuit challenging the tight control maintained over the media during the Gulf War, however, was unsuccessful.[16]

In the military operations launched against Afghanistan following the September 11, 2001, attacks, the media were initially not permitted access to the actual ground operations, restricted instead to offshore stationing on U.S. military vessels in the Arabian Sea. The Pentagon subsequently determined that both its interests and the interests of the press might best be served by "embedding" reporters with selected military units. In 2004, the RAND Corporation, a think tank, concluded that this embedding of reporters with the military in Iraq had worked well, that the media's objectivity had not been compromised by their close relationship with soldiers.

Equal Access to News as a First Amendment Right

Although courts have been very reluctant to find in the First Amendment an implicit right to gather news, several courts have held that once the government *chooses* to provide access to the news media, it may not discriminate among friendly and unfriendly media outlets. In one case, a federal judge held that a sheriff in the New Orleans area, who at the time was involved in libel litigation with the *Times-Picayune* newspaper, had trampled on the First Amendment when he announced that reporters for that particular media company would no longer receive advance word of upcoming press conferences and would be turned away at the door if they attempted to participate in any such press conferences. The sheriff further advised his staff not to provide any information to or answer any questions from employees of the newspaper, except through a highly restricted process in writing through his public information office.[17]

A similar result was reached in Hawaii, where Honolulu mayor Frank Fasi sought to bar one particular *Honolulu Advertiser* reporter from official press conferences. That the mayor described it as a personal grudge against only one man (reporter Richard Borreca) and that he was willing to welcome any reporter from the same newspaper other than Borreca made no difference to the federal judge. Granting access to individual reporters on the basis of compatibility with the mayor is as much an act of censorship, Judge King concluded, as would be requiring a newspaper to submit its proposed news stories for prepublication clearance.[18] A similar result would likely obtain if Kathleen Baydala or her employer, the *Clarion-Ledger*, ever sought a

---

16. *Nation Magazine v. U.S. Department of Defense*, 762 F. Supp. 1558 (S.D.N.Y. 1991).

17. *Times-Picayune Publishing v. Lee*, 15 Media L. Rep. (BNA) 1713 (E.D. La. 1988).

18. *Borreca v. Fasi*, 369 F. Supp. 906 (D. Haw. 1974).

judgment against Jackson, Mississippi, mayor Frank Melton, who refused her entry to a generally open press conference in early 2006.[19] Perhaps it is a measure of poetic justice that Baydala's byline continues to be seen by Jackson residents reading about the mayor's being sentenced to jail for violating parole conditions related to misdemeanor gun charges.[20]

Even the White House is not relieved of the obligation to treat media representatives evenhandedly. Reporter Robert Sherrill from the *Nation* magazine brought suit against the Secret Service for denying him access to the White House as a "security risk." Although the D.C. Circuit Court of Appeals did not require that the Secret Service's decision be reversed, it did insist that the Secret Service give any reporter denied a pass written notice and an opportunity to rebut whatever evidence was used to support the government's decision. The court made clear, however, that its decision should not be read to require "that the White House must open its doors to the press, conduct press conferences, or operate press facilities."[21]

Politicians might not be able to deny individual reporters access to press conferences or similar events open to large numbers of media representatives, but this does not mean that public officials must grant special access to any particular reporter. Indeed, at least in some circumstances the reporter's calls need not even be returned. Thus, Governor Robert Ehrlich of Maryland was within his rights to instruct state agencies to refuse any contact beyond that required by law (such as to answer inquiries made under the state's Public Information Act) with two specific *Baltimore Sun* reporters whom he disliked.[22] Similarly, the mayor of Youngstown, Ohio, did not violate the law, a federal judge held, by refusing to do one-on-one interviews with disfavored reporters.[23]

Hearing from Criminals and Bureaucrats

In two instances, the Supreme Court has struck down laws aimed squarely at reporters' potential sources rather than at media outlets themselves, at least in part because of the laws' effect on the "public's right to know." The term "news gathering" appears nowhere in either case, yet the philosophical bases for the decisions are very consistent with the media's often-repeated argument that the news-gathering process deserves special protection precisely because the public will otherwise be deprived of important information about weighty political matters.

---

19. Chris Joyner, "Mayor Kicks C-L Out of News Conference," *Clarion-Ledger* (Jackson, Mississippi), April 12, 2006, 1B.

20. Kathleen Baydala, "Jailed," *Clarion-Ledger* (Jackson, Mississippi), March 8, 2007, 1A.

21. *Sherrill v. Knight*, 569 F.2d 124 (D.C. Cir. 1977).

22. *Baltimore Sun Co. v. Ehrlich*, 437 F.3d 410 (4th Cir. 2006).

23. *Youngstown Publishing Co. v. McKelvey*, 2005 U.S. Dist. LEXIS 9476 (N.D. Ohio 2005). The case was later vacated by an appellate court, which refused to rule on the merits because the mayor had already left office. 189 Fed. Appx. 402 (6th Cir. 2006).

The first of these cases involved New York State's "Son of Sam" law, named after the Son of Sam serial killer, David Berkowitz. The law required that any profits derived from writing about criminal wrongdoing be placed in a special escrow account for a period of five years, during which time the identifiable victims of any such crimes would be able to seek payment from that fund in partial compensation for their injuries. Justice O'Connor's majority opinion struck down the law as classic content-based censorship, finding that a financial disincentive to publish, when aimed only at some topics of discussion, is just as odious as an outright ban on the speech. Her opinion argues that such statutes also can deprive the public of important information, that such classic works as *The Autobiography of Malcolm X* (which describes crimes committed by the civil rights leader before he became a public figure) and Henry David Thoreau's *Civil Disobedience* might never have been written if such a law had been in place.[24] Although most states have a Son of Sam law on the books, those that have been challenged in the courts have generally not fared well.[25] In 2002, for example, the California Supreme Court struck down its law, even though the legislature had tried to cure what it saw as the New York law's main weaknesses.[26]

The second Supreme Court decision was handed down in 1995, invalidating portions of the federal Ethics Reform Act that prohibited the vast majority of federal employees from receiving honoraria for writing or lecturing in their spare time, even if the topic of their communications was not at all related to their official duties. Here too, the Court emphasized the law's effect on the public's right to know. "Federal

Son of Sam laws are designed to prevent this kind of profiteering from crime, but they have generally been found unconstitutional when challenged.

---

24. *Simon & Schuster, Inc. v. New York State Crime Victims Board*, 502 U.S. 105 (1991).

25. Melissa Malecki, "Son of Sam: Has North Carolina Remedied the Past Problems of Criminal Anti-profit Legislation?" 89 *Marquette Law Review* 673 (2006).

26. *Keenan v. Superior Court*, 40 P.3d 718 (Cal. 2002).

employees who write for publication in their spare time have made significant contributions to the marketplace of ideas," wrote Justice Stevens for the Court. "They include literary giants like Nathaniel Hawthorne and Herman Melville, who were employed by the Customs Service; Walt Whitman, who worked for the Departments of Justice and Interior; and Bret Harte, an employee of the mint."[27]

Note, however, that neither of these cases seeks to establish an affirmative constitutional right to *compel* criminals or government employees to share their wisdom with us. In this sense, perhaps, they are best thought of as anticensorship decisions that happen to include a bit of pro-news-gathering dicta.

Access to Public Information: The Statutory Framework

Although the First Amendment does not provide the media an affirmative right to obtain government documents, the federal government and all state governments have passed laws that give varying degrees of such access. The federal and state laws often cover similar kinds of information and provide similar exemptions from disclosure. Even though forty states had freedom of information laws on the books before passage of the federal legislation in 1966, for convenience, we begin here with a detailed examination of the federal Freedom of Information Act.

The Federal Freedom of Information Act

Congress passed the **Freedom of Information Act** (**FOIA**, pronounced "foy-uh") in 1966, although it has been amended several times since. The philosophy undergirding the act, as interpreted by the federal courts, is that government works best when its work is open to public inspection. By exercising their rights accorded by the act, reporters and activists have helped us learn about issues such as the dangerous Ford Pinto gas tank and the carcinogenic Red Dye #2, why the Hubble space telescope initially failed, and how the federal savings and loan crisis developed. Although the initial shocking photos from the Abu Ghraib prison in Iraq were released spontaneously by a soldier, the government was forced to release additional photos and details of detainee abuse as a direct result of a FOIA request made by the American Civil Liberties Union.

The act requires federal agencies, upon request, to make available any records that do not fit one of the law's nine exemptions. Most of the exemptions tell agencies only what they *may* withhold; government officials can usually choose to reveal more than the FOIA demands. Each year several million FOIA requests for government information are made. Because requesters who are denied the information they seek are ex-

---

27. *United States v. National Treasury Employees Union*, 513 U.S. 454, 464–465 (1995).

The fact that Congress chose to prohibit certain federal employees from making money by giving speeches or writing was a fatal flaw, the Court held in the *National Treasury Employees Union* case.

---

plicitly given the right to bring suit in federal court, hundreds of federal FOIA cases are decided annually.

These cases typically involve the process of statutory construction introduced in chapter 1, as the courts' main role is to decide what the act means and whether a specific federal agency has conducted itself in ways consistent with the act. The courts generally do not look to the First Amendment to decide these cases, because there is no *constitutional* obligation for the government to open its records to the public.

It is also important to note that the act depends very much on the goodwill of the various federal agencies and the executive branch in fostering an atmosphere of openness. Each administration has interpreted the FOIA in ways consistent with the president's own philosophies. There are myriad ways for agencies to violate the spirit of the act: they may interpret the various exemptions broadly; they may not hire enough staff for their agencies' FOIA units; or, even if they have sufficient staff, they may create an incentive system that rewards the staff for maintaining secrecy rather than for fostering openness. As reporter Carl Stern once explained, although the act includes nine statutory exemptions to the presumption of disclosure, in fact there always has been a tenth unwritten exemption: the individual bureaucrat who has decided that "I don't want to give it to you, so I won't give it to you."

In response to the terrorist attacks of 2001, the federal government took numerous actions consistent with its belief that more secrecy was needed to minimize the likelihood of future incidents. Potentially sensitive information was removed from government websites. Then attorney general John Ashcroft circulated a memo in October 2001 to agency heads telling them to err on the side of nondisclosure of information requested under the FOIA and promising them the government's resources to defend them in any resulting litigation, just so long as there is "any sound legal basis" for a refusal to release information. In 2003 the General Accounting Office (now the Government Accountability Office) reported that one-third of federal agency officers responsible for FOIA requests admitted that the memo had already resulted in their holding back information on requests they would have granted in the past.

In more than twenty cases since 2001, the government has asked courts to dismiss a plaintiff's suit—such as when a German citizen sought damages for having been kidnapped by the CIA and tortured—on the grounds that by defending itself, the government would be forced to reveal classified and otherwise sensitive information.[28] Although this latter phenomenon is not directly relevant to the FOIA, it nonetheless serves as a reminder that we may be in for a cycle of relatively secret government, and given that we have no way of knowing when a "war against terror" might be over, it is hard to predict how long that cycle might run.

We now continue our look at the federal FOIA by examining how courts have interpreted such basic issues as the definition of an "agency record" and the scope of the statutorily prescribed exemptions from disclosure.

---

28. *El-Masri v. Tenet*, 437 F. Supp. 2d 530 (E.D. Va. 2006).

What Is an "Agency"?   The FOIA defines a federal agency as "any executive department, military department, Government corporation, Government controlled corporation, or other establishment in the executive branch of the Government (including the Executive Office of the President), or any independent regulatory agency." Conspicuously missing from this list are Congress and the federal judiciary. The president is also not considered an "agency," nor is the presidential staff or any group whose sole function is to advise the president. Thus, for example, President Reagan's Task Force on Regulatory Relief was deemed an advisory board whose records were properly withheld from a FOIA request, notwithstanding that *individual members* of the task force (including Vice President Bush and several cabinet officers) certainly had functions beyond that of simply advising the president.[29] Similarly, the National Security Council has been held to be beyond the reach of the FOIA. The council's function, as set forth in the National Security Act, is "to *advise* the President with respect to the integration of domestic, foreign, and military policies relating to the national security."[30]

The definition of "agency" in the act does cover many entities, however. It includes the departments of government headed by the various cabinet officers, such as the Department of the Treasury and the Department of Defense. The act also covers the various agencies that report to cabinet members; for example, the FBI, which reports to the attorney general, is covered. The many agencies whose work is especially relevant to communication industries, such as the Federal Communications Commission, the Federal Trade Commission, and the Food and Drug Administration, are also covered by the act.

What Is a "Record"?   The FOIA does not define the word *record*, but the case law makes clear that it is to be interpreted broadly to include papers, reports, manuals, letters, and computer files, as well as audiotapes and other sound recordings, films, and photos. One thing that all these categories of materials have in common is their reproducibility. Physical objects that do not share this quality are generally beyond the scope of the FOIA. Thus, a reporter might obtain ballistic records from the FBI but will not be given access to actual guns and bullets. You may get reports on the efficacy of competing diet pills from the FDA, but you will not get samples of the pills studied by the agency.

In determining whether requested information is an agency record within the meaning of the act, courts often focus on whether the information was created by the agency, or at least obtained by the agency in the course of its normal duties. A 1980 Supreme Court decision, *Kissinger v. Reporters Committee for Freedom of the Press*, is instructive.[31] The Reporters Committee had requested transcripts of some of former

---

29. *Meyer v. Bush*, 981 F.2d 1288 (D.C. Cir. 1993).
30. *Armstrong v. Executive Office of the President*, 90 F.3d 553 (D.C. Cir. 1996) (emphasis added).
31. 445 U.S. 136 (1980).

secretary of state Henry Kissinger's conversations. Although such materials might otherwise have been within the scope of the FOIA, the Supreme Court held that the fact that Kissinger donated them to the Library of Congress prior to the filing of the committee's FOIA request meant that the transcripts were no longer "agency re-cords." Because the Library of Congress is not covered by the FOIA and Kissinger's agreement with the library included substantial limitations on public access to the donated materials, this decision effectively prevented the disclosure of the requested transcripts.

That same case also included a request by *New York Times* columnist William Safire for some written notes made by Kissinger about his phone conversations. Be-cause the notes were made while Kissinger was an adviser to the president rather than the secretary of state, they would not normally be treated as agency records covered by the FOIA. Safire, however, hoped that they would be released anyway because they were housed at the State Department, which is within FOIA's scope. The Supreme Court refused Safire's request, however, holding that the physical location of materials cannot alone make them into "agency records." To be considered agency records, materials must be created by a covered agency or otherwise obtained in the course of carrying out its official functions. For example, the Department of Justice was ordered to release numerous records of federal court decisions involving tax laws. Although the department does not create such records—they are created by the trial courts themselves—it keeps them on file because it provides the attorneys to represent the government in court on tax matters. This fact was enough to have the opinions con-sidered Department of Justice agency records for the purposes of a FOIA request.[32]

A quirky case in 2006 put government officials on notice that if they don't want their appointment calendars to be treated as agency records, they should not share them too widely within their agencies. A consumer group wanted to see the desk calendars of six Department of Agriculture administrators to learn with which indi-viduals and groups they had met before they loosened some meat-testing standards. A federal appellate court held that the appointment books for five of the six employ-ees should be disclosed. They were agency records rather than merely personal re-cords, the court found, because they were created on company time and the employees had found it helpful to make their calendar entries available on a central-ized computer system (apparently to keep coworkers and superiors appraised of their activities). The one employee whose calendar entries were shared only with his secre-tary was allowed to keep his data secret. But the five employees whose appointment books were subject to disclosure were told they could delete truly personal entries (dental appointments?) prior to complying.[33]

---

32. *U.S. Department of Justice v. Tax Analysts*, 492 U.S. 136 (1989).

33. *Consumer Federation of America v. U.S. Department of Agriculture*, 455 F.3d 283 (D.C. Cir. 2006).

Making a FOIA Request.   Perhaps the most difficult part of making a request under the FOIA is identifying the federal agency most likely to house the information sought. There is no single government-wide FOIA clearinghouse, so a fairly thorough understanding of the kinds of functions performed by the various agencies is needed. If you are interested in learning whether a particular toy is suspected by the government of being a safety hazard, for example, the Consumer Product Safety Commission is a logical place to start. A reporter desiring the latest report on the conditions at a specific nursing home that receives Medicare payments would likely contact the local Social Security office. If you are unsure which agency to contact, a good place to begin your research is the *Federal Register*, where each agency provides a description of its functions, as well as any FOIA contact information. Many federal agencies also have websites that provide varying degrees of helpfulness to potential FOIA requesters. The website of the Reporters Committee for Freedom of the Press (http://www.rcfp.org) also provides help in using the FOIA, including sample letters of request.

Once you identify the specific agency most likely to house the information you seek, a short letter to that agency's freedom of information (FOI) officer is the next step. Indicate early on (probably in the opening paragraph) that you are making a request "pursuant to the federal Freedom of Information Act" and, in as much detail as you possibly can, specify the precise information you seek. Mention if you are a representative of the news media, because the FOIA instructs agencies to give special consideration to reporters who intend to disseminate the information they gather. Perhaps most important is that agencies are supposed to charge such requestors only the cost of duplicating the records (waiving the often much larger cost involved in researching and organizing the records). Indeed, the act provides that *all* fees may be waived if the release of the information sought will be in the public interest. So add a sentence or two explaining why you believe the articles you intend to write will indeed benefit the public.

Because we are living in a digital age, indicate also in what form you would like the information (old-fashioned paper, CD-ROM, etc.). The FOIA was amended in 1996 by the Electronic Freedom of Information Act Amendments, which require that agencies comply with such instructions as long as the records sought are "readily reproducible" in the format requested. In other words, an agency FOI officer will not be required to *create* a database according to the parameters you prefer, but if the database has already been created, it is considered an agency record every bit as much as is the hard paper version of the same data.

The FOIA requires that agencies respond to requests for information within twenty days of receipt. This requirement, however, does not necessarily mean you will have the information you seek in twenty days. Often the response is in the form of a request for additional specificity or an alert that the request is a huge one that will take a fair amount of time to fill. If the agency's FOI officer concludes that the information you seek falls within the scope of one of the nine exemptions enumerated in the act, your request may be denied. Or some material may be deemed releasable, and other portions subject to withholding. In that case, a redacted version of your request will be released, which often takes the decidedly low-tech form of sheets of paper with the exempted information blacked out. Agencies that deny requests either in whole or in part are generally required to provide descriptions of the kinds of documents being withheld, together with precise reasons for the withholding.[34] This detailed listing of the kinds of documents in the agency's possession that are and are not being released is often referred to in the case law and commentary as a **Vaughn index**, named after an appellate decision from 1973.[35] If, however, an agency can demonstrate that the mere listing of the kinds of information available in the file will itself result in the same kind of serious harm that disclosure of the full documents would cause, the agency may be permitted to answer a request by refusing to indicate even whether the requested documents exist. Such answers are called **Glomar responses**, named after a commercial vessel, the records for which had been the subject of a FOIA request in a 1976 decision.[36]

Exemptions from Disclosure.

The Freedom of Information Act provides nine exemptions from the presumption that requests for information should be honored. Except for exemption 3, these exemptions are discretionary: FOI officers who conclude that a requested record falls within the scope of an exemption *may* withhold the information, but they are *not obligated* to withhold it.

THINGS TO REMEMBER

Fundamentals of the Federal FOIA

- Passed in 1966 and amended several times since, the Freedom of Information Act tells government officials that they must make their agency records available to requestors, unless the requests fall within the scope of a handful of statutory exemptions.
- Under the act, "agencies" include departments headed by or reporting to cabinet officials, as well as many other kinds of executive offices; the president, Congress, and the judiciary are exempted, as are entities whose sole function is to advise the president.
- Virtually any reproducible data can be considered a "record" under the act, whether in the form of paper, film, photos, or computer records.
- Agency records must have been created by a covered agency or otherwise obtained in the course of carrying out its official functions.
- The act specifies the time frame in which FOI staff must respond to requests for information, as well as fees to be charged for searching and photocopying.

---

34. *King v. U.S. Department of Justice*, 830 F.2d 210, 224 (D.C. Cir. 1987).
35. *Vaughn v. Rosen*, 484 F.2d 820 (D.C. Cir. 1973).
36. *Phillippi v. CIA*, 546 F.2d 1009 (D.C. Cir. 1976).

Exemption 1: National Security.   This first exemption permits agencies to withhold records that are "specifically authorized under criteria established by an Executive order to be kept secret in the interest of national defense or foreign policy" if the records are properly classified.[37] Not surprisingly, some agencies, such as the CIA and the NSA, are in effect given virtual carte blanche to withhold information under this exemption. In 2004 a federal appellate court denied a law professor's request to see what documents the CIA had accumulated about him. The agency was willing to say only that they had a file. The court allowed this, reminding us the FOIA does not permit agencies to take into account the identity of a requestor. "Any information available to [Professor] Bassiouni is available to North Korea's secret police and Iran's counterintelligence service too," Judge Easterbrook explained.[38] On the other hand, the American Civil Liberties Union succeeded in compelling the CIA to reveal some photos of detainee abuse by coalition forces in Iraq and Afghanistan.[39]

Federal judges who hear exemption 1 appeals are permitted to review the classified material to determine if the decision to classify was a proper one. In practice, judges very rarely exercise their right to perform such in camera reviews, relying instead on detailed affidavits from the government explaining why the material has been kept secret. An exception to this generalization is seen in a 2006 decision in which U.S. district court judge Ellen Segal Huvelle performed an independent review of dozens of documents sought by the American Civil Liberties Union concerning FBI surveillance activities, the release of which was opposed by the agency on national security grounds. The judge determined that all but one of the documents were properly withheld; the one remaining document apparently was pretty innocuous, naming attendees at a University of California, Irvine forum sponsored by the Muslim Public Affairs Council.[40]

Exemption 2: Internal Agency Personnel Rules.   This exemption covers records of two very different kinds. FOIA attorneys often refer to them as the "low 2" and "high 2" categories.

The "low 2" exemption covers records "related solely to the internal personnel rules and practices of an agency." This part of exemption 2 is designed to protect some admittedly trivial materials from disclosure, such as the agency's rules for coffee or cigarette breaks and personal leave days. This exemption does not exist to protect delicate information, the kind that would violate employees' privacy. (Exemption 6 covers the more personal kinds of personnel files.) The Supreme Court has held that this part of exemption 2 seeks to "relieve agencies of the burden of assembling and

---

37. *Baez v. U.S. Department of Justice*, 647 F.2d 1328 (D.C. Cir. 1980).

38. *Bassiouni v. CIA*, 392 F.3d 244 (7th Cir. 2004). In general, the court was right about the irrelevance of a FOIA requestor's identity, but there are exceptions, especially concerning prisoners' presentencing reports. See the discussion of this issue on pages 303–4.

39. *American Civil Liberties Union v. U.S. Department of Defense*, 2006 U.S. Dist. LEXIS 40894 (S.D.N.Y. 2006).

40. *American Civil Liberties Union v. FBI*, 429 F. Supp. 2d 179 (D.D.C. 2006).

maintaining for public inspection matter in which the public could not reasonably be expected to have an interest."[41] By contrast, the "high 2" portion of exemption 2 is designed to protect internal agency data that may very well have some public interest but that could make it difficult for the agency to function if it were publicly disseminated.

Let us look at an example of each kind of exemption 2 withholding. In *Sinsheimer v. U.S. Department of Homeland Security*, an accountant in the Department of Homeland Security who had a pending employment-discrimination suit and who had himself been a defendant in a couple of sexual-harassment complaints sought a memo that apparently gave supervisors instructions as to how to resolve sexual-harassment complaints.[42] If this document were publicized, the department warned, future complainants and defendants might be able to foil an ongoing investigation. Here was a perfect example of a "high 2" exemption. Our "low 2" example is a bit older. In *Schiller v. National Labor Relations Board*,[43] a private citizen had filed an FOIA request seeking documents related to the Equal Access to Justice Act, by which plaintiffs who successfully sue government agencies may sometimes receive court costs and attorney's fees. This may sound a bit too weighty to be a "low 2" case, but some of the documents withheld or at least blacked out in part by the National Labor Relations Board included references to information the court felt was fairly trivial and of primary interest only as internal personnel matters. Included were the agency's internal deadlines for completing various tasks, names of persons individuals at the agency sometimes call for assistance, and even instructions to employees about how to keep records.

Some federal agencies have taken the position that *any* information in their files that can assist the agency's employees in performing their duties should fall within exemption 2. Courts have generally rejected such a broad interpretation of the exemption. In two similar cases from 1997, for example, the Ninth and Tenth Circuits rejected the U.S. Forest Service's somewhat comical assertion that maps showing the nesting sites of certain birds were the kinds of internal personnel files encompassed by exemption 2.[44]

Exemption 3: Withholding Mandated by Other Federal Laws. Perhaps this part of the FOIA should be known as the "We bow down to other laws" exemption. It is sometimes referred to as the "catchall" exemption, and it is the only one of the nine wherein nondisclosure of requested files may be mandatory rather than discretionary. Agencies seeking to withhold data under this exemption must point to a specific federal law that either demands that this kind of information be kept secret or

---

41. *Department of Air Force v. Rose*, 425 U.S. 352, 369–370 (1976).

42. 2006 U.S. Dist. LEXIS 39684 (D.D.C. 2006).

43. 964 F.2d 1205 (D.C. Cir. 1992).

44. *Audubon Society v. U.S. Forest Service*, 104 F.3d 1201 (10th Cir. 1997); *Maricopa Audubon Society v. U.S. Forest Service*, 108 F.3d 1082 (9th Cir. 1997).

establishes clear criteria for determining whether the material must be withheld. Often courts are called on to referee what might be described as a "dance of deference," as some federal statutes generally calling for nondisclosure include provisions rendering that presumption inoperable if another law (such as FOIA) would otherwise mandate disclosure. Thus, for example, a group seeking Internal Revenue Service documents about how the agency decided to extend tax-exempt status to Pat Robertson's Christian Broadcasting Network was unsuccessful, in large part because sections of the Internal Revenue Code required that such records remain confidential.[45]

Dozens of federal laws sometimes are interpreted to require nondisclosure under FOIA's exemption 3. Among these are the Family Educational Rights and Privacy Act (FERPA, sometimes called the Buckley Act), the Health Insurance Portability and Accountability Act (HIPAA), and the more recently enacted Homeland Security Act of 2002, a section of which provides that information submitted to the government concerning "critical infrastructure" should be withheld from FOIA disclosure. Senator Patrick Leahy of Vermont has pointed out that such a broad exemption is easily subject to abuse, as companies can shield from public scrutiny damaging information about their own inadequate performance with a "disclose [to the government] and immunize [from further disclosure]" strategy.

Perhaps the federal law FOIA requestors most frequently confront is the Privacy Act of 1974, which grants a qualified right to find out what information the government has about us, to correct such information where necessary, and to limit the ways in which the government may use that information (and to whom it may release it). In 1984 Congress amended the Privacy Act to clarify that the FOIA's presumption in favor of openness should prevail whenever the two laws might seem to conflict. Nonetheless, agencies will sometimes err on the side of nondisclosure, because persons may bring suit under the Privacy Act against any government agency that improperly reveals personal information about them to others. Such suits, if successful, can result in payment not only of court costs and attorney's fees but also of compensatory damages. By contrast, an FOIA requestor who sues an agency for improperly withholding data cannot receive damages.

A good example of exemption 3 at work is found in *CIA v. Sims*, decided by the Supreme Court in 1985.[46] At issue was a FOIA request for information about "MKULTRA," a multifaceted initiative in the 1950s and 1960s through which the CIA sought data on "the use of biological and chemical materials in altering human behavior," or "brainwashing." Part of the experiments had the government administering consciousness-altering drugs such as LSD to unwitting subjects, two of whom died during the course of the studies. The FOIA request sought copies of the grant proposals and contracts awarded under the MKULTRA program as well as the names of the individuals, research universities, and other institutions that had performed the research. In denying that request, the CIA pointed to the National Security Act of

---

45. *Tax Analysts v. IRS*, 410 F.3d 715 (D.C. Cir. 2005).
46. 471 U.S. 159 (1985).

1947, which instructs the director of the agency to "protect intelligence sources and methods."

The Supreme Court ruled unanimously in favor of the CIA and had no difficulty in determining at the outset that the National Security Act was precisely the kind of law to which Congress intended agency FOI officers to defer when it wrote exemption 3. The legislative history of the FOIA indicated that Congress knew the act's sponsors intended that the National Security Act would trigger FOIA's third exemption. Lower courts called on to rule on the issue had also so held.

The more complicated part of the Court's deliberations concerned whether this particular FOIA request was covered by the National Security Act's call for nondisclosure, that is, whether the names of the individuals and institutions sought should be categorized as "intelligence sources." The lower court fashioned a definition limited to sources of information that the agency "could not reasonably expect to obtain without guaranteeing confidentiality," but Chief Justice Burger's majority opinion concluded that the decision as to when promises of confidentiality are necessary should be left to the director of the CIA, not to the courts.

Exemption 4: Confidential Commercial Information.   Often, in the course of conducting an investigation of a company or an industry (such as in deciding whether to approve a merger or to block it on antitrust grounds[47]), the government will learn things about one company that its competitors would love to learn but have no right to know. Exemption 4 reflects Congress's belief that neither competing companies nor the public in general necessarily have a right to learn such information, which after all had not started off as *government* information at all. For a FOIA request to be denied on the grounds that it includes such confidential commercial or financial information, the agency must conform to either of two rules set forth in a pair of decisions from the D.C. Circuit Court of Appeals. These rules are often referred to as the *National Parks* test,[48] as modified by the more recent *Critical Mass* decision.[49] The *National Parks* test governs information that a company has been *required* to provide to the government. When another entity makes a FOIA request for such data, an agency that seeks to deny the request under exemption 4 must be able to demonstrate that disclosure will either make it more difficult for the government to obtain such data in the future (because corporations will be less forthright) or do substantial harm to the competitive stance of the company that originally made the data available to the government. In *People for the Ethical Treatment of Animals v. U.S. Department of Agriculture*, for example, the animal rights group sought financial data obtained by the Department of Agriculture from the Hunte Corporation, a "puppy distributor,"

---

47. *Inner City Press v. Board of Governors of the Federal Reserve System*, 380 F. Supp. 2d 211 (S.D.N.Y. 2005).

48. *National Parks and Conservation Association v. Morton*, 498 F.2d 765, 770 (D.C. Cir. 1974).

49. *Critical Mass Energy Project v. NRC*, 975 F.2d 871 (D.C. Cir. 1992).

in support of its application for a loan from the department.[50] Judge Suzanne Conlon performed an exhaustive line-by-line review of the contested documents, allowing the department to withhold those she concluded would damage Hunte's competitive posture but requiring disclosure of the rest. She also rejected the department's assertion that disclosure would make it more difficult for the government to obtain similar information from other companies in the future. This kind of financial data is *required* in order to qualify for the kind of loan Hunte sought and received, the judge pointed out, so any future applicants would also be likely to provide it.

Data that a company has *voluntarily* submitted to the government are administered instead under the rule set forth in the *Critical Mass* decision. There, the D.C. Circuit Court of Appeals applied the first prong of the *National Parks* test but substituted for the second prong a new test: that the information sought be of a kind that would not "customarily" be revealed by a corporation to the public in general.

Exemption 4 also provides for the withholding of "trade secrets," which the D.C. Circuit Court of Appeals defines as innovative and "commercially valuable" formulas or processes.[51] Examples are KFC's combination of spices in its fried chicken and the formula for Coca-Cola syrup.

Exemption 5: Internal Agency Policy Discussions and Memoranda. The philosophy behind exemption 5 of the FOIA—often called the "working papers" or "executive privilege" exemption—is that the public has a right to know what policies a government agency has adopted but not all details of the discussions that helped shape the completed policy. Such revelations would "chill" the speech of agency employees and advisors—who will fear that their words may come back to haunt them—and thus jeopardize the quality of decision making. The exemption is also consistent with a sense that public servants "should be judged by what they decided, not for matters they considered before making up their minds."[52]

Exemption 5 also permits withholding data related to a government agency's legal consultations with its own or outside attorneys (the "attorney-client privilege")[53] as well as, more generally, any strategizing done by attorneys who are contemplating litigation on behalf of a government agency (the "attorney work-product privilege").[54] This latter privilege reflects the belief that the FOIA should not result in disclosure of information that would not normally be revealed to an adversary in litigation through the discovery process. In 1988, the Supreme Court issued a ruling on this facet of the exemption, in the context of a FOIA request by a group of federal prisoners for their "**presentencing reports,**" which are made at the request of probation officers to the district court judge and which often include testimony from neigh-

---

50. 2005 U.S. Dist. LEXIS 10586 (D.D.C. 2005).
51. *Public Citizen Health Research Group v. FDA*, 704 F.2d 1280, 1288 (D.C. Cir. 1983).
52. *Jordan v. U.S. Department of Justice*, 591 F.2d 753, 773 (D.C. Cir. 1978).
53. *Mead Data Central v. Department of the Air Force*, 566 F.2d 242 (D.C. Cir. 1977).
54. *FTC v. Grolier*, 462 U.S. 19 (1983).

bors, therapists, and others who may have some knowledge about the circumstances surrounding a defendant's crimes. In a 5-3 vote, the Court determined that such reports might be withheld under exemption 5 from release to third parties but that the data should be given to the prisoners themselves.[55]

In 2005 the D.C. Circuit Court of Appeals found it helpful to distinguish the "working papers" and "attorney privilege" components of exemption 5.[56] At issue was a FOIA request made to the Department of Justice seeking a small number of e-mail messages sent within the department as it was considering whether to intervene in an unusual case in which Americans were suing a group of foreign associations they blamed for the death of their son in Israel.[57] Intra-agency discussions that fall into the "working papers" category might be disclosed, at least in part, the court found, because some utterances concerned relatively uncontroversial factual questions (e.g., "Has this kind of litigation ever been attempted before?" or, "How many attorneys do we have who know anything about the group Hamas?"), rather than the kinds of nascent proposals or statements of personal opinion the exemption seeks to protect. Conversations between agencies and their attorneys, however, should be deemed completely and inarguably subject to withholding.

Exemption 6: Personnel, Medical, and Similar Files. As seen earlier, exemption 2 permits the nondisclosure of the kinds of trivial personnel matters (parking space allocations, coffee break policies) in which the public has no interest. Exemption 6 also provides for the nondisclosure of personnel matters, but those of a more personal nature. The latter exemption is not restricted to information about government personnel but extends to any individual about whom highly private information is included in a file.

The specific wording of the exemption tells FOI officers they may withhold information from "personnel and medical files and similar files the disclosure of which would constitute a clearly unwarranted invasion of privacy." There are thus two steps in adjudicating disputes arising under exemption 6: first, a court must determine whether the file is indeed a personnel or medical or "similar" file; second, a court must assess how "unwarranted" the privacy invasion would be if the file were disclosed.

Concerning the initial inquiry, it is not surprising that the word *similar* has been problematic. The key to determining relevant similarity is that the information sought is "of the same magnitude, as highly personal, or as intimate in nature, as that at stake in personnel and medical records."[58] In other words, the law does not care if the

---

55. *U.S. Department of Justice v. Julian,* 486 U.S. 1 (1988).

56. *Judicial Watch v. U.S. Department of Justice,* 432 F.3d 366 (D.C. Cir. 2005).

57. *Boim v. Quranic Literacy Institute,* 291 F.3d 1000 (7th Cir. 2002).

58. *Board of Trade of the City of Chicago v. Commodity Futures Trading Commission,* 627 F.2d 392, 398 (D.C. Cir. 1980).

record physically resembles a medical chart; rather, it asks whether the record includes information as personal as might be seen in a medical chart.

Using this framework, the First Circuit Court of Appeals found that the names of scientists who had submitted unsuccessful proposals for National Cancer Institute grants would not be as "personal" a revelation as is envisioned by the exemption. The court pointed out that being rejected for such grants was "not so rare an occurrence as to stigmatize the unfunded applicant." Moreover, those in a position to affect the careers of these applicants would tend to be rather sophisticated themselves about the scientific grant-making process and would thus know that failure to obtain a particular kind of funding is not necessarily a negative reflection on the objective merits of a proposal.[59]

Probably one of the most closely watched instances of exemption 6 litigation involved the explosion of the *Challenger* space shuttle, which killed all the astronauts aboard, including high school teacher Christa McAuliffe. The *New York Times* sought from NASA the audiotape of the shuttle voice recorder. One of the threshold issues the courts had to confront was whether, given that NASA had already released what it claimed were the full transcripts of the tapes, the release of the tapes themselves would provide enough *additional* "personal" information to trigger exemption 6. In an en banc ruling, the D.C. Circuit Court of Appeals found that the tapes were in fact covered by the exemption. "While the taped words do not contain information about the personal lives of the astronauts," Judge Douglas Ginsburg wrote for the majority, "disclosure of the file would reveal the sound and inflection of the crew's voices during the last seconds of their lives." He went on to compare the *Challenger* disaster with the *Apollo One* cockpit fire that claimed the lives of three astronauts back in 1967. The transcripts of that tragedy ended with Roger Chaffee yelling, "We're on fire! Get us out of here!" As Ginsburg explains: "The description alone is chilling. One can hardly doubt that the horror in the voices on the tape would convey additional information that applies to the astronauts in the throes of their deaths."[60]

The second exemption 6 inquiry asks whether the feared privacy invasion will be "unwarranted." The *Challenger* tapes were ultimately withheld from the *New York Times* because of the feared privacy invasion that would be suffered by the families of the perished astronauts.[61]

Records need not be nearly as dramatic as in the *NASA* case to still be "personal" enough to be covered by exemption 6. In 1994 the Supreme Court adjudicated a FOIA request by union affiliates who wanted to organize federal workers in several agencies and thus sought workers' home mailing addresses. Disclosure of this information would constitute an unwarranted invasion of privacy, Justice Thomas concluded for the majority, because it would lead to an "influx of union-related mail,

---

59. *Kurzon v. Health and Human Services*, 649 F.2d 65 (1st Cir. 1981).
60. *NASA v. New York Times Co.*, 920 F.2d 1002 (D.C. Cir. 1990).
61. *NASA v. New York Times Co.*, 782 F. Supp. 628 (D.D.C. 1991).

and, perhaps, union-related telephone calls or visits" that at least some employees would prefer to avoid.[62]

Exemption 7: Law Enforcement. The purpose of exemption 7 is to prevent the premature disclosure of materials that would jeopardize criminal or civil investigations or cause some kind of demonstrable harm to informants who have assisted law enforcement personnel. This is the wordiest of the FOIA exemptions. Because it is set forth within the statute as subsections (A) through (F), it is often thought of as six exemptions in one. Courts called on to adjudicate exemption 7 claims engage in a two-part analysis. First, they must determine whether the requested information was "compiled for law enforcement purposes." If the answer is yes, the courts must next ask if disclosing the information will interfere with law enforcement proceedings, jeopardize someone's right to a fair trial, constitute an invasion of privacy rights, reveal a confidential source's identity, reveal investigatory techniques, or endanger someone's life or physical safety.

Courts have generally been very deferential in their handling of the first inquiry, the question of whether the information sought was "compiled for law enforcement purposes." In 1982, for example, the Supreme Court held that the FBI files and other possibly derogatory materials that the Nixon administration had gathered to hurt persons on Nixon's famous "enemies list" should be considered exempt from FOIA disclosure. Even though the immediate reason for compiling the information may have been for rather shallow, and perhaps even illegal, political ends, the data had originally been gathered for legitimate law enforcement purposes.[63]

In another case, the Court held that materials not initially gathered for a law enforcement purpose can be exempted from FOIA disclosure if later used for such a purpose.[64] As part of a routine government audit—*not* as part of a law enforcement investigation—Grumman Aircraft made financial data available to the Defense Contract Audit Agency in 1978. Several years later the government was investigating Grumman for allegedly fraudulent practices, and the company sought from the government the data it had provided earlier, hoping the information would help in its defense.

The government refused the FOIA request. Emphasizing that the statute demands only that the information had been "compiled," not necessarily "*originally* compiled," for law enforcement purposes, Justice Blackmun concluded for the majority that exemption 7 is appropriately invoked as long as the information requested has been "compiled" for such a purpose at any time prior to the filing of the FOIA request itself.

Recall that one of the negative results that exemption 7 tries to avoid is violation

---

62. *U.S. Department of Defense v. Federal Labor Relations Authority*, 510 U.S. 487, 501 (1994).
63. *FBI v. Abramson*, 456 U.S. 615, 631–632 (1982).
64. *John Doe Agency v. John Doe Corp.*, 493 U.S. 146 (1989).

of the privacy interests of the person to whom the records refer. In its 2003-2004 term, the Court had to consider a novel issue—must the person objecting to disclosure be the subject of the files, or can that person's survivors also inject themselves into the litigation? You may recall Vincent Foster, who was deputy counsel to President Clinton and whose death shocked the Washington establishment and provided fodder for conspiracy theorists of many persuasions, despite the unanimous conclusions of the U.S. Park Police, the Senate, the House, the FBI, and independent counsels Robert Fiske and Kenneth Starr that his death was, in fact, a suicide. At issue in the case before the Supreme Court were photographs of the death scene in a park outside of Washington, D.C., including pictures of Foster's body.

Allan Favish of the group Accuracy in Media was unconvinced that Foster's death was suicide and sought disclosure of the official police photos under the FOIA. When the case—actually a handful of consolidated related cases—reached the Supreme Court, Justice Kennedy concluded for a unanimous Court that the privacy interests of Foster's surviving family members were strong enough to outweigh Favish's interest in disclosure. It would be different if the family members were merely arguing as a proxy for Foster's own privacy interests, Kennedy admitted, but they had their own independent claims, in that continued media attention would cause his family additional grief and lead to further hounding of family members by the media.[65]

Not surprisingly, the law enforcement exemption has been cited frequently in our post-9/11 world as a barrier to FOIA requests seeking information about our government's treatment of detainees and related responses to terrorist threats. In *Center for National Security Studies v. U.S. Department of Justice*, the plaintiff's request for information about the number of detainees held on immigration or criminal charges, or as material witnesses, was denied.[66] Thus remaining secret were detainees' names and citizenship, the charges filed against them, and the names of their attorneys (if any). Any First Amendment interests in opposition to the government's interest in preserving an ongoing law enforcement investigation were minimal, the court found, in that detainees or their attorneys were always free to contact the press, should they so wish.

Exemption 8: Financial Institutions. The purpose of the rather infrequently used exemption 8 is to foster continued public confidence in banks, trust companies, securities exchanges, and similar entities. Experience has shown, after all, that an unsupported belief in a financial institution's insolvency can become a self-fulfilling prophecy. Yet the exemption also covers institutions that do not receive deposits and are not subject to mass withdrawals in the way ordinary banks are. For example, the consumer group Public Citizen was unsuccessful in its FOIA request for the annual credit examinations of the National Consumer Cooperative Bank, chartered by Congress to provide "specialized credit and technical assistance to nonprofit coopera-

---

65. *National Archives and Records Administration v. Favish*, 541 U.S. 1057 (2004).
66. 331 F.3d 918 (D.C. Cir. 2003).

tives." Deposits made to that bank are not subject to withdraw on demand, thus undermining the governmental interest in avoiding a "run on the bank." The D.C. Circuit Court of Appeals, however, concluded that the phrase "financial institutions" as used in exemption 8 is not limited to depository institutions.[67]

Exemption 9: Geological and Geophysical Data.   Exemption 9 is designed to protect the financial interests of companies that have filed with the government data concerning oil wells and natural gas deposits. It is the least used of all the nine FOIA exemptions; it has been cited in only a handful of court cases. Moreover, claims under this exemption often overlap with arguments made under other exemptions, such as exemption 8 (financial data)[68] or exemption 4 (trade secrets).[69]

The Government in the Sunshine Act

In 1976, Congress passed the Government in the Sunshine Act (also known as the federal open-meetings law), which requires generally that certain federal agencies conduct their meetings in public. Most of the agencies covered by FOIA are covered by the Sunshine Act; to be subject to the open-meetings requirement, an agency must be covered by the FOIA and at least two of the agency's governing body members must be appointed by the president (with Senate approval).

That a federal body's leadership is composed of rather high-powered government officials, however, is not alone sufficient to trigger the Sunshine Act. For example, the ad hoc Chrysler Loan Guarantee Board—its name is a reminder of its function, to administer the federal government's "bail out" of the financially troubled auto manufacturer—was exempt from the law, even though it boasted the chairman of the Federal Reserve and the secretary of the Treasury among its leadership, and even though

---

THINGS TO REMEMBER

The Nine FOIA Exemptions

1. National Security
2. Routine Personnel Records
3. Deference to Other Federal Laws
4. Confidential Commercial Information
5. Internal Agency Discussions

6. Personnel, Medical, or "Similar" Files
7. Law Enforcement
8. Confidential Data from Financial Institutions
9. Geological and Geophysical Data

---

67. *Public Citizen v. Farm Credit Administration*, 938 F.2d 290 (D.C. Cir. 1991).

68. *National Broadcasting Co. v. Small Business Administration*, 836 F. Supp. 121 (S.D.N.Y. 1993).

69. *Black Hills Alliance v. U.S. Forest Service*, 603 F. Supp. 117 (D.S.D. 1984).

all members of the board had been appointed to their more permanent federal positions via presidential appointment and Senate approval.[70] To be covered by the Sunshine Act, a governing body must also have some policymaking powers. Thus, the Council of Economic Advisers—again, the name suggests the function—is exempt from the act, precisely because its role is only to *advise* the president on economic matters.[71]

Agencies that are covered by the Sunshine Act must conduct their meetings in public. A "meeting" is defined in the act as any gathering of a quorum of its members to talk together about their official business. A meeting can thus be in a government hearing room or in a coffee shop. It can be live or via telephone conference call. Future litigation will likely hold that "chat room" consultations can also be considered meetings.

Under the act, agencies must announce upcoming meetings at least one week in advance. Should an agency determine that an upcoming meeting need not be open to the public because its subject matter is listed among the act's explicit exemptions, that determination must be included in the announcement. Persons who wish to appeal the agency's proposed closing can immediately bring suit in federal district court. Aggrieved parties can also sue after a closed hearing has been held, although such suits must be filed within sixty days. Although the burden of proof is always on the agency to justify closure, even a successful suit will typically result only in release of a transcript or tape recording of the closed hearing. (Agencies are always required to produce such records and to retain them for at least two years.) There is no provision for damage awards, and the awarding of attorneys' fees and court costs is infrequent.

The statutory exemptions to open meetings are designed for the most part to mirror FOIA exemptions, including exemptions for meetings at which trade secrets will be discussed or where an open meeting would jeopardize a national security interest. A few of the Sunshine Act's exemptions are different from those of the FOIA, however. For example, the Sunshine Act includes an exemption for meetings that "involve accusing any person of a crime, or formally censuring any person." Meetings can also be closed if companies or individuals likely to be subject to a proposed regulation would want to attend only to learn ways of evading the law.[72]

The Federal Advisory Committee Act

"Vote for me, and you get two for one!" So said Bill Clinton during the 1992 presidential campaign, as a way of reminding voters that Hillary Rodham Clinton would be the nation's first First Lady reared in the feminist era and that she would spearhead important policy initiatives in a Clinton White House. Some voters undoubtedly ap-

---

70. *Symons v. Chrysler Corporation Loan Guarantee Board*, 670 F.2d 238 (D.C. Cir. 1981).
71. *Rushforth v. Council of Economic Advisors*, 762 F.2d 1038 (D.C. Cir. 1985).
72. *Common Cause v. Nuclear Regulatory Commission*, 674 F.2d 921 (D.C. Cir. 1982).

plauded this new kind of First Lady, while others were wary. As it turned out, her status as First Lady helped her prevail against a lawsuit brought under an infrequently used federal law.

Not long after Inauguration Day in 1993, President Clinton appointed his wife as chair of the President's Task Force on National Health Care Reform, a small group consisting mostly of cabinet-level officers. With the exception of one high-profile public hearing, the task force conducted its work in closed session. This fact disturbed a coalition of doctors and allies who thought that the meetings should be open to the public. Their suit against Mrs. Clinton was unsuccessful, however. As the D.C. Circuit Court of Appeals pointed out, the Federal Advisory Committee Act (FACA) was designed to open to the public the meetings of groups composed of private citizens. The act specifically exempts committees "composed wholly of full-time, or permanent part-time, officers or employees of the Federal Government." Despite Mrs. Clinton's unpaid status, the court emphasized, she must be considered the equivalent of a federal employee for at least two reasons. First, elsewhere in the federal code, Congress had specifically authorized presidents to pay their spouses out of the Treasury funds for providing assistance in the carrying out of presidential duties. Second, to rule otherwise would have absurd and unwanted effects on the functioning of the executive branch. Were a First Lady to attend and participate in cabinet meetings regularly, suddenly the entire cabinet would be converted to a FACA "advisory group," and would thus not be able to conduct its deliberations in private.[73]

The Clinton administration produced another headline-making Federal Advisory Committee Act precedent when it set up the Presidential Legal Expense Trust to collect private donations toward the Clintons' private legal expenses from the Whitewater investigations and the Paula Jones sexual-harassment suit.[74] When a private citizens' committee brought suit, alleging that the trust was not behaving in accordance with the FACA, the federal district court determined that the act was not implicated, that "a trust established by a government officer in his personal capacity without use of public funds, and which renders absolutely no advice on official government policy, simply is not within FACA's scope."[75]

More recently, Vice President Cheney was able to use the Federal Advisory Committee Act to avoid disclosing information about his leadership in the National Energy Policy Development Group, created by President George W. Bush shortly after his inauguration in 2001. In June 2004, the Supreme Court sent the case back to the district court to first ensure that the vice president had a full opportunity to argue why disclosure might encroach upon the separation of powers between the judicial

---

73. *Association of American Physicians and Surgeons, v. Clinton*, 997 F.2d 898 (D.C. Cir. 1993); *Association of American Physicians and Surgeons v. Clinton*, 989 F. Supp. 8 (D.D.C. 1997).

74. Ruth Marcus, "Clintons Establish Fund to Meet Legal Expenses," *Washington Post*, June 29, 1994, A1.

75. *Judicial Watch v. Clinton*, 880 F. Supp. 1, 8 (D.D.C. 1995), *aff'd*, 76 F.3d 1232 (D.C. Cir. 1996).

and executive branches. The immediate result of the Supreme Court decision was to interrupt the discovery process set in motion by the federal district court on behalf of plaintiffs, the Sierra Club and Judicial Watch.[76] In later proceedings, the plaintiffs' complaint was dismissed entirely.[77]

State Freedom of Information Acts

All fifty states and the District of Columbia have some form of legislation providing for access to government records. Although there are many similarities between the state laws and the federal FOIA, in fact the states were the leaders here, with over forty states having some kind of freedom of information law on the books before the federal law was adopted in 1966. In any event, it is not at all unusual for state supreme courts to cite federal case law interpreting the federal FOIA as precedents when they are called on to interpret their own state statutes.

State statutes typically define records rather broadly to include not only papers but also most other methods in which information might be retained, including computer databases. Several state laws make an explicit distinction between the information contained in a database (revealable) and the computer software that helps organize that information (not necessarily revealable). Perhaps the most dramatic example of a state freedom of information law at work in recent years has been the application of Florida's law to include the individual ballots from the 2000 election, thus enabling a consortium of news media to conduct a postelection statewide recount of all ballots not able to be processed by vote tally machines. Unused Florida ballots from that same election, however, were not deemed public records.[78]

THINGS TO REMEMBER

Federal Open-Meetings Laws

- The Government in the Sunshine Act of 1976 generally requires meetings conducted by agencies covered by FOIA to be open to the public.
- Meetings need not be in person nor in formal meeting rooms.
- Exemptions generally mirror FOIA's own exemptions.
- Agencies wishing to meet in private must first alert the public of this intention, which is itself appealable.
- The Federal Advisory Committee Act, which also requires that certain meetings be open to the public, was deemed inapplicable to Hillary Rodham Clinton's Health Care Reform group and Vice President Cheney's National Energy Policy Development Group.

---

76. *Cheney v. U.S. District Court*, 542 U.S. 367 (2004).
77. *In re Cheney*, 406 F.3d 723 (D.C. Cir. 2005).
78. *Rogers v. Hood*, 906 So. 2d 1220 (Fla. Dist. Ct. App. 2005).

A few states restrict informational access to citizens of that particular state. However, in 2005 a federal court in Delaware invalidated such a restriction there, in part because of the disproportionate number of major national and multinational corporations that are incorporated in Delaware or set up their official headquarters in the tax-friendly state.[79]

Most states do not allow agencies to base access decisions on the requestors' motives (personal, educational, commercial), although several states do provide for a higher fee structure in the case of purely commercial uses. Within this framework, reporters seeking information for dissemination to the public are not considered commercial users, the profit motive of their employers notwithstanding. In 1999, the Supreme Court saw no constitutional impediment to a California statute permitting the release by law enforcement agencies of arrestees' home addresses only to persons willing to declare that the information would not be used for commercial purposes. (The company challenging the law routinely made the addresses available to attorneys, who would presumably contact the individuals named to solicit business.)[80] Although most states charge requestors only for photocopying costs, some also assess a fee for the agency's expenditure of human and other resources in researching a request. Overall fee waivers are common when requestors are able to demonstrate a public benefit from the release of the information sought. In practice, the result is that the media often do not have to pay fees.

Not surprisingly, all state access laws provide exceptions to the general presumption of openness. Often these exemptions are part of the statute itself, as is the case with the federal FOIA. Sometimes it has instead fallen to the state courts to create categories of exemptions. Whether an exemption requires or merely permits nondisclosure varies from state to state. Although many states have fashioned their own lists of exemptions after the federal statute, clearly some FOIA provisions make little sense in the context of a state law. The national security exemption, for example, is much more likely to be relevant to requests for federal than for state information.

Requestors who are dissatisfied with a state agency's response may appeal, either initially via some administrative process or directly to state court. Many states provide for an expedited appeals process, so that these kinds of cases can be moved to the front of a court's calendar. Successful litigants will generally receive only the information they sought, not money damages, although attorneys' fees may be awarded under some circumstances.

Requests for certain categories of information have generated substantial public interest and litigation under state law. One such recurring issue has been the need to balance the public's right to know the details of searches to fill high-level job vacancies against the danger of discouraging the candidacies of applicants who fear publicity.

---

79. *Lee v. Minner*, 369 F. Supp. 2d 527 (D. Del. 2005).

80. *Los Angeles Police Department v. United Reporting Publishing Corp.*, 528 U.S. 32 (1999).

State universities want to attract the very best candidates to become administrators and often argue that the most attractive candidates might not want to have their current employers know that they are considering moving.[81]

There has also been a fair amount of litigation seeking the disclosure of test results on exams used for identifying candidates for promotion within state or local civil service systems. Generally, state courts have ruled in favor of disclosing test scores in the aggregate but not scores of any individual employee. The exams themselves have generally not been subject to disclosure, to help maintain their integrity and to permit the reuse of items in future testing.[82] Some courts have required even more disclosure. In Wisconsin, for example, test scores on a physician licensing exam were ordered disclosed, as were the scores of individual physicians asked to retake the exams because questions had been raised about their professional skills.[83]

An appellate decision from Kentucky found that the state's Open Records Act applied to supervisors' evaluations of public employees' performance. The suit stemmed from the theft of hundreds of pairs of athletic shoes from the Louisville Metro Parks. Since a particular individual had been implicated in the incident, there was significant media interest in seeing what that employee's supervisors had said about him.[84]

Individuals' medical records and birth certificates are generally not disclosable under state FOIA provisions. Coroners' records, however, are generally revealable (unless they are part of an ongoing police investigation), on the grounds that our privacy rights expire along with us. The Florida legislature, in response to the media's voyeuristic appetite for photos of deceased NASCAR racer Dale Earnhardt, passed a law declaring that autopsy photos should generally be withheld under the state's public records act.[85] The Delaware Supreme Court also held that autopsy results should not be made public (even though in this particular case the local police wanted them revealed, apparently to clear up speculation that the police department had been involved in a cover-up of the circumstances surrounding the death of a businessman).[86]

The increasingly common phenomenon of states contracting out traditional government functions—for example, the operation of schools, prisons, and other institutions and programs—to private companies has often meant that the records of those private companies are treated as public records covered by state freedom of information laws. This happened in Tennessee, when the records of a private company that

---

81. *Arizona Board of Regents v. Phoenix Newspapers*, 806 P.2d 348 (Ariz. 1991); *Wood v. Marston*, 442 So. 2d 934 (Fla. 1983); *Booth Newspapers v. Board of Regents*, 507 N.W.2d 422 (Mich. 1993).

82. *DeLamater v. Marion Civil Service Commission*, 554 N.W.2d 875 (Iowa 1996).

83. *Munroe v. Braatz*, 549 N.W.2d 451 (Wis. Ct. App. 1996).

84. *Cape Publications v. City of Louisville*, 191 S.W.3d 10 (Ky. Ct. App. 2006).

85. *Campus Communications v. Earnhardt*, 821 So. 2d 388 (Fla. Dist. Ct. App. 2002).

86. *Lawson v. Meconi*, 897 A.2d 740 (Del. 2006).

provided day care programs for the state were treated as public records.[87] A similar concern has been expressed about federal government privatization.[88]

Until 1994 it had been left to each state's discretion whether to keep information found in driver's license records open to the public. The public policy implications of this question had become controversial for at least two reasons. First, there was growing resentment in some quarters at the states' profiting from selling their motor vehicle license databases to commercial users, such as in letting Toyota have a list of the state's Honda owners. To many this policy was seen as an unwarranted invasion of privacy. Second, a great deal of concern was also expressed that states that made driver's license records available to any requestor were acting as unwitting accomplices to criminal wrongdoing. An actress in California was murdered by a stalker who was able to obtain her address from the state because he knew the woman's license plate number. Antiabortion protesters can similarly obtain names and addresses not only of clinic physicians and staff but often of their clients as well, which has sometimes led to harassing mail and phone calls.

Concerns such as these led to passage of the federal Drivers Privacy Protection Act in 1994, which requires that states give motorists the option of keeping their data confidential. The Supreme Court upheld the law in 2000.[89]

State Open-Meetings Laws

All fifty states and the District of Columbia also have some kind of legislation providing for the opening up of governmental meetings to the press and public. The majority of these laws predate the federal government in the Sunshine Act of 1976, which was itself modeled after the law in Florida. These statutes also require that some form of advance public notice be provided of an upcoming meeting, often in the form of a formal announcement in the local newspaper. In some states, openness means not only that the public and press may attend but also that citizens may address the meeting during a public comment period. Some statutes also explicitly provide for a right to broadcast meetings live. Typically, state-level laws govern meetings held by city, county, and town entities as well. Whether a group is covered by an open-meetings law depends on a number of factors, including whether the group performs government-like functions or has policymaking authority, whether it was created by state law (or the state constitution), whether its membership consists mostly of public officials, and whether its expenses are paid out of public funds.

Reporters often complain that public officials will try to skirt their state's open-meetings law by having informal or "spontaneous" gatherings over lunch or in some other

---

87. *Memphis Publishing Co. v. Cherokee Children and Family Services*, 87 S.W.3d 67 (Tenn. 2002).

88. Craig Feiser, "Privatization and the Freedom of Information Act," 52 *Federal Communication Law Journal* 21 (1999).

89. *Condon v. Reno*, 155 F.3d 453 (4th Cir. 1998), *rev'd*, 528 U.S. 141 (2000).

THINGS TO REMEMBER

State Freedom of Information and Open-Meetings Laws

- All fifty states and the District of Columbia have FOI and open-meetings laws.
- State FOI laws, although generally modeled after the federal law, vary greatly in terms of who may obtain information and for what purposes and whether any statutory exemptions require, or merely permit, nondisclosure.
- Most state open-meetings laws predate the federal law, and many give the public the right not only to attend but also to speak.
- States have often been called on to apply their laws to "spontaneous, off-the-record" meetings.

seemingly social milieu. State laws and judicial interpretations vary in the zeal with which they will try to prevent such abuses. Most open-meetings laws provide that any gathering of a quorum (the smallest number needed to take official action) of a governmental body will be considered a "meeting," wherever such gatherings may take place, as long as some official business is discussed. The Texas Supreme Court held that when two of the state's three water commissioners discussed a case before them while in the men's room on recess, they held a "meeting" that should have been open to the public (although not necessarily in the men's room, one can assume).[90] Another popular way of trying to evade the law's demand for openness is the use of "serial communication," a succession of private communications, each one of which involves a number of participants fewer than necessary to trigger the statute, but where the cumulative effect is to conduct via this "telephone game" the equivalent of a prohibited meeting of the whole. Some state statutes specifically prohibit this procedure, and in other states the judiciary has stepped in to accomplish the same thing.

Not surprisingly, state statutes provide exceptions to the assumption of openness. Public bodies can meet in secret "executive session" when the matters they intend to discuss fall into certain specified categories, such as consultations with an attorney about ongoing litigation or internal personnel matters that would likely result in an unwarranted invasion of privacy. Typically, the decision to move into executive session must itself be in the form of a motion that is made and voted on in open session. Moreover, many states dictate that executive sessions are designed for discussions only, that any formal actions taken by the government body after participating in such private discussions must then again be voted on in public.

Although the kinds of matters that can justify an executive session vary from state to state, a good rule of thumb is that the more general the discussion, the more likely

---

90. *Acker v. Texas Water Commission*, 790 S.W.2d 299 (Tex. 1990); *Newspaper Guild v. Sacramento County Board of Supervisors*, 69 Cal. Rptr. 480 (Ct. App. 1968) (a luncheon at the Elks Club deemed a "meeting" under the state law).

it is to be kept open—closed sessions tend to deal with specific individuals. Thus, discussion of welfare reform would be public, but fact-finding about a specific welfare recipient's alleged abuse of benefits is more likely to be done in private.

States vary in the kinds of sanctions to be applied against public officials who hold closed meetings that should have been open to the public. Some statutes provide for criminal fines and even imprisonment, but these penalties are rarely invoked. It is also possible in several jurisdictions to have a state court nullify any government actions that were taken in an improperly convened executive session.

Private "Censorship" of Information

The famous *New York Times* masthead boasts that the paper includes "All the news that's fit to print"; it does not say, "All the news we know."

When media organizations make judgments about whether to report or withhold information on the basis of its perceived news value or on the editors' comfort level concerning the reliability of a reporter's sources, few eyebrows are raised. For example, in the reporting of the Monica Lewinsky saga, Jackie Judd of ABC News was virtually the only employee from a mainstream news organization who reported on the existence of the infamous "blue dress"—long before special prosecutor Kenneth Starr's report confirmed such evidence—even though the artifact was common knowledge within the Washington press corps. Such "should we go with it or hold it?" decisions are the essence of editorial judgment.

Suspicions are often aroused, however, when a news organization's decision to withhold information from the public seems to be based on criteria other than ordinary news judgment. In this concluding section we discuss four categories of such criteria that often lead to controversy. Each can be described as behavior that appears to some observers as bowing to pressure—from advertisers, from sources, from the news organization's owners, or from reporters' possibly competing financial incentives. It should be admitted at the outset that virtually none of the situations to be described here involves media *law* per se; rather the situations reflect problems in media *ethics*. They are presented here because, from the consumers' perspective, it often does not matter whether information is being withheld by the government or by the media themselves.

Pressure from Advertisers

Writing in the *Columbia Journalism Review*, Russ Baker reported that Chrysler's advertising agency had put dozens of major magazines on notice that it must be alerted in advance about any content in news and editorials "that might be construed as provocative or offensive." Apparently the car manufacturer feared having a major advertising piece appear in a magazine issue that produced too much controversy of any kind. The memorandum had dramatic repercussions at *Esquire* magazine, which killed a short story by writer David Leavitt at the last minute, out of fear that the piece's somewhat risqué content might offend Chrysler. The magazine's literary editor submitted his resignation in protest.[91]

Clearly, news and advertising content are interdependent. In a small town, the opening of a major department store is legitimate news, even though feature stories about the opening may do more for the store's bottom line than its initial paid advertising. We also would not expect a newspaper or magazine that had just run a favorable review of a restaurant to *refuse* to run an ad from the eatery touting excerpts from the review as reasons for patronizing the place. Ethical questions arise, however, when news and editorial judgments seem to be based primarily on the need to please advertisers. Thus, for example, the *Columbia Journalism Review*'s "Darts and Laurels" column, which exists to raise an eyebrow at ethically questionable media practices, expressed concern at the *Sacramento Bee*'s having run a huge front-page story about a new supermarket chain's low prices. Was it a coincidence that the chain had taken out a full-page four-color ad in the same issue?[92]

It used to be that respected news outlets considered the separation of editorial and commercial functions a mantra akin to the constitutionally mandated separation of church and state. But the walls have been permeated so often in recent years that we have become a bit jaded, as if we expect the news to be tainted by crassly commercial considerations far beyond ratings or circulation. We seem to take for granted the "synergy" of using news programs to plug entertainment programming, as in the CBS *Early Show*'s daily extended interviews with the previous night's outcast from the latest installment of the *Survivor* series. More generally, a 2001 report from the Project for Excellence in Journalism showed that 33 percent of stories on morning network news programs were devoted to selling something, disproportionately books, movies, and other products owned by the same company that produced the news show. Perhaps the breakdown between commercial and editorial departments reached its zenith with the 2006 premier of *Amazon Fishbowl with Bill Maher*, the former *Politically Incorrect* host's online interview program, where it is an open secret that most of his guests are hawking some kind of product on the Amazon.com website.

Pressure from News Sources

It is not at all unusual for a person interviewed for a news story to try to kill the story prior to publication. Sometimes the request may be quite reasonable; for example, the news outlet may have the facts wrong, or the narrative it is planning to present may be libelous. At other times there may be no allegation at all as to the untruth of

91. Russ Baker, "Some Major Advertisers Step Up the Pressure on Magazines to Alter Their Content. Will Editors Bend?" *Columbia Journalism Review*, September/October 1997, 30.

92. Darts and Laurels, *Columbia Journalism Review*, September/October 2005, 12.

a planned story, although some legal action other than libel may be threatened. Such was the case when former tobacco company executive Jeffrey Wigand's 1995 interview on CBS's *60 Minutes* was canceled because Wigand's former employer (Brown and Williamson) threatened CBS with a multibillion-dollar lawsuit for "tortious interference." Wigand had a confidentiality agreement with Brown and Williamson, and CBS feared that it could be held liable for inducing Wigand to break that agreement. After details of one of Wigand's depositions in a Mississippi suit against the tobacco giant were published in the *Wall Street Journal*, CBS decided its own potential liability was greatly diminished, and it finally aired a version of the original interview three months after it was originally scheduled to air. The story formed the basis for the 1999 feature film *The Insider*.

More mundane pressure from sources to postpone publication of news comes in the form of "news embargoes." Often, an organization will widely disseminate a press release with some presumed news value and ask that the information in the mailing not be published until a specific date in the near future. This typically occurs when an organization does not want the substance of the story to leak prior to its own planned press conference but recognizes that the story is too complex to expect accurate coverage without giving the media some lead time to do their own research. News outlets that violate the terms of the embargo will not have committed any crime; nor will the organization that drafted the press release have any legal cause of action against them. The main incentive for obeying the embargo is to stay on the organization's mailing list for future announcements.

An ethical dilemma emerges when the news sought to be embargoed is so important that it might literally be a matter of life and death. In 1998, for example, several news outlets pleaded unsuccessfully with the British medical journal *Nature Medicine* for permission to publish immediately details about a dietary supplement sold in health food stores that might have been contaminated with a highly dangerous chemical.[93] The *New England Journal of Medicine* has also been the source of highly controversial news embargoes. It has a rather strict policy to the effect that media outlets violating the terms of their embargo will be cut off for an indefinite period from future announcements and researchers scheduled to be published in the journal who dare to discuss their findings prematurely with the media may have their manuscripts killed at the last moment. In the 1980s, the policy was enforced against physicians who wanted to go public with their data showing the efficacy of aspirin in reducing the risk of second heart attacks.[94] The *New England Journal of Medicine* waived this

---

93. Howard Kurtz, "Journal Resisted Calls to Lift News Embargo," *Washington Post*, September 1, 1998, A2.

94. I. Herbert Scheinberg, "When a Medical News Embargo Caused Harm," Letter to the Editor, *New York Times*, April 30, 1994, 22.

policy in the case of a 1997 report on the potentially fatal cardiac complications associated with taking a particular combination of prescription diet pills."[95]

The medical news embargo phenomenon finds professional journals serving as the "news source" for the mainstream media. But before anything gets published in those medical journals in the first place, scientific researchers who submit their data to the editors are the news sources, and the journals are the media. Now consider that as much as 70 percent of clinical research on new drugs is paid for by individual pharmaceutical companies. Most people probably don't know that. There is always the danger that researchers may be beholden to the companies, loath to report data about a drug's *in*effectiveness. In 2001 over a dozen major medical journals jointly published an editorial elaborating on this concern. The immediate impetus seems to have been an article from the *Journal of the American Medical Association* that touted the effectiveness of the painkiller Celebrex by selectively omitting data unfavorable to the drug. Scientists who submit studies to most of the leading medical journals must now attest in writing that their sponsoring companies have not infringed on their scientific independence or attempted to exercise any control over publication.

Sometimes a scientist's motivation for fudging data might simply be to get published and to establish a reputation. This seems to have been at issue when Dr. Hwang Woo Suk falsely reported in the journal *Science* that he had cloned human cells. As Dr. Lawrence Altman suggests in a 2006 *New York Times* column, perhaps the ethical problem here is that editors of medical journals need to be more forthright with their readers about the shortcomings of their own "vetting" of submissions.[96]

Pressure from Management

A. J. Liebling once wrote in the *New Yorker* that "freedom of the press is guaranteed only to those who own one." Judicial interpretation of the First Amendment has generally been consistent with this appraisal. Reporters and editors who are terminated because their work angers their bosses do not have any legal recourse, at least not under the First Amendment. In the 1990s, for example, it was widely reported that Michael Kelly was fired from his position as editor of the *New Republic* because he was too critical in print of Vice President Al Gore, a personal friend of Martin Peretz, the magazine's publisher. *Philadelphia Inquirer* reporter Ralph Cipriano claimed that he was fired because his reporting about financial improprieties within the local Catholic archdiocese was making life a bit too uncomfortable for his bosses.[97] In neither situation would the aggrieved employee have a First Amendment claim

---

95. Kenneth Walker, "Pills Never the Best Way to Reduce Weight," *Chicago Sun Times*, November 23, 1997, 47.

96. Lawrence Altman, "For Science's Gatekeepers, A Credibility Gap," *New York Times*, May 2, 2006, F1.

97. Howard Kurtz, "Crossed Agendas: Church vs. Reporter," *Washington Post*, June 13, 1998, E1.

against the former employer. Actually, Cipriano did sue the *Inquirer*—though not on First Amendment grounds—and the case was settled out of court in late 2000.

More troublesome are allegations of a media outlet's institutional self-censorship aimed at preventing negative publicity about the outlet itself. Such allegations have been on the rise ever since large conglomerates whose major assets are not journalism holdings have bought media companies. Thus, for example, concerns are often expressed that the NBC network is especially reluctant to criticize its parent company, General Electric, and that Disney films and Disney company practices are very unlikely to be panned on ABC, which it is owned by Disney. Indeed, in 1998, ABC's *20/20* killed a planned exposé of unfair labor practices at Disney World.[98] When NBC forced reporter Bob Costas to apologize for mentioning China's human rights abuses on air during the 1996 Olympics, critics wondered if the network's motivation was that its parent company, GE, has enormous investments in China.[99]

Management at the *Los Angeles Times* had to conduct an extraordinary business meeting in the fall of 1999 to apologize to its staff for having kept them, and thus the public, in the dark about one of the paper's financial interests. It seems that the newspaper, unbeknownst to any of its own editors, had entered into a financial arrangement with the owners of the city's new sports arena whereby the two entities would split the advertising revenues from the Sunday magazine supplement devoted to coverage of the arena's opening. As one media critic put it: "Journalists are not supposed to have financial arrangements with the people or institutions they cover. That's a conflict of interest, clear and simple."[100]

Finally, sometimes allegations of financial conflicts are made against the media industry as a whole. Perhaps, for example, you have jumped on the HDTV band wagon recently and purchased a high-definition television. There is a good chance, however, that you did not hear or read much about the enormous lobbying campaign that the mass media waged in Washington to ensure that the new electromagnetic spectrum bandwidths needed to transmit in HDTV—worth scores of billions of dollars—would be *given away* to the holders of more traditional TV licenses. If you have not heard about the spectrum giveaway, or if you did not know much about the issue before, might it be because media companies preferred that you not know? The issue was never featured on any of the nightly news program segments that focus on the wasting of government dollars, such as NBC's "The Fleecing of America" or ABC's "It's Your Money."

---

98. Lawrie Mifflin, "An ABC News Reporter Tests the Boundaries of Investigating Disney and Finds Them," *New York Times*, October 19, 1998, C8.

99. "Muzzled by Murdoch," *Boston Globe*, March 6, 1998, A18.

100. Richard Cohen, "No Way to Do Business," *Washington Post*, November 11, 1999, A43.

Pressure from Reporters' Competing Financial Interests

Government officials are required by a wide array of federal, state, and local regulations to file highly detailed public documentation of their financial holdings. The purpose behind such laws, of course, is to help the public ensure that their elected (and, in many cases, appointed) representatives do not abuse their positions of power by making decisions that will benefit them financially. Indeed, officials are often called on to put their financial holdings into a blind trust, so that they will not *know* when their decisions may help or hurt their own financial health. Not surprisingly, then, the question has often arisen as to whether similar concerns about potential conflicts of interest should be applied to our "representatives" in the fourth estate, the news media.

Sometimes the concerns may seem mundane, such as when travel reporters accept free trips to vacation spots. Will they not feel compelled to report positively about the locales they visit, the inns where they stay, the area's restaurants and other diversions? The number of raised eyebrows aimed at reporters' financial dealings has undoubtedly increased with reports of the media superstars' multimillion-dollar contracts and speaking fees in the tens of thousands of dollars. When such reporters are called on to write stories that in some way affect the interests of the industry groups that have paid these fees, their own credibility might be jeopardized. Financial reporters have been subject to a special measure of scrutiny, the danger being that they, or the "experts" they interview, might tout a stock in part because they hope their own holdings in the company will rise in value.

Sometimes a concern has been expressed about reporters who are working on longer book-length manuscripts without taking a leave of absence from their employers. Might such reporters be tempted to withhold from their newspaper audience the most truly newsworthy facts they uncover, out of fear that they will steal their own thunder and undermine the eventual market for their upcoming book? On more than one occasion, questions have been raised about the divided loyalties of the *Washington Post*'s Bob Woodward, who in the 1980s was working on a book about the CIA and managed to obtain some rather intimate access to the agency's former director, William Casey. Those interviews led to some startling revelations about the CIA's role in various covert operations, but *Post* readers did not learn the details until Woodward's book appeared. The news media were abuzz with allegations that Woodward's dual roles as reporter and author may have done journalism a disservice. More recently, Woodward came under fire in 2005 for failure to tell his *Post* superiors that a government source had leaked to him two years earlier the fact that Valerie Plame was a CIA agent. Plame has filed suit against Vice President Cheney and his former assistant Lewis "Scooter" Libby for leaking her status to the press in presumed retaliation for her husband's criticism about President Bush's claims that Iraq had obtained materials for the production of weapons of mass destruction. Libby himself, it will be

THINGS TO REMEMBER

Private "Censorship"

- The line between "censorship" and "editorial discretion" can be hard to draw.
- Ethical questions arise when the decision to withhold information is based on pressures from advertisers, inappropriate use of news embargoes, or financial conflicts of interest within the media themselves.

recalled, was convicted in 2007 of perjury and obstruction of justice charges related to his conversations with reporters about Plame.

Chapter Summary

Although Supreme Court decisions have often included dicta to the effect that the First Amendment has some relevance to the news-gathering process, the Supreme Court has held that there is no constitutional right to obtain information from the government. Congress and the state legislatures, however, have created a limited statutory right through the passage of freedom of information and open-meetings laws. These laws all provide categories of exemptions from disclosure, which have in turn resulted in a voluminous case law seeking to determine if a specific information request is exempted.

From the media consumer's perspective, it often matters not whether information is withheld by the government or by the media themselves, and the line between improper self-censorship (stemming from identifiable sources of conflicts of interest) and ordinary editorial judgment is sometimes hard to discern.

Chapter 8

REPORTING ON THE JUDICIARY

Y ou may wonder why there is a separate chapter on media coverage of the courts. Shouldn't the judiciary be treated as just one more topic of government information to which the press would want to gain access? In other words, couldn't the subject matter of this chapter have been handled in the previous chapter instead, the one dealing with access to information?

The main reason is one of happenstance: the law in this area has developed separately from the "access to information" case law. Also, the kinds of issues encountered in this chapter concern not only access to judicial venues and information but also the core right to publish what the press already knows.

A Clash of Rights

In many legal disputes concerning information about the judiciary, both litigants favoring disclosure and those seeking secrecy have constitutional arguments on their side. Indeed, these disputes are often referred to as "First versus Sixth Amendment" clashes, reflecting the fact that the free press guarantee is pitted against the various "fair trial" rights—the right to a speedy trial, the right to an impartial jury of one's peers, and so forth—enumerated in the Sixth Amendment. Although presidents may occasionally argue that the Constitution itself—rather than just a Freedom of Information Act exemption—gives them the right to withhold information, the case law examining the constitutional underpinnings of such an "executive privilege" is scant. By contrast, the U.S. Supreme Court has handed down dozens of cases involving the clash between the First and Sixth Amendments. Thus, the case law from the previous chapter dealt mostly with statutory construction, the process of figuring out what laws mean. By contrast, litigation involving access to and freedom to report information about a court case is at its core a battle over competing constitutional rights. The Supreme Court's interpretation of these competing claims has resulted in more of a constitutional right of access to judicial venues and documents than to other public spaces and information. Thus, there is a constitutional right to attend a criminal suspect's trial, even though there is not a right (as we saw in chapter 7) to interview that same suspect in jail. On the other hand, media are often prohibited from publishing what they already know about a judicial proceeding, whereas such a restriction on publishing information about other governmental proceedings is almost unthinkable.

The Contempt Power

It is especially important for professional communicators to understand their obligations under the Sixth Amendment because those who disobey orders from a trial judge risk being issued a contempt citation. To be held in **contempt of court** means to be fined or imprisoned for taking any action that a trial judge perceives as disobedient or disrespectful. The judiciary is not the only branch of government that can hold an offender in contempt. Congress held in contempt several uncooperative witnesses called before it during the McCarthy era and has often threatened to hold presidential appointees in contempt for failing to give complete and accurate testimony. The contempt power, however, is wielded most often by the judiciary. Most forcefully, too, in that the founders borrowed from the English common law the power of judges to issue **summary contempt** orders, through which persons disrupting the courtroom can be cited and punished on the spot, without a right to any further due process.

The law recognizes two broad categories of contempt citations: civil and criminal. **Civil contempt citations** are designed to persuade ("coerce" might be a better word) a reluctant party to do something she or he has thus far failed to do. In the case of reporters, this most typically means to reveal the identity of one's sources. Many reporters have incurred daily fines and have even been imprisoned as part of a judge's efforts to compel disclosure. So important is the overall issue of reporters' relationships with their confidential sources that it is the subject of the next chapter.

Reporters have not been alone in having to do jail time for failing to do the bidding of the judicial branch. In 2006 Barry Bonds's personal trainer, Greg Anderson, was jailed for fifteen days for refusing to testify in front of the grand jury investigating whether Bonds had committed perjury when he denied using steroids.

Criminal contempt citations are issued as punishment for actions already taken. Overzealous attorneys may incur the wrath of trial judges if they disobey orders. The order might be to "stop badgering a witness" or to accept an adverse ruling from the bench without any vocal complaints. On at least one occasion, Judge Lance Ito warned the attorneys in the O. J. Simpson criminal trial, "Get out your checkbooks— Now!" One of the attorneys in the 1998 Tawana Brawley defamation case (Tawana

Brawley apparently concocted a story about having been gang raped) was sentenced to a short jail term by the trial judge after an especially heated courtroom exchange. The judge presiding over a trial stemming from the 1993 bombing of the World Trade Center threatened an unusual contempt citation—ultimately thrown out on appeal— against attorneys who might disobey his order not to talk to the press: $200 for the first offense, $40,000 (200 squared) for the second, and one can assume $1.6 billion for the third, and so on.[1]

When media professionals are found in criminal contempt of court, it is most frequently for publishing information that had been subject to a judge's gag order prohibiting such publication.[2] Reporters have gotten into trouble in other ways as well. In Louisiana, a cameraman was held in contempt for disobeying an order prohibiting filming in the halls of the criminal justice building.[3] In Texas, a cameraman was arrested after having filmed jurors leaving the courtroom.[4]

Trial Judges' Burden of Proof

In the law the phrase "burden of proof" often comes up. Usually we think in terms of a prosecutor's burden of proof in a criminal case, to establish the defendant's guilt "beyond a reasonable doubt." In First versus Sixth Amendment conflicts, there is another kind of burden of proof involved, imposed by appellate courts (and especially by the U.S. Supreme Court) on trial judges who wish to rein in press coverage of trial proceedings. Sometimes judges try to do so by explicitly forbidding the dissemination of particular facts related to a trial. Such gag orders (judges usually prefer to call them restrictive orders) might be imposed directly on the media or on the trial participants—lawyers, witnesses, jurors—from whom the media might gather news. Judges often instead determine that the best way to retain some control over courtroom proceedings is to close the trial and deny the press and the public access to the courtroom altogether. **Closure orders** may apply to a trial itself or to any of several steps in the pretrial process. Trial judges may also deny press access to certain categories of court documents.

As it turns out, the Supreme Court has heard numerous cases involving closure orders, and a small number of cases involving gag orders. To varying degrees, the doctrines that emerge from those cases give trial judges a sense of the burden of proof they incur when they contemplate issuing such orders. Sometimes it is the press that brings suit against the trial judge, either because they have been "gagged" or closed out of the courtroom or because gag orders placed on trial participants arguably in-

1. *United States v. Salameh*, 992 F.2d 445 (2d Cir. 1993).
2. See, e.g., *In re Court Order Dated October 22, 2003*, 886 A.2d 342 (R.I. 2005).
3. *State v. Angelico*, 328 So. 2d 378 (La. 1975).
4. *Duffy v. State*, 567 S.W.2d 197 (Tex. Crim. App. 1978).

fringe on the press's right to *gather* news. Sometimes the trial participants themselves, most frequently attorneys or witnesses, will seek to have a gag order lifted. Sometimes criminal defendants will argue that their convictions should be overturned because a judge's closure order (or refusal to issue a closure order) resulted in an unfair trial. Whatever the specific legal posture of a case, it makes sense to think in terms of the trial judge's burden of proof when answering to a higher judicial authority.

What's a Judge to Do?
The Supreme Court and the Fugitive

Sometimes First and Sixth Amendment values work well together. The First Amendment, of course, includes among its provisions the constitutional guarantees of freedom of speech and freedom of the press. The Sixth Amendment promises criminal defendants the right to "a speedy and public trial, by an impartial jury." The Sixth Amendment's guarantee of a public trial seems wholly consistent with freedom of the press. To the extent that unfettered public and press access to the workings of the judiciary can uncover governmental abuses, such access would seem also to be at least one means of giving breath to the Sixth Amendment's promise of a trial by "impartial" jurors.

Yet the two amendments do sometimes conflict. Before enumerating the types of conflicts that arise, a bit of perspective is in order. The vast majority of criminal cases nationwide attract little or no media attention. In the absence of a pretrial media spectacle, there is no conflict between First Amendment values and the equally compelling interest in impaneling an impartial jury. Further, more than 90 percent of criminal prosecutions do not result in a trial at all. Rather, the typical defendant, after having been given a sense of the kinds of evidence the state will be able to present should a trial be held, will choose instead to plea bargain. In return for saving the

---

THINGS TO REMEMBER

An Overview of First versus Sixth
Amendment Controversies

- Conflicts in which the press is prevented from learning or reporting information about the judiciary usually pit the First Amendment against the Sixth Amendment.
- Judges may hold reporters in contempt of court for violating their orders:
  - Civil contempt citations are designed to produce compliance.
  - Criminal contempt citations are designed to punish noncompliance.
- Trial judges assume a "burden of proof" when they consider either closing their courtrooms or placing gag orders on those who are permitted in.

state the time and expense of a full-blown trial, the district attorney's office, with the cooperation of the presiding judge, will accept a guilty plea to some lesser offense or promise to seek a lesser penalty than might otherwise be requested. The infamous Unabomber, Theodore J. Kaczynski, for example, reached a plea agreement with federal prosecutors that resulted in successive life terms instead of the death penalty.

We should realize, then, that the discussion of conflicts between the First and Sixth Amendments involves a tiny portion of criminal prosecutions. That being said, what are some of the ways that media coverage of the criminal justice system may make it difficult for a suspect to receive a fair trial? Consider the plight of Dr. Sam Sheppard, whose conviction for the murder of his wife provided the basic source material for the TV series and later movie *The Fugitive*. After several unsuccessful appeals in the Ohio state court system, and after he had spent a dozen years in jail, the U.S. Supreme Court overturned Sheppard's conviction on the grounds that the media circus surrounding his prosecution made a fair trial impossible.[5]

Within a few days of Marilyn Sheppard's death, newspaper stories made clear that the doctor was the prime suspect and that local police were frustrated by his refusal to take a lie detector test or to be injected with "truth serum." Such accounts were followed by what Justice Clark's majority opinion referred to as the "editorial artillery," the first of which asserted boldly that Sheppard was "getting away with murder." Prejudicial pretrial publicity continued. One story reported a detective's assertion that "scientific tests" had "definitely established" a particular trail of blood that would conflict with Sheppard's account of the murder. Yet no such evidence was produced at trial. Other articles reported on Sheppard's alleged extramarital affairs with numerous women, although only one such relationship was ever discussed at trial. Sheppard's difficulties with the media followed him into the courtroom as well; the press were seated so close to him that he and his attorney often needed to leave the room to confer in confidence.

It was not difficult for the Supreme Court to conclude that jurors had been tainted by both pretrial publicity and by events in the courtroom. Justice Clark thought it highly relevant that the jurors' photographs and life stories showed up frequently in the media and that they were not questioned about their own media consumption habits once they were chosen.

Justice Clark's majority opinion amounted to a public scolding of the trial judge. He had allowed the courtroom to become a circus, Clark charged, and failed to take any meaningful actions to minimize the effects of pretrial publicity on the jury pool or of media coverage of the trial itself on the jurors. The Court also made clear that the vast majority of avenues available to trial judges seeking to ensure that defendants receive a fair trial do not infringe on the First Amendment at all. Before examining the development of Supreme Court doctrine concerning closures and gag orders, we consider some of these other remedies.

---

5. *Sheppard v. Maxwell*, 384 U.S. 333 (1966).

Remedies That Do Not Infringe upon Freedom of the Press

As we shall see, the Supreme Court has imposed a rather strict burden of proof on trial judges who seek to further Sixth Amendment interests in a fair trial by using methods such as courtroom closures or gag orders. With respect to the latter kind of remedy, there exists a problem above and beyond any First Amendment counterweights to be applied. Most of the truly damaging material, from the defendant's perspective, is likely to emerge long before a trial is held, long before a trial judge is even selected. Trial judges cannot prevent dissemination of such TV images as the defendant being handcuffed and arrested, often juxtaposed with "sound bites" of community members expressing outrage at the heinousness of the crime. Let us consider some of the actions trial judges can take to remedy the effects of pretrial publicity.

Continuance

A fair amount of social science evidence suggests that news stories are rather ephemeral and soon forgotten.[6] Defendants who seek a **continuance** (i.e., a delay) of their trial are banking on the forgetfulness of community members from whom the jury pool will be drawn. Any harmful effects of prejudicial pretrial publicity should diminish, the reasoning goes, as citizens cease to focus on the sordid details of any particular crime and return to their normal day-to-day concerns.

Courts are reluctant to grant motions for a continuance. Delaying a trial places a burden on the judicial system. Witnesses may become unavailable and their memories may fade, records may be lost or otherwise become less usable. Another problem with trial delay is that the Sixth Amendment provides that defendants should be granted a "speedy" trial. The Speedy Trial Act of 1974 provides quantitative definitions of "speedy" judicial proceedings, at least for defendants in the federal courts. The act requires, with some flexibility, that defendants generally be indicted within thirty days of arrest and brought to trial within seventy days of indictment. The Supreme Court reaffirmed in 2006 that the proper remedy for violations of the act is dismissal of charges against the defendant.[7]

Change of Venue

In extraordinary circumstances, where a community is so saturated with prejudicial publicity that a trial judge concludes it will be impossible to impanel an impartial jury, the trial may be moved to another jurisdiction. While state trials may generally

---

6. See sources cited in Laura Donnelly, "Proximity, Not Story Format, Improves News Awareness among Readers," 26 *Newspaper Research Journal* 59, 64 n.1 (2005).

7. *Zedner v. United States*, 126 S. Ct. 1976 (2006).

only be moved to another county within the state, federal trials can be moved just about anywhere. For example, the trial of Timothy McVeigh for the bombing of the Alfred P. Murrah Federal Building in Oklahoma City took place in Denver, Colorado. The court had considered moving the trial instead to Tulsa but determined that pretrial publicity had been so intense that a fair trial was unlikely anywhere in the state.[8]

The McVeigh example notwithstanding, trial judges very rarely grant defendants' motions for a **change of venue**. Most Americans probably assume the practice is much more commonplace than it is, because the few successful motions for a change of venue tend to be, not surprisingly, in media-saturated cases—for example, the trial of Scott Peterson for the killing of his wife, Laci, and their unborn child, the trials of D.C. snipers Lee Boyd Malvo and John Allen Muhammad, and the trial of the Los Angeles police officers accused of beating Rodney King.

It is a very difficult thing for judges to make a ruling admitting they are powerless to ensure a fair trial in their own jurisdiction. Even the judge presiding over the original trial of Jack Ruby for murdering accused JFK assassin Lee Harvey Oswald refused to grant the defendant a change of venue, despite the fact that so many millions had seen Ruby shoot Oswald on television. This decision weighed heavily in an appellate

---

8. *United States v. McVeigh*, 918 F. Supp. 1467, 1474 (W.D. Okla. 1996).

court's decision to overturn the conviction.[9] A change of venue is also an extremely expensive remedy. The transportation, housing, and boarding expenses for attorneys, court personnel, and an often large group of witnesses can be staggering.

There is an additional problem associated with changes of venue: defendants who accept a new venue as a means of maximizing their chances of obtaining a fair trial must waive their Sixth Amendment right to a trial of their peers, at least as the Constitution's drafters envisioned it. The Sixth Amendment promises the accused a jury of "impartial" citizens "of the State and district wherein the crime shall have been committed." Defendants are thus guaranteed both an impartial jury and a *local* one, and often they must choose between the two guarantees.

Finally, trial judges may be incorrect in their faith that the news media in the new locale will avoid the kind of sensationalist coverage that prompted the defense to seek the change. Because there is typically a delay of several weeks or even months between the granting of a venue change request and the actual commencing of a trial, the problem of pretrial publicity may simply start all over again.

Some of these problems can be avoided through a **change of venire** instead of a change of venue: the trial is conducted in the locale where the crime was committed, but the jury is imported from another jurisdiction. A change of venire is generally less costly than a change of venue, although the living and traveling expenses of the jury have to be considered. It also is no less violative of the Sixth Amendment guarantee of a local jury than is a change of venue. Whether the imported jurors will themselves be bombarded by prejudicial publicity back in their hometowns will be a function of both media interest and the delay between the trial judge's decision to change the venire and the actual seating of the jurors.

Sequestration of the Jury

Sequestration is a remedy that does not prevent bias caused by *pre*trial publicity but does effectively shield jurors already impaneled from any ongoing news coverage of the trial itself. To sequester jurors is to house them in seclusion, at the government's expense, monitoring their media consumption to make sure that the trial itself is their only source of information. The O. J. Simpson homicide jury was sequestered; the jury in his later civil trial was not. Neither was the Timothy McVeigh jury sequestered.

The life of a sequestered juror resembles that of an inmate in a minimum-security prison. Long trials can take a hefty toll on jurors' morale, mental health, and family relationships. Juror pay is minimal, and although employers are generally required to make their workers available for jury duty, they are not typically required to pay them their full salaries during the trial. Because sequestration is a remedy disproportion-

---

9. *Rubenstein v. State*, 407 S.W.2d 793 (Tex. Crim. App. 1966). Ruby died of cancer while awaiting retrial.

ately used in trials that are predicted to be quite lengthy, the financial burden on individual jurors can be immense. In addition, jurors may come to blame the defendant for the inconveniences to which they are being subjected and thus become more prone to convict.

In some states sequestration of the jury is mandatory in cases that might lead to capital punishment, although even here the procedure can be waived by the defendant (or, in a subset of states, if both the state and the defense agree to waive the right to a sequestered jury).[10]

Voir Dire

Mark Twain once quipped that the U.S. criminal jury system is the best in the world, its only blemish being "the difficulty of finding twelve everyday men who don't know anything and can't read." Twain was commenting on excesses in the **voir dire** process. The term "voir dire" refers to the process of questioning potential jurors in an effort to identify any sources of bias. It is by far the most frequently employed technique for ensuring that defendants—and the state—receive a fair trial. Voir dire is also used in civil trials.

The process may be as simple as a judge addressing the entire group of potential jurors, asking them if there is any reason they will not be able to render a verdict based solely on the evidence to be presented in the trial itself. Or potential jurors may be asked to fill out a lengthy questionnaire drafted jointly by counsel for both sides, under the judge's supervision.

Twain and other critics notwithstanding, voir dire, when conducted properly, does not need to result in the impaneling of ignoramuses as jurors. Indeed, the Supreme Court has made clear on a number of occasions that jurors need not be ignorant of the matter before them. As long ago as 1878, in refusing a convicted bigamist's appeal, the Court found that the seating of a juror who had admitted during voir dire that he had an "opinion" about the defendant's guilt or innocence was not a violation of the defendant's rights, because the juror also indicated that he would be able to set aside his opinion and make his final judgment based on the evidence to be presented.[11] Chief Justice Waite even cautioned trial judges that potential jurors will not infrequently feign bias to avoid having to serve. (Conversely, contemporary critics have suggested that potential jurors may intentionally hide their biases in order to serve in especially notorious trials.)

In a more recent case, the Court suggested that because we live in an era of "swift, widespread and diverse methods of communication"—these words were written in the early 1960s, so the point is surely even more true today—it is unrealistic to expect to find many jurors who have heard nothing about a particularly notorious crime. All

---

10. Marcy Strauss, "Sequestration," 24 *American Journal of Criminal Law* 63 (1996).
11. *Reynolds v. United States*, 98 U.S. 145 (1878).

that is necessary to ensure a fair trial, Justice Clark wrote, is that a juror be able to "lay aside his impression or opinion and render a verdict based on the evidence presented in court."[12] In a 1991 decision, the Supreme Court held that trial judges need not ask each potential juror about his or her exposure to media accounts of the case. It is sufficient, Chief Justice Rehnquist wrote, that jurors be questioned about their ability to render a verdict based solely on the courtroom evidence.[13]

What happens when a potential juror's bias is uncovered? An attorney for either side can have that juror removed **for cause** if the trial judge is persuaded of the likely bias. Attorneys are granted an unlimited number of such motions for removal. In addition, attorneys for both sides are permitted to seek the exclusion of other jurors whose bias is not alleged. These **peremptory challenges** form the art of jury selection. Those who can afford it often hire highly paid jury consultants to help identify the kinds of jurors, in terms of demographic variables or patterns of answers to specific questions, who are likely to be predisposed either for or against the defendant. In addition to the limit on the number of such challenges, which varies from venue to venue and among types of cases, the Supreme Court has said that attorneys may not systematically use their peremptory challenges to exclude jurors based on either race[14] or gender.[15] The Court has also held that a defendant's Sixth Amendment rights are violated by a racially discriminatory pattern of jury foreperson selection.[16] The case came from Louisiana, where such selections are made by trial judges.

It would be constitutionally permissible for peremptory challenges to be forbidden altogether, and many critics have so suggested. As one proponent of such reform has put it, the whole process encourages "trivializing gamesmanship," whereas "trials are [supposed to be] about truth detection, not about whose lawyer is the cleverest."[17]

The voir dire process is designed to work hand in hand with the use of clearly worded instructions to the jurors by the trial judge. Except in the rare cases where juries are sequestered, judges must rely on juror compliance with admonitions such as "Do not discuss the case with friends or family members" and "Do not permit yourselves to view any news accounts of this trial." Judges may insist that jurors not read newspapers or magazines at all, for fear that a headline alone will prove prejudicial. Although jurors probably take such admonitions quite seriously, social science evidence suggests that the more forceful the instructions from the judge, the *less* likely jurors will be able to ignore "evidence" from beyond the courtroom.[18] This reaction

12. *Irvin v. Dowd*, 366 U.S. 717, 722, 723 (1961).

13. *Mu'Min v. Virginia*, 500 U.S. 415 (1991).

14. *Batson v. Kentucky*, 476 U.S. 79 (1986).

15. *J. E. B. v. Alabama*, 511 U.S. 127 (1994).

16. *Campbell v. Louisiana*, 523 U.S. 392 (1998).

17. Morris Hoffman, "Unnatural Selection," *New York Times*, March 7, 2006, A1.

18. Geoffrey P. Kramer, Norbert L. Kerr, and John S. Carroll, "Pretrial Publicity, Judicial Remedies, and Jury Bias," 14 *Law and Human Behavior* 409 (1990); J. Alexander Tanford, "The Law and Psychology of Jury Instructions," 69 *Nebraska Law Review* 71 (1990).

THINGS TO REMEMBER

Traditional Sixth Amendment Interventions

- In *Sheppard v. Maxwell*, the Supreme Court expressed displeasure with a trial judge's failure to keep control over the courtroom.
- Traditionally, trial judges have numerous strategies at their disposal to minimize the effects of prejudicial publicity:

Continuance	Change of Venue	Change of Venire
Sequestration of the Jury	Careful Voir Dire	Instructions to Jurors

might be a function of what social psychologist Jack Brehm calls *reactance*: if we coerce people into doing things that they were planning to do anyway, resentment and noncompliance may result.[19] A perhaps more benign explanation is that focusing on the instruction itself necessitates focusing on what the instruction forbids: an adult version of the childhood admonition "Don't think of pink elephants."

Preventing Prejudicial Publicity: Gag Orders

There are at least some disadvantages to each of the traditional remedies trial judges may use to minimize the effects of prejudicial publicity. It is not surprising, then, that judges have sometimes tried to employ the seemingly more efficient strategy of simply forbidding the press to report potentially prejudicial information. Judges call these instructions restrictive orders, although the decrees are often referred to as gag orders. Judges also sometimes impose gag orders on trial participants. This section considers both kinds of restrictions.

Gag Orders Applied to the Press

One autumn evening in 1975, police in the town of Sutherland, Nebraska (population 850), found six members of the Henry Kellie family murdered in their home. Suspect Erwin Charles Simants was arraigned the next morning. Both the prosecutor's office and Simants's attorney asked the court to issue a gag order to minimize the extent of pretrial publicity. The county judge issued a rather broad one, forbidding the press from publishing "any testimony given or evidence adduced." A group of media entities appealed the order. The Nebraska Supreme Court modified and narrowed the order but continued to prohibit discussion of the suspect's confession to

---

19. Jack Brehm, *A Theory of Psychological Reactance* (New York: Academic Press, 1966).

police, as well as of any other matter that would be "strongly implicative of the accused"—in other words, that would imply his guilt.

The court emphasized that specific provisions of Nebraska criminal law made it difficult for the trial judge to entertain remedies other than a gag order. A continuance would be improper, because state law required a trial be held within six months of a suspect's arrest. Similarly, a change of venue would be ineffective, in that Nebraska trial judges could move proceedings only to contiguous counties, and the extraordinary pretrial publicity in this case had already permeated the neighboring counties.

The U.S. Supreme Court held unanimously that the restrictive order, even as construed by the state's highest court, violated the First Amendment.[20] Chief Justice Burger's opinion emphasized that gag orders, although they sometimes seem the best way to ensure a fair trial, are still prior restraints on communication, which come to the Court with a presumption of their unconstitutionality. In this particular case, the trial judge failed to demonstrate that less restrictive remedies—such as careful voir dire coupled with clear and strict judicial instructions to the jurors—could not have produced a fair trial. Burger also rejected the state's refusal to consider a change of venue. The Nebraska practice of restricting such changes to neighboring counties may have had to give way to the larger Sixth Amendment interests.

The gag order in the Simants case was especially troublesome for three other reasons, Burger concluded. First, the amended order's prohibition on stories containing "implicative" information was plainly too vague. Second, the order prohibited discussion of the suspect's confession, which had been presented in a preliminary hearing open to the press and public. It is a "settled principle," he wrote, that "once a public hearing [has] been held, what transpired there [cannot] be subject to prior restraint." Finally, the gag order was likely to be ineffective. This homicide took place, after all, in a town of 850 residents, where "rumors would travel swiftly by word of mouth."

Chief Justice Burger's opinion was a relatively narrow one, emphasizing again and again the particular facts of the case before the Court. If only the trial judge had more systematically entertained less restrictive remedies, if only the gag order had been worded more clearly, if only the order's likely success could have been better predicted, the outcome might have been different. "Of necessity," Burger cautioned, the Court's holding should be "confined to the record before us."

Several justices wrote separate concurring opinions that, taken together, depicted a majority of the Court at least flirting with an *absolute* ban on gag orders. Over time, the most influential of all the *Nebraska Press* opinions was the concurrence offered by Justice Powell. Whereas Chief Justice Burger's opinion emphasized the unique features of this particular gag order, Powell went out of his way to offer lower court judges what they hunger for from the high Court—a set of rules to apply in future cases. A gag order would only be permitted, Powell suggested, if there is a "clear

---

20. *Nebraska Press Association v. Stuart*, 427 U.S. 539 (1976).

threat" to a fair trial posed by precisely the narrowly crafted categories of publicity the order seeks to contain, and if no less restrictive alternatives are available. At least some courts have quoted portions of Powell's concurrence as if it were majority doctrine.[21]

The *Nebraska Press* decision has been interpreted by lower courts as a requirement that trial judges demonstrate a "clear and present danger" to the fairness of a trial before a gag order on the press can be entertained. It is now very rare for an appellate court to uphold restrictive orders applied against the media.

For example, the Third Circuit Court of Appeals in 2005 invalidated a gag order that prohibited the press from reporting about former state police officer John Shingara's suit alleging that his firing was in retaliation for his having publicly revealed that the state was using faulty radar speed detectors. Shingara's suit raised important questions of public interest, the appellate court held, in that it alleged misconduct by high-ranking public officials.[22] Also in 2005, the Rhode Island Supreme Court threw out contempt citations issued against WLNE-6 TV for broadcasting, in violation of an earlier-imposed gag order, the faces of at least two witnesses in the trial of convicted murderer Charles Pona for, among other things, murdering an eyewitness who had been scheduled to testify against him at his first trial. One can readily see why the trial judge wanted to protect witnesses' identities. Still, the state's high court found that application of the gag order here would violate basic notions of due process because the specific reporters involved had not themselves been aware of the gag order.[23] And in 2006 the Second Circuit Court of Appeals invalidated a gag order that had prohibited the press from revealing the names of jurors in a securities fraud case who had already spoken them aloud in open court.[24]

Knowing that they are likely to be overturned on appeal, wise trial judges will be very loath to accept even the most sympathetic arguments in favor of imposing a gag order against the press. Thus, for example, in early 2007, in a bizarre federal trial involving charges of sadomasochistic sex trafficking, U.S. district judge Allyne Ross denied a defense motion for a gag order prohibiting the press from revealing some of the witnesses' identities. The judge, while admitting that witnesses would be testifying about some very sensitive and unpopular kinds of behaviors and could be jeopardizing (at least) their livelihoods, determined that a remedy less restrictive than a gag order should be employed. The solution ultimately embraced by the court was to allow the witnesses to testify using only their first names.[25]

In only a tiny handful of instances in recent years have appellate courts upheld gag orders applied to the press itself. Certainly the best-known example involved Manuel

---

21. See, e.g., *Sherrill v. Amerada Hess Corp.*, 504 S.E.2d 802 (N.C. Ct. App. 1998).
22. *Shingara v. Skiles*, 420 F.3d 301 (3d Cir. 2005).
23. *In re Court Order Dated October 22, 2003*, 886 A.2d 342 (R.I. 2005).
24. *United States v. Quattrone*, 402 F.3d 304 (2d Cir. 2005).
25. *United States v. Marcus*, 2007 U.S. Dist. LEXIS 7226 (E.D.N.Y. 2007).

Noriega, the former leader of Panama who was brought to the United States to face drug-trafficking charges. When Judge William Hoeveler learned that prison officials had surreptitiously taped conversations between Noriega and his attorneys and that CNN had copies of the tapes, he ordered the cable network not to broadcast any excerpts from them. An appellate court upheld Judge Hoeveler's order, and the U.S. Supreme Court, by refusing to hear the case, let the gag order stand.[26] After listening to the tapes and satisfying himself that Noriega's rights to a fair trial would not be jeopardized by their dissemination, Judge Hoeveler rescinded his own order.[27] CNN had already aired English translations of some of the tapes while Hoeveler's gag order was still in place. As a result, the network was held in contempt of court, which was eventually settled in 1995 when it ran an on-air apology and reimbursed the government the approximately $85,000 incurred in prosecuting the case.

The CNN case is but one example of a body of case law that places the media on warning: disobey a judge's order at your own peril. Even if the original judicial decree is later found unconstitutional, the contempt of court citation issued to punish the press for disobeying the judge may be upheld. This is called the **collateral bar rule**, or the "*Dickinson* rule," referring to a federal appellate decision from 1972 concerning two reporters for a Baton Rouge, Louisiana, newspaper who disobeyed a local judge's order by printing details of a federal hearing convened to examine an indictment for conspiracy to kill the city's mayor.[28] This rule has been accepted in some jurisdictions and rejected in others. In a 1987 decision, another federal appellate court determined that disobeying a "transparently invalid" court order could not serve as the basis for a contempt citation,[29] but a later en banc ruling emphasized that the press would be far wiser to obey even a blatantly unconstitutional ruling while appealing it to a higher court.[30]

Gag Orders Applied to Trial Participants

As we have seen, the U.S. Supreme Court has placed a very high burden of proof on trial judges who seek to ensure a fair trial by imposing restrictive orders on the media. The Court's *Nebraska Press* decision, however, had very little to say concerning the appropriateness of imposing gag orders instead on the media's most likely news sources: lawyers, witnesses, litigants, and jurors. Indeed, the Supreme Court has never dealt with a case involving this precise issue, and lower courts are in disagreement as to the burden of proof to be imposed on trial judges who contemplate the use of gag orders aimed at trial participants rather than the media. At least in some jurisdictions,

26. *United States v. Noriega*, 752 F. Supp. 1032 (S.D. Fla.), *aff'd sub nom, In re Cable News Network*, 917 F.2d 1543 (11th Cir. 1990), *cert. denied*, 498 U.S. 976 (1990).

27. *United States v. Noriega*, 752 F. Supp. 1045 (S.D. Fla. 1990).

28. *United States v. Dickinson*, 465 F.2d 496 (5th Cir. 1972).

29. *In re Providence Journal Co.*, 820 F.2d 1342, 1347 (1st Cir. 1986).

30. *In re Providence Journal Co.*, 820 F.2d 1354, 1355 (1st Cir. 1987).

a trial judge's showing of a "reasonable likelihood" of an unfair trial is often sufficient to support the issuance of such a gag order.[31] Other courts, emphasizing the First Amendment right to hear, have concluded that gag orders imposed on those likely to speak to the press are indistinguishable from those imposed on the press directly.[32] In this section we look first at gag orders imposed on attorneys and then at orders targeted at other trial participants (such as jurors and witnesses).

Attorneys.   Although the U.S. Supreme Court has never heard a case involving a gag order issued against an individual attorney, it did, in 1991, assess the constitutionality of a state supreme court rule governing the out-of-courtroom speech of Nevada lawyers. The appellant in that case was Las Vegas criminal defense attorney Dominic Gentile, who had been disciplined for holding a press conference in which he not only proclaimed his client's innocence but also suggested that the guilty party may have been a police detective who Gentile had concluded was a cocaine addict. Although the U.S. Supreme Court held that the state rule was improperly applied to Gentile's speech, it did not find the rule itself unconstitutional.[33]

Most states have such rules, modeled after the rules of professional conduct of the American Bar Association (ABA), which warn lawyers not to make any "extrajudicial statement that a reasonable person would expect to be disseminated by means of public communication if the lawyer knows or reasonably should know that it will have a substantial likelihood of materially prejudicing an adjudicative proceeding."[34] The ABA rules offer several categories of statements that might result in such prejudice, including references to a suspect's confession or refusal to take a polygraph test or the possibility of a plea bargain. It is not surprising, then, that trial judges' gag orders aimed at attorneys are a far more acceptable part of the legal landscape than similar orders targeting the press directly. Attorneys, after all, are often referred to as "officers of the court," a label that emphasizes their special responsibility to avoid behaving in ways that will likely result in an unfair trial. Thus it was seen as relatively unremarkable when Judge Richard Matsch prohibited attorneys and other court personnel in the Timothy McVeigh and Terry Nichols Oklahoma City bombing trials from engaging in categories of communications closely paralleling those enumerated in the ABA rules.[35] Similarly, a gag order was upheld as applied against attorney Bruce Cutler, who at the time was representing Mafia figure John Gotti.[36]

None of this discussion is meant to suggest that trial judges issue gag orders against attorneys whenever one or both parties in litigation request it. Thus, for example,

---

31. *In re Dow Jones & Co.*, 842 F.2d 603, 610 (2d Cir. 1988).

32. *Journal Publishing Co. v. Mechem*, 801 F.2d 1233 (10th Cir. 1986); *CBS, Inc. v. Young*, 522 F.2d 234 (6th Cir. 1975); *Connecticut Magazine v. Moraghan*, 676 F. Supp. 38 (D. Conn. 1987).

33. *Gentile v. State Bar of Nevada*, 501 U.S. 1030 (1991).

34. *ABA Model Rules of Professional Conduct* Rule 3.6 (1994).

35. *United States v. McVeigh*, 931 F. Supp. 756 (1996).

36. *United States v. Cutler*, 58 F.3d 825, 838 (2d Cir. 1995).

when entertainer Bill Cosby was accused by Andrea Constand of drugging and raping her, the trial court judge refused a request to impose a broad gag order on the parties' attorneys that would forbid them to speak to the press. Yes, there had been sensational coverage in the media, but that coverage was based on the actual pleadings filed by Cosby and Constand, not on anything an attorney had said to the press.[37]

Jurors and Witnesses. Often restrictive orders are targeted at jurors and witnesses instead of—or more frequently, in addition to—attorneys. There is no U.S. Supreme Court majority opinion giving trial judges clear guidelines as to whether restrictions placed on witnesses and jurors should be granted more or less deference than those aimed at attorneys. In the *Gentile* case involving the Nevada attorney, Justice Kennedy argued that trial judges should be able to "require an attorney's cooperation to an extent not possible of nonparticipants," but that section of his opinion was joined by only three other justices. Jurors and witnesses are not "officers of the court" in the same way that attorneys are, and thus one might suppose that gag orders aimed at trial participants other than attorneys would be less likely to be upheld on appeal.

With respect to jurors, however, such a supposition would ignore the long tradition in this country of *secret* jury deliberations. Part of what it means to have a fair trial is that jurors feel comfortable expressing themselves openly and candidly during their deliberations. If jurors fear that their statements and their votes will be revealed publicly by other jurors, might their candor be thus diminished? Keep in mind, of course, that we are considering restrictions on the *post*-trial statements of jurors. During trials, jurors are always required not to speak to anyone about the case before them. The other side of the equation is that jurors are uniquely qualified to set the record straight about controversial trials. Several jurors from the O. J. Simpson criminal trial felt the need to explain their not-guilty verdict. Indeed, three of them coauthored a book toward that end.[38]

Typically, gag orders aimed at jurors in completed cases are really directed at the press, telling reporters whether they may contact jurors and, if so, what they may or may not ask them. As a general rule, broadly worded gag orders prohibiting jurors in completed trials from ever being interviewed by the press or prohibiting such interviews from eliciting jurors' broad impressions about their experiences have been invalidated.[39] By contrast, orders prohibiting former jurors from talking about how they or others on the jury voted, or from characterizing the jury room discussions, have been upheld.[40]

---

37. *Constand v. Cosby*, 232 F.R.D. 486 (E.D. Pa. 2006).

38. Armanda Cooley, Carrie Bess, and Marsha Rubin-Jackson, *Madam Foreman: A Rush to Judgment?* (Beverly Hills, Calif.: Dove Publishing, 1996).

39. See, e.g., *Journal Publishing Co. v. Mechem*, 801 F.2d 1233 (10th Cir. 1986); *United States v. Sherman*, 581 F.2d 1358 (9th Cir. 1978).

40. See, e.g., *United States v. Cleveland*, 128 F.3d 267 (5th Cir. 1997); *United States v. Antar*, 38 F.3d 1348 (3d Cir. 1994); *United States v. Harrelson*, 713 F.2d 1114 (5th Cir. 1983).

THINGS TO REMEMBER

Gag Orders

- In the *Nebraska Press* case, the Supreme Court ruled that trial judges may impose gag orders on the media only when
  - there is a clear threat to the fairness of trial;
  - the gag order is narrowly tailored, to remedy just that threat;
  - more traditional means of ensuring a fair trial would not work; and
  - it is not too late for the gag order to be effective.
- Gag orders placed on the press are likely to be invalidated or at least limited.
- In most jurisdictions, trial judges have a far lower burden of proof when they impose a gag order on trial participants rather than on the media.
- This lower burden of proof applies especially to attorneys, whose own ethical code demands that they refrain from out-of-court utterances likely to make a fair trial more difficult.
- Contempt citations issued against reporters who disobey even an obviously unconstitutional order from a trial judge may still be upheld by an appellate court.

If a first trial resulted in a hung jury and a second trial of the same defendant is about to begin, stricter restrictions on press contacts with the first trial's jurors are likely to be upheld.[41] The logic here, of course, is to avoid tainting the second jury pool.

Trial witnesses are rarely singled out for gag orders; rather they tend to be covered by global orders affecting all trial participants. Witnesses will generally not be restricted in the same way that former jurors are; after all, they will not have had access to such traditionally confidential proceedings as jury deliberations. A state appellate court in Georgia threw out an unusually prescriptive gag order in a case involving allegations of child cruelty and assault made against a local church. The gag rule had instructed all trial participants, if contacted by the press, to say either "no comment," or "whatever I have to say will be said in court."[42] And a federal court in New York held a gag order in mob figure John Gotti's trial inapplicable to Curtis Sliwa, well known for forming the Guardian Angels anticrime group, perhaps less well known for having a radio talk show.[43] Sliwa was almost certain to be called as a witness because he alleged that Gotti had tried to kill him. Two years later, litigation against Gotti was still going on, and broad gag orders were issued against many trial participants, but not against Sliwa.[44] Finally, some state courts, Montana's among them,[45]

41. *State v. Neulander*, 801 A.2d 255 (N.J. 2002).

42. *Atlanta Journal-Constitution v. State*, 596 S.E.2d 694 (Ga. Ct. App. 2004).

43. *United States v. Gotti*, 2004 U.S. Dist. LEXIS 24192 (S.D.N.Y. 2004).

44. Thomas Zambito, "Judge Orders Junior Gotti to Zip It," *Daily News*, July 6, 2006, 8.

45. *The Missoulian v. Montana Twenty-First Judicial District Court*, 933 P.2d 829 (Mont. 1997).

have found in their state constitutions a public "right to know" beyond that implicit in the First Amendment and have thus held that even gag orders aimed only at trial participants (rather than the press) can survive only if violation of such orders would produce a "substantial probability" of an unfair trial.

Barring Reporters from the Courtroom

Restrictive orders seek to prevent the media from reporting what they already know. Sometimes judges have instead tried to ensure a fair trial by preventing the media from learning potentially prejudicial information in the first place. Language from two Supreme Court decisions handed down not long after the *Nebraska Press* case may have emboldened some trial judges to issue such closure orders. In the first case, decided in 1978, the Court ruled that a Virginia newspaper had a right to publish a story identifying a state judge whose conduct had been the subject of hearings conducted by the state's judicial review committee. A gag order was not at issue in *Landmark Communications, Inc. v. Virginia*, but rather a state statute specifically prohibiting dissemination of information concerning the committee's investigations.[46] Writing for the Supreme Court's majority, Chief Justice Burger allowed that the committee certainly had the right to conduct its business secretly but concluded that the press could not be forbidden to publish whatever it learns about the committee's work (even if the source who "leaked" the material may have violated the statute). The majority decision seems to be telling the states, "If you want to keep certain judicial proceedings secret, make sure that they are indeed secret."

The second case, *Smith v. Daily Mail Publishing Co.*, also concerned a state statute rather than a gag order.[47] West Virginia law prohibited the publication of juvenile defendants' names without prior written approval of the juvenile court. When newspapers in Charleston published the name of a fourteen-year-old accused of killing a junior high school classmate—the information was obtained by interviewing witnesses at the scene—the state prosecuted them for violation of the statute. When the appeal reached the Supreme Court, Chief Justice Burger concluded that the statute violated the First Amendment. Yet he added that this ruling was a narrow one, in that the Court had not been asked to determine whether the state could legitimately close juvenile proceedings to the press and public, nor was this case one of a newspaper reporter somehow gaining "unlawful access" to such proceedings.

This section examines judicial closure orders as applied to trials and to various kinds of pretrial hearings. We also look at orders sealing court documents from press and public inspection. In addition, we consider the history and current status of televising trials.

---

46. 435 U.S. 829 (1978).
47. 443 U.S. 97 (1979).

Closing the Trial Itself

The U.S. Supreme Court has given trial court judges fairly clear guidance concerning when closing an actual criminal trial to the press and public can be permitted. The burden of proof demanded by the Supreme Court is a rather strict one, especially considering the circumstances surrounding the closure order at issue in the leading precedent, *Richmond Newspapers, Inc. v. Virginia*.[48] The unusual feature about the case was that this murder trial was defendant John Stevenson's *fourth*. His first trial had resulted in a conviction, but the judgment was reversed on the grounds that some inadmissible evidence had been presented to the jury. His second and third trials ended in mistrial. If ever a trial judge could be excused for a bit of zealotry in his attempt to ensure a fair trial, this case would seem to be such a situation, especially because the defense sought the closure order and the prosecution had no objection to it. But when two newspaper reporters demanded a hearing on the closure order, the trial judge determined that the hearing should be considered a part of the trial itself, and thus subject to the closure order. As a result, and somewhat ironically, the reporters were closed out of their own hearing! Their interests were represented at the hearing by their attorneys.

Chief Justice Burger announced the judgment of the Court, a 7-1 decision that the public and the press have a First Amendment right to attend criminal trials. Only two other justices joined Burger's opinion. Although it was not a majority opinion, it has been treated as such, because the pattern of concurring opinions suggests that a clear majority actually did support his reasoning, as far as it went. "The right to attend criminal trials," Burger wrote, "is implicit in the guarantees of the First Amendment; without the freedom to attend such trials, which people have exercised for centuries, important aspects of freedom of speech and the press could be eviscerated." Could criminal trials ever be closed? Burger maintained that trial judges must have an "overriding interest" in doing so and that the interest must be "articulated in findings" that include an inquiry as to whether remedies less intrusive on First Amendment interests might have sufficed. The various concurring opinions revealed the Court's lack of consensus as to whether the right to a *public* trial is a Sixth Amendment right, a First Amendment right, or both, and whether the right should extend to civil trials as well.

The only other case in which the Supreme Court has dealt with the closure of a criminal trial was in the context of a closure order issued by a Massachusetts judge presiding over a sex-crime trial. The trial judge was required by state law to issue such an order, in that the victims were juveniles. When the *Boston Globe* appealed the order, the state supreme court interpreted the statute to require clearing the courtroom only during times when a juvenile victim was actually testifying. That interpretation would not help the *Globe* in this particular instance, because the rape trial had

---

48. 448 U.S. 555 (1980).

already been completed, with the press and the public completely closed out of the proceedings. The newspaper pursued the litigation to the U.S. Supreme Court, which held that statutes *requiring* closure violate the First Amendment. Writing for the majority, Justice Brennan admitted that although at least one of the state's interests involved—"the protection of minor victims of sex crimes from further trauma and embarrassment"—was a compelling one, it did not justify a broad statutory requirement of closure. Rather, he said, the trial judge must be permitted to determine these matters case by case, taking into account the victim's willingness to testify in open court, tempered by his or her age and psychological maturity.[49]

Overall the impact of the *Richmond Newspapers* and *Globe Newspaper* cases together is that actual trials are almost always kept open to the press and the public, except when the trial is part of the juvenile justice system. At least since the 1820s, juvenile law in the United States has been premised on the belief that youthful offenders can and should be rehabilitated.[50] Several differences between the adult and juvenile justice systems have thus been part of the U.S. legal landscape throughout much of the country's history. Although juveniles are incarcerated, we send them to separate detention centers rather than prisons. The residents of such facilities are typically referred to as "delinquents" or "juvenile offenders" rather than "criminals." Punishment for crimes committed as a juvenile typically ends at the attainment of the age of majority, at which time the individual's record is expunged. Seen in this light, that trial proceedings involving juvenile defendants have traditionally been conducted in secret is but just one more difference.

It is possible for an individual to be tried as a *federal* juvenile delinquent under the provisions of the Federal Juvenile Delinquency Act, as in the case of underage defendants charged with violating federal hate-crimes laws. Although the act does not clearly set forth whether proceedings conducted within its scope should be open to the press, several courts have interpreted the act to provide discretion in this regard to the trial judges.[51]

Juvenile proceedings are more typically a matter of state law. In most states, anyone who does not have a "direct interest" in the outcome of a juvenile proceeding, or at least in the judicial operations of the court, is excluded from the courtroom. There is tremendous variation across jurisdictions, however, as to whether the media are considered to have such an interest. Many statutes explicitly invite trial judges to make this determination on a case-by-case basis. The wording of other statutes seems to suggest to judges that, when in doubt, they should exclude the media. Media representatives would thus be wise to become familiar with the applicable statutes and judicial interpretation of those statutes in their own jurisdictions.

---

49. *Globe Newspaper Co. v. Superior Court*, 457 U.S. 596 (1982).

50. Sanford J. Fox, "Juvenile Justice Reform: An Historical Perspective," 22 *Stanford Law Review* 1187 (1970).

51. *United States v. L. M.*, 425 F. Supp. 2d 948, 952 (N.D. Iowa 2006).

THINGS TO REMEMBER

Closing Actual Trials

- In the *Richmond Newspapers* case, the Supreme Court told trial judges that they may close the courtroom to the press and public only for an "overriding interest."
- Later, in the *Globe Newspaper* case, the Court indicated that even in highly sensitive sex-crime trials, closures must be made on a case-by-case, perhaps even a moment-by-moment, basis; they cannot be mandated by statute.
- Actual trials, other than juvenile trials, are very rarely closed to the public these days.

Closing Pretrial Hearings

Most of what the Supreme Court has had to say about conflicts between First and Sixth Amendment rights emerges from a handful of its decisions governing public and press access to pretrial hearings. Because it is important to understand the evolution of that case law, in this section the cases are discussed in chronological order.

The Defendant Seeks Closure: *Gannett Co. v. DePasquale.* The

Court's doctrine concerning when pretrial hearings can be closed began with its 1979 decision in *Gannett Co. v. DePasquale.*[52] At issue was whether the press had a right to attend a pretrial suppression hearing, even when the defendant has asked that it be closed and the prosecution and trial judge have agreed. The case stemmed from a homicide trial in the Rochester, New York, area; the trial judge, Daniel DePasquale, excluded the public and the press from the suppression hearing and further denied the local newspapers' request to be provided immediately with a transcript of that hearing. The homicide case ended quickly with a plea bargain, at which point the transcript to the suppression hearing was released. The newspapers decided to press the constitutional issue further, however, which ultimately resulted in a 5-4 vote by the Supreme Court upholding Judge DePasquale's original closure order.

Writing for the majority, Justice Stewart concluded that the most important right at stake in the dispute was that to a public trial. Such a right is granted by the Sixth Amendment to the accused, not to the press and the public. In situations such as this one, where the defendant specifically requests closure, the Sixth Amendment inquiry would be concluded. None of this discussion is to deny that the public may have interests that generally coincide with the rights enumerated in the Sixth Amendment. A public trial benefits the public in many ways, Justice Stewart admitted, but that does not mean that the public has a Sixth Amendment *right* to a public trial.

---

52. 443 U.S. 368 (1979).

Justice Stewart allowed that the press and the public *might* be able to argue under the First Amendment for an open suppression hearing, but he was not ready to commit himself to the proposition that such a right exists. Even if such a right does exist, Stewart continued, the defendant's Sixth Amendment rights would prevail, at least in this case. After all, the press was granted a hearing to present through counsel its interests in keeping the hearing opening. Also, the closure did not amount to a permanent denial to the press and public of information about the judiciary, in that the transcript of the suppression hearing was released immediately upon the entering of the defendant's plea bargain.

The majority opinion was thus a narrowly written one from two perspectives. First, Stewart did not commit himself one way or the other as to whether a First Amendment right to attend pretrial hearings exists. Second, he felt no need to create a general rule to the effect that a defendant's Sixth Amendment interest in having a closed hearing would always trump whatever First Amendment interest the public may have in keeping the hearing open.

Justice Powell wrote a separate concurring opinion, destined to become majority doctrine a few years later.[53] Although agreeing with the majority that the defendant's wishes must prevail in this particular case, Powell went one step further than Stewart, committing himself to the view that there *is* a First Amendment right on the part of the press and the public to attend even pretrial hearings. Access to suppression hearings is especially deserving of protection, Powell asserted, precisely because such hearings are often the only trial; depending on their outcome, they most often lead either to a defendant very anxious to plea bargain or to a district attorney dropping the prosecution in frustration. Powell's concurring opinion also provided lower courts with a set of guidelines to use in determining whether a suppression hearing should be closed to the press and public. Upon receiving a defendant's motion for closure, trial judges should consider whether any of the more traditional means of preserving a fair trial might work as well as closure. Should they be leaning toward closure, they must make sure that the closure order extends no further than necessary. They must also permit any press representatives present to express their views on the matter. Although these suggestions were not majority doctrine, many lower courts have since quoted the "Powell standard" with approval, and it has been adopted by both the Judicial Conference of the United States, which makes rules governing the federal judiciary, and the Department of Justice.

As it turns out, there had been a newspaper reporter in the courtroom when Judge DePasquale entertained the defense motion for closure, and she did not object to the motion. Largely as a result of that reporter's acquiescence—she was not an attorney, after all, and may not have felt comfortable rising to object—mass media companies soon got into the habit of providing their reporters on the "courtroom beat" a carefully worded statement that would enable them to object immediately and more effec-

---

53. *Press-Enterprise Co. v. Superior Court II*, 478 U.S. 1 (1986).

tively to any proposed courtroom closure. Printed on what are often called "**Gannett cards**," these statements are designed to prevent a closure order from being instituted before the media's attorneys have had a chance to make legal arguments against it. Typically, the reporter will make clear in delivering the statement that he or she is not prepared to make the necessary arguments and will request a short break so that attorneys can be called in. In at least one case involving a motion to close a suppression hearing, the reading of the Gannett card backfired. The Kansas Supreme Court upheld a trial judge's decision to close a suppression hearing in a homicide case, partly on the basis that the judge had conducted a hearing on the matter. That "hearing" consisted of a *Kansas City Times* reporter standing up and reading her Gannett card to the judge![54]

Voir Dire Hearings: *Press-Enterprise Co. v. Superior Court I.* Technically, the process of jury selection and questioning (voir dire) is the beginning of a trial. Still, the Supreme Court's case law concerning motions to close voir dire proceedings has developed separately from cases involving closure of trials themselves. The first of two otherwise unrelated pretrial closure cases bearing the same name, *Press-Enterprise Co. v. Superior Court I*, stemmed from a racially tinged (white victim, black defendant) rape and homicide trial in Riverside, California.[55] In this case, it was the prosecution that sought to close the voir dire proceedings, fearing that media presence would make it difficult for potential jurors to answer candidly the highly personal questions likely to be posed to them. The trial judge decided to close virtually the entire voir dire hearing, which lasted six weeks, to the press and public.

Immediately after the selection of the jury, the *Press-Enterprise* sought a transcript of the hearing. The trial judge denied this request, on the grounds that the privacy of individual jurors would be compromised. A second request for the transcripts, made after the trial itself had concluded—the defendant had been convicted and sentenced—was similarly denied. The newspaper then commenced litigation to obtain the transcripts and have the original closure order ruled unconstitutional. By a unanimous vote, the Supreme Court sided with the press on both counts. Chief Justice Burger wrote the opinion for the Court. In it he reviewed the available historical evidence dating back to even before the Norman conquests to demonstrate that the jury-selection process had been a presumptively open one under English law for many centuries. "The process of juror selection is itself a matter of importance," he explained, "not simply to the adversaries but to the criminal justice system." Openness helps the community see "that offenders are being brought to account for their criminal conduct by jurors fairly and openly selected."

Because the defendant in this case had wanted the voir dire hearing open as much as the press did, Burger did not need to determine whether the right to this openness

---

54. *Kansas City Star Company v. Fossey*, 630 P.2d 1176 (Kan. 1981).
55. 464 U.S. 501 (1984).

was enjoyed only by the accused (as a Sixth Amendment right) or by the press and the public as well (whether as a Sixth Amendment or a First Amendment right). He did, however, feel the need to give trial judges some kind of guidance as to their burden of proof should they contemplate closing a voir dire hearing: "The presumption of openness may be overcome only by an overriding interest based on findings that closure is essential to preserve higher values and is narrowly tailored to serve that interest. The interest is to be articulated along with findings specific enough that a reviewing court can determine whether the closure order was properly entered."

Much of this language is familiar, but at least one thing is new. Notice the deliberately vague reference to "higher values," rather than a more concrete reference to "a fair trial." The protection of individual jurors' privacy rights may itself constitute such a "higher value." Although the trial judge's desire to produce an impartial jury and to protect participants' privacy was laudable, Burger concluded, the closure order was overkill. A more narrowly tailored closure might have been permissible, he added. For example, if a juror were to tell the judge and attorneys of her own or a loved one's experience as a rape survivor, that specific part of the voir dire might legitimately be held in the judge's chambers, away from the press and public. As part of the voir dire process, the trial judge could explicitly invite any jurors who have any reluctance about answering specific questions in the open courtroom to request the same level of privacy. The closure of virtually the entire hearing to the press and public, however, was a far greater encroachment on the presumption of openness than was warranted.

Chief Justice Burger's suggestions to trial courts should be seen as just that. In several instances since *Press-Enterprise I* was handed down,[56] trial judges have succeeded in closing most or all of the voir dire process without being overturned on appeal. When boxing promoter Don King was on trial for wire fraud, the trial judge sealed the questionnaires filled out by prospective jurors, as well as transcripts of follow-up questions posed in the judge's chambers. Media plaintiffs protested, arguing that at a bare minimum, the burden should have been on individual jurors to request having their follow-up questioning be conducted in private. The Second Circuit Court of Appeals disagreed. The trial judge's goal here was not the protection of juror privacy, as was the case in *Press-Enterprise I*; rather, the judge wanted to ensure a fair trial in a highly charged atmosphere. An HBO movie highly critical of King had just come out. There had already been a mistrial, which local press headlines blamed on the defendant's having "played the race card," when all King had done was to challenge the prosecution's alleged use of peremptory challenges to get rid of a disproportionate number of African-American jurors. One of the New York newspapers, reacting angrily to the earlier mistrial, referred to King as "another Teflon Don," thus analogizing him to Mafia kingpin John Gotti. The appellate court ruled that *Press-Enterprise I* requires only that trial judges "make supportable findings, consider alter-

---

56. See also *United States v. Koubriti*, 252 F. Supp. 2d 424 (E.D. Mich. 2003).

natives, and frame a limited form of relief." They need not follow each and every one of Chief Justice Burger's suggestions.[57]

Still, trial judges must demonstrate more than conjecture if they wish to have their voir dire closures upheld by an appellate court. The judge in Martha Stewart's securities law trial closed the voir dire hearing, an action later ruled unconstitutional by the Second Circuit Court of Appeals. True, the appellate panel agreed, many potential jurors will have prejudged the defendant, but that is true of any high-profile trial, and there was no reason to assume that the members of the jury pool would be loath to admit their biases during an open voir dire hearing.[58]

Closures Ignoring the Defendant's Wishes: *Waller v. Georgia*.

A few months after the *Press-Enterprise I* case was decided, the Court handed down an unusual decision in which the appeal for an open pretrial hearing came to the Court from the criminal defendant himself rather than from the press. Guy Waller appealed his conviction on commercial gambling charges on the grounds that the closing of the pretrial hearing convened to assess the admissibility of wiretap evidence was a violation of his constitutional right to a fair trial.[59] It was the state that had moved for closure, on two grounds. First, publicly playing some of the wiretap tapes would invade the privacy of innocent persons whose names or voices could be heard. Conversely, other persons identified on the tapes had been indicted but not yet tried, and the playing of the tapes in open court might, under Georgia law, make it difficult or impossible for the state to use such "tainted" evidence in later trials with other defendants. The suppression hearing was closed for its entire seven-day duration, even though only a few hours were taken up in actually playing tapes from the wiretaps.

Writing for a unanimous Court, Justice Powell concluded that Waller's constitutional rights had indeed been violated. Powell's opinion emphasizes the importance of suppression hearings in the overall judicial system. He repeated the point he had made in his concurring opinion from *Gannett Co. v. DePasquale*: such hearings are often the only "trial" a suspect will experience because suppression hearings usually end in either plea bargains or the dismissal of charges, with no trial to follow.

Perhaps the most interesting part of the *Waller* case was the Court's struggle to fashion an appropriate remedy. To set Waller free seemed a bit extreme, as did the suggestion that he be granted a new trial. Principles of equity demanded only that Waller be given what he had been denied: a new suppression hearing, this time open to the press and public. If and only if that new hearing were to result in the suppression of significant evidence that had earlier been deemed admissible would Waller be granted a whole new trial.

---

57. *United States v. Don King Productions*, 140 F.3d 76 (2d Cir. 1998).
58. *ABC, Inc. v. Stewart*, 360 F.3d 90 (2d Cir. 2004).
59. *Waller v. Georgia*, 467 U.S. 39 (1984).

In 2004, the Washington Supreme Court went a step further and actually over-turned a murder conviction because a voir dire hearing was improperly closed to the public.[60] The decision, which resulted in a new trial rather than just a new voir dire hearing, was based on state constitutional guarantees of openness.

Closing a Preliminary Hearing:
Press-Enterprise Co. v. Superior Court II

Two years after the first case bearing the same name, the Court ruled in what has come to be known as *Press-Enterprise Co. v. Superior Court II*.[61] The case stemmed from a multiple homicide case involving a nurse named Robert Diaz, who was ac-cused of killing a dozen patients in California by administering overdoses of a heart drug. The defendant's preliminary hearing was closed to the press and public at his own request. In California's penal system, these hearings function very much like full-blown trials; the prosecution produces evidence and witnesses, and the defense is in-vited to do so also. Witnesses can be cross-examined by either side. Indeed, almost the only differences between the preliminary hearing and the trial is the absence of a jury and the lower standard of proof of guilt ("probable cause" to proceed to trial compared to "beyond a reasonable doubt" to convict).

By a 7-2 vote, the U.S. Supreme Court ruled that the standard employed in decid-ing to close Diaz's preliminary hearing was not sensitive enough to the public's First Amendment interest and that, in any event, a transcript of the proceedings should have been made available to the press at the first possible moment.

Chief Justice Burger's majority opinion is notable for at least three reasons. First, he committed the Court for the first time to the principle that the interest in keeping judicial proceedings open to the press and public is primarily a *First* Amendment issue.

Second, the Court came about as close as it possibly could to overturning the *Gan-nett* case without explicitly doing so. *Gannett*, it will be recalled, also involved a mo-tion from the defendant to close a pretrial hearing. No doubt Burger did not feel compelled to overturn *Gannett*, precisely because the majority decision in that 1979 case, by leaving open the possibility that there *might* be a First Amendment right to attend pretrial hearings that *might* in some circumstances outweigh a defendant's wish for closure, left future Court majorities enough "wiggle room." Still, if *Gannett* ever stood for the principle that a defendant's wish for closure necessarily trumps the media's desire for openness, that notion was rejected in *Press-Enterprise II*.

Finally, and perhaps most important, *Press-Enterprise II* represents the Court's first attempt to give trial judges a rule that should cover *all* kinds of judicial hearings. This attempt is all the more important when we consider that the Supreme Court to date

---

60. *In re Personal Restraint Petition of Orange*, 100 P.3d 291 (Wash. 2004).
61. 478 U.S. 1 (1986).

has only reviewed cases involving three kinds of judicial hearings beyond trials themselves: voir dire proceedings, suppression hearings, and the kind of quasi trial that California's preliminary hearings resemble. Trial judges, however, have to deal with all sorts of other hearings as well, such as bail hearings, competency hearings, plea bargain hearings, post-trial hearings alleging prosecutorial or jury misconduct, and increasingly in the wake of the September 11, 2001, attacks, detention and deportation hearings.

The *Press-Enterprise II* test asks trial judges to consider first whether the category of hearing involved is one that should be considered "presumptively open." To be considered presumptively open, a category of hearings must meet at least one half of what the Court calls the "experience and logic test": either the category of hearings has historically been conducted in public (i.e., openness has been our practice, our "experience"), or we reason (logically?) that openness will make for a better hearing (i.e., it will enhance the hearing's "function in the judicial process.").

Once it is determined that a category of judicial hearing is, in fact, presumptively open, then a burden of proof applies to any persons seeking to close the proceeding. Before approving a motion for closure, a trial judge must be able to demonstrate that there is a *substantial probability* of jeopardizing a "higher value" and that the closure is narrowly tailored to preserve that higher value.

In 1993, the Supreme Court had occasion to consider application of the *Press-Enterprise II* test to preliminary hearings conducted in the Commonwealth of Puerto Rico.[62] The hearings were structured very similarly to those in California, but local law explicitly stated that they were to be conducted in secret unless the defendant requested otherwise. Puerto Rico's highest court upheld this provision against a challenge by local newspaper reporters, having concluded that the hearings function differently in the commonwealth's "unique history and traditions, which display a special concern for the honor and reputation of the citizenry." The court also emphasized that the openly conducted preliminary hearings were far more likely to result in biased trial juries, given the commonwealth's small size and dense population. In a relatively short, per curiam opinion, a unanimous U.S. Supreme Court rejected Puerto Rico's analysis, emphasizing that when the *Press-Enterprise II* test asks that trial courts look at whether certain categories of hearings have historically been "presumptively open," that inquiry is to be based on U.S. history as a whole, not the history of any smaller jurisdiction within.

Lower Courts Apply the *Press-Enterprise II* Test

As we have seen, the Supreme Court has heard closure cases involving only suppression hearings, voir dire hearings, and the kind of elaborate preliminary hearings

---

62. *El Vocero de Puerto Rico v. Puerto Rico*, 508 U.S. 147 (1993).

conducted in California and some other jurisdictions. In this section we examine the pattern of lower court case law in which other kinds of hearings were at issue.

One-Sided Preliminary Hearings.

Recall that the preliminary hearing conducted in the *Press-Enterprise II* case from California was itself very similar to a trial, especially in that both sides were permitted to present evidence and to question each other's witnesses, and that the defendant had an absolute right to such a hearing. In most states, however, preliminary hearings are far more one-sided. They provide an opportunity for the prosecution to present a truncated version of its case to a magistrate, who will then decide if probable cause exists to hold the defendant over for trial. Given the kinds of damaging evidence often heard in such hearings, it is no surprise that defendants often move for closure. The pattern of post–*Press-Enterprise II* lower court decisions suggests, however, that trial judges are very reluctant to approve these motions, in part because the preliminary hearing, like a suppression hearing, typically results in either a plea bargain or in the dismissal of charges and may thus be the only opportunity for the press and the public to monitor the criminal justice system. The Idaho Supreme Court feared that closure denies the public "the opportunity to observe the criminal justice system at work."[63] "Public access to the preliminary hearing," the Iowa Supreme Court has similarly emphasized, functions as "a curb on prosecutorial and judicial misconduct."[64] The First Circuit Court of Appeals has held that preliminary hearings in Puerto Rico must generally be open to the press and public, even though the tradition of that particular jurisdiction is more consistent with closure.[65] And in a fascinating case from Washington, that state's highest court granted a new trial to convicted drug dealer Ricko Fernandez Easterling because his codefendant's guilty plea to a lesser charge in exchange for offering testimony against him was delivered in a closed preliminary hearing. The court emphasized that it was not only Easterling's but also the public's right to an open proceeding that had been violated.[66]

Hearing on a Motion to Disqualify a Judge.

In the 1980s, officers of the Teamsters union being prosecuted on embezzlement charges moved to disqualify Judge Ann Aldrich from hearing the case, alleging that her past conflicts with one of their attorneys would bias her. Defendants requested further that the hearing on this motion be conducted in secret, and a district court judge chosen to hear the motion agreed. The Sixth Circuit Court of Appeals overturned this ruling, finding that disqualification hearings met both parts of the *Press-Enterprise II* test for presumed openness. First, the court reviewed many decades of history within the circuit and

---

63. *Cowles Publishing Co. v. Magistrate Court*, 800 P.2d 640 (Idaho 1990).
64. *Des Moines Register & Tribune Co. v. District Court*, 426 N.W.2d 142 (Iowa 1988).
65. *Rivera-Puig v. Garcia-Rosario*, 983 F.2d 311, 323 (1st Cir. 1992).
66. *State v. Easterling*, 137 P.3d 825 (Wash. 2006).

found that all such hearings had been open in the past. Writing for the appellate panel majority, Judge Lively concluded also that openness served a valuable societal function. "The background, experience, and associations of the judge are important factors in any trial," Lively wrote. "When a judge's impartiality is questioned, it strengthens the judicial process for the public to be informed of how the issue is approached and decided."[67] As of 2007, the Sixth Circuit was still the only court to have issued a ruling on the openness of disqualification hearings.

Bail Hearings.   Probably some of the most dramatic recurring media narratives about the judiciary are tales of violent criminal acts committed by persons out on bail while awaiting trial on wholly unrelated charges. Thus there is tremendous public interest in at least the end results, if not the mechanics, of bail hearings, and courts have often held that such hearings are presumptively open.

The Court of Appeals for the First Circuit has emphasized that just as pretrial hearings are often a defendant's only trial, a bail hearing may represent the public's only chance to witness a suspect's interaction with the criminal justice system. This situation would occur, of course, if bail is granted, and the suspect then flees. Conversely, the decision not to grant bail, or to set it so high as to effectively ensure that suspects will remain in jail pending trial, necessarily deprives defendants of their liberty before they have been convicted of any crime.[68] The First Amendment right to attend bail hearings is not absolute. Limited closure has often been permitted when inadmissible evidence, such as tapes or transcripts from improperly conducted wiretaps, is to be presented as part of the prosecution's argument for denying bail.[69]

Competency Hearings.   Although there have not been many cases involving the issue of closing competency hearings, courts that have addressed the matter have generally found a First Amendment interest in favor of openness. Some of these cases predate the *Press-Enterprise II* rule.[70] Not surprisingly, post–*Press-Enterprise II* cases have continued the trend toward openness of competency hearings. "Given [the] strong public policy against trying an incompetent person for a criminal offense," the Utah Supreme Court wrote in an 1987 case, "it seems plain that the proceeding at which competency is determined is a significant one in the criminal process."[71] More recently, a state appellate court in Virginia held that the press must be given access to a videotape of the competency hearing already held for a multiple homicide defendant. "Public access can play a significant positive role in criminal competency hear-

---

67. *In re National Broadcasting Co.*, 828 F.2d 340, 345 (6th Cir. 1987).

68. *In re Globe Newspaper Co.*, 729 F.2d 47 (1st Cir. 1984).

69. See, for example, *United States v. Giordano*, 158 F. Supp. 2d 242 (D. Conn. 2001); *United States v. Leonardo*, 129 F. Supp. 2d 240 (W.D.N.Y. 2001).

70. *Westchester Rockland Newspapers Corp. v. Leggett*, 399 N.E.2d 518, 523 (N.Y. 1979); *Miami Herald Publishing Co. v. Chappell*, 403 So. 2d 1342 (Fla. Dist. Ct. App. 1981).

71. *Society of Professional Journalists v. Bullock*, 743 P.2d 1166, 1178 (Utah 1987).

ings," the court wrote, in that such hearings "can postpone, sometimes indefinitely, the trial of an accused."[72] Consistent with these decisions, a federal court in Ohio in 2005 decided that the report from mental health professionals called in to determine if a convicted murderer was competent to waive further appeals could not be sealed.[73]

"Show Cause" Hearings.   In October, 2005 an underage patron of a bar in Lawrence, Massachusetts, was a stabbing victim. Consistent with Massachusetts law, to aid the state in deciding whether to initiate any proceedings against the bar owner, indeed whether even to arrest the bar owner, what is known as a "show cause" hearing was held. A local newspaper unsuccessfully sought access to the hearing, and the state's highest court upheld the closure.

Show-cause hearings are very different from trials, the court found. Presiding over such hearings is a "clerk-magistrate" who need not even be a lawyer. The purpose of show-cause hearings is to weed out minor cases from the full-blown criminal justice system, using counseling, discussion, or perhaps the *threat* of prosecution, in an effort to bring about an informal settlement of grievances. Such hearings, the Massachusetts Supreme Judicial Court held, have not traditionally been open to the press and the public. Indeed, opening them may impair their function, the court found, because the glare of publicity might inflame the animosities of the involved parties, making the hoped-for amicable settlement less likely.[74]

Deportation Hearings.   In response to the September 11, 2001, terrorist attacks, the federal government sought and obtained many new law enforcement investigatory powers; it also sought to increase the level of secrecy surrounding its use of those powers. Some of these changes in law and in everyday practice by the executive branch have been challenged in the courts.

One of the key issues likely to be resolved ultimately by the Supreme Court is whether deportation hearings should be open to the press and the public. Two federal appellate courts have reached opposite conclusions. The Sixth Circuit ruled that they should be open,[75] but the Third Circuit decided in favor of closure.[76] The latter decision minced no words when it came time to articulate the higher values at stake: "This case arises in the wake of September 11, 2001, a day on which American life changed drastically and dramatically. The era that dawned on September 11, and the war against terrorism that has pervaded the sinews of our national life since that day, are reflected in thousands of ways in legislative and national policy, the habits of daily living, and our collective psyches." In May 2003 the Supreme Court denied review to the Third Circuit decision.

---

72. *In re Times-World Corp.*, 488 S.E.2d 677, 682 (Va. Ct. App. 1997).
73. *Ashworth v. Bagley*, 351 F. Supp. 2d 786 (S.D. Ohio 2005).
74. *Eagle-Tribune Publishing Co. v. Clerk-Magistrate*, 863 N.E.2d 517 (Mass. 2007).
75. *Detroit Free Press v. Ashcroft*, 303 F.3d 681 (6th Cir. 2002).
76. *North Jersey Media Group, Inc. v. Ashcroft*, 308 F.3d 198 (3d Cir. 2002).

Access to Judicial Documents

Some of the same Supreme Court precedents that have established a qualified First Amendment right to attend judicial proceedings have also had something to say about access to judicial documents. The transcript of a voir dire proceeding is, after all, a judicial document. In *Press-Enterprise Co. v. Superior Court I*, one of the issues before the Supreme Court was whether the press should have at least been given a transcript of the voir dire proceeding in a timely fashion. The Court's majority came out strongly in favor of such disclosure. Similarly, in *Press-Enterprise Co. v. Superior Court II*, the Supreme Court concluded that by denying the press's repeated requests for a transcript of the elaborate preliminary hearing, the trial judge had frustrated "the community therapeutic value of openness."[77]

If voir dire hearings are presumptively open, should additional information about jurors—such as their names, addresses, occupations, or even the questionnaires they may have had to complete about their knowledge and attitudes—be revealed to the media? Whether the media have a constitutional right to the data is a matter that has never reached the U.S. Supreme Court, and the lower court case law is mixed.[78] Note, however, that the media likely have no right to private communications between jurors and trial judges, such as when jurors seek clarification of instructions,[79] though sometimes the gist of conversations between a judge and a juror can be revealed at the end of the trial.[80]

Trial judges have a burden of proof when they seek to close judicial records that closely mirrors the burden of proof for closing judicial hearings. Often this means demonstrating that there is not a history of openness with respect to a particular category of judicial documents (such as details of the negotiations that may lead to a plea agreement). Sometimes the judge meets the burden of proof by identifying reasons for closure compelling enough to override whatever common-law or constitutional interests may exist in openness.

Given the traditional secrecy surrounding grand jury proceedings, it is no surprise that judges overseeing such matters are given great deference should they wish to deny media access to related documents. This became painfully clear to the array of media outlets that conducted a daily stakeout of the courthouse in Washington, D.C., where the grand jury was looking into whether Monica Lewinsky should be tried for suborning perjury and otherwise obstructing justice in Paula Jones's suit against President Clinton. Although it was obvious to all concerned that the press had no First Amendment right to observe grand jury proceedings themselves, the media thought

---

77. 478 U.S. 1, 13 (1986).

78. Marcus M. Wilson, Jr., "Juror Identities in High Profile Trials: The Case for a First Amendment Right of Access," 3 *First Amendment Law Review* 437, 451 n.68 (2005).

79. *United States v. Kemp*, 366 F. Supp. 2d 255 (E.D. Pa. 2005).

80. *United States v. Edwards*, 823 F.2d 111 (5th Cir. 1987).

they should be given access to documents related to several "ancillary proceedings" flowing from the grand jury.

Several witnesses called before the grand jury had decided to challenge their subpoenas. President Clinton's attorneys filed papers asking that Kenneth Starr's Office of the Independent Counsel be compelled to show cause why it should not be held in contempt of court for leaking confidential materials to the press and thus compromising the grand jury's function. Should the press have been granted access to paperwork associated with such matters? The D.C. Circuit Court of Appeals, in two separate decisions, ruled against the press.[81] The First Amendment, and relevant federal and local rules of judicial procedure, dictated that the press could be denied not only full-text copies of any grand jury documents but also a docket of the kinds of motions before the judge overseeing the grand jury. The appellate court threw one bone to the plaintiff media organizations, however: if the trial judge refused a formal request for a docket of matters related to a specific grand jury proceeding, that denial must include a clear justification that "must bear some logical connection to the individual request." The court cannot simply claim that the "administrative burdens" would be too cumbersome; unsubstantiated and general fears of leaks would be insufficient to justify denial.

Often, the media are granted access to judicial documents under the *Press-Enterprise II* test. But what if those "documents" are in the form of audio or video recordings? Do the media then have a corollary right to copy and broadcast those recordings? The Supreme Court has given us one ruling on the issue, but because the facts of that case are intertwined with a unique federal statute, the value of the precedent is somewhat limited. The case was the trial of former attorney general John Mitchell for Watergate-related offenses.[82] The Supreme Court denied a request made by the media for the right to broadcast and sell copies of the several hours of Oval Office tape recordings that had been admitted in evidence. This case was unusual, Justice Powell admitted, in that Congress had already instituted a process for orderly release of the Nixon tapes to the public when it passed the Presidential Recordings Act. Lower courts have thus been free to find a right—most frequently a common-law right based on tradition rather than a First Amendment right—for the media to copy and broadcast copies of audiotapes or videotapes played as evidence in court.

And indeed the general rule seems to be that if tapes are played in open court and if the media are permitted into the court, the materials can be copied and broadcast.[83] There are exceptions, however. For example, just as portions of bail and detention hearings during which evidence likely to be inadmissible at trial is presented may be

---

81. *In re Motions of Dow Jones & Co.*, 142 F.3d 496 (D.C. Cir. 1998); *In re Sealed Case*, 199 F.3d 522 (D.C. Cir. 2000).

82. *Nixon v. Warner Communications, Inc.*, 435 U.S. 589 (1978).

83. *In re National Broadcasting Co. (United States v. Criden)*, 648 F.2d 814 (3d Cir. 1981); *In re National Broadcasting Co. (United States v. Myers)*, 635 F.2d 945 (2d Cir. 1980).

THINGS TO REMEMBER

Closure of Other Court Proceedings

- In 1979, in *Gannett v. DePasquale*, the Court ruled that a defendant's wish to exclude the press from a pretrial hearing might outweigh whatever rights the press may have to attend.
- In *Press-Enterprise Co. v. Superior Court I* (1984), the majority ruled that voir dire hearings may be closed only when an "overriding interest" is established, and closure is determined to be "essential" by "findings" (i.e., the judge must prove it, not just say it). The "overriding interest" might be something other than a fair trial; it might be to protect jurors' privacy.
- In *Press-Enterprise Co. v. Superior Court II* (1986), the Court instructed trial judges to consider whether the kind of hearing they are considering closing has historically been open and whether the function of the hearing will be enhanced by openness.
- Presumptively open categories of hearings may be closed only if the closure is narrowly tailored to ward off a "substantial probability" of jeopardizing a "higher value."
- This *Press-Enterprise II* test has since been applied by lower courts to several additional categories of pretrial hearings.
- Lower courts have fashioned similar rules to determine whether judicial documents may be sealed.

closed to the press and public, so too access to, and permission to broadcast, such inadmissible evidence (often tapes from "wired" informants) may be denied.[84] Also, if a witness makes a request to provide testimony via videotape, rather than live in the courtroom, the resulting video will not necessarily be considered a judicial record, even if it is played in open court. Thus when President Clinton provided a videotape deposition in the Arkansas trial of his Whitewater associate Jim McDougal, the media were not permitted to copy and broadcast the tape.[85] After all, the Eighth Circuit Court of Appeals reasoned, cameras are generally not permitted into federal courtrooms—more about that later—so why should the media be given a video record of this one witness's testimony?

TV Cameras in Court

The question of whether electronic media should be permitted in courtrooms—to date all the case law in this area has involved television cameras—is quite different from the issues of gag orders and closure discussed above. Unlike a judge's decision to issue a gag order or close a hearing, a trial judge's discretionary decision to prohibit

---

84. *United States v. Andreas*, 1998 U.S. Dist. LEXIS 11347 (N.D. Ill. 1998).
85. *United States v. McDougal*, 103 F.3d 651 (8th Cir. 1996).

cameras in the courtroom is generally not appealable. From the perspective of those who favor televised coverage of the judiciary, even this state of affairs represents a major step forward from the 1960s.

It was in 1965 that the Supreme Court overturned the fraud conviction of Billie Sol Estes, a friend of President Johnson's who had apparently "sold" farmers imaginary tanks of fertilizer and other agricultural equipment.[86] The majority accepted Estes's argument that his constitutional rights had been violated by the introduction of TV cameras into the courtroom. Writing for a 5-4 majority, Justice Clark expressed dismay over the cables and wires that "snaked across the courtroom floor," and the "considerable disruption" caused by the dozen cameramen and their equipment.

Clark dismissed the argument made in the amicus briefs filed by the National Association of Broadcasters and the Radio and Television News Directors Association. The First Amendment would not be violated by the discriminatory exclusion of *broadcast* media from the judicial process, Clark wrote. TV reporters would be allowed into courtrooms; they simply would not be permitted to bring their cameras, just as print reporters are not permitted to bring their typewriters.

Only four of the five justices in the *Estes* majority felt that TV cameras in courtrooms necessarily violated criminal defendants' rights. Justice Harlan, who provided the majority with its needed fifth vote, made clear that the *Estes* decision should be read narrowly as a suggestion that bringing cameras into criminal trials generating "great notoriety" could be violative of the defendant's rights.

Thus the individual states felt free to experiment cautiously with television in the courtroom. By 1980, twenty-eight states had already permitted some trials to be televised, and another dozen states were studying the issue. In 1982, the American Bar Association abandoned its own decades-long opposition to TV cameras in courtrooms.

The amount of such experimentation increased dramatically after a second Supreme Court decision handed down sixteen years after *Estes*. *Chandler v. Florida* involved two Miami Beach police officers appealing their burglary conviction on the grounds that the trial judge's decision to permit the televising of portions of their trial had violated their constitutional rights.[87] In a unanimous ruling, the Supreme Court upheld the conviction and determined that the televising of a trial, even over a defendant's objections, is not itself a violation of the right to a fair trial. *Chandler* was not an outright overturning of the earlier *Estes* doctrine, however. Using the vocabulary from chapter 1, we might say that the 1981 decision is best thought of as having *modified* the 1965 precedent. The introduction of TV cameras into the courtroom was no longer deemed inherently violative of a defendant's rights because something in the real world had changed—technology had improved to the point that TV cameras were no longer automatically intrusive. They had become smaller, as well as quieter, and they were now less dependent on the glare of high-intensity lighting.

---

86. *Estes v. Texas*, 381 U.S. 532 (1965).
87. 449 U.S. 560 (1981).

If anything, the pace with which state judiciaries have introduced TV cameras into courtrooms since *Chandler* has been so fast that it no longer makes sense to even speak of "experimentation" with the technology. All fifty states now permit cameras in civil appellate courts, and most states permit television coverage in both trial and appellate courts in connection with both civil and criminal litigation.

But even in state courts that permit TV cameras, broadcast media do not have a free rein. Trial judges are the ultimate arbiters in this arena. *Chandler* stands only for the principle that trial judges *may* have cameras in court; it does not instruct them to do so. The various state supreme court rules that govern audio and video technologies in courtrooms typically provide rather strict guidelines. Jurors are not to be shown, nor may private consultations among attorneys and the judge be broadcast. There may also be strict limitations on the number and positioning of cameras, which may not bear the name or logo of any particular network or station.

Some states have even permitted televised coverage of that traditionally secret venue, the jury room. Thus PBS was able to produce a documentary in the 1980s, *Inside the Jury Room*, focusing on jury deliberations in a Milwaukee case involving a mentally retarded ex-felon accused of violating parole when, following the instructions from a correspondence course for security guards, he purchased a firearm. But when PBS sought permission more recently to televise the jury at work in a capital murder trial in Texas, a state appellate court nixed the idea as a violation of state law prohibiting any person from "being with" the jury during their deliberations.[88]

Several news outlets over the years have sought judicial permission to film an execution, but none have prevailed.[89] Most recently, the Eighth Circuit Court of Appeals upheld the State of Missouri's policy against cameras in or around the execution chamber. The court agreed that there was a strong public interest in just about every aspect of the capital punishment debate but concluded that First Amendment rights were not implicated by the state's policy.[90]

While state courts are generally very open to the electronic media, in federal courts the story is quite different. In the early 1990s the Judicial Conference of the United States, which promulgates rules governing the federal judiciary, initiated a three-year experiment, allowing cameras in two federal appellate courts as well as district courts in a handful of states. Although the Judicial Conference staff report was highly positive, the Judicial Conference decided to continue the long-standing tradition against permitting cameras in federal courtrooms. The ultimate decision was left up to each

---

88. *State ex rel. Rosenthal v. Poe*, 98 S.W.3d 194, 201–202 (Tex. Ct. App. 2003).

89. *Garrett v. Estelle*, 556 F.2d 1274 (5th Cir. 1977), *cert. denied*, 438 U.S. 914 (1978); *Entertainment Network, Inc. v. Lappin*, 134 F. Supp. 2d 1002 (S.D. Ind. 2001); *Lawson v. Dixon*, 446 S.E.2d 799 (N.C. 1994); *Halquist v. Department of Corrections*, 783 P.2d 1065 (Wash. 1989). The Ninth Circuit has held that executions must be open to the public (though not necessarily televised). *California First Amendment Coalition v. Woodford*, 299 F.3d 868 (9th Cir. 2002).

90. *Rice v. Kemker*, 373 F.3d 675 (8th Cir. 2004).

> **THINGS TO REMEMBER**
>
> ### TV in Courts
>
> - There is no First Amendment right to have a trial televised.
> - Nonetheless, all states permit cameras in at least some courts, and most states permit cameras at both the trial and appellate levels in both civil and criminal cases.
> - State trial judges retain complete discretion to refuse a request to televise a trial.
> - TV is highly unusual in federal courtrooms, despite generally positive feedback from an experimental program in the 1990s.

circuit court, and at present only the Second and Ninth Circuits permit cameras into appellate proceedings.[91]

Most observers agree that the U.S. Supreme Court itself is unlikely to permit cameras to cover its oral arguments anytime soon, although it does sometimes permit immediate release of audiotapes after some high-profile cases. The majority of the justices seem to be against inviting cameras in, some for fear that the incessant replaying of emotionally charged sound bites will diminish the Court's stature, others likely because they relish wielding as much power as they do without having to suffer the inconvenience of celebrity. (How many of the current Court's members would you be able to recognize on sight, without using their group photo in chapter 1 as a guide?)

Chapter Summary

Reporters covering the judiciary often confront a clash between First Amendment and Sixth Amendment values. If a trial judge issues an order that unconstitutionally restricts the press, wise reporters obey the order even while taking an appeal to a higher court, lest a contempt citation be upheld.

Trial judges have many strategies at their disposal to minimize the damage caused by pretrial publicity. Among these options are issuing a continuance, granting a change of venue or of venire, or sequestering the jury. By far the most common techniques are a carefully conducted voir dire and clear instructions to the jurors.

Sometimes trial judges also embrace one of two other strategies: either preventing the press from publishing what it already knows (a "gag" order) or barring the press and the public from the judicial proceedings at which they might learn potentially prejudicial information. In a number of decisions handed down since the late 1970s,

---

91. Audrey Maness, "Does the First Amendment's 'Right of Access' Require Court Proceedings to be Televised? A Constitutional and Practical Discussion," 34 *Pepperdine Law Review* 123, 149–151 (2006).

the Supreme Court has set forth rules governing the burden of proof trial judges assume if they choose to use either strategy.

Although the Court has said that there is a qualified First Amendment right to attend and report about judicial proceedings, there is no such constitutional right to bring TV cameras into courtrooms. Nonetheless, the states do permit cameras in their courtrooms (as long as the trial judge does not object). Cameras are virtually unheard of, however, in federal courts.

Chapter 9

PROTECTING NEWS SOURCES

In the summer of 2006, a grand jury was convened in Virginia, apparently looking into whether the *Washington Post* and the *New York Times* violated federal law—including the Espionage Act—by breaking two sensational stories the year before about the "war on terrorism."[1] The *Post*'s story revealed that the CIA was maintaining several secret prisons in as many as eight countries, where its officers could presumably use interrogation techniques that would lead to political embarrassment if conducted in settings subject to more oversight. Reporter Dana Priest cited "current and former intelligence officials and diplomats from three continents" as her sources.[2]

The *Times* story informed readers that President Bush had secretly authorized the National Security Agency to eavesdrop on Americans' international phone calls without going through the usual procedure for obtaining a special warrant for such surveillance activities. Reporters James Risen and Eric Lichtblau cited "nearly a dozen current and former officials, who were granted anonymity because of the classified nature of the program." Those sources talked to the *Times* because of "their concerns about the operation's legality and oversight," the reporters added.[3]

That this particular grand jury was even considering a finding that the *Post* and *Times* reporters may have been guilty of violating the Espionage Act is itself noteworthy. The Espionage Act, which you may recall is a World War I–era piece of legisla-

---

1. Scott Shane, "Leak of Classified Information Prompts Inquiry," *New York Times*, July 29, 2006, A10.

2. Dana Priest, "CIA Holds Terror Suspects in Secret Prisons," *Washington Post*, November 2, 2005, A1.

3. James Risen and Eric Lichtblau, "Bush Lets U.S. Spy on Callers without Courts," *New York Times*, December 16, 2005, A1.

tion, has been used against persons who leak classified documents but not against reporters who reveal information that might have been classified. It is more likely that the reporters will be asked by the grand jury to reveal the names of their confidential sources for their articles. Failure to comply could lead to a citation for contempt of court, and even to imprisonment.

Another *New York Times* reporter—Judith Miller—was imprisoned for three months in 2005 for failing to reveal her confidential sources related to a story she never even wrote. But newspaper columnist and frequent TV pundit Robert Novak did write the story, two years earlier, in which he cited "two senior administration officials" in revealing that Valerie Plame, wife of former U.S. ambassador to Iraq Joseph Wilson, was a CIA operative.[4] In 2006 Novak revealed that presidential adviser Karl Rove was one of his sources for the Plame story. (It later emerged that his other source, former deputy secretary of state Richard Armitage, was the first leaker and that Rove was used to confirm the story.) Numerous Washington insiders have suggested that Rove may have intended to retaliate against Wilson for his public statements contradicting the Bush administration's insistence that Saddam Hussein had obtained materials from the African nation of Niger that could assist him in making nuclear weapons. Whereas Novak apparently cooperated with the grand jury investigating the Plame leak, Judith Miller and *Time* magazine reporter Matthew Cooper were held in contempt for refusing to cooperate, and the D.C. Circuit Court of Appeals upheld the contempt citation.[5] Unlike Miller, Cooper avoided jail time because his source (also Karl Rove) released him from his promise of confidentiality, allowing him and the magazine to obey Judge Thomas Hogan's orders to testify. Only after Judith Miller had served eighty-five days in jail did her source, former vice presidential chief of staff I. Lewis "Scooter" Libby, release her from her promise of confidentiality, paving the way for her release. Libby himself, of course, was convicted in 2007 on perjury and obstruction of justice charges related to the Plame leak.

While going to prison is not part of a reporter's usual job description, it should be pointed out that Judith Miller is hardly unique in this regard. A quick phone call to the Reporters Committee for Freedom of the Press revealed that at least seventeen reporters went to jail for failure to testify (most often about confidential sources) between 1984 and 2006. The journalist with the unhappy distinction of having been jailed longest is freelance photojournalist and political activist Josh Wolf, who began serving a jail term in August 2006 after refusing to turn over video footage he had taken of political demonstrations in San Francisco the year before that resulted in a police officer being seriously injured. Wolf was released in April 2007 after serving 226 days in jail. As part of the agreement leading to his release, he uploaded all the

---

4. "The Mission to Niger," *Chicago Sun-Times*, July 14, 2003, 31.

5. *In re Grand Jury Subpoena (Judith Miller)*, 397 F.3d 964 (D.C. Cir. 2005), *reh'g denied*, 405 F.3d 17 (D.C. Cir. 2005).

video outtakes sought by prosecutors to his website, and he stated under oath that he had no firsthand information about how or by whose hand the officer was injured.[6]

Wolf's time behind bars broke the record previously held by Vanessa Leggett, a part-time college teacher in Texas who had been conducting research for a book about the murder of Houston-area socialite Doris Angleton. The State of Texas charged Doris's husband Robert with hiring his brother Roger to kill her. While the case was pending, Roger Angleton committed suicide in jail. He left notes behind taking full responsibility for the killing and admitting that he framed his brother, who was later acquitted of the murder in state court.

The federal government was considering filing its own charges against Robert Angleton (he was ultimately convicted on tax evasion charges). The federal grand jury subpoenaed notes from Leggett, who had conducted interviews with Roger Angleton. She argued that the First Amendment and the Texas Constitution together create a strong enough reporters' shield to protect her from being forced to produce her notes or testify in front of the grand jury. Federal judge Melinda Harmon held Leggett in contempt of court, and the Fifth Circuit Court of Appeals, in an unpublished opinion, upheld the citation. The Supreme Court later denied review.[7] Leggett was sent to jail on July 20, 2001, and was not released until the grand jury was dismissed in January 2002—she spent 168 days in jail.

Reporters and Confidential Sources

In this chapter we look at what happens when the government seeks information from reporters. Whether reporters will have to turn over information to the government depends on a number of factors. One consideration is the kind of information sought. Is the reporter merely being asked to tell what he or she has seen firsthand as a witness to an event, or does the government instead want the reporter to repeat information that an informant has provided? Other factors include whether the government seeks disclosure of an informant's identity and whether the reporter explicitly promised anonymity to his or her source.

This area of law is complicated, since whatever rights reporters may have to avoid compelled disclosures come from a patchwork of federal and state case law interpreting First Amendment and state constitutional provisions, state "reporter shield laws," judicial rules, and even attorney general guidelines.

Look in any major newspaper, especially one well known for doing investigative reporting, and you will find frequent references to "sources in a position to know," "highly placed sources," "administration sources," and sources who spoke "upon a

---

6. Joe Mozingo, "Imprisoned Blogger Is Freed in Deal with Federal Prosecutor," *Los Angeles Times*, April 4, 2007, B3.

7. *Leggett v. United States*, 535 U.S. 1011 (2002).

THINGS TO REMEMBER

Reporters and Confidential Sources

- Reporters, especially in Washington, D.C., have a love-hate, interdependent relationship with confidential sources.
- Journalists and writers have occasionally gone to jail to protect the confidentiality of their sources.
- A special lexicon exists describing the degree of anonymity demanded by a source, including such phrases as speaking "off the record," "on background," and "on deep background."

---

promise of anonymity." Often the passive voice is used to avoid even suggesting the existence of a source. Thus we may hear only that "CNN has learned . . ." (from intense meditation?) some important news.

It is fair to say that the media have a love-hate relationship with confidential sources. The dangers of overreliance on such sources are obvious; it is equally obvious, however, that many important stories would never be reported without promises of anonymity. Perhaps the best example in modern American journalism is "Deep Throat," Bob Woodward's Watergate source, who remained anonymous for thirty-plus years and finally "outed" himself in 2005 as W. Mark Felt, once the second in command at the FBI. Consider for a moment if you would prefer that the Watergate break-in and cover-up, or the more recent stories about CIA secret prisons and warrantless government wiretaps of Americans' phone conversations, had never been reported. Without reporters' freedom to promise their sources confidentiality, stories such as these likely would never be revealed.

A whole lexicon has developed governing the degree of anonymity a source may expect when conversing with a reporter. There is no ambiguity about the meaning of talking "on the record"—the reporter is free to use everything the source says and to quote the source directly. "Off the record" means, minimally, that the source is not to be quoted. Some assume that it also means that paraphrases are equally forbidden, and still others think that the reporter should pretend that off-the-record conversations never took place.

If a source insists on speaking "on background," the reporter can repeat everything that is said and attribute it, although somewhat vaguely. Certainly the source's name should not be associated with any quotes. Sources sometimes will speak only "on deep background," which most reporters take to mean that paraphrasing is permitted, but not attributions, even to such vague entities as "informed sources."[8]

---

8. Mark Feldstein, "Leak Riddle: Who's Playing Whom?" *Washington Post*, July 24, 2005, B1; Jo Mannies, "The Background on Sources," *St. Louis Post-Dispatch*, February 17, 1993, C1.

Most of the remainder of this chapter concerns the legal conflicts that arise when government officials ask reporters to break their bonds of confidentiality with their sources. We begin that exploration by looking closely at the one time the U.S. Supreme Court has issued an opinion addressing whether the U.S. Constitution protects reporters who wish to protect the identity of their confidential sources.

The First Amendment and Confidential Sources: *Branzburg v. Hayes*

It all began with a story written by reporter Paul Branzburg of the Louisville *Courier-Journal* in November 1969 about a pair of local residents—given the pseudonyms Larry and Jack—and their partnership in the synthesis of hashish from marijuana plants. Not surprisingly, the local district attorney was interested in learning the subjects' true identities. Thus Branzburg was subpoenaed to appear before a Jefferson County grand jury. Although the reporter did appear as ordered, he refused to answer any questions he felt would tend to reveal the identities of his sources.

The *Courier-Journal* published another Branzburg article, this one about marijuana use by residents of Frankfort, Kentucky, and here also the reporter's work attracted the attention of local law enforcement officials. This time Branzburg refused to testify at all before the grand jury. It is a very difficult thing, Branzburg argued, for a reporter to build trust between himself and informants with firsthand information about the extent of illicit drug use in a community. Such sources would never trust him again were he to appear before a grand jury. Because grand jury proceedings are traditionally sealed, the moment it became known that he had appeared before the grand jury, he would have no way of persuading his informants that he did *not* betray them.

The Supreme Court consolidated the two disputes involving Paul Branzburg with two other appeals involving stories written by reporters Paul Pappas and Earl Caldwell about the Black Panther Party, items that also attracted the attention of local law officials.

Counting the Votes

Branzburg v. Hayes resulted in a 5-4 split among the justices.[9] Much of Justice White's opinion for the Court was majority doctrine, joined by Chief Justice Burger as well as Justices Blackmun, Powell, and Rehnquist. Yet the odd nature of Justice Powell's separate concurring opinion leads to the conclusion that, although Powell officially voted with the majority, some sections of Justice White's opinion really commanded only a plurality of four votes. Moreover, because Justice Powell's concurring opinion shared some common ground with those of the four dissenters, *Branz-*

---

9. 408 U.S. 665 (1972).

Could Be a Pot of Gold
THE HASH THEY MAKE ISN'T TO EAT
By Paul M. Branzburg

(excerpts from the Louisville *Courier-Journal* article, November 15, 1969)

Larry, a young Louisville hippie, wiped the sweat off his brow, looked about the stuffy little room and put another pot on the stove over which he had been laboring for hours. For over a week, he has been proudly tending his pots and pans. . . . Larry and his partner, Jack, are engaged in a weird business that is a combination of capitalism, chemistry, and criminality.

They are operating a makeshift laboratory in south-central Louisville that may produce them enough hashish, or "hash," a concentrate of marijuana, to net them up to $5,000 for three weeks of work. . . .

"I don't know why I'm letting you do this story. . . . To make the narcs (narcotics detectives) mad, I guess. That's the main reason. . . ."

"The trouble we're having is finding the right base," Larry said, as he continued to chop stems. "The hash we've produced gets you stoned, but it doesn't smoke the same as foreign hash. I tried to use incense as a base, but it gives too much of a sweet taste. In the Middle East they use camel manure, so I'm thinking of going out to the zoo. . . ."

burg represents one of those quirky situations in which lower courts have followed the dissenting opinion more than the majority opinion.

Looking first at the majority opinion, we note that Justice White rejected the reporters' claim that confidential sources whose identities reporters are compelled to reveal to a grand jury "will be measurably deterred from furnishing publishable information, all to the detriment of the free flow of information protected by the First Amendment." Only when reporters' sources are suspected of criminal wrongdoing would the question of compelled testimony surface. To rule for the reporters here would send the message that "it is better to write about crime than to do something about it."

The imposition placed on the reporters in these cases by the respective grand juries was minimal, Justice White concluded. The reporters were not prohibited from publishing, nor were they told that they had to eschew the use of confidential sources. "The sole issue before us," he wrote, "is the obligation of reporters to respond to grand jury subpoenas as other citizens do and to answer questions relevant to an investigation into the commission of crime." Reporters, he added, "are not exempt from the normal duty of appearing before a grand jury and answering questions relevant to a criminal investigation." The majority thus made clear that it did not see this as a First Amendment case at all. Indeed, White added, for the judiciary to find a constitutional right on the part of reporters to refuse to testify in front of grand juries would create a logistic nightmare. "Sooner or later," he warned, "it would be necessary to define those categories of newsmen who qualified for the privilege, a questionable procedure in light of the traditional doctrine that liberty of the press is the right of the lonely pamphleteer who uses carbon paper or a mimeograph just as much as of the large metropolitan publisher who utilizes the latest photo composition methods." As we see later in this chapter, state legislatures have had to deal with this precise issue—defining who is a "reporter"—in connection with the enactment of reporter shield laws. Congressional committees pondering a federal law—none has yet been enacted—have had to deal with the same issue.

Let us examine the dissenting opinions. Justice Douglas, writing only for himself, argued that reporters should enjoy an *absolute* right to refuse to testify in front of grand juries. In those rare circumstances in which reporters themselves are suspected of criminal wrongdoing, the Fifth Amendment's guarantee against self-incrimination would provide the protection. The First Amendment should serve as a reporter's security against forced disclosure about any other matters, Douglas concluded.

The other three dissenters were not willing to go quite as far as Justice Douglas. Justice Stewart, writing for himself as well as for Justices Brennan and Marshall, offered lower courts a set of principles by which to balance a reporter's interest in keeping information confidential with the grand jury's interest in compelling disclosure. The reporter's interest should prevail, Justice Stewart suggested, unless the government can prove three elements:

- There is probable cause to believe that the reporter possesses information relevant to a criminal investigation.
- The government has a compelling need for this information (i.e., its disclosure or nondisclosure will likely affect the outcome of the case).
- The reporter is the only identifiable source of the needed information.

Why, though, should the government have to meet such a high burden of proof? For Justice Stewart, the special interdependent relationship between informants and reporters provides the answer. "The promise of confidentiality," he proposed, is "a necessary prerequisite" to the nurturance of that relationship. The institutionalized press needs such informants "if it is to perform its constitutional mission." Without them the media will be reduced to "print[ing] public statements" and "publish[ing] prepared handouts."

Justice Powell's brief concurring opinion in *Branzburg* is the key to understanding how and why the three-part test from Justice Stewart's dissenting opinion has been so very influential. Powell cautions that the majority "does not hold that newsmen, subpoenaed to testify before a grand jury, are without constitutional rights." Should a reporter called before a grand jury conclude that "the investigation is not being conducted in good faith," that the information sought has "only a remote and tenuous relationship to the subject of the investigation," a motion to quash (i.e., to invalidate) the subpoena would appropriately be sought. A court asked to intervene in this way would make its decision by "striking a proper balance" between the reporter's First Amendment claims and competing state's interests.

At its core, Justice Powell's opinion was far more consistent with the philosophy espoused by the dissenters than that of the majority. He, unlike the majority, accepted that the First Amendment is implicated when reporters are called on by the government to reveal confidential information. Like Justice Stewart, he argued for a balancing test. Perhaps it should not be surprising, then, that many lower court judges counted up the *Branzburg* votes and concluded that a majority of the Court—the four dissenters plus Justice Powell—insisted that reporters' First Amendment claims of confidentiality be taken seriously.

The Lower Courts Apply *Branzburg*

In the decades since *Branzburg* was decided, most courts that have confronted the issue have recognized at least a limited First Amendment privilege for reporters who wish to avoid compelled disclosure of information in their possession. The two exceptions are the Sixth and Seventh Circuits, but even these exceptions do not represent a complete repudiation of a reporters' privilege.

The Seventh Circuit, covering Illinois, Indiana, and Wisconsin, rejected in 2003 a First Amendment privilege for reporters, but Judge Richard Posner suggested that his ruling might have been different had the identity of a confidential source been at

---

THINGS TO REMEMBER

Branzburg v. Hayes

- In *Branzburg v. Hayes* (1972) the Supreme Court held that even if reporters do enjoy First Amendment protection, their claims must yield to the need of grand juries investigating criminal wrongdoing.
- Justice Stewart's dissenting opinion—which has proved more influential than the majority opinion—argued that states wishing to compel reporter testimony must prove that (1) there is probable cause to believe that the reporter possesses information relevant to a criminal investigation; (2) the government has a compelling need for this information (i.e., its disclosure or nondisclosure will likely affect the outcome of the case); and (3) the reporter is the only identifiable source of the needed information.

issue.[10] And at least one lower court judge in that circuit has since extended First Amendment protection to a reporter's confidential sources.[11] A 1987 decision from the Sixth Circuit, which includes Kentucky, Michigan, Ohio, and Tennessee, seemed to reject the reporters' privilege,[12] but later cases from the same circuit have interpreted the decision very narrowly and have allowed that reporters do have some constitutional confidentiality rights,[13] or at least that a "balancing of interests" must be conducted.[14]

Because the Supreme Court has never clarified the confusing array of opinions from the *Branzburg* case and has never heard a similar dispute, lower courts have fashioned their own assessments as to the scope of any First Amendment protection for journalists' sources. How much protection courts grant is a function of three variables: (1) Is the judicial proceeding at issue a grand jury? (2) Is the information sought truly "confidential"? and (3) Is the person being asked to testify really a "reporter"?

Before reaching the constitutional issue, courts often find it helpful to determine whether a subpoena issued to a reporter comports with Rule 17(c) of Federal Rules of Civil Procedure, which tells us that subpoenas must have three characteristics to be proper: relevancy, specificity, and admissibility. *Relevancy* is clear enough: the information sought must be relevant to the legal proceeding in which the litigant claims to need the reporter's help. *Specificity* is another way of saying that the motion cannot be part of the kind of "fishing expedition" Justice Powell warned against in *Branzburg* itself. *Admissibility* means that the subpoena must seek information that would itself be admissible in the court where the litigant's ongoing case is being adjudicated. If any of these criteria are not met, the subpoena will be quashed without any need to address whether the reporters' privilege exists in the jurisdiction where the dispute arises.

If, however, the subpoena is well constructed and properly executed as per Rule 17(c), courts will generally next consider whether and to what extent *Branzburg v. Hayes* provides reporters with a privilege not to produce documents or not to testify in court. The first factor that may inform such an inquiry is the kind of legal proceeding in which information is being sought.

What Type of Judicial Proceeding?   Lower courts have applied the *Branzburg* precedent in three different circumstances: when a reporter is compelled to testify in a criminal trial; when civil litigants seek information from a reporter; and when

---

10. *McKevitt v. Pallasch*, 339 F.3d 530 (7th Cir. 2003).

11. *Solaia Technology v. Rockwell Automation*, 2003 U.S. Dist. LEXIS 20196 (N.D. Ill. 2003).

12. *Storer Communications v. Giovan*, 810 F.2d 580 (6th Cir. 1987).

13. *Southwell v. The Southern Poverty Law Center*, 949 F. Supp. 1303 (W.D. Mich. 1996); *Marketos v. American Employers Insurance Co.*, 460 N.W.2d 272 (Mich. Ct. App. 1990); *King v. Photo Marketing Association International*, 327 N.W.2d 515 (Mich. Ct. App. 1982).

14. *In re Daimler Chrysler AG Securities Litigation*, 216 F.R.D. 395 (E.D. Mich. 2003).

a reporter is compelled to testify before a grand jury, the same situation that was at issue in *Branzburg*.

Criminal Trials.   In chapter 8 we considered conflicts between the media's First Amendment interest in reporting on judicial proceedings and the accused's Sixth Amendment right to a fair trial. Those two constitutional provisions are again in conflict here. Reporters claim a First Amendment privilege in keeping information from the judiciary, but criminal suspects also have a Sixth Amendment interest in compelling disclosure of such information. The relevant portion of the Sixth Amendment says that the accused has a right "to have compulsory process for obtaining witnesses in his favor."

Because criminal defendants enjoy an explicit constitutional right, some courts have been especially skittish about recognizing a confidentiality privilege for reporters seeking to quash a subpoena to testify at criminal trials. When John Phillip Walker Lindh, dubbed "the American Taliban" because he was captured by U.S. forces during their post-9/11 invasion of Afghanistan, was facing trial, his attorneys subpoenaed freelance journalist Robert Young Pelton. Pelton's interviews with Lindh during his hospital stay in Afghanistan had appeared on CNN, and Lindh contended that Pelton's testimony at his suppression hearing would be invaluable. Even assuming that a First Amendment privilege might apply to Pelton in this circumstance, "Lindh's Sixth Amendment right to prepare and present a full defense" would have to prevail, Judge T. S. Ellis III held.[15]

Another celebrated defendant, former vice presidential chief of staff Lewis "Scooter" Libby, was similarly permitted to compel disclosure of some key documents from numerous media sources when he was charged with perjury and obstruction of justice charges in connection with the media "outing" of CIA operative Valerie Plame. Libby sought notes from NBC and correspondent Andrea Mitchell, *Time* magazine and reporter Matthew Cooper, and the *New York Times* and reporter Judith Miller. Since charges of perjury against Libby stemmed from possible falsehoods told by him to law enforcement officials about his conversations with these and other journalists, the journalists' own notes about the conversations were highly relevant. Judge Reggie Walton compared Libby's situation to the factual situation in *Branzburg v. Hayes* itself. Unlike Paul Branzburg, who merely "report[ed] on alleged criminal activity," here the reporters being subpoenaed "were personally involved in the conversations with the defendant that form the predicate for several charges in the indictment." Although the *Branzburg* case concerned a grand jury and this case involved an actual criminal proceeding, the same logic that compelled Branzburg to testify would apply here. If reporters must testify in front of grand juries, Judge Walton reasoned, they surely may not "invoke the First Amendment to stonewall a criminal

---

15. *United States v. Lindh*, 210 F. Supp. 2d 780 (E.D. Va. 2002).

defendant who has been indicted by that grand jury and seeks evidence to establish his innocence."[16] Libby, it will be recalled, was convicted, in 2007.

In an unusual 2005 decision from New York, that state's highest court overturned a criminal manslaughter conviction and granted a new trial because the defendant's pretrial motion to compel disclosure of some documentary TV footage had been denied. It seems that Brooklyn's North Homicide Task Force had given Court TV "unprecedented access" to its work and that the cable network had videotaped (but never aired) the defendant's entire police interrogation. Although the prosecution only used the last fourteen minutes of that interrogation in court, the defendant claimed that the earlier moments were the ones where he had made a good case that he had acted in self-defense. What makes the case unusual is that the cable TV network was functioning in a quasi-governmental function. Had the police themselves videotaped the whole interrogation (as police are now required to do in many jurisdictions), they would have been compelled to give the defense a copy of the entire tape.[17]

In most American jurisdictions, however, at least a qualified reporters' privilege has been recognized even in the context of criminal trials, though not always based on the First Amendment. The Supreme Court of Washington, for example, has held that the tradition of that state's common law provides for a qualified reporters' confidentiality privilege, even with respect to criminal trials.[18]

In the criminal realm, some of the federal circuits apply a balancing test not too different from that proposed by Justice Stewart's *Branzburg* dissent. In *United States v. Burke*, which involved charges of conspiring to "fix" college basketball games, the Second Circuit held that media representatives may be compelled to reveal confidential information in criminal proceedings only when the information cannot be obtained from any other source. The material sought must also be "highly material and relevant," and "necessary or critical" to the trial outcome.[19] At least one judge on the D.C. Circuit suggests that no balancing test in this context would be complete without considering "the public's interest in protecting the reporter's sources against the private interest in compelling disclosure."[20]

In the Third Circuit, the press has been told that its qualified confidentiality privilege applies with equal force in civil and in criminal proceedings. The relevant ruling emerged from a case involving a subpoena of statements made to CBS's *60 Minutes* program by likely government witnesses in a fraud prosecution against the owners of a chain of fast-food restaurants in the Newark, New Jersey, area. As the appellate court put it, "the interests of the press that form the foundation for the privilege are not diminished because the nature of the underlying proceeding out of which the

16. *United States v. Libby*, 432 F. Supp. 2d 26 (D.D.C. 2006).

17. *People v. Combest*, 828 N.E.2d 583 (N.Y. 2005).

18. *State v. Rinaldo*, 689 P.2d 392 (Sup. Ct. Wash. 1984).

19. *United States v. Burke*, 700 F.2d 70 (2d Cir. 1983).

20. *In re Grand Jury Subpoena (Judith Miller)*, 405 F.3d 17, 18 (D.C. Cir. 2005) (Tatel, J., concurring in the denial of rehearing en banc).

request for the information arises is a criminal trial"[21] Criminal defendants' Fifth Amendment due process rights and Sixth Amendment right to compel the testimony of witnesses could be weighed against the press's First Amendment rights, case by case, but they did not count as reasons for denying the existence of the journalistic privilege.

Civil Proceedings.   When the person seeking to compel a reporter to testify is a civil litigant rather than a criminal defendant, there is no Sixth Amendment right to balance against the journalist's asserted First Amendment interests. As a result, we find that courts are especially likely to embrace the media's qualified privilege and apply some form of the test suggested in Justice Stewart's dissenting opinion from *Branzburg*. Moreover, the case-by-case application of such a test is more likely to result in a finding for the press when a civil litigant is involved. Judges are less likely to find that the private interests of civil litigants rise to a level of "compelling interest" manifested by a criminal suspect seeking to avoid a prison term. To the extent that the larger public interest factors into the judge's reasoning, disputes among private parties are unlikely to tip the scales against reporters quite as easily as the societal interest in ensuring that all criminal defendants obtain a fair trial.

A qualified privilege against disclosure in civil litigation was recognized very soon after the *Branzburg* decision was handed down. The precipitating incidents were the Watergate break-in and the Democratic National Committee's (DNC's) subpoena issued against several media outlets seeking information that would help the DNC in its civil suit against the burglars. A federal district court in the District of Columbia quashed the subpoena.[22]

Several years later the U.S. Court of Appeals for the District of Columbia produced a decision very strongly supportive of the reporters' privilege. In the early 1970s *Detroit News* reporter Seth Kantor published a series of articles about organized crime's influence on that city. Local residents Anthony T. Zerilli and Michael Polizzi, whose phones had been illegally tapped by the Justice Department, concluded that some of the factual assertions in those articles could only have been obtained from transcripts of their recorded conversations. To aid them in their civil lawsuit against the Justice Department, the plaintiffs sought the identity of Kantor's sources. The D.C. Circuit Court of Appeals denied the request. Although the information sought was unquestionably crucial to their case, the court reasoned, the plaintiffs had not exhausted all other possible ways of obtaining it, especially since the Justice Department had already provided them with a list of other persons who had had access to the transcripts. The court also concluded that when balanced against civil litigants' interests, the reporters' privilege should prevail in "all but the most exceptional cases."[23]

---

21. *United States v. Cuthbertson*, 630 F.2d 139, 147 (3d Cir. 1980).

22. *Democratic National Committee v. McCord*, 356 F. Supp. 1394 (D.D.C. 1973).

23. *Zerilli v. Smith*, 656 F.2d 705 (D.C. Cir. 1981).

One such exceptional case, also from the D.C. Circuit, involved former Department of Energy scientist Wen Ho Lee, who had been investigated as a possible spy for the People's Republic of China and who eventually pled guilty to one count of mishandling classified computer files. Articles about the ongoing investigation appeared in the *New York Times*, the *Washington Post*, and the *Wall Street Journal*. In 2005 the D.C. Circuit Court of Appeals upheld contempt citations issued against these media outlets for failing to reveal their confidential sources to Lee, who needed that information in order to go forward with his civil suit against the Department of Justice. Lee's suit alleged that the federal government had violated his rights under the Privacy Act, and the appellate court held that the identity of the government leakers was absolutely essential to his suit.[24]

Still, as a general rule, reporters will not be compelled to disclose confidential information to civil litigants unless it can be shown that the material sought is of clear relevance to the litigation, that the case's outcome will likely be determined by the disclosure, and that the information is not available from any other source. Again, these criteria parallel closely the guidelines offered by Justice Stewart in his *Branzburg* dissent.

A bit more complicated are those civil cases in which reporters are themselves litigants. Most typically this situation occurs in a libel suit stemming from an article that relied on one or more anonymous sources. We already know from *Herbert v. Lando* (discussed in chapter 4) that libel plaintiffs who need to prove actual malice will be granted access to reporters' notes and outtakes as part of the pretrial discovery process.[25] The same logic often requires that the media reveal the identity of their confidential sources to libel plaintiffs. Thus, comedian Rodney Dangerfield finally got some respect when he sued the publishers of the *Star* tabloid, which quoted several unnamed employees of Caesars Palace in Las Vegas in an article that depicted the comic as quite a party animal. He trashed his hotel room, the article said, breaking a marble shower; he was wildly drunk in his flooded hotel room, standing in ankle-deep water with two naked girls and chasing a female employee around his room with ice tongs, saying he wanted to rip her clothes off. The court granted Dangerfield's request to compel disclosure of these confidential sources because challenging the very existence of the sources, or demonstrating their lack of credibility, would have to form the heart of his proof of actual malice.[26]

Media outlets that find themselves as libel defendants and that refuse to reveal the name of a confidential source may be subject to a specially fashioned sanction. The court adjudicating the libel claim may rule, as a matter of law, that no such source exists. The logical conclusion of such an assumption is that the media simply made up whatever libelous statements had been attributed to the unnamed source. To do

---

24. *Lee v. U.S. Department of Justice*, 413 F.3d 53 (D.C. Cir. 2005).
25. 441 U.S. 153 (1979).
26. *Dangerfield v. Star Editorial*, 817 F. Supp. 833 (C.D. Calif.), *aff'd*, 7 F.3d 856 (9th Cir. 1993).

so would clearly be to publish a "knowing falsehood." In other words, refuse to reveal your source, and you admit that you published with actual malice.[27] This assumption that no source exists is not embraced in most jurisdictions, however, and state reporter shield statutes may provide explicit protections against the assumption.[28]

Grand Jury Proceedings. Courts are least likely to recognize a confidentiality privilege when the forum seeking information from a reporter is a grand jury. This generalization is somewhat counterintuitive. One would think that reporters would be more likely to be compelled to testify at criminal trials than at grand jury proceedings. After all, the Sixth Amendment's explicit right of the accused to compel witness testimony applies to trials, not to grand juries. The seeming logical inconsistency can be explained by the principle of stare decisis introduced in chapter 1. Supreme Court precedents, to the extent they offer clear guidance, should be followed. The *Branzburg* case itself dealt with reporters whose grand jury testimony was sought—by the local district attorneys, as it turns out, rather than by a criminal defendant. Because the majority ruled against the journalists, the decision provides little "wiggle room" to lower court judges who might otherwise be inclined to recognize a journalistic privilege against compelled grand jury testimony. Indeed, a general rule has developed, consistent with the majority and concurring opinions in *Branzburg*, that reporters must testify unless the grand jury is engaged in a bad faith "fishing expedition" or is otherwise intent merely on harassing the media.

Perhaps the strongest reaffirmation in recent years of the principle that reporters must share what they know with grand juries comes from the D.C. Circuit Court of Appeals 2005 decision ordering journalists Judith Miller (eventually jailed for several months for disobeying) and Matthew Cooper to reveal the identities of whoever told them that Valerie Plame was a CIA operative.[29] Judge Sentelle's decision makes clear his view, shared by the lower court judge whose ruling he affirmed, that there is no First Amendment privilege to refuse to testify before a grand jury. The thrust of the holding is worth repeating. He did not say that there might be such a privilege, but that it is outweighed in this particular instance. He said that there is no such privilege, period.

In a Second Circuit Court of Appeals decision the next year, also involving *New York Times* reporter Judith Miller, Judge Winter concluded for a 2-1 panel majority that the phone records from Miller and one of her *Times* coworkers were properly compelled by a grand jury investigating leaks related to an investigation of two Islamic charities. The *Times* reporters learned from confidential sources that the FBI was planning to search the offices of the charities and to freeze their assets. Both their published articles and calls placed by the reporters to the charities likely diminished

27. See, e.g., *Downing v. Monitor Publishing Co.*, 415 A.2d 683 (N.H. 1980).

28. *Maressa v. New Jersey Monthly*, 445 A.2d 376 (N.J. 1982).

29. *In re Grand Jury Subpoena (Judith Miller)*, 397 F.3d 964 (D.C. Cir. 2005).

the effectiveness of both the searches and the freezing of assets, the government asserted. In ruling for the government, Judge Winter stopped short of holding that *Branzburg* offered no First Amendment protection to reporters seeking to withhold information from grand juries. Rather, he found that even the exacting demands imposed by Justice Stewart's *Branzburg* dissent would be met in this specific situation. Clearly the reporters knew who leaked the information (and the phone records might reveal the leakers' identities), and indeed they were likely the only people who knew. Moreover, the government's need to avoid alerting targets of investigation of imminent FBI actions aimed at them was compelling.[30]

What Kind of Information? Whether courts will recognize a qualified reporter's privilege is also in large part a function of whether the information sought is truly *confidential* information. Generally, confidential information is what a source tells a reporter under an agreement of anonymity. Certainly this also includes the confidential source's identity.

Nonconfidential information refers to things that reporters witness for themselves firsthand, as well as any other materials gathered without a promise of confidentiality. Thus, for example, if an interview with a nonconfidential source is aired on a TV news program, the footage that was shot but not aired is no more confidential than what was broadcast. Similarly, information found in a print reporter's notes that did not survive the editor's red pen are no more confidential than the words that were actually printed. (The notes may be considered confidential, however, if they could be used to reveal the identity of an anonymous source.)

United States v. Libby, cited in our earlier discussion of *Branzburg* applied to criminal cases, involved nonconfidential information, in that Libby had already outed himself as at least one source for some media's reporting that Valerie Plame was a CIA

THINGS TO REMEMBER

Applying *Branzburg* to Various Judicial Proceedings

- As a general rule, reporters are most likely to succeed in their efforts to keep information confidential when confronting a subpoena to testify in an ordinary civil proceeding; a bit less likely to succeed if the proceeding is a criminal trial; and least likely to succeed when they wish to keep information from a grand jury.
- In some jurisdictions, reporters who refuse to reveal a confidential source when they are sued for libel risk a judicial determination that no such source exists; such a declaration virtually ensures that the plaintiff will prevail.

---

30. *New York Times Co. v. Gonzales*, 459 F.3d 160 (2d Cir. 2006).

operative.[31] At issue in the 2006 decision was whether reporters would have to testify on Libby's behalf at his trial for obstructing the investigation of the leak about Plame. It will be recalled that the court ordered the reporters and media outlets involved to make available to Libby much of the materials he sought.

The defendants in the *Branzburg* case sought to keep *confidential* information—the identify of their sources—from the grand jury. That facet of the case figured prominently in all of the justices' separate opinions. Thus, whatever First Amendment confidentiality right reporters enjoy is most likely to be outweighed by competing state interests when the information sought from the journalist is not truly confidential.

A January 1997 episode of NBC's *Dateline* television newsmagazine featured an exposé of how a deputy sheriff on highway patrol in part of Louisiana had a reputation for pulling over out-of-state motorists and trumping up charges against them, resulting in huge fines and sometimes in confiscation of the "offending" vehicles. Albert and Mary Gonzales, in pursuit of their lawsuit against a Louisiana deputy sheriff who they alleged pulled them over on Interstate 10 and detained them for an overly long time in a discriminatory fashion—a "driving while Hispanic" offense, they claimed—sought NBC's outtakes from the program. They had reason to assume the material would be especially helpful because the network story featured the very same deputy named in their lawsuit. NBC refused, but the Second Circuit Court of Appeals ruled for the plaintiffs. The court concluded that there is no First Amendment privilege in withholding this kind of *non*confidential material. At least some of the media's traditional arguments in favor of a privilege have little validity with respect to nonconfidential material, the court emphasized. Almost by definition, after all, there is no danger that "the well of confidential sources will run dry." Also, because on-the-record sources have no way of knowing, at the time they are interviewed, what portions of the dialogue will be aired and what portions will become outtakes, they have no recognizable privacy interests in the unaired material.[32] In some jurisdictions, federal appellate courts stop short of concluding categorically that reporters enjoy no First Amendment rights in challenging a subpoena for nonconfidential information, asserting that there is a First Amendment interest to be placed in the balance. One court has enumerated four plausible interests raised by reporters seeking to protect even nonconfidential information: (1) the threat of intrusion into the news-gathering and editorial processes; (2) fear that the media will seem to become an investigative arm of the government; (3) concern that media will have a disincentive to compile and preserve outtakes; and (4) the burden on journalists' time and resources in responding to subpoenas.[33] Even in those jurisdictions favoring a balancing test, how-

---

31. 432 F. Supp. 2d 26 (D.D.C. 2006).
32. *Gonzales v. National Broadcasting Co.*, 194 F.3d 29 (2d Cir. 1999).
33. *United States v. La Rouche Campaign*, 841 F.2d 1176, 1182 (1st Cir. 1988).

ever, the scales are weighted a bit more against the press when the information sought is nonconfidential.[34]

From Whom Is the Information Sought? *"It would be unthinkable to have a rule that an investigative journalist, such as Bob Woodward, would be protected by the privilege in his capacity as a newspaper reporter writing about Watergate, but not as the author of a book on the same topic."*[35]

If the lesson of *Branzburg* and subsequent cases is that there exists at least a limited First Amendment reporters' privilege, we should ask the question that the Supreme Court avoided in that case—what does it mean to be a reporter?

The question has been addressed by several courts, dating back to the 1970s. *Apicella v. McNeil Laboratories, Inc.* stemmed from a damages suit against the manufacturer of Innovar, an anesthetic used during operations.[36] The defendant sought to compel testimony from the editor of a bimonthly professional medical journal called the *Medical Letter on Drugs and Therapeutics*, which had run an article critical of Innovar. That article included anonymous testimony from a physician claiming to have seen three patients die from heart problems as a result of using the drug. The federal district court denied the defendant's request, finding that the journal performed as valuable a public service as any general-circulation newspaper and that the reporters' confidentiality privilege would thus apply to the publication's contributors.

The reporters' privilege was also extended to documentary filmmaker Buzz Hirsch, who was researching the suspicious death of Karen Silkwood, the whistle-blower who had alleged various public-safety violations at a nuclear generating plant. That the Kerr-McGee Corporation (the target of Silkwood's complaints) was making such a "major legal effort" to obtain Hirsch's testimony was seen by a panel of the Tenth

---

THINGS TO REMEMBER

Applying *Branzburg* to Various Kinds of Information

- Whereas the *Branzburg* case involved reporters' *confidential* information, courts are very loath to recognize a media right not to testify about *non*confidential information.
- The usual press arguments in favor of nondisclosure do not apply to such situations, courts reason; there is, for example, no danger of "the well of confidential sources running dry" when there is no *confidential* source at all.

---

34. *Shoen v. Shoen*, 5 F.3d 1289 (9th Cir. 1993); *von Bulow v. von Bulow*, 811 F.2d 136 (2d Cir. 1987).

35. *Shoen v. Shoen*, 5 F.3d 1289, 1293 (9th Cir. 1993).

36. 66 F.R.D. 78 (E.D.N.Y. 1975).

Circuit Court of Appeals as evidence that he must have been doing serious reporting.[37]

A 1987 case involving another notoriously suspicious turn of events led the Second Circuit Court of Appeals to devise a set of guidelines to determine what categories of persons may claim the reporters' confidentiality privilege. The case was an offshoot of the criminal prosecution and later civil litigation against Claus von Bulow alleging that he assaulted his wife, Sunny, with intent to kill by injecting her with insulin and other drugs. (He was acquitted of the criminal charges.) In the civil litigation, Sunny von Bulow's family members sought testimony and document disclosures from Andrea Reynolds, a longtime friend of Claus von Bulow's, who was at the time writing a book based on the criminal case. The court determined that a "reporter" need not be an employee of a newspaper or other traditional media outlet; all that was required was that she intended, at the time she was gathering information, to disseminate it to the public. Reynolds herself, however, failed even this test. Her primary motivation at the outset of her fact gathering, the court determined, was to clear Claus von Bulow's name, not to write a book.[38]

The test suggested by the *von Bulow* court has been accepted in at least two other circuits. The Ninth Circuit adopted the test in *Shoen v. Shoen*, which involved the tragicomic family feud among the owners of the privately held U-Haul truck-rental company.[39] One side of the family sought disclosures from Ronald J. Watkins, who had interviewed patriarch Leonard Shoen as part of his research for *Birthright: Murder, Greed, and Power in the U-Haul Family Dynasty*, the book in which he deconstructs the family's travails. The court ruled in favor of Watkins, emphasizing that the reporters' privilege applies to book authors. The court singled out Upton Sinclair, Rachel Carson, and Ralph Nader as examples of authors who brought more "newsworthy" information to the public than most "reporters" ever do.

The Third Circuit, although rejecting a claim of journalistic privilege made by World Championship Wrestling (WCW) employee Mark Madden, also embraced the test proposed by the *von Bulow* court. *In re Madden* flowed from an unfair trade practices suit between the two major producers of professional wrestling events in the United States. One of the litigants sought to depose Madden, whose job for the WCW was to produce tongue-in-cheek tape recordings for the company's 900-number phone lines. The *von Bulow* test requires that "reporters" have an intention to publish at the time they gather news and that they be involved in activities traditionally associated with the gathering and dissemination of news. Madden did not pass the test, because the information he was to use in his phone recordings was provided directly by his employers. "Madden's primary goal," the court held, was "to provide advertisement and entertainment—not to gather news or disseminate information."[40]

37. *Silkwood v. Kerr-McGee Corp.*, 563 F.2d 433 (10th Cir. 1977).
38. *von Bulow v. von Bulow*, 811 F.2d 136 (2d Cir. 1987).
39. 5 F.3d 1289 (9th Cir. 1993).
40. *In re Madden (Titan Sports v. Turner Broadcasting)*, 151 F.3d 125 (3d Cir. 1998).

THINGS TO REMEMBER

Applying *Branzburg* to Various Kinds of Writers

- The First Amendment "reporters' privilege" has been applied not only to employees of well-known media outlets but also to writers for professional journals with far more limited circulation, to book authors, and to documentary filmmakers.
- Many courts will apply the privilege to any persons who, at the time of gathering information or "news," intended to disseminate their findings to the public eventually. Such individuals need not be employees of media organizations.

Finally, in an unpublished opinion from 2001, the Fifth Circuit Court of Appeals skirted the issue of whether Vanessa Leggett, the Texas writer jailed for almost half a year for refusing to reveal her confidential sources, should be considered a journalist for purposes of applying whatever reporters' privilege is found in the *Branzburg* precedent. The appellate panel deemed it unnecessary to decide this question, because the fact that a grand jury was the entity seeking disclosure would outweigh whatever privilege might exist. Still, the judges went out of their way to describe Leggett as a "virtually unpublished freelance writer, operating without an employer or a contract for publication,"[41] thus hinting that the determination of whether the reporters' privilege applied to her likely would have focused on whether her ultimate goal while she was collecting information about the underlying homicide case was to publicly disseminate such information.

State Reporter Shield Laws

Reporters who wish to avoid testifying before judicial proceedings are not limited to making First Amendment arguments. In 1972, when *Branzburg v. Hayes* told the press that any First Amendment claims would necessarily be limited by the judiciary's needs, seventeen states already had statutes on the books providing reporters with a limited right to keep their confidential sources confidential. The first such law was enacted by Maryland in 1896.

Thirty-two states plus the District of Columbia have some form of reporter shield law on the books, the most recent one having been enacted in Connecticut in 2006. The majority of the remaining states that do not have an actual statute still provide some protection for confidential sources through judicial interpretation of either state

---

41. Petition for Writ of Certiorari, *Leggett v. United States*, 535 U.S. 1011 (2002) (No. 01-983).

constitutions[42] or the common law.[43] In only a handful of remaining states—Hawaii, Mississippi, Utah, and Wyoming—has the state supreme court not produced a ruling committing itself to at least some kind of reporters' privilege.

Specific provisions of state shield laws vary in ways that generally parallel the three criteria already seen with respect to the federal constitutional privilege: whether the reporter is asked to testify before a civil proceeding, a criminal trial, or a grand jury;[44] the nature of the information being sought; and who should be considered a reporter.

What Type of Proceeding?

For the press, one advantage of living in a state with a strong shield law is that such statutes need not be constrained by the specific holding from *Branzburg v. Hayes* that there is no First Amendment right to refuse to testify in front of a grand jury. Still, several states do provide more protection to reporters seeking to quash a subpoena emerging from civil litigation than from a criminal prosecution. The logic here is much the same as that offered by the various federal courts that have adjudicated the issue from a constitutional perspective. A criminal defendant's right to a fair trial figures prominently in the balance. The shield law in Michigan, for example, requires reporters to produce subpoenaed materials when sought by a criminal defendant facing a possible life sentence.[45] The New Jersey statute offers absolute protection from compelled testimony in civil cases, but only qualified immunity in criminal cases.[46] Similarly, in Ohio, an otherwise absolute immunity from having to reveal one's confidential sources must yield when a criminal defendant's Sixth Amendment rights would suffer.[47]

What Kind of Information?

Shield statutes vary as to the kinds of information that are protected. Some jurisdictions—Arizona, Maryland, and the District of Columbia among them—provide absolute immunity from compelled disclosure of a source's identity.[48] The Illinois statute provides a qualified privilege to shield a source's identity, but no other protec-

---

42. See, e.g., *O'Grady v. Superior Court*, 139 Cal. App. 4th 1423 (Cal. Ct. App. 2006); *In re Contempt of Wright*, 700 P.2d 40 (Idaho 1985); *Winegard v. Oxberger*, 258 N.W.2d 847 (Iowa 1977); *In re Letellier*, 578 A.2d 722 (Me. 1990); *Opinion of the Justices*, 373 A.2d 644 (N.H.1977).

43. See, e.g., *Sinnott v. Boston Retirement Board*, 524 N.E.2d 100 (Mass. 1988).

44. Laurence B. Alexander and Ellen M. Bush, "Shield Laws on Trial: State Court Interpretation of the Journalist's Statutory Privilege," 23 *Journal of Legislation* 215 (1997).

45. Mich. Comp. Laws Ann. § 28.945(1) (1998).

46. N.J. Rev. Stat. § 2A:84A-21.1 (1998).

47. Ohio Rev. Code Ann. §§ 2739.04, 2739.12 (1998).

48. See, e.g., Ariz. Rev. Stat. Ann. §§ 12-2214, 12-2237 (1998); D.C. Code Ann. §§ 16-4701 to 16-4704 (1998); Md. Code Ann. Cts. & Jud. Proc. § 9-112 (1998).

tions.[49] New York's statute provides absolute immunity for both a source's identity and for any information obtained from that source in confidence.[50] California and Florida do not distinguish between confidential and nonconfidential information.[51] The privilege in New Jersey extends also to reporters' notes and outtakes in general—the statute has been interpreted to protect the news-gathering process itself.[52]

Although one might assume that New York and California, the two states in which media industries are especially concentrated, would boast the most far-reaching shield statutes, laws in some of the other states actually offer more protection. New Jersey, for example, provides reporters absolute immunity from having to testify in civil cases. Reporters in that state are sometimes required to testify when called before criminal proceedings, but only if they have witnessed a crime taking place or an accident happening. The privilege will remain intact, in other words, if the reporter arrived on the scene so late as to only see the *aftermath* of the crime or the accident.[53] The Nevada statute is also quite extensive, providing absolute protection for source identity and other information, even in cases where a media outlet is defending itself in a libel suit.[54]

Who Is Protected?

Most state shield laws define *reporter* fairly narrowly, limiting protection to those who are "employed by" such traditional media outlets as newspapers, magazines, and broadcast stations.[55] Such wording seems to exclude freelance writers. The Florida statute explicitly excludes from its scope "book authors and others who are not professional journalists."[56] Other statutes more broadly protect not only persons employed by the media industry but also those "connected with" the media.[57] The Delaware statute lists "scholars," "educators," and even "polemicists" among those who enjoy the reporters' privilege,[58] whereas the law in Nebraska provides immunity to anyone "engaged in procuring, gathering, writing, editing, or disseminating news *or other information* to the public.[59]

Oddly, the Alabama shield law protects reporters for newspapers (and radio and TV outlets) but not magazines. That quirky feature of the statute was most unfortu-

---

49. 735 Ill. Comp. Stat. Ann. 5/8-901 to 5/8-909 (1998).

50. N.Y. Civ. Rights Law § 79-h (1998).

51. Cal. Const. art. I, § 2 (1998); *Davis v. State*, 720 So. 2d 220 (Fla. 1998).

52. N.J. Stat. Ann. §§ 2A:84A-21, 2A:84A-21.9, 2A:84A-29 (1998).

53. *In re Woodhaven Lumber and Mill Work*, 589 A.2d 135, 143 (N.J. 1991).

54. Nev. Rev. Stat. Ann. §§ 49.275, 49.385 (1998).

55. Anthony L. Fargo, "Analyzing Federal Shield Law Proposals: What Congress Can Learn From the States," 11 *Communication Law and Policy* 35, 56 (2006).

56. Fla. Stat. § 90.5015 (1998).

57. See, e.g., Ala. Code § 12-21-142 (1998).

58. Del. Code Ann. tit. 10, §§ 4320–4326 (1998).

59. Neb. Rev. Stat. Ann. §§ 20-144 to 20-147 (1998) (emphasis added).

nate from the perspective of *Sports Illustrated* reporter Don Yaeger, who tried to withhold information about a confidential source from University of Alabama football coach (and libel plaintiff) Mike Price, who Yaeger's article claimed had manifested "boorish" behaviors since assuming his duties, including hanging out in strip clubs and hiring the "dancers" there for sex.[60] Judge Edward Carnes looked to several dictionaries to justify his conclusion that a defining distinction between newspapers and magazines is that the former tend to be printed on folded, unstapled sheets of paper, while magazines such as *Sports Illustrated* tend to be stapled or bound. He also noted that the Pulitzer Prize for newspaper journalism, the guidelines for which never actually *define* "newspaper," nonetheless has never been awarded to any publication we would normally think of as a magazine.

Often the question of whether freelance writers are protected is not spelled out clearly in the statute itself, requiring state courts to weigh in with their interpretations of the law's wording. An appellate court in Arizona, for example, refused to apply its shield law to author Dary Matera, who at the time was writing a book about undercover "sting" operations that had resulted in the prosecution of several state officials.

COLLEGE SPORTS

BAD BEHAVIOR

Associating with strippers and carousing with coeds proved costly for Alabama's Mike Price and Iowa State's Larry Eustachy, respectively, as they lost their jobs, embarrassed their schools and stoked the debate over the duty of college coaches to set a good example on and off the field

How He Met His Destiny at a Strip Club
BY DON YAEGER

MIKE PRICE: FIRED

ON APRIL 23 an Auburn fan with the screen name EagleKlaw visited autigers.com, a website for Tigers boosters, and posted a message that may well have marked the beginning of the end of Mike Price's brief tenure as football coach at bitter rival Alabama: "Someone told me the night before the [Emerald Coast Classic Pro-Am]

The Party Ends for an Admitted Alcoholic
BY GRANT WAHL WITH REPORTING BY GEORGE DOHRMANN

LARRY EUSTACHY: FORCED OUT

LARRY EUSTACHY'S slow dance with alcohol began on a warm spring evening in the 11th grade. He remembers all the details: how he and his friends stood outside an Arcadia, Calif., liquor store and coaxed a stranger to buy beer for them; how they took their treasure to a nearby backyard; and how he drank three cans that night, unleashing a rush like nothing he'd ever felt before. "The sensation was, *Wow, this is where it's at,*" Eustachy re-

The *Sports Illustrated* reporter responsible for this cover story was not offered any protection by the Alabama reporter shield law, which covers newspapers but not magazines.

---

60. *Price v. Time*, 416 F.3d 1327 (11th Cir. 2005).

One of those state officials subpoenaed Matera for materials he thought would help him in preparing his defense. Although the statute was worded broadly, the court noted that *Webster's Ninth New Collegiate Dictionary* defined "news" as "material reported in a newspaper or news periodical or on a newscast." Matera's motion to quash the subpoena was thus denied.[61]

It is likely but not certain that freelance reporters are protected by California's shield law. A 1982 lower court case held that authors who have not yet entered into a contract with a news organization or book publisher cannot claim the reporters' privilege.[62] A decade later, however, the state supreme court declined to review a lower court ruling that had extended the privilege to a freelance writer. The lower court had made much of the fact that the freelancer in question had many years of experience as a regular media employee, however, so it is not entirely clear what the state supreme court would do with a less seasoned freelancer who had never been a salaried media professional.[63]

Although we again have no definitive word from the California state supreme court on the matter, in 2006 an appellate court applied the shield law to an "online news magazine,"[64] which would seem logically consistent with a trend toward a liberal interpretation of the law.

U.S. Department of Justice Guidelines

In the wake of *Branzburg*, several bills were introduced in Congress that sought to provide some measure of protection for reporters' confidential sources, but none

---

THINGS TO REMEMBER

State Reporter Shield Laws

- Thirty-two states, plus the District of Columbia, have reporter shield statutes, and the majority of the remaining states recognize a reporters' privilege either in their state constitutions or in the common law.
- Many reporter shield statutes give the media a stronger presumption in favor of nondisclosure of information in civil, as opposed to criminal, proceedings.
- The statutes vary widely with respect to what kinds of information are protected and who is considered a reporter.

---

61. *Matera v. Superior Court*, 825 P.2d 971 (Ariz. Ct. App. 1992).

62. *In re Van Ness*, 8 Media L. Rep. (BNA) 2563 (Cal. Super. Ct. 1982).

63. *People v. Von Villas*, 13 Cal. Rptr. 2d 62 (Cal. Ct. App. 1992).

64. *O'Grady v. Superior Court*, 139 Cal. App. 4th 1423 (Ct. App. 2006).

passed. The attorney general's office has, however, promulgated guidelines imposing certain restrictions on the federal government's ability to obtain information from reporters. The guidelines, which have been in the *Federal Register* in their current form since 1973, are in some ways modeled after Justice Stewart's dissenting opinion from *Branzburg v. Hayes*.[65] Department of Justice officials are instructed in the guidelines to make "all reasonable attempts" to obtain needed information elsewhere before seeking a subpoena against the news media. Moreover, the information must be deemed "essential" to building the government's case. There has not been a lot of litigation stemming from the guidelines, however, in large part because they provide no judicial remedy against a Justice Department official who violates them.[66]

It should also be emphasized that the guidelines govern only the Department of Justice, which is not the only federal entity empowered to issue subpoenas. In one case from Charleston, West Virginia, a federal district court granted a temporary injunction against enforcement by the National Labor Relations Board of a subpoena issued in seeming violation of the attorney general's guidelines to a local newspaper reporter, but the Fourth Circuit Court of Appeals vacated this ruling.[67]

Newsroom Searches

From a law enforcement perspective, issuing a subpoena to a reluctant informant— whether a reporter or anyone else—can be a rather inefficient means of obtaining data. If the subpoena's recipient is well heeled or well insured or both, the motions to modify or quash a subpoena can be time consuming and expensive for both sides. No wonder, then, that police sometimes find it more expedient to knock on the media's door with search warrant in hand.

No Constitutional Immunity: *Zurcher v. Stanford Daily*

Stanford University enjoys an international reputation as a top-ranked institution with a beautiful campus of bicyclists, inline skaters, and mission revival–style sandstone buildings with red tile roofs, the essence of "West Coast laid back." On one particular Friday afternoon in April 1971, however, the Stanford campus was the site of a violent political demonstration pressing several employee demands and protesting the firing of a janitor by the university hospital. When local police were brought in to remove the protesters, there were twenty-two arrests, several injuries, and over $100,000 in damages. The incident also resulted in a major Supreme Court decision and an important piece of federal legislation aimed at undoing that decision.

---

65. 28 C.F.R. § 50.10 (1999).

66. *In re Grand Jury Subpoena (Judith Miller)*, 397 F.3d 964 (D.C. Cir. 2005).

67. *Maurice v. National Labor Relations Board*, 7 Media L. Rep. (BNA) 2221 (S.D. W. Va. 1981), *vacated and remanded*, 691 F.2d 182 (4th Cir. 1982).

The campus newspaper published a special Sunday edition focusing on the demonstration. The very next day, the local district attorney obtained and executed a warrant to search the offices of the *Stanford Daily* in hopes of recovering photo negatives that might serve to identify those demonstrators who had engaged in violence or vandalism. The police affidavits accompanying the application for the warrant made clear that the newspaper staff itself was not suspected of any wrongdoing.

The search was unsuccessful; only photographs already published in the newspaper were on hand. The newspaper staff, upset that the search could have laid bare reporters' notes that had been gathered from confidential sources, brought suit against the Palo Alto police chief James Zurcher, alleging that the search violated the First and Fourth Amendments.

When the case reached the Supreme Court, it resulted in a 5-3 vote (Justice Brennan did not participate) rejecting the newspaper's claims. Justice White disposed of the Fourth Amendment argument first. That this was a "third-party search"—the newspaper staff was not itself under investigation—was of no constitutional consequence, he concluded. "Under existing law," he wrote, "valid warrants may be issued to search any property, whether or not occupied by a third party, at which there is probable cause to believe that fruits, instrumentalities, or evidence of a crime will be found."[68]

The plaintiffs had also argued that whatever Fourth Amendment protections might apply to third-party searches in general, the First Amendment interests that come into play when the site to be searched is a newspaper office necessitated judicial recognition of an added measure of privacy. Justice White expressed sympathy for the media's First Amendment claims. Newsroom searches are often physically disruptive, he admitted, thus jeopardizing "timely publication" of the news. In addition, confidential sources might dry up if things they tell a reporter in confidence may be revealed to the police by coercion. The proliferation of such searches might give reporters an incentive toward sloppy journalism, because they will be reluctant to maintain detailed notes or recordings. Important though these interests might be, White concluded, there was no need to create any special measure of Fourth Amendment protection for the press against third-party searches. "Properly administered," he wrote, "the preconditions for a warrant—probable cause, specificity with respect to the place to be searched and the things to be seized, and overall reasonableness—should afford sufficient protection against the harms that are assertedly threatened by warrants for searching newspaper offices."

The Privacy Protection Act

The *Zurcher* case prompted media industries to lobby Congress for some legislative remedy. In response, Congress passed the Privacy Protection Act of 1980, which provides that law enforcement officials at any level of government who seek testimony

---

68. *Zurcher v. Stanford Daily*, 436 U.S. 547, 554 (1978).

from reporters or from anyone "reasonably believed to have a purpose to disseminate" information to the public, should generally use subpoenas rather than search
warrants. Subpoenas are far preferable from the media's perspective. They invite a
chance to argue, through counsel, why some or all of the sought materials should not
be turned over. More important, they do not result in the ransacking of a newsroom,
which disrupts the reporting operation and often turns up confidential materials not
at all related to the specific law investigation at hand.

The use of the word *newsroom* in the previous sentence carries perhaps more
meaning than you might think at first blush. Although litigation under the Privacy
Protection Act is scant, it is clear that not every law enforcement seizing of media
materials such as film, videotape, reporters' notes, and the like is considered a search
at all. In one case, an animal rights group sought to document what they feared would
be cruel practices in an Ohio park's use of expert marksmen to cull a local deer over-
population. The group hid video cameras in the park during evening hours when the
area was closed to the public. But the cameras must not have been hidden very well,
because the park's rangers stumbled upon them in the course of their workday. When
the rangers confiscated the cameras, the animal rights group sued, alleging a Privacy
Protection Act violation. The federal district court held the act wholly inapplicable
because the rangers' having inadvertently found the cameras did not constitute a
search, nor was it part of law enforcement activity.[69]

The Privacy Protection Act provides that there will be occasions when law enforcement *will* need to conduct a search of the newsroom. These exceptions to the general
rule that a subpoena should be issued instead vary according to what kinds of materials are sought. The act recognizes two broad categories: **work product** and **documentary materials**.

To help distinguish between these two categories, let us imagine that you are a
reporter assigned to cover a recurring story in the United States—the competing political protests that take place each year in late January, the anniversary of the Supreme Court's famous abortion decision, *Roe v. Wade*. As you prepare to do the story,
you will likely gather together many materials that have been written by others. These
might include position statements from both pro-life and pro-choice organizations,
excerpts from any of the scores of books and thousands of articles that have been
written about abortion, and the Supreme Court opinion itself (and later abortion
opinions that have cited *Roe* as a precedent). These are all examples of documentary
materials, as defined in the Privacy Protection Act.

Your story will likely also flow from materials you produce yourself. These might
include transcripts of interviews you conduct with leaders on both sides of the abortion debate, notes you make to yourself as you observe the street demonstrations, and
any early drafts of your article. These materials all fit into the work product category.

---

69. *S.H.A.R.K. v. Metro Parks Serving Summit County*, 2006 U.S. Dist. LEXIS 40027 (N.D. Ohio
2006).

Work product is the more protected of the two categories; after all, your work product is unique to you and is not as easily reproducible as the documentary materials you gather. Hence there will be fewer exceptions to the "get a subpoena, not a search warrant" rule if law enforcement officials seek your work product. Indeed, under the act, when seeking a reporter's work product, law enforcement may obtain a search warrant only in two situations. The first situation is if the police can demonstrate that someone is likely to die or suffer serious bodily harm should the sought material not be immediately uncovered. The second situation is a bit more complicated. The reporter must personally be suspected of criminal wrongdoing; in other words, this situation does not involve the kind of third-party search that was conducted on the Stanford University campus.

In one case, the producers of a community-access cable TV news program in Maplewood, Minnesota, tried to attend and film a banquet honoring a few retiring members of the city council. But the cable producers balked at paying the nominal fifteen-dollar admission fee to this private event, and they were turned away. When they refused to leave, a short scuffle with local police ensued, which the producers dutifully filmed. The police then confiscated the tape, an action that led the producers to sue the police for an alleged violation of the Privacy Protection Act. The federal district court held that the act could offer the cable crew no relief because the ostensible reason for confiscating the tape was for use as evidence in a possible disorderly conduct prosecution against, you guessed it, the cable crew. In other words, this was not a third-party search. The "reporters" were holding work product that documented their own alleged criminal acts.[70]

The "not a third party search" exception to the Privacy Protection Act is limited a bit further. The criminal wrongdoing of which the reporter is suspected cannot simply be the possession of the materials the law enforcement officials want. Rather, the investigators must persuade the magistrate from whom a search warrant is sought that the work product will provide independent evidence of some *other* kinds of wrongdoing. Now, just to complicate things even further, there is an exception to the exception. It is sufficient proof of suspected criminal wrongdoing if the police can show that the reporter has in his or her possession classified materials or similarly restricted data, or any similar "information relating to the national defense." Similarly, suspected possession of child pornography is sufficient to obtain a search warrant.

When law enforcement officials seek a reporter's documentary materials (rather than his or her work product), the same two exceptions already articulated still apply, plus two more. First, the police will be permitted to search a newsroom if using a subpoena would likely result in the "destruction, alteration, or concealment" of the materials. Alternatively, if the reporter has disobeyed a subpoena seeking the production of the material in question, a search of the premises may be justified. Prior to

---

70. *Bergland v. City of Maplewood*, 173 F. Supp. 2d 935 (D. Minn. 2001).

the authorization of such a search, however, the reporter must be given a chance to submit an affidavit arguing why the materials in question should not be subject to seizure.

There is yet one additional complication we need to consider, and it can be applicable to work product and documentary materials alike. Section 215 of the Patriot Act, passed by Congress in the aftermath of the 2001 terrorist attacks, lowered the federal government's burden of proof when seeking a warrant (from the FISA court, a special entity created decades earlier in the Foreign Intelligence Surveillance Act) to search the records of a business. Department of Justice officials have testified before Congress that media outlets are not exempted from this change in law. As a result, there may be a new exception to the Privacy Protection Act's general rule to use a subpoena, rather than a search warrant—that is, if the government asserts to the FISA court that it needs to obtain media records in order to further an investigation relevant to terrorist activity. We do not yet have any litigation in this area, only speculation.

Ignoring the FISA complication for the moment, what remedies are available to news media representatives whose premises have been searched in violation of the Privacy Protection Act? The act gives aggrieved parties the right to sue the government for the improper conduct of any law enforcement official. This could mean suing the federal government, or state or local governments, with one caveat: the Eleventh Amendment to the U.S. Constitution tells individual states that they need not permit citizens to sue them. Because the Constitution supersedes any individual piece of federal legislation, the individual states may be sued for Privacy Protection Act violations only with their consent.

Plaintiffs may obtain damage awards either large enough to reimburse them for actual losses or up to $1,000, whichever is larger. Attorneys' fees and other related litigation costs are also recoverable. No damages will be paid, and the plaintiff's suit will fail, if the state is able to show that its agents acted in the "good faith" belief that they were not, in fact, violating the law.

If the specific facts of a case might permit a search under the act, a failure on the part of police to state clearly in their application for a search warrant which of the act's provisions support issuance of the warrant will not itself constitute a violation of law. This lesson was learned in a case involving WDAF-TV in Kansas City, which purchased from a tourist one evening in August 1994 a videotape depicting a brutal murder that had been committed earlier in the day. (The tourist was not himself suspected of any criminal activity; apparently he and his wife had been videotaping a local park from the Liberty Memorial Tower and "stumbled" upon the crime in progress from that vantage point.) The local police were able to make an arrest in the homicide, but they would not be able to hold the suspect very long without the additional evidence they presumed the videotape could provide. It is at least arguable that the act's exception aimed at preventing death or serious injury would apply to this situation; after all, here is a person suspected of homicide, who may very well commit additional crimes if released. The majority of a federal appellate court panel ruled that the district attorney should be permitted to defend herself against the station's Privacy Protection Act suit by citing this exemption, despite the defectiveness of the affidavit in support of the search warrant application.[71]

One might suppose that a search conducted in violation of the Privacy Protection Act is, by definition, an *unconstitutional* search. The act itself, however, makes clear that the question of whether a search is constitutional or not—that is, whether it is in keeping with the Fourth Amendment's prohibition against unreasonable searches and seizures—is a completely separate issue. This point is important because it means that the fruits of a search conducted in violation of the Privacy Protection Act are not by that fact alone subject to the exclusionary rule of Fourth Amendment jurisprudence. Such evidence is not automatically suppressed; it can still be used in a criminal prosecution.

The federal Privacy Protection Act clearly gives media industries important rights vis-à-vis law enforcement officials. Reporters should also know that a handful of states boast their own such laws and that some of these give protections beyond those provided in the federal law. Wisconsin's statute, for example, does not contemplate the use of search warrants against news media except when the staff there is itself suspected of criminal wrongdoing.[72]

THINGS TO REMEMBER

Newsroom Searches

- Although there is no federal reporter shield law, the Department of Justice has issued guidelines to its own agents that greatly limit the circumstances in which media representatives should be compelled to reveal their sources or other confidential information.
- In *Zurcher v. Stanford Daily* (1978), the Supreme Court ruled that the First Amendment does not protect the media from a newsroom search that is conducted in the furtherance of a properly issued warrant.
- In response to the *Zurcher* case, Congress passed the Privacy Protection Act of 1980, which creates a general presumption that law enforcement officials at all levels of government should use subpoenas instead of searches to compel testimony from reporters.
- The act is especially protective of a reporter's work product (things the reporter created, such as notes or interview tapes) and a bit less protective of documentary materials gathered by the reporter from other sources.
- Searches conducted in violation of the act are not necessarily unconstitutional under the Fourth Amendment.

---

71. *Citicasters DBA WDAF-TV v. McCaskill*, 89 F.3d 1350 (8th Cir. 1996).
72. Wis. Stat. § 968.12 (2006).

Betraying a Pledge of Confidentiality

Thus far this chapter has focused on reporters' efforts to protect the identity of their confidential sources and the information obtained from them. In 1991 the Supreme Court ruled in a dispute that turned the usual relationship between the media and their sources on its head.[73] The case emerged out of a hotly contested gubernatorial election in Minnesota.

Dan Cohen, who had been working in 1982 as a public relations consultant for the gubernatorial campaign of Independent-Republican Wheelock Whitney, brought to the attention of several Twin Cities–area reporters the fact that the Democratic-Farmer-Labor candidate for lieutenant governor, Marlene Johnson, had been convicted many years earlier of petty larceny. With each reporter he approached, Cohen performed a ritual of sorts. Prior to opening the envelope containing Johnson's court records, Cohen would indicate that he had "some documents which may or may not relate to a candidate in the upcoming election" and offer to hand them over only if the reporter promised "that I will be treated as an anonymous source, that my name will not appear in any material in connection with this," and that "you're not going to pursue me with a question of who my source is."

Some of the reporters shooed Cohen away, concluding that Johnson's criminal act was too minor and too long ago to be newsworthy. Reporters for the *St. Paul Pioneer Press Dispatch* and the *Minneapolis Star and Tribune*, however, felt otherwise and decided to write articles incorporating Cohen's information. They both readily agreed to their source's request for confidentiality.

The two papers, in independent editorial meetings, determined that the news about Johnson's petty larceny conviction was sufficiently newsworthy to be placed before their readers on the eve of this hotly contested election. The editors also decided that Cohen's identity was too integral to the story to be omitted. The *Minneapolis Star and Tribune* unmasked Cohen it its very first paragraph. The article carried Wheelock Whitney and his campaign manager's denial of having prior knowledge of Cohen's intentions; both nonetheless told the reporter that "such information about a candidate's past ought to be available to the public before an election."

On several occasions in the next few years—in depositions, at trial, and in other court documents—the *Minneapolis Star and Tribune* staff was called on to describe the editorial process that day. In their brief before the U.S. Supreme Court, the newspaper's publishers noted that several options had been open to them. They could publish no article at all, but that would be unacceptable. Not only were the allegations themselves newsworthy, but, because other local media had gone forward with the story, for the *Minneapolis Star and Tribune* not to publish would open it to charges

---

73. *Cohen v. Cowles Media Co.*, No. 79-8806 (Minn. Dist. Ct.), *rev'd*, 457 N.W.2d 199 (Minn. 1990), *rev'd*, 501 U.S. 663 (1991).

of being biased in favor of the Democratic candidate (whom the paper had endorsed editorially a few days earlier). Attributing the charge in a deliberately vague way, such as to a "Whitney supporter," was also deemed unacceptable because the Whitney campaign denied (falsely, as it later turned out) any involvement in the dissemination of the information.

So it was that two newspapers in the Twin Cities decided to override their own reporters' promises of confidentiality to Cohen, who lost his job with a public relations firm almost immediately upon publication, and who promptly brought suit in a Minnesota state court for fraudulent misrepresentation and for breach of contract. A jury awarded damages totaling $700,000 on both claims. The trial judge determined that the First Amendment had nothing to say about this dispute, that it was governed instead by the purely commercial relationship between reporter and source.

The Minnesota Supreme Court overturned both judgments against the newspapers. Writing for the majority, Justice Simonett concluded that the agreement between Cohen and the two reporters was never a formal contract but merely an "I'll scratch your back if you scratch mine" accommodation. The court noted in particular that the dispute arose "in the classic First Amendment context of the quintessential public debate in our democratic society, namely, a political source involved in a political campaign." To permit the awarding of damages for such promises, he added, "chills public debate."[74]

The U.S. Supreme Court reviewed the case, allowing at the outset that there was indeed no formal contract between Cohen and either of the reporters. The legal doctrine known as **promissory estoppel**, however, dictates that if failure to enforce an agreement would be inequitable or would otherwise be against the public interest, the state may enforce the agreement, even in the absence of a contract. From the justices' point of view, the *Cohen* case asked whether the First Amendment should preclude the state from applying promissory estoppel against the press. Justice White, writing for the majority, concluded that the First Amendment does not bar application of the doctrine in situations such as these. Newspaper publishers have "no special immunity from the application of general laws," he wrote. They must obey the National Labor Relations Act and the Fair Labor Standards Act, as well as laws against breaking and entering. Application of such general laws to the media, White wrote, "is not subject to stricter scrutiny than would be applied to enforcement against other persons or organizations."[75]

Nothing in the *Cohen* decision limits the application of promissory estoppel to guarantees of confidentiality. Reporters who mislead their sources in other ways can also incur liability. In 2000, the First Circuit Court of Appeals permitted a truck driver to sue NBC because the network's *Dateline* producers falsely promised the source that the story they were preparing would not include testimony from a group called Par-

---

74. 457 N.W.2d 199, 205 (Minn. 1990).
75. 501 U.S. 663, 670 (1991).

ents Against Tired Truckers. The producers' more general promise to the effect that the broadcast would depict the driver in a positive light was deemed too vague to be actionable.[76] A reporter can also be sued simply for asking specific questions during an interview if an earlier agreement had included a guarantee that certain subject matters would be off-limits.[77]

Dan Cohen's case was unusual, in that his attorneys were able to use arguments traditionally embraced by the media *against* the local newspapers. If confidential sources are so important to the media, Cohen's argument proceeded, anything that would dissuade such sources from telling their tales would necessarily jeopardize core First Amendment values. Cohen's Supreme Court brief pointed to studies showing that "eighty percent of national news magazine articles and fifty percent of national wire service stories . . . rely on confidential sources" and that the *Washington Post* often uses more than a hundred such sources in a single day's paper.

The media in general were not quite sure what to make of the *Cohen* case. On one hand, editorials appeared in newspapers across the country, distancing their own practices from those of the two Twin Cities papers. The *Baltimore Sun*'s Supreme Court reporter argued that the conduct of the two newspapers was "unforgivable" and amounted to "a straightforward, bald-faced ethical violation." Media attorney Floyd Abrams called the newspapers' betrayal of Cohen "reprehensible and damaging to all journalists."[78]

This does not mean that the media were happy with the Supreme Court's decision. Long Island's *Newsday* editorialized that "if disgruntled sources are free to sue under state laws because they don't like the way their stories came out in print, the media's First Amendment protection is in serious jeopardy."[79] The *Chicago Tribune* added that "there is no compelling public interest in suddenly formalizing the relationship" between newspapers and their sources "through the threat of lawsuit."[80] And the *St. Petersburg Times* concluded that "the government is on the wrong side when a newspaper can be punished for publishing the truth to inform voters about an election, even if it has to break a promise to do so."[81]

The *Cohen* case represents a cry for improved communication between reporters and editors. If reporters are not truly empowered to make promises of confidentiality to their sources, such promises should not be made, or at least they should be made conditionally. This solution is not wholly satisfying, of course. There is no way of knowing how many important stories will be lost because sources are not sufficiently

---

76. *Veilleux v. National Broadcasting Co.*, 206 F.3d 92 (1st Cir. 2000).

77. Kyu Ho Youm and Harry W. Stonecipher, "The Legal Bounds of Confidentiality Promises: Promissory Estoppel and the First Amendment," 45 *Federal Communication Law Journal* 63, 77–78 (1992).

78. Cited in Petition for Writ of Certiorari, *Cohen*, 501 U.S. 663 (No. 90-634), 7.

79. "Don't Punish the Media When They Tell the Truth," *Newsday*, June 27, 1991, 64.

80. "A Bad First Amendment Case," *Chicago Tribune*, July 1, 1991, C16.

81. "Voters Had a Right to Know," *St. Petersburg Times*, June 25, 1991, 10A.

THINGS TO REMEMBER

Betraying a Source

- In *Cohen v. Cowles Media Co.* (1991), the Supreme Court relied on the principle that the media are not exempt from obeying laws applied to all, and thus upheld a damage award against newspapers that published a source's name after having promised confidentiality.
- The situation can occur whenever reporters on the beat are in the habit of offering unconditional confidentiality when in fact they are authorized only to offer such promises contingent on their editors' agreement.

comforted by a promise of confidentiality that is "contingent on my editor's signing off on it later."

At least one court has concluded that a *Cohen*-like promise is not binding on a reporter when the source is a liar. The CBS television newsmagazine *60 Minutes* conducted an interview with former White House employee Kathleen Willey, who claimed that President Clinton had "groped" her in the Oval Office when she came to speak with him about a personal problem. Seeking to bolster her credibility, Willey apparently asked longtime friend Julie Steele to tell a *Newsweek* reporter, falsely, that Willey had confided in her immediately after the incident with Clinton. Steele agreed to do so only on the condition that her name never appear in print. When Steele later confessed to the *Newsweek* reporter that she had lied, the magazine felt relieved of any moral responsibility to keep its promise of confidentiality. A federal district court in Washington, D.C., concluded that the publication was also relieved of any legal contractual obligation to keep its promise under these circumstances.[82]

Chapter Summary

In *Branzburg v. Hayes* (1972), the Supreme Court ruled that whatever First Amendment rights reporters might enjoy regarding the confidentiality of their sources, such rights do not extend so far as to outweigh a grand jury's demand for testimony. Because five members of the Court agreed that the First Amendment is at least implicated, however, lower courts in many jurisdictions have concluded that there is a qualified reporters' privilege to confidentiality. How much protection that privilege provides is a function of what type of judicial proceeding is involved (grand jury, or criminal or civil proceeding), what kind of information is being sought (sources' identities, other confidential information, or nonconfidential information witnessed

---

82. *Steele v. Isikoff*, 130 F. Supp. 2d 23 (D.D.C. 2000).

firsthand by the reporter), and whether the person from whom the material is being sought is considered a "reporter." Several jurisdictions have openly embraced a test endorsed by Justice Stewart in his dissenting opinion from *Branzburg*. Reporters should be compelled to testify, Stewart argued, only if they are the only identifiable source of information relevant to a criminal investigation and for which the government has a compelling need. The vast majority of the states either have a reporter shield law in their statute books or recognize a confidentiality privilege as a matter of state constitutional or common law. Here too, the same three factors tend to determine how much protection is provided.

Although there is no federal reporter shield law, the Department of Justice has created guidelines for its own agents that emphasize a preference for negotiating with media representatives rather than creating an adversary relationship by using a subpoena or a search warrant.

In *Zurcher v. Stanford Daily* (1978), the Supreme Court held that the First Amendment does not provide reporters with any special measure of protection against newsroom searches, that the Constitution requires only that such searches be conducted in accordance with standard Fourth Amendment limitations. The Privacy Protection Act of 1980, designed to undo the effects of the *Zurcher* decision, proceeds on the general assumption that law enforcement officials seeking information from reporters should use subpoenas instead of search warrants. Exceptions may be made under certain specified circumstances, depending on whether the material sought was created by the reporters themselves (their work product) or was created by others and gathered by the reporters (documentary materials).

A promise of confidentiality made and then broken to a news source was the impetus for the 1991 case *Cohen v. Cowles Media Co.* There the Court held that media employees, like other citizens, may be sued for violating their promises, in accordance with the principle of promissory estoppel. That doctrine holds that the state may find it in the public interest to enforce promises even if they were not part of a formal contract.

Chapter 10

REGULATION OF ADVERTISING

It has been an ongoing joke in Hollywood for decades that those newspaper ads touting the latest movies with uniformly glowing accolades from film critics are to be taken with a grain of salt. If a critic writes, "It is unbelievable that anyone but an idiot would think this sequel was as good as or better than the original," the marketing folks will cleverly excerpt, "Unbelievable! Better than the original!" But Sony took this chicanery to a new level in 2001 when, in ads for several of its films, it created a fictional reviewer called David Manning, who touted Heath Ledger as "this year's hottest new star," told us that *Hollow Man* boasted "the summer's best special effects," and said of *The Animal* that "the producing team of *Big Daddy* has delivered another winner."

Perhaps the movie studio never would have been caught had they not assigned their imaginary critic to a real newspaper (the *Ridgefield Press* in Connecticut). In any event, a number of filmgoers were significantly miffed by the incident that they brought a class-action suit against Sony. After an appellate court in California ruled that the case could go forward,[1] the international entertainment goliath settled out of court. While aggrieved parties who sent off completed affidavits in timely fashion could recoup up to $20 (ostensibly the price of four movie tickets), the vast majority of the settlement was approximately equally split among the plaintiffs' attorneys and an AIDS charity.[2]

---

1. *Rezec v. Sony Pictures*, 116 Cal. App. 4th 135 (2004).
2. William Booth, "Big Payday for Lawyers in Sony Fake-Blurb Deal," *Washington Post*, September 10, 2005, C1.

The fact that movie critic David Manning never existed prompted a lawsuit against Sony Corporation alleging that the company fraudulently encouraged moviegoers to part with their money.

There was a dissenting opinion from that California appellate court, in which Justice Ortega chastised plaintiffs' attorneys for bringing what he characterized as "the most frivolous case" he had ever encountered. Ortega's protests notwithstanding, the case reminds us that we Americans sometimes see ourselves as consumers more than we do as citizens. We expect to encounter misleading ads in political campaigns and expect that the proper remedy will be to watch competing ads (or to seek out nonpartisan "truth brigades" to sort things out for us). We don't expect laws or courts to protect us from false or misleading political speech, and by and large, that feeling is consistent with what the First Amendment demands. The Supreme Court of Washington, for example, found unconstitutional a state law designed to punish false political speech, in the context of a challenge to clearly false advertising by a group opposed to Initiative 119, a failed attempt at creating a "death with dignity" law.[3] The court's decision is consistent with a maxim we saw back in chapter 2—Justice Brandeis's suggestion from *Whitney v. California* that the proper remedy when we confront bad speech is "more speech, not enforced silence."[4]

We Americans have a love-hate relationship with advertising. We express dismay at the ubiquity of commercial messages on shopping carts, on movie screens, and even in public toilet stalls. Yet we also cannot help but admire the art of the sell. Super Bowl viewers are often more likely to talk the next day about the commercials premiered during that annual event than about the game itself, which should not be surprising given the production and airtime costs associated with a thirty-second commercial seen by so many hundreds of millions of eyeballs.

One of the major themes of this chapter is that society's legal response to advertising manifests the same love-hate relationship. Perhaps nowhere has that ambivalence been more pronounced than in the development of the U.S. Supreme Court's own commercial speech doctrine. The first part of this chapter examines the evolution of that doctrine. Supreme Court pronouncements, however, are intended only to tell the other branches of government how much regulation is consistent with the First Amendment. It is also important to understand how the government regulates advertising day to day. The second part of the chapter therefore considers statutory and regulatory approaches. That section begins by considering state and local regulation of advertising and then moves to an extensive discussion of the most important regulatory body in this area, the Federal Trade Commission (FTC). Next is a discussion of the federal Lanham Act—which allows a company to sue a competitor it feels has hurt its market share through deceptive advertising—and a short discourse on industry self-regulation. The chapter concludes with a discussion of political campaign advertising.

---

3. *State v. 119 Vote No! Committee*, 957 P.2d 691 (Wash. 1998).
4. 274 U.S. 357, 377 (1927) (Brandeis, J., concurring).

The Supreme Court and Commercial Speech

Just as there are many sources of communication law in general, there are also many sources of law affecting the practice of advertising. Congress, the states, and local governments may all pass laws governing some kinds of commercial speech, such as regulating the size and distance from the highway of roadside billboards. Various federal and state agencies promulgate regulations dealing with the advertising, marketing, and labeling of commercial goods. Ultimately, all these laws and regulations must comport with the First Amendment, a determination that can be made definitively only by the Supreme Court.

Beyond the First Amendment?

"See how men live in a hell diver! Popular prices: adults 25 cents and children 15 cents." So read the brochure that colorful entrepreneur F. J. Chrestensen handed out on New York City streets to attract paying customers for a tour of his surplus Navy submarine. But it was not to be. Chrestensen was forbidden by police commissioner Lewis Valentine to dock his submarine. The problem was not the submarine but the brochure, which would put Chrestensen in violation of a city ordinance that forbade the distribution of *commercial* handbills.

Chrestensen went back to the printing press—quite literally—and reprinted his leaflets, this time on two sides. The reverse side boasted a political message (protesting the fact that he was not allowed to distribute a purely commercial message!). Would the distribution of this leaflet similarly be prohibited? Writing for a unanimous Supreme Court, Justice Jackson concluded that even the reprinted leaflet was "purely commercial" in nature. For the Court to rule otherwise, Jackson feared, would mean that "every merchant who desires to broadcast advertising leaflets in the streets need only append a civic appeal, or a moral platitude, to achieve immunity from the law's command."[5]

Even nowadays, when commercial speech does enjoy much First Amendment protection, litigants often try to infuse their advertising message with political elements in order to enhance the message's legal status. And just as Justice Jackson was not impressed, neither are more contemporary jurists. Frequently these more recent cases have involved litigants packaging and selling kits designed to teach consumers how to avoid paying income tax (illegally); the political element is often a suggestion that the federal income tax is unconstitutional. As one court, in upholding the issuance of an injunction, put it: "Packaging a commercial message with token political commentary does not insulate commercial speech from appropriate restrictions."[6]

---

5. *Valentine v. Chrestensen*, 316 U.S. 52, 55 (1942).

6. *United States v. Bell*, 414 F.3d 474 (3d Cir. 2005); see also *United States v. Schiff*, 379 F.3d 621 (9th Cir. 2004).

Protecting All But "Pure" Advertising?

It took the Court more than thirty years to decide that advertising should in fact receive First Amendment protection. Along the way, the justices dealt with issues such as editorial advertisements placed by political activists, the classified pages' "help wanted" ads, and one state's prohibition against ads for a product or service that is legal in other states.

Revisiting *New York Times Co. v. Sullivan.*

The Supreme Court's next examination of advertising's place in the system of free expression came in the 1964 libel case *New York Times Co. v. Sullivan.*[7] Recall that what prompted Montgomery, Alabama, police commissioner L. B. Sullivan to sue the newspaper was a paid advertisement. One of Sullivan's arguments at trial was that the newspaper should be prohibited from raising any constitutional defenses at all, because this material was commercial speech, wholly unprotected by the First Amendment. Yet it was not a "*commercial* advertisement," Justice Brennan replied, noting that it "communicated information, expressed opinion, recited grievances, protested claimed abuses, and sought financial support on behalf of a movement whose existence and objectives are matters of the highest public interest and concern."

Even today courts wrestle with the distinction between commercial and political speech. The distinction was very much at issue in a case alleging that Nike had engaged in deceptive advertising.[8] Nike had embarked on a major public relations campaign aimed at countering criticism of working conditions in the overseas factories where many of its products are manufactured. A California court found that Nike's assertions were advertisements because they "were directed by a commercial speaker to a commercial audience and because they made representations of fact about the speaker's own business operations for the purpose of promoting sales of its products." On the last day of its 2002-2003 term—months after having heard oral arguments in the case—the U.S. Supreme Court determined that it had too hastily taken on the case and sent it back to the lower courts to develop a full trial record.[9] There will be no additional adjudication, however. In September 2003, it was reported that Nike had entered into a $1.5 million out-of-court settlement with the citizen-activist who had initially brought the lawsuit.

Job Hunting in Pennsylvania.

Consider next a case from 1973 involving the classified advertising pages of the *Pittsburgh Press.*[10] As was the case with many newspapers of the day, the *Press*'s "help wanted" ads were separated by gender into sections headed "HELP WANTED—MALE" and "HELP WANTED—FEMALE."

---

7. 376 U.S. 254 (1964).
8. *Kasky v. Nike, Inc.,* 45 P.3d 243 (Cal. 2002).
9. *Nike, Inc. v. Kasky,* 539 U.S. 654 (2003).
10. *Pittsburgh Press Co. v. Pittsburgh Commission on Human Relations,* 413 U.S. 376 (1973).

The newspaper disavowed any discriminatory purpose, justifying the organization of the ads by pointing out that "most jobs generally appeal more to persons of one sex than the other."

The National Organization for Women filed a complaint against the newspaper with the Pittsburgh Human Relations Commission, which found that both the advertisers and the newspaper were in violation of the Pittsburgh Human Relations Ordinance. When the case finally reached the Supreme Court, it produced a 5-4 ruling against the newspaper. Justice Powell's majority opinion makes clear that the advertisements here were purely commercial speech, unlike the political advertisement at issue in the *New York Times Co. v. Sullivan* libel case. That should have been enough to resolve the case: if the ads were purely commercial, they enjoyed no First Amendment protection at all, thus making almost any challenge to the Human Relations Commission's findings meritless. Justice Powell, however, emphasized that these ads were incitements to "illegal commercial activity" (employment discrimination).

The press can also be held liable for more subtle communications of an intention to discriminate. Some courts have found that the disproportionate use of white faces in display ads for housing developments can itself be a violation of the federal Fair Housing Act, in that the practice visually implies that some housing opportunities are still for "whites only." The Court of Appeals for the Second Circuit permitted a suit to go forward against the *New York Times* for an alleged long-term pattern of publishing real estate ads that either excluded black models altogether or used them only when dressed as maids and doormen.[11] Most such suits tend to name the real estate advertisers themselves as defendants, however, rather than the newspaper or magazine in which such ads appear.[12] Indeed, in the Sixth Circuit a formidable obstacle has been placed in the way of plaintiffs seeking to recover damages from media outlets for pictorially discriminatory advertising. Only a campaign of several ads over time by a single advertiser can be actionable, this court has held. Neither a newspaper's decision to publish a particular ad nor its many individual decisions over time to publish ads from many different advertisers would constitute a campaign.[13] This area of the law will likely require Supreme Court resolution.

The 1973 *Pittsburgh Press* decision says that an employer's use of discriminatory language in a help-wanted ad is inseparable from the act of employment discrimination itself. What about ads placed by job *seekers*? Consider the following examples of such ads that ran in the *Pittsburgh Press* and were at issue in a 1979 Pennsylvania Supreme Court decision:

---

11. *Ragin v. New York Times Co.*, 923 F.2d 995 (2d Cir. 1991).

12. *Arkansas Acorn Fair Housing v. Greystone Limited*, 160 F.3d 433 (8th Cir. 1998); *Tyus v. Urban Search Management*, 102 F.3d 256 (7th Cir. 1997); *Ragin v. Harry Macklowe Real Estate Co.*, 6 F.3d 898 (2d Cir. 1993); *Spann v. Colonial Village, Inc.*, 899 F.2d 24 (D.C. Cir. 1990).

13. *Housing Opportunities Made Equal v. Cincinnati Enquirer*, 943 F.2d 644 (6th Cir. 1991).

SITUATION WANTED

- **College Grad—Born Again Christian with Bachelor's Degree and seven years sales and marketing management experience seeking work with Christian business or organization.**
- **White Woman—desires day work, office cleaning.**
- **Parolee—White, needs employment to be released. Licensed steam boiler and engineer.**
- **Salesman, age 30, looking for career in Pittsburgh, start immediately, 15 years selling experience.**

Justice Manderino concluded for the court that the newspaper could accept these ads with impunity because they "proposed no illegal transactions, [but] simply ask that prospective employers hire the respective individual advertisers." That the advertisers sought to bring to employers' attention such "prohibited employment criteria" as age, race, and gender was irrelevant, the court majority concluded; after all, employers could easily obtain that same information simply by scheduling a job interview.[14]

Out-of-State Abortion Services.

Jeffrey Bigelow was the editor of a weekly "underground" newspaper focusing on events in the University of Virginia community. In February 1971, two years before the Supreme Court's *Roe v. Wade* abortion decision, Bigelow accepted a paid advertisement from the Women's Pavilion in New York City, an abortion referral center. At the time of the ad's placement, not only was abortion illegal in Virginia, but the state also forbade any communications that might "encourage" or "prompt" women to receive abortions anywhere. Bigelow was successfully prosecuted under the statute and appealed his conviction all the way to the Supreme Court. Writing for a 7-2 majority, Justice Blackmun found for Bigelow, holding that the abortion ad was reminiscent of the advocacy advertisement in *New York Times Co. v. Sullivan*. In the context of a highly contentious national debate about reproductive freedom, this simple ad "conveyed information of potential interest and value," and was thus "newsworthy."[15]

The *Bigelow* decision created much confusion concerning the place of commercial speech in the system of free expression. Surely the Court did not mean to suggest that advertisements only for controversial products and services were to enjoy First

---

14. *Commonwealth v. Pittsburgh Press Co.*, 396 A.2d 1187 (Pa. 1979). In 2007, the Ninth Circuit Court of Appeals ruled that an online service called roommates.com was not immune from liability when it allowed and even encouraged clients to post notices indicating preferences for roommates and/or living situations based on such characteristics as race, gender, and sexual orientation. *Fair Housing Council of San Fernando Valley v. Roommates.com*, 2007 U.S. App. LEXIS 11350 (9th Cir. 2007). See generally, Helen Norton, "You Can't Ask (or Say) That: The First Amendment and Civil Rights Restrictions on Decisionmaker Speech," 11 *William and Mary Bill of Rights Journal* 727 (2003).

15. *Bigelow v. Virginia*, 421 U.S. 809, 822 (1975).

Amendment protection. It would have been so much easier had the Court simply admitted that its real goal was to overturn *Chrestensen*, bringing advertising as a broad category of speech within the First Amendment. The Court, however, would consider a case in the next term that demanded a more candid overturning of the decades-old precedent.

Bringing Commercial Speech under the First Amendment Umbrella

The State of Virginia forbade not only advertising for abortions but also advertising by pharmacists of prescription drug prices. A successful court challenge of this latter provision led the Supreme Court to finally overturn the 1942 *Chrestensen* decision, holding that the First Amendment does cover even purely commercial speech. Justice Blackmun's majority opinion pointed out that the case was postured as a right to hear issue, in that the plaintiffs were consumers rather than pharmacists. "Freedom of speech presupposes a willing speaker," Blackmun wrote; the First Amendment protects "the communication," both its source and its recipient. Predictably, the state felt its most powerful argument was that this was purely commercial speech, wholly unprotected by the First Amendment. Blackmun admitted that the "idea" sought to be communicated here—"I will sell you the X prescription drug at the Y price"—was a purely commercial one. The Court must thus finally answer whether such a message is "wholly outside the protection of the First Amendment. . . . Our answer is that it is not."[16]

Thus the Court overturned *Chrestensen* and brought commercial speech within the protection of the First Amendment. It is understandable that Blackmun felt a need to provide some justification for the Court's having simply changed its mind after thirty-four years. It was not difficult to do. Surveys of local prescription drug prices provided to the trial court uncovered tremendous disparity among drug dispensers, as much as 650 percent for some drugs. Keeping consumers ignorant as to who in town offered the best prices served only to bilk the poor. Surely that would have been enough, but Blackmun went further and in so doing, demonstrated the Court's continuing ambivalence about *pure* advertising by purposely blurring the line between commercial and political speech. "So long as we preserve a predominantly free enterprise economy," he wrote, "the allocation of our resources in large measure will be made through numerous private economic decisions. It is a matter of public interest that those decisions, in the aggregate, be intelligent and well informed." What better way to ensure that this public benefit is achieved than through "the free flow of commercial information?" Seen this way, advertising must be protected even by a First Amendment narrowly construed to apply only to speech that "enlightens public decisionmaking in a democracy." *Virginia Pharmacy*, then, says that commercial speech

---

16. *Virginia State Board of Pharmacy v. Virginia Citizens Consumer Council*, 425 U.S. 748, 761–762 (1976).

is protected even if it has no political elements. Yet the reason for this change of heart seems to be precisely because commercial speech has very strong political elements. Hasn't Justice Blackmun, after all, equated smart shopping with patriotism?

In its next term, the Court continued its tendency to emphasize the political elements of commercial messages, even though it had already extended First Amendment protection to purely commercial speech. At issue was a Willingboro, New Jersey, town ordinance—designed to curb "white flight" and retain its integrated community—which forbade the use of For Sale and Sold signs on residential lawns. The Court unanimously struck down the ordinance, in part because it stifled the flow of information "of vital interest to Willingboro residents, since it may bear on one of the most important decisions they have a right to make: where to live and raise their families."[17] Here too we see the elevation of the commercial ("I have a house for sale here") to the political (a statement about racial harmony?). Justice Marshall's opinion is especially ironic because in a racially charged atmosphere of unscrupulous real estate agents inducing panic selling, the presence of a For Sale sign would not necessarily signal to a black family that this was, indeed, a place where *they* could live.

Those For Sale signs we often seen in automobiles by the side of the road were at issue in a 2006 case from the Sixth Circuit. The court upheld a Glendale, Ohio, rule against such signage (unless the car was parked in the seller's driveway). The state's interests in traffic safety and aesthetics (if only cars that are truly part of traffic flow are on roadways, those roadways will be less congested) were enough to carry the day.[18]

How Much Protection? The *Central Hudson* Test

The *Virginia Pharmacy* case says that commercial speech enjoys at least some First Amendment protection, but not how much. The answer to that question emerged a few years later in a case involving a New York law, borne of the 1970s energy crisis, prohibiting advertising by any electric company that would tend to promote the increased use of electricity.[19] Writing for an 8-1 majority, Justice Powell struck down the law as unconstitutional. In so doing, he established the four-part *Central Hudson* test, intended to give lower courts guidance as to how to adjudicate disputes involving the regulation of commercial speech. In step one, courts ask if the advertisement is misleading, or if it is promoting an illegal product or service. If so, then a law regulating or prohibiting it is constitutional. If not, courts pose three queries about the state's interest in regulating this kind of speech: (1) Is that interest a substantial one?

---

17. *Linmark Associates v. Township of Willingboro*, 431 U.S. 85, 96 (1977).
18. *Pagan v. Fruchey*, 453 F.3d 784 (6th Cir. 2006).
19. *Central Hudson Gas & Electric v. Public Service Commission of New York*, 447 U.S. 557 (1980).

THINGS TO REMEMBER

Commercial Speech Doctrine: Early History

- *Valentine v. Chrestensen* (1942). The Supreme Court holds that commercial speech is wholly unprotected by the First Amendment.
- *New York Times Co. v. Sullivan* (1964). That the offending material in this landmark libel case appeared in a paid advocacy *advertisement* did not make it any less protected by the First Amendment than any other political speech.
- *Pittsburgh Press Co. v. Pittsburgh Commission on Human Relations* (1973). Although the Court begins to suggest that it might be ready to overturn *Chrestensen*, this case would not be the right one. The help-wanted ads at issue here were held to be an inextricable part of illegal activity (employment discrimination).
- *Bigelow v. Virginia* (1973). As in the *New York Times* case, the Court here also emphasizes the political elements in an ad for an out-of-state abortion clinic. We know that the Court is closer to being ready to overturn *Chrestensen*, in that this was an advertisement for a service—admittedly, a very controversial service. It was not an advocacy ad like the one the civil right workers paid to have the *New York Times* publish.
- *Virginia State Board of Pharmacy v. Virginia Citizens Consumer Council* (1976). Forced finally to determine whether *Chrestensen* is still good law, the Court overturns the 1942 precedent, holding for the first time that even purely commercial speech is protected by the First Amendment.

(2) Does the regulation really further that interest? and (3) Does the regulation abridge no more speech than necessary?[20]

Applying the test to the law before it, Justice Powell found initially that electricity is a legal product and that Central Hudson's ads were not misleading. Moving to the second inquiry, he allowed that the state did in fact have a substantial interest at stake—energy conservation. Did the law under review further that substantial interest, as the third inquiry demands? Powell felt so. Common sense suggests that advertising for a product will result in more demand for that product. Why would Central Hudson contest the advertising ban unless it believed it could increase its own sales via advertising?

The fourth inquiry, regarding how extensive the regulation, whether it abridged more speech than necessary to achieve the state's legitimate goals, proved to be the state's downfall. The prohibition on advertising was more extensive than necessary for two reasons, Powell concluded. First, the ban covered *all* promotional advertising, thus even prohibiting utility companies from marketing energy-*saving* devices. Second, the state's interest was in saving *energy*, not electricity, yet some people (depend-

---

20. In 1989, the Court substituted a less stringent final query, asking only that there be a "reasonable fit" between the regulation and the state's interest. *Board of Trustees of the State University of New York v. Fox*, 492 U.S. 469 (1989).

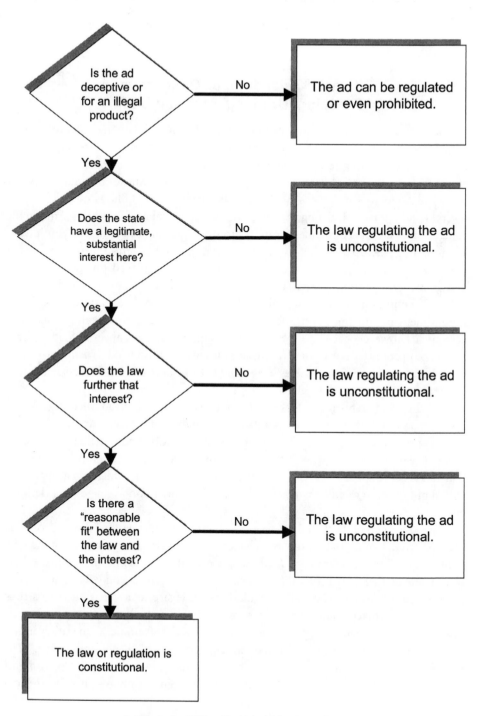

A Model of the *Central Hudson* Test

ing on what systems they already were using) might waste less energy overall by switching to electricity.

Illegal, Misleading, or *Dangerous*? Smoking, Drinking, and Gambling

The late 1990s saw a tremendous flurry of legal activity involving tobacco companies. Dozens of states' attorneys general prepared lawsuits against the big tobacco conglomerates, seeking reimbursement for billions of dollars in health care costs. In early 2000, the major tobacco companies entered into a "Master Settlement Agreement" that put to rest dozens of those suits in return for billions of dollars, plus several concessions concerning the future marketing of tobacco products. Among the concessions were the companies' promises to stop targeting the underage youth market, to cease using cartoon figures such as Joe Camel, and to refrain from any further outdoor advertising (such as highway billboards or ads placed on the exterior of buses). By signing the agreement, the tobacco companies hoped to avoid judicial resolution of a question that has stymied jurists and scholars for decades: would the First Amendment permit the government to forbid tobacco advertising altogether? The agreement, however, could not resolve all outstanding issues concerning advertising of tobacco products. For example, although it covers outdoor advertising placed by the tobacco companies themselves, it is mute with respect to such advertising placed by retail establishments that sell tobacco products.

Into this void stepped the State of Massachusetts, which established regulations affecting both the advertising and point-of-sale conduct of retailers. Among the regulations' provisions was a prohibition against any outdoor advertising for tobacco products within one thousand feet of schools and parks. The regulations also insisted that retailers eschew self-service displays of tobacco products, which must instead be placed out of reach of customers, available to them only upon asking a sales clerk for help.

Toward the end of its 2000-2001 term, the Supreme Court handed down a complex decision from a combination of cases challenging the various regulations. Some portions of *Lorillard Tobacco Co. v. Reilly* were decided by a unanimous Court; others commanded either of two very different six-justice majorities, and still other sections produced a 5-4 vote.[21] The state's regulations on cigarette advertising were struck down on **Supremacy Clause** grounds because Congress had already made clear its own intention to regulate cigarette advertising (by, for example, demanding health warning labels on packages and removing cigarette ads from TV and radio). (The Supremacy Clause of the U.S. Constitution prohibits state and local governments from enacting laws that conflict with federal law.) Since Congress had been silent

---

21. 533 U.S. 525 (2001). The decision includes the Court's handling of *Consolidated Cigar Corporation v. Reilly*.

about its intentions concerning advertising for cigars and smokeless tobacco, the Court turned to the *Central Hudson* test. The advertising regulations were struck down on the grounds that they failed the fourth prong of the test—there was not a "reasonable fit" between the rules and the state's interest. Put another way, the regulations prohibited much more speech than was warranted. In many very urban areas in Massachusetts, the Court found, the rule prohibiting outdoor advertising within one thousand feet of schools and parks would effectively ban virtually *all* outdoor advertising for tobacco products. Adult smokers have an interest and a right to see such advertising, the majority emphasized, just as the retailers have a right to reach such potential customers. Rules demanding that in-store "point of sale" advertisements for tobacco products be placed at least five feet above the ground also failed the *Central Hudson* test. These rules, Justice O'Connor wrote for the majority, could not even be said to further the state's interest in keeping minors from smoking. "Not all children are less than 5 feet tall," she reminded us, "and those who are certainly have the ability to look up and take in their surroundings." The regulations providing that tobacco products must be placed out of reach behind the counter so that customers must first ask a clerk for help were the only ones at issue here to survive the Court's scrutiny. These regulations were plainly beyond the scope of the First Amendment, O'Connor held.

In 2006, federal district judge Gladys Kessler, in a case stemming from the Clinton administration, enjoined the tobacco industry from making any future claims to the effect that smoking "low tar" or "low nicotine" or "light" cigarettes might be less harmful than other kinds of cigarettes and ruled that tobacco companies must pay for **corrective advertising**.[22]

Whereas tobacco advertising has been banned from the airwaves for several decades, the absence of hard liquor ads on TV is a function of long-standing self-restraint by both broadcasters and distilleries. That pattern of self-restraint, dating back to 1948, began to unravel in 2001, especially on cable television. In 2006 the Center on Alcohol Marketing and Youth reported that the number of hard liquor ads on TV had increased dramatically in just a few short years.[23]

Unless you are more than a bit older than the typical undergraduate student, your only familiarity with TV commercials for tobacco products will be through archival footage. Yet tobacco companies were among the biggest spenders on TV and radio airtime until the early 1970s. Indeed, in decades past, broadcast personalities often stepped out of role for a few moments to hawk cigarettes on their own programs. Lucille Ball and Desi Arnaz did it, as did the voices behind the Flintstones. That all stopped with the passage of the Public Health Cigarette Smoking Act, which as of 1971 forbade the advertising of cigarettes on TV and radio. A special three-judge panel of the federal district court for Washington, D.C., upheld the constitutionality

---

22. *United States v. Philip Morris USA, Inc.*, 449 F. Supp. 2d 1 (D.D.C. 2006).
23. "Findings," *Washington Post*, September 1, 2006, A8.

of that act, and the Supreme Court, without writing an opinion, upheld the lower court's ruling.[24] Although the decision was based on the government's unique relationship to the electronic media, the district court majority added in dicta that "Congress has the power to prohibit the advertising of cigarettes *in any media*."

How much weight this statement should be given is unclear. That broader question was not presented to the lower court. Moreover, the decision was written prior to the *Virginia Pharmacy* ruling, at a time when lower courts had no reason to expect that advertising enjoyed *any* First Amendment protection.

Those who support a complete ban on tobacco advertising across all media took solace from a 1986 Supreme Court decision. Recall that the first part of the *Central Hudson* test from 1980 asks whether an advertisement is misleading or is for an illegal product or service. The 1986 ruling in *Posadas de Puerto Rico Associates v. Tourism Co.* prompted many to wonder whether the justices had secretly added a third prong to that inquiry.[25] The decision seemed to say that a very diluted version of the commercial-speech doctrine would apply when the product or service being advertised was a *dangerous* (although legal) one. At issue was a Puerto Rico law that forbade some forms of advertising for casinos. More specifically, ads aimed at Puerto Ricans were banned, but ads aimed at tourists from elsewhere were permitted.

Writing for a 5-4 majority, Justice Rehnquist made clear that the governmental interests—avoiding increases in prostitution and in other local and organized crime—were substantial. Rehnquist went on to find that the law directly advanced the governmental interest, employing the same common-sense rationale used in *Central Hudson* itself: that advertising tends to increase consumption. The law was not overly restrictive, he said, precisely because it was applicable only to ads aimed at island residents.[26]

The most puzzling part of the Rehnquist opinion was his addition of another reason, beyond the mechanics of the *Central Hudson* test, for upholding the statute. Rehnquist placed gambling in the category of products and services—he included cigarettes, alcoholic beverages, and prostitution—that governments may legitimately "deem harmful." Puerto Rico could surely have prohibited its residents from engaging altogether in such a harmful activity as casino gambling, Rehnquist suggested, and this broad power must surely include "the lesser power" to ban advertising designed to stimulate demand for the casinos.

Did Rehnquist thus mean to suggest that governments would be given carte blanche to regulate (or indeed, to prohibit) advertising for any "products or activities

---

24. *Capital Broadcasting Co. v. Mitchell*, 333 F. Supp. 582 (D.D.C. 1971), *aff'd mem.*, 405 U.S. 1000 (1972).

25. 478 U.S. 328 (1986).

26. The *Posadas* case has turned out to be an aberration in many ways, including its treating Puerto Rico residents differently from other Americans. See *El Dia, Inc. v. Puerto Rico Department of Consumer Affairs*, 413 F.3d 110 (1st Cir. 2005).

deemed harmful"? Two more recent cases indicate that the *Posadas* decision is perhaps best seen as an aberration, even though it has not yet been explicitly overturned.

The first of these involved Coors Brewing Company, which industry analysts suggest has been plagued by a reputation that its products have too *low* an alcohol content. The company sought permission from the Bureau of Alcohol, Tobacco, and Firearms (BATF), which seemed empowered by relevant sections of the Federal Alcohol Administration Act (FAAA) to interact with the states[27] in the regulation of both labeling and advertising of alcoholic beverages, to inform consumers of the percent of alcohol content in its beer through both means of communication. The BATF concluded that the act required it to deny both requests. The Tenth Circuit Court of Appeals upheld the BATF with respect to advertising, but held that application of the FAAA to beer labeling violated the First Amendment.

Writing for a unanimous Court, Justice Thomas admitted that the government has a substantial interest in discouraging liquor companies from engaging in "strength wars," trying to lure potential customers to their brands by dint of their high alcohol content. But forbidding beer distributors from labeling their products' alcoholic content would not further that state's interest (as the *Central Hudson* test demands), he concluded.

Since the vast majority of states permit advertising of alcohol content—the federal law, interestingly, is not triggered unless a state itself prohibits the advertising of this information—the net effect of the lower court ruling was that brewers were still allowed in most regions to disclose alcohol content in advertisements, but not on labels. "The failure to prohibit the disclosure of alcohol content in advertising, which would seem to constitute a more influential weapon in any strength war than labels," Thomas concluded, "makes no rational sense if the government's true aim is to suppress strength wars."[28]

Thomas also found suspect the overall pattern of federal regulation of liquor labeling, in that the law treats wines and spirits in precisely the opposite manner as it treats beer. Not only *may* distilled spirits containers include statements about alcohol content, but such disclosures are *required* in the case of both spirits and wines that have more than 14 percent alcohol: "If combating strength wars were the goal," Thomas wrote, "we would assume that Congress would regulate disclosure of alcohol content for the strongest beverages as well as for the weakest ones."

The *Rubin* decision struck down regulations on advertising for one of the "harmful" products listed by Rehnquist in his *Posadas* opinion. If *Rubin* represents a step back from *Posadas*, a decision from the Court's very next term looks more like a full-throttle retreat. At issue in *44 Liquormart v. Rhode Island* were two state statutes, both dating back to 1956.[29] The first prohibited licensed vendors of alcoholic products

---

27. The Twenty-first Amendment, which ended federal Prohibition, gave the states much freedom to regulate alcoholic beverages.

28. *Rubin v. Coors Brewing Co.*, 514 U.S. 476, 488 (1995).

29. 517 U.S. 484 (1986).

from advertising their prices (except in the form of in-store displays not visible from the street), and the other prohibited the media in Rhode Island from publicizing liquor prices, even prices offered by out-of-state retail outlets.

Although the Supreme Court unanimously struck down the statutes, the justices could not agree on a single rationale and thus did not produce a majority opinion. Some parts of Justice Stevens's plurality opinion speak for one group of four justices, some parts for another four, and some parts for only three. Stevens expressed skepticism as to whether the laws would further the state's legitimate interest in encouraging temperance. Even accepting the common-sense assumption that the regulations here will drive prices up and demand down, temperance may not be the result, in that the most abusive drinkers are not much swayed by price.

Stevens also argued that the *Central Hudson* test does not sufficiently protect speech from state regulations that completely ban a truthful message about a legal product. Such rules "rest solely on the offensive assumption that the public will respond irrationally to the truth," that it is a legitimate function of government to keep the citizenry ignorant. Regulations that manifest this kind of paternalism, Stevens suggested, should be subject to a level of scrutiny approaching that applied to laws abridging political speech.

Stevens showed an awareness that the *Posadas* decision seems to argue for upholding the Rhode Island statutes for two reasons. First, alcohol is one of the harmful products or services mentioned in *Posadas*, the market for which the state should be free to damper, even if its strategy includes regulation of advertising. Second, just as Puerto Rico could have banned casino gambling altogether, so also Rhode Island could have chosen to become a dry state, and in both situations, *Posadas* stands for the principle that regulating advertising for the product or service is less restrictive than banning the activity itself.

Instead of honoring the precedential value of *Posadas*, however, Stevens wrote that he and the three justices who joined this section of his opinion were "persuaded that *Posadas* erroneously performed the First Amendment analysis." Moreover, his reading of the various concurring opinions persuaded him that "the entire Court apparently now agrees [that] the statements in the *Posadas* opinion on which Rhode Island relies are no longer persuasive." None of the other justices expressed disagreement with this sentiment, which at least on the surface seems to be the death knell for *Posadas*.

What does all this bode for restrictions on tobacco advertising beyond those that might survive *Central Hudson* scrutiny anyway, or even for an outright ban on advertising for this still-legal product? The question cannot be answered with total certainty, but it would seem that the *Rubin* and *44 Liquormart* cases together signal the Court's reluctance to permit the censoring of true commercial information based on the fear that readers will act on the information.[30] The argument could be made, of

---

30. Such an inference finds further support in *Greater New Orleans Broadcasting Association v. United States*, 527 U.S. 173 (1999).

course, that most tobacco advertising either does not impart any information or imparts mostly a kind of nonverbal misinformation. Do not most print ads for tobacco products, after all, seek to create a mental association of the product with athletic endeavors engaged in by healthy, young models with impeccably white teeth? Surely this is quite different from such mundane and verifiable kinds of information as the price of a bottle of beer or its alcohol content. Whether that difference is one that makes a difference in First Amendment analysis is a question for possible future litigation.

Advertising by Lawyers and Other Professionals

Back in the landmark *Virginia Pharmacy* decision, which first held that purely commercial speech is protected by the First Amendment, some of the justices tried carefully to limit the ruling to pharmacists only. In his majority opinion, Justice Blackmun went out of his way to say that he would "express no opinion as to other professions." He hinted, however, that lawyers and doctors would likely be treated differently because they "do not dispense standardized products" but rather "render professional services of almost infinite variety and nature."[31] Chief Justice Burger's concurring opinion emphasized that he was voting with the majority only because he predicted it would be possible to restrict this ruling to pharmacists. He pointed to data showing that 95 percent of prescriptions are already in dosage units when they arrive at the pharmacy, thus implying that pharmacists spend most of their time simply pouring pills from big bottles into little bottles.

Not Only Pharmacists.   Only Justice Rehnquist's crystal ball seems to have been working. He alone, in his *Virginia Pharmacy* dissenting opinion, argued that

---

THINGS TO REMEMBER

Posadas de Puerto Rico v. Tourism Company

- Justice Rehnquist seemed to add two very new rationales, above and beyond the *Central Hudson* test, for upholding the Commonwealth's ban on casino advertising:
  - The state's inarguable freedom to ban the activity altogether surely includes the "lesser" right to ban advertising for the activity.
  - Governments should have a large amount of leeway in regulating advertising for products or services deemed harmful, such as gambling, smoking, drinking, and the like.
- *Posadas* has since been discredited, though not explicitly overruled.

---

31. *Virginia State Board of Pharmacy v. Virginia Citizens Consumer Council*, 425 U.S. 748, 773 n.25 (1976).

there would be no way to avoid opening the door to advertising by all categories of professionals, including lawyers. "I cannot distinguish," he taunted his colleagues, "between the public's right to know the price of drugs and its right to know the price of title searches or physical examinations." Why "title searches" and "physical examinations"? Clearly this was his way of throwing the majority's words back at Justice Blackmun. Pharmacists are not the only professionals who render "standardized products."

It did not take very long for Justice Rehnquist to be proved right. In its very next term after deciding *Virginia Pharmacy*, the Court ruled 5-4 to strike down Arizona's law banning lawyer advertising. A Phoenix law firm called Bates and O'Steen placed an ad in a local newspaper describing itself as a "legal clinic" offering "very reasonable rates." The ad went on to indicate the actual rates charged for services such as uncontested divorce or separation, adoption, change of name, and bankruptcy.

Among the state's arguments in defense of the law were that lawyer advertising would have an adverse effect on attorney professionalism and that lawyer ads are inherently misleading. With respect to the first concern, Justice Blackmun likened it to a prediction that a client who perceives that the lawyer is motivated by profit will lose confidence that the attorney is acting out of a commitment to the client's welfare. How absurd, Blackmun exclaimed, given that the ABA's code of ethics explicitly advises attorneys to "reach a clear agreement" with clients about fees as early on as possible. If the obvious fact that the attorney-client relationship is at least in part a commercial one must be disclosed once the client is in the office, how can the state condemn "the candid revelation of the same information" in advertising, prior to the client's arrival?[32]

Justice Blackmun took the state's second argument to mean that lawyers could not possibly advertise without deceiving potential clients "because such services are so individualized with regard to content and quality as to prevent informed comparison on the basis of an advertisement." In response, he admits that it would be rare for an attorney to advertise a fixed price for a nonroutine service ("No matter what crime you have committed, I will keep you out of jail, for $5000 or less!"). After all, attorneys know they cannot predict how much work, and of what variety, such complicated cases will require. If and when attorneys do choose to include their price lists in their ads, Blackmun contended, the state's only concern should be that they do "the necessary work at the advertised price," that they keep whatever promises they make.

"High-Quality" Professionals?

Having determined that the state could not forbid attorney advertising across the board, Blackmun next had to consider whether this particular law firm's advertising campaign was deceptive. Despite the state's allegation to the contrary, he found that the lawyers' calling themselves a "legal clinic" was not necessarily misleading, that the phrase does not suggest some kind of

---

32. *Bates v. State Bar of Arizona*, 433 U.S. 350, 369 (1977).

When Justice Blackmun, in his *Bates* majority opinion, suggested that lawyers and clients should come to a mutual understanding at the outset about legal fees, this is likely not what he had in mind.

government subsidy is at work here to keep prices down. Nor was it unreasonable for Bates to call his fees "reasonable." Indeed they were toward the low end of the Phoenix market at the time. The majority cautioned, however, that lawyers should be very careful about making global pronouncements in their ads about the "quality" of their services, because such claims would not be "susceptible to measurement by verification."

In two more recent decisions, the Court elaborated on, and perhaps stepped back a bit from, its concern about advertisements touting a professional's "quality" of service. In 1990, by a 5-4 vote, the Court overturned the censuring of Illinois attorney Gary Peel for having advertised, on his personal letterhead, that he held a "Certificate in Civil Trial Advocacy from the National Board of Trial Advocacy."[33] Although Peel did hold such certification, the state was concerned that readers would assume (incorrectly) that the National Board of Trial Advocacy (NBTA) is a government agency. The state also argued that Peel's boasting of his certificate was an impermissible statement, at least implicitly, about the quality of his services. Four of the five justices ruling in favor of Peel emphasized the difference between unsubstantiated promises of quality based on nothing more than a lawyer's own assessment of how wonderful he or she is and statements of objective facts that may support an inference of quality. Although Justice Marshall did not join in the plurality opinion, his separate opinion did not contradict the plurality on this point.

---

33. *Peel v. Attorney Registration and Disciplinary Commission of Illinois*, 496 U.S. 91 (1990).

Whether touting that one has been judged a "super lawyer" by one's peers counts as such an unsubstantiated promise was at least implicitly at issue in a 2006 decision by a committee appointed by the Supreme Court of New Jersey. The committee held it improper for attorneys to advertise their services in a special "Super Attorneys" supplement to *New Jersey Monthly* magazine. Most of the ads in the supplement congratulated those members of a particular law firm who had been recognized by the magazine's survey. The court's committee determined that any such ads, in this particular context, violated state rules against making comparisons between the quality of one's own legal expertise and that offered by the competition. The ads also ran afoul of a rule against assertions "likely to create an unjustified expectation about results the lawyer can achieve."[34] In April 2007, the state supreme court asked a retired state appellate judge to mediate the dispute; in the meantime, the 2007 special issue of *New Jersey Monthly* hit the proverbial newsstands, with several ads again touting individual attorneys' status as Super Lawyers.

Four years after the U.S. Supreme Court's *Peel* decision, a similar case presented

The New Jersey Supreme Court's Committee on Attorney Advertising told attorneys that they may not advertise in this magazine's "Super Lawyers" section, whether or not their ad calls attention to this accolade. Presumably the ad here, which did appear in the 2006 Super Lawyers supplement, would have been perfectly fine if run instead in, say, the Yellow Pages.

---

34. Committee on Attorney Advertising, Opinion 30 (N.J. 2006) (Advertisements Touting Designations as "Super Lawyer" or "Best Lawyer in America"). The decision was stayed, pending review by the justices themselves.

itself. Florida attorney Silvia Safille Ibanez, who also happened to be both an accountant and a certified financial planner, advertised these latter qualifications in her Yellow Pages advertisement (under "Attorneys").[35] The state agency regulating the practice of accountancy took issue with her listing her certification as a financial planner on the grounds, reminiscent of the *Peel* case just discussed, that readers would incorrectly presume such certification came from the state itself. This time a clear majority of the Court, with Justice Ginsburg writing, concluded that there was nothing inherently misleading in Ibanez's description of her qualifications.

State-Prescribed Wording. The Court had more to say about lawyer advertising in a case involving a St. Louis attorney—identified in the court proceedings only as RMJ—who had been disciplined by the Missouri Supreme Court's Advisory Committee for placing advertisements containing text that deviated from the committee's strict guidelines.[36] Chief among RMJ's sins were his having deviated from the precise wording demanded by the state to describe his practice—"personal injury" instead of "tort law" and "real estate" instead of "property law"—and his having indicated that he was a member of the U.S. Supreme Court Bar. Writing for a unanimous Court, Justice Powell overturned the reprimand issued against RMJ, telling the states that they may not "place an absolute prohibition" on whole categories of "*potentially* misleading information," but must instead target advertising practices that are, in fact, deceptive.

RMJ's use of slightly different wording to describe his areas of specialty from what the state prescribed was not inherently misleading and was thus protected by the First Amendment. The fact that the attorney indicated his membership in the Bar of the Supreme Court of the United States was "somewhat more troubling," Powell admitted. Consider for a moment what it would mean to *you* to learn that an attorney had such membership. Would you be impressed? You probably should not be, at least not very much. Membership in the Supreme Court Bar means that you are permitted to make oral arguments in front of the nation's highest court, but there is no test to take or interview to pass. One must simply have been a practicing attorney for three years, pay a fee, and obtain a statement of "good character" from a current member of the bar. That RMJ chose to include this relatively uninformative fact about his qualifications was "at least bad taste," Powell concluded, but the Missouri rules did not specifically prohibit the disclosure, and in any event the state did not present clear evidence to support its contention that this particular boast was deceptive. Moreover, as RMJ's attorneys argued in his defense, potential clients with a case that raises federal constitutional issues may want to seek out a member of the Supreme Court Bar to represent them, and such membership is routinely listed in the kinds of legal directories available at public libraries.

---

35. *Ibanez v. Florida Department of Business and Professional Regulation, Board of Accountancy*, 512 U.S. 136 (1994).

36. *In re R. M. J.*, 455 U.S. 191 (1982).

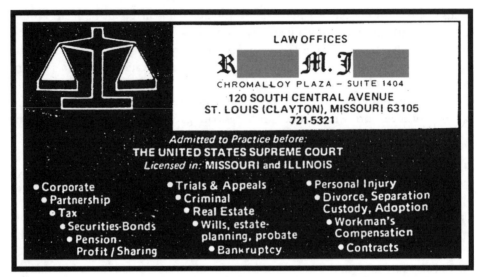

This ad from *West End Word* resulted in the *R. M. J.* case. Notice that the lawyer mentions, although not in an especially dramatic way, that he is a member of the Supreme Court bar.

Shifting for a moment from the practice of law to that of optometry, consider the plight of Dr. N. Jay Rogers, a Texas optometrist who unsuccessfully challenged a state rule prohibiting members of his profession from doing business under a trade name. A trade name in this context would mean virtually any wording on the shingle other than "N. Jay Rogers, O.D." You are probably familiar with numerous trade names used by optometrists; sometimes they are clever puns such as "For Eyes" or "Make a Spectacle." Rogers's chosen trade name was the more mundane "Texas State Optical."

Writing for a 7-2 majority, Justice Powell upheld the constitutionality of the state's prohibition, contrasting the Texas rule here with the Virginia rule that had prohibited pharmacists from advertising their prescription drug prices. It is difficult to imagine any commercial information more crucial to consumers than the prices of goods and services, Powell suggested. The speech Texas prohibits here, by contrast, is not valuable information, and indeed "has no intrinsic meaning" at all. Moreover, Powell pointed out, trade names are at least as likely to deceive consumers as to inform them. A company can continue to use a trade name even after one or more optometrists whose reputation first attracted the public to the practice have departed. Conversely, an optometrist with a terrible reputation, perhaps owing to his or her own "negligence or misconduct," can simply change the name of the practice. A single optometrist could even, "by using different trade names at shops under his common ownership, give the public the false impression of competition among the shops." None of these situations should be seen as whimsical hypotheticals, Powell warned.

Indeed, they came from the pages of a real investigation of a Texas optometrist by the state's Board of Examiners.[37]

In 1985, the Court dealt with two incidents stemming from a Columbus, Ohio, attorney's having advertised for DUI defendants and IUD plaintiffs (please forgive the forced symmetry).[38] In the first advertisement, attorney Philip Zauderer promised potential clients that "your full legal fee will be refunded if you are convicted of drunk driving." The deceptiveness in this ad, Ohio claimed, was its failure to inform readers that most criminal cases ripe for trial end in plea bargains. Any of Zauderer's clients who chose to plead guilty to a lesser offense would have to pay his full fee. As soon as the state expressed its displeasure to Zauderer, he withdrew the ad and pledged not to take on as clients any person who might respond to it.

The second instance involved Zauderer's elaborate ad seeking women who had been hurt by intrauterine devices (IUDs). The ad featured a drawing of the Dalkon Shield and the caption, "Did you use this IUD?" The text went on to enumerate the many health problems that had been associated with this particular IUD, admonish possible victims that it is "not too late to take legal action," and inform them that "our law firm is presently representing women on such cases." The ad also promised that "no legal fees" will be owed unless a suit is successful.

The Dalkon Shield ad attracted the attention of the Supreme Court of Ohio's Office of Disciplinary Counsel for several reasons. First, the state had a clear rule against drawings or any other illustrations in lawyer advertisements. Second, Ohio had an anti-"ambulance chasing" rule that it interpreted as forbidding attorneys to recommend themselves to any potential client who has not specifically sought out their advice. In other words, attorneys were forbidden to give unsolicited legal advice, including the messages "You need an attorney" and "You ought to consider hiring *me*." Third, Zauderer's promise that "if there is no recovery, no legal fees are owed" seemed vague. Apparently the client would not have to pay the attorney his fee. But what about fees due to the court itself, such as filing fees, or fees for photocopying official documents? Moreover, if the client wins—and thus has to pay the attorney's fee—will that fee be calculated as a percentage of the gross amount awarded to the client, or the net (after the client pays all court costs out of pocket)?

Writing for the Court, Justice White had no trouble overturning the state's blanket prohibition against drawings or illustrations. "The use of illustrations or pictures in advertisements," he wrote, "serves important communicative functions: it attracts the attention of the audience to the advertiser's message, and it may serve also to impart information directly."

Concerning the issue of contingency fees, Justice White's opinion upheld the judgment of the state, in a manner very consistent with Justices Holmes and Brandeis's

---

37. *Friedman v. Rogers*, 440 U.S. 1, 13 (1979).
38. *Zauderer v. Office of Disciplinary Counsel*, 471 U.S. 626 (1985).

famous dicta—see the discussion of *Whitney v. California* in chapter 2—that the proper remedy to be applied to bad speech is "more speech rather than enforced silence." The Court's ruling might have been different had Ohio prohibited attorneys from advertising that they are willing to accept clients on a contingency-fee basis, but all that Ohio demanded of Zauderer was that he clarify what the fee arrangement truly would be. The reprimand on this point would therefore remain in force, because to laypeople unaware of the distinction between "legal fees" and "costs," the ad would falsely suggest "that employing Zauderer would be a no-lose proposition."

Solicitation, Advertising, and the Mails.   One key issue remained in the *Zauderer* case: the state's application of its antisolicitation rules to Zauderer for having suggested to readers both that they might need an attorney *and* that he might be a good one to hire. "All advertising is at least implicitly a plea for its audience's custom," Justice White reminded the Ohio Supreme Court. More to the point, there was nothing deceptive either in the ad's suggesting that women who have been hurt by the Dalkon Shield might need an attorney to help them recover damages or in its reporting that Zauderer's firm was experienced in this particular kind of litigation. Justice White made clear that it is quite legitimate for state regulations to protect the public from *in-person* attorney solicitations (from true "ambulance chasers"). Print advertising is different, however, in that it lacks "the coercive force of the personal presence of a trained advocate," and thus is "more conducive to reflection."

A few years later, the Court revisited the distinction between in-person solicitation of business by attorneys and attorney advertising. The case concerned a Louisville, Kentucky, attorney named Richard Shapero who was in the habit of culling through public records for lists of persons whose homes were being foreclosed. He would then write to these individuals and offer his services. The Kentucky Bar Association had strict rules forbidding most kinds of direct-mail advertising, and its logic was interesting. States can surely prohibit attorneys from mailing an individually targeted letter of solicitation to a specific individual, Kentucky reasoned, in that such a communication is very similar to in-person solicitation. As the science of information retrieval and direct-mail list development grows more precise, lawyers may know so much about the persons on a carefully created mailing list that writing a letter to the entire list might also come to approximate in-person self-promotion. The Kentucky Bar Association therefore prohibited attorneys from sending direct mailings to any group of people who are somehow systematically different from the general public because of some "specific event or occurrence" (such as an auto accident or, indeed, a home foreclosure).

The wording of the rule was not terribly clear, which is part of the reason the Supreme Court struck it down. The rule prohibited mailings to persons "known to need legal services of the kind provided by the lawyer in a particular manner," but permitted mailing to persons "who are so situated that they *might* in general find such services useful." Perhaps, then, Shapero could have mailed to whole zip codes in the poorer parts of town? Justice Brennan's opinion for the Court, like Justice White's in the earlier *Zauderer* case, emphasizes the key difference between in-person solicitation and direct-mail appeals. "A letter, like a printed advertisement (but unlike a lawyer)," Brennan wrote, "can readily be put in a drawer to be considered later, ignored, or discarded."[39]

Brennan admitted that a targeted mail campaign does carry with it the danger that recipients will overestimate the lawyer's qualifications—"He knows so much about me, he must be a good attorney!"—but this danger counts as a reason for carefully monitoring direct mail, not for banning it altogether. The Court suggests here that states may require all attorneys who wish to send direct mailings to have them pre-screened by an appropriate regulatory body.

If the *Shapero* decision tells attorneys that it is all right to target for direct mail someone who may need their services because of a specific catastrophic life event, a 1995 decision cautions that they may have to wait a suitable period of time before sending any letters. In a 5-4 ruling, the Court upheld a Florida statute prohibiting attorneys from sending targeted direct-mail solicitations to accident or natural catastrophe victims or their relatives for thirty days following the event. Justice O'Connor applied the *Central Hudson* test on behalf of the Court. The state's purported interest in "protecting the privacy and tranquility of personal injury victims and their loved ones against intrusive, unsolicited contact by lawyers" was clearly substantial.[40] Moreover, the state's regulation served to further that interest in a narrowly tailored way. After all, attorneys do not have to wait thirty days to do other kinds of outreach, such as newspaper ads, billboard placements, or broadcast spots.

A pair of federal appellate decisions, one in 2005, the other in 2006, tried to apply the Supreme Court's lawyer-solicitation cases to chiropractors. In the Fifth Circuit, a Louisiana statute forbidding chiropractors to solicit individuals on targeted lists, such as victims of recent auto accidents, was struck down.[41] But in the Seventh Circuit, the State of Illinois was allowed to prevent a chiropractor from similar solicitations.[42] The difference? In the Illinois case the chiropractor intended to use paid telemarketers (as opposed to his own office staff, or making calls himself).

The whole issue of in-person solicitation was treated somewhat differently by the Supreme Court when the professional involved was an accountant rather than an attorney. Florida was one of a tiny handful of states that forbade accountants to engage in "direct, in-person, uninvited solicitation" to obtain new clients. Accountant Scott Fane wanted to do just that and so sought a declaratory judgment on the rule's constitutionality. Writing for an 8-1 majority, Justice Kennedy rejected the state's argument

---

39. *Shapero v. Kentucky Bar Association*, 486 U.S. 466, 475–476 (1988).

40. *Florida Bar v. Went For It, Inc.*, 515 U.S. 618, 624 (1995).

41. *Speaks v. Kruse*, 445 F.3d 396 (5th Cir. 2006).

42. *Goodman v. Illinois Department of Financial and Professional Regulation*, 430 F.3d 432 (7th Cir. 2005).

THINGS TO REMEMBER

Advertising by Lawyers and Other Professionals

- The 1977 *Bates* case first opened the door to lawyer advertising.
- The Court has since *said* it would be very leery of attorneys whose ads were designed to tout the high quality of their services, yet the justices have never upheld any state sanction against an attorney for doing just that.
- The only sanctions the Court has upheld were for advertising in potentially deceptive ways with respect to fees.
- There is a long history of forbidding in-person solicitation by attorneys; neither traditional mass media advertising nor direct-mail appeals are considered solicitation.
- States may, however, insist that attorneys wait a suitable time after an accident or other catastrophic event before sending a mailing to the victims.
- States may not constitutionally prohibit accountants (nor, presumably, other professionals who are not "trained in the art of persuasion") from engaging in in-person solicitation.
- States may prohibit professionals from doing business under a trade name.

that any accountant who solicits clients in that manner "is obviously in need of business" and might be a bit too willing to bend the rules when it comes time each year to certify that the client's accounting practices are appropriate. Indeed, the opposite—that accountants with *long-standing* clients would be most likely to bend reality a bit at certification time—is equally plausible. Despite the Court's often-expressed fears about in-person solicitation *by attorneys*,[43] Kennedy had some rather laudatory comments about the benefits of commercial solicitation in general. Only in-person solicitations, after all, permit "direct and spontaneous communication between buyer and seller." Why, then, should in-person solicitation by attorneys be considered dangerous? Because attorneys are almost unique among professionals, in that they are "trained in the art of persuasion," and because their clients are very often "unsophisticated, injured, or distressed lay persons." Initial contacts between attorneys and potential clients often occur "at a moment of high stress and vulnerability." By contrast, most accountants' clients are "experienced business executives," and meetings between accountants and such businesspeople tend to take place "in their [the client's] offices at a time of their choosing."[44]

Statutory and Regulatory Approaches

The First Amendment, as interpreted by the Supreme Court in such landmark decisions as *Virginia Pharmacy* and *Central Hudson*, puts the government on notice as to

43. See, e.g., *Ohralik v. Ohio State Bar Association*, 436 U.S. 447 (1978).
44. *Edenfield v. Fane*, 507 U.S. 761, 766, 774–776 (1993).

how much regulation of advertising will be permissible. One thing that has remained constant throughout and even before the development of the Supreme Court's commercial-speech doctrine is the common-sense notion that government should protect us from deceptive advertising. Not surprisingly, most of the ongoing regulatory interactions between the government and advertisers are aimed at identifying and eliminating deceptive statements from commercial messages. This section looks first at state and local regulation of advertising, then at the most important source of federal regulation—the Federal Trade Commission (FTC). We then examine the federal Lanham Act, which permits one competitor to sue another for damages, without having to persuade the FTC to intervene. After considering nongovernmental efforts at self-regulation by media and by the advertising industry, we conclude with a brief look at Supreme Court decisions concerning corporate advertising that seeks to "sell" political candidates rather than products and services.

State and Local Regulation

In recent years dozens of states and even more individuals have been engaged in litigation against the nation's major tobacco companies, attempting to recover billions of dollars of health care–related expenses as well as other kinds of damage awards. One argument made in several of these cases is that the tobacco companies had used deceptive advertising—failing to disclose the addictive nature of their products—in violation of relevant state laws.

None of this should be surprising. State regulation of advertising predates any meaningful intervention by the federal government. A magazine based in New York, reacting to an array of newspaper and magazine exposés of medical quackery, proposed in 1911 that individual states draft laws criminalizing the use of deceptive advertising. Such **Printers' Ink statutes**, named after that magazine, were eventually passed by the majority of states.

Many state laws governing advertising practices are fashioned after federal laws and regulations, and some explicitly instruct state courts to consider FTC and federal court rulings. Some go further. Massachusetts, for example, makes it easier than most states for plaintiffs alleging deceptive advertising to bring a class-action suit. In 2006 the Center for Science in the Public Interest announced its intention to bring suit under the state law against Kellogg Company for using cartoon characters such as Nickelodeon's SpongeBob SquarePants on packaging of unhealthy foods marketed to young children, including Pop-Tarts. In June 2007, Kellogg was reportedly planning to voluntarily impose new restrictions on its marketing to children, in order to ward off what was likely to be a $1 billion lawsuit.

At times state laws have been found to violate the federal Constitution's Supremacy Clause, which prohibits state and local governments from enacting laws that conflict with federal law. While a detailed examination of the circumstances under which federal law can preempt state and local law is beyond the scope of this book, suffice

The Center for Science in the Public Interest's formal letter to Kellogg complained that the use of popular cartoon characters to sell sugary foods to young children is a violation of Massachusetts' consumer protection law.

it to say that the issue has been a hot issue in recent years. A representative of the Council of State Governments was able to point to seventy-two pieces of pending federal legislation in April 2006 that would preempt state and local laws.[45] In 1992 the Supreme Court prevented a group of state attorneys general from enforcing their own guidelines governing price advertising by airlines. The federal Airline Deregulation Act of 1978, the Court held, explicitly preempted state regulation in this area.[46] In another case, the Supreme Court held that the State of Oklahoma could not enforce a law prohibiting wine advertising on cable television stations, because doing so would conflict with federal laws and regulations.[47]

Where state provisions do not conflict with or usurp federal regulations—and again, courts often have to make that determination—the Supremacy Clause does not apply, and the individual states therefore do often take actions against advertisers that for whatever reasons the federal government is slow to take. To cite just a few examples from 2006:

■ Sun Country Travel was ordered to pay $64 million in penalties and restitution in a lawsuit brought by the attorney general of Texas, which alleged that the company had fraudulently advertised "completely free" vacation packages to lure potential customers to a sales presentation.

■ The State of Florida settled a handful of suits against lenders it alleged had used deceptive advertising practices to lure Orlando area residents into dubious mortgage refinancing plans.

■ A hearing aid company was the target of a nineteen-count lawsuit brought by the attorney general of Pennsylvania, one count of which alleged that the company fraudulently advertised that it would provide free batteries for life.

---

45. Sheryl Harris, "States Resisting Pre-emption Trend," *Cleveland Plain Dealer*, July 16, 2006, G1.

46. *Morales v. Trans World Airlines*, 504 U.S. 374 (1992).

47. *Capital Cities Cable v. Crisp*, 467 U.S. 691 (1984).

Often, the federal government takes its lead from the states. In 1998, for example, American Family Publishers had to pay damages totaling over $1 million to several states that had sued the magazine subscription service best known for its annual sweepstakes using Ed McMahon and Dick Clark as pitchmen. The large print in mailings from the company trumpeted that the recipient "has won" millions of dollars; only by reading the very fine print would one learn that this joyful event will only have come to pass if "you have and mail in the winning number." Some recipients of the mail piece, convinced that they were millionaires, had flown cross-country at their own expense to pick up their prizes![48] Publicity generated from state prosecutions spurred the federal government into action. In December 1999, President Clinton signed into law the Deceptive Mail Prevention and Enforcement Act; among its provisions is a requirement that qualifying language contradicting the bold assertion that the recipient "has won" must be "clearly and conspicuously displayed." The law also requires sweepstakes mailings to make clear that participants' odds of winning are not affected by whether they purchase the promoter's products, such as magazine subscriptions.

Municipal governments have also gotten involved in the regulation of commercial messages. The *Pittsburgh Press* case discussed earlier in this chapter concerned *local* statutes forbidding discriminatory advertisement for employment. In another case, the City of Cincinnati required news racks on city streets to be used only for the distribution of "real" newspapers rather than the "commercial" newspapers one often finds publicizing local real estate offerings, alternative "learning exchange" educational institutions, or even dating services.[49] That the Supreme Court struck down this particular local law is not surprising. After all, the factual situation was very similar to that of *Valentine v. Chrestensen* (involving handbills inviting folks to pay a few pennies to come aboard a submarine), which had itself been overturned in the landmark *Virginia Pharmacy* decision. In addition, many cities and towns have some kind of regulations governing the placement of signs and billboards. A San Diego statute was struck down by the Supreme Court in part because it, ironically enough, provided *more* freedom of speech for commercial messages than for political ones.[50] Some anti-billboard laws in other locales that did not include this fatal flaw have been upheld.[51]

---

48. Diane Bell, "Sweeping Changes in Sweepstakes," *The San Diego Union-Tribune*, May 12, 1998, B1.

49. *City of Cincinnati v. Discovery Network*, 507 U.S. 410 (1993).

50. *Metromedia v. City of San Diego*, 453 U.S. 490 (1981).

51. *Granite State Outdoor Advertising v. Cobb County*, 2006 U.S. App. LEXIS 21092 (11th Cir. 2006); *Advantage Media v. City of Eden Prairie*, 2006 U.S. App. LEXIS 19291 (8th Cir. 2006); *Messer v. City of Douglasville, Georgia*, 975 F.2d 1505 (11th Cir. 1992); *National Advertising Co. v. City of Denver*, 912 F.2d 405 (10th Cir. 1990); *Major Media, Inc. v. City of Raleigh*, 792 F.2d 1269 (4th Cir. 1986).

THINGS TO REMEMBER

State and Local Regulation of Advertising

- State Printers' Ink statutes were adopted early in the twentieth century to protect consumers from deceptive advertising.
- The Supremacy Clause of the U.S. Constitution prevents states or localities from passing regulations that conflict with federal law.

The Federal Trade Commission

The main vehicle for the day-to-day federal regulation of advertising is the FTC, created appropriately enough by the Federal Trade Commission Act of 1914. The FTC has five commissioners, who are appointed by the president with the consent of the Senate, and who serve for seven-year staggered terms. The FTC was originally empowered only to police business practices that could unfairly hurt a competing company's bottom line. Congress's passage of the Wheeler-Lea amendments to the Federal Trade Commission Act, in 1938, gave the commission the broader power to protect consumers from unfair and deceptive business practices as well.

A word is in order about that phrase from the preceding sentence—"unfair and deceptive." Much of what the FTC does is not actually concerned with deceptive advertising. The commission's definition of *unfairness*, as laid down by Congress, points to any business practice that "causes or is likely to cause substantial injury to consumers which is not reasonably avoidable by consumers themselves and not outweighed by countervailing benefits to consumers or to competition." There is nothing in the act that restricts the commission to considering only issues related to advertising messages. Thus, for example, in 1973 Philip Morris, which even then was a conglomerate that sold many kinds of products other than cigarettes, got into trouble with the FTC for giving away free razor blades as part of newspaper inserts. The commission had no trouble concluding that the serious safety hazard inherent in the practice constituted the kind of "substantial injury to consumers" Congress sought to prevent.[52]

Deceptive Advertising. The FTC uses a three-step process to determine whether it should take action against an allegedly deceptive advertisement. The first step involves a textual analysis of the ad and its context to determine just what it is saying and whether it appears on the surface to be deceptive. The second step, almost inseparable from the first in practice, requires the commission to consider whether a

---

52. *Philip Morris, Inc.*, 82 F.T.C. 16 (1973). Notice that citations to FTC opinions most frequently name only the company involved. Only if and when a company appeals an FTC decision to a federal court does the citation then acquire the form "Company X v. FTC."

reasonable consumer would be deceived by the ad. Assuming that there is some deception at work, the last inquiry is whether that inaccuracy is *material*—that is, whether it is likely to affect the purchasing decision. Let us examine these three inquiries in turn.

Finding the Meaning of the Ad.   Some advertisements, such as one that falsely claims the surgeon general has endorsed a product, are obviously deceptive. More typically, deceptive messages are implied rather than expressly stated. Professor Ivan Preston of the University of Wisconsin, one of the country's most prolific writers on FTC policies, has suggested that advertisers who study commission decisions carefully will discover that there are recurring categories of implied deception employed by the agency. Preston identifies fifteen such categories.[53] Although the pages that follow owe much to Preston's work, several of his categories have been collapsed together and renamed to make them easier to remember. Four categories of implied deception result: "And I can prove it!" "More than I can say," "Did I hear that right?" and "Who said that?"

   "And I can prove it!"   At one level, almost all advertising copy includes the implication "And I can prove it!" Make virtually any factual claim about your product, and consumers will assume that you have some reasonable basis for making the claim, that you can prove it. Sometimes ads teasingly go a step further, hinting at a particular kind of proof for their claims. Suppose an advertiser said that "90 percent of all teachers surveyed recommended the Grok Reading Program." That seems like pretty compelling testimony, doesn't it? But what if the 90 percent figure refers, literally, to nine out of ten teachers, and that all ten were employees of the company? The deceptiveness then becomes apparent. The moment survey data or other statistical evidence are offered as proof for a claim, consumers have a right to expect that the figures were gathered in a scientifically valid way. Thus, for example, the makers of Fleishmann's margarine were told by the FTC to stop advertising that twice as many doctors recommended their margarine as any other brand. The manufacturer failed to include the sobering caveat that almost 70 percent of the physicians surveyed did not express a preference for any particular brand.[54]

   Frequently the FTC is just not satisfied that a company's purportedly scientific evidence is sufficient to back up its claims. Thus in 2005, Tropicana was told to stop making dramatic claims about how its Healthy Heart orange juice formula could raise good cholesterol and lower bad in a few short weeks. The studies cited by the company had been based on too few subjects for too short a time.[55]

   When a company offers "proof" of its product effectiveness in the form of an ac-

---

   53. Ivan Preston, "The Federal Trade Commission's Identification of Implications as Constituting Deceptive Advertising," 57 *University of Cincinnati Law Review* 1243 (1989).

   54. *Standard Brands, Inc.*, 97 F.T.C. 233 (1981).

   55. *In re Tropicana Products*, 2005 F.T.C. LEXIS 128.

tual demonstration, the FTC requires that the demonstration not be rigged in any material way. Campbell Soup Company, for example, concerned that the solid chunks of meat and vegetables in their product would tend to sink to the bottom of the bowl over time, dropped a number of marbles into soup bowls so that the TV camera would not make it seem as if the soup was merely broth. The FTC charged Campbell's with making a visually deceptive claim.[56]

Probably the most famously deceptive advertising demonstration to attract the FTC's attention was that engaged in by the makers of Rapid Shave, who wanted to show viewers that their lather made shaving so effortless that it could strip sandpaper of its grain. Apparently, it would have been possible for the product to shave very fine sandpaper if the paper had been soaking long enough in advance of the demonstration. Fine sandpaper, however, does not "read" like sandpaper at all on TV—you can't see the grain. Very coarse sandpaper would produce the right picture for the cameras, except that it would be impossible to actually shave. So the manufacturer instead affixed grains of sand onto a piece of Plexiglas. The announcer then informed the audience that the purpose of the demonstration was "to prove Rapid Shave's super-moisturizing power," and that the process was as simple as "apply, soak, and off in a stroke." The FTC ordered the company to take the ads off the air, and the manufacturer appealed all the way to the Supreme Court, which upheld the commission's decision. The commercial included three misrepresentations, the Court held: that sandpaper could be shaved by Rapid Shave, that an experiment had been conducted verifying this claim, and that viewers were seeing this experiment for themselves.[57]

"More than I can say!" Advertisements fit into the "More than I can say" category when their text is cleverly crafted to imply erroneous conclusions. For a tire company to claim that its tires passed all the manufacturer's inspections, for example, would seem to imply that the product must be wholly without defects. It is not what the text *says*, but the message is surely implied.[58] The makers of Geritol, who for many years sponsored Ted Mack's *Original Amateur Hour* on television, touted its product as a miracle dietary supplement for those who suffer from the lethargy caused by "iron-poor blood." Such a claim, the commission concluded, was misleading in its failure to point out that very few cases of fatigue are caused by anemic blood.[59]

Sometimes a disclaimer is provided in a commercial specifically asking consumers *not* to jump to the erroneous conclusions that the rest of the advertisement's text would otherwise imply. The commission, however, will still need to determine if that qualification or disclaimer is adequate to prevent the consumers' leap of faith. Thus, when in the 1970s Ford Motor Company used a dramatic advertising campaign, in-

---

56. *Campbell Soup Co.*, 77 F.T.C. 150 (1970).
57. *FTC v. Colgate-Palmolive Co.*, 380 U.S. 374 (1965).
58. *Firestone Tire & Rubber Co. v. FTC*, 481 F.2d 246 (6th Cir. 1973).
59. *J. B. Williams & Co. v. FTC*, 381 F.2d 884 (6th Cir. 1967).

Actually, since there likely is not a reasonable way for humans to determine if the new dog food really has an "improved" flavor, the only claim the FTC would likely require this company to prove is that it had indeed changed the formula.

cluding a test drive from Phoenix to Los Angeles, to show that cars get excellent mileage, the commission felt that the company's disclaimer—"the mileage you get may be less or even more depending on many factors"—was inadequate.[60]

Sometimes, by touting a specific property inherent to its product, an advertiser may suggest that this brand is the only one on the market with that quality. For example, Whirlpool got the commission's attention when it boasted that its air conditioners had a "special Panic Button to cool you off extra fast." The FTC found that such a button was hardly unique to Whirlpool's products, but was "merely a control which activates the highest of the three fan speeds, substantially similar to controls on comparable air conditioners made by other companies."[61]

60. *Ford Motor Co.*, 87 F.T.C. 756 (1976).
61. *Whirlpool Co.*, 83 F.T.C. 1830 (1974).

Sometimes the way a company emphasizes an advantage its product truly does have may create a "halo effect," implying falsely that the product has other related benefits. When Anacin is touted as having more of a specific but unnamed pain reliever (aspirin) than the competition, isn't it likely that consumers will infer that the product is superior overall as a painkiller? The inference may not be logical. It ignores the possibility that competing brands' formulas, which may include some aspirin plus some other drugs, might produce better results. Yet the inference is a likely one and one that the Anacin ad almost demands we make.[62] Another example is found in the ad campaign run by Sun Oil Company (now known as Sunoco) for its high-octane Sunoco 260 gasoline. In meticulous detail, the ads explained how there were two kinds of gasoline stored underground at Sunoco stations, the regular 190 octane and the high-premium 260 octane. Customers could pump gasoline labeled 190, 200, 210, and so on, all the way to 260, and for the intermediate grades an appropriately proportioned blend from the two tanks would be delivered. The company's transgression, from the commission's perspective, was emphasizing that all its blends except pure 190 would thus have "260 action." Were consumers thus not being led to conclude that whatever sterling qualities pure 260 gas had would somehow also be enjoyed by those pumping lesser grades?[63] Indeed, Professor Ivan Preston found that 80 percent of students he surveyed had inferred precisely that.[64]

A related type of distortion occurs when advertisers offer, often in a dramatic way, true but not terribly important information about their product. One of the best-known examples was when the makers of Carnation Instant Breakfast emphasized in their ads that their product has "as much mineral nourishment as two strips of crisp bacon." How many consumers realized that bacon has very few mineral nutrients, so that the comparison was not terribly meaningful?[65]

In a 2005 action "about firm abs and phony ads," the FTC found that the manufacturer of the Ab Force belts had engaged in deceptive advertising, even though its ads never directly said what the product does. Instead, the ads reminded consumers of competing companies' ads that touted wearing similar belts, which administer small electric shocks to the abdominal muscles, as "the latest fitness craze." Those other companies promise that their units will "get our abs into great shape—without exercise." Although the Ab Force ads never said what its own machines were supposed to do, the commission determined that touting the units as "just as powerful and effective" (but less expensive) was to promise, without substantiation, that they would help consumers shed inches and pounds. Since the commission had never been

---

62. *American Home Products Corp.*, 98 F.T.C. 136 (1981).

63. *Sun Oil Co.*, 84 F.T.C. 247 (1974).

64. Ivan L. Preston, *The Great American Blowup: Puffery in Advertising and Selling* (Madison: University of Wisconsin Press, 1996), 106–108.

65. *Carnation Co.*, 77 F.T.C. 1547 (1970).

persuaded that any of these kinds of machines work, the Ab Force manufacturers could not be let off the hook by seeming not to promise anything.[66]

"Did I hear that right?"   Advertisers will often choose their words carefully, perhaps even injecting new words into the lexicon, to lead consumers to make conclusions based on a kind of auditory confusion. If you heard that a sweater was made of "cashmora," for example, isn't it likely that you will think of "cashmere?"[67] Or consider "plyhide" as a descriptive name for an upholstery material. Does it not suggest some kind of leather, or at least the hide of some unnamed animal, rather than the vinyl it really was?[68]

Advertisers do not have to invent new words to create linguistic ambiguity. Thus, the commission's suspicions were aroused by America Online's ubiquitous offers of "ten free hours" of online time. Consumers would easily miss the barely visible warnings that the hours must all be used in one month, that any use exceeding the ten hours or going beyond the one-month trial would result in automatic charges to their credit card, and that users needed to take the affirmative step of contacting the company to cancel their membership prior to the month's passage or they would begin to incur hourly fees.[69]

If advertisers can get into trouble for offering their wares "free," they certainly can attract the FTC's attention when they offer merchandise at sale prices. Look at the typical full-page department store ad in your local newspaper, telling readers that this or that product is now "on sale" for a hefty "percent off." What does this wording mean? The commission demands that the percentage shown be a comparison with a bona fide "regular" price and that the regular price shall have been in place for a reasonable period of time prior to the beginning of the special sale days. Ideally too, a substantial number of sales will have occurred at the regular price. If not, this very fact must be affirmatively disclosed in the ad. Thus, if you look at the fine print of such ads, you will often see words to the effect that "our regular and original prices are offering prices only and may or may not have resulted in sales."[70]

"Who said that?"   Advertisements often rely just as heavily on the attributed source for their message as on the text itself. Madison Avenue is constantly on the lookout for appropriate spokespersons, celebrity or otherwise, to endorse their clients' goods and services. FTC regulation in this area is rather complex.

The commission does not consider all instances of people saying nice things about products in commercials "endorsements." Advertising narratives in which one character teaches another about a product, whether food storage bags or laxatives, would not usually be of commission concern. Viewers understand that these are fictional

---

66. *In re Telebrands*, 2005 F.T.C. LEXIS 9313.
67. *Elliot Knitwear*, 59 F.T.C. 893 (1961).
68. *Robbin Products*, 62 F.T.C. 1461 (1963).
69. *America Online*, 1998 F.T.C. LEXIS 25 (1998).
70. *Home Centers, Inc.*, 94 F.T.C. 1362 (1979).

relationships depicted by paid actors. Nor does a spokesperson who does not enjoy any special brand of notoriety beyond appearing in a commercial typically count as an endorser. The "Dude, you're getting a Dell" commercials would not make actor Ben Curtis an endorser, nor would Verizon's "Can you hear me now?" spots do so for actor Paul Marcarelli, for purposes of FTC policies.

An endorsement must represent the genuine beliefs and experiences of the person or group to whom it is attributed. In a classic case, a cigarette company's advertisements implied that a *Reader's Digest* article had endorsed its product line. The appellate court that upheld the FTC's order to cease the advertisement campaign referred to the ads as "a perversion of the meaning of the *Reader's Digest* article." Whereas the article itself emphasized that the differences in tar and nicotine levels of competing cigarette brands were so negligible that a smoker could be confident that any of them could "effectively nail down his coffin," the manufacturer made it seem as if the magazine had endorsed Old Gold cigarettes as an especially healthful brand.[71]

Endorsers who claim to be users of products they advertise must in fact be users. Thus, singer Pat Boone's hawking of Acne-Statin skin medication was seen as deceptive because, among other reasons, he claimed falsely that all his daughters used it.[72] Advertisers have the responsibility to keep in touch with endorsers periodically, to make sure that they still are users of products they endorse for as long as the campaign runs.

If an endorser's experience with a product is more dramatically positive than most consumers should expect, that fact must be disclosed. In 1998, the FTC filed a complaint against Jenny Craig, Inc., asking that it clearly indicate that the "success story" testimonials appearing in the company's ads are unusual, that most people will not lose so many pounds so quickly, and that many people regain the weight they lose on such plans.[73]

When an advertisement purports to be using ordinary consumers rather than paid actors, that representation must itself be truthful. In its guide to advertisers, the FTC uses the example of a company seeming to have a hidden camera catch real consumers in a candid scene at a cafeteria giving spontaneous testimonials about a new brand of breakfast cereal. Such a production technique would be deceptive if the on-screen spokespersons are instead paid actors.

The commission employs a special measure of scrutiny concerning the use of "experts" giving testimonials. When an advertisement either expressly or implicitly states that an endorser has some special expertise vis-à-vis a product, FTC policy is that "the endorser's qualifications must in fact give him the expertise that he is represented as possessing." Beatrice Foods, makers of Milk Duds candies, got into a bit of trouble with the commission for its TV ads depicting baseball player Lou Brock getting a base

71. *P. Lorillard Co. v. FTC*, 186 F.2d 52 (4th Cir. 1950).

72. *Cooga Mooga*, 92 F.T.C. 310 (1978).

73. *Jenny Craig*, 1998 F.T.C. LEXIS 13 (1998).

hit, catching an opponent's fly ball, and stealing second base. The voiceover interviewer asks Brock his "secret for stealing second," and Brock replies that as soon as the pitcher winds up, "I take off like a sprinter. I take off running like I'm going for the last box of Milk Duds in town."

The FTC forced Beatrice Foods to stop using this narrative. From the commission's perspective, the commercial implied that the consumption of Milk Duds "is linked to and necessary for the instilling, improving and maintaining of athletic ability and performance." The implication is untrue, the commission held, and Brock, despite his inarguable athletic abilities, was not qualified as an expert to make such a claim.[74] Interestingly, the FTC has not gotten involved in advertising campaigns exploiting the "expertise" attached to actors because of particular roles with which they are best associated. The commission never asked the Sanka people to refrain from using actor Robert Young to tout the benefits of drinking decaffeinated coffee, yet it is clear that the manufacturer was primarily interested in exploiting the public's identification of Young as the title character on *Marcus Welby, M.D.* Similarly, American Express embarked on its famous "Don't leave home without it" campaign with actor Karl Malden, best known at the time for playing a cop on the television show *The Streets of San Francisco.*[75]

Deceptive to a "Reasonable" Consumer?   In fulfilling its mission to protect the consumer against deceptive advertising, the FTC has at times presumed complete gullibility on the part of the citizenry. In one often-criticized case, the commission refused to permit a cosmetics company to advertise that its product could "color hair permanently." The commission felt this was misleading because hair that had not yet grown in would emerge in one's natural color.[76] The commission abandoned that entirely paternalistic approach some years later. In 1963, for example, it determined that a company marketing a device called Swim-Ezy to help novice swimmers stay afloat had not advertised deceptively by describing the small device as "invisible"; obviously, the product was not "invisible or impalpable or dimensionless," the FTC allowed, and consumers would be no more likely to think so than they would be to assume that "Danish pastry" must, as a matter of law, come from Denmark.[77]

Whether a reasonable consumer—the language currently favored by the commission is "consumers acting reasonably under the circumstances"—is likely to be misled can sometimes become a numbers game. What percentage of consumers need to be led astray before an ad will be found deceptive? Indeed, sometimes the commission has entertained survey or experimental research data to determine whether an ad is

---

74. *Beatrice Foods,* 81 F.T.C. 830 (1972).

75. Michael Schudson, *Advertising: The Uneasy Persuasion: Its Dubious Impact on American Society* (New York: Basic Books, 1986), 212–213; Michael Madow, "Private Ownership of Public Image: Popular Culture and Publicity Rights," 81 *California Law Review* 125 (1993).

76. *Gelb v. FTC,* 144 F.2d 580 (2d Cir. 1944).

77. *Heinz W. Kirchner,* 63 F.T.C. 1282 (1963).

deceptive. In recent years, however, the courts have been more deferential to the commission, in essence saying that its staff's educated guesses as to whether an ad is likely to deceive will be sufficient justification.[78]

The commission recognizes also that some ad campaigns are targeted to very specific markets. If the persons targeted are likely to be particularly vulnerable, the FTC may employ a more fluid definition of what it means to be "reasonable" or to be "likely to deceive." In 1975 the commission forced a company to stop advertising travel packages to the Philippines to undergo "psychic surgery," a kind of faith healing purported to be a treatment by which the body is entered without surgical instruments, using only bare hands. The FTC complaint charged that these ads "prey upon and exploit the frustrations and hopes of people who are seriously ill," that such people are "vulnerable to the influence" of the promotions because they "hold out a tantalizing hope which the medical profession, by contrast, cannot offer."[79] And in 1998 the commission indicated its concern about companies that aggressively market loans to persons who may have very poor credit histories but lots of equity built up in their homes. Such persons may be in need not only of money but also the chance to improve their credit ratings. Often these "predatory" mortgage companies, as the FTC calls them, make loans that they surmise will lead to default, thus allowing them to foreclose on their clients' homes.[80]

Not surprisingly, the commission has often expressed concern about children as an especially vulnerable target audience. Youngsters are, in the commission's words, "unqualified by age or experience to anticipate or appreciate the possibility that representations may be exaggerated or untrue."[81] Perhaps you have noticed that TV spots for toys often include the disclaimer that this or that accessory is "sold separately." That practice is very much in keeping with an FTC complaint filed against Lewis Galoob Toys, Inc., whose ads visually implied, falsely, that the "Transport Chopper," "Aircraft Carrier," and "Air Cargo" playsets came prepackaged with all the accessories depicted in the commercials. The commission also expressed its concern that the ad's depiction of a toy missile launcher made it appear that the missile would travel a great distance at a high speed and that the company's "Bouncin' Kids Ballerina" was deceptively depicted to "stand on one foot and twirl by herself without human assistance." Future disclaimers in the company's ads would have to be written "in language understandable to children."[82]

In 1998 Congress passed the Children's Online Privacy Protection Act, designed to protect children from the gathering of personal information about them without their

---

78. Dennis P. Stolle, "The FTC's Reliance on Extrinsic Evidence in Cases of Deceptive Advertising: A Proposal for Interpretive Rulemaking," 74 *Nebraska Law Review* 352 (1995).

79. *Travel King, Inc.*, 86 F.T.C. 715 (1975).

80. "FTC Charges D.C. Mortgage Lender with Deception and Unfairness against Borrowers," press release, January 30, 1998, http://www.ftc.gov/opa/1998/01/capcity.htm.

81. *Ideal Toy Corp.*, 64 F.T.C. 297 (1964).

82. *Lewis Galoob Toys*, 1991 F.T.C. LEXIS 74 (1991).

parents' explicit consent. The law instructed the FTC—which had already expressed concern back in 1997 about websites that entice children to input personal information about themselves and their families[83]—to create and enforce specific rules in furtherance of the act's goals. The commission decided upon what it called a "sliding scale" rule, imposing the heaviest consent requirements for companies that intended to disclose information about children under thirteen to third parties, and less stringent consent requirements if the information was to be used only internally. In 2006 the commission revisited its body of rules and found no need to change them.[84]

"Material" Information.　Not all potentially deceptive marketing messages are actionable. Only those that are material, that will likely affect the consumer's purchasing decision, will catch the FTC's attention. In practice, the FTC considers any factual claim about a product expressed in words to be material. The logic seems to be that if the advertiser chooses to make a claim, it is likely doing so to influence the consumer's purchasing decision. That is the whole point of running the ad in the first place.

Nontextual, visual elements become a bit trickier. If your product line is children's sportswear and your TV ads depict kids running around having fun while wearing your product, the FTC will not be terribly concerned that the ice cream cones the child actors seem to be consuming with such glee are actually filled with colored mashed potatoes. Ice cream just does not hold up very well to the hot lights in the TV studio. Indeed, even if you are selling ice cream itself, you will be able to use mashed potatoes in your ads, as long as you do nothing special to make the switch material. Thus, for example, if your ad touts the large number of flavor choices your company offers, there is no problem. If, however, your ad instead emphasizes the rich color and texture of the ice cream and the "fact" that it will help keep your kids neat and clean because it does not melt as quickly as other brands, you will have serious problems with the commission.

The finding of materiality must come from the ads themselves. Thus, for example, in a 2000 case Pizza Hut was able to demonstrate that many consumers believed Papa John's advertising claim that its pies have "better ingredients than other national pizza chains." Pizza Hut claimed this was a deceptive claim, in that its competitor's ads suggested that a small handful of differences in the two companies' production techniques was why Papa John's was "better," even though consumers apparently had no taste preferences for pies made with the one or the other set of techniques. Even if the claims were deceptive, however, Pizza Hut failed to prove materiality, the court held, because consumers' beliefs might have been based on their firsthand experiences with the two companies' products, rather than on the ad campaign.[85]

---

83. Chris Brewster, "FTC Issues Guidelines for Marketers Targeting Kids Online," *Marketing News*, December 8, 1997, 7.

84. Children's Online Privacy Protection Rule, 16 C.F.R. § 312 (2006).

85. *Pizza Hut, Inc. v. Papa John's International, Inc.*, 227 F.3d 489 (5th Cir. 2000).

Since the label "action figure" has become so common (perhaps as a way of allowing boys to play with dolls without being teased), the FTC would likely not bring a complaint against the toy depicted here.

There is a special category of assertions about products that the commission has determined would not be used by reasonable consumers in making purchasing decisions. This is called **puffery**, those unsubstantiated statements of opinion about a product's overall quality that consumers theoretically listen to with only one ear and do not take very seriously. We buy Hallmark greeting cards when we "care enough to send the very best." We are told that Carnival cruises are "the most popular in the world." If we "bring out the Hellmann's" mayonnaise, we "bring out the best." The FTC presumes that such claims about products serve no higher purpose than to keep the brand names alive in the collective consciousness, that they do not affect purchasing decisions in a material way. That Papa John's was permitted to advertise that its pies had "better ingredients" than the competition (in the case cited earlier) is another clear example of puffery.

Procedures and Powers of the FTC.

The totality of the FTC's powers and responsibilities goes far beyond the subject matter of this book. Over the years, Congress has asked the agency to enforce no fewer than three dozen federal statutes, many

The FTC would not get involved in this kind of advertising claim but would treat the labeling of an "all-day" lollipop as an example of puffery, protected speech precisely because no reasonable consumer would take the claim literally.

of which have nothing to do with communication. We limit the consideration here to the commission's actions against deceptive advertising.

How does the FTC decide which cases to pursue? It often makes these determinations independently, after its own staff has monitored a specific ad campaign or concluded that a whole industry could benefit from the commission's guidance concerning consumers' likely inferences from the claims made in a category of advertising. Or the commission may first learn about a potentially deceptive practice from a company's competitors, or even from a member of the public.

However an advertising campaign comes to the commission's attention, the FTC staff may, if it believes a violation of the law has occurred, attempt to obtain voluntary compliance. The staff will thus seek to enter into what is called a **consent order** with the company. This is similar to a **consent decree**, except that there is no judge and no court of law in charge of enforcing the order. A company that signs a consent order need not admit that it violated the law, but it must agree to stop the disputed practices, which the commission will have outlined in an accompanying complaint. Most FTC actions against particular advertisers are such consent orders. Skeptics often point out that the FTC succeeds in getting this level of agreement from the targets of its investigations because the commission takes so long to act that the offending ad campaign is likely already over, or at least soon scheduled to be retired.

Sometimes a company is unwilling to sign a consent order. It may dispute the FTC's findings, believing that its advertising is not deceptive and should not be subject to any governmental sanctions. In this event, the commission staff will often issue an **administrative complaint**, which leads to a formal proceeding that is much like a court trial, except that the judge hearing the dispute is not an ordinary federal district judge but rather an **administrative law judge** (ALJ). Should the ALJ determine that the advertisement in dispute is indeed deceptive, a **cease and desist order**—the term is self-explanatory—will typically be issued.

If the defendant advertiser is dissatisfied with the ALJ's initial ruling, it may appeal to the five FTC commissioners themselves. These commission rulings are also appealable, first to a federal appellate court (usually the one for the District of Columbia) and ultimately to the Supreme Court (if it chooses to hear the case).

The FTC may in some circumstances opt to circumvent the often laborious administrative process of seeking a consent order and going to an ALJ. It can instead apply directly to a federal district judge for an injunction ordering the advertising to cease. The direct adjudicative route has the advantage of surprise, in that offending advertisers will not learn of the FTC's interest in them until the suit is actually filed. The commission typically reserves this action for egregious and continuing ad campaigns, as well as for those that may have direct and immediate implications for consumers' health.

The FTC is empowered not only to stop the use of an advertisement's deceptive wording but also to require advertisers to insert specific language, called **affirmative disclosures**, into future advertisements. Consent orders (agreements between the FTC and an advertiser) and consent decrees (issued by a federal court at the commission's request) frequently include such a requirement. In 1997, for example, the FTC reached an agreement with a maker of sunscreen that the commission's staff felt had made unrealistic claims about its product's ability to protect users from dangerous rays. The final order required, among other things, that the company's future advertising include such caveats as "tanning in sunlight or under tanning lamps can cause skin cancer and premature skin aging—even if you don't burn," and (with respect to lotions not having at least an SPF value of 2) that "this product does not contain a sunscreen and does not protect against sunburn."[86]

Many disclaimers found in commercial messages, however, are offered voluntarily by the individual advertiser, with no direct input from the FTC or any other regulatory body. As a practical matter, marketers know that consumers are often unable to make sense of such disclaimers, especially in TV ads, since they flash on the screen too quickly and in print far too small to read.[87]

---

86. *California Suncare*, 1997 F.T.C. LEXIS 24 (1997).

87. Paul Farhi, "The Big Business of Small Type," *Washington Post*, March 6, 2000, C4; Darrel D. Muehling and Richard H. Kolbe, "Fine Print in Television Advertising: Views from the Top," 26 *Journal of Advertising* 1 (1997); "Seeing Is Believing: False Advertising Should Be Investigated by

In rare circumstances, an advertiser will be required to insert specific language into future advertising to undo a long history of past deceptions. Such **corrective advertising** has been required by the FTC only twice since its creation. The first case involved Warner-Lambert Company, makers of Listerine mouthwash, which had for many years suggested in its advertisements that the product could prevent the common cold. In 1975 the FTC ordered the company to insert into its next $10 million worth of advertising the admission that the mouthwash "will not help prevent colds or sore throats." The commission also wanted the company to precede that admission with the words "contrary to prior advertising"—thus forcing Warner-Lambert to explicitly admit that it had lied in the past—but the federal appellate court held that this latter language was unnecessarily punitive.[88] When the corrective ads eventually ran on TV, Warner-Lambert cleverly deemphasized the forced disclaimer by making it the dependent clause in a compound sentence, thus turning a negative into a positive: "Although Listerine will not help prevent colds or sore throats or lessen their severity, it kills germs on contact, the germs that can cause bad breath."[89]

In May 1999, the FTC voted to require that the manufacturer of Doan's pills, which the commissioners felt had implied falsely for many years that their product was superior to other analgesics for the relief of back pain, insert in its next $8 million of advertising a candid admission that there is no such evidence. The ruling was a vehicle for the commission to assert that corrective advertising is an appropriate remedy whenever prior advertising has "substantially created or reinforced a misbelief, and the misbelief is likely to linger into the future."[90]

The commission need not wait until a specific company's advertising campaign comes to its attention. Often the agency acts prospectively, offering general guidelines concerning advertising of particular products or within a particular industry. Such **industry guides**, as they are called, offer highly specific instructions concerning the proper use of product claims and may have relevance for manufacturers of many kinds of products rather than just one. In 1998, for example, the commission issued a lengthy policy statement explaining when products may legitimately be marketed as "recyclable" or "made from recycled materials."[91] A related kind of prospective action is the **trade regulation rule**, which looks very much like an industry guide but carries the force of law. The commission is therefore required to follow elaborate public notice procedures in advance of issuing such rules. In 2006 the commission began the elaborate process of creating such a rule governing the relationship between corpora-

Federal Trade Commission, but Some Ads Still Run with Only Small Changes and May Still Mislead Consumers," *Dateline NBC* (NBC Transcripts), November 16, 1997.

88. *Warner-Lambert Co. v. FTC*, 562 F.2d 749 (D.C. Cir. 1977).

89. "Turning Warner-Lambert into a Marketing Conglomerate," *Business Week*, March 5, 1979, 60.

90. *In re Novartis Corporation and Novartis Consumer Health, Inc.*, 1999 F.T.C. LEXIS 63 (1999).

91. Guides for the Use of Environmental Marketing Claims, 16 C.F.R. §§ 260.1–260.8 (1998).

tions and their franchisees.[92] (McDonald's is probably the nation's best-known franchise. The home corporation does not own each and every restaurant; rather, individual restaurant owners have a contract with McDonald's to buy the company's foodstuffs and process them in approved ways for sale, while the owners then benefit from the value of the trademark and the huge worldwide advertising and marketing supporting that trademark.) The rule would establish that a corporation disclose to potential franchisees (who typically have to invest a few hundred or a few thousand dollars upfront) matters such as the business background of its leadership and their litigation and bankruptcy histories; statistical analyses of existing franchised and company-owned outlets; the names and addresses of at least ten purchasers nearest the prospective buyer; and audited financial statements.

The Lanham Act: Suits by Competitors and Consumers

The FTC investigates what it wishes and passes on any issue for which it does not have sufficient resources or the enthusiasm to pursue. Bringing a claim of deceptive advertising to the attention of the commission, however, is not the only remedy available to aggrieved parties. The federal Lanham Act, adopted in 1946 and initially designed to protect against trademark infringements, also includes prohibitions against

---

THINGS TO REMEMBER

The Federal Trade Commission

- When created in 1914, the commission was only able to protect competing companies from each other's excesses; today the FTC is also empowered to protect consumers from unfair and deceptive practices.
- To determine if an advertisement is deceptive, the commission first performs a textual analysis of the ad, then determines whether a reasonable consumer is likely to be misled, and finally decides whether any such deception would be material to the purchasing decision.
- Deceptiveness can be explicit or implicit; it can appear in text or in visual demonstrations.
- Remedies available to the FTC include the consent order (whereby the FTC staff itself typically requires, at a bare minimum, that the offending company cease making a particular claim that the commission has decided is deceptive), the cease and desist order (issued by an administrative law judge after a full hearing), and a demand that the advertiser engage in affirmative disclosures or corrective advertising in future commercial messages.
- The commission can also issue industry guides and trade regulation rules, both of which put companies on notice about the kinds of claims the FTC staff is likely to find deceptive.

---

92. Business Opportunity Rule, 71 Fed. Reg. 19,054 (April 12, 2006).

deceptive advertising. Section 43(a) of the act forbids advertisers to "misrepresent the nature, characteristics, qualities, or geographic origin of [their] or another person's goods, services, or commercial activities."[93] Perhaps the section's most important feature is that it allows "any person who believes that he or she is or is likely to be damaged" by the misrepresentation to sue. Certainly this means that competing companies may bring suit. In some jurisdictions the courts have interpreted the act to give individual consumers a right to sue as well. Consumers rarely litigate under the Lanham Act, however. Indeed, they rarely take advantage of state or common-law remedies against deceptive advertising, because the harm they might be able to prove generally is not large enough to justify the expense of hiring an attorney.[94]

Perhaps the most frequent category of Lanham Act advertising claims concern comparative advertising, in which one company's commercials mention and criticize the competition by name. Will you get the best value on your cell phone from Verizon, Sprint, or Cingular? Faster and more reliable delivery service from UPS, FedEx, or DHL? It would be hard to find a definitive answer by observing the companies' multimillion-dollar national advertising campaigns. All one learns from the ads is that corporations vying for consumers' dollars are not at all shy about naming or (visually alluding to) and criticizing their competitors.

Sometimes the named competitor is an entire product line. The maker of Listerine was sued under the Lanham Act in 2005 by a company that makes dental floss, not because Pfizer's ads for the leading mouthwash criticized that company by name, but because Pfizer claimed swirling and gargling its product is "is as effective as floss in fighting plaque and gingivitis." After determining that the claim was false, federal district judge Denny Chin enjoined Pfizer from continuing to make such a claim. One result of

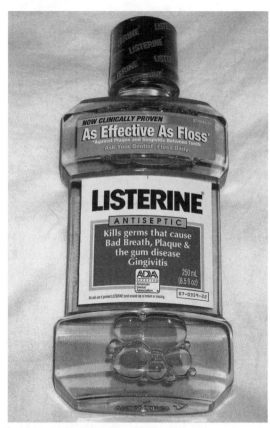

As a result of a suit brought under the Lanham Act, you will no longer see this label's claim about flossing.

---

93. *Groden v. Random House*, 61 F.3d 1045, 1051 (2d Cir. 1995). Section 43(a) of the Lanham Act is codified at 15 U.S.C. § 1125(a) (2000).

94. Lee Goldman, "The World's Best Article on Competitor Suits for False Advertising," 45 *Florida Law Review* 487, 505 (1993).

THINGS TO REMEMBER

The Lanham Act

- Created in 1946, the act permits a company to sue a competitor for deceptive advertising.
- A successful suit can result in forfeiture of profits attributable to the deception, damages, court costs, attorneys' fees, and compelled corrective advertising.

the suit was that Pfizer spent a few million dollars sending folks to drug stores and other outlets nationwide to remove the "as effective as floss" labels from bottles.

Lanham Act suits can result in an injunction against the defendant company's ads. Damage awards can also be made and can include the defendant's full profits attributable to the deception, the plaintiff's damages (such as lost market share), and court costs. In especially egregious cases the award can be triple the actual amount of damages and can include attorneys' fees. Corrective advertising can be ordered as well.

Industry Self-Regulation

Companies that think their competitors are engaged in deceptive advertising campaigns but that wish to avoid the costs and long delays inherent in litigation and governmental intervention may instead choose to bring a complaint to the National Advertising Division (NAD). The NAD is a self-regulatory system created by major advertising associations and the Council of Better Business Bureaus in 1971 to hear such complaints. Comparative advertising cases have always been a large part of the NAD's docket.

The procedure for bringing an NAD complaint is in some ways very similar to that of going to court. After the complaint is filed, an investigation ensues, and a process like pretrial discovery takes place. The NAD's inquiry will generally be limited to determining whether the company whose advertising is the target of the complaint can offer sufficient substantiation of the claims made in the advertisement. If the NAD determines that the ad lacks substantiation, it will request that the campaign be stopped or changed. For example, in 2006 the NAD requested that the maker of HeadOn stop claiming that the product provided "fast, safe, effective" headache relief. Thus the next wave of TV spots, which have frequently been parodied, say only "HeadOn—Apply directly to the forehead" (and do not give any indication *why* one should do so).[95]

---

95. Theresa Howard, "Headache Commercial Hits Parody Circuit, Well, 'Head-On,'" *USA Today*, July 31, 2006, 1B.

This quasi "cease and desist order" is the only remedy available to those filing a complaint with the NAD. There are no money damages to be awarded, no attorneys' fees, no court costs. Of course, because the NAD regularly publishes the results of its hearings in periodicals such as the *Wall Street Journal* and *Advertising Age*, adverse publicity must also be considered a remedy inherent in this self-regulatory process. If either party is dissatisfied with the ruling, it can appeal to the next and final level of decision making, the five-member National Advertising Review Board (NARB). This is a relatively infrequent occurrence. If a company refuses to adhere to an NAD or NARB ruling, these industry self-regulation groups may choose to turn the matter over to the FTC for possible investigation.

Compared with litigation or waiting for ultimate FTC action, the NAD/NARB process is timely, informal, and relatively inexpensive. Advertisers also often prefer to use this procedure because the decision makers are all experts in the fields of advertising and marketing. The industry self-regulatory procedure is not a panacea, however. The NAD restricts its inquiries to national advertising campaigns and reserves the right to refuse to hear any complaint that does not raise issues of public interest. That one company is losing market share to another is usually insufficient to trigger an investigation.

Regulation of Political Campaign Advertising

Not all advertising by corporate America is designed to sell a particular product or service. Exxon Mobil's frequent *New York Times* "advertorials," through which the company expresses its opinion on various political issues—not all directly related to the oil industry—are studied in university business schools and public relations programs nationwide. It is perfectly legal for corporations to use the advertising space or time they pay for to participate in the nation's political dialogue. Some legal restrictions apply, however, when the focus of the speech is on a particular election, whether on behalf of a candidate or of a public referendum issue. Before discussing those legal

THINGS TO REMEMBER

Industry Self-Regulation

- The National Advertising Division was created in 1971 to provide a forum to address complaints about competitors' allegedly deceptive national advertising campaigns.
- The NAD can request that an offending advertiser cease and desist and publishes its findings in media outlets that reach the advertising community, as well as the general public.

restrictions, three preliminary points need to be made about the limited scope of that discussion. First, we need to understand that there is a body of case law governing political campaign advertising that applies only to television and radio, largely as a result of specific provisions of the legislation that set up the Federal Communications Commission. We postpone a discussion of that case law until chapter 12, which deals with content regulations of the broadcast media. Second, although there is also a body of case law based on the Federal Election Campaign Act (and parallel state laws) that addresses the issue of limitations on financial *contributions* to political campaigns[96]—as well as cases dealing with contributions to committees set up to work for or against referendum proposals[97]—that area of law is beyond the scope of this book. After all, even though candidates do spend a high proportion of contributions on political advertising, they might also spend donations on travel expenses or on any number of other things not directly related to communication. Suffice it to say that in general there are far more restrictions on contributions to political campaigns than on independent expenditures in support of those campaigns.

At least one Supreme Court decision in this area deserves mention because it dealt directly with the timing and structure of political campaign messages. In *McConnell v. Federal Election Commission*, the Court upheld much of the Bipartisan Campaign Reform Act of 2002, popularly known as the McCain-Feingold campaign finance law.[98] Two of the provisions that the Court upheld are related directly to the act of communication: (1) the law requires that candidates who wish to qualify for the lowest ad rates from broadcasters include in their ads a clear message indicating that the candidate approves of the communication—for example, "I'm Hillary Clinton, and I approved this ad"; and (2) the law forbids TV and radio stations from airing ads from special interest groups (i.e., from anyone other than candidates or parties themselves) within sixty days of an election (thirty days of a primary) if those ads mention the name of any candidate for federal office. Although the Supreme Court upheld this latter provision against a full-scale attack (suggesting, among other things, that the provision was "facially" unconstitutional, that is, unconstitutional in all instances), in a later ruling the justices said they were open to arguments from plaintiffs who might allege that the law was unconstitutional in its application to their specific ads.[99] In December 2006 just such an argument persuaded a special panel of federal judges that the law had been unconstitutionally applied to radio and TV ads run by Wisconsin Right to Life in the 2004 election cycle expressing disfavor with the Senate's likely filibuster of President Bush's judicial appointees. Although those ads used the name of Senator Russ Feingold, who was then running for reelection, they did so only in the context of suggesting to Wisconsin voters that they contact both their senators

---

96. *Nixon v. Shrink Missouri Government PAC*, 528 U.S. 377 (2000).

97. *Citizens Against Rent Control v. Berkeley*, 454 U.S. 290 (1981).

98. 540 U.S. 93 (2003).

99. *Wisconsin Right to Life v. Federal Election Commission*, 546 U.S. 410, 411–412 (2006).

(Feingold and Herb Kohl, who was not up for reelection in 2004) to "tell them to oppose the filibuster." Such ads were not aimed at affecting the upcoming election, a 2-1 majority of the lower court panel held.[100] The Supreme Court heard oral arguments on the case in February 2007, with a decision still pending as we were going to press.

The third preliminary matter to keep in mind is that the discussion of *corporate* expenditures in this section refers to monies taken directly from a company's treasury. Restrictions on such political expenditures have generally been upheld, but corporations and other entities are free to establish and solicit contributions for separate funds, often called political action committees (PACs), and to use such funds in the furtherance of political causes or candidates.[101]

---

100. *Wisconsin Right to Life v. Federal Election Commission*, 446 F. Supp. 2d 195 (D.D.C. 2006).

101. *McConnell v. Federal Election Commission*, 540 U.S. 93 (2003); *Federal Election Commission v. Akins*, 524 U.S. 11 (1998); *Colorado Republican Federal Campaign Committee v. Federal Election Commission*, 518 U.S. 604 (1996); *Federal Election Commission v. National Conservative Political Action Committee*, 470 U.S. 480 (1985); *Buckley v. Valeo*, 424 U.S. 1 (1976).

We focus now on the rights of corporations to pay (from their general treasuries) for advertising aimed at swaying public opinion concerning either upcoming referendum issues or the relative merits of competing political candidates. In general, the Supreme Court has been more deferential to governmental restrictions on expenditures related to candidacies than to citizen referenda. In part this is because of the fear that candidates, if successful, will be inappropriately beholden to the interests of corporations that have used their general funds to advertise on their behalf.

Approximately half the states permit some form of direct referendum, whereby citizens can circumvent their legislatures and create law themselves. State referenda have in recent years covered matters such as gay marriage, term limits, and the right to die. Several states embracing the referendum process enacted laws that prohibit corporations from spending money to try to influence the outcome of referenda. The Supreme Court ruled on such a statute in 1978, when the First National Bank of Boston wanted to buy newspaper ads opposing a referendum that would amend the state constitution to permit the creation of a graduated personal income tax in Massachusetts. The proposed ads would have violated a state law prohibiting corporate expenditures on referenda not directly related to the specific company's area of business. In overturning this state law, the Court focused primarily on the rights of the citizens to hear what the bank's officers had to say. Justice Powell wrote for the majority that information about a tax referendum is "indispensable to decision-making in a democracy" and that "the inherent worth of the speech in terms of its capacity for informing the public does not depend upon the identity of its source, whether corporation, association, union, or individual."[102] Nowhere did the Court suggest, however, that the right to free speech enjoyed by corporations would necessarily be equal to that enjoyed by the citizens themselves. If the state had successfully demonstrated that corporate speech was likely to dominate the referendum process and thus to jeopardize the integrity of the electoral process itself, the decision would have been a different one.

The Court has also on occasion ruled on the matter of corporate expenditures in the furtherance of particular candidates for elected office. In a 1986 decision, the Court held that a portion of the Federal Election Campaign Act prohibiting expenditures "in connection with" (supporting or opposing) any candidate for federal office was unconstitutional as applied to Massachusetts Citizens for Life (MCFL). In advance of the September 1978 primary elections, MCFL had spent approximately $10,000 to distribute over 100,000 copies of a special edition of its newsletter. The thrust of the group's message is apparent from the newsletter's front-page headline— "Everything You Need to Know to Vote Pro-life." The newsletter included a coupon intended to be clipped and taken to the polls to remind voters of the names of all of the pro-life candidates.

Writing for the majority, Justice Brennan allowed that the Federal Election Cam-

---

102. *First National Bank of Boston v. Bellotti*, 435 U.S. 765, 776 (1978).

paign Act, as applied to ordinary for-profit companies using their general funds in support of candidates, furthered the compelling state interest of protecting the electoral process from corporations' aggregated wealth, especially since most people who invest in corporations do so to make money, not to have their investments used for political purposes. Such a government interest is greatly diminished or absent, Brennan concluded, when the expenditures are made by organizations such as MCFL, which are more similar to voluntary political associations than they are to business firms. How much money groups such as MCFL have on hand to pay for political speech is a direct reflection of the popular support enjoyed by the committee's positions. By contrast, the resources available in the coffers of for-profit corporations is a function only of how many widgets the company sells. The main reason the act was held unconstitutional as applied to MCFL, then, was that those who contributed to the pro-life group clearly knew that their money would be used for very specific political ends.[103]

Even though such politically oriented nonprofit groups may spend money to educate voters, the groups may still be covered by restrictions on their own direct contributions to candidates. In 2003 the Supreme Court ruled that the Federal Election Campaign Act applied to North Carolina Right to Life, prohibiting the group from actually contributing to individual political campaigns.[104]

A slightly different kind of corporate entity was involved in *Austin v. Michigan Chamber of Commerce*, a 1990 case in which the Supreme Court upheld a state law prohibiting corporate expenditures on behalf of candidates. At first blush one would think that the Chamber of Commerce would be treated the same as MCFL: both are nonprofit corporations, and both seem to have predictable political agenda such that their financial supporters would be on notice about the kinds of causes espoused by the groups. The Supreme Court, however, concluded that the Michigan statute could be constitutionally applied to the Chamber of Commerce, thus preventing the group from buying newspaper advertisements in support of a candidate for state office. Whereas MCFL "was formed for the express purpose of promoting political ideas," the Michigan Chamber of Commerce's bylaws "set forth more varied purposes, several of which are not inherently political."[105]

The Court emphasized also that there were no persons whose association with MCFL could be analogized to that of a shareholder to a corporation. Such a relationship creates an "economic disincentive for disassociating" with a company (i.e., for selling one's holdings) if one "disagree[s] with its political activity." Members of the Chamber of Commerce, although not shareholders as such, would nonetheless be reluctant to end their membership in the organization, even if the group did support causes or candidates with which they disagreed. The resultant loss of ties with the

103. *Federal Election Commission v. Massachusetts Citizens for Life*, 479 U.S. 238 (1986).
104. *Federal Election Commission v. Beaumont*, 539 U.S. 146 (2003).
105. *Austin v. Michigan Chamber of Commerce*, 494 U.S. 652, 662 (1990).

THINGS TO REMEMBER

Regulation of Corporate Expenditures on Political Advertising

- There are generally far more restrictions on contributions to candidates' campaigns than on independent expenditures in support of candidates or issues.
- Corporations are generally free to spend their own monies on advertising concerning upcoming citizen initiative (referendum) issues.
- Corporations are less free to spend their own monies on advertising for or against specific candidates for office, unless such corporations function more like political associations.
- The Supreme Court has focused in this area of law on whether contributors to the corporate general funds would expect their monies to be used to support candidates and whether the contributors might be reluctant to disassociate themselves from a corporation espousing political views with which they themselves disagree.
- Special interest groups' broadcast ads mentioning specific candidates may be prohibited very close to elections.
- Broadcast ads placed by candidates themselves must include the candidate's name and an indication that the candidate approved of the ad.

business community, as well as forfeiting numerous other membership services provided by the Chamber of Commerce, would be too high a price to pay.

The Chamber of Commerce was also different from the MCFL in that its membership consisted primarily of for-profit businesses; approximately three-quarters of its eight thousand or so members fit into this category. Thus, to the extent that the Michigan Campaign Finance Act was designed to diminish the ability of *corporations* to influence the political process, the Chamber of Commerce was an appropriate target of the legislation, in that it is simply a large group of corporations. MCFL, by contrast, was funded entirely by individual donors, accepting no corporate contributions.

Chapter Summary

The Supreme Court currently uses the *Central Hudson* test to determine whether a regulation on commercial speech is consistent with the First Amendment. The test requires that we ask whether the product or service being offered is itself legal or the advertisement deceptive, whether the state has a legitimate interest in this regulation, and whether there is a reasonable fit between the regulation and the interest.

The Court has on a number of occasions dealt with the issue of advertising by attorneys and other professionals. In general, the rule seems to be that we should focus on the first *Central Hudson* question: is the advertisement inherently deceptive? If not, the Court has been very reluctant to allow much state intrusion on the content of communications between professionals and potential clients.

Although individual states and even municipalities are in the business of regulating advertising, by far the most active agent in this area is the Federal Trade Commission. To determine if a given ad is deceptive, the commission first examines the text of the ad and then considers whether a reasonable consumer would likely be deceived and whether any such deception would be material to the purchasing decision. The majority of commission investigations go no further than the consent order stage, at which time the offending company agrees to meet certain requests by the commission staff, such as to stop making a deceptive claim. The FTC also is empowered to require advertisers to insert specific wording into future ads. Companies can also sue competitors for deceptive advertising under the federal Lanham Act.

As a general rule, corporations are free to engage in political speech but are regulated when they seek to comment on particular upcoming elections. Corporations generally have more freedom to spend monies from their own treasuries to comment on upcoming referendum issues than to comment on competing candidates for office.

Chapter 11

SEXUALLY ORIENTED SPEECH

I n an episode of the HBO series *Curb Your Enthusiasm*, Larry and Jeff are planning to view the racy *College Girls Gone Wild* video together, an event they refer to as their private "*Auto Focus* party." The reference is to the 2002 biographical film about Bob Crane, star of the long-running TV series *Hogan's Heroes* (and as true TV sitcom trivia junkies may know, a supporting actor a few years earlier on *The Donna Reed Show*). The film depicts Crane's pathological friendship with the tech-savvy John Carpenter, who set up elaborate video systems so he and Crane could document their various sexual exploits with starstruck young women. The film posits that Carpenter bludgeoned Crane to death because VCRs and video camcorders had become so user-friendly and ubiquitous that the TV personality no longer needed Carpenter to facilitate his debauchery.

Americans are often described as oversexed. The pornographic film industry makes much more money than its mainstream Hollywood counterpart.[1] Candid and highly emotional discussions of every imaginable sexual variation and fetish are the mainstay of daytime TV talk shows. The communication technologies we embrace most swiftly are those—such as self-developing film, VCRs and camcorders of course, and more recently, the Internet—that allow an indulgence in sexual imagery.

Somewhat paradoxically, we Americans are also seen as highly puritanical in our approach to sexual matters. Award-winning European film directors often produce a toned-down print for distribution in the U.S. market to obtain an "R" rather than the dreaded "NC-17" rating. Emotional debates in the United States over what to tell youngsters about sex and morality regularly consume the time and energy of school boards nationwide.

In the 1940s the U.S. Supreme Court, in one of the most often-quoted passages in

---

1. Douglas Brown, "Pornopolis," *Denver Post*, July 9, 2006, L1.

the history of First Amendment jurisprudence, placed "the lewd and obscene" at the head of its list of categories of speech deemed "of such slight social value" as to be outside the Constitution's protection.[2] Sexual speech that meets the current legal definition of **obscenity** can be criminalized. Even nonobscene sexual expression can be regulated in several ways. It can be banned from TV and radio[3] or zoned into certain restricted parts of town.[4] Communicators of sexual messages might not be permitted to use their chosen mode of presentation; the state can insist, for example, that they keep their clothes on.[5]

Thinking about the Obscene

Although this chapter is primarily about *obscenity* and the law, a few related constructs that often produce confusion need to be defined first. The word **pornography** refers to any printed text, drawing, picture, film, or other communication in which the explicit depiction or description of sexual conduct occurs. Although journalists, scholars, and even lawyers and judges often use the word to refer to sexual materials, it has no *legal* definition, nor does its publication carry any legal penalty.

When the word *child* is added however, the phrase **child pornography** results, and it does have legal definitions under both federal[6] and state[7] law. A later section of this chapter is devoted to the law regarding child pornography. For now suffice it to say that depictions of real children in sexually provocative poses, even if partially clothed, are generally what the courts have in mind when they adjudicate child pornography cases.

Indecency is a word used to describe a wider set of sexual materials that meet some but not all of the components of the Supreme Court's current definition of obscenity.[8] Although it would be unconstitutional for the government to ban writings that are merely indecent, such materials may not generally be broadcast during daytime hours on radio and TV stations that use the public airwaves. **Profanity** has been defined by courts as "vulgar, irreverent, or coarse language, . . . personally reviling epithets . . . so grossly offensive as to amount to a nuisance."[9] Because the law regarding indecent and profane speech is restricted to the broadcast media, we postpone a more extensive discussion of these matters until chapter 12, which deals with regulation of the elec-

---

2. *Chaplinsky v. New Hampshire*, 315 U.S. 568, 571 (1942).

3. *FCC v. Pacifica Foundation*, 438 U.S. 726 (1978).

4. *Young v. American Mini Theatres*, 427 U.S. 50 (1976).

5. *City of Erie v. Pap's A.M.*, 529 U.S. 277 (2000); *Barnes v. Glen Theatre*, 501 U.S. 560 (1991).

6. *United States v. Frabizio*, 2006 U.S. App. LEXIS 20931 (1st Cir. 2006).

7. *Osborne v. Ohio*, 495 U.S. 103 (1990).

8. *FCC v. Pacifica Foundation*, 438 U.S. 726 (1978).

9. *In re Complaints against Various Broadcast Licensees Regarding Their Airing of the "Golden Globe Awards" Program*, 199 F.C.C. Rcd. 4975 (2004).

tronic media. As we see in chapter 13, the government has also attempted, mostly unsuccessfully, to outlaw indecent speech on the Internet.

What does it mean to be obscene? In everyday parlance, the word can attach to anything deemed outrageous or offensive, from the high price of funerals to the exorbitant salaries paid to professional sports figures. For most of us, the label is not limited to matters of sex. The philosopher Harry Clor has suggested that the term *obscenity* refers to making offensively public that which should be private, which is consistent with some etymologists' belief that the word *obscene* is derived from Greek words referring to that which happens "off the stage."[10] Certainly the notion of obscenity as graphic depictions of others' sexual behavior would fit within this definition, but there can also be obscene depictions of such physical acts as eating, scratching, grooming, or picking one's nose while driving. For Clor, the key is that the persons depicted are degraded by having their humanity reduced to animalistic behaviors. If "dining" is too genteel a word to describe the way you might attack that lamb chop when no one is watching, you can surely understand Clor's point.[11]

Development of Obscenity Law in America

There are no recorded prosecutions in the United States for obscenity until 1815, when a Philadelphia merchant named Jesse Sharpless was accused of exhibiting "a certain lewd, wicked, scandalous, infamous . . . painting" depicting a man and woman in "an obscene, imprudent, and indecent posture."[12] Six years later, in the first U.S. obscenity case involving the printed word, Peter Holmes was prosecuted for publishing an edition of John Cleland's famous *Memoirs of a Woman of Pleasure*, more com-

---

THINGS TO REMEMBER

Thinking about Obscenity

- Under the law, obscenity is viewed as something other than speech, thus wholly outside the First Amendment's protection.
- In everyday conversation, obscenity seems to refer to anything outrageously offensive, not narrowly to sexual matters.

---

10. Michel W. Pharand, "Sexual and Cultural Theatrical Dissidence," 49 *English Literature in Translation* 201 (2006).

11. Harry M. Clor, *Obscenity and Public Morality: Censorship in a Liberal* Society (Chicago: University of Chicago Press, 1966), 225.

12. *Commonwealth v. Sharpless*, 2 Serg. & Rawle 91 (Pa. 1815).

monly known as *Fanny Hill.*[13] The book had first appeared in England in 1748 with no government opposition.

Both the Sharpless and Holmes prosecutions were made under the common law, because there were no applicable obscenity statutes on the books at the time. The first such written law did not show up until 1821, in Vermont. Connecticut and Massachusetts enacted obscenity laws in the 1830s, and several other states followed suit in the years leading up to the Civil War. These laws typically criminalized not only the publication of obscene materials but also the use of profane language and such offenses as public lewdness and indecent exposure.

The first federal obscenity statute did not appear until 1842, in the form of amendments to the customs laws that forbade the importing of obscene materials. In 1865, it first became illegal to send obscene works through the U.S. mails; then the Comstock Act, enacted in 1873, more explicitly gave post office officials the authority to open and confiscate such disapproved mailings.

The *Hicklin* Rule

For many decades, U.S. obscenity law was modeled after a British case from the 1860s called *Regina v. Hicklin*, which involved a defendant who had distributed a pamphlet highly critical of the Catholic Church.[14] In a famous bit of dicta accompanying a decision that upheld the defendant's obscenity conviction, Lord Chief Justice Cockburn established two important points of law that together constitute the "*Hicklin* rule." The first point was that an entire work may be found obscene even if only relatively small, isolated passages are punishable. The second point concerned a work's possible effects on its audience. As Lord Chief Justice Cockburn put it, obscenity would be judged by the work's potential "to deprave and corrupt *those whose minds are open to such immoral influences* and into whose hands a publication of this sort may fall" (emphasis added). In the nonsexual arena, this would be akin to prosecuting director Martin Scorsese because his award-winning film *Taxi Driver* seemed to be the impetus for John Hinckley, in his deranged mind, to conclude that killing President Reagan would make actress Jodie Foster fall in love with him.

The Supreme Court first stated its approval of the *Hicklin* rule—although it did not mention the case by name—in *Rosen v. United States*, decided in 1896.[15] Lew Rosen's offense was having sent through the mails pictures of women whose clothing consisted of a kind of opaque but removable substance—similar to that used today on "scratch and win" lottery tickets—such that the models' covering could be "erased with a piece of bread." Writing for the Court's majority, Justice Harlan expressed

---

13. *Commonwealth v. Holmes*, 17 Mass. 336 (1821).

14. 3 Q.B. 360 (1868). Some U.S. cases embracing the *Hicklin* rule include *United States v. Bennett*, 24 F. Cas. 1093 (C.C.S.D.N.Y. 1879); *United States v. Clarke*, 38 F. 732 (E.D. Mo. 1889); and *United States v. Chesman*, 19 F. 497 (C.C.E.D. Mo. 1881).

15. 161 U.S. 29 (1896).

approval for the judge's instructions to the jury, which encouraged them to consider whether the pictures would "suggest or convey lewd thoughts and lascivious thoughts to the young and inexperienced."

U.S. obscenity law in the first half of the twentieth century was characterized by conflicting trends, although overall by a tendency toward liberalization. On one hand, prosecutors were zealous in their pursuit of sexual materials and were often not concerned whether their targets were "dirt for dirt's sake" or literary classics. Thus, such noteworthy books as Radclyffe Hall's *The Well of Loneliness*,[16] Theodore Dreiser's *An American Tragedy*,[17] and Henry Miller's *Tropic of Cancer* and *Tropic of Capricorn*[18] were all successfully prosecuted. Yet other courts began slowly to reject aspects of the *Hicklin* rule and to set the stage for the Supreme Court's ultimate repudiation, in 1957, of the British precedent. Lower courts, both state and federal, began to take steps such as taking into account a book's literary merits (and often accepting expert testimony on the matter), viewing works in their entirety (instead of condemning them for isolated passages), and considering a work's likely effect on a "reasonable" or "average" person or on the author's intended audience (rather than on the "depraved" and "susceptible" consumers envisioned in the *Hicklin* rule). Although this more liberal pattern of cases was by no means consistent across jurisdictions or over time, it did permit the Supreme Court to make it seem as if it were saying nothing dramatic or unprecedented when it articulated a new constitutional framework for obscenity.

THINGS TO REMEMBER

Early Obscenity Law in the United States

- The first state obscenity law (in Vermont) was passed in 1821; the first federal obscenity law (prohibiting the importation of obscene materials from overseas) was enacted in 1842.
- For many years U.S. courts embraced the British *Hicklin* rule, which held that a work's obscenity could be determined based on its most salacious passages' potential effects on particularly susceptible consumers.
- In the first half of the twentieth century, many prosecutors zealously brought obscenity charges cases against even accepted literary works; there was also a contradictory trend in other courts toward slowly rejecting the *Hicklin* rule and making it more difficult for the government to obtain convictions.

---

16. *People v. Friede*, 233 N.Y.S. 565 (1929).

17. *Commonwealth v. Friede*, 171 N.E. 472 (Mass. 1930).

18. *United States v. Two Obscene Books*, 99 F. Supp. 760 (N.D. Cal. 1951), *aff'd sub nom. Besig v. United States*, 208 F.2d 142 (9th Cir. 1953).

The *Roth* Test

Samuel Roth was a New York–based entrepreneur convicted of mailing obscene books and periodicals with titles such as *Wanton by Night* and *Wild Passion*. Unlike most convicted pornographers, Roth appealed his conviction on straightforward constitutional grounds, arguing that the Comstock Act violated the First Amendment. The gist of Roth's argument was that sexual communication should be treated no differently from other categories of messages, such as political or religious speech, that the government should have a right to prohibit such speech only if a "clear and present danger" of a "substantive evil" was on the horizon. Traditionally, obscenity laws had been predicated on a felt need to avoid the encouragement of lustful thoughts by the consumers of pornography. Roth argued that this is not a legitimate state's interest, that Americans have a right to feel sexy.[19]

Here, Roth's argument was a rearticulation of traditional civil libertarian theory, the notion that some categories of personal conduct are plainly not the government's business. In his opinion for the Court, Justice Brennan rejected Roth's invitation to bring obscene writings within the protection of the Constitution, whether on First Amendment or privacy grounds. Rather, the *Roth* decision says that obscenity is "utterly without redeeming social importance," and therefore "not within the area of constitutionally protected speech or press."[20] Nonetheless, even obscene works may enjoy other kinds of legal protection. For example, you may not sell bootleg copies of obscene films without running afoul of copyright laws.[21] Similarly, the fact that there is clearly a market for sanitized versions of popular Hollywood films does not give you the right to edit out the scenes that might be deemed offensive, then sell the edited versions to the squeamish.[22]

The argument that sexual communications should be wholly beyond the reach of the law reemerged in 2005, when a federal judge in Pennsylvania applied what he saw as the Supreme Court's logic in overturning sodomy laws[23] to the issue of whether obscenity laws are constitutional. Judge Lancaster read the Supreme Court's sodomy decision as saying that the government may not criminalize conduct merely because the behavior offends a "moral code"; since this was the only reason the judge could intuit for continued enforcement of obscenity laws, he struck down much of federal obscenity law. Judge Lancaster was overturned a few months later, however.[24]

---

19. Some argued that the state's interest was really to prevent rape or other criminal behaviors. But Roth countered that there was no evidence that reading pornographic books and magazines causes an increase in such antisocial conduct.

20. *Roth v. United States*, 354 U.S. 476, 484, 485 (1957). Mr. Roth's case was decided together with another case, *Alberts v. California*, in which David Alberts appealed his conviction for violating a state obscenity statute.

21. *Nova Productions v. Kisma Video*, 2004 U.S. Dist. LEXIS 24171 (S.D.N.Y. 2004).

22. *Clean Flicks of Colorado v. Soderbergh*, 433 F. Supp. 2d 1236 (D. Colo. 2006).

23. *Lawrence v. Texas*, 539 U.S. 558 (2003).

24. *United States v. Extreme Associates*, 352 F. Supp. 2d 578 (W.D. Pa. 2005), *rev'd*, 431 F.3d 150 (3d Cir. 2005).

Justice Brennan's *Roth* opinion, even while upholding the convictions, makes clear that sex and obscenity are not the same thing. "The portrayal of sex . . . in art, literature and scientific works" should not incur the wrath of the law, he wrote. To be obscene, a work must be aimed at readers' "prurient interest"—an "itching," a "lascivious longing," or "a shameful or morbid interest in nudity, sex, or excretion."[25]

Despite Justice Brennan's words, we do often act as if anything sexual, or even anything unclothed, is pornographic. In the fall of 2006, for example, a Texas schoolteacher was suspended after taking her students to the Dallas Museum of Art, apparently because one parent complained that the children had seen "nude" statues and paintings.[26]

Justice Brennan's opinion moved next to a more explicit repudiation of the *Hicklin* rule. While some courts had embraced that "early standard," which "allowed material to be judged merely by the effect of an isolated excerpt upon particularly susceptible persons," the Court now preferred the following test for defining obscenity: "whether to the average person, applying contemporary community standards, the dominant theme of the material taken as a whole appeals to prurient interest."[27]

It was not clear what the Court meant by the phrase "contemporary community standards." Certainly "contemporary" suggests an awareness that societal values and sexual mores change over time. But what size "community" did the Court intend? Is the entire United States one large community? Would each state set its own standard? Or could that which is obscene in one county be accepted for distribution in a contiguous county? The Court grappled with this question in 1964, in *Jacobellis v. Ohio*, but could not produce a majority opinion.[28] The plurality opinion argued for a nationwide standard. (This case was also the vehicle for Justice Stewart, in a separate concur-

---

THINGS TO REMEMBER

The *Roth* Test

- In *Roth v. United States* (1957), the Supreme Court explicitly rejected the *Hicklin* rule.
- The majority opinion provided these guidelines for determining whether a work is obscene:
  - The work must be judged as a whole.
  - It must appeal to the "prurient interest" in sex.
  - It is to be judged by "contemporary community standards."
  - The work's likely effect on the *average* community member must be considered.

---

25. *Roth*, 354 U.S. at 487 & n.20, 488.

26. Ralph Blumenthal, "Museum Field Trip Deemed Too Revealing," *New York Times*, September 30, 2006, A1.

27. *Roth*, 354 U.S. at 489.

28. 378 U.S. 184 (1964).

ring opinion, to issue his famous admission that, although he was unable to articulate a coherent definition of obscenity, "I know it when I see it!") The Court finally resolved the "*community* standard" issue in 1973, when it handed down a decision that altered the *Roth* test somewhat and produced the test for obscenity that, in slightly amended form, still governs today.

The *Miller* Test

The Supreme Court of 1973 was very different from the one that produced the *Roth* decision back in 1957. Only two justices who had participated in *Roth*—Douglas and Brennan—remained on the Court. Perhaps more important is that four new justices—Blackmun, Burger, Powell, and Rehnquist—had been appointed by President Nixon, whose disdain for permissive sexuality was well known. In 1970, when the Commission on Obscenity and Pornography, which had been appointed by President Johnson, issued a report calling for the repeal of virtually all laws against sexual communications, Nixon issued a statement in which he "categorically reject[ed]" the group's "morally bankrupt" conclusions. "So long as I am in the White House," he promised, "there will be no relaxation of the national effort to control and eliminate smut from our national life."

The Court accepted many obscenity cases for consideration in its 1972-1973 term and handed down eight of them in June 1973. By far the most important one was *Miller v. California*,[29] which represented the first time since 1957 that a majority of the Court would grapple with the actual definition of obscenity.

The factual situation was an unusual one. Most obscenity convictions involved the selling or mailing of materials to willing recipients, or at least to undercover police officers masquerading as such willing recipients. Here the defendant instead had mailed unsolicited brochures advertising books bearing titles such as *Intercourse* and *Sex Orgies Illustrated*. The brochure itself was not for the squeamish, consisting primarily of "pictures and drawings very explicitly depicting men and women in groups of two or more engaging in a variety of sexual activities, with genitals often prominently displayed." The prosecution commenced after a restaurant owner in Newport Beach opened the brochure (in the company of his mother) and complained to the police. The Supreme Court, by a 5-4 vote, upheld Miller's conviction.

Chief Justice Burger's majority opinion is a reminder that the Court, despite having heard dozens of obscenity cases in the interim, had been unable to agree about the definition of obscenity since the *Roth* formulation sixteen years earlier. Although the *Miller* decision does not provide a single comprehensive definition, it does give the individual states several important guidelines. Most fundamentally, the chief justice told the states that "the permissible scope" of their regulations must be limited to "works which depict or describe sexual conduct," and that the regulations themselves,

29. 413 U.S. 15 (1973).

whether in statutes or in judge-made common law, must "specifically define" what is prohibited. The First Amendment requires also that government regulations prohibit only "works which, taken as a whole, appeal to the prurient interest in sex, which portray sexual conduct in a patently offensive way, and which, taken as a whole, do not have serious literary, artistic, political, or scientific value."

Some features of the *Miller* test represent significant breaks with *Roth*. First is the added requirement that a work must be "patently offensive." Stanford University law professor Kathleen Sullivan has suggested that the dual requirements of appealing to the prurient interest *and* being patently offensive together mean only materials that both turn us on and gross us out can be found obscene.[30]

Another feature that was changed, or at least clarified, from the earlier *Roth* test is the nature of the "community" in the phrase "contemporary community standards." The *Roth* decision itself was silent on this point, but many courts since had assumed that a single nationwide standard was intended for the purposes of determining whether a work appealed to the prurient interest. The *Miller* jury, however, had been asked to apply *statewide* standards, and Chief Justice Burger agreed with this instruction, suggesting that a smaller "community" might also be invoked.

Asking jurors to apply a *local* community standard has important implications, depending in part on the technology involved. If a book or a magazine is found obscene in only a few venues in relatively conservative areas of the country, distribution can still proceed in the rest of the country. Suppose, though, that the work at issue is a film, distributed using direct broadcast satellite. The cost of maximizing the number of viewers who can see the film (and maximizing profits) while ensuring that potential viewers who live in parts of the country where the film has been judged obscene will not be able to access it can be large. In 1990, a New York–based film distributor called Home Dish Satellite was effectively put out of business by one successful obscenity prosecution in Alabama. The State of Alabama requested further that the company's executives be extradited from New York to stand trial, but Governor Mario Cuomo

30. Quoted in Jeffrey Rosen, "*Miller* Time," *New Republic*, October 1, 1990, 17.

refused to do so.[31] As we shall see in chapter 13, the whole notion of what constitutes a "community" has important implications too for companies marketing sexually oriented messages on the Internet.

Local communities' judgments must sometimes be kept in check by appellate review, however, as the Supreme Court made clear in its very next term after handing down *Miller*. The State of Georgia had ruled that the film *Carnal Knowledge*, starring Jack Nicholson, Art Garfunkel, Candice Bergen, and Ann-Margret was obscene. This story of two male college roommates' difficulties in relating to women (after years of marriage, Garfunkel's character wonders aloud if sex is "just not supposed to be fun anymore when you love her") made many critics' "best ten films of the year" lists, and resulted in an Academy Award nomination for Ann-Margret. The film did include brief bits of nudity. There were also several instances where the characters seemed to be engaging in sexual activity—notably in the final scene, where Nicholson's character can achieve orgasm only through a highly ritualized act of fellatio performed by a high-class call girl played by Rita Moreno—but all of these acts were only hinted at, with the camera focused elsewhere. The Supreme Court held that this film was plainly not obscene, that no reasonable jury could have found it patently offensive.[32]

Perhaps the *Miller* Court's most significant departure from the earlier *Roth* test was Chief Justice Burger's reference to the limiting of obscenity laws to works lacking *serious* value, whether literary, artistic, political, or scientific (the SLAPS test). States were now given far more leeway than before; the *Roth* test, you will recall, defined the obscene as that which lacks *any* redeeming value.

In a decision handed down in 1987, the Supreme Court clarified that jurors' adjudication of the "serious value" question—unlike the questions concerning whether a work is "patently offensive" and whether it appeals to the "prurient interest"—should be based on a national standard. Moreover, when determining whether a work boasts enough serious value to be protected from an obscenity charge, jurors should conjure up as best they can their image of what a "reasonable" person would say, rather than an "average" person.[33] This latter point may on its surface seem a bit insulting, as if the Court is suggesting that the "average" American is not very reasonable. It also makes an already confusing set of legal instructions even more so. In any event, the clear intent of the decision is in the direction of making obscenity convictions a bit more difficult to obtain against works of value.

Fine-Tuning the Legal Definition of Obscenity

The Supreme Court has offered additional guidelines for states trying to fashion constitutional obscenity statutes. Some of these guidelines can be culled from *Miller*

---

31. Sam Howe Verhovek, "Cuomo Turns Down Request to Extradite Cable Officials," *New York Times*, June 21, 1990, B4.

32. *Jenkins v. Georgia*, 418 U.S. 153 (1974).

33. *Pope v. Illinois*, 481 U.S. 497 (1987).

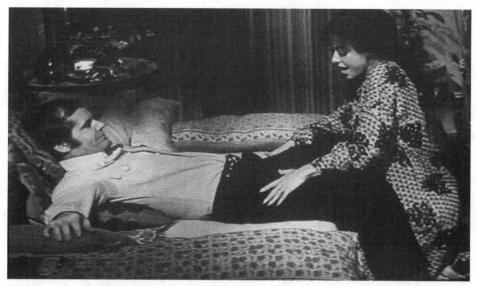

In part because the sexual activity in scenes such as this one between Jack Nicholson and Rita Moreno, playing a high-class prostitute, was only hinted at rather than depicted on-screen, the U.S. Supreme Court found that the film *Carnal Knowledge* was not "patently offensive" enough to be obscene.

THINGS TO REMEMBER

The *Miller* Test

- In *Miller v. California* (1973), the Supreme Court created a new test for obscenity, retaining some features and rejecting others from the earlier *Roth* test.
- Under the *Miller* test, a work is obscene if
  - the average person, applying contemporary community standards, would find that the work, taken as a whole, appeals to the prurient interest;
  - the work depicts or describes specified sexual conduct in a patently offensive manner; and
  - the work lacks serious literary, artistic, political, or scientific value.

---

itself, others from new interpretations of previous cases, and others still from cases decided in more recent years.

What Kind of Sexual Conduct?
Under *Miller*, obscenity prosecutions can succeed only against "patently offensive" works aimed at our "prurient" interests. Neither phrase is self-defining. Even while cautioning that "it is not our function to propose regulatory schemes for the states," that is in fact what the *Miller* majority

did. A constitutionally acceptable statute might be one, Burger wrote, that prohibits either "representations or descriptions of ultimate sexual acts, normal or perverted, actual or simulated," or "representations or descriptions of masturbation, excretory functions, and lewd exhibition of the genitals."[34] Not surprisingly, many states simply quote this language in their statutes.

The *Miller* Court also required that obscenity laws "specifically define" what was to be prohibited. A few years later, however, the Court made clear that whatever due process guarantees seemed to flow from such a requirement would not be strictly enforced. Defendants in *Ward v. Illinois* had been convicted for selling magazines that depicted sadomasochistic sexual practices.[35] By a vote of 5-4, the Court upheld Ward's conviction, even though the state law nowhere mentioned sadomasochistic practices. Justice Stevens's dissenting opinion lamented what he saw as the majority's having "abandon[ed] one of the cornerstones of the *Miller* test," the requirement that states put citizens on notice as to precisely what kinds of sexual expression would be criminalized.

Thematic Obscenity.   States may not use obscenity law to stifle debate *about* sexual matters. The leading case on this issue is from 1959, when the Supreme Court told the State of New York that it could not deny a distribution license for the showing of a film version of D. H. Lawrence's *Lady Chatterley's Lover*. One of the state's arguments had been that the film glorifies the commission of adultery, which is "contrary to the moral standards, the religious precepts, and the legal code of its citizenry." Writing for the Court, Justice Stewart chided the state for "misconceiving what the Constitution protects." The First Amendment "protects advocacy of the opinion that adultery may sometimes be proper," as well as all sorts of other views not necessarily shared by the majority of citizens.[36]

The doctrine of **thematic obscenity** established in the 1959 decision means that artistic works with a sexual theme or thesis cannot be the targets of government sanctions in this country unless actual sexual depictions in the films meet the *Miller* definition of obscenity. Martin Scorcese's 1988 film *The Last Temptation of Christ* posited a sexual relationship between Jesus and Mary Magdalene. Kevin Bacon's performance in the 2004 independent film *The Woodsman* offers a humanizing, almost heroic depiction of a pedophile. Both films were highly controversial. But neither could be held obscene by dint of their provocative themes.

The Privacy of the Home.   Georgia state police suspected Robert E. Stanley of being a small-time bookmaker and obtained a search warrant for his home. They did not find any helpful evidence on the gambling charge, but while looking through

---

34. *Miller v. California*, 413 U.S. 15, 25 (1973).
35. 431 U.S. 767 (1977).
36. *Kingsley International Pictures Corp. v. Regents*, 360 U.S. 684 (1959).

a desk drawer in an upstairs bedroom, they found three reels of film. Using Stanley's own film projector, they examined the films, which they concluded were obscene. Stanley was placed under arrest for possession of obscene materials, in violation of state law. The state obtained a conviction, which was upheld by the Georgia Supreme Court. The U.S. Supreme Court, however, unanimously overturned Stanley's conviction. Justice Marshall's opinion for the Court articulated a fusion of First and Fourth Amendment values, emphasizing that the government "has no business telling a man, sitting alone in his own house, what books he may read or what films he may watch."[37]

Some lower courts, citing *Stanley*'s emphasis on a right to receive information, reasoned that the right should have a life beyond one's own four walls. Thus, for example, one federal court ruled that obscenity laws could not reach the patrons (or the owner) of a movie theater showing the film *I Am Curious (Yellow)*, which the judges assumed to be obscene under the relevant local statute. "If Stanley has a constitutional right to view obscene films," the judges reasoned, it makes no sense that he can exercise that right only at the expense of a criminal prosecution against the theater owner, "the only logical source" of such films for most patrons.[38] Similarly, a federal court in California assumed that the Supreme Court's emphasis in *Stanley* on the right to own obscene films must include a right to receive them, and so struck down the federal statute against importation of such materials. The Supreme Court disagreed and reinstated the federal law.[39]

Another court used *Stanley* to strike down a federal law prohibiting the interstate transport of obscene materials. Writing for a 5-4 majority, however, Chief Justice Burger vacated the lower court ruling, rejecting the notion that "the right to possess obscene material in the privacy of the home . . . creates a correlative right to receive it [or] transport it."[40] The Supreme Court similarly vacated a lower court ruling that had cited *Stanley*'s logic in striking down a federal law permitting the U.S. Customs Service to seize obscene works at the border.[41] This line of cases led Justice Black to comment on what he saw as the illogic of construing *Stanley* too narrowly. "The right to read and view any literature and pictures at home is hollow indeed," Black lamented, "if it does not include a right to carry that material privately in one's luggage when entering the country."[42] Justice Douglas added, in another case, that he "fail[ed] to comprehend how the right to possession enunciated in *Stanley* has any meaning

---

37. *Stanley v. Georgia*, 394 U.S. 557, 565 (1969).

38. *Karalexis v. Byrne*, 306 F. Supp. 1363, 1366 (D. Mass. 1969).

39. *United States v. Thirty-Seven Photographs*, 309 F. Supp. 36 (C.D. Cal. 1970), *rev'd*, 402 U.S. 363 (1971).

40. *United States v. Orito*, 413 U.S. 139, 141 (1973).

41. *United States v. 12 200-Foot Reels of 8 MM Film*, 413 U.S. 123 (1973).

42. *United States v. Thirty-Seven Photographs*, 402 U.S. 363, 381 (1971) (Black, J., dissenting).

when States are allowed to outlaw the commercial transactions which give rise to such possession."[43]

Perhaps the death knell for broad interpretations of *Stanley* occurred in 1973, when, on the same day the Supreme Court produced the *Miller* test, it also handed down *Paris Adult Theatre I v. Slaton*, upholding the constitutionality of an obscenity prosecution against a pair of adult-movie-theater owners in Atlanta.[44] The theater owners argued that their patrons were consenting adults, each of whom would, under *Stanley*, have a right to view the same films at home that they saw at the theater. The entrance to the theater, which the Court described as "conventional" and "inoffensive," boasted signs saying, "Atlanta's Finest Mature Feature Films" and "Adult Theatre—You must be 21 and able to prove it. If viewing the nude body offends you, Please Do Not Enter." A 5-4 Court rejected the "consenting adults" defense and made clear that *Stanley* "was hardly more than a reaffirmation that 'a man's home is his castle,'" not the creation of a "zone of privacy that follows a distributor or a consumer of obscene materials wherever he goes."

It should also be noted that a parolee's freedom can be rescinded for having otherwise legal pornography in the privacy of his home. This was a lesson learned by convicted sex offender Christopher Farrell, who argued that conditioning his parole on his not possessing any "pornographic" material was both vague (what is pornography?) and overbroad (in that the construct clearly includes materials he would have a perfect right to own were he not on parole). The Third Circuit Court of Appeals disagreed in a 2006 decision that does not even mention the *Stanley* case.[45]

Variable Obscenity.   On occasion the Supreme Court has recognized that its definition of obscenity has to be adjusted or modified—sometimes making it stricter, sometimes making it more relaxed—depending on a pornographer's intended audience or the manner in which he advertises his wares. Collectively, such instances have come to be called the doctrine of **variable obscenity**.

There is a practical problem in using the views of an "average" member of a community as the standard for defining obscenity, as do both the *Roth* and *Miller* tests. Much of the typical adult bookstore's and movie outlet's wares are aimed not at the average consumer but at consumers with sexual interests that deviate from the statistical norm. Fetishes may run from leather to lace, from diapers to latex, and one will be able to find pornographic materials aimed at all of them and many more. To the hypothesized "average" citizen, such erotica might not appeal to the prurient interest at all. These more specialized images also may or may not be patently offensive to

43. *Carlson v. Minnesota*, 414 U.S. 953, 954 (1973) (Douglas, J., dissenting).

44. 413 U.S. 49 (1973). The "I" in the name of the case is not an indication that there is a later court decision by the same name, but rather that there were two theaters, side by side, the Paris Adult I and the Paris Adult II.

45. *Farrell v. Burke*, 449 F.3d 470 (2d Cir. 2006).

that same average person; they might instead simply confuse or amuse. How does one define obscenity and instruct a jury in such situations?

The general rule the Court has fashioned, intuitively enough, says to focus on the average member of the intended target audience. Consider the case of Edward Mishkin, who was convicted in New York of selling numerous books depicting practices such as sadomasochism, spanking, and flagellation. Mishkin's novel argument on appeal was that his publications could not possibly meet the Supreme Court's definition of obscenity, because the average person, rather than being sexually stimulated by this material, would be disgusted and sickened. Justice Brennan, writing for the Court, rejected Mishkin's argument and held instead that "when the material is designed and primarily disseminated to a clearly defined deviant sexual group, rather than the public at large, the prurient appeal requirement . . . is satisfied if the dominant theme of the material taken as a whole appeals to the prurient interest in sex *of the members of that group*."[46] Of course, ordinary jurors who are not themselves adherents to the particular fetishes exploited by an obscenity defendant's wares may be at somewhat of a loss trying to discern what such persons would find sexually stimulating. Trial courts tend to handle this problem by being a bit more open to expert testimony than they might be in more "mainstream" obscenity prosecutions.

The government claims a special interest in seeing to it that obscene materials do not fall into the hands of children. Thus another instance of variable obscenity concerns materials that are marketed to children or at least where the purveyors do not take sufficient steps to block access by children. The leading case on this point is *Ginsberg v. New York*. The defendant's and his wife's troubles began when they sold two "girlie magazines," as the Court put it, to a sixteen-year-old patron of their stationery store and luncheonette on Long Island. Although no one claimed that the magazines were obscene for an adult audience, the sale of the magazines to the sixteen-year-old was found to violate a state law prohibiting the distribution to minors of photos showing "female buttocks . . . or female breasts with less than a fully opaque covering." The Supreme Court upheld Ginsberg's conviction, with Justice Brennan finding that it is "altogether fitting and proper for a state to include in a statute designed to regulate the sale of pornography to children special standards, broader than those embodied in legislation aimed at controlling dissemination of such material to adults."[47]

A few clarifying points about the *Ginsberg* case are in order. First, it is important to remember that Ginsberg actually sold to a minor. That is the offense for which he was prosecuted, not for publishing or selling materials that would be deemed harmful to a hypothetical minor who *might* come across them. Similarly, in 2005 an appellate court in Illinois upheld Clinton Jackson's conviction for "distributing harmful materials to a minor" when he, an employee of a residential home for boys in the juvenile

---

46. *Mishkin v. New York*, 383 U.S. 502, 508 (1966).
47. *Ginsberg v. New York*, 390 U.S. 629, 640 (1968).

justice system, brought to work a home video of himself engaging in sexual intercourse with a woman cooperative enough to say on cue for the camera, "This is for my boys at the JJP [Juvenile Justice Program]."[48]

The Supreme Court has made clear, however, that states may not, in pursuit of the laudable goal of protecting children, create obscenity laws so restrictive that adults are limited to what would be suitable for children.[49] Thus, for example, in 2002, a federal court in Ohio invalidated a "harmful to minors" section of the state obscenity statute because it covered material not generally thought of as obscene, such as depictions of extreme violence or repeated use of foul language.[50]

The *Ginsberg* case did, however, put managers of bookstores and magazine stands on notice that it would be in their interests to take certain actions to prevent minors from accessing sexually explicit materials. In recent years statutes have sprung up in numerous locales requiring such businesses to cover up titillating magazine covers or to keep such materials where minors can't see them (such as behind the counter). When these statutes have narrowly and carefully specified the kinds of materials within their scope, they have generally been upheld.[51] The U.S. Supreme Court has yet to rule on such a statute, however.

A final point about the *Ginsberg* case concerns how the Supreme Court asks us to interpret the decision. From Justice Brennan's perspective, the New York statute used against Ginsberg was upheld precisely because it demanded a finding of obscenity, albeit a modified or watered-down version of obscenity. States may, Brennan wrote, "adjust the definition of obscenity to social realities by permitting the appeal of this type of material to be assessed in terms of the sexual interests . . . of such minors."[52] Thus, the *Ginsberg* case did for minors what the *Mishkin* case did for fetishists and others whose sexual interests are beyond the mainstream: it said that obscenity statutes may take into consideration the sexual material's audience. This is probably a legal fiction, of course; fetishist films and magazines really are targeted toward narrow groups of consumers, whereas "girlie magazines" are read by minors and adults alike. As applied to children, then, "variable obscenity" probably does not really mean obscenity at all, although the Supreme Court does not admit as much.

The doctrine of variable obscenity also permits states to take into account the manner in which sexual materials are marketed, specifically whether the defendant has

---

48. *People v. Jackson*, 832 N.E.2d 418 (Ill. App. Ct. 2005).

49. *Butler v. Michigan*, 352 U.S. 380 (1957).

50. *Bookfriends, Inc. v. Taft*, 223 F. Supp. 2d 932 (S.D. Ohio 2002).

51. *M.S. News Co. v. Casado*, 721 F.2d 1281 (10th Cir. 1983); *Upper Midwest Booksellers Association v. City of Minneapolis*, 602 F. Supp. 1361 (D. Minn. 1985); *American Booksellers Association v. Rendell*, 481 A.2d 919 (Pa. Super. Ct. 1984). But see *American Booksellers Association v. Virginia*, 792 F.2d 1261 (4th Cir. 1986); *Rushia v. Town of Ashburnham*, 582 F. Supp. 900 (D. Mass. 1983); *American Booksellers Association v. McAuliffe*, 533 F. Supp. 50 (N.D. Ga. 1981); *Tattered Cover, Inc. v. Tooley*, 696 P.2d 780 (Colo. 1985).

52. *Ginsberg*, 390 U.S. at 638.

engaged in what is called "pandering." The leading case is *Ginzburg v. United States*[53] (do not confuse this with the *Ginsberg* case discussed earlier). Ralph Ginzburg appealed his Comstock Act convictions for having used the U.S. mails to distribute three issues of his magazine, *Eros*, which consisted of articles, essays, and photos. Some of the material in one of the issues had appeared previously in professional journals. That same issue also included "an interview with a psychotherapist who favors the broadest license in sexual relationships." In other words, this was not the sort of material one usually considers hard-core pornography.

One reason the Supreme Court upheld Ginzburg's conviction was that he had engaged in pandering, "the business of purveying textual or graphic matter openly advertised to appeal to the erotic interest of [one's] customers." The mailed advertisements, Justice Brennan wrote, "stressed the sexual candor of the respective publications, and openly boasted that the publishers would take full advantage of what they regarded as an unrestricted license allowed by law in the expression of sex and sexual matters." That Ginzburg had tried unsuccessfully to obtain mailing privileges for his wares from the postmasters of Blue Ball, and Intercourse, Pennsylvania—in the end, he had to settle for the post office in Middlesex, New Jersey—also merited the Court's mention.

The *Ginzburg* case did not create a separate cause of action or enhanced punishment for pandering (as the dissenting justices claimed). One cannot be prosecuted for advertising *non*obscene materials in a sexy manner, unless the advertisements themselves are obscene. Pandering is an indicator of crime; it is not itself a crime. In essence, the decision means that a purveyor's having marketed sexy wares in a pandering manner may be used only as one piece of evidence "in determining the ultimate question of obscenity."

Child Pornography

The variable obscenity doctrine, as we have seen, is in part a manifestation of society's desire to protect children from sexually explicit messages. That protectiveness is apparent even more clearly in the existence of child pornography laws. These statutes, which began to spring up in the late 1970s and 1980s, generally prohibit the use of minors as actors or models in the production and later distribution of sexual images. Clearly then, one of the government's interests in criminalizing the production of "kiddie porn," as it is often called, is to prevent the sexual abuse of children. Whereas the traditional impetus behind obscenity laws is to safeguard the morals of pornography's consumers, child pornography laws are designed to protect the actors.

It matters not, then, if child pornography meets all the components of the *Miller* test. Child abuse is child abuse, whether the photographic record of the event appeals

---

53. 383 U.S. 463 (1966).

THINGS TO REMEMBER

Fine-Tuning Obscenity

- In *Ward v. Illinois* (1977), the Court told states that their obscenity statutes need not spell out every possible component of what might make a sexual depiction obscene.
- The doctrine of "thematic obscenity" says that works cannot be found obscene because they seem to glorify or condone immoral sexual practices or values.
- The Court's decision in *Stanley v. Georgia* (1969) gives Americans the right to *own* obscene material (but not to buy it, or import it, or transport it across state lines).
- The mere fact that the only attendees at a viewing of obscene materials are consenting adults does not protect the proprietor of that establishment from prosecution.
- The "variable obscenity" doctrine says that the definition of obscenity can be modified to reflect the specific audience targeted (e.g., persons with unusual sexual interests or children) or to reflect the manner in which materials are marketed (e.g., that a pornographer has marketed his or her wares in a "pandering," leering way).

to consumers' prurient interests, regardless of a lack of patent offensiveness, and despite whatever serious literary or other value the work as a whole may possess. Therefore, most child pornography statutes do not require that these issues be addressed to justify a conviction. Similarly, the finished product need not be judged as a whole, for what difference would it make whether a scene involving child abuse takes up 5 percent or 75 percent of a film's total running time?

If the only state interest in prosecuting child pornography cases were the prevention of the child abuse inherent in the production of the materials themselves, it would at least be open to debate whether such statutes should reach beyond the producers to the distributors and to individual consumers. Governments argue, however, that they have other related interests as well. The Supreme Court, in a 1982 decision upholding New York's child pornography law, pointed to several harms flowing from the production and distribution of these materials.[54] Sexually exploited children, Justice White pointed out, are often unable to develop healthy affectionate relationships in later life and are likely to become sexual abusers themselves. The existence of a photographic or film record of an episode of sexual abuse continues to victimize the child participants by invading their privacy as adults.

Justice White concluded that the state may legitimately criminalize not only the production but also the distribution of child pornography. One of the most efficient ways of providing a disincentive for the production of such pornographic images designed for commercial distribution is to choke off the distribution network itself. It is much easier for the state to go after marketers because the production of this kind of material tends to be a "low-profile" and "clandestine" enterprise.

---

54. *Ferber v. New York*, 458 U.S. 747 (1982).

Virtually the only portion of the *Miller* obscenity test that the Court did apply to child pornography statutes is the due process requirement that such laws clearly specify precisely what kinds of representations or depictions are covered. The only guidance the majority opinion provides to the states is that the laws criminalize only "works that visually depict sexual conduct by children below a specified age" and that the phrase "sexual conduct" itself needs to be "suitably limited and described." The New York statute's definition of sexual conduct included "actual or simulated sexual intercourse, deviate sexual intercourse, sexual bestiality, masturbation, sado-masochistic abuse, or lewd exhibition of the genitals," which the Court found precise enough to withstand constitutional challenge.

That the courts take very seriously the state's interest in protecting children from the production and dissemination of child pornography is apparent from a number of later decisions, which together establish the following principles:

- Despite the lofty language in *Stanley v. Georgia* about the right to enjoy even obscene works in the privacy of our own homes, we have no such right to own child pornography.[55]
- Journalists will not be immune from prosecution by claiming that they were viewing child pornography only in order to write about its evils.[56]
- Pictures of fully clothed children may still be deemed child pornography.[57]
- Although federal laws are supposed to be triggered only by interstate commerce, the mere fact that pornographic photos depicting children in the possession of a Florida man were printed on Kodak paper (produced in New York) was sufficient to permit application of federal law.[58]

There have been government excesses in this area of law. In one notorious instance, child pornography was found in words alone, without pictures. Brian Dalton, on probation for possession of photographs of children in compromising positions, was found to keep a diary that included fantasies of sexually abusing children. Dalton was pressured to plead guilty to new charges that could have resulted in a seven-year prison term. He was eventually permitted to rescind his guilty plea, and the new charges were dropped.[59]

Also, in 2002 the Supreme Court struck down the "virtual porn" portions of the Child Pornography Prevention Act of 1996, which would have criminalized the production, distribution, and possession of images that even *appear* to depict children engaged in sexual acts. The law was so broad, Justice Kennedy wrote for the majority, that it would seem to outlaw such popular films as *American Beauty* and *Traffic*, both

---

55. *Osborne v. Ohio*, 495 U.S. 103 (1990).
56. *United States v. Matthews*, 209 F.3d 338 (4th Cir. 2000).
57. *United States v. Knox*, 32 F.3d 733 (3d Cir. 1994).
58. *United States v. Smith*, 2006 U.S. App. LEXIS 20572 (11th Cir. 2006).
59. *State v. Dalton*, 793 N.E.2d 509 (Ohio Ct. App. 2003).

of which included scenes with minors appearing to have sex. Even some film versions of *Romeo and Juliet* could have been banned, he added.[60] Justice O'Connor, in a separate concurring opinion, suggested that the government's interest will become stronger as technology improves to the point where computer-generated images of children become "virtually indistinguishable" from real children, at which point pedophiles might use the images to lure very real children into engaging in sexual practices. Even in the few years since this case was decided, technology does seem to be progressing rapidly in this direction;[61] it is anyone's guess what the Court may do if forced to reassess the issue.

In response to the 2002 decision, Congress passed the "PROTECT" Act (the acronym stands for "Prosecutorial Remedies and Other Tools to End the Exploitation of Children Today") as an amendment to the Child Pornography Prevention Act. The Eleventh Circuit Court of Appeals in 2006 struck down a portion of the amendment that focused on "pandering." The law's fatal flaw was apparently Congress's failure to restrict its scope to purely commercial transactions. As the amendment was written, the appellate court found, it would cover even "an outright liar" who claimed falsely to have child pornography to share, but might in fact have only "a video of 'Our Gang,' a dirty handkerchief, or an empty pocket."[62] The Supreme Court accepted the decision for review in its 2007-2008 term, with a ruling expected by summer of 2008.

THINGS TO REMEMBER

Child Pornography

- Child pornography laws are aimed at sexually oriented materials that use children as actors or models.
- Such laws differ from obscenity statutes in that
  - works need not be judged as a whole;
  - there is no exemption for works with serious value;
  - the works need not appeal to the prurient interest, nor be obscene; and
  - the state may criminalize the mere possession of child pornography.
- Even photos of fully clothed youngsters may be child pornography if the children are engaged in lewd poses or conduct, or if the focus is on the genital area.
- It is a violation of the First Amendment to criminalize images that merely *appear to be* of children in sexual poses.

---

60. *Ashcroft v. Free Speech Coalition*, 535 U.S. 234 (2002).

61. Sharon Waxman, "Cyberface: A New Technology Makes Animated Figures as Expressive as SAG Members," *New York Times*, October 15, 2006, section 2, 1.

62. *United States v. Williams*, 444 F.3d 1286 (11th Cir. 2006).

Pornography as a Civil Rights Issue: The Feminist Response

In the early 1980s, the feminists Andrea Dworkin and Catherine MacKinnon drafted a model ordinance that would take a novel approach to sexually explicit communications. The ordinance sought to define *pornography* rather than *obscenity* as a legal construct. It provided for civil actions rather than criminal prosecutions. Most crucially, the purported state interest in providing for such civil actions was the promotion of equal rights rather than a desire to foster a traditional view of morality.

Pornography, the law's feminist sponsors argued, harms women in several ways. The women who appear in pornography are often physically and sexually abused in the course of producing films. As MacKinnon has written, pornography "forces, threatens, blackmails, pressures, tricks and cajoles women into sex for pictures."[63] Proponents of the civil rights approach also point to the plethora of social science research showing that people who are exposed to many pornographic images develop misogynist attitudes and beliefs (for example, that women enjoy pain or that they want to be raped). There is also considerable evidence that those who commit sex crimes are disproportionately likely to have been voracious consumers of pornography.[64]

The city council in Minneapolis passed the model ordinance, but the law was promptly vetoed by the city's mayor. Then, conservative organizations in Indianapolis cleverly co-opted the feminist model and succeeded in passing a similar ordinance. The law was challenged in court by a coalition of groups and individuals headed by the American Booksellers Association. A federal district court, affirmed by the Seventh Circuit Court of Appeals, held the statute unconstitutional.[65]

The statute defined pornography as "the graphic sexually explicit subordination of women, whether in pictures or in words" when such depictions also include any of several specified exacerbating features. Depictions of women enjoying pain or humiliation would trigger the law, as would depictions of them tied up, mutilated, or penetrated by objects or animals. More broadly, the law also would reach depictions of "degradation"—of women as "inferior" or in "postures or positions of servility or submission."

Writing for the appellate panel, Judge Easterbrook emphasized that the statute lacked many of the constitutional protections provided under the *Miller* test. First, there was no requirement that works be judged as a whole. Also conspicuously absent

---

63. Catherine A. MacKinnon, *Only Words* (Cambridge, Mass.: Harvard University Press, 1993), 15.

64. Gail Dines, Robert Jensen, and Ann Russo, *Pornography: The Production and Consumption of Inequality* (New York: Routledge, 1998).

65. *American Booksellers Association v. Hudnut*, 598 F. Supp. 1316 (S.D. Ind. 1984), *aff'd*, 771 F.2d 323 (7th Cir. 1985).

THINGS TO REMEMBER

Pornography and Feminism

- Some feminists joined forces with conservative groups in the 1980s to lobby for laws giving women the right to sue pornographers for depicting women in sexually degrading ways.
- An Indianapolis ordinance that took this approach was held unconstitutional.

from the ordinance was an exception for works of serious value, akin to *Miller*'s SLAPS test. In addition, the statutory definition required neither a finding of patent offensiveness nor of the work's appeal to the prurient interest. The statute's more fundamental constitutional flaw, however, was that it prohibited the expression of specific *ideas* about women. Speech that portrays women in positions of equality or superiority, Easterbrook pointed out, would be beyond the law's reach, no matter how graphic the content, whereas speech that presents women in submissive roles would be subject to civil actions, no matter how tame. Such legislation seeks to establish "an approved view of women," and thus amounts to "thought control."[66]

Although the Indianapolis statute is often characterized as *the* feminist answer to sexually explicit images, in fact many women who describe themselves as feminists are strong opponents of any government censorship in this arena. Nadine Strossen's book *Defending Pornography* is probably the best-known articulation of the feminist civil libertarian view. Members of a group called the Feminist Anti-Censorship Task Force (FACT) also oppose obscenity laws.

Other Means of Regulating Sexual Materials

As we have seen, the Supreme Court defines obscenity as categorically beyond the protection of the First Amendment, as if it were not speech at all. There is also a wide variety of sexual texts and images that do not necessarily fit the definition of obscenity but that the government has been permitted to regulate in numerous ways. In this section, we examine several kinds of such regulations, including the zoning of adult businesses (sometimes called "sexually oriented businesses," and yes, cities often refer to them as SOBs for short),[67] declaring such businesses to be "public nuisances," and treating pornographers as practitioners of organized crime. Also included here are discussions of movie censorship, government funding of the arts and humanities, and

---

66. *American Booksellers Association v. Hudnut*, 771 F.2d 323, 328 (7th Cir. 1985).
67. *Fantasy Ranch v. City of Arlington*, 459 F.3d 546 (5th Cir. 2006).

U.S. Postal Service regulations governing the mailing of adult-oriented materials. We conclude with a brief discussion of nongovernmental actions against sexual images, either by private citizen groups or through industry self-regulation.

Zoning Laws

Government zoning commissions wield tremendous power in the United States. They can decide where you may live, tell you that you may not convert your attic into a separate apartment, and even dictate what colors you may or may not paint your home's exterior. Many communities have used zoning ordinances either to cluster all "adult businesses" into a single red-light district or to disperse them widely so that they do not become too big an eyesore for any one neighborhood. Generally the courts have upheld such zoning plans if they further a clearly articulated and substantial state interest, are aimed at the "secondary effects" of adult businesses (not at the adult content itself), provide for expedited judicial review,[68] restrict no more speech than necessary, and do not have the real-world effect of forcing the targeted businesses to go *out of* business[69] (though it might be permissible to force one of two adult-oriented businesses operating under the same roof to move to another part of town).[70]

The Supreme Court first ruled on this kind of zoning law in 1976. At issue were Detroit statutes requiring that adult movie theaters—defined in the statute as those that present material "characterized by an emphasis" on any of a list of "sexual activities" or "anatomical areas" enumerated in the law itself—obtain a city license to operate and prohibiting them from locating within a thousand feet of any two other adult theaters (or adult bookstores, cabarets, bars, or hotels). Clearly, then, Detroit's aim was to prevent the creation of a red-light district. Equally clear is that the definition of affected businesses was not at all related to obscenity itself; a theater could be subject to the licensing and zoning scheme without ever having been accused of showing obscene movies. Justice Stevens's majority opinion upholding the ordinances rested in part on his assertion that nonobscene sexual speech, although it may enjoy some First Amendment protection, is not nearly as central to our system of freedom of expression as is political speech. "Few of us would march our sons and daughters off to war," Stevens wrote, "to preserve the citizen's right to see 'Specified Sexual Activities' exhibited in the theaters of our choice."[71]

The City of Detroit had presented considerable evidence about the "secondary effects" of these kinds of movie houses. The Court found this significant. It would not

---

68. *City of Littleton, Colorado v. Z.J. Gifts D-4*, 541 U.S. 774 (2004). The expedited review provision need not be in the licensing scheme itself. Colorado, for example, already provided for expedited review of any complaints involving weighty constitutional claims.

69. *Executive Arts Studio v. City of Grand Rapids*, 391 F.3d 783 (6th Cir. 2004).

70. *City of Los Angeles v. Alameda Books*, 535 U.S. 425 (2002).

71. *Young v. American Mini Theatres*, 427 U.S. 50, 70 (1976)

do, the majority ruled, for a government to say that its substantial interest in zoning X-rated theaters is that it does not like such places or finds them immoral. Rather, the government must be able to articulate some additional negative impact that is not itself related to the content of the films. In the case of Detroit, this took the form of showing that "neighborhood decay" is a predictable result of allowing too many of these kinds of businesses in a limited area.

Five years later, the Court struck down a zoning ordinance in Mount Ephraim, New Jersey. Although the defendant was in the business of providing coin-operated booths through which patrons could watch live nude dancers perform, the applicable ordinance was worded so broadly as to preclude *any* live entertainment from the entire downtown area. The Court's decision was based in large part on the borough's failure to clearly articulate a substantive state interest in preventing its citizens from partaking of such a wide variety of protected expression.[72]

Then in 1986, the Court upheld a zoning law from Renton, Washington, that forbade adult movie houses from locating within a thousand feet of any residential area, church, park, or school. It is in this decision that the Court most clearly articulated the criteria to be used in assessing the constitutionality of such zoning schemes. Justice Rehnquist (he had not yet been elevated to Chief Justice) admitted at the outset that these kinds of laws constitute a unique category. In a way, they are based on the content of the theater owners' message, in that only movie houses that predominantly show "adult" films are affected. Traditional First Amendment jurisprudence dictates that content-based regulations come to the Court with a presumption of unconstitutionality, unless the state can show a *compelling* interest furthered by the regulation. However, since these zoning ordinances are aimed at the adverse "secondary effects" of adult businesses on neighborhood children and on attempts at urban development, rather than at the content of any specific film, the laws will be judged by a far less exacting standard.[73] Using that standard, the Court has also allowed communities to ban (not merely zone) nude-dancing clubs as long as the statute aims at secondary effects.[74]

Concerning this whole notion of secondary effects, social science research makes clear that municipalities' assumptions about how adult-oriented businesses will increase crime rates are not supported. Indeed, quite the opposite happens, perhaps in part because proprietors of such businesses have so much at stake that they willingly incur additional costs to maintain well-lit parking areas and to hire security guards.[75]

---

72. *Schad v. Mount Ephraim*, 452 U.S. 61 (1981).

73. *Renton v. Playtime Theatres, Inc.*, 475 U.S. 41 (1986).

74. *City of Erie v. Pap's A.M.*, 529 U.S. 277 (2000).

75. Bryant Paul, Daniel Linz, and Bradley J. Shaffer, "Government Regulation of 'Adult' Businesses through Zoning and Anti-nudity Ordinances: Debunking the Legal Myth of Negative Secondary Effects," 6 *Communication Law and Policy* 355 (2001); Daniel Linz, Kenneth Land, Jay Williams, and Bryant Paul, "An Examination of the Assumption that Adult Businesses Are Associated with Crime in Surrounding Areas," 38 *Law and Society Review* 69 (2004).

An interesting twist on zoning ordinances emerged in New York in 1999, when a number of businesses featuring strippers decided to avoid the impact of local laws simply by admitting minors. They could thus no longer be considered adult-oriented businesses, or so they argued. A state judge in New York City agreed with one club's owners, whose attorney argued that if "you could take your 15-year-old to see the movie 'Striptease,'" you should also be able to take him to see a live striptease. The state's highest court disagreed, however, finding that the state may legitimately base its definition of "adult" establishments on the nature of the entertainment provided within, regardless of whether admission is limited to those who have achieved the age of majority.[76]

Public-Nuisance Laws

For many years communities have attempted, through the use of public-nuisance laws, to protect citizens from having unwanted sexual images thrust at them. These laws have not always demanded that the images be obscene ones. A Dallas ordinance, for example, prohibited the public display of photos depicting human genitals or buttocks. Newsstand workers thus had to paste over a famous *Newsweek* magazine cover in 1975 that showed a Vietnamese mother carrying her young, wounded, *nude*, daughter. In 1975, the Supreme Court struck down the Jacksonville, Florida, public-nuisance law, which had been applied to a drive-in movie theater showing nonobscene films that included nudity and could be seen from a nearby church parking lot. Those who might be offended by these images could always avert their eyes, the Court held.[77]

At the other extreme, businesses that happen to sell books or rent or sell videotapes cannot find First Amendment protection when the government seeks to enjoin activ-

---

THINGS TO REMEMBER

Zoning Ordinances

- Some local governments have decided to control the proliferation of adult-oriented businesses through the use of zoning ordinances, intended either to cluster all such businesses together into a red-light district or to disperse them to avoid the creation of such a zone.
- Such laws have generally been upheld if they further a clearly articulated and substantial state interest, are aimed at regulating the "secondary effects" of adult businesses, restrict no more speech than necessary, and do not make it impossible for such businesses to exist.

---

76. *City of New York v. Stringfellows*, 749 N.E.2d 192 (N.Y. 2001).
77. *Erznoznik v. Jacksonville*, 422 U.S. 205 (1975).

474   CHAPTER 11 ■ SEXUALLY ORIENTED SPEECH

ity that is inarguably prohibitable as a public nuisance. Thus, the operators of the Village Books and News Store in Kenmore, New York, were put out of business for violating the state's public-nuisance statute by permitting their premises to be used by patrons for masturbation, oral sex, and solicitation of prostitution. Writing for the Supreme Court majority, Chief Justice Burger chided the defendants for making the "ludicrous" argument that closing the bookstore was an unconstitutional sanction. Such an assertion, he wrote, is akin to "a thief who is sent to prison . . . complain[ing] that his First Amendment right to speak in public places has been infringed because of the confinement."[78]

Some courts, however, have concluded that the First Amendment requires that a company's "expressive activity" be permitted to continue even while activity that truly is a public nuisance is enjoined or punished. Thus, an adult establishment in Allen County, Ohio, that included a bookstore and an arcade of private booths in which patrons would masturbate while viewing films was allowed to retain its inventory and stay in business (although the arcade area was shut down).[79] Similarly, rules in Chattanooga, Tennessee, requiring that viewing booths not provide enough privacy to engage in sex and that establishments with such booths not be permitted to remain open twenty-four hours a day were upheld, although other rules affecting the owners and investors in the bookstore in which such booths were located were struck down.[80]

Under some local nuisance laws, once a business has been found to have sold or distributed obscene material, the government may issue an injunction, often referred to as a **standards injunction**, forbidding the further dissemination of those *or similar* materials. The case law on these kinds of statutes is mixed, often turning on whether the court concludes that the law is aimed at punishing pornographers for past sins or at trying to prevent future dissemination of possibly obscene materials.[81] When judges conclude that the latter motivation is involved, statutes tend to be struck down as unconstitutional prior restraints on speech.[82] Some courts also look more favorably on "padlock laws," which force offending businesses to close shop for a specified period of time, than on those that include the complete revocation of the defendant's license to conduct business as part of the punishment.[83]

78. *Arcara v. Cloud Books*, 478 U.S. 697, 706 (1986).

79. *Ohio v. Elida Road Video & Books*, 696 N.E.2d 668 (Ohio Ct. App. 1997).

80. *Broadway Books v. Roberts*, 642 F. Supp. 486 (E.D. Tenn. 1986); see also *Ellwest Stereo Theater v. Boner*, 718 F. Supp. 1553 (M.D. Tenn. 1989) (concerning similar rules in Nashville).

81. Steven T. Catlett, "Enjoining Obscenity as a Public Nuisance and the Prior Restraint Doctrine," 84 *Columbia Law Review* 1616 (1984).

82. *Cohen v. City of Daleville*, 695 F. Supp. 1168 (M.D. Ala. 1988).

83. *City of Paducah v. Investment Entertainment, Inc.*, 791 F.2d 463 (6th Cir. 1986); *Krontz v. City of San Diego*, 136 Cal. App. 4th 1126 (2006).

THINGS TO REMEMBER

Public Nuisances

- Some communities have used public nuisance statutes to close down adult businesses.
- Not all such laws require a finding that a business has sold obscene literature.
- Nuisance laws vary with respect to whether they result in businesses losing their licenses or being shut down for a specified period of time.
- These laws are most likely to be found constitutional if they are perceived as punishments for past offenses, rather than as prophylactic measures designed to prevent future wrongdoing (thus falling into the category of "prior restraints" on speech).

Racketeering Statutes

Both the federal government and many states have embraced a new and controversial weapon against pornographers, similar to public-nuisance laws but with a few twists. The federal Racketeer Influenced and Corrupt Organizations Act, popularly known as RICO, was enacted in 1970 as a way of curtailing the influence of organized crime on otherwise legitimate businesses. Today, RICO is used against many different kinds of activities that at first blush might not seem the stuff of the Mafia. For example, the Supreme Court has held that RICO can be used against pro-life protestors at abortion clinics to the extent that they are involved in organized conspiracies to shut down the clinics through illegal means.[84] In addition, state and federal prosecutors nationwide have used RICO and similar state laws against persons who peddle pornography. It has been assumed for some time that organized crime has a hand in pornography industries. Still, RICO and similar state statutes are worded and interpreted broadly enough to reach even relatively mainstream publishers and bookstores. All that is usually required to obtain a conviction is to show that the accused has sold obscene materials at least two times over a ten-year period.

As in the case of public-nuisance statutes, the fact that a defendant has engaged in the peddling of obscenity is used as a means of triggering a legal action other than enforcement of an ordinary obscenity statute. Under racketeering laws, defendants face punishments not contemplated in the typical obscenity law or public-nuisance statute. A racketeering conviction can result in a twenty-year jail sentence and hundreds of thousands of dollars in fines. Moreover, any property used by the defendant in racketeering activities or purchased with the profits from such activities is often forfeitable. Not only can the defendant's place of business and entire inventory (obscene and nonobscene) be seized, but the seizure might extend to personal property

---

84. *National Organization for Women v. Scheidler*, 510 U.S. 249 (1994).

such as a place of residence. After all, placing a phone call to order a supply of magazines or videotapes for the store or giving instructions to employees—activities often conducted from a store owner's private residence—are both "associated with" committing the crime of selling obscene materials.

The Supreme Court has twice had occasion to rule on the application of racketeering laws to pornography. In 1989, it held that the State of Indiana violated the First Amendment when, under its state racketeering law, it seized an adult bookstore's inventory before any convictions had been obtained. The Court gave its approval, however, to the use of racketeering statutes and their forfeiture provisions, as long as no confiscation occurs prior to a conviction.[85] Four years later, in *Alexander v. United States*, the Court made a similar ruling concerning RICO, emphasizing that the forfeiture here of the defendant's entire business and approximately $9 million in profits was not a prior restraint on feared future pornography peddling, but rather permissible punishment for past violations of the law.[86] The majority sent the case back to the lower courts, however, to determine if this huge forfeiture violated the Eighth Amendment's prohibition against cruel and unusual punishment. On remand, the lower courts upheld the forfeiture amount, and the Supreme Court declined to review the case again.[87]

Movie Censorship

When motion pictures first came on the scene around the end of the nineteenth century, audiences were spellbound by the technology itself, by the optical illusion of

---

THINGS TO REMEMBER

Sex and Racketeering

- The federal Racketeer Influenced and Corrupt Organizations Act (RICO), originally enacted in 1970, has been amended to provide for the prosecution of pornographers as one would prosecute organized crime figures.
- Many states have passed their own racketeering laws as well.
- These laws provide for hefty fines and lengthy prison terms, as well as forfeiture of any and all possessions purchased with proceeds from the commission of such racketeering crimes or that have been used in the furtherance of the criminal activity.
- The Supreme Court has upheld the constitutionality of such forfeitures as long as they do not happen before any convictions are obtained.

---

85. *Fort Wayne Books v. Indiana*, 489 U.S. 46 (1989).
86. 509 U.S. 544 (1993).
87. *United States v. Alexander*, 32 F.3d 1231 (1994) (remanding case back to district court on the Eighth Amendment question); 108 F.3d 853 (1997) (upholding district court's finding that forfeiture was constitutional), *cert. denied sub nom. Schlidt v. Souval*, 522 U.S. 869 (1997).

THINGS TO REMEMBER

Movie Censorship

- Although they are not common today, for many years cities nationwide required film distributors to permit local censor boards to preview movies.
- The Supreme Court has never explicitly struck down the use of such censorship boards, but it has imposed certain restrictions on the way they function.

having multiple, successive still shots of a subject seem to present the subject in motion. The idea of using the technology to tell stories did not come about until years later. The Supreme Court, when first asked to rule on the matter in 1915, decided that movies were entertainment and nothing more, and were beyond the protection of the First Amendment.[88] That decision, even though disavowed by the Court in 1952,[89] set a tone for many years thereafter consistent with treating movies as a bit more dangerous, a bit less deserving of constitutional consideration, than print media.

For many years, cities nationwide required film distributors to present their products to local censorship boards prior to their public exhibition. This practice hardly ever happens anymore, although the Supreme Court has never explicitly said that it is unconstitutional. Rather, the Court has, in a number of decisions, created a set of rules by which any such commissions must operate.[90] The reviewing board must act swiftly (generally within two weeks) either to grant permission to show the movie or to begin litigation to stop the exhibition. In the event that litigation is commenced, there must be expedited review of the case (i.e., within two months or so). Finally, the burden of proof will always rest with the censors, rather than with the movie's distributors. The same standards have been applied by the Court to prior restraints for alleged obscenity in other settings as well, from seizures of goods by the U.S. Postal Service[91] and the U.S. Customs Service[92] to live theatrical performances.[93]

Government Sponsorship of the Arts

There is a long and complicated body of case law on the question of what First Amendment limitations apply when the government itself is the speaker. It is clear

---

88. *Mutual Film Corp. v. Industrial Commission of Ohio*, 236 U.S. 230 (1915).

89. *Burstyn v. Wilson*, 343 U.S. 495 (1952).

90. *Teitel Films v. Cussak*, 390 U.S. 139 (1968); *Freedman v. Maryland*, 380 U.S. 51 (1965); *Times Film Corporation v. City of Chicago*, 365 U.S. 43 (1961); *Superior Films v. Department of Education*, 346 U.S. 587 (1954); *Gelling v. Texas*, 343 U.S. 960 (1952).

91. *Blount v. Rizzi*, 400 U.S. 410 (1971).

92. *United States v. Thirty-Seven Photographs*, 402 U.S. 363 (1971).

93. *Southeastern Promotions v. Conrad*, 420 U.S. 546 (1975).

that the government as speaker may engage in viewpoint-based discrimination that would be impermissible in other contexts. The state may not censor private speech arguing for or against drug legalization, but when was the last time you saw a government-sponsored public service announcement on the issue calling for anything other than complete abstinence? In another context, the Supreme Court has said that when the federal government pays for health care, the professionals delivering that care can be prohibited not only from performing abortions but also from even mentioning the topic.[94]

The National Endowment for the Arts (NEA) was created in 1965. Since then it has made over 100,000 grants, totaling over $3 billion, to artists and arts organizations. Only a tiny number of the grants have resulted in political controversies. Two such controversies from 1989, however—one involving photographer Robert Mapplethorpe's sadomasochistic and homoerotic images, the other Andres Serrano's photograph "Piss Christ," in which a crucifix is immersed in urine—were intense enough to prompt congressional response. That action took the form of an amendment to the National Foundation on the Arts and Humanities Act forbidding the use of federal funds "to promote, disseminate, or produce" any materials that the NEA believes might be obscene. That provision was struck down by a federal court, not because the government should be forced to fund obscene art, but because the statute placed too much administrative discretion within the NEA itself. In other words, judges determine what is obscene, not government bureaucrats.[95]

Congress tried its hand once more at amending the act, this time instructing the NEA that it should make grants not only on the basis of artistic excellence but also "taking into consideration general standards of decency and respect for the diverse beliefs and values of the American public." Four performance artists with reputations for creating feminist, gay, and other provocative works—Karen Finley, John Fleck, Holly Hughes, and Tim Miller—challenged the new provision. Each had previously received an NEA grant, and each had a pending proposal accepted by an endowment advisory panel but ultimately disapproved by the director. Two lower federal courts held the "decency" amendment unconstitutional, but the Supreme Court, in an 8-1 ruling, overturned these judgments in 1998. Justice O'Connor's majority opinion was based on the rather narrow grounds that the amendment was merely "hortatory," that it told the NEA director what the grants application *should* look like, rather than explicitly prohibiting the funding of indecent art. Had the NEA in fact developed an unwritten policy against funding art espousing specific political messages, the decision might have been different.[96]

Washington is not the only source of government funding for the arts, of course. From time to time state and local governments create their own First Amendment

---

94. *Rust v. Sullivan*, 500 U.S. 173 (1991).

95. *Bella Lewitzky Dance Foundation v. Frohnmayer*, 754 F. Supp. 774 (C.D. Cal. 1991).

96. *National Endowment for the Arts v. Finley*, 524 U.S. 569 (1998).

nightmares. In 1999 the Brooklyn Museum included as part of an exhibit entitled *Sensation* a painting by Chris Ofili—an impressionistic rendering of the Virgin Mary created from, among other materials, elephant dung. Outraged by what he perceived as the artist's desecration of the Catholic faith, New York City mayor Rudolph Giuliani promptly withheld funds already appropriated to the museum for operating expenses and maintenance. He also commenced litigation seeking to eject the museum from the city-owned land and building in which its collections had been housed for over a hundred years. Federal district judge Nina Gershon enjoined the city from imposing any such tangible sanctions against the museum.[97]

Postal Regulations and Sexually Oriented Junk Mail

Earlier in the chapter we examined the federal laws making it illegal to send obscene materials through the mails and giving post office investigators the right to open and seize obscene materials. In this section we see two additional pieces of federal legislation that, taken together, can save individuals the embarrassment or inconvenience of receiving any "adult" mailings.

Under section 3010 of title 39 of the U.S. Code, known as the Goldwater amendment to the Postal Reorganization Act, individuals who do not wish to receive sexually oriented mail of any kind may fill out a form at their local post office informing the postmaster of this wish. The U.S. Postal Service in turn alerts all companies that it has previously determined to be in the business of sending such mail to purchase the list—updated monthly—of all such mail patrons who have filled out the requisite paperwork. These companies are then required by law to remove the names and addresses of all those on the list from any mailing lists and to never mail *anything* to those individuals (whether the companies think a particular mailing is "adult" or not). The constitutionality of this provision has been upheld. That the mailings cov-

THINGS TO REMEMBER

Government Sponsorship

- A small handful of the thousands of grants made by the National Endowment of the Arts has been very controversial and have led Congress to demand that the funding agency include general notions of "decency" into its decision making.
- The Supreme Court has upheld this provision but has warned the NEA that it must not engage in flagrant viewpoint-based discrimination.

97. *Brooklyn Institute of Arts and Sciences v. City of New York,* 64 F. Supp. 2d 184 (E.D.N.Y. 1999); see also *Cuban Museum of Arts and Culture, Inc. v. City of Miami,* 766 F. Supp. 1121 (S.D. Fla. 1991).

ered by the statute were not obscene and were thus protected by the First Amendment, Judge Judd wrote for a special three-judge panel, "does not mean that the mailer's right to communicate ideas supersedes the right of the addressee to be let alone."[98]

More wide-reaching is section 3008, usually referred to as the Pandering Advertisements Statute. Under this provision, mail patrons who fill out a different form at the post office indicating their belief that a specific company's mailing was "erotically arousing" will thus put that company on notice that it may no longer send mail to those patrons. Notice the difference. The U.S. Postal Service does not decide that the mailing is sexually oriented or that the mailer is a company in the business of sending such mailings. Only you may make that determination, and your judgment is final and unappealable. Yes, this means that you may use this law to avoid getting those bulky mail-order catalogs that take up so much room in your mailbox. The catalog need not be from Victoria's Secret; it can be from Radio Shack. Section 3008 was also found constitutional in a 1970 Supreme Court decision. As Chief Justice Burger wrote for the Court, "whether measured by pieces or pounds, Everyman's mail today is made up overwhelmingly of material he did not seek from persons he does not know, and all too often it is matter he finds offensive."[99]

Private Pressure and Industry Self-Regulation

Our freedom of speech has always included the right to persuade others to shut up—as long we do so peaceably. Because the Supreme Court's legal definition of obscenity covers only a tiny portion of the sexual imagery that many people may find

---

THINGS TO REMEMBER

Sex and the Mails

- In addition to laws criminalizing the mailing of obscene materials, the U.S. Postal Service is empowered by two other congressional provisions to control the mailing of nonobscene, but sexually oriented, messages.
- Title 39, section 3010 of the U.S. Code requires companies that mail "adult" materials to purchase, and respect, a periodically updated list from the U.S. Postal Service of all mail patrons who do not want to receive any such mailings.
- Section 3008 gives mail patrons themselves the absolute right to determine that a given mailing is "sexually arousing" and to notify the post office of this determination. The U.S. Postal Service will then notify the offending company that it may not send any mail to that patron again.

---

98. *Pent-R-Books v. U.S. Postal Service*, 328 F. Supp. 297 (E.D.N.Y. 1971).
99. *Rowan v. U.S. Post Office Department*, 397 U.S. 728, 735 (1970).

offensive, it is no surprise that private citizen action often fills the vacuum, in an effort to shame the pornographer. Most such efforts are local and attract little or no national media attention. A typical scenario may find a citizens' group pressuring the owner of a strip shopping mall not to lease space to adult-oriented businesses; sometimes a video rental store will be persuaded to decrease or eliminate its X-rated offerings.

Sometimes more organized citizens' efforts intertwine with government action. As we shall see in chapter 12, the Federal Communication Commission generally waits until viewers or listeners complain before beginning an investigation into whether a broadcast station has run afoul of its indecency rules. In recent years there have been numerous letter-writing campaigns aimed at spurring the FCC to adopt stricter regulations.

Sexual imagery and narratives found offensive by some groups may become the impetus for an organized boycott. Disney—owner of Capital Cities/ABC—has often become the target of boycotts in recent years. When ABC aired the famous "coming out" and subsequent episodes of the TV show *Ellen*, several groups called for a boycott of the network and of *Ellen*'s advertising sponsors. The program did indeed experience a noticeable drop in viewership not long after its title character's emergence as a lesbian icon, but by most accounts, that was more a reflection of stale writing than of the boycott. A group called the American Family Association has often threatened boycotts of retailers that carry racy magazines or movies such as the gay-themed *Brokeback Mountain*.[100] Public protests regarding what many viewed as soft-core pornography also compelled youth-oriented clothier Abercrombie and Fitch to stop distributing its Christmas 2003 catalog. More recently, a hastily instigated but far-reaching call for a boycott by the Catholic League resulted in the Lab Gallery, an art gallery located in the Roger Smith Hotel in New York City, cancelling a planned exhibition of sculptor Cosimo Cavallaro's *Sweet Jesus*, a depiction of the crucifixion in which the Christ figure is constructed of over two hundred pounds of chocolate. The League's call for a boycott of the hotel emphasized not only the timing of the planned display (during Easter week) but the fact that Christ was shown nude and "anatomically correct."[101]

One of the most dramatic examples of citizen action in the past generation was aimed at music. The Parents Music Resource Center, among whose founders was Al Gore's wife, Tipper, joined forces in the mid-1980s with the PTA and other groups to pressure the recording industry to help parents prevent their children from gaining access to music with sexually explicit and otherwise offensive lyrics. The Recording Industry Association of America responded by instituting a system of parental advisory labels affixed to cassette and CD packaging.

---

100. Julie Bosman, "Wal-Mart Resists Pressure in 'Brokeback' DVD Sales," *New York Times*, April 10, 2006, C6.

101. Peter Kadushin, Nicole Lyn Pesce, and Michael Saul, "No Room at the Inn: Chocolate Nude Jesus Gets Booted from Hotel's Gallery amid Torrent of Complaints," *Daily News* (New York), March 31, 2007, 5.

Former secretary of education William Bennett, together with Senator Joe Lieberman, used to offer their "Silver Sewer" awards to mass media companies they saw as "purveyors of cultural filth." The pair usually did not succeed in eliminating offensive products, but they did manage to shame many companies. Time Warner, for example, was pressured to sell its financial interests in Interscope Records, among whose artists was the group Nine Inch Nails, whose sexually explicit lyrics were harshly criticized by Bennett, Lieberman, and then-senator Bob Dole.

The motion picture industry has for many years exercised self-regulation in the form of the Motion Picture Association of America's movie rating system—the G, PG, PG-13, R, and NC-17 labels so familiar to us all. Self-regulation in the industry far predates this particular rating system. In the 1930s, the Motion Picture Producers and Distributors Association, led by former Republican Party chairman Will Hays, created a code to monitor movie content. The Hollywood Production Code dealt with violent and other kinds of antisocial images but reserved its most detailed guidelines for depictions of sexual relationships. The code, which remained in effect for over thirty years, prohibited—among hundreds of other images—on-screen kisses longer than thirty seconds or with open mouths, and exposure of the female leg above the knee.

Similar rating systems exist for broadcast and cable television as well as videogames, indicating not only the appropriate age levels for viewers (or players, in the case of videogames) but also whether the program or videogame includes violence, nudity, "adult situations," and the like. With respect to videogames, since 1994 the Entertainment Software Association's Entertainment Software Rating Board (ESRB) has labeled games from EC (for "early childhood") all the way to AO (for "adults only"). In 2006 the ESRB announced that it would spend more on training raters and would send undercover shoppers to retailers to ensure compliance.[102]

Chapter Summary

The Supreme Court has said that obscenity is not speech and is thus wholly outside of the First Amendment's protection. For many years, U.S. law followed the British *Hicklin* rule, which said that pornography should be judged by its potential effects on society's most susceptible members and that even an isolated obscene passage could be enough to find an entire book obscene. The *Hicklin* rule was rejected in favor of the *Roth* test in 1957, which in turn gave way to the *Miller* test, first articulated in 1973.

The *Miller* test provides that allegedly obscene works should be judged as a whole, not by isolated passages, and by their likely effects on average, or reasonable, commu-

---

102. Brian Crecente, "Game Board Builds Its Rating Muscle," *Rocky Mountain News*, July 21, 2006, 29D.

nity members. To be judged obscene, a work must describe or depict sexual matters in a patently offensive way and in a way that appeals to the prurient interest. Whether a work meets that definition is a determination to be made using contemporary community standards (not a single national standard). Moreover, works that have serious literary, artistic, political, or scientific value—as judged by a national standard—cannot be found obscene. Materials cannot be found obscene merely because they seem to condone or glorify immoral sexual values.

There exists a right to privacy in the home that extends far enough to protect an individual's right to possess obscene materials but not so far as to permit an individual to import such materials, carry them across state lines, or use the mails to ship them.

Child pornography laws are aimed at sexually oriented materials that use children as actors or models. Such laws differ from obscenity statutes in many ways: works need not be judged as a whole; they are not exempted from the law by dint of having serious value; and they need not appeal to the prurient interest, nor be obscene. Moreover, the state may criminalize the mere possession of child pornography.

In the 1980s a feminist response to pornography developed, emphasizing the material's degrading depiction of women rather than its overall effect on a society's moral tone. An Indianapolis ordinance based on this new theory was struck down as unconstitutional.

In recent years, communities have embraced legal strategies beyond a reliance on obscenity laws per se to stem the proliferation of adult-oriented businesses. These include zoning ordinances, public-nuisance statutes, and the use of federal and state racketeering laws. In addition, individuals have rights under laws governing the U.S. Postal Service to avoid receiving unwanted sexual mailings, whether obscene or not.

Governmental regulation of sexual content is augmented by citizens' groups, as well as by industry self-regulation.

Chapter 12

BROADCAST, CABLE, AND SATELLITE TV REGULATION

To link me to George Bush is like linking me to an Oscar.

—California governor Arnold Schwarzenegger to Jay Leno
on *The Tonight Show*, Wednesday, October 11, 2006

The governor's self-deprecating humor was in response to a question from Leno about negative ads by Phil Angelides, the Democratic challenger for governor, that sought to associate Schwarzenegger with a highly unpopular (especially in California) president. Angelides complained about the free publicity given to his opponent's reelection bid by that *Tonight Show* appearance. As we shall see later in this chapter, Angelides had at least a plausible (though ultimately unsuccessful)[1] legal argument, one that he never would have had if, say, the *Los Angeles Times* editorial board invited Schwarzenegger but not his challenger to meet them. The reason Angelides could even raise a claim with respect to *The Tonight Show* but not with respect to the *Times* is that broadcast media are subject to regulations not applicable to print media.

In this chapter we review the complicated regulatory framework governing the electronic media—chiefly, broadcast radio and TV, but also cable, satellite, and microwave means of delivery. Then chapter 13 explores the new and challenging field of Internet law.

A sense of humility should accompany us as we try to make sense of the rapid changes that have characterized the regulation of electronic media. New court cases and new Federal Communications Commission rules (or more often, the discarding of old rules) emerge on the scene every week. Also of relevance are the frequent announcements of mergers among major players in the telecommunications industry

---

1. *In re Equal Opportunities Complaint Filed by Angelides for Governor Campaign against 11 California Television Stations*, 21 F.C.C. Rcd. 11,919 (2006).

and the new ways of playing out old turf wars among broadcast, cable, satellite, local and long-distance telephone, and Internet companies. The primary characteristic of U.S. media outlets is largeness. A tiny handful of companies own not only the four major TV networks but also the majority of cable TV networks.[2] A single company, Clear Channel Communications, owns more than 1,200 radio stations nationwide.[3] More generally, fewer than two dozen companies control almost the entirety of our media culture.[4]

We are often reminded that we live in an era not only of rapid deregulation of the electronic media industry but also of **convergence**. Industry analysts use the word to describe as best they can the not-too-distant future of telecommunications. They predict that in a few decades or sooner, the average middle-class household will not have televisions, radios, telephones, cable decoders, computers, and newspapers and magazines, but instead one single apparatus that will perform all these media functions and more. It will likely also be our home alarm system and our monitoring system to ensure we use gas and electricity efficiently, and it may perform several other functions not yet imagined.

Although there is broad consensus that the industry is headed in this general direction, no one knows what that single apparatus will look like or exactly how it will gather, store, and transmit data. Necessarily, we are therefore also looking toward a highly fluid and unpredictable regulatory environment. Traditionally, we have been content with a small handful of neatly defined and separate categories of communications media. The print media are governed by one body of law, and the broadcast media have had additional laws and regulations imposed on them. Cable TV systems have been subject to a body of regulations somewhat more restrictive than those applied to the print media but less restrictive than those applied to over-the-air TV and radio. Rather separate has been the body of law governing telephone companies, often called "common carriers" because their traditional function has been to serve as a mere conduit for others' transmissions—anyone able and willing to pay the price (the hook-up costs, the monthly phone bill) gets to send messages. Which model shall we use, then, to regulate this yet-unseen single home appliance that will perform all our communications functions? The short answer is that no one knows. All these cautions should be kept in mind as you read these final two chapters.

In the next section we explore the history and general structure of electronic media regulation. The most prominent feature of that structure is the Federal Communications Commission (FCC), which governs through its rule-making authority and through its interactions with Congress, the courts (especially the D.C. Circuit Court of Appeals), and industry trade groups.

---

2. http://stopbigmedia.com/=threat (accessed October 17, 2006).

3. James Granelli, "Consolidation in Media Is Called Stifling," *Los Angeles Times*, October 4, 2006, C2.

4. Robert McChesney, "A Media Deal with Plenty of Bad News," *San Diego Union-Tribune*, January 19, 2000, B7.

THINGS TO REMEMBER

A Changing Media Landscape

- Traditionally, media in the United States have been regulated by one of three models: print, broadcasting, and "common carrier" (e.g., telephone and telegraph), with cable TV treated as something in between print and broadcasting.
- Media analysts, however, predict that diverse media technologies will soon converge, so that most people will have one as-yet-unnamed appliance that will perform the functions now associated with all of these media and more.
- Because it is impossible to know what model of communication law will apply to that single appliance, the body of law presented in these final two chapters must be regarded as a work in progress.

This chapter next considers the traditional rationales used by the FCC, Congress, and the courts for treating print and electronic media differently. The government has regulated electronic media more strictly because of the scarceness of available frequencies (not everyone who wants to obtain a broadcast license may get one), the pervasiveness of TV and radio in our daily lives, and the electronic media's unique power to influence the young.

We next focus on three broad categories of regulations governing TV and radio: those affecting the licensing of individual stations, those aimed at improving the technical and engineering aspects of broadcasting (including the goal of making signals accessible to the hearing impaired and the visually impaired), and those more directly aimed at specific kinds of content. As we shall see, electronic media are subject to regulations concerning political content (especially with respect to speech by and about political candidates), sexually oriented messages, and programming aimed at children. Content regulations that apply uniquely to public broadcasters, such as NPR and PBS stations, are also discussed.

Then we examine the complicated development of laws and regulations affecting the cable industry. Even to this day, the Supreme Court has refused to commit itself to a determination of how much free speech cable TV operators should enjoy, save to say that it will be an "intermediate" amount, somewhere between the free speech accorded to the print media and that accorded to the electronic media. We will also see how the law has affected the direct broadcast satellite (DBS) industry, which thus far has been the cable industry's chief competition.

The Birth of Broadcast Regulation

Social historians have often pointed out that two seemingly contradictory features of radio's early history together ensured that electronic media would be treated differently from print and that radio (and later, television) would not enjoy the full protection of the First Amendment. One of these forces was radio's emergence as a hobbyist's toy. The other is radio's ability, proven very early on, to save lives.

The social histories of radio and of motion pictures were very similar in that both began as media whose main function was to entertain. The first commercially produced films had no narrative, no tale to tell. Their selling point was merely the novelty of seeing images appear to move. So it was that the Supreme Court decided early on, in *Mutual Film Corp. v. Industrial Commission of Ohio*[5]—a decision it would not repudiate for many years[6]—that motion pictures were wholly outside the protection of the First Amendment. The logic underlying the *Mutual Film* decision, that this medium was designed for entertainment, or "spectacle," and thus not "to be regarded . . . as part of the press of the country or as organs of public opinion," was fresh in the minds of lawmakers in the 1920s, when the first comprehensive legislation governing the broadcast media was drafted. It seemed only natural to also deny radio the full measure of First Amendment protection granted to print media. Radio, like motion pictures, existed primarily for its entertainment value.

Sometimes, however, the specific message sent by radio was a matter of life and death. The timely transmission and retransmission of an SOS saved many lives in January 1909, when the RMS *Republic*, a 600-foot luxury liner owned by the White Star Shipping Company, collided with a smaller ship, the *Florida*. There were over fifteen hundred passengers and crew aboard the two ships, yet only six perished. The event marked the first use of a distress signal at sea; the *Republic*'s radio operator was hailed as an international hero. It also led Congress to pass the Wireless Ship Act of 1910, which required any steamer large enough to carry fifty or more passengers and sailing to or from a U.S. port on a journey of two hundred miles or more to have radio equipment and a trained operator on board. The law also required that operators answer and retransmit ship distress signals.

White Star also owned the *Titanic*, whose sinking taught us that radio distress signals save lives only if they are timely received. An ocean liner called the *California* was fewer than twenty miles away when the *Titanic* hit the iceberg. The *California*'s radio operator, however, had gone off duty. Indeed, its captain had turned off the ship's engines. Without an auxiliary power system, the radio would not have worked. The *Titanic*'s distress signal did reach a Marconi company outpost in Newfoundland, but that station's retransmissions were blocked by interference from amateur hobbyists. The hobbyists' interference may also serve to explain how the *Titanic* failed to receive warnings from vessels that had traversed the same route a bit earlier and had spotted numerous icebergs.[7]

---

5. 236 U.S. 230 (1915).

6. *Burstyn v. Wilson*, 343 U.S. 495 (1952).

7. Susan J. Douglas, *Inventing American Broadcasting: 1899-1922* (Baltimore: Johns Hopkins University Press, 1987).

Congress then passed the Radio Act of 1912, which provided that all radio operators had to be licensed by the federal government and which authorized the secretary of commerce to administer the license system and ensure twenty-four-hour staffing of ship radio equipment. The act had many unfortunate omissions. It provided no mechanism for choosing among competing applicants for a specific radio frequency, nor was the commerce secretary permitted to turn down a request for a license. Because the law lacked teeth, it was common for licensees to take it upon themselves to broadcast at frequencies other than those assigned to them or at hours when they were not permitted to broadcast. There were also instances of licensees moving operations to new cities, thus directly interfering with other operators already authorized there to use a certain frequency. When Secretary of Commerce Herbert Hoover tried to bring order from chaos and sanctioned a Chicago radio station that had been broadcasting in a manner inconsistent with its license, a federal judge determined that Hoover had exceeded his authority.[8] Hoover certainly was not happy; neither were radio listeners, because they often received only the cacophony of competing signals. Radio manufacturers General Electric and Westinghouse were perhaps the least happy, recognizing that the market for their product would stagnate unless a meaningful system of regulations allowed the authorized signals to get through. As Hoover himself remarked, "This is probably the only industry in the United States that is unanimously in favor of having itself regulated."[9]

Congress's response was the Radio Act of 1927, the first comprehensive piece of legislation aimed at the electronic media. The act not only provided for a far more elaborate licensing scheme but also established a "public trustee" model to govern radio in America. Because the electromagnetic spectrum, which includes not only radio waves but also X-rays, gamma rays, and both infrared and ultraviolet light, is inherently limited, not every applicant who would like to obtain a broadcasting license can do so. Congress therefore asserted that the airwaves belong to the public and that individual licensees, in their roles as trustees of that valuable public resource, must use their broadcasting licenses in a manner consistent with the "public interest, convenience, and necessity." The act also created the Federal Radio Commission (FRC), a five-member board granted broad powers not only to issue licenses but also to deny applications and to revoke licenses already granted. As interpreted by the Supreme Court in a 1933 decision, the 1927 act also clarified that regulation of the radio spectrum must take place at the national rather than at the state level, because "no state lines divide the radio waves."[10]

In 1934 Congress entered further into the regulation of electronic media with the passage of the Federal Communications Act which, as amended over the years, still

---

8. *United States v. Zenith Radio Corp.*, 12 F.2d 616 (N.D. Ill. 1926).

9. Quoted by Sidney Head, *Broadcasting in America: a Survey of Television and Radio*, 3d ed. (New York: Houghton Mifflin, 1976), 126.

10. *Federal Radio Commission v. Nelson Brothers*, 289 U.S. 266, 279 (1933).

THINGS TO REMEMBER

Early Broadcast Regulation

- Radio's early history virtually guaranteed that it would enjoy less First Amendment protection than print for two reasons:
  - It was a hobbyist's toy.
  - If properly regulated, it could be used to save lives in emergencies.
- The Radio Act of 1912 authorized the secretary of commerce to dole out licenses but did not authorize the secretary to impose any sanctions against stations that violated the terms of their licenses.
- The Radio Act of 1927 created the Federal Radio Commission and first authorized the federal government to rescind licenses from those who were not operating "in the public interest."
- In 1934, Congress passed the Federal Communications Act, which, as modified over the years, is the basis for government regulation of electronic media as well as telecommunications.

governs American broadcasting. The 1934 act disbanded the FRC and created in its stead the Federal Communications Commission, aptly named in that its seven commissioners (since reduced to five) were to be charged with regulating not only radio but also the common-carrier technologies of the day (telephone and telegraph).

Structure and Powers of the FCC

The Federal Communication Commission's five commissioners are appointed by the president with the consent of the Senate. They serve five-year staggered terms. No more than three of the five commissioners may be registered in the same political party. The president designates one of the five to serve as the commission's chairman. Kevin Martin is currently the chairman of the FCC and is scheduled to serve until 2011. A graduate of Harvard Law School, Martin served as an assistant to a previous FCC commissioner, as special assistant to the president for economic policy, and as deputy general counsel for the Bush campaign.

The FCC's Bureaus

As with any large bureaucracy, most of the nuts-and-bolts work in the FCC is done by its professional staff, who are primarily attorneys, engineers, and economists. The staff is organized into seven divisions or "bureaus." The Media Bureau regulates AM and FM radio, and both broadcast and cable television. The Wireless Telecommunica-

tions Bureau deals with private land mobile,[11] aviation, marine, and personal and amateur wireless transmissions; this FCC entity also oversees cellular telephone and
personal communication services, as well as paging systems. The Wireline Competition Bureau deals with, among many other related matters, the policy initiative
needed to maximize our access to high-quality old-fashioned phone service and new-
fangled broadband Internet service. The Public Safety and Homeland Security Bureau, as its name implies, addresses national security and emergency-preparedness
issues related to communication. The International Bureau represents the commission at international conferences involving telecommunications matters and adminis-
ters any relevant provisions of treaties and other international agreements. The
Consumer and Governmental Affairs Bureau deals with public inquiries and informal
consumer complaints, maintains relationships with all levels of government, and
makes policy recommendations concerning disability access. Finally, the Enforcement
Bureau's responsibilities cut across the other bureaus' domains for the purpose of
investigating alleged violations of law or FCC policies by licensees. In this bureau
agents quite literally bring out the hatchets when they hear of unauthorized, "rogue"
radio transmitters.

Rulemaking and Enforcement

The process of creating new FCC regulations typically begins when the commission's professional staff—sometimes on their own initiative, sometimes after complaints by external constituencies—brings to the commissioners an outline of a
problem and its proposed solution. That solution is usually in the form of a "notice
of proposed rule making." If accepted by the commissioners, the notice is then widely
disseminated to the affected industries and, through publication in the *Federal Register*, to the public at large. Public comments are sought over a period of months, and
the text of those comments is also made available for review by any interested parties,
which typically results in a second round of comments. At that point, the commissioners review staff reports and the public's feedback and articulate their final decision, called a "report and order."

The FCC not only creates new policies, of course; it must also enforce existing
policies and relevant statutes. One might suppose that the most frequent impetus for
the commission to commence an investigation against a broadcast licensee would be
a complaint from an offended viewer or listener. The FCC, however, requires that a
pattern of abuse be demonstrated before it will take on a case for review, and the
average consumer simply does not have the time and resources to monitor a station

---

11. Private land mobile, according to the FCC, is "used by companies, local governments, and
other organizations to meet a wide range of communication requirements, including coordination
of people and materials, important safety and security needs, and quick response in times of emergency." http://wireless.fcc.gov/services/index.htm?job = service_home&id = private eland_radio
(accessed April 1, 2007).

for a long enough period to meet this standard. More typical, therefore, are complaints from organized interest groups or from licensees whose own economic interests are tangibly affected by another station's alleged wrongdoing.

If a matter brought to the FCC's attention is seen as warranting investigation, a typical next step is to draft a letter of inquiry (LOI) to the licensee against whom a complaint has been brought, seeking additional information. This initial inquiry is popularly known as "regulation by raised eyebrow" and is often sufficient to bring licensees' behaviors into compliance with FCC policies. The licensee's written response to the LOI might elicit a slight escalation from the FCC staff, in the form of a notice of apparent liability. Sometimes too, the "raised eyebrow" does not consist of singling out individual stations at all but instead takes the form of a speech or other formal statement by the chairman or other commissioners criticizing an overall industry practice. In the 1970s, the FCC followed this strategy in expressing dismay over radio stations whose play lists included songs thought to glorify the drug culture.

The commission is also empowered to issue cease and desist orders and to levy fines against offending licensees. As we will see a bit later in this chapter, the commission has in recent years issued huge fines against stations for broadcasting indecent speech at times when children were likely to be in the audience.

The most extreme measures available to the commission include granting a license renewal on a probationary basis—for a shorter time than the usual eight years—and refusing to renew a license altogether. This latter action is very rarely taken and in recent decades, almost never on the basis of broadcast content itself. Licensees found to have engaged in fraud, however, may very well lose their licenses. The FCC has revoked licenses when licensees have purposely overbilled advertisers or have been untruthful in dealings with the commission itself. In 1999, for example, the commission revoked the Trinity Broadcasting Network's license for WHFT-TV in Miami. The licensee had apparently set up a "puppet," ostensibly minority-owned company, to qualify for more licenses than to which it would have otherwise been entitled.[12]

Ancillary Powers

Technically, the FCC is empowered only to regulate government licensees; with respect to broadcast regulation, that means the FCC may regulate only the individuals and companies who have been granted a license to run specific local TV or radio stations. Even more narrowly, because Congress's right to establish the FCC in the first place flows from the Constitution's Commerce Clause (which gives Congress the power to regulate *interstate* commerce), one might expect that a station with a small broadcast radius capable of only *intra*state transmissions would be beyond the commission's purview. Enter the **ancillary powers** doctrine, through which the courts have granted the FCC authority to regulate matters not specifically enumerated in the

---

12. Harry Martin, "FCC Revokes Trinity License," *Broadcast Engineering*, June 1999.

THINGS TO REMEMBER

FCC Structure and Powers

- The FCC has five commissioners, each appointed by the president with the consent of the Senate, and no more than three of whom may be of the same political party; they serve for staggered five-year terms.
- The FCC is empowered to enforce existing regulations as well as to promulgate new regulations consistent with federal law.
- To punish stations found in violation of relevant regulations, the FCC is empowered to use any of several sanctions, including the rarely invoked revocation of a license.
- The ancillary powers doctrine has been used to extend the commission's authority to TV and radio networks, cable systems, and small stations with wholly *intra*state signals.

Federal Communications Act but which the commission must oversee if it is to effectively regulate interstate transmissions by individual licensees.

The doctrine has been invoked to permit regulation of purely intrastate signals, on the theory that such transmissions could interfere with neighboring broadcast stations whose *interstate* transmissions inarguably bring them into the commission's domain.[13] The FCC has also been permitted to maintain some oversight of radio and TV *networks*, which are not themselves licensed entities. In this instance, two theories are involved. First, although networks are mostly composed of far-flung individual stations (affiliates) that they do not own, each network also does have a number of "O&O" (owned and operated) stations within its portfolio. Second, the contractual relationships between networks and their affiliate stations necessarily have an impact on local broadcasting.[14] The doctrine was also used to give the FCC some limited jurisdiction over cable television, even before Congress passed its first piece of legislation specifically governing that industry.[15]

Why Treat Broadcast and Print Media Differently?

A whole host of laws and regulations that govern the broadcast media would be clearly unconstitutional if applied to newspapers, books, magazines, or other print media. Some of these rules determine who may own a station license, others impose highly specific restrictions on message content. Over the years, several rationales have been offered in support of the differential treatment of print and broadcast media.

---

13. *Nelson Brothers*, 289 U.S. 266.
14. *National Broadcasting Co. v. FCC*, 319 U.S. 190 (1943).
15. *United States v. Southwestern Cable Co.*, 392 U.S. 157 (1968).

The chief rationale has always been, as was seen in the earlier discussion of the Radio Act of 1927, Congress's assertion that the airwaves belong to the public. There have been other reasons offered as well. We look here at three of them: spectrum scarcity, pervasiveness, and accessibility to children.

Spectrum Scarcity

As we have already seen, spectrum scarcity forced the government to regulate radio broadcasting from the very beginning of the industry. It makes no sense to speak of a "right" to a broadcast license when there are not enough licenses to go around.[16]

The spectrum-scarcity rationale is not without its critics. Many argue that the government creates, or at least exacerbates, the scarcity by *giving away* licenses worth tens or even hundreds of millions of dollars. If scarcity is determined by the ratio of the supply of and demand for a product, then giving away licenses, which increases demand, does much to exacerbate the scarcity of licenses. In recent years Congress has instructed the FCC to experiment with the use of auctions, rather than government giveaways, to distribute new kinds of licenses. The commission has since raised tens of billions of dollars auctioning off licenses to use portions of the spectrum for personal communication systems and other wireless telephone and radio services.

Clearly the government can affect demand for spectrum by selling rather than giving away licenses. The supply side of the equation is also at least somewhat in the government's control. As we move to digital broadcasting, for technological reasons that go beyond both the scope of this book and your nonengineer author's expertise, there will be no spectrum scarcity to speak of. The main limitation on the number of commercially viable broadcast stations in any given market will be the finite number of advertising dollars attracted to that market, not the potential for signal interference. The FCC itself, although still accepting the notion that there is not enough room on the spectrum for all who want a broadcast license to have one, has in recent years downplayed the significance of that reality. We should examine the issue from the consumer's perspective, the commission contends. Whereas most TV viewers had a choice of only three or four TV stations a few decades ago, the advent of cable and satellite options has increased that number to dozens, even hundreds.[17]

Pervasiveness

Long before there was "Web surfing," we spoke of "channel surfing." The phrase is a handy way of emphasizing that TV viewers often do not have a specific program in mind when they turn on the set. They are settling in to watch *TV* itself. We bring TV sets and radios into our homes and elsewhere and have little control over what

---

16. *Red Lion Broadcasting v. FCC*, 395 U.S. 367, 388–389 (1969).

17. *FCC v. League of Women Voters of California*, 468 U.S. 364, 376 (1984); *Syracuse Peace Council v. WTVH*, 867 F.2d 654 (D.C. Cir. 1989).

kinds of messages might then be transmitted to us. For these reasons and more, broadcast media are often described as pervasive.[18] (Some critics have suggested that "intrusive" would have been a more appropriate word to express the government's real concerns.)

Viewers change channels so often that even well-intentioned disclaimers to the effect that a specific program might be offensive or upsetting may be ineffectual. To be sure, TVs and radios are all equipped with tuners and on-off switches, and the argument is often made that they are the best defense against offensive messages. As Justice Stevens once wrote, however, this argument "is like saying that the remedy for an assault is to run away after the first blow."[19]

Protecting the Children

Closely related to the pervasiveness rationale is the concern that the broadcast media are especially accessible (and therefore dangerous) to children. If we think in terms of young preliterate children, the broadcast media necessarily have an impact on this audience that the print media cannot. That is one reason why we try to use TV to help build pro-social values in youngsters or to help teach them to read. Indeed, from the FCC's perspective, these functions are defining characteristics of "children's programming." Yet we often seek to regulate the electronic media precisely because of the harm we believe they can do to children. When we express concerns about the level of violence or sexual banter on TV, it is the potential effect on children that most irks us. As we shall see, the FCC's definition of "broadcast indecency" includes a reference to the likelihood that there are large numbers of children in the audience. Moreover, the hard-fought compromise over how to regulate broadcast indecency, the creation of a "safe harbor" for such programming late at night and early in the morning, was settled on with children in mind.

THINGS TO REMEMBER

Rationales for Broadcast Regulation

The three most frequently invoked reasons for regulating broadcast media more strictly than print are the scarcity of the electromagnetic spectrum, the pervasiveness or intrusiveness of TV and radio, and the stronger potential for these media to reach children.

---

18. *In re WUHY-FM*, 24 F.C.C. 2d 408, 411 (1970).
19. *FCC v. Pacifica Foundation*, 438 U.S. 726, 748–749 (1978).

Broadcast Regulation: Licensure and Ownership

Certainly the most fundamental difference between communication law as applied to the print media and as applied to the broadcast media is that one needs a federal *license* to engage in broadcasting. The requirements for licensure discussed below may seem like common sense and thus unremarkable; consider, however, how odd it would seem if the same criteria were applied to the print media. Indeed, application of almost any of these criteria to publishers of books, magazines, or newspapers would seem very reminiscent of the old British system of monopolistic licensing with consent of the Crown.

Requirements for Licensure

Licensees must be "of good character," which in recent years has generally meant only that they not be convicted felons or have a history of lying in previous dealings with the FCC. Applicants for a broadcast license must also be citizens of the United States. A corporate applicant may qualify if at least 75 percent of its assets are American owned. This latter rule was waived by the FCC to permit Rupert Murdoch's News Corporation (an Australian company) to retain licenses for several TV stations that formed the core of the Fox network.

Broadcast license applicants must have, or be able to hire people who have, the requisite engineering skills to run such a complicated operation. The applicant must also demonstrate sufficient financial resources to remain in business for three months even without one penny of advertising revenue coming in.

How Much Can You Own?

The age of deregulation that began in the early 1980s has all but eliminated limits on the total number of stations that any one individual or company may own. There are currently no limits on the number of radio stations a single entity can own nationwide. San Antonio–based Clear Channel Communications alone owns over 1,200 stations (which may seem a lot, the company's website acknowledges, but that represents less than 9 percent of all the radio stations in the United States). As for television stations, the rules governing nationwide ownership are not based on the number of stations owned but on how many people those stations can reach. Currently a single company can own as many stations as it would like, as long as those stations, taken together, do not reach more than 39 percent of America's TV households.

The commission still has on the books an array of rules governing how many media companies one can own in the same local market, which is a function of how competitive that market is (i.e., how many other stations operate there). Generally only two TV stations in even the most competitive markets can be owned by the same company (though the FCC would like to raise this limit to three). The FCC would also like to permit a single company, again only in the most competitive markets, to own its usual allotment of broadcast stations, as well as the local newspaper. The FCC's proposals to deregulate in the ways suggested here were put on hold by a 2004 decision from the Third Circuit Court of Appeals, which demanded that the commission explain more thoroughly its rationale for these proposals.[20] The Third Circuit's decision represented an intriguing break with recent tradition, which found the FCC challenged several times by the D.C. Circuit Court of Appeals to deregulate the broadcast media at a quicker pace.[21] As the *Chicago Tribune* editorialized, the commission "is caught between one appellate court ordering full speed ahead and another cautioning not so fast."[22]

As of the summer of 2007 the commission was still working on a response to the Third Circuit decision, and most observers believe that whatever new proposals emerge will themselves be challenged in court. The commission was also revisiting the wisdom of retaining a rule forbidding any of the four major TV networks (ABC, CBS, NBC, and Fox) to buy one of the competing networks. Indeed, the FCC is instructed by Congress to conduct a biennial review (in even-numbered years) of all of its regulations restricting station ownership and to propose the elimination of any rule deemed no longer effective or necessary in an era of convergence and increased competition.

In 2000 the FCC began issuing licenses for noncommercial low-power FM (LPFM) stations, which operate at up to 100 watts of power with a broadcast antenna no higher than thirty meters, and which generally are designed to have a broadcast radius of only about three and a half miles. A search of the FCC's website in October 2006 revealed that 761 such licenses had already been issued.

Preferences for Minority Ownership

One additional issue related to ownership and licensure is whether the federal government could require or encourage broadcast licensees to embrace affirmative action or minority-hiring preferences. For decades the FCC has assumed this would be the most feasible way to foster a diversity of viewpoints on the air. However, the courts

---

20. *Prometheus Radio Project v. FCC*, 373 F.3d 372 (3d Cir. 2004). Interestingly, the court also questioned the commission's decision to retain rules limiting how many radio stations (a maximum of eight) a single company could own in the same market.

21. See, e.g., *Fox Television Stations v. FCC*, 280 F.3d 1027 (D.C. Cir. 2002); *Sinclair Broadcast Group v. FCC*, 284 F.3d 148 (D.C. Cir. 2002). A third decision in the direction of deregulation, though striking down a congressional rather than an FCC action, was *Ruggiero v. FCC*, 278 F.3d 1323 (D.C. Cir. 2002).

22. "Confusion in the Air," *Chicago Tribune*, July 17, 2004, C20.

have usually restrained the commission,[23] just as they have expressed an overall disfavor with affirmative action in most other settings.[24] In one of the cases ruling against the FCC, Judge Edward Tamm of the D.C. Circuit Court of Appeals—joined by Judge Antonin Scalia prior to his elevation to the high court—questioned the commission's logic. To expect that a black owner would play hip-hop music and would somehow embrace a "black editorial viewpoint," Tamm suggested, would be akin to assuming that "an Italian station owner would primarily program Italian operas, or would eschew Wagner in favor of Verdi."[25] There is reason to doubt that the current Supreme Court would support any attempts by the FCC to do more than it does now in furtherance of racial diversity among owners,[26] which is simply to require that licensees report to the commission the degree of female and minority ownership every two years.

Broadcast Regulation: Consumers and Technology

The FCC, sometimes in direct response to a specific congressional mandate, at other times on its own initiative, has frequently taken steps to improve the technological aspects of broadcasting. Clearly technological considerations are always part of the licensing process. The management of a radio station with a history of engineering glitches that result in extended periods of "dead air" will find it harder to renew its broadcast license. We can also identify times in the history of broadcasting when the FCC has stepped in to bring the entire industry up to a higher standard. For example, over a period of more than twenty years—pursuant to the 1962 All Channel Receiver Act—the commission promulgated rules requiring that TV sets be able to receive UHF stations as conveniently as they did VHF stations. Two noteworthy ongoing examples of FCC regulations governing technical broadcast standards are digital high-definition television and signal accessibility for persons with hearing or visual impairments.

The Switch to HDTV

After many years of internal debates about competing formats, the federal government in 1997 embarked on a long-term commitment to bring the U.S. system of TV

---

23. *MD/DC/DE Broadcasters Association v. FCC*, 236 F.3d 13 (D.C. Cir. 2001); *Lutheran Church, Missouri Synod v. FCC*, 141 F.3d 344, 350 (D.C. Cir. 1998), *reh'g en banc denied*, 154 F.3d 494 (D.C. Cir. 1998).

24. *Gratz v. Bollinger*, 539 U.S. 244 (2003).

25. *Steele v. FCC*, 770 F.2d 1192, 1198 (D.C. Cir. 1985).

26. Leonard M. Baynes, "Making the Case for a Compelling Governmental Interest and Reestablishing FCC Affirmative Action Programs for Broadcast Licensing," 57 *Rutgers Law Review* 235, 252 n.127 (2004).

In recent years the courts have expressed skepticism about predicting the diversity of radio station formats from the diversity (in terms of gender, race, ethnic background, etc.) of licensees.

THINGS TO REMEMBER

Licensure and Ownership Issues

- Basic requirements for obtaining a broadcast license include U.S. citizenship, "good character," technical expertise, and financial solvency.
- Many long-standing limits on the number of TV and radio stations any one person or company can own have been eliminated; other FCC moves toward deregulation were still on hold in early 2007.
- The courts have generally been very skeptical of the FCC's various plans to enhance minority ownership of stations.

transmission into the digital age. Existing TV license holders were granted a second frequency, gratis, to start making the transition to high-definition television (HDTV). The plan calls for stations to complete the switch from analog to digital broadcasting in early 2009 (three years later than the original deadline). By March 2009, all TVs for retail sale should be capable of receiving digital signals. The federal government is committed to subsidizing the purchase of converter boxes for poorer households not ready to make the switch to digital TV receivers. As of October 2006, the FCC reported that over 1,100 TV stations nationwide were offering at least some content in HDTV format.

Accessibility to Audio and Video Signals

Millions of Americans have limited visual or auditory acuity. They may have been born deaf or hard of hearing, or blind, or they may have lost some of their sense modalities with age. In recent years Congress has intervened to ensure that television programming is as accessible as practicable to all.

Closed Captioning.   The Television Decoder Circuitry Act of 1990 (TDCA) mandated that as of July 1, 1993, all TV sets with thirteen-inch or larger screens would have to be capable of receiving closed-captioning signals. Thus most American TV households have access to captioning. Although the most obvious market for the service is persons who are deaf and hard of hearing, the technology can also benefit other identifiable groups, such as children learning to read and adults learning English as a second language.[27] You have probably also seen TVs with captions on and volume off in commercial establishments such as bars and health clubs.

Section 713 of the Telecommunications Act of 1996 instructed the FCC to conduct a study of the current level of closed captioning and to "prescribe such regulations as are necessary" to significantly increase that level. After following the usual procedure of issuing a notice of proposed rule making and gathering comments, in September 1997 the commission issued an order, which, as amended the next year, required that virtually 100 percent of new programming, whether delivered on broadcast TV, cable systems, or direct broadcast satellite systems, be captioned by January 1, 2006.[28] The transition has been largely successful, and the FCC's website offers clear procedures for filing a complaint against any errant programmer.

Some categories of programming will be permanently exempted from the captioning requirement. Included among the exemptions are such commonsense categories

---

27. Senate Committee on Commerce, Science and Transportation, *Hearing on S. 1822, the Communications Act of 1994*, 103d Cong., 2d sess., 1994, 614 (testimony of Mark L. Goldfarb).

28. A slightly longer phase-in would be applied to repeat showings of older programs that had not been captioned; also, Spanish-language programming would not have to be fully captioned until 2010.

as primarily textual programs (e.g., community bulletin boards) and programs consisting mostly of instrumental music. Advertisements are also exempted, as are "interstitial announcements" (e.g., "How did the city council vote go? News at 11."). Programs airing only between 2 a.m. and 6 a.m. need not be captioned, nor do locally produced and distributed nonnews programs with limited repeat value (such as local parades, local high school or nonprofessional sports and community theater productions.) Exemptions would also apply to TV channels or networks that can demonstrate that providing closed captioning would impose an undue financial burden.

Video Descriptions.

It is one of the most famous scenes from contemporary American cinema: young Elliott (played by Henry Thomas) befriends the creature we will all soon know as "E.T." The scene lasts for almost five minutes. The audio is limited to some pleasant but mysterious background music, a bit of breathing and chewing, the sound of something crashing to the floor and of a door slamming, and only one word spoken: Elliott's barely whispered "Wow!" In other words, if you were a blind child encountering the Spielberg film for the first time, you would have no idea what was going on.

Enter now the power of video description, the artistically complex method of adding a second audio track, a voice describing the action, to TV programs as well as to films, whether on the big screen or in home video format. WGBH-TV in Boston has been a pioneer in this area, with its trademarked Descriptive Video Service (DVS).

As you can appreciate from the elaborate nature of the *E.T.* video-description text, legislation placing on broadcasters the same kinds of demands for the service that the commission has imposed for closed captioning would likely be subtitled something along the lines of "The English Majors' Full Employment Act."[29] The Telecommunications Act of 1996, however, required only that the FCC "commence an inquiry" as to the extent of available programming with video descriptions. The act does not prescribe a closing date for any such inquiry, nor does it indicate what, if any, regulations should emerge from such an inquiry. When the FCC promulgated fairly modest rules requiring that network affiliate stations in the twenty-five largest markets provide fifty hours of video-described programming quarterly (about four hours weekly), a coalition of broadcasters and cablecasters successfully challenged those rules.[30]

---

29. Advisory Committee on Public Interest Obligations of Digital Television Broadcasters, January 16, 1998, transcript of meeting, 130 (statement of Peggy Charren, Action for Children's Television), *available at* http://www.ntia.doc.gov/pubintadvcom/janmtg/transcript-all.htm (commenting on the description video services group of WGBH, "It's an extraordinary place for unemployed English majors.").

30. *Motion Picture Association of America v. FCC*, 309 F.3d 796 (D.C. Cir. 2002).

Video Description from *E.T.*

Elliott stands at the top of the staircase on the second floor. Holding a bag of candy in one hand, he drops a pile of Reese's Pieces onto the carpeted landing. He backs away to the door of his room, crouches on the floor, and keeps his eyes locked on the candy. The alien's long, pencil-thin fingers reach over the top of the stairs to pick up one of the pieces. . . . A faint smile spreads across Elliott's mouth.

The alien grabs the rest of the candy, leaving one piece behind. He steps onto the landing to get it. Elliott dumps more Reese's Pieces in the doorway of his room. The alien eagerly reaches for them and scoops them into his hands. . . .

As the creature stands in the light, we see him clearly for the first time. He has wrinkly, light-brown skin, his stubby torso rests on squat, inch-high legs connected to his webbed feet. Completely bald, he has a broad face, shaped like a squashed heart, with a button nose and great big blue eyes. . . .

THINGS TO REMEMBER

Technology and Access Issues

- TV stations are mandated by federal law to make the switch to HDTV by 2009.
- The Television Decoder Circuitry Act of 1990 mandated that TVs larger than thirteen inches be capable of reading closed captioning, and the Telecommunications Act of 1996 instructs the FCC to create rules that will result in full captioning on broadcast and cable TV. The commission issued an order requiring full captioning by January 1, 2006.
- With respect to video descriptions for the blind, the 1996 act requires only that the FCC study the issue. The commission has thus far not been permitted to actually require video descriptions.

Broadcast Regulation: Content

Section 326 of the Federal Communications Act reads:

> Nothing in this Act shall be understood or construed to give the [FCC] the power of censorship over the radio communications or signals transmitted by any radio station, and no regulation or condition shall be promulgated or fixed by the Commission which shall interfere with the right of free speech by means of radio communication.

"*No* regulation or condition"? This is very reminiscent of the First Amendment's admonition that Congress shall pass "*no* law abridging . . . freedom of speech." Yet if that latter admonition were interpreted literally, this book would have been much shorter. Similarly, both Congress and the FCC frequently legislate and regulate the actual content of media messages. In this section we look at several categories of restrictions on broadcast media content. Included are the regulation of political speech and sexually oriented speech; children's programming; the V chip as an answer to TV violence; special regulations applied to PBS and NPR stations; and some other miscellaneous content regulations.

Regulation of Political Speech

As a result of the deregulation fervor of the 1980s and beyond, just about the only broadcast regulations governing political speech apply exclusively to times when political campaigns are underway. Chief among these are the **candidate-access rule** and the **equal-time rule**.

The Candidate-Access Rule.   Section 312(a) of the Federal Communications Act authorizes the FCC to revoke the license of any TV or radio station that fails to "allow reasonable access to or to permit purchase of reasonable amounts of time . . . by a legally qualified candidate for Federal elective office on behalf of his candidacy." Section 312 further dictates that as an election grows near, stations must charge candidates the lowest rates they make available to their best commercial customers.[31] Although the act refers only to candidates for *federal* office, station managers understand that an absolute refusal to sell ads to candidates for state and local offices would be seen by the FCC as an abrogation of their overall obligation to broadcast "in the public interest."[32]

---

31. Under the McCain-Feingold campaign finance law, upheld in relevant part by the Supreme Court in 2003, candidates must now include their faces in their TV ads, saying something to the effect that they "approved this message," in order to qualify for the lowest ad rates. *McConnell v. Federal Election Commission*, 540 U.S. 93 (2003).

32. *CBS, Inc. v. FCC*, 453 U.S. 367 (1981).

The candidate-access rule does not indicate its own triggering mechanism; when, exactly, has a campaign begun? In 1981, however, the Supreme Court offered some guidance. The impetus for the decision was the Carter-Mondale campaign's request to purchase a thirty-minute spot on all three major networks in December 1979. None of the networks agreed to the specific request. The campaign complained to the FCC and ultimately obtained a 6-3 victory in the Supreme Court. Chief Justice Warren Burger's majority opinion indicates that the 1980 presidential campaign was in full swing at the time the Carter-Mondale campaign sought airtime. More than a dozen candidates had formally announced that they were running. Both major parties had already begun the process of convention delegate selection. Moreover, the Iowa caucuses were barely a month away.

Look again at the precise wording of section 312. It requires stations to "allow reasonable access to" airtime *or* "to permit purchase of . . ." airtime. Does this mean that a willingness to sell airtime precludes any responsibility to cover a candidate's campaign in other ways? Does "reasonable access" mean turning one's studio over to candidates for their own use, unedited by station management, unquestioned by the station's reporters? Or can such access mean simply covering the candidate's activities during the course of the campaign? That same 1980 presidential race resulted in two separate federal appellate decisions, both flowing from complaints lodged with the FCC by Senator Edward Kennedy, who was then challenging President Carter for the Democratic Party's nomination.[33] In February and March 1980, President Carter's carefully timed press conferences and speeches were carried in their entirety by all three networks. Kennedy, pointing out that one of the press conferences took place on the eve of the New Hampshire primary and was very much in keeping with what pundits called Carter's "Rose Garden" strategy of looking as presidential as possible and not "lowering himself" to campaigning for reelection, requested that a similar parcel of time be *given* to his campaign. The networks refused, the FCC upheld the networks' decision, and the D.C. Circuit Court of Appeals supported the FCC. Writing for the three-judge panel, Judge Robinson concluded that section 312 was never intended to require TV stations to *give* their airtime to candidates. The law is written with the disjunctive "or," so that stations can meet their obligations by *selling* airtime. Because Kennedy never even asked to buy time, he was not in a position to demand that free time be given him. Although Judge Robinson did *not* suggest that a station could point to its own news coverage of a candidate as a substitute for meeting its section 312 obligations, he emphasized that Kennedy's campaign was hardly being ignored by the major networks: "CBS had televised Senator Kennedy's response to the press conference on its news programs, PBS had invited him to appear on its McNeil/Lehrer Report, and NBC had proposed an appearance on its 'Today' program on the morning after the conference."

---

33. *Kennedy for President Committee v. FCC*, 636 F.2d 432 (D.C. Cir. 1980); *Kennedy for President Committee v. FCC*, 636 F.2d 417 (D.C. Cir. 1980).

The Equal-Time Rule.

Although section 312 litigation has been sparse, candidates have frequently challenged FCC rulings concerning a station's obligations under section 315 of the Federal Communications Act. Often referred to as the equal-time rule (even though the statutory language is "equal *opportunities*"), section 315 has been part of the Federal Communications Act since its passage in 1934. Indeed, it was born as section 18 of the 1927 Radio Act. The essence of the rule is found in 315(a): anytime a "legally qualified candidate for any public office" is permitted to "use" a broadcasting station, the station's owner must "afford equal opportunities to all other such candidates for that office." The rule also prohibits stations from exercising the "power of censorship over the material broadcast under the provisions of this section." An important corollary: broadcast licensees are immune from liability, such as for defamation, stemming from the content of candidate-placed political ads over which the licensees, after all, have no control.[34]

Note two differences between the equal-time rule and the candidate-access rule discussed earlier. Unlike section 312, section 315 applies to candidates for office at all levels of government, from local dog catcher to president of the United States. Also, candidates earn a right to access under section 315 only if another candidate for the same office has already been permitted to "use" the station's airwaves. That a political campaign has begun is not sufficient to trigger the rule.

What Is a "Legally Qualified" Candidate?

The FCC employs four guidelines to determine if an individual is a "legally qualified" candidate for purposes of applying Section 315. First, the candidate must have publicly announced his or her intention to run for office. This rule seems straightforward enough, although candidates are often quite coy about whether they are in fact running for office or reelection. The longer they can avoid making the official announcement, the longer they can continue to appear on camera in various capacities without triggering the equal-time rule.

Second, the candidate must be legally qualified to hold the particular office. Winning enough votes is a necessary but not a sufficient condition to be elected to public office. For example, the president must be a natural-born citizen and must be at least thirty-five when assuming office. Anyone who has already served two terms as president can no longer be a legally qualified candidate for that office. Senators must be at least thirty years old, representatives at least twenty-five; members of both houses must be residents of the districts or states they represent. Similar age and residency requirements, and in some cases, term limits, apply to many state and local offices as well.

Third, the candidate must be qualified for a place on the ballot (or as a write-in candidate). In most circumstances, simply announcing that you are a candidate does not earn you a place on the ballot come Election Day. You must file a petition con-

---

34. *Farmers Educational & Cooperative Union of America v. WDAY*, 360 U.S. 525, 530 (1959).

taining a sufficient number of qualified voters' signatures with the Board of Elections or similar governmental entity to meet local rules for ballot placement. If the office for which you are running is permitted to have write-in candidacies, you can be a legally qualified candidate for the purposes of section 315 by meeting whatever qualifications are prerequisite to that status.

Finally, candidates must have been nominated for the office by a recognized political party, or at least must have made a "substantial showing" of their candidacy. Making a "substantial showing" in this context does not necessarily mean that your polling numbers suggest that you have a good chance of winning the race. Rather, this part of the test for determining a candidate's status should be thought of as more of a "looks like a duck, quacks like a duck" yardstick. What kinds of behaviors do candidates generally engage in? the FCC asks itself. They make speeches about political topics, they establish a campaign headquarters (for low-budget candidates vying for minor offices, this might be their own home or the home of a supporter), they distribute campaign literature, they assemble a committee to help them with their campaigns. These are the kinds of behaviors that count as making a "substantial showing."

"Using" the Airwaves.   The equal-time rule is triggered when a broadcast station permits a candidate for elected office to use its airwaves. But what does it mean to *use* a station's airwaves? First, the appearance must be a "positive" one, which does not mean that the candidate has to come off well on camera, or say clever things. Rather, the rule is intended to exempt such scenarios as when candidate A, in the course of a media appearance, uses the voice or picture of opposing candidate B while criticizing the opponent. Such a scenario would not constitute a "use" by candidate B.

Use of the airwaves does not have to be for the purpose of delivering political messages at all. Indeed, TV stations had to be careful about showing old Arnold Schwarzenegger or Ronald Reagan movies at election time. When in 1994 NBC broadcast the movie *Necessary Roughness*, which included an appearance by lawyer-turned-actor-turned-politician Fred Thompson, it had to give free airtime to Democrat Jim Cooper, Thompson's opponent in the Senate race in Tennessee. As the FCC has ruled in numerous cases, Cooper was not entitled to an amount of time equivalent to the entire running time of the film, but only to the amount of time that Thompson appeared on screen—four minutes and thirteen seconds. Only if a candidate is in charge of the TV broadcast does "equal time" mean "equivalent to the entire broadcast's length."

Even a tongue-in-cheek candidate's appearances constitute a use for purposes of the equal-time rule. Comedian Pat Paulsen, who made his own mock candidacy for president a running gag on the *Smothers Brothers Comedy Hour*, continued the joke in the 1972 campaign and actually filed as a candidate for the Republican nomination. A problem emerged, however. He was also to appear as a guest on a decidedly nonpolitical program called *The Mouse Factory*, owned by Disney. The FCC ruled that stations airing that episode would indeed incur the usual section 315 obligations, and a federal appellate court upheld the commission. The court rejected Paulsen's argument that the commission's ruling applied to entertainers as a class denied them the Constitution's promise of equal protection under law, because only they would have to choose between running for office and their usual way of making a living.[35]

Similar claims of unfair treatment were rejected years later when made by a more serious candidate for lesser office. When William Branch, a general-assignment reporter for KOVR-TV in Sacramento, decided to run for a seat on the Town Council of Loomis, California, a community of about four thousand residents within his station's viewing area, his employer insisted that he take an unpaid leave of absence for the duration of the campaign, with no guarantee of continued employment thereafter. The station management feared that section 315 would require it to give many hours of free airtime to other candidates for the Loomis Town Council. The FCC, and later the D.C. Court of Appeals, concluded that section 315 would indeed apply in such a situation and that none of Branch's constitutional rights had been violated.[36]

Courts have generally interpreted the language in section 315 warning broadcast licensees not to censor "material broadcast under the provisions of this section" as applicable to more than just one candidate's free use of airtime to respond to another candidate's triggering "use." Rather, courts assume that the provision applies to all candidate speech during an election campaign, including political ads candidates place on TV and radio stations.[37]

The "no censorship" rule has frequently caused grief for station managers. In 1972, one of the candidates for the Democratic Party's nomination for U.S. senator from Georgia, J. B. Stoner, used a campaign ad that was as overtly racist as one can imagine: "The main reason why niggers want integration" is that they "want our white women," he charged. Stoner further disparaged all of his opponents for office as "race mixers," warning that "you cannot have law and order and niggers too." The NAACP and the mayor of Atlanta sought a declaration from the commission that stations could not be forced to run such an ad, in part because reactions to it could jeopardize public safety. But the commission rejected this argument and asserted that "a contrary conclusion here would permit anyone to prevent a candidate from exercising his rights under section 315 by threatening a violent reaction."[38]

In 1980, the Citizens Party ran a radio ad on behalf of its presidential candidate, Barry Commoner, that began with an exasperated male voice shouting "Bullshit! . . . Carter, Reagan, and Anderson. It's all bullshit!" Commoner's voice then took over, with the candidate lamenting that he had to use "such strong language" to get any-

---

35. *Paulsen v. FCC*, 491 F.2d 887 (9th Cir. 1974).

36. *In re William H. Branch*, 101 F.C.C. 2d 901 (1985), *aff'd*, *Branch v. FCC*, 824 F.2d 37 (D.C. Cir. 1987).

37. *Hammond for Governor Committee*, 69 F.C.C. 2d 946, 947 (1978).

38. *Letter to Lonnie King*, 36 F.C.C. 2d 635 (1972).

one's attention. When NBC initially refused to run the ad, Commoner appealed to the FCC, which ruled in his favor.[39]

In the 1990s, several pro-life candidates sought to run ads that included highly graphic images of aborted fetuses. The management of WAGA-TV in Atlanta agreed to run such ads from congressional candidate Daniel Becker, but only at times of day when the number of children in the audience would be small. The FCC sided with the station, but the D.C. Circuit Court of Appeals reversed the commission's decision and held that even such "channeling" of offensive messages to late-night hours was a violation of both section 312(a) and section 315.[40]

Statutory Exemptions to the Equal-Time Rule.   In 1959, largely in response to FCC decisions that it saw as applying equal-time requirements too strictly to a Chicago station,[41] Congress amended section 315 to exempt certain categories of candidate appearances from triggering stations' obligations to opposing candidates. The amendments cover candidate appearances on newscasts, news interview programs, and documentaries, as well as appearances in on-the-spot coverage of news events. Let us look at each of these in a bit more detail.

The newscast exemption covers not only such obvious kinds of programs as *NBC Nightly News* or *ABC World News Tonight* but also newsmagazines such as *20/20*, *Primetime Live*, and *Dateline NBC*, as well as the networks' morning news/variety programs, such as *Today* and *Good Morning America*. As part of its responsibility for the day-to-day administration of section 315, the FCC has also granted exemptions, on a case-by-case basis, to various syndicated talk shows, such as the old *Phil Donahue Show*, *Geraldo*, and *Sally Jesse Raphael*.[42] In 1989, the commission ruled that some but not all of the weekly *McLaughlin Group* was beyond section 315's reach. At the time of the FCC ruling, the typical *McLaughlin* program consisted of a short news clip, often borrowed from another network, followed by a few minutes of discussion about that event by the show's four panelists. This "news clip, then discussion" format was repeated two or more times during the course of the program. The FCC ruled that a candidate appearance on one of the prerecorded news clips was exempt from the equal-time rule but that the same candidate's appearance in the studio, participating in a panel discussion with the small group of journalists, might not be exempt.[43] The D.C. Circuit Court of Appeals upheld the FCC's decision.[44]

News interview programs are exempt if they are regularly scheduled programs, rather than ad hoc "meet the candidates" events. (If a network or a local station pre-

39. *In re Complaint of Barry Commoner and LaDonna Harris against NBC Radio*, 87 F.C.C. 2d 1 (1980).

40. *Becker v. FCC*, 95 F.3d 75 (D.C. Cir. 1996).

41. *In re CBS, Inc. (Lars Daly)*, 26 F.C.C. 715 (1959).

42. *Multimedia Entertainment, Inc.*, 56 Rad. Reg. 2d (P & F) 143 (1984).

43. *In re Oliver Productions, Inc.*, 4 F.C.C. Rcd. 5953 (1989).

44. *Telecommunications Research and Action Center v. FCC*, 26 F.3d 185 (D.C. Cir. 1994).

empted regular programming to interview one candidate for an hour, however, all other bona fide candidates for the same office would be able to make an equal-time claim.) Thus, any of the well-known Sunday morning programs on the various networks, such as *Meet the Press*, *This Week*, and *Face the Nation*, can invite one candidate for office on to the show without having to invite all other announced candidates onto that or later editions of the program. Regularly scheduled programs only part of which involve the host interviewing political figures have also been exempted from section 315. Included in this mix have been programs conducted by Jerry Springer, Sally Jesse Raphael, Bill Maher, and even Howard Stern.[45] Thus it was no surprise when the FCC, less than two weeks before the 2006 election, dismissed California gubernatorial candidate Phil Angelides's complaint stemming from Arnold Schwarzenegger's appearance on *The Tonight Show*, reference to which opened this chapter. Of course, California TV stations would still have to be careful not to show any non-exempt Schwarzenegger appearances—notably any of the governor's old movies—in the days and weeks before the election.

Documentary programs are exempt from section 315's provisions only if the candidate's appearance is "incidental" to the subject matter of the program. The candidate cannot *be* the subject matter. The commission has offered several criteria to help determine whether a candidate appearance is truly "incidental": the program should not have been designed to aid or advance the candidate's campaign; the decision to have the candidate appear in the documentary should have been made on the basis of "bona fide news judgment"; and the candidate should not have had any control over the format or the production of the broadcast.

The on-the-spot news exemption covers a wide range of situations, most of which tend to favor the interests of incumbents seeking reelection. A public official might show up at the scene of a natural disaster or at a ribbon-cutting ceremony for a new shopping center. Both would be news events. So too would press briefings and press conferences. Indeed, in the post-CNN era of twenty-four-hour news coverage, the real difference between the newscast and on-the-spot coverage exemptions is whether the candidate participates in an event deemed sufficiently newsworthy for the TV news not just to cover but to cover *live* instead of waiting for the evening news.

Under what circumstances a staged debate between political candidates is exempted as an on-the-spot news event has been a long-running and complicated question for the FCC, Congress, and the courts. In 1960 Congress passed special legislation formally suspending section 315 insofar as it might have prevented the broadcasting of debates between Senator John F. Kennedy and Vice President Richard Nixon unless they invited every imaginable minor party candidate on the same stage with them. Partly because of section 315 fears, and partly because the individual candidates in

---

45. See, respectively, *Request of Multimedia Entertainment*, 9 F.C.C. Rcd. 2811 (1994); *Request of Multimedia Entertainment*, 6 F.C.C. Rcd. 1798 (1991); *Request of ABC*, 15 F.C.C. Rcd. 1355 (1999); and *Request of Infinity Broadcasting*, 18 F.C.C. Rcd. 18603 (2003).

the interim saw no real advantage to them, there were no head-to-head debates between the two major parties' presidential candidates again until the 1976 campaign.

In the interim the FCC had decided that debates were exempt from section 315, as long as they were sponsored by an outside group other than the TV networks or the candidates themselves. Further, the debates would have to be covered live, and media decisions whether to air the debates would have to be based on sound news judgment rather than favoritism for any particular candidate.

Thus it was that League of Women Voters sponsored debates between Ford and Carter in 1976, and Carter and Reagan in 1980. If the philosophy underlying the commission's outside-sponsorship requirement was that the debate should be a news event that would take place regardless of the TV networks' independent decisions to cover the event, the notion was exposed as a fiction when, during a Ford-Carter debate in Philadelphia, the audio feed to the networks went dead. The live audience in the auditorium could hear just fine; if the event had not been staged for the cameras' benefit, the debate would have continued uninterrupted. That did not happen of course. The candidates sat or stood, silently, for twenty-seven minutes!

In any event, the FCC lifted its restriction on network sponsorship in 1983.[46] The 1984 debates between Ronald Reagan and Walter Mondale were still sponsored by the League of Women Voters which, along with the networks and the candidates themselves, was named as a defendant in a suit brought by Citizens Party candidate Sonia Johnson. The D.C. Circuit Court of Appeals denied her request for inclusion in the debates, finding "no basis for disturbing" the FCC's judgment.[47]

More recently, rules governing sponsorship of debates were loosened further, as the FCC decided that even the candidates themselves may serve as sponsors. The TV stations involved, however, would have to retain ultimate control as to the amount and type of coverage of the debate.[48]

Regulation of Sexually Oriented Speech

It was the wardrobe malfunction seen around the world. And in this country, the effects on the broadcast industry of Justin Timberlake's baring of Janet Jackson's breast during their halftime performance at the 2004 Super Bowl have been profound. The FCC received over 500,000 complaints about the event—mind you, the vast majority of these were organized mailings by a single public interest group, but still, no government agency can afford to ignore that kind of outpouring. CBS itself was fined $550,000 for that Super Bowl moment. More significantly, after several false starts, in 2006 Congress increased the statutory fine for broadcast indecency tenfold, from $32,500 to $325,000 per incident.

---

46. *In re Petitions of Henry Geller et al.*, 95 F.C.C. 2d 1236 (1983).
47. *Johnson v. FCC*, 829 F.2d 157 (D.C. Cir. 1987).
48. *In re Request for Declaratory Ruling by WCVB-TV*, 2 F.C.C. Rcd. 4778 (1987).

THINGS TO REMEMBER

Broadcast Regulation and Political Campaigns

- The candidate-access rule tells stations that they must make their airwaves available to persons running for federal office and that any advertising time they sell to candidates must be at the lowest rates available.
- The equal-time rule provides that stations who permit one candidate (for *any* elected office) to "use" their airwaves must provide a comparable time slot to all other candidates for the same office. Not all appearances are "uses," however; among the exemptions are appearances on news and news interview programs, and on documentaries whose subject matter is something other than the candidate.
- Stations are not permitted to censor candidates' speech, whether on unpaid news programs or on paid advertisements.

Notice that reference was made to *indecency* in the preceding paragraph, not *obscenity*. To be sure, the U.S. Code also has a provision (section 1464) forbidding the use of the airwaves to broadcast obscenity. Such a prohibition has been part of our broadcasting system since the adoption of the Radio Act of 1927. But section 1464 also warns radio and TV station licensees that they may not broadcast either "indecent" or "profane" speech. There is virtually no case law concerning the latter, and indeed the FCC seems only to have rediscovered profanity in the last few years. But the courts have had much to say about indecency. The leading Supreme Court case, *FCC v. Pacifica Foundation*, resulted from an FM radio station in New York broadcasting on a Tuesday afternoon in October 1973 a George Carlin routine called "Filthy Words." The monologue might be described as a popular sociolinguistic treatise on the function of sexual language.

The FCC received one complaint about the broadcast from a father who was taken by surprise while listening to the radio in the car with his son. After investigating, the commission determined that the station had violated section 1464's prohibition against indecent broadcasting. The broadcast was not obscene in that it was not designed to appeal to "the prurient interest," and it may very well have had "serious literary, artistic, political, or scientific value." The commission's definition of broadcast indecency, however, did not include these two features of the *Miller* obscenity test (see chapter 11 for a review of the test). It was enough that the monologue described sexual or excretory functions in a patently offensive way and that children were likely to be listening. But when are enough children likely to be listening to make an otherwise acceptable program indecent? After several years of sometimes comic wrangling among Congress, the FCC, and the federal judiciary, in 1995 it became clear that broadcast licensees must refrain from airing indecent programming during the hours from 6 a.m. to 10 p.m.[49] The remaining hours are referred to in the industry as broadcasting's "safe harbor."

The commission's chosen sanction was not to revoke the Pacifica station's license, nor to fine it, but only to place in its file a letter describing the incident, which presumably would inform the commissioners' deliberations when license renewal time came around. The station's parent association decided to appeal that ruling, an appeal that produced a Supreme Court decision in 1978. Most but not all of Justice Stevens's opinion carried enough votes to be majority doctrine. Stevens emphasized the propriety of regulating broadcast media more strictly than other modes of communication, emphasizing radio's "pervasiveness" (especially its ability to intrude on one's privacy at home) and its accessibility to children, "even those too young to read."[50] The *Pacifica* decision tells the FCC that it *may* impose sanctions against licensees who broadcast indecent, nonobscene speech; it does not tell the commission that it must or should do so.

---

49. *Action for Children's Television v. FCC*, 58 F.3d 654 (D.C. Cir. 1995).
50. *FCC v. Pacifica Foundation*, 438 U.S. 726 (1978).

After the *Pacifica* decision, the commission's enforcement of indecency restrictions on licensees was virtually nonexistent for a decade or so. Then, in 1987, the FCC imposed sanctions against a handful of licensees, including a station that had broadcast excerpts from a radio play called *Jerker*, which at the time was enjoying a critically acclaimed off-Broadway run. The play's theme was a deadly serious one—gay men redefining the meaning of eroticism in the midst of the AIDS epidemic—but its language was a bit too graphic for the airwaves, the commission concluded.[51] One of the commission's other 1987 actions was taken against the highly successful Howard Stern radio program.[52] Actually this was one of several cases the FCC brought against Stern's employers, who eventually settled with the commission in 1995 for a lump-sum payment of approximately $1.7 million. Years later Stern moved to the Sirius satellite radio network, a medium that, unlike old fashioned over-the-air TV and radio, is free to broadcast indecent speech at any time of day or night.

The Super Bowl wardrobe malfunction incident has resulted in a dramatic increase in FCC activity aimed at broadcast indecency. Not long after the $550,000 fine was levied against CBS for Mr. Timberlake's overreaching, the commission fined the Fox network $1.2 million for an episode of the reality series *Married by America* that featured some electronically obscured nudity.

The broadcast industry has complied, or cowered, depending on your perspective. TV writers and producers have admitted that they have been toning down their racier narratives. PBS complained to the FCC that it was afraid even an episode of its *Antiques Roadshow* might get it into trouble, because the show focused for a while on a lithograph of a nude Marilyn Monroe.[53] Even its award-winning documentary series *Frontline* was seen as vulnerable, evidenced by PBS's decision to delete soldiers' spontaneous utterances while on patrol in Iraq—"instead of cursing during an ambush or sniper attack, there is bleeping," one critic noted.[54] Dozens of TV stations nationwide balked at airing Steven Spielberg's *Saving Private Ryan* on Veterans Day 2004, for fear of liability stemming from the fictional soldiers' occasional use of indecent language. In retrospect, the fears about the film were unfounded. The FCC did indeed receive complaints but concluded that the movie was not indecent.[55]

It is unlikely that the ABC affiliates who took a pass on *Saving Private Ryan* were engaged in a publicity stunt. The FCC had given every indication that even a fleeting

---

51. *In re Pacifica Foundation*, 2 F.C.C. Rcd. 2698 (1987).

52. *In re Infinity Broadcasting Corp. of Pennsylvania*, 2 F.C.C. Rcd. 2705 (1987).

53. Jacques Steinberg, "Eye on FCC, TV and Radio Watch Words," *New York Times*, May 10, 2004, A1.

54. Kay McFadden, "PBS Feels Heat of Indecency Debate, Bleeps Iraq War Piece," *Seattle Times*, February 18, 2005, A1.

55. *In re Complaints against Various Television Licensees Regarding Their Broadcast on November 11, 2004, of the ABC Television Network's Presentation of the Film Saving Private Ryan*, 20 F.C.C. Rcd. 4507 (2005).

instance of a single "fuck" could result in a hefty fine.[56] When rock star Bono, in receiving an award at the 2003 Golden Globes, spontaneously exclaimed that "this is *fucking* fantastic," the commission overruled its own staff and, in an opinion that would surely make linguists cringe, held that "any use of the word or any of its variants necessarily carries a sexual connotation. . . . Its use invariably invokes a coarse sexual image."[57]

In February 2006 the commission released a huge document covering indecency complaints against various programs that aired between 2002 and 2005. We learn that the word "shit" will be treated by the commission as presumptively indecent and profane. Profanity, the commission tells us, consists of language so "vulgar and coarse," so "grossly offensive to members of the public who actually hear it as to amount to a nuisance."[58]

Broadcasters continue to fear FCC action against them for indecent or profane speech. In 2006 the commission decided to issue a fine of over $3 million against CBS for an episode of its series *Without a Trace*. It also issued a fine against a PBS station for airing a documentary about and including interviews with blues musicians, a group of people known for frequent use of salty language. Confusion in the industry

---

56. In *Saving Private Ryan*, not only do we find the expected expletives uttered by young men viewing the horrors of war, but there is also a running joke early on as to the meaning of "FUBAR," which we soon learn is an acronym for "fucked up beyond all recognition."

57. *In re Complaints against Various Broadcast Licensees regarding Their Airing of the "Golden Globe Awards" Program*, 19 F.C.C. Rcd. 4975 (2004). Linguists would point to Bono's use of "fucking" as an "intensifier," performing the same function as "really" or "very."

58. *In re Complaints regarding Various Television Broadcasts between February 2, 2002, and March 8, 2005*, 21 F.C.C. Rcd. 2664 (2006). "Shit," and its variants, the FCC tells us, "invariably invokes a coarse excretory image." Again, linguists would cringe at the notion that the word itself always refers literally to excrement. Most frequently it serves as an "exclamation," as in "Shit! I burnt the pot roast!" The next year, the Second Circuit Court of Appeals vacated the FCC's ruling, pointing to much-publicized uses by President Bush and Vice President Cheney of "fuck" and "shit." *Fox TV, Inc. v. FCC*, 2007 U.S. App. LEXIS 12868 (2d Cir. 2007).

THINGS TO REMEMBER

Sexually Oriented Broadcasts

- Section 1464 of the U.S. Code prohibits broadcasting of obscene, indecent, and profane programming.
- Nonobscene sexual programming (even if it includes indecency and, presumably, profanity) may be broadcast between 10 p.m. and 6 a.m.
- There has been a huge increase in FCC actions against indecent and profane broadcasts since the infamous 2004 Super Bowl "wardrobe malfunction."
- In response to that same incident, Congress increased tenfold the statutory fine for a single instance of broadcast indecency, to $325,000.
- Although the FCC intended in a lengthy 2006 document to clarify its standards, in fact broadcasters claimed to be cowering with uncertainty as to what leeway they enjoy, even when broadcasting weighty documentary programming.

as to what the FCC really intends seems justified. A fictional group of soldiers cursing (*Saving Private Ryan*) results in no fine. A real-life group of musicians cursing does result in a fine. So it is no surprise that a number of stations bleeped out an expletive uttered by civil rights leader James Forman in the long-awaited PBS re-airing of the documentary series *Eyes on the Prize*. What will happen with depictions of real soldiers' cursing in Ken Burns's forthcoming documentary series *The War*, a seven-part documentary about World War II, broadcasters wonder?[59]

Regulation of Children's Television

Given that the electronic media's unique ability to reach children has been one of the most frequently raised arguments in favor of government regulation, it is no surprise that the government has long expressed a special interest in children's television. Former FCC chairman Newton Minow's dismay at the state of children's TV was one of the chief reasons he titled his famous 1961 speech "The Vast Wasteland." Even today, concerns about the effects of the electronic media on children have permeated public discourse about broadcast regulation in general. If consuming electronic media programming were an adults-only activity, the ongoing debates about sexual and violent imagery would likely have a very different tone, if conducted at all. In this section we review government regulations of those parts of the commercial broadcast day specifically aimed at children.

For the first several decades of commercial radio and TV, there were virtually no legal requirements concerning children's programming, save for general statements from the FCC to the effect that meeting the needs of children was one of the many items included in broadcasters' overall obligation to function "in the public interest."

59. Dusty Saunders, "Industry Is Bleeping Scared," *Rocky Mountain News*, October 12, 2006.

The FCC also imposed limits on the numbers of commercials that could be aired during, as well as immediately before and after, a children's program, but these were rescinded in the 1980s, in keeping with the commission's fervor for deregulation.

Congress, by passing the Children's Television Act in 1990, reimposed limits on the number of commercial minutes that could be aired during children's programming (defined as programs aimed at viewers age twelve and younger). Current maximums are ten and a half minutes per hour on weekends and twelve minutes per hour on weekdays. The act's requirement that broadcasters provide programming designed to further the "development" of children was, however, often criticized for its vagueness. It was not at all unusual for TV stations to petition the FCC to accept as evidence of their having met the law's requirements their airing of cartoon programs such as *The Flintstones*, *The Jetsons*, and *Yogi Bear*.[60] The FCC insisted that licensees take the act more seriously; in 1996 the commission adopted rules, still in place, specifying that all commercial stations must air an average of at least three hours per week of programming designed to foster the development of children's cognitive and social growth. The Spanish language network, Univision, ran afoul of the requirements in a big way, and in 2007 had to pay $24 million in fines for repeated attempts to have various *telenovelas* (soap operas) count as children's programming.[61]

In 2006 the commission required further that broadcasters provide some kind of on-air icon or similar notice to parents that a given program is designed specifically to educate children. The commission admitted that this might prove counterproductive, that children might go out of their way to avoid any program so "tainted." If empirical evidence bears out the notion that calling something "educational" ensures kids will turn the channel, the commission will revisit the issue.

Federal law, then, imposes limits on the number of minutes per hour broadcasters may insert commercials into children's programming and sets extremely modest requirements on the number of hours of programming that must be dedicated to "core" educational TV. A third noteworthy limitation resulted from lobbying and litigation by a group called Action for Children's Television (ACT), which back in the 1980s highlighted the issue of "program-length commercials"—children's shows such as *G.I. Joe*, *Teenage Mutant Ninja Turtles*, *Super Mario Bros.*, *The Smurfs*, and *Gummi Bears* that were conceived of primarily as vehicles for marketing "action figures" and other toys. ACT won a ruling from the D.C. Circuit Court of Appeals that, while stopping short of demanding any specific new rules, ordered the FCC to provide a more persuasive rationale for much of its deregulation of children's TV.[62] In 1992, the commission decided that there was nothing wrong with program-length commercials as long as no paid advertisements for merchandise associated with the characters on

---

60. Dale Kunkel, "They Call This Educational?" *Broadcasting and Cable*, September 13, 2004, 36.

61. "FCC Lets Univision Go Private," *UPI*, March 28, 2007.

62. *Action for Children's Television v. FCC*, 821 F.2d 741 (D.C. Cir. 1987).

a specific program aired during the program. G.I. Joe action figures can still be advertised on *The Smurfs*, and vice versa.[63]

One of the most dramatic changes in broadcast regulation in the 1990s was introduced in a section of the Telecommunications Act of 1996 requiring that all TV sets with thirteen-inch or larger screens have a microchip, often called the V-chip, preinstalled. The chip is designed to read electronic signals embedded in specified TV programs, thus enabling parents to screen out material they think inappropriate for their children. Under considerable pressure from Congress and from the executive branch, the major networks created a rating system that indicates each program's age appropriateness and offers warnings about specific features of a particular episode—V for violence (with FV for fantasy violence in children's shows), S for sexual situations, L for coarse language, and D for suggestive dialogue. Although much praised from many quarters, the V-chip has also been criticized from both left and right. Some fear that the technology will embolden TV executives to place ever more violent images on the screen, because they now have a ready answer to any parents who might complain. Conversely, since the rating system cannot distinguish between gratuitous violence and the kinds of violence in such critically acclaimed films as *Schindler's List* or *Saving Private Ryan*, many critics fear that TV fare will grow more and more bland, that networks will self-censor out of fear that parents will unthinkingly block broad categories of programs. Another concern is that the V-chip works only on entertainment programming; news programs often carry considerable violence and gore, as evidenced by the old adage supposedly governing the daily decision making of local TV news directors: "If it bleeds, if leads." In any event, a 2004 study from the Henry J. Kaiser Family Foundation reported that only about 15 percent of parents ever used the V-chip to filter their children's TV viewing.

---

63. *Children's Television Programming*, 56 Fed. Reg. 19,611 (April 29, 1991).

THINGS TO REMEMBER

Children's Television

- TV stations must air, on average, at least three hours of pro-social programs for children per week.
- Advertising on children's programs (those aimed at viewers aged twelve and younger) is limited to ten and a half minutes per hour on weekends and twelve minutes per hour on weekdays.
- Ever since 1998, most TV sets in the United States have been equipped with a V-chip to help parents filter out undesired categories of programs, but it appears that very few parents use the technology.

Special Regulations Imposed on PBS and NPR

Questions about how to fund public television and radio in the United States and what their programming should consist of have been matters of ongoing debate ever since the passage of the Educational Television Facilities Act of 1962, which first provided federal funding for noncommercial stations, and the Public Broadcasting Act of 1967, which created the Corporation for Public Broadcasting (CPB) as the system's funding mechanism. In the 1960s, the Carnegie Commission on Educational Television suggested that the United States should adopt the United Kingdom's practice of funding public broadcasting through a predictable, renewable source, such as a tax on the sale of each TV and radio set. This idea was rejected, however, thus setting up a system of oversight in which public broadcast representatives must appear before Congress regularly to justify their budget requests. In recent years, Congress has pressed public broadcasters to reduce their dependence on government monies by obtaining more favorable merchandising contracts with producers of its most popular programs.

Conservatives charge that too much of the programming on National Public Radio (NPR) and the Public Broadcasting Service (PBS) is left leaning. Liberals also have their gripes with the programming, such as the network's high reliance on government spokespersons. Viewers of all political persuasions complain that during PBS's periodic fund-raising drives, programs with a proven track record of bringing in the pledge calls are repeated ad nauseam.

The Public Broadcasting Act of 1967 gives the CPB responsibility for maintaining "strict adherence to objectivity and balance in all programs or series of programs of a controversial nature." No such restrictions are imposed on commercial broadcasters. The law also dictates the manner in which the corporation's board of directors will be appointed.

Some of the legal differences between public and commercial broadcasting in the United States are directly related to program content. Perhaps most obviously, we do

not talk about "advertisers" on PBS and NPR but instead of "underwriters." Messages alerting us as to which individuals, foundations, or corporations have underwritten a program may resemble commercials in some ways, but the legally prescribed purpose of these messages is to inform viewers, not to persuade them.[64] A corporate sponsor can say who it is and display its logo. It can say what products it makes, which is especially important if its product line and its corporate name are not one and the same. A sponsor's message, however, may not tout the quality of the company's products or services the way most commercials do.

There are additional differences between the regulation of commercial and noncommercial broadcasters. Recall the earlier discussion of statutory exemptions to the equal-time rule. One exemption, for "on-the-spot" coverage of news events, has been applied to candidate debates. In recent years, the FCC has held that this exemption applies even when the TV networks, or the candidates themselves, are the sponsors.

This rule has not applied automatically to debates sponsored by PBS stations, however. Especially in the case of PBS stations owned by the state, which is not an unusual circumstance, candidates who are excluded from a debate can make a First Amendment attack on such editorial decisions. This lesson is apparent from a 1998 Supreme

---

64. *Commission Policy Concerning the Noncommercial Nature of Educational Broadcasting Stations*, 97 F.C.C. 2d 95 (1984).

THINGS TO REMEMBER

Public Broadcasting

■ Public broadcasting stations are governed by rules not applicable to commercial stations:
  • Each program or series is supposed to be objective and balanced.
  • Public stations may not have on-air "advertising" per se, although sponsors' names and products or service lines are mentioned in "enhanced underwriting" messages at the beginning or end of each program.
  • Station management may not endorse candidates for office.

Court decision concerning Arkansas congressional candidate Ralph Forbes, an Independent who was not invited to join his Republican and Democratic counterparts in a debate sponsored by that state's public broadcasting network in 1992. Writing for a 6-3 Court, Justice Kennedy used public-forum analysis (see chapter 2) and determined that the proposed debate constituted a nonpublic forum. When the government sponsors such a forum, it is permitted to choose who may and may not participate as long as such decisions are not based on favoritism for some speakers' messages over other speakers' messages. The state broadcasting system prevailed, but only by demonstrating that its decision to exclude Forbes had been based on sound journalistic concerns: the shortage of airtime and the belief that Forbes was a perennial candidate with little or no chance of winning. The commercial networks would not have had to make such a showing.[65]

Another difference between public and commercial broadcasting stations is the management's freedom to editorialize on the air. Unlike their commercial counterparts, PBS and NPR stations are not permitted to endorse political candidates. As a result of a Supreme Court decision from 1984, however, additional regulations forbidding public broadcasting stations from editorializing about political issues and ballot initiatives were struck down.[66]

Regulation of Cable TV

When the earliest forms of cable television came on the scene in the 1940s, they were viewed by broadcasters as their natural allies. Called community antenna television systems (CATV), their main function was to pick up and retransmit local TV signals

---

65. *Arkansas Educational Television Commission v. Forbes*, 523 U.S. 666 (1998).

66. *FCC v. League of Women Voters of California*, 468 U.S. 364 (1984). This case is also discussed briefly in chapter 2.

to homes in rural communities otherwise too remote to receive high-quality signals with their own roof antennas. Broadcasters became a bit wary of the new industry in the 1950s, however, when cable systems began using microwave technology to import more distant TV stations. Local stations could thus lose market share.

The FCC Begins to Regulate Cable

The danger posed by cable systems to local broadcast stations' bottom lines was the rationale embraced by the Supreme Court in 1968 in support of the FCC's authority—asserted haltingly and tentatively—to regulate cable. Any industry that could interfere, technically or economically, with local broadcast stations was logically of interest to the commission.[67] At issue in this particular case were FCC restrictions on the ability of CATV systems to import distant signals into another market. The commission was afraid that distant stations would fragment local UHF stations' natural audience base.

In the 1960s, when cable companies began to create their own programming, a phenomenon emerged that is now taken for granted: use of the home television set to receive programs that had never been "broadcast." Suddenly the traditional rationale for regulating electronic media differently from print—the use of the public's airwaves—had to be rethought. This situation is even more true today, when the vast majority of U.S. homes are hooked up to cable or satellite systems and no longer have TV roof antennas.

In 1972 a 5-4 Supreme Court majority upheld FCC regulations, soon thereafter abandoned voluntarily by the commission, requiring that cable systems produce a certain percentage of their own programming rather than serve only as retransmitters of others' signals.[68] But the FCC went too far, a 6-3 majority held in 1979, when it required cable systems to open some of their channel capacity to public, educational, and local government uses, as well as for leased access by independent programmers.[69] The FCC was trying to regulate cable systems as if they were common carriers (like telephone and telegraph companies) that must send messages provided by anyone willing to pay the cost. Congress had decided long ago that over-the-air broadcasters could not themselves be regulated in this manner. Since whatever authority the FCC has to regulate cable stems from the industry's relationship to broadcasting, such authority could not allow common-carrier status to be imposed on cable.

Although cable systems do not necessarily use the public's airwaves, they inevitably use the public's telephone poles and streets to lay the miles of coaxial cable needed to connect each subscriber's home to the system's "head-end" (its main switching area). Typically, a cable system will sign a long-term contract with a city or similar local

---

67. *United States v. Southwestern Cable Co.*, 392 U.S. 157 (1968).
68. *United States v. Midwest Video*, 406 U.S. 649 (1972).
69. *FCC v. Midwest Video*, 440 U.S. 689 (1979).

government for the right to lay the cable, and the cities have predictably expected much in return, such as annual franchise fees, promises about the quality of customer service, and the inclusion of certain kinds of programming or leased network access (e.g., a station for airing city council hearings and other government events). In 1984, the Supreme Court placed significant restraints on state and local governments' claimed right to regulate cable programming. *Capital Cities Cable, Inc. v. Crisp*,[70] however, was not as much a victory for the cable industry as for the doctrine of federal preemption, pursuant to which valid federal laws trump state or local laws. At issue was an Oklahoma law forbidding advertising for alcoholic beverages. The state's attorney general had determined that this statute was applicable to out-of-state TV signals imported by Oklahoma-based cable systems. Writing for a unanimous Court, Justice Brennan found that the state's law was in conflict with legitimate FCC policies governing the relationship between broadcast stations and cable franchisees and thus struck down the Oklahoma law.

Congressional Actions

The Cable Communications Policy Act of 1984 was seen by the cable industry as its own Bill of Rights. Largely in response to a public perception that the cable industry abused those rights, however, Congress created the Cable Television Consumer Protection and Competition Act of 1992 to rein the industry in a bit. Under these two laws, as well as FCC and judicial interpretations of them, the federal government is given considerable power to regulate the cable industry, but local governments are given the authority to regulate individual cable system operators. A complication has arisen in recent years, as telephone companies—which have begun to offer video services—by 2007 had persuaded about a dozen states to allow the companies to negotiate at the state rather than local level.

Thus, for example, cable system operators are assured by federal statute that their contracts with local governments for the ongoing right to use local streets, utility poles, and the like will carry at least a presumption of being renewed. At the same time, however, cities cannot artificially create a cable monopoly. Other companies that wish to compete may do so if they can afford to. The economic reality is such that a municipality with more than one cable system is highly unlikely (although in most areas of the country consumers now have a choice between a cable system and a direct broadcast satellite (DBS) system).

Cities cannot dictate that the local cable system carry any specific network, although they can require that cable systems carry certain broad categories of programming, including public-access, educational, and government channels, sometimes "PEG" for short. Thus we find, for example, that most cable systems carry C-SPAN and likely too the channel that carries the state legislature and the local city and county governmental bodies. True public-access channels are made available to any

---

70. 467 U.S. 691 (1984).

interested community members on a first-come, first-served basis. Often the local cable system will train interested community groups on how to run cameras and in whatever other skills are necessary to get a program on air. Federal law dictates that neither the government nor the cable system may censor such public-access programming.

During cable's early decades, there was no question that your cable system would carry the local broadcast signals as part of their offerings. Indeed, retransmission of the broadcast signal was cable's main function. But as time went on and as the cable industry began creating its own programming, some cable systems balked at carrying less lucrative broadcast signals. Thus the FCC, Congress, and the courts struggled for many years with various versions of **"must carry" rules**, requiring that cable systems carry local stations. As a general rule, cable systems now indeed must carry any local stations that request such carriage and must carry them as part of the "basic tier" rather than as part of a premium level of service. Moreover, the local stations that request carriage must appear on the cable system as if they had been received over the air. That is, "channel 7" must appear as channel 7 on the cable system. When a cable system carries a local station that requests to be on the system, no payment is made by the cable company to the local station.

Local stations may, however, opt not to be carried for free by a cable system and may instead negotiate a fee for the cable system to have the privilege of carrying them. This is known as exercising the right to **retransmission consent**. Typically such negotiations are less likely to involve a demand for payment as a demand that the cable system also carry other cable networks in which the local station's parent company owns an interest. The overall system of "must carry," or retransmission consent, was upheld by the Supreme Court in 1997.[71]

To a large extent the Cable Television Consumer Protection and Competition Act of 1992, as its name implies, was designed to curb cable industry excesses that led to numerous consumer complaints. The law requires, for example, that cable systems answer their phones within thirty seconds of the first ring and that they maintain some kind of telephone response system 24/7. Installation requests must be honored within one week, and there must be a system of rebating appropriate portions of monthly fees in response to system outages or similar malfunctions.

Not all of the 1992 act dealt with such minutiae, however. The law also explicitly empowered the commission to impose two kinds of ownership limits on cable companies: horizontal limits placed a cap on the total percentage of U.S. households receiving some kind of multichannel programming (whether cable or satellite) that any one cable company could service; vertical limits capped the percentage of channels on a cable system that could be owned by the system operator. In early 2001, the D.C. Circuit Court of Appeals vacated the rules, sending them back to the commission for additional fact-finding and justification.[72] As of summer 2007, the commission was

---

71. *Turner Broadcasting System, Inc. v. FCC (II)*, 520 U.S. 180 (1997).
72. *Time Warner Entertainment Co. v. FCC*, 240 F.3d 1126 (D.C. Cir. 2001).

still gathering information to help it address the court's concerns, and individual commissioners had begun to point out that some cable systems were growing sufficiently large to approach the ownership limits the commission had originally proposed.[73]

The Telecommunications Act of 1996, generally intended to foster competition among communications industries, also had some direct impact on cable. It eliminated some regulation of consumer cable fees immediately and provided for a phaseout of the remaining regulations. Also, the law eliminated most barriers that had prevented cable companies, long-distance phone companies, and local phone companies from competing in each other's domains. Many critics have concluded that the main effect of the Telecommunications Act of 1996 has been not the fostering of genuine competition in most markets but "merger (and acquisition) mania." To be fair, the move toward greater and greater consolidation in the media industry had begun long before the 1996 act went into effect; still, by most accounts the legislation has accelerated the rate of mergers and acquisitions.

Cable TV and the First Amendment

As we have seen, the reasons traditionally offered for regulating broadcast media more strictly than print media are spectrum scarcity (not everyone who would like a broadcast license could be given a frequency on "the people's airwaves") and the power of TV and radio to intrude on the privacy of the home and to influence young children.

Does cable television manifest these same features of electronic media, and what are the First Amendment implications of the answer to that question? The Supreme Court has had a number of occasions to address this issue and has always approached it with caution. The Court's opinions have not always offered clear guidance, nor have they been completely consistent. In 1986, in the course of ruling that the City of Los Angeles could not sign an exclusive cable contract with one company, the Court majority granted that cable operators perform an "editorial" role like "the traditional enterprises of newspapers and book publishers" when they decide which cable networks to include on their systems.[74] In the very next sentence, however, Chief Justice Rehnquist equated cable's First Amendment rights with those of "wireless broadcasters." The Court thus did not say which model of regulation it would use in cable cases: print, broadcast, or some kind of hybrid created especially for the new industry.

A few years later the Court was asked to rule on the constitutionality of a broad-based sales tax in Arkansas, from which the state decided to exempt the sales of subscriptions to magazines and newspapers. A local cable system and a cable subscriber sued on free speech and equal protection grounds since monthly cable bills were not

---

73. "FCC Approves Adelphia/Time Warner/Comcast Transfer," 2006 FCC LEXIS 3842 (statement of Commissioner Adelstein).

74. *City of Los Angeles v. Preferred Communications*, 476 U.S. 488, 194 (1986).

also exempt from the tax. The Court held that there was no constitutional defect in the tax system, because it did not discriminate on the basis of taxpayers' speech.[75]

In 1994, the Supreme Court took its first look at the "must carry" rules imposed by the 1992 cable act and instructed a lower court on remand to subject the rules to a level of scrutiny somewhere between the strict scrutiny used for print media and the far more lax standards applied to broadcast regulations.[76] The lower court then found the rules constitutional, and the Supreme Court, hearing the case a second time, agreed.[77]

In 1996 the Court had occasion to decide what level of scrutiny should apply to regulations that directly affect cable content. At issue were three related sections of the Cable Television Consumer Protection and Competition Act of 1992 that all governed how cable systems might deal with sexually indecent material on leased-access and public-access stations. Justice Breyer, in an opinion that only at some points commanded enough votes to constitute a majority, refused to commit the Court to any of the competing models—print, broadcast, or common carrier—for analyzing laws regulating cable content.[78]

Even while eschewing the temptation to embrace any one model, Breyer found it helpful to analogize to broadcast regulation. He called to mind the *Pacifica* decision involving George Carlin's comedy routine. The Court suggested in that case that one of the main reasons for restricting broadcast indecency was to protect children. Many courts and commentators have suggested in the intervening years that the rationale carries diminished force in a cable environment. After all, parents have more control over which cable stations to allow into their homes. They do not have to subscribe to the Playboy channel or to similar adult fare. For Breyer, however, the state's interest in protecting children weighs more heavily today than when *Pacifica* was decided. Cable systems boast dozens, often over a hundred, channels, compared with the mere handful to which most homes had access in the 1970s. Moreover, because cable subscribers tend to "channel surf" more than do nonsubscribers, children in cable households are more "susceptible to random exposure to unwanted materials."

In 2000, a Supreme Court majority applied the same kind of strict scrutiny to a cable regulation that it would normally apply to the print media. At issue were sections of the Telecommunications Act of 1996 requiring "sexually oriented" cable channels (a cable channel is considered "sexually oriented" if the majority of its programming is sexually oriented), and the local cable systems that retransmit their programming to subscribers, to "fully scramble" their signals or to limit their transmissions to between 10 p.m. and 6 a.m. The impetus for the regulation was that existing scrambling technologies were generally imperfect, resulting in "bleeding" of

---

75. *Leathers v. Medlock*, 499 U.S. 439 (1991).
76. *Turner Broadcasting System, Inc. v. FCC (I)*, 512 U.S. 622 (1994).
77. *Turner Broadcasting System, Inc. v. FCC (II)*, 520 U.S. 180 (1997).
78. *Denver Area Educational Telecommunications Consortium v. FCC*, 518 U.S. 727 (1996).

THINGS TO REMEMBER

Cable Regulation

- Cable regulation was at first accomplished through a combination of sometimes conflicting FCC policies and rules set forth by local franchising authorities. Congress did not pass the first law governing cable until 1984. The 1984 act was very industry friendly.
- Charges of poor service and inordinately high monthly fees led Congress to create new legislation in 1992, which reimposed some controls and established minimal levels of acceptable service.
- The Telecommunications Act of 1996, however, eliminated most cable rate regulations; it also permitted cable companies, and local and long-distance phone companies, to compete in each other's industries.
- Currently, many of the best-known regulations regarding broadcast speech apply with equal force to cable programming.
- The Supreme Court has not yet decided what level of scrutiny should be applied to cable content regulations, although in recent decisions a majority is moving more and more toward the print model.

the video or audio messages to other channels; households not subscribing to and not interested in "adult" programming might receive it anyway. Most cable franchises carrying signals affected by this provision chose the path of least resistance, restricting their hours of transmission to eight overnight hours daily.

In striking down the regulation, the majority found that the degree of self-censorship imposed on the cable industry was plainly unacceptable. Writing for the majority, Justice Kennedy suggested that the Court's decision to employ the strictest level of review in such a case was more a reflection of the regulation's structure than a judicial statement about the overall level of First Amendment protection due the cable industry. The regulation, after all, not only was triggered by the content of messages (sexually oriented ones) but also was limited only to certain speakers (sexually oriented cable channels). That is, HBO or Showtime, even if they aired an occasional program that might otherwise be covered by the rule, would escape liability, precisely because such programs are not their usual content. Far better, Kennedy said, for cable operators to fully block unwanted channels from a given household upon written request from the subscriber.[79]

When, then, are cable systems exempt from the kinds of regulations that are regularly imposed on the broadcast media but that would be clearly unconstitutional if applied to print media? Although the Court has not yet articulated a clear answer to this question, we can intuit a pattern emerging from relevant cases and statutes. In general, in the case of regulations aimed at indecent speech—sexual programming

---

79. *United States v. Playboy Entertainment Group*, 529 U.S. 803 (2000).

that the print media may disseminate freely but that can be highly regulated if appearing on broadcast stations—cable is treated more like print. When regulations force broadcast licensees to speak or to otherwise take action—think in terms of speech about political campaigns or rules demanding accessibility for the disabled—cable is subject to the same controls, even though these regulations could not be applied to the print media.

As a general rule, Congress has in recent years included the cable industry within the purview of any new statutes governing broadcast content. Thus, for example, those sections of the Telecommunications Act of 1996 mandating closed captioning apply with equal force to broadcast and cable signals. Some of the older broadcast rules have been amended to apply to cable as well, such as the equal-time rule and the candidate-access rule.

Direct Broadcast Satellite Services

While most Americans get their TV signals these days from their local cable companies, about 27 million or so instead subscribe to one of the two major direct broadcast satellite (DBS) services, EchoStar and DirecTV. The history of DBS regulation is a bit different from that for cable, in that the satellite industry never had to deal with the problem of getting public rights of way to run cables underground or on utility poles. They beam their signals to orbiting satellites which then bounce the signals back directly to home subscribers' satellite dishes.

Although the FCC at first tried to exempt the satellite industry from those federal regulations governing the broadcast industry that have been applied to the cable industry, the courts[80] and Congress[81] insisted otherwise. As it stands, the candidate-access rule and the equal-time rule, the various nonduplication rules[82] designed to protect local over-the-air broadcasters, and the limits on the total number of commercial minutes per hour on children's television all apply not only to cable but to satellite as well. Additionally, a special kind of "must carry" rule applies to DBS systems. Aptly named "carry one, carry all," the rule dictates that if a DBS system chooses to carry at least one of the local stations in a given community, it must carry all of them. This latter provision was upheld in a 2001 federal appellate ruling.[83]

---

80. *National Association of Broadcasters v. FCC*, 740 F.2d 1190 (D.C. Cir. 1984); *Daniels Cablevision v. United States*, 835 F. Supp. 1 (D.D.C. 1993); *rev'd sub nom, Time Warner Entertainment Co. v. FCC*, 93 F.3d 957 (D.C. Cir. 1996).

81. The 1992 cable act instructed the FCC to create mechanisms through which to apply the candidate-access rule and the equal-time rule to DBS systems.

82. Nonduplication rules permit local broadcasters to demand that cable or satellite operators that import distant stations carrying a specific program that a local station is carrying at the same time (say, a specific episode of a series now in syndication) block out the duplicated program.

83. *Satellite Broadcasting and Communications Association v. FCC*, 275 F.3d 337 (4th Cir. 2001).

THINGS TO REMEMBER

DBS

- DBS systems transmit signals directly from satellites to subscribers' home satellite dishes.
- Although the FCC was at first reluctant to regulate DBS, the courts and Congress insisted that the industry be subject to the same kinds of political content regulations and children's TV regulations as are broadcasters.

Chapter Summary

The traditional reliance on distinctions between print, broadcast, cable, and other "new media" is very much in flux as we enter an era of media convergence, wherein communication services will likely soon be provided to us by a single wire.

The Federal Communications Act of 1934 created the FCC; it still provides the basic framework for regulation of electronic media. A major overhaul of the law was accomplished in the Telecommunications Act of 1996, through which Congress sought to encourage competition among and across segments of the communications industry.

The general trend since the early 1980s has been toward deregulating electronic media. Virtually all limits on the number of stations any single person or company may own have been eliminated; so too have several regulations governing media content. The FCC is mandated to report to Congress biennially as to the wisdom of even further deregulation.

Some rules do still apply only to electronic media, however; among them are the candidate-access rule, the equal-time rule, prohibitions against indecent programming, and a requirement to provide at least three hours of weekly programming designed to aid youngsters' cognitive and social development. TV stations have also been mandated to switch to high-definition digital broadcasting by 2009.

Special rules apply to NPR and PBS stations, which must strive for balance and objectivity in every single program they broadcast and, unlike their commercial counterparts, may not use their airwaves to endorse candidates for public office.

Cable television, once only a means of retransmitting broadcast signals to rural areas otherwise cut off from television service, has emerged as the primary delivery system for video in the United States. Regulations governing cable have historically been a confusing and sometimes contradictory array of actions by the FCC, Congress, the courts, and local governments. The Supreme Court in 1996 explicitly refused to indicate what standard of review should be used to evaluate regulations aimed at cable content.

Other means of delivering video programming have emerged in recent years, chief among these being direct broadcast satellite (DBS) service. The FCC, Congress, and the courts have struggled to decide which, if any, regulations normally applied to broadcast stations should apply to DBS as well.

Chapter 13

COMMUNICATION LAW
AND THE INTERNET

Many people use the word **Internet** to describe the totality of the millions of websites and other content to which anyone with a computer and a modem has access. To "go online" is to "use the Internet." But actually the word *Internet* was coined to refer to the technical ways in which the innumerable computer networks worldwide connect to each other. The history of the Internet is intertwined with the cold war (itself a quaint, anachronistic notion since the collapse of the Soviet Union and the new focus on the so-called war on terrorism).

In 1969 the Department of Defense created the Advanced Research Projects Agency Network (ARPANET), a complex array of computer connections designed to ensure that the military could continue to carry on sensitive communications even in the event of nuclear war. Two features of the system were especially relevant to that goal. The first was a purposefully high degree of redundancy so that messages could be relayed even if some of the network became inoperable. Thus, a message that could not be sent directly from Washington, D.C., to Palo Alto, California, might be sent on a circuitous route from Washington, D.C., to Philadelphia, to Pittsburgh, then to Chicago, Denver, and Salt Lake City, and finally to Palo Alto. The second feature was a reliance on "packet switching," which breaks down large and complicated messages into manageable chunks (or "packets") that are sent independently to the ultimate destination, where they are reassembled into a meaningful whole. If you have ever visited a website and noted that the textual elements pop up on the computer screen almost immediately but that you may have to wait for the more colorful graphics to appear, you have seen packet switching at work.

At the same time that the now-defunct ARPANET was maturing, other similar computer networks, including BITNET, CSNET, FidoNet, and Usenet developed to link universities, research facilities, businesses, and individuals. The multiple layers of linkages of these and numerous other computer networks to each other formed the basis for the Internet.

The Internet is often thought of as a place, though of course this is a metaphor. It is rather the result of our all having agreed to hook our computers together. Indeed, it is not as much a bunch of computers as it is the way the computers talk to each other. Still, the word *cyberspace* is often used as a synonym for the Internet, and we will sometimes be guilty of that practice here as well.

The whole notion of the Internet as an imaginary place cannot help but call to mind the discussion of the U.S. Supreme Court's public-forum analysis (see chapter 2). There we learned that the Court recognizes that freedom of speech does not translate into a right to say anything we please anywhere and anytime we please. Some times and places are more conducive to communication than others. It is perfectly acceptable to deliver an impassioned and spontaneous political speech on a street corner, but not in a hospital emergency room. That the Court has singled out public streets and parks as the quintessential public forums is something to keep in mind as we explore the still-nascent body of Internet law. After all, parks may be fine for speech making, but they are also used for flying kites, jogging, and picnicking. Public street corners are also places we have historically expected to encounter speakers, but that is not their only or even primary function. By contrast, the Internet may be the first "place" whose *only* function is to facilitate communication. Some commentators have therefore argued that this new medium is the ultimate public forum, purer than pure, and that government would properly permit more freedom of speech in this place than in any other.

Cyberspace attorney Lance Rose argues that a full appreciation of the Internet requires us to recognize that communication events throughout history have been of three kinds: one-to-one, one-to-many, and many-to-many. Prior to the Internet, only the first two levels of communication had been stretched beyond the context of actual participants in one room. One-to-one conversations can take place at a party, but also by telephone between persons thousands of miles apart. One-to-many conversations happen at parties, such as when one person makes a toast to the crowd, but they are also the essence of radio and TV broadcasts. Prior to the Internet, Rose suggests, many-to-many conversations took place almost exclusively—a telephone conference call would be an exception—among persons sharing a common time and place, such as the small group at a party that might talk among themselves in the kitchen. Online talk has finally brought this third category of communication within the scope of electronic mass media. Unlike television and radio, however, consumers are not restricted to messages sent by huge mass media companies. In cyberspace, "anyone can be heard by many others, either in his or her own town or across the globe," says Rose. The Internet not only "allows groups of all kinds to organize effectively," it also "enables those who don't fit in where they live to find hundreds or thousands of kindred souls across the world."[1]

---

1. Lance Rose, *Netlaw: Your Rights in the Online World* (Berkeley, Calif.: Osborne McGraw-Hill, 1995), 5–6.

THINGS TO REMEMBER

Some Internet Basics

- Begun by the Department of Defense in the 1960s, the Internet was designed as a means of ensuring that government communications could continue even after a nuclear attack.
- It is the first medium to bring many-to-many communication (akin to a small group of friends having an informal discussion) into the electronic age.
- There is a high degree of redundancy in data transmissions among the computer networks that constitute the Internet; thus, it is impossible to know at any one time how many computer networks are involved, or which path any particular message or portion of a message (a "packet") has taken.
- The Internet is often thought of as an imaginary place called "cyberspace," leading some theorists to suggest it should be considered the purest of "pure public forums," subject to less government regulation than any other communications medium.

The next section of this chapter discusses a handful of unique characteristics of cyberspace communication, always with the goal of at least musing over the implications of these features for the structure and application of communication law. Then, we examine the relevant Internet case law to date, including libel, trademark and copyright, invasion of privacy, and the sending of sexual messages. Within each area of the law, we are especially interested in those opinions in which judges say exactly what they think this new medium is and which analogies to more traditional media best describe it.

What Makes the Internet Different?

Many theorists and jurists who have examined the issue agree that the Internet boasts several unique communication features, each of which has significant implications for the application of communication law to this new technology.

An Infinite Number of Information Sources

This feature of the Internet is important because it helps us distinguish cyberspace from the electromagnetic spectrum that governs more traditional electronic media, such as radio and television. As seen in chapter 12, one of the chief arguments used to justify regulations of broadcast media that would be unconstitutional as applied to the print media is "spectrum scarcity." Only so many TV or radio stations can fit onto the spectrum, so not everyone who wishes to obtain a broadcast license can get one. In 1997, the Supreme Court was asked to uphold the Communications Decency Act, which would have made it a criminal offense to transmit indecent sexual messages on the Internet. (A more detailed discussion of the act appears later in this chapter). One of the government's arguments in favor of the law was that the Federal Communications Commission prohibits the broadcasting of such messages on TV and radio. The Supreme Court, however, refused to equate the Internet with the more traditional broadcast media. "Unlike the conditions that prevailed when Congress first authorized regulation of the broadcast spectrum," Justice Stevens wrote for the Court, "the Internet can hardly be considered a 'scarce' expressive commodity. It provides relatively unlimited, low-cost capacity for communication of all kinds."[2]

A Lack of "Gatekeepers"

Cultural critics and jurists alike have often expressed frustration with the enormous difficulty that ordinary speakers have in trying to reach audiences of meaningful size. Intellectual property attorney Edward Cavazos, one of the most prolific writers on Internet law, reminds us how high this "speaker burden" is in the traditional media. If we wish to reach a large audience, we must either have a lot of money or have friends in high places in media industries. Potential book authors, for example, must find someone willing to incur the cost of publishing and distributing their words. Even if they succeed, they face the additional constraint of editorial control. Such control is not limited to books, of course. Only the most established Hollywood movie directors obtain the rights to make the "final cut" on their films. Whatever the medium, rarely do a writer's unfiltered ideas make their way to the audience.

According to many social theorists, all that changed with the advent of the Internet. No matter what size audience you seek to reach, there is no editor from whom to seek approval. Your message is made instantaneously available to an individual (e-mail), to a select group of like-minded souls of whatever size (via a "listserv"), or to anyone with access to the Internet (through your website or "blog").[3] Clearly there are significant exceptions to this Internet feature. Many listservs are organized by a human moderator, who may choose not to permit the posting of messages deemed irrelevant to the subscribers' common interest. In addition, Internet service providers such as America Online (AOL) do enforce a set of rules aimed at preventing subscribers from abusing one another, and AOL will impose sanctions against those who violate the rules. But even these counterexamples do not negate the Internet's extraordinary openness. After all, if a listserv's moderator "censors" some postings, it is only because the list's subscribers have decided for themselves the scope of their discourse. A listserv dedicated to tracking civil rights bills pending in Congress will likely not be much interested in postings expressing adoration for the teen heartthrob of the moment. With respect to rules of discourse imposed by AOL, they tend to be

---

2. *Reno v. American Civil Liberties Union*, 521 U.S. 844, 870 (1997).

3. Edward A. Cavazos, "The Idea Incubator: Why the Internet Poses Unique Problems for the First Amendment," 8 *Seton Hall Constitutional Law Journal* 667 (1998).

limited to personally abusive or fraudulent conduct. The general rule that any subscriber who wants to write to any other subscriber may do so is still in force.

Many theorists argue that it is naive to think of cyberspace as lacking gatekeepers, especially when one considers how hard it is to get noticed among the millions of blogs and websites. The problem of the Internet is not a lack of information, these critics point out; it is too much information, and thus a need to depend on search engines such as Google and Yahoo! to create order from chaos. What happens if the sophisticated mathematical calculations those search engines perform result in a somehow "biased" search? (This sometimes happens when sophisticated Web users learn to game the system, sometimes employing the services of "search engine optimizer" consultants who help clients get their sites listed early on in a Google search.)[4] From the perspective of the individual blogger seeking an audience, the attempt to reach an audience can seem as stifled on the supposedly gatekeeper-less Internet as it might if trying to get onto network TV. Litigation in this area is scant, but it seems fair to say that legislation would be needed before plaintiffs could have a cause of action against a search engine that is alleged to have "discriminated" against some sites in favor of others.[5]

Still, to the extent that the Internet is relatively devoid of traditional gatekeepers, such a state of affairs carries an important implication. In chapter 2, we encountered Elisabeth Noelle-Neumann's "spiral of silence" theory. Noelle-Neumann argued that the political and social perspectives that mass media industries depict are rather middle-of-the-road, that anything too far left, right, or otherwise removed from established norms would not play well, would not garner much of an audience. As a result, she argued, our own interpersonal discourse comes to manifest the same relative blandness, as persons with outlandish ideas will be loath to share them with their neighbors.

The Internet, and especially the phenomenon of the chat room, seems to be pushing things in the opposite direction. One of the defining characteristics of Internet chatter is that companions are chosen on the basis of shared interests rather than on the accident of proximity.[6] As a result, chat rooms can serve, for better or worse, as incubators for unpopular ideas, with participants egging each other on to adopt yet more extreme viewpoints. Chat rooms thus can create a new kind of "spiral" of discourse, but it is hardly a spiral of *silence*.

Parity among Senders and Receivers

Internet discourse forces us to rethink some of our most basic distinctions between broad categories of communication events. Perhaps most fundamentally, it is no

---

4. Jefferson Graham, "How to Get Google to Notice You: Tips to Push Your Site to Top of Heap," *USA Today*, January 17, 2007, 3B.

5. *Kinderstart.com v. Google, Inc.*, 2007 U.S. Dist. LEXIS 22637 (N.D. Cal. 2007).

6. Andrew L. Shapiro, "The Net That Binds: Using Cyberspace to Create Real Communities," *Nation*, June 21, 1999, 20.

longer quite clear what "mass" communication means on the Internet. Traditionally, mass communication is thought of as having a fairly large corporation as the source of messages. When we watch a TV network newscast, we realize that the "speaker" is a highly complex organization, that scores of people had a direct hand in deciding what would be included in the broadcast, and that these staff members were trying in turn to reflect the collective interests of management, stockholders, and advertisers.

Because traditional mass media speakers often have the backing of huge corporate structures, we all know instinctively the difference in "production values" between a network broadcast or a big city newspaper compared with home videos or a neighborhood association newsletter. The Internet seems to have changed much of this. Put plainly, there are only so many things one can do to a website to make it slick and professional, and most of these tricks of the trade are equally available to a huge media corporation or to talented, motivated individuals with limited funds. This is why, for example, political parodists have had so much fun with the World Wide Web; they often set up websites that look on the surface to be a presidential candidate's official site, but their purpose is to make fun of the candidate. Several such online comics made quite a name for themselves with their parody websites. Sometimes the content of the sites seems to cross the line between satire and political dirty tricks, attributing to the candidate outlandish stances likely to dissuade potential supporters.[7]

It has often been suggested that the growth of the Internet means that we are *all* publishers now. This admittedly glib assertion may come to have important long-term effects on the structure of U.S. communication law. Consider the many times throughout this book's earlier chapters that we saw the courts treat members of the institutional press differently from the rest of us. In chapter 9, for example, we saw the difficulty in deciding who is a "reporter" covered by state reporter shield laws. Should such laws, or a possible new federal law, protect Internet "bloggers" along with employees of the traditional media?[8] Certainly there have been numerous times in recent years when nontraditional cyberspace reporters, or bloggers, have scooped, or at least led, the mainstream media. It was bloggers who first pointed out that the memos used by former CBS news anchor Dan Rather ostensibly proving that George W. Bush failed to fulfill his military obligations were likely forgeries. A blogger simi-

---

7. Marc Lifsher, "'Yes On Prop 87' Group Sued over Cyber No-No," *Los Angeles Times*, August 23, 2006, C1; Jon Oram, "Will the Real Candidate Please Stand Up? Political Parody on the Internet," 5 *Journal of Intellectual Property Law* 467 (1998); Ben White, "Parody Site Wins at FEC," *Washington Post*, April 20, 2000, A4.

8. Joseph Alonzo, "Restoring the Ideal Marketplace: How Recognizing Bloggers as Journalists Can Save the Press," 9 *NYU Journal of Legislation and Public Policy* 751 (2005); Anne Flanagan, "Blogging: A Journal Need Not a Journalist Make," 16 *Fordham Intellectual Property, Media, and Entertainment Law Journal* 395 (2006).

larly was the impetus for the mainstream media to begin reporting on former congressman Mark Foley's attraction to young male congressional pages.[9]

There are also times when media industries are more protected from libel suits than other defendants.[10] Again, when will or should an Internet "publisher" be considered a mass media outlet? Consider also that the Privacy Protection Act (see chapter 9), the federal law that was enacted in response to the Supreme Court decision in *Zurcher v. Stanford Daily* and which requires in most circumstances that law enforcement officials issue a subpoena rather than searching newsrooms, is worded rather broadly. Rather than restricting the act's provisions to, for example, full-time employees of bona fide media outlets, Congress instead made reference to all persons "reasonably believed to have a purpose to disseminate to the public a newspaper, book, broadcast, or other similar form of public communication." Does not the advent of the Internet mean that virtually *everyone* fits this definition?[11]

Extraordinarily Low Cost

Chapter 10 included discussion of a Supreme Court decision involving a ban on residential For Sale signs in Willingboro, New Jersey. One of the reasons Justice Marshall gave for overturning the statute was that it precluded homeowners from using the least expensive traditional means of letting people know they are looking for a buyer. To be sure, Marshall allowed, Willingboro residents were still free to advertise in the newspaper's real estate section or to hire a professional real estate agent, but both those options are more expensive than placing a sign on one's lawn.[12]

Although it would be overstating Marshall's point to suggest that the "free" in "free speech" means free from financial cost, his opinion reminds us that the vigor of our First Amendment rights should not depend on the size of our wallets. This logic suggests that speech on the Internet should enjoy a special measure of protection. After all, the For Sale signs in Willingboro would reach the eyes only of those walking or driving by a specific home in the course of their daily activities; depending on the home's location, that could mean only a few dozen audience members. By contrast, the Internet permits speakers to reach an audience of thousands, even millions, at little or no cost.

That it is so inexpensive to reach huge audiences online can be a rationale for either furthering Internet speech or for inhibiting it. On the one hand, Internet speakers seem to be the modern-day equivalent of the "lone pamphleteers" whose outrage at the Crown's imposition of the stamp tax created at least part of the impetus for the

---

9. Stephen Watson, "Blogs Give Reynolds Story Longer Legs," *Buffalo News*, October 6, 2006, A1.

10. *Philadelphia Newspapers, Inc. v. Hepps*, 475 U.S. 767 (1986).

11. Mark Eckenwiller, "Constitutional Issues Involving Use of the Internet: Applications of the Privacy Protection Act," 8 *Seton Hall Constitutional Law Journal* 725 (1998).

12. *Linmark Associates v. Township of Willingboro*, 431 U.S. 85, 93 (1977).

American Revolution. The great ease with which Internet publishers can disseminate their messages, however, often irks their audiences in ways not often seen with other media. Perhaps the best example is the phenomenon called "spam," or junk e-mail. This issue is discussed at more length later in this chapter; for now suffice it to say that Internet service providers have gone to court to try to eliminate such unwanted commercial messages from their systems.

The dramatic implications of the low cost of Internet transmission are apparent from a scenario that played out in late 2000 and early 2001. A protester of Nike's alleged use of exploited labor in Asia and South America went to the company's website and followed the directions there for ordering a customized pair of athletic shoes. The activist requested that the shoes be emblazoned with a single word: *sweatshop*. Nike refused the request, initially claiming that the word fell into the category of "inappropriate slang," and later admitting that their basis for refusal was an escape clause they had purposely included on their website, which gave the company the right to refuse to embroider any slogan it considers "inappropriate."

The activist sent copies of his lengthy e-mail exchange to friends, and that is where the explosion of what he calls the "micromedia" of the Internet began. Friends forwarded the e-mail to friends of friends, and suddenly the notion of "six degrees of separation" seemed anachronistically quaint, as millions of people worldwide saw the exchange, which proved highly embarrassing to Nike. Eventually more traditional media began to feed on the story as well, resulting in articles in publications such as *USA Today*, the *Wall Street Journal*, and *Business Week*, as well as a personal appearance by the activist on the *Today* show.[13]

Jurisdictional Ambiguity

Perhaps you recall from chapter 4 the discussion of the lawsuit pursued by Kathy Keeton against *Hustler* magazine. The plaintiff was a New York resident, the magazine's corporate headquarters were in Ohio, and yet her lawsuit was heard by a federal district court in New Hampshire. Keeton chose that forum because of the state's unusually long statute of limitations, and the Supreme Court decided she could do so because *Hustler* distributed some copies of its magazines to New Hampshire residents.

The *Keeton* case was actually a special case of the more general issue of **personal jurisdiction**, which helps courts decide when one state may adjudicate claims involving nonresidents of that state. In 1945, the Supreme Court articulated a general rule to the effect that there must be some kind of "minimum contacts" between a defendant and the "forum state" (the state in which personal jurisdiction is sought). The issue is really one of due process, because it would be fundamentally unfair for citizens of one state to be dragged into the courts of another state in which they had not and never intended to do business.[14] In a 1985 case, the Court ruled that the requisite

---

13. Jonah Peretti, "My Nike Media Adventure," *Nation*, April 9, 2001, 19.
14. *International Shoe v. Washington*, 326 U.S. 310 (1945).

minimum contacts can be found even if the defendant rarely, if ever, had set foot in the forum state: "It is an inescapable fact of modern commercial life that a substantial amount of business is transacted solely by mail and wire communications across state lines," Justice Brennan wrote for the Court, "thus obviating the need for physical presence within a State in which business is conducted." Courts can exercise jurisdiction over a resident of another state as long as the potential defendant has engaged in some commercial enterprise "purposefully directed toward" residents of the forum state.[15] A plurality decision from 1987 offers several factors that may be used as evidence that a company has engaged in such "purposeful" activity. These criteria include "designing the product for the market in the forum State, advertising in the forum State, establishing channels for providing regular advice to customers in the forum State, or marketing the product through a distributor who has agreed to serve as the sales agent in the forum State."[16]

How should these principles apply on the Internet? The matter is complicated by the fact that websites, once they have been uploaded to the Internet, are accessible in every state (and indeed, around the world). Internet speech would be unfairly stifled, many commentators have suggested, if the simple posting of a website opened one up to nationwide liability.

In Internet cases a general rule has emerged that is not at all inconsistent with cases that have involved earlier communication media.[17] The rule is that the creation of a website is not itself sufficient to create personal jurisdiction, especially if it is a "passive" site that does not function interactively—for example, it does not have "leave feedback" or "contact us" options, and it does not offer any products for sale online.

It is an easy thing to engage in anonymous speech on the Internet. (Perhaps you have several different highly idiosyncratic screen names yourself.) What happens if a defendant in a communication lawsuit (or indeed any lawsuit) has to be named "John Doe" because of the anonymity of cyberspace? Some federal courts are very reluctant to accept jurisdiction in these cases, unless there is an allegation of a violation of federal law. Why? Because federal courts are only supposed to adjudicate state law claims when the plaintiff and defendant are from different states—when the court has diversity of citizenship jurisdiction. When the defendant is a "John Doe" hiding behind an Internet screen name, there is no way of knowing whether the litigants are from different states.[18]

The Internet is not merely a nationwide but rather a worldwide communication medium, however, which leads to some unusual jurisdictional and enforcement issues. Later in this chapter we discuss *Reno v. American Civil Liberties Union*, the 1997 case that produced the Supreme Court's very first Internet decision. The issue in-

---

15. *Burger King Corp. v. Rudzewicz*, 471 U.S. 462, 476 (1985).

16. *Asahi Metal Industry Company v. Superior Court*, 480 U.S. 102, 112 (1987).

17. Andrew E. Costa, "Minimum Contacts in Cyberspace: A Taxonomy of the Case Law," 35 *Houston Law Review* 453 (1998).

18. *McMann v. Doe*, 460 F. Supp. 2d 259 (D. Mass. 2006).

volved was the constitutionality of the Communications Decency Act, which sought to protect children from unsolicited transmission of sexual materials online. For now, it is worth noting that one of the problems involved in such legislation is that sexually oriented websites can originate halfway around the world just as easily as they can from the next state or the next block. How can we possibly enforce American obscenity law against a website operator doing business halfway around the globe?

More generally, that the Internet is such a decentralized and uncontrollable international medium of communication often frustrates government gatekeepers. With varying degrees of success, China tries to block access to sites about Tibet, Taiwan, democratic movements, and dissident groups; and Saudi Arabia censors sites critical of its royal family. At least twenty countries have some kind of formal Internet censorship policy, although such rules are virtually unenforceable, at least in the sense that information will get through anyway. Some websites may be effectively blocked, some high-profile prosecutions may take place, but "netizens" will still be able to communicate via e-mail, chat rooms, and even new websites with code names designed to

The truly global nature of Internet communication makes it somewhere between difficult and impossible to enforce one nation's laws against "renegade" websites based in other countries.

fool blocking software.[19] The uncontrollable Internet can even negate a government's efforts to silence more traditional media. During the Kosovo crisis, the politically and ethnically independent Belgrade radio station, B92, although banned by the government, continued to broadcast intermittently via a Netherlands-based Internet site. It was on the Internet that the Chinese people heard of NATO's apology for bombing that country's embassy in Belgrade, this part of the story having initially been banned by China's official media.[20]

Still, international media companies, both traditional and on the Internet, often do act in deference to the sensibilities of nations whose laws are more restrictive than those in the United States. The Paris edition of the *International Herald Tribune*, for example, which is owned by The New York Times Company, subjects itself to regular legal review to ensure compliance with libel laws of those nations in which it is distributed.[21] That review no doubt intensified after the paper settled a libel suit—over a piece that surely would have been considered protected opinion under U.S. law—with two government officials in Singapore for over $200,000.

One of the better-known early examples of this phenomenon in the online world occurred in December 1995 when a Bavarian prosecutor notified CompuServe that it was under criminal investigation for making available the uncensored Internet, including sexually oriented sites whose content could be banned under German law. CompuServe responded by blocking access—by all of its subscribers, both children and adults—to several hundred possibly offensive websites and online newsgroups. The move led many Internet enthusiasts to cry "Censorship!" A few weeks later, the company backed away from its original stance, restoring access to all but a handful of discussion groups, while making software available to its subscribers that would effectively block their children's access to offensive portions of the Internet.

More recently, Yahoo! was sued in France by a couple of antidefamation groups complaining that several merchants could be found on the Internet company's website auctioning Nazi memorabilia and materials written by Holocaust deniers, in violation of French law. When Yahoo! countersued in a U.S. federal court, seeking a judgment that French law could not be applied to the company, a highly fractured Ninth Circuit Court of Appeals skirted the issue, with a majority of the judges concluding that the case should be dismissed, either because the court lacked personal jurisdiction or because the case was not ripe (since the French courts had not made any effort to collect the fine they had imposed on Yahoo!).[22] The U.S. Supreme Court denied review.

19. David L. Marcus, "Nations Strive to Limit Freedom of the Internet," *Boston Globe*, December 28, 1998, A1.

20. Sarah Marriott, "Fighting the Cybercensors," *Irish Times*, May 24, 1999, 8.

21. Floyd Abrams, "Cyberspace and the Law," 11 *St. John's Journal of Legal Commentary* 693 (1996).

22. *Yahoo! Inc. v. La Ligue Contre Le Racisme*, 433 F.3d 1199 (9th Cir. 2006).

THINGS TO REMEMBER

Unique Features of the Internet

- It is theoretically possible to carry an infinite amount of information on the Internet.
- Its basic structure does not require the use of "gatekeepers"; anyone who wants to post messages can do so.
- Users tend to choose their online "friends" on the basis of shared interests, rather than physical proximity.
- On the Internet, consumers and "publishers" are the same people.
- Even on a humble budget, individuals can make their online presence appear as slick and professional as that of a multibillion-dollar corporation.
- This parity among all Internet users challenges traditional legal privileges accorded to the institutionalized press, because we no longer can say what it means to be a "reporter."
- Because information posted on the Internet is available to anyone nationwide (and worldwide), courts have had to rethink the matter of personal jurisdiction (i.e., when it is appropriate for one state's courts to accept jurisdiction over a nonresident of that state).
- In general, the more interactive a website, the more likely its manager can be sued anywhere; operators of more passive sites do not incur this liability.
- The Internet also poses significant challenges to the flow and control of information across international boundaries.

Developments in Communication Law Online

Although the Internet is still in its infancy, a fair amount of relevant communications case law and legislative activity has already accumulated. Indeed, many attorneys around the country make their living in the practice of cyberspace law, which is also the focus of full courses at law schools. In this chapter we examine five separate areas of communication law as applied to cyberspace: libel, trademark and copyright, privacy, regulation of advertising, and the transmission of sexually oriented messages.

Libel Online

If one subscriber to an online service such as Prodigy or CompuServe uses the Internet to engage in defamatory speech, should the plaintiff be able to recoup damages from the service provider, or only from the individual speaker? Two relatively early decisions from New York produced opposite results; soon thereafter, Congress weighed in on the issue and may have effectively settled this specific question.

In *Cubby, Inc. v. CompuServe, Inc.*, a federal district court ruled that the defendant could not be held liable for defamatory statements made in an electronic newsletter (called *Rumorville*) for subscribers who participated in a discussion forum focusing on trends in journalism and mass media. The service CompuServ offered its subscribers, the court observed, was like "an electronic, for-profit library that carries a vast number of publications." The company cannot possibly have advance knowledge of the contents of all those publications, any more than can "a public library, bookstore, or newsstand."[23] Imposing liability on CompuServe would be especially inappropriate, the court emphasized, in that the company's relationship with the offending newsletter was rather tenuous, with three layers of contractors and subcontractors.

Contrast this decision with a New York state court's ruling in *Stratton Oakmont, Inc. v. Prodigy Services Co.* Here, an anonymous bulletin board participant on Prodigy accused the plaintiff company of fraudulent practices in its handling of its clients' initial public offerings of stocks. The resulting libel suit could proceed against Prodigy, the court held, because, unlike CompuServe in the earlier case, the defendant here "held itself out as an online service that exercised editorial control over the content of messages posted on its computer bulletin boards."[24] The company's marketing scheme at the time was predicated on positioning itself as the most "family friendly" of the major online service providers. Prodigy would put its own subscribers on notice that they had an obligation to be civil to each other and not post insulting messages; the company also used blocking software designed to weed out especially offensive language. In short, the company proudly exercised the kinds of editorial controls that make more traditional publishers liable for their content.

Thus a rule seemed to be developing that to determine an online company's potential liability in a defamation suit, one must look to whether the company's relationship with its own online content was more akin to that of a library or bookstore, on one hand, or an actual publisher, on the other.

A portion of the Telecommunications Act of 1996, however, says that "no provider or user of an interactive computer service shall be treated as the publisher or speaker of any information provided by another information content provider." This law has resulted in Internet service providers (ISPs) escaping liability for their subscribers' transgressions, even when the Internet company clearly intended to benefit from the rhetorical excesses of those subscribers. No case makes this point more clearly than *Blumenthal v. Drudge*, which resulted when online columnist Matt Drudge accused journalist-cum-presidential adviser Sidney Blumenthal of physically abusing his wife. Blumenthal filed suit against both Drudge and AOL, but AOL's motion to be released as a defendant was readily granted by the court, even though the company had signed a contract with the columnist for the rights to include the "Drudge Report" on its system, touted this relationship in some of its marketing materials, and retained the right to edit Drudge's content. The court admitted that the close relationship between AOL and Drudge was certainly more akin to that of publisher and journalist than

---

23. *Cubby, Inc. v. CompuServe, Inc.*, 776 F. Supp. 135, 140 (S.D.N.Y. 1991).

24. *Stratton Oakmont, Inc. v. Prodigy Services Co.*, 23 Media L. Rep. (BNA) 1794 (N.Y. Sup. Ct. 1995).

bookstore and author. "Why is this different from AOL advertising and promoting a new purveyor of child pornography or other offensive material? Why should AOL be permitted to tout someone as a gossip columnist or rumor monger who will make such rumors and gossip 'instantly accessible' to AOL subscribers, and then claim immunity when that person, as might be anticipated, defames another?"[25] Federal district Judge Paul Friedman even went so far as to say that he would agree with Blumenthal, if he were "writing on a clean slate." Congress, however, had made it clear that ISPs were not to be held liable for their customers' postings.

AOL also escaped liability in a disturbing case involving Kenneth Zeran, a young man with an anonymous yet highly persistent enemy. In April 1995, a prankster posted a notice on an AOL bulletin board ostensibly offering for sale T-shirts with any of a number of highly offensive slogans—for example, "Visit Oklahoma . . . It's a Blast!"—making reference to the bombing that month of the Murrah Federal Building in Oklahoma City. The completely fictional posting instructed readers to call "Ken" at Zeran's home phone number in Seattle. Not surprisingly, Zeran received many hateful phone calls, including death threats. When Zeran complained to AOL, the company promised to remove the posting promptly. Similar notices continued to appear on the bulletin board for several days, however. Finally, in response to further complaints from Zeran, AOL promised to close the account from which the postings were being generated. Zeran sued AOL, claiming that the company unreasonably delayed removing the defamatory messages, refused to post retractions to those messages, and subsequently failed to screen for similar postings.

The Court of Appeals for the Fourth Circuit granted summary judgment to AOL. Unlike Judge Friedman in the *Blumenthal* case, here the court expressed its strong support for the relevant portion of the Telecommunications Act. Since ISPs serve millions of users, processing a "staggering" amount of information, they should not "face potential liability each time they receive notice of a potentially defamatory statement." To hold otherwise, the court emphasized, "would create an impossible burden in the Internet context."[26]

By immunizing ISPs from most liability, Congress has thus answered at least one of the Internet's challenges for traditional libel law. Other issues must await future resolution. Consider, for example, the distinctions among categories of libel plaintiffs. In *Gertz v. Robert Welch, Inc.*, covered at length in chapter 4, the Supreme Court offered two reasons why the First Amendment demands that public officials and public figures have a difficult time obtaining a libel judgment. One of those rationales was that such persons "usually enjoy significantly greater access to the channels of effective communication and hence have a more realistic opportunity to counteract false statements than private individuals normally enjoy."[27]

---

25. *Blumenthal v. Drudge*, 992 F. Supp. 44, 51 (D.D.C. 1998).

26. *Zeran v. America Online*, 129 F.3d 327, 330, 331, 333 (4th Cir. 1997); see also *Zeran v. Diamond Broadcasting*, 203 F.3d 714 (10th Cir. 2000); but see the discussion of the roommates.com case from 2007 in note 14 on page 401.

27. *Gertz v. Robert Welch, Inc.*, 418 U.S. 323, 344 (1974).

Does this reasoning apply with full force on the Internet, one of whose defining characteristics is a relative equality of access for all, as both consumers and "publishers"? Persons who are maligned online can and do respond in kind. Flaming begets flaming. Moreover, the aggrieved individuals can reach an audience as large as the one exposed to the original defamation. Some commentators have suggested that the new communication dynamics of the Internet will soon require a rethinking of the *Gertz* doctrine. Might it not make more sense, some argue, for all Internet participants to be considered public figures?[28]

As we have already seen in our discussion of personal jurisdiction issues online, defendants in Internet-based lawsuits are often anonymous. At least one state supreme court has held that a libel plaintiff who is a public official carries a heavy pretrial burden of proof merely to unmask a "John Doe" defendant. Defendant Doe had placed remarks highly critical of Smyrna, Delaware, city councilman Patrick Cahill on a website run by a local news service. Cahill has numerous "character flaws," Doe charged, and manifests obvious "mental deterioration." The Delaware Supreme Court, after weighing the pluses and minuses of anonymous online speech, determined that public officials or public figures who seek disclosure of a potential libel defendant's identity must first alert the defendant that a motion for compelled disclosure is pending. (This could be done by posting to the same website where the allegedly libelous statements appeared.) Then the plaintiff must meet the same standard of proof he or she would have to meet to prevail over a libel defendant's motion for summary judgment. Such plaintiffs would have to make a prima facie case; that is, they must demonstrate to the judge's satisfaction that they are likely to prevail if the case is brought to full trial. Cahill could not meet such a burden, Justice Steele wrote, in that the most inflammatory remarks posted about Cahill were almost certainly protected opinion. Who is to say any of us lack "character flaws"? And even "mental deterioration," at least in the context of an emotionally charged web posting, is in the eye of the beholder.[29]

Trademark and Copyright Online

Cyberspace forces us to rethink some of the most basic tenets of intellectual property law. In the online world, we are not certain what it means to make a "copy" of a work, nor is the relationship clear between traditional trademarks and the Internet "addresses" called universal resource locators, or URLs. That the Internet is a computer-mediated form of communication where messages are sent digitally has enormous implications for intellectual property law for three related reasons. First, the Internet makes the mass production of protected works so effortless. Second, unau-

---

28. Aaron Perzanowski, "Relative Access to Corrective Speech: A New Test for Requiring Actual Malice," 94 *California Law Review* 833 (2006). But see Michael Hadley, "The *Gertz* Doctrine and Internet Defamation," 84 *Virginia Law Review* 477, 494 (1998).

29. *John Doe #1 v. Cahill*, 884 A.2d 451 (Del. 2005).

THINGS TO REMEMBER

Libel Online

- A common-law principle seemed to be developing to the effect that Internet service providers that exercise editorial control over messages sent by and among subscribers could be liable for damages stemming from a subscriber's defamatory postings.
- A portion of the Telecommunications Act of 1996, however, negated that presumption by giving ISPs virtually complete immunity from such liability.
- Some commentators have suggested that the traditional distinctions between public figures and private plaintiffs be discarded for Internet libel suits, that all persons who engage in "cyber chatter" should be considered public figures.
  - Public officials and public figures may have a high burden of proof if they seek to unmask "John Doe" online libel defendants.

thorized copies can be distributed worldwide in a matter of seconds. Finally, the enormous volume of copying makes it virtually impossible to track down the original infringer in a chain of Internet piracy;[30] some have even argued that this fact alone will be looked back on as the beginning of the end of copyright law.[31]

"Copying" in a Digital World.   Traditional copyright law does not seem to fit well with the Internet. In the physical world, we recognize the difference between reading something and copying it. You might have seen a funny cartoon or a provocative article in your local newspaper, and perhaps you chose to show it to a friend or clip it and paste it on your door for any passersby to enjoy. You have not *copied* it. On the Internet, however, to read *is* to copy, because we access digital expression by *reproducing* it (in RAM, or on a hard drive, CD, or similar medium). Thus, the simple act of reading an online file "violates the copyright holder's exclusive right to reproduce."[32]

Many commentators have pointed to a fundamental irony here. The Internet is often touted as a revolutionary vehicle for the unlimited exchange of information, yet its infrastructure would seem to give copyright holders a veto over what will be seen and where, power far in excess of what Congress had ever intended. If you cannot even read a protected work on your computer screen without permission, what will happen to the fair-use doctrine? After all, in virtually all protected works, some subset of the text consists of the recounting of historical facts, which are themselves not copyrightable.

---

30. Jack E. Brown, "New Law for the Internet," 28 *Arizona State Law Journal* 1243 (1996).

31. John Perry Barlow, "The Economy of Ideas: A Framework for Rethinking Patents and Copyrights in the Digital Age," *Wired*, March 1994, 84.

32. Fred Cate, "Law in Cyberspace," 39 *Howard Law Journal* 565, 575 (1996).

What does all this mean for the individual netizen? We may violate copyright law when we incorporate text or graphics created by others on our own websites, and perhaps even when we point visitors to others' protected works with hyperlinks. Will copyright holders sue you for these kinds of transgressions, or for simply reading their works on your computer screen? Usually not, because you are either "under the radar screen" or the cost of going after you is prohibitive. But the balance between the rights of copyright holders and the rights of users who may wish to read and to comment on others' works seems to have shifted.

Surely, if the technology itself seems to be tilted a bit too much toward rights holders, laws would be passed to reset the balance. Ah, but no. In fact, there has been a strong legislative trend toward strengthening the copyright holders' control over Internet content even more. The Digital Millennium Copyright Act (DMCA), enacted in late 1998, has been especially vexing for librarians. That statute contains a provision making it a criminal offense to circumvent any technological locking device that might be used by copyright holders to prevent unauthorized copying.

At one level, such a provision makes sense. If we envision a future in which virtually all intellectual products—books, music, films, and so forth—will be transmitted primarily via the Internet, it is not surprising that movie studios, for example, would want to install devices permitting downloaders to view a film only once. Otherwise every video rental becomes a video sale. In 2001 the Second Circuit Court of Appeals upheld an injunction issued two years earlier against a group of computer hackers posting software that would enable users to circumvent the encryption device used on many DVDs (and thus permitting unauthorized copying).[33] The encryption device is called CSS (for "content scrambling system"). The hackers, who called themselves MORE (Masters of Reverse Engineering), have achieved a kind of cult status. Source code for their software, aptly enough named DeCSS, has appeared on T-shirts distributed worldwide.

How should the relevant section of the DMCA apply to digitally transmitted books and periodicals? In the physical world, libraries are permitted to make copies of articles from journals in their collections for any number of purposes, such as for interlibrary loans. Individual library users have been similarly accustomed to making photocopies of library materials for their own use, often for research projects. If, however, all knowledge comes to us on the Internet in a "locked" format and librarians are prohibited from unlocking it, we will have entered what a *Washington Post* editorial called a "pay-per-view world."[34]

Peer-to-Peer Websites.

In the "old days," if you owned a phonograph record coveted by a friend of yours, you might make her a copy of the record by playing

---

33. *Universal City Studios v. Reimerdes*, 111 F. Supp. 2d 346 (S.D.N.Y. 2000), *aff'd sub nom. Universal City Studios v. Corley*, 273 F.3d 429 (2d Cir. 2001).

34. "A Pay-Per-View World," *Washington Post*, August 4, 1998, A14.

the LP with the phonograph linked to a cassette tape deck. Technically this would likely have been a violation of copyright law, but none of the record companies would find it worth their while to sue you. It is also worth noting that if your friend wanted to make a copy of that cassette for another person, the resulting second-generation copy would be of audibly inferior quality. Third- and fourth-generation copies would manifest yet further deteriorated sound. In short, there would not be much of an incentive or opportunity for the casual copyright infringer to do much damage.

Enter the digital age, and things change markedly. Many Internet users have installed on their computers software that permits them to make compressed copies of any and all tracks from a CD and to upload this musical data to a website, ready for anyone who wishes to download the performances for themselves. Multiple copies and multiple generations of copies using this "MP3" technology lose little, if any, of the fidelity of the original.

In 1999 there were over half a million MP3 websites, virtually all of which boasted pirated copies that were unauthorized by the copyright holders.[35] Napster's website, a clearinghouse for members sharing MP3 music files with each other (in the industry, this is called peer-to-peer file sharing), attracted considerable attention. Many universities blocked access to napster.com, lest their entire information infrastructures be crippled by heavy student use of the site. Not surprisingly, a consortium of the largest recording companies sued Napster. In early 2001, the Ninth Circuit Court of Appeals handed down a preliminary ruling to the effect that the plaintiffs would likely succeed in proving Napster guilty of contributing to copyright infringement on the part of its millions of users. The three-judge panel handed the case back to a lower court, which issued an injunction ordering Napster to block access within three days after the plaintiffs assert their copyright ownership. Napster went out of business in response to the ruling, then, with the contractual cooperation of major recording companies, reemerged as a legal site whose users pay to download songs.

Numerous other peer-to-peer sharing sites have been involved in copyright-infringement suits since the Napster case. Most notably, the Supreme Court ruled in 2005 that movie studios and recording labels may sue services such as Grokster and Morpheus.[36] Even though clients of those and similar websites might use them to share perfectly legal material not protected by copyright, the companies themselves were guilty of "actively inducing" users to share protected movies and music. The unanimous Court thus distinguished its earlier *Sony* decision (see chapter 6), even while admitting that Sony's ads for its VCRs decades ago also encouraged purchasers to "record favorite shows" and even to "build a library" of recorded programs. Within a few months of the adverse ruling, Grokster went out business, with a terse message on its site: "There are legal services for downloading music and movies. This service is not one of them."

---

35. Alice Rawsthorn, "Internet Fast Becoming Copyright Battleground," *Stuart News/Port St. Lucie News* (Stuart, Fla.), March 28, 1999, D2.

36. *MGM Studios v. Grokster, Ltd.*, 545 U.S. 913 (2005).

The D.C. Circuit Court of Appeals made it a bit more difficult for major recording labels when it ruled in 2003 that the companies are not empowered under the Digital Millennium Copyright Act to compel ISPs to reveal names and addresses of members who the labels believe are violating copyright law.[37] The record labels' response was to file hundreds of suits using a new strategy—naming defendants by their Internet protocol (IP) addresses rather than their names, under the assumption that the actual identities would be revealed later on as part of the normal pretrial discovery process.

Most observers agree that the end game to the threat posed by MP3 websites to traditional copyright interests will find the major companies buying (or at least contracting with) rather than fighting the sites. The writing is on the wall, they say. Young people hardly ever buy music from stores anymore, preferring to download it instead. Internet guru Ian Clarke tells the music labels to consider an analogy: if you make your money by selling water in the desert and then it starts to rain bloody murder, you had better change your business model.

Sysop/ISP Liability. Just as was the case with libel law, the question of whether ISPs or system operators (sysops) can be held liable for an individual subscriber's copyright infringement has been the focus of both litigation and federal legislation. It is also a source of considerable confusion among sysops themselves.[38] One of the early cases was *Playboy Enterprises, Inc. v. Frena.*[39] George Frena was the sysop of a computer bulletin board called "Techs Warehouse," whose content included "adult-oriented" graphics and photos. The impetus for the lawsuit was the plaintiff's discovery that about 170 of those images were photos from *Playboy* magazine and other publications to which it owned the rights.

Frena denied that he himself had ever uploaded any of the photos in question, maintaining that his subscribers were the direct infringers. He testified further that the moment *Playboy* attorneys alerted him about the infringements, he deleted the unauthorized images from his system and began to carefully monitor subscriber uploads. Although that testimony was not directly contested in court, it is apparent that Judge Harvey Schlesinger was unconvinced of Frena's truthfulness because the defendant had removed the plaintiff's trademarked logo from the photos, substituting his own name and phone number. The plaintiff's motion for summary judgment was granted. Judge Schlesinger emphasized that it really did not matter whether Frena knew of the infringements prior to having been officially notified of them by the plaintiff. "Intent to infringe" is not an element of copyright suits. If Frena were truly an "innocent infringer," that fact may be taken into account later, when damages are assessed.

---

37. *RIAA v. Verizon Internet Services*, 351 F.3d 1229 (D.C. Cir. 2003).

38. Ashley Packard, "Infringement or Impingement: Carving Out an Actual Knowledge Defense for Sysops Facing Strict Liability," *Journalism and Mass Communication Monographs*, December 1998, 1–46.

39. 839 F. Supp. 1552 (M.D. Fla. 1993).

The Religious Technology Center, which owns the copyrights to the writings of Church of Scientology founder L. Ron Hubbard, has been an especially litigious plaintiff. One of the suits brought by the group was against Netcom, an Internet service provider. Judge Ronald White noted that courts in his jurisdiction (the Northern District of California) had never dealt with the issue presented, namely, "whether the operator of a computer bulletin board service ('BBS'), and the large Internet access provider that allows that BBS to reach the Internet, should be liable for copyright infringement committed by a subscriber of the BBS."[40] The subscriber was Dennis Erlich, once a minister within the Church of Scientology and now one of its harshest critics. Erlich used an Internet discussion group of his design (alt.religion.scientology) to disseminate his views. From the church's perspective, he crossed the line when he began posting to his online group lengthy, nearly verbatim excerpts from some of Hubbard's works.

At first the church contacted Erlich directly, asking that he cease the online copyright infringement. When he refused, the plaintiff contacted Thomas Klemesrud, the operator of the larger computer bulletin board of which Erlich's was a part, and Netcom, which provided the BBS's access to the Internet. Klemesrud made clear that he would not take any action until the church provided some *evidence* that Erlich had infringed on their copyrights. For its part, Netcom also refused to simply kick Erlich off the Internet; because of the way the BBS was structured, this could not be accomplished without also denying access to every one of Klemesrud's subscribers.

Judge White determined that Netcom was not responsible for directly infringing on the church's copyrights, because the ISP did not exercise any immediate control over subscribers' postings. He agreed that Netcom itself had made "copies" of the works in question, but only to the extent that "copying" and "posting" data on the Internet are part of the same action—that one cannot read anything online unless it has been "copied." The judge agreed with Netcom's assertion that it should be no more liable for direct copyright infringement here than a telephone company "for carrying an infringing facsimile transmission or storing an infringing audio recording on its voice mail," or no more liable than a highway toll booth operator for whatever criminal activities might take place on the roads.

Judge White cautioned, however, that Netcom might be held accountable for *contributory* infringement of the church's copyrights and for that reason did not fully grant the company's motion for summary judgment. A defendant can incur such liability if "with knowledge of the infringing activity, [it] induces, causes or materially contributes to the infringing conduct of another." White rejected Netcom's assertion that the notice it received from the plaintiff lacked sufficient evidence that one of its subscribers had indeed been infringing on a valid copyright. He admitted that copyright-infringement cases on the Internet more commonly concern unauthorized

---

40. *Religious Technology Center v. Netcom On-Line Services*, 907 F. Supp. 1361, 1365 (N.D. Cal. 1995).

copying of computer software, a product category with which Internet service providers have special expertise and can thus more easily ascertain for themselves if an infringement has taken place. That this case involved old-fashioned text instead, however, would not excuse Netcom from all liability. Although he allowed the lawsuit to go forward on this point, Judge White set up a high barrier for the plaintiffs. Netcom would ultimately prevail even against a claim of contributory infringement, White told the parties, if it could show even a plausible suspicion that Erlich's postings constituted a fair use of the church's otherwise protected works.

Sega, the video game manufacturer, has also had to go to court to protect its copyrighted materials from online infringements. In one case, the company brought suit against Chad Sherman, an online BBS operator whose subscribers uploaded and downloaded dozens of Sega video games. In addition, Sherman marketed a product called "The Super Magic Drive," computer hardware designed to facilitate the copying of video game cartridges onto floppy disks for convenient uploading to the BBS. As in the *Netcom* case, the defendant here could not be charged with direct infringement, although his conduct did fall squarely within the definition of contributory infringement. That finding was bolstered by Judge Wilken's conclusion that the BBS subscribers' conduct here was so clearly violative of copyright law that the fair-use defense would never work for them. Their primary motivation for participating in the BBS was to download illegal copies and avoid having to buy products directly from Sega.

One fascinating feature of this case is that Sega had itself helped gather evidence to support a search warrant. The company did so by having one of its employees log on to the defendant's BBS to observe firsthand the extent of unauthorized copying. The defendant cried foul—Sega had "unclean hands" and should not benefit from such conduct—but to no avail. Whatever merit the argument would normally have, Judge Wilken concluded, it has none in the context of Internet discourse. The typical computer BBS is, after all, "open to the public, and *normally* accessed by use of an alias or pseudonym."[41]

A portion of the Digital Millennium Copyright Act, adopted in 1998, addresses the issue of liability for systems operators stemming from their subscribers' content. In effect the law adopts a stance not too different from that seen in the line of cases reviewed here, although it is a bit friendlier to Internet service providers than was the *Frena* court. The DMCA exempts service providers and systems operators from liability if they do not know of their subscribers' infringing conduct. The exemption will hold also if the provider, once made aware of the existence on their systems of unauthorized copyrighted material, "acts expeditiously to remove or disable access to the material." The law further protects the service provider from lawsuits that might be brought by subscribers distraught over their noninfringing content having been re-

41. *Sega Enterprises v. Maphia*, 948 F. Supp. 923 (N.D. Cal. 1995); see also *Sega Enterprises v. Sabella*, 1995 U.S. Dist. LEXIS 20470 (N.D. Cal. 1995).

moved from the system without their consent, as long as the provider believed in good faith that the materials had been posted in violation of copyright law. It is also important that the service provider not gain financially as a direct result of the users' infringing activities.

Trademark, URL Addresses, and Website Interactions.   One of the most fascinating—and for those directly involved, perplexing—ways in which cyberspace has affected communication law concerns Internet domain names, which are the heart of a website's URL. In the real world many companies can use the same trademark for very different products or services. Thus we have Life cereal and also Life the board game, Thrifty Car Rental and Thrifty Drug Stores, Universal Van Lines and Universal Pictures. In trademark law, this is called **concurrent registration** of marks. Concurrent registration is the norm as long as two businesses are not in direct competition or marketing complementary products that consumers would presume must come from the same source.[42] In cyberspace, however, there can be only one www.life.com, one www.thrifty.com, and so on.

This restriction on the naming of Internet URLs is actually more a convention than an insurmountable technological barrier. It has been suggested, for example, that "master domain name masks" be created so that there would not be just one McDonalds.com, but rather McDonalds1.com, McDonalds2.com, McDonalds3.com, and so forth; such a system would be akin to finding *the* "John Smith" of interest from among a long list of John Smiths in the phone book.[43] At least for now, though, one and only one entity can be assigned the "space" of a particular URL address.

Since there is no universal Yellow Pages to help consumers associate domain names with company names—and Internet search engines such as Yahoo! and Google can produce overwhelmingly large numbers of "hits" in response to a request for one specific site—consumers are often left guessing. The wise company seeking an Internet presence needs to predict as best it can whatever addresses consumers will *guess* might be theirs. Such domain names are thus very valuable commodities and have been the impetus for a flurry of litigation.

Internet domain names are actually series of numbers that computers read in order to "talk" to each other; they are sometimes called Internet protocol, or IP, addresses. But humans do not remember numbers very well, so the IPs are translated into more mnemonic devices. The names consist of two parts. Starting on the right, the portion of a name that appears after the "dot" is called the top-level domain (TLD) name. Sometimes they are called gTLDs, the "g" standing for "generic." In the United States, six TLDs have been most commonly used: ".com" (for profit-making compa-

---

42. *Aunt Jemima Mills Co. v. Rigney & Co.*, 247 F. 407 (2d Cir. 1917).

43. Rosanne T. Mitchell, "Resolving Domain Name–Trademark Disputes: A New System of Alternative Dispute Resolution Is Needed in Cyberspace," 14 *Ohio State Journal on Dispute Resolution* 157 (1998).

nies), ".org" (for nonprofit organizations), ".net" (for computer networks), ".edu" (for educational institutions), ".gov" (for government agencies), and ".int" (for international organizations such as NATO). More recent additions have included ".aero" (for aerospace companies), ".biz" and ".info" (serving the same function as .com), ".coop" (for business cooperatives) ".museum" (self-evident, no?), ".name" (for personal websites), and ".pro" (for individual professionals such as doctors and lawyers).

Moving from right to left, we come to the second-level domain name. In "MyBusiness.com," "MyBusiness" is the second-level domain name. Whoever owns the rights to use "MyBusiness.com" as an Internet address might find it helpful to subdivide the second level a bit more. Thus we might find "Billing_MyBusiness.com" functioning alongside "Jobs_MyBusiness.com," "NewProducts_MyBusiness.com," and so on.

There have been at least three identifiable categories of disputes between trademark holders and URL address holders. First are those situations in which the URL registrant legitimately is doing business under a name that just happens to be the cherished trademark of another company. In one often-cited case, a nightclub in Columbia, Missouri, used a URL that included the phrase "BlueNote," which is also the name of a well-known night club in New York City.[44] In that case, the court in New York refused to accept jurisdiction, because the smaller club's website was a "passive" one not set up for such interactions as actually buying tickets online. Had the site been more interactive, and especially if it could have been shown that some customers from the New York area had purchased tickets in preparation for a trip to the Midwest college town, the court would have been forced to address the conflict between one company's legitimately obtained URL address and the other's federally protected trademark.

A second kind of legal dispute, especially vexing from a trademark holder's perspective, involves "**cybersquatters**." These are folks who never actually intend to do business using the URL addresses for which they apply; rather, they make money by thinking a few steps ahead of large businesses that for whatever reasons, did not establish an early Internet presence. One particularly well-known squatter is Dennis Toeppen, who received authorization for hundreds of domain names with familiar rings, from "aircanada.com" and "neiman-marcus.com" to camdenyards.com."[45] Even though the legal climate is shifting against the squatter—Congress enacted the Anticybersquatting Consumer Protection Act in 1999, which makes clear that an Internet address can be the basis of a trademark-infringement suit—corporations often will settle with squatters out of court to avoid the expense and delay of litigation.

A third category of conflict involves URL addresses maintained by companies or individuals who intend to prevent consumers from reaching the "natural" owners of

---

44. *Bensusan Restaurant Corp. v. King*, 937 F. Supp. 295, 299 (S.D.N.Y. 1996), *aff'd*, 126 F.3d 25 (2d Cir. 1997).

45. *Panavision International v. Toeppen*, 945 F. Supp. 1296 (C.D. Cal. 1996).

the addresses, either because they are business competitors or because they have some ideological conflict with the trademark holders. For example, The Princeton Review began using "kaplan.com" as its domain name; site visitors would be treated to a comparison between Princeton's test-prep courses and those offered by its competitor Kaplan. An arbitrator ultimately awarded the domain name to Kaplan. Or consider the antics of Steven C. Brodsky, who was personally very opposed to the organization Jews for Jesus. His website could be found at "jewsforjesus.org," where visitors would find text highly critical of the group. Jews for Jesus eventually obtained an injunction against Brodsky's further use of the URL address.[46] In 2001 the Fourth Circuit Court of Appeals upheld a lower court ruling instructing the registered owner of "www .peta.org," whose website was designed to make fun of the animal rights group People for the Ethical Treatment of Animals, to relinquish his URL.[47] Prior to the courts' intervention, visitors to that address had been introduced to the fictitious "People Eating Tasty Animals."

Many large companies have tried to stay a step ahead of their cyber-enemies by buying up URL addresses that might be used to disparage their good names. Thus, for example, UPS owns the rights to UPSBites.com, UPSstinks.com, IhateUPS.com, and some more X-rated addresses as well.[48]

---

46. *Jews for Jesus v. Brodsky*, 993 F. Supp. 282 (N.J. 1998).

47. *People for the Ethical Treatment of Animals v. Doughney*, 113 F. Supp. 2d 915 (E.D. Va. 2000), *aff'd*, 263 F.3d 359 (4th Cir. 2001).

48. David Streitfeld, "Making Bad Names for Themselves," *Washington Post*, September 8, 2000, E1.

Another mingling of trademark law and the Internet concerns the use of hyperlinks from one website to another.[49] When website A is linked to website B, visitors to A can move to B by clicking on highlighted text or graphics; they need not know B's Internet address. Indeed, they might not even know that they have been moved to site B; this is especially true if the link is accomplished through **framing** or **deep linking**, as described below.

Linking raises questions of trademark law in a number of ways. To begin with, site A's link to site B might include an unauthorized use of B's logo. Without an appropriate disclaimer, visitors may be misled to believe that B not only has permitted this use but also has in some way endorsed A's products or services. For example, an injunction issued against the defendant in *Playboy Enterprises, Inc. v. Universal Tel-A-Talk, Inc.*, which had made several infringing uses of the Playboy name and its famous bunny logo, included a prohibition against any further linking of its own adult website with the plaintiff's site.[50] In another case, Playboy unsuccessfully sought to enjoin a former Playmate of the Year from mentioning this biographical tidbit on her personal website; the court emphasized, however, that its ruling might have been different had the defendant also used the bunny logo.[51] Courts are perhaps more sensitive to the use of logos on websites than in other communication forums because of the very nature of "cybersurfing," which is typically done at such a rapid rate that there is no time to sort out mentally the implicit endorsements.[52]

The linking techniques called framing and deep linking can raise special problems. Framing occurs when site B pops up as a window within site A, thus not making clear to visitors that they have indeed moved from one site to another. The practice was at issue in a 1999 case involving the company that owns the Hard Rock Cafes and one of its founders, Peter Morton, who had earlier sold most of his interest in the company. Under the sale agreement, Morton retained ownership of the Hard Rock Hotel and Casino in Las Vegas and a right to open additional hotels in specified locations, but he was precluded from using the Hard Rock name or logo in other commercial enterprises. The suit was prompted by Morton's "framing" of a music seller's website on his Hard Rock Hotel and Casino website. Enjoining Morton from engaging in this practice, Judge Robert Patterson explained that this framing resulted in computer users' not knowing when they have been shifted from one website to another, because "the domain name appearing at the top of the computer screen, which indicates the location of the user in the World Wide Web, continues to indicate the domain name of Hard Rock Hotel."[53]

Deep linking takes the visitor, upon clicking on the appropriate button, from site

---

49. Glenn Mitchell and Craig S. Mende, "Internet Links Raise Issues of Trademark, Other Liability," *New York Law Journal*, May 17, 1999, 51.

50. 1998 U.S. Dist. LEXIS 17282 (E.D. Pa. 1998).

51. *Playboy Enterprises, Inc. v. Terri Welles*, 7 F. Supp. 2d 1098 (S.D. Cal. 1998).

52. *Digital Equipment Corp. v. Altavista Technology, Inc.*, 960 F. Supp. 456 (D. Mass. 1997).

53. *Hard Rock Cafe International v. Morton*, 1999 U.S. Dist. LEXIS 8340 (S.D.N.Y. 1999).

A to a page *within* site B, rather than to B's home page, thus further increasing the chances that the visitor will not know of the switch and will assume that this new page is simply another part of site A. As the Internet world becomes more and more commercialized, these practices can give the manager of site A and that site's advertisers a "free ride" on site B's content. The practice also effectively bypasses site B's advertisers, thus costing site B's operators revenue (the fewer eyeballs that visit, the less you can charge for ads). In one highly publicized lawsuit, Ticketmaster sued Microsoft over the latter's deep linking to a page within Ticketmaster's site. Interestingly, Microsoft agreed, in an out-of-court settlement, to link its own visitors directly to Ticketmaster's home page.[54]

Yet another trademark problem posed by the Internet is the matter of "**meta tags**," the keywords that site owners embed in their websites using hypertext markup language (HTML), invisible to the casual visitor, to help search engines locate relevant sites. Sometimes companies have been known to use competitors' trademarks among their meta tags. For example, suppose that two commercial websites are maintained by competing discount travel agencies, the aggressively marketed "cheapestfare.com" and the far more obscure "cheapflights.com." If Cheapflights includes "cheapestfare" among its meta tags, consumers who use "cheapestfare" as a search engine keyword will also "hit" the Cheapflights website. The smaller company will be unfairly riding the coattails of the larger company in this scenario, which trademark lawyers call "**initial interest confusion**." Even if the consumer eventually figures out she was directed to a site other than the one she thought she wanted, she might still make a purchase if finding the site in which she was initially interested is too much trouble.

In one early case of this kind, *Brookfield Communications Inc. v. West Coast Entertainment Corp.*, a company that marketed online information about the entertainment industry designed both for trivia fans and for Hollywood professionals learned that a competing company had been attracting business to its own website by using the word *moviebuff* (the name of a software package marketed by Brookfield) among its meta tags. Although the court allowed that the defendant's larger sin was using the word as part of its domain name, the meta tag caused additional problems. By fooling search engines to bring unwary customers to westcoastvideo.com instead of to moviebuff.com, the defendant was "improperly benefit[ing] from the goodwill that Brookfield developed in its mark. Using another's trademark in one's metatags is much like posting a sign with another's trademark in front of one's store."[55]

More recent cases have involved search engines as defendants, rather than (or in addition to) direct competitors. Thus, for example, in 2004 GEICO sued Google,

---

54. Bob Tedeschi, "Ticketmaster and Microsoft Settle Suit on Internet Linking," *New York Times*, February 15, 1999, C6.

55. *Brookfield Communications Inc. v. West Coast Entertainment Corp.*, 174 F.3d 1036 (9th Cir. 1999); see also *Faegre & Benson v. Purdy*, 367 F. Supp. 2d 1238 (D. Minn. 2005); *J.K. Harris & Co. v. Kassel*, 253 F. Supp. 2d 1120 (N.D. Cal. 2003).

which had allowed competing insurance companies to pay for pop-up ads that would emerge whenever an Internet user input "GEICO" as a search term. The case poses an intriguing question—can trademark infringement result from the fact that the trademarked word "GEICO" is what triggers the ads, even though it is the end user (rather than the defendant) who is typing in the word? Upon a motion for summary judgment by Google, U.S. district court judge Leonie Brinkema ruled that GEICO's Lanham Act and unfair-competition (under state law) claims could go forward.[56]

A similar case from 2006 involved the "pay for priority" search engine called GoTo.com. The plaintiff was a cigar manufacturer named Junior Cigar, some of whose competitors were bidding with the search engine to receive priority placement of their listings as "hits" when Internet surfers input some variation of the plaintiff's protected trademarks. Judge John Lifland determined that GoTo.com likely had violated federal trademark law, but since there were some remaining factual disputes as to whether consumers would actually be confused by the practice, he refused to grant summary judgment to the cigar maker.[57]

This area of the law is a bit of a mess at present. There is no Supreme Court ruling, and the federal court rulings, almost entirely at the trial level, go in both directions. Google has sometimes prevailed in cases with facts highly similar to those in which it has lost.[58] More generally, some courts have pointed out that it is not at all unusual in the brick-and-mortar world for lesser-known brands to try to capitalize on the industry leaders, even to the point of obtaining retail shelf placement right next to those leaders. Thus, for example, we all know that a drug store's own brand of amber-colored mouthwash will be next to the Listerine, the green next to Scope, and the red next to Lavoris. This certainly resembles initial interest confusion.

And the plot thickens. Not all unauthorized uses of another entity's meta tags are actionable trademark infringements. Courts are especially unlikely to shut down a website designed to make a critical commentary on another company or individual, since that is the essence of political speech. Thus, for example, a federal district court in Minnesota refused to enjoin an individual from unauthorized use of meta tags referring to a local realty company, because his purpose was apparently to direct Internet users to his own site, which criticized the company's practices. Indeed, the defendant even included a disclaimer on his site's home page, making clear that it "is intended as a criticism" of the plaintiff's company and its president and is (unsurprisingly), "not endorsed or affiliated with [the plaintiff's company] in any way."[59] To make matters even more complicated, there might be an exception to the exception. If your "gripe site" not only comments on a company you hate but also directs users

---

56. *GEICO v. Google*, 330 F. Supp. 2d 700 (E.D. Va. 2004); see also *Google v. American Blind and Wallpaper Factory*, 2005 U.S. District LEXIS 6228 (2005).

57. *800-Jr Cigar v. GoTo.com*, 437 F. Supp. 2d 273 (D.N.J. 2006).

58. See, e.g., *Rescuecom v. Google*, 456 F. Supp. 2d 393 (N.D.N.Y. 2006).

59. *Gregerson v. Vilana Financial*, 2006 U.S. Dist. LEXIS 81731 (D. Minn. 2006).

to websites of the company's competitors, there may be an actionable trademark infringement.[60]

Databases and Authors' Rights.

Another novel issue posed by the Internet is whether publishers, having contracted to purchase the rights to distribute an author's work in traditional print media, may, without further payment or permission, redistribute the work in computer databases. A rather elaborate explication of the issue is found in *Tasini v. New York Times Co.*[61] At issue was whether specific permission must be sought from freelance journalists who had been paid by the *Times* (and other publications) for their work when the paper wished to make those writings available as part of the NEXIS database. When one uses NEXIS's highly sophisticated search engine, the database groups together the articles that meet the searcher's chosen parameters. A *New York Times* article might be on the list alongside a transcript from an *ABC News* broadcast, a *Newsweek* editorial, and perhaps even some congressional testimony or other such Washington event covered by any of the exclusively online "magazines" that are part of the database. What you will not see is a mockup of, for example, the full page of the *New York Times* where the article of interest to you had initially appeared.

The litigation focused on section 201(c) of the Copyright Act, which describes the rights retained by the publisher of a "collective work" (you may recall from chapter 6 that this is a compilation of smaller works, each one of which is separately copyrightable). A compilation of poems by different poets is a collective work, as is your daily newspaper. Since section 201(c) gives publishers the right to create, without obtaining further permission, "any revisions of the collective work"—such as a final edition of a given day's paper—the question became whether inputting the individual articles into the NEXIS database was consistent with the *Times*' right to publish a "revision."

The courts first had to determine exactly what it is about each day's edition of the *Times* that constituted the creative element added by the paper's editors to what the individual writers had already provided. Then they had to determine whether that element of creativity was preserved when the authors' writings were transferred into the NEXIS database.

Writing for the majority in a 7-2 decision, Justice Ginsburg ruled for the freelancers. The level of creativity the *Times* adds to its own writers' work goes no further than its selection, arrangement, and formatting of reporters' individual contributions. But this modest amount of added creativity is stripped away when articles pop up in response to NEXIS searches, she concluded. Whatever "hits" result "appear to a user

---

60. *Bihari v. Gross*, 119 F. Supp. 2d 309 (S.D.N.Y. 2000).

61. 972 F. Supp. 804 (S.D.N.Y. 1997), *reconsideration denied*, 981 F. Supp. 841 (S.D.N.Y. 1997), *rev'd and remanded*, 206 F.3d 161 (2d Cir. 1999), *aff'd*, 533 U.S. 483 (2001); see also *Random House v. Rosetta Books*, 283 F.3d 490 (2d Cir. 2002) (holding that publisher needs to obtain explicit rights to create an interactive "e-book" from a freelancer's work).

without the graphics, formatting, or other articles with which the article was initially published."[62] Thus, she concluded, the databases do not constitute a "revision" of the original day's newspaper (which the publishers would have been permitted to distribute without obtaining the freelancers' permission).

The Supreme Court decision, of course, merely establishes the "default" position, which can always be overridden by language written into individual contracts. Indeed, numerous media companies have already begun to ask their freelancers to sign away their digital rights as a matter of course. As is always the case in such conflicts between writers and publishers, the winner in any specific instance will be the one with the larger measure of clout.

Privacy Online

The Internet's impact on users' privacy dramatically demonstrates the complex and contradictory nature of this new medium. Certainly the Internet can be, for better or worse, a privacy-enhancing means of communication. Many pundits have suggested that 1993 will be looked back upon as the year the Internet finally "arrived" as a cultural phenomenon. That is when it first became the subject of a *New Yorker* car-

---

THINGS TO REMEMBER

Trademark and Copyright Online

- The simple act of reading a file on a computer screen cannot help but also involve making a "copy" of the file; this fact alone poses a serious complication for traditional copyright law.
- The Digital Millennium Copyright Act makes it a criminal offense to circumvent any software attached to a work by the copyright holder; librarians fear that it will have the effect of jettisoning the whole idea of fair use.
- The DMCA also immunizes Internet service providers and sysops from liability for infringements made by their subscribers if they were unaware of such infringements.
- Many suits have been brought in recent years alleging that an Internet domain name is too similar to the plaintiff's trademark. Sometimes the defendant is a cybersquatter, someone who obtained the rights to the domain name only to sell it back to the more legitimate owner at a higher price.
- Trademark law is also implicated by the unauthorized linking of one's own website to another, especially if the latter company's logo is used as the link.
- Links that do not fully move a visitor from site A to site B, but rather "frame" B within A, cause special problems; the use of inappropriate meta tags can also be an infringement.
- The Supreme Court has ruled that in the absence of a specific contract clause one way or the other, media outlets may not upload their freelancers' work into a database such as NEXIS without the freelance authors' permission.

---

62. *New York Times Co. v. Tasini*, 533 U.S. 483, 500 (2001).

toon, which showed two dogs sitting together, interacting intently with a computer screen; one, winking, advised the other that "on the Internet, no one *knows* you're a dog.

Shielding one's personal identity while online, such as by using a screen name unrelated to one's real name, has become a cyberspace norm. Sophisticated software also exists for shielding the identity of the computer and the network from which e-mail is sent. The programs do this by stripping off the identifying information on an e-mail and substituting an anonymous code number or term. Some kinds of software also route messages through many different relay computers around the world, leaving no record of the path a message traveled.

Even to the extent that cyberspace increases our level of privacy, it is both a blessing and a curse. Privacy—perhaps "anonymity" is a better word in this context—is usually seen as a societal good; it permits us to try out new ideas without having to commit prematurely to those ideas. Personal and group privacy have been essential components of the American brand of liberty from the very beginning. Surely Thomas Paine would have been hanged if he had published *Common Sense* under his own name. Yet privacy can be a dangerous thing too, perhaps more so on the Internet than ever before. Cyberspace anonymity enables organized crime and terrorist networks to conspire and can make it far easier for petty crooks to defraud the unwary and abscond with their profits long before their nefarious deeds have been detected.

The digitized world also diminishes our personal privacy in dramatic ways. By its very infrastructure, as a worldwide interconnected network of countless smaller computer networks, the Internet both makes the gathering of personal information much less expensive than ever and facilitates sophisticated cross-referencing of data to create highly detailed dossiers on us all.

E-mail is highly susceptible to being intercepted and read while it is being transmitted or while it is sitting on the mail server of either the sender's or the recipient's computer network. To minimize the likelihood of such snooping, privacy experts advise senders to use purposefully bland headings. As one consultant warns, "an e-mail message with a subject like 'CONFIDENTIAL,' 'Don't Let Anyone Else Read This,' or 'Our Secret Rendezvous' is likely to spark the interest of even the most trustworthy system administrator."[63]

In this section, we explore how the Internet affects your privacy interests vis-à-vis your job, the government, and the private sector in general.

Online Privacy at Work.   In the workplace, your employer may have installed software that allows him or her to monitor every single keystroke you make at your own office computer terminal. Inexpensive software abounds for companies wishing to keep track of every e-mail message employees send and every website they visit.

---

63. Kim Komando, "Ways to Protect Your Privacy on the Internet," *Arizona Republic*, March 22, 1999, E2.

Employers offer several reasons for using such software: they want to ensure that their employees are doing what they are being paid to do; workplace e-mail systems may become bogged with huge amounts of personal e-mail and server-slowing attachments; companies want to protect sensitive or even classified information from being duplicated and shared; and employers are afraid that they will be held liable for employees who send coworkers sexually harassing communications.[64]

The law is clearly on the side of employers; after all, they own the office and the hardware. The Electronic Communications Privacy Act (ECPA), which under many circumstances prohibits anyone from eavesdropping on both voice telephone conversations and digitized transmissions such as e-mail, does not apply to your employer. The pattern of case law makes clear that as long as employers put their workforce on notice that they intend to monitor e-mail transmissions, employees will generally not have legal recourse.[65] Some courts also emphasize that wise employees have no realistic expectation of privacy in their e-mails, even in the absence of an explicit workplace policy to that effect. Workplace anecdotes abound of e-mails sent accidentally to multiple recipients when the sender wanted the message to go to only one person. In the spur of the moment, who among us has not hit "REPLY ALL" when we intended to hit "REPLY"?

Online Privacy and the Government.

Although the Electronic Communications Privacy Act now prohibits unauthorized interceptions of voice and digital messages by both governmental and private agents, the law was originally conceived of as an anti-wiretapping statute aimed only at law enforcement officials.

The ECPA protects newer e-mail messages more fully than it does older ones. If a message has been stored on an online system for fewer than 180 days, law enforcement officials must obtain a search warrant to read it. To read messages that have been on a server longer than that, only an "administrative subpoena" is required. Such subpoenas can be issued within a law enforcement agency without having to obtain an independent judge's approval.

Separate portions (or "titles") of the ECPA prohibit the interception of e-mail messages while they are actually being sent (Title I) and while they are in storage on a server waiting for a subscriber to access them (Title II). Significantly, plaintiffs who are unable to prove actual damages stemming from a law enforcement officer's transgressions are entitled to up to ten times the amount of statutory damages ($10,000 per incident versus $1,000) under Title I as they are under Title II. In one case from Austin, Texas, the Secret Service admitted that it had violated Title II when it seized computers operated by a bulletin board operator who was suspected of unauthorized copying of sensitive files about emergency call systems. At the time, the computers'

---

64. Meir S. Hornung, "Think Before You Type: A Look at Email Privacy in the Workplace," 11 *Fordham Journal of Corporate and Financial Law* 115 (2005).

65. *TBG Insurance Service Corp. v. Superior Court*, 96 Cal. App. 4th 443, 451–453 (2002).

hard drives contained hundreds of undelivered e-mail messages for many of the system's more than three hundred subscribers. No evidence of wrongdoing was found, and the BBS company then sued the government for violation of both Titles I and II of the ECPA. The plaintiff argued that the Secret Service had violated Title I because e-mail messages stored on a server, if prevented from being delivered (the Secret Service had read and deleted the private mail), have been "intercepted" within the meaning of the ECPA. Writing for a three-judge appellate panel, Judge Rhesa Hawkins Barksdale disagreed. She emphasized the logic of having two separate bodies of law, one for interception of live transmissions, and one for reviewing of stored messages, noting that the first kind of intervention is far more intrusive. Agents will have no idea when a "real-time" message being sent is relevant to their investigations; the privacy invasion will thus be greater, because irrelevant discussions among innocent participants cannot help but being intercepted. With respect to stored e-mail, however, "technology exists [such as keyword searches] by which relevant communications can be located without the necessity of reviewing the entire contents of all of the stored communications."[66]

The Patriot Act, passed swiftly by Congress in response to the 9/11 terrorist attacks, amended the ECPA to give the government more power to monitor e-mail. Specifically, section 216 of the Patriot Act lets the government monitor the addresses to which a computer sends e-mail, the digital-age equivalent of a "pen register" search pursuant to which the government could obtain a list of phone numbers dialed from a specific phone but could not actually listen to the telephone conversations.

Online Privacy and the Private Sector.   Look up the phrase "double whammy" in the dictionary and perhaps you will encounter a photograph of Timothy McVeigh. The highly decorated U.S. Navy senior chief petty officer no doubt had it hard enough sharing the same name as the infamous Oklahoma City bomber. On top of that, he became a tangible reminder to us all that the privacy we seem to enjoy in our online interactions can be taken from us in an instant. Perhaps you heard the story. Like many AOL subscribers, McVeigh posted a profile of himself on the system using a provocative screen name—in his case, "Boysrch." Gay but relatively closeted, in keeping with the military's "don't ask, don't tell" policy, McVeigh used only his first name in the profile, which included among his hobbies "driving, boy watching, collecting pictures of other young studs." A naval investigator contacted AOL, one of whose employees—in violation of the company's published policy respecting the privacy interests of subscribers unless actually subpoenaed for information—readily divulged McVeigh's full identity. Predictably, McVeigh was promptly discharged from the navy. In 1998, McVeigh's lawsuit against AOL was settled out of court. As is usual in such settlements, no public disclosures were made concerning the amount of

---

66. *Steve Jackson Games, Inc. v. U.S. Secret Service*, 36 F.3d 457, 463 (5th Cir. 1994). But see *Warshak v. U.S.*, 2007 U.S. App. LEXIS 14297 (6th Cir. 2007), holding that even stored, older e-mail messages enjoy a measure of Fourth Amendment protection greater than granted by Congress.

money paid to McVeigh. It is known that AOL, as part of the agreement, was to provide more rigorous staff training in how to preserve subscribers' privacy interests. It is unlikely, by the way, that AOL's treatment of McVeigh would have been found in violation of federal law. The naval representative who had contacted AOL apparently presented himself as one of McVeigh's regular online correspondents, and the Electronic Communications Privacy Act explicitly excludes ISPs from liability for divulging the contents of a subscriber's e-mail message, including the subscriber's identity, to the intended recipient.[67]

The government was given a stronger hand in seeking personal data about ISP clients in section 225 of the Homeland Security Act, a section sometimes referred to as the Cyber Security Enhancement Act. This section provides ISPs with immunity from lawsuits for privacy invasion by clients dismayed to learn that their provider has given the government data about them, just so long as the ISP can demonstrate a "good faith" belief that some serious harm (a death, an injury, etc.) would result otherwise.

Even ISPs that seek to maintain their subscribers' privacy may be forced to disclose personal data. Obviously that would be the case when an ISP is handed a valid subpoena, but there is more. In recent years there has been an increase in "John Doe" defamation suits, wherein companies that have been criticized by individuals engaged in online chatter seek to compel the intermediary ISP to divulge the true identity of the otherwise anonymous subscribers, who would then presumably be named as defendants.[68] Often what happens instead is that the offended company will immediately drop the defamation suit upon obtaining the names, thus making clear that the real purpose of the litigation was to "out" their online critics. If those critics happen to be disgruntled employees of the company, no one is surprised when they soon become *ex*-employees.

One of the defining characteristics of the Internet is the interconnectedness of the countless computer networks that constitute it. Two important privacy concerns flow from this feature. First, the gathering, compiling, and cross-referencing of users' personal identification has become dramatically more efficient and less expensive than at anytime in the past. Second, in some kinds of environments, it is possible, using "cookies," to track a user's every keystroke and mouse click. The two concerns are clearly interdependent, in that your online behavior is an important component of your personal marketing profile.

Concerns about how much personal information is shared readily within the corporate world are hardly new. Perhaps you have done your own unscientific test of this phenomenon by purposely misspelling your name on a magazine subscription form and then seeing that same misspelling pop up repeatedly in future "junk mail,"

---

67. Clifford T. Karafin, "'Don't Ask, Don't Tell': A Discussion of Employee Privacy in Cyberspace in Light of *McVeigh v. Cohen, et al*," 3 *Virginia Journal of Law and Technology* 7 (1998).

68. Scot Wilson, "Corporate Criticism on the Internet: The Fine Line between Anonymous Speech and Cybersmear," 29 *Pepperdine Law Review* 533 (2002).

thus enabling you to get a sense of who is buying mailing lists from whom. The Internet's contribution to this kind of privacy issue is a difference of both degree and kind. That the compiling of information about us has now become so inexpensive means that mailing-list vendors can offer ever more narrowly tailored groupings of names. Thus, a list broker may know not only such basic demographic information about you as name, age, gender, race, zip code, and so forth but also your political party affiliation, your favorite breakfast cereal, your taste in music and movie rentals, how often you use an ATM, how much red meat and alcohol you consume, and whether you are taking antidepressant drugs.[69]

The interconnectedness of computer networks also permits a netizen of even moderate sophistication, under some circumstances, to learn much more in "real time" about other users than they likely would have chosen to reveal. At the touch of one function key, you can see with whom someone else online is e-mailing or chatting or even what newsgroup that person is reading. A few more clicks and you can gather personal information such as the individual's name, address, occupation, and date of birth.[70]

If ordinary consumers can obtain such details, it is not difficult to imagine how easily corporate users who make it their business to deal in personal information may collect relevant data. Personify, a company in San Francisco, helps businesses not only monitor their customers' visits to their website but also make personalized real-time pricing decisions to avoid losing a sale.[71] Thus, for example, Virtual Vineyards might notice a site visitor clicking here and there but not committing to anything. A message will pop up on the customer's screen: "So, we notice you have been here for 15 minutes but have not bought anything. Suppose we offered you free shipping today. Would that help?" In that such Internet dialogue resembles live behavior at outdoor markets around the world, with sellers trying to size up buyers' interest in their wares by observing relevant nonverbal cues, the phenomenon has been dubbed a "cyberbazaar."[72] In another development, Internet advertising company DoubleClick, in response to innumerable protests and threats of congressional action, backed off in the spring of 2000 from its plan to merge its huge name and address data to track consumers' online activities. The company had hoped to create a highly detailed and individualized database that could then be marketed to other advertisers.

Much outrage has been expressed in recent years by citizens' groups about commercial websites that have been used to gather information from children. In response, Congress passed the Children's Online Privacy Protection Act, which requires that websites targeted at children gain parental permission before collecting person-

---

69. "Big Brother, Big Business," CNBC documentary (first aired November 2006).

70. Lawrence Lessig, "The Path of Cyberlaw," 104 *Yale Law Journal* 1743, 1748 (1995).

71. Andrew Celli and Kenneth Dreifach, "Postcards from the Edge," 20 *Cardozo Arts and Entertainment Law Journal* 53 (2002).

72. Elizabeth Weise, "Online 'Cyberbazaars' Practice Fluid Pricing: Web Prices May Depend on Factors That Raise Serious Privacy Issues," *Detroit News*, May 17, 1999, S3.

THINGS TO REMEMBER

Privacy Online

- The Internet both enhances and diminishes privacy.
- State wiretapping statutes have generally been interpreted to protect the privacy of e-mail only at the exact moment of transmission.
- The federal Electronic Communications Privacy Act covers both e-mail in transmission and in storage, but damages for unauthorized access are potentially much higher when the intrusion occurs at the time of transmission.
- There has been an increase in the incidence of "John Doe" suits filed by potential libel plaintiffs in an effort to unmask persons who had been maligning them in online discourse.
- The Children's Online Privacy Protection Act prevents websites from gathering information from youngsters under thirteen without parental permission.

ally identifiable information from anyone under thirteen years old. The Federal Trade Commission has been empowered to enforce the law and has done so aggressively. In September 2006, for example, the operators of a social-networking website called Xanga.com reached a settlement with the FTC that included a $1 million civil penalty. Although the site's posted online privacy policy seemed to be in accordance with the law, in fact the site permitted users to post highly personal information about themselves even after inputting birth dates making clear they were under thirteen.[73]

Advertising Online: Spam and Deceptive Meta Tags

Internet users express concerns not only about how information is gathered about them but also about the intrusion on their privacy by large numbers of unwanted commercial messages, or "**spam**." Online mailboxes can quickly fill up with such junk mail, which is often disguised as personal messages rather than advertisements, a practice called "**spoofing**."

Federal legislation aimed at protecting computer users from unwanted commercial e-mail was signed into law by President Bush in December 2003. The law prohibits the use of misleading subject lines and false identities on the part of commercial e-mailers. Sexually oriented e-mail must be clearly labeled as such. Violators may be fined up to $250 per violation, subject to a cap of $2 million. Especially egregious violators may have their fines tripled and may be subject to up to five years' imprisonment. Further, the FTC is empowered by the law to at least study the idea of creating

---

73. "Xanga.com to Pay $1 Million for Violating Children's Online Privacy Protection Rule," press release, September 7, 2006, http://www.ftc.gov/opa/2006/09/xanga.htm (accessed November 17, 2006).

a "do not spam" list akin to the recently created (and still controversial) "do not call" list aimed at more traditional telemarketers. In June 2004, however, the FTC announced that it would not create such a list; not only would it be ineffectual, the commissioners felt, but the leaked names of persons who signed the list might open such individuals up to a substantial amount of "revenge spam."

Critics point out that the so-called CAN-SPAM Act ("CAN-SPAM" is actually an acronym for Controlling the Assault of Non-Solicited Pornography and Marketing) is not as strict as some of the thirty or so state laws it may preempt, notably a California statute that prohibits almost all commercial e-mail to e-mail account holders who did not give explicit permission to send them spam (i.e., an "opt in," rather than an "opt out," system). Whether in fact CAN-SPAM preempts state and local law is still an open question, however. In 2005 a federal appellate court held that the University of Texas's own elaborate antispam regulations were not preempted by the federal law.[74]

That computer users have been clamoring for laws with teeth is no surprise. By some estimates, about 40 percent of e-mail messages are spam, and about 15 percent of Internet service providers' budgets are earmarked for protecting subscribers from spam (costs necessarily passed on to those same subscribers). As columnist Ellen Goodman has put it, "SPAM has become cheap, portable, and as indigestible as its namesake."

Spam is annoying to most of us, even when not it is not deceptive. As we learned in chapter 10, materially deceptive advertising is illegal in any communication medium. Thus it is no surprise that the FTC has been vigilant in bringing complaints against deceptive online advertisers.

There is also, however, an issue related to deceptive advertising that is unique to the Internet. We have already seen how Internet search engines produce "hits" at least in part on the basis of hidden meta tags created by website managers to describe their own sites. Can there be deception in meta tags alone, even if the readily visible portions of the website itself are wholly truthful? Suppose a desperate medical patient inputs "breast cancer alternative treatments." Suppose further that a website pops up touting the many health benefits of garlic (never suggesting that it has any efficacy as a cancer cure) among the first few "hits." If the search engine located that website because the site's meta tags touted garlic as a cancer cure, has the Internet user been deceived? While the vast majority of case law and scholarly commentary about the legal problems associated with meta tags have focused on the role they play in trademark-infringement cases, this generally invisible Internet indexing system can also be the stuff of deceptive advertising. The Federal Trade Commission has ruled in a tiny handful of cases, but these cases are inconclusive as to this narrower issue because the visible portions of defendants' websites in these cases also included deceptive claims.[75]

---

74. *White Buffalo Ventures v. University of Texas at Austin*, 420 F.3d 366 (5th Cir. 2005).

75. I am indebted to Professor S. Camille Broadway of the University of Texas at Arlington for bringing this issue to my attention.

THINGS TO REMEMBER

Advertising Online

- Precisely because the cost of disseminating e-mail widely is so low, spam has become a major problem on the Internet.
- The federal CAN-SPAM Act is designed to enable computer users to opt out of getting a particular company's messages and offers some protection from unwanted sexually oriented messages, but it may preempt a number of stricter state laws already on the books.
  - A unique and unsettled issue posed by the Internet is whether deceptive messages in websites' meta tags are actionable when the text of the visible portions of a site are not deceptive.

Sexual Messages Online

"The Internet is for porn!" So exclaims Trekkie Monster, a lovable but worldly puppet character in the Tony Award–winning musical, *Avenue Q*. Regardless of whether you agree with Trekkie Monster, the fact is that "adult-oriented" websites were among the first to turn a profit (although evidence began to emerge in 2007 that online professional pornography was no longer a growth industry, in that so much free smut was available from amateurs).[76] When sexual messages are too easily accessed by minors, or indeed when minors are the target of online predators, however, the state has a compelling interest to intervene.

In 2006 Justin Berry testified before Congress about how he was induced, when he was as young as thirteen, by online chat room participants to make money by posing nude in front of his webcam. At first a viewer paid him $50 to take off his shirt. Over the years the young man made hundreds of thousands of dollars by engaging in numerous sexual practices for the entertainment of over 1,500 online voyeurs. The webcam has been the online pedophile's friend, federal investigators explained in a *New York Times* article that first brought Berry's story to light.[77] Often Berry's own online fans posed initially as teenage girls, only to slip up in later conversations and be forced to reveal their true status. To paraphrase the caption of the famous *New Yorker* cartoon, "On the Internet, they don't know you're a child molester."

The desire to protect children from inappropriate sexual messages and content online led Congress to enact the Communications Decency Act (CDA), which was actually Title V of the Telecommunications Act of 1996. The CDA criminalized the use of

---

76. Matt Richtel, "For Producers of Pornography, Internet's Virtues Turn to Vices," *New York Times*, June 2, 2007, A1.

77. Kurt Eichenwald, "Through His Webcam, a Boy Joins a Sordid Online World," *New York Times*, December 19, 2005, A1. In the article Berry reports how he also prostituted himself or was molested by several men he initially met online.

a computer network to knowingly transmit any obscene or indecent message to a child under eighteen years of age. Also prohibited was the posting of any such message in a manner that would be "available" to minors, as well as permitting a minor in one's charge (presumably including one's own child) to have access to such online messages.

In 1997, however, the Supreme Court overturned key sections of the CDA. That decision is worthy of our attention for several reasons, not the least of which is that it represented the Court's first opportunity to deal with Internet communications.[78]

Writing for the Court, Justice Stevens emphasized the extraordinary breadth of the CDA's prohibitions against sending sexual messages that are merely indecent, rather than obscene. First, he contrasted this statute with the Federal Communications Commission's broadcast indecency policy that had been upheld in its application to the George Carlin monologue in *FCC v. Pacifica Foundation* (discussed in chapter 12). The FCC's policy was narrower; it proscribed the broadcasting of indecent material only at hours when substantial numbers of children were likely to be in the audience. By contrast, the CDA "prohibits a particular category of speech from being disseminated *every hour of every day.*" In addition, the only penalty incurred by the radio station playing the Carlin monologue was the equivalent of a "raised eyebrow" from the FCC, whereas CDA violators could go to jail for up to two years. Equally offensive was the CDA's usurping of parental authority in that the law could reach

---

78. *Reno v. American Civil Liberties Union*, 521 U.S. 844 (1997).

even parents who sent their seventeen-year-old college freshman e-mail about birth control.

The Court subjected the CDA to its most exacting scrutiny. Use of this standard of review, however, was not a preordained conclusion. Justice Stevens spent a considerable amount of time comparing the Internet with broadcasting, and he determined that there were several significant distinctions. That determination was crucial because, as we saw in chapter 12, the broadcast media are subject to many regulations that would be unconstitutional if applied to the print media. Perhaps the most controversial of the distinctions Stevens drew between broadcasting and the Internet was the former's "pervasiveness," especially its accessibility to children. The moment a radio is turned on, all within earshot risk being bombarded by sexual messages best restricted to only adult ears. Web browsing is different, Stevens claimed. A child cannot surf the Web without "some sophistication and some ability to read to retrieve material and thereby to use the Internet unattended." Sexually oriented material is "seldom encounter[ed]" by accident, he argued, asserting that "receipt of information on the Internet requires a series of affirmative steps more deliberate and directed than merely turning a [radio] dial."

In truth, the contrast between the radio and the Internet is not quite as clear as Stevens posits. If booting up one's computer is the analogue for turning on the radio, then Stevens is surely right. Doing the latter, but not the former, can alone result in being subjected to inappropriate sexual content. But Stevens' reference to turning the dial of the radio is telling. The proper computer analogy to that behavior is clicking a mouse, and that is all one need do to uncover inappropriate materials, at least after a Web search has been conducted.

Obviously Stevens was right about the near impossibility of a preliterate child finding much sexual (or other) content online. The CDA's protections did not stop with literacy, however, but with attaining the age of majority. Older children who input the most innocuous words—"boy," "girl," "teen," "nurse," and so forth—into a search engine will find numerous X-rated sites among their "hits."

In his opinion Stevens also pointed out, correctly, that on-screen warnings usually appear in huge letters on the home page of a sexually oriented site. Yet often that same home page already includes sexual imagery. Moreover, as many commentators have pointed out, those warnings may serve to entice rather than dissuade older children.

In the end, Stevens stopped short of concluding that the Internet should *always* enjoy the full amount of First Amendment protection enjoyed by the print media, that *no* law aimed at Internet indecency could possibly be constitutional. Still, after reviewing and distinguishing several relevant precedents, he determined that there is "no basis" for diluting "the level of First Amendment scrutiny that should be applied to this medium."

The CDA soon begat the "son of CDA," as Congress passed the Children's Online Protection Act, which would have taken effect in November 1998 had it not been

Whether children are likely to inadvertently encounter "adult-oriented" websites was a factual question with which the Supreme Court had to wrestle in *Reno v. American Civil Liberties Union*, its first Internet case.

challenged successfully in federal district court,[79] a ruling followed by two trips up to the Supreme Court. COPA, as it was popularly called, was designed to eliminate some of the flaws the Supreme Court identified in the earlier Communications Decency Act. The law covered only certain kinds of online sexual materials defined within the statute as "harmful to minors." Companies whose websites include such materials could escape liability if they sought to screen out minors by requiring all visitors either to pay by credit card or to cooperate with the company in the creation of some form of adult access code.

In its second and final ruling on the matter, the Court's 5-4 majority was represented by Justice Kennedy, who, while stopping short of actually invalidating the stat-

79. *American Civil Liberties Union v. Reno*, 31 F. Supp. 2d 473 (E.D. Pa. 1999), *aff'd*, 217 F.3d 162 (3d Cir. 2000), *vacated and remanded sub nom. Ashcroft v. American Civil Liberties Union*, 535 U.S. 564 (2002), *aff'd*, 322 F.3d 240 (3d Cir. 2003), *aff'd and remanded*, 542 U.S. 656 (2004).

ute outright, suggested that parental use of any of the filtering software on the market might be a more suitable means of protecting children from sexual messages. Not only would filtering software be less intrusive of the First Amendment, he concluded, but it also might be more effective than federal legislation, which cannot reach the huge number of sexually oriented websites that originate in other countries. As a result of the ruling, the case was sent back to the district court for the purpose of, among other things, updating the factual record concerning the performance of filtering software. In 2007, Judge Lowell Reed, of the same federal district court in Pennsylvania that had issued the 1999 ruling preventing COPA from taking effect, found the act unconstitutional in several respects—vagueness, overbreadth, underinclusiveness—and issued a permanent injunction against the law's enforcement.[80]

Many commentators have pointed out the irony of expecting the baby boomer generation to depend on computer software to prevent their far more computer-literate offspring from having free reign on the Internet. Still, blocking software has become very popular in recent years. A 2005 study from the Pew Internet and American Life Project found that 54 percent of Internet households with teens in residence were using some kind of filtering software such as CyberPatrol, Cybersitter, and Surf-Watch. Such software will likely never be perfect, but, as both the Supreme Court majority and Judge Lowell Reed agreed, the First Amendment demands that parents, not the government, decide how much access to the Internet their children should enjoy.

Although parents certainly have a right to limit their children's Internet access with blocking software, do public libraries and public schools have a similar right to filter their students' and patrons' access? In 1997, the Loudoun County, Virginia, public library system adopted a "Policy on Internet Sexual Harassment," aimed at least as

---

80. *American Civil Liberties Union v. Gonzales*, 478 F. Supp. 2d 775 (E.D. Pa. 2007).

much at protecting one computer station patron from being offended at what pops up on a neighbor's screen as at limiting any individual's Internet access. The board implemented the policy by installing X-Stop software on all its patron computers. Adult patrons were free to "appeal" the software's "decisions" by providing their name and address and their reason for wanting access to a specific site blocked by the software to the librarian on duty, who would then make a case-by-case determination.

Several individuals and organizations, including some whose websites were blocked by the library's software, challenged the county's policy. Judge Leonie Brinkema determined that the county's conduct was unconstitutional in that it was not the least restrictive means of achieving its laudable goals.[81] She did not offer any opinion as to which, if any, of the less restrictive means proposed by plaintiffs, such as using blocking software only on computer terminals reserved for juveniles or permitting any adult patron to turn off the blocking software without having to go through an appeals mechanism, would themselves be found constitutional.

Brinkema's characterization of the Internet was itself a fascinating feature of the case. The library had claimed that the Internet is akin to a "vast Interlibrary Loan system," arguing that "restricting Internet access to selected materials is merely a decision not to acquire such materials rather than a decision to remove them from a library's collection." The library pressed this point because the Supreme Court had, in *Board of Education v. Pico*[82] (see the discussion of this case in chapter 2), suggested that library books, once purchased, acquire a kind of "squatter's right" to remain on the shelf, at least insofar as they should not be removed because of their content. Judge Brinkema rejected the library's argument, however, finding instead that the Internet, "unlike a library's collection of individual books," is a "single, integrated system." She analogized the library's use of blocking software to its buying a set of encyclopedias and then "laboriously redact[ing] portions deemed unfit for library patrons."[83]

Congress's next foray into the oversexed Internet was the Children's Internet Protection Act (CIPA), which requires all schools and libraries receiving special earmarked federal monies—a $2.25 billion expenditure aimed at "wiring" them to the Internet—to install blocking software to block sexually oriented websites whenever their juvenile patrons go online. The ACLU and the American Library Association filed suit against the government in the spring of 2001, alleging that the new law was unconstitutional. In 2003 the Supreme Court concluded that the act did not violate the constitution, marking the first time the Court had upheld a congressional action aimed at protecting children from sexually charged Internet content.[84]

81. *Mainstream Loudoun v. Board of Trustees of the Loudoun County Library*, 2 F. Supp. 2d 783 (E.D. Va. 1998) (rejecting motion to dismiss), 24 F. Supp. 2d 552 (E.D. Va. 1998) (granting summary judgment to plaintiffs).

82. 457 U.S. 853 (1982).

83. *Mainstream Loudoun*, 2 F. Supp. 2d at 793–794.

84. *United States v. American Library Association*, 539 U.S. 194 (2003).

Writing for a four-justice plurality, Chief Justice Rehnquist determined that a heightened level of scrutiny was not called for, because the government was merely asserting its right to decide what its monies would be used for. Moreover, any inconvenience to library patrons wishing full access to the Web was minimal, since the law required library staff to disable the filtering software for any individual adult user upon request. He also rejected plaintiffs' assertion that librarians establish a public forum of sorts when they make the Internet available to patrons. The Internet is but one more way to organize a library's offerings, Rehnquist replied. It is in this sense not much different from a bookshelf.

In his concurring opinion, Justice Kennedy suggested that if patrons could demonstrate at a later date that they were not able to persuade libraries to disable the blocking software (or if the disable utility itself did not work), such defective applications of the law might be unconstitutional. But he expressed discomfort with the plaintiffs' call for a broad ruling that the statute was unconstitutional on its face. Justice Breyer also wrote a separate concurrence, arguing that the Court should have at least applied an intermediate level of scrutiny to the law, but he hastily added that the law would still have survived such review. Justices Ginsburg, Stevens, and Souter dissented.

Regulation of sexual messages on the Internet raises at least one more novel issue beyond that of how best to protect children from harmful websites and chat rooms. Recall the mechanics of the Supreme Court's *Miller* test for defining obscenity, described in more detail in chapter 11. The test depends upon reference to "contemporary *community* standards," and the Court has made clear that this refers to a statewide or local standard, not a nationwide one. If sexual images are made available on a computer bulletin board, can its operators therefore be prosecuted anywhere, using the standards of a much more conservative community rather than their home state?

The Sixth Circuit Court of Appeals concluded that the answer is "yes"—at least under the circumstances presented in the case before the court in *United States v. Thomas.*[85] Robert and Carleen Thomas managed an adult-oriented bulletin board from their home in Milpitas, California. Acting on a citizen's complaint, an investigator in Tennessee assumed an alias to subscribe to the Thomases' BBS, view sexually explicit materials online, and purchase several videotapes advertised on the system. As a result, the Thomases were charged with violating relevant federal statutes prohibiting the interstate transfer of obscenity and were eventually sentenced to over three years in prison. Two of the defendants' arguments in their unsuccessful appeal are of particular interest.

First, the defendants argued that it was inappropriate for a federal court in Tennessee to have assumed jurisdiction of their case and thus for the Memphis jury to have been instructed to use its own community's standards to determine if the images involved were truly obscene. Obscenity prosecutions involving the Internet, they claimed, demand "a new definition of community, i.e., one that is based on the

85. 74 F.3d 701 (6th Cir. 1996).

THINGS TO REMEMBER

Sexual Messages Online

- The Communications Decency Act, Congress's first attempt to protect children from inappropriate sexual messages and content in cyberspace, was struck down by the Supreme Court in 1997.
- Justice Stevens said that he saw no reason to make Internet speech less protected than print speech.
- The Children's Online Protection Act also has never been permitted to take effect; the federal judge whose injunction was eventually upheld by the Supreme Court suggested parents use some form of Internet blocking device instead.
- Some communities began installing blocking software on public library computers, a practice found unconstitutional by a federal district court in Virginia.
  - To date, the only federal law designed to protect children from sexual messages online to be upheld by the Supreme Court is the Children's Internet Protection Act, which requires libraries receiving certain kinds of federal grants to use filtering software on any computers used by minors.

broad-ranging connections among people in cyberspace rather than the geographic locale of the federal judicial district of the criminal trial." In the absence of such a bold new definition, BBS operators "will be forced to censor their materials so as not to run afoul of the standards of the community with the most restrictive standards."

But the Thomases were not the ideal poster children for such creative adjudication, the court found. Theirs was a restricted BBS; visitors had to pay a fee and fill out an application form, including their address, before being granted full access to the system or being allowed to purchase materials. The undercover agent may have lied about his name, but he truthfully indicated that he was from Memphis. The Thomases would have been wise to reject the application. Writing for the appellate panel, Judge Nancy Edmunds chose not to express an opinion about whether a BBS open to all, where the operators would not know who had visited or where they lived, could lead to this same kind of criminal liability.

The Thomases also argued that when a computer in one state downloads an image (in this case, a .gif file) from a computer in another state, nothing obscene, indeed nothing *tangible*, has really crossed state lines. How could they be convicted of interstate transfer of a series of 1's and 0's? Very easily, the court replied, in the same way that money laundering schemes can be prosecuted at the federal level, even if only electronic funds transfers are involved.

Chapter Summary

The Internet, developed as part of a Department of Defense program aimed at ensuring the survival of intragovernmental communications in case of nuclear war, has revolutionized the exchange of information. It boasts a number of unique features—a lack of gatekeepers (a not entirely uncontroversial assertion, given our new dependency on search engines), the potential for carrying infinite amounts of data, a kind of parity between content provider and consumers, an extraordinarily low cost of data transmission—and each poses challenges to traditional legal doctrines.

Cyberspace law is in its infancy. There have been only a handful of Supreme Court cases, but there has been a fair amount of congressional activity in this area, and a body of case law has begun to develop at the lower courts.

Among some of the communication law issues posed by the Internet are the following open questions:

- Are bloggers "reporters" within the meaning of reporter shield laws?
- Who has a right to send us e-mail? To monitor our e-mail?
- What does it mean to be a public figure in cyberspace for the purpose of libel law?
- How much of a right to anonymous speech should be respected online?
- How should courts determine if they even have jurisdiction to hear an Internet dispute?
- How should we balance the interests of copyright holders against those who envision a more free-form kind of communication online, in which we all build on each other's work?

Perhaps most fundamentally, because the United States still has different models of regulation applied to different types of media (print, broadcast, cable), netizens need to know which model will apply to the Internet. Although the print model has thus far been embraced for the most part, it is not clear that this will always be the case. Moreover, as we move to a truly convergent media system, in which all our "messaging" is done with or by one yet-to-be-developed appliance, which model will govern a more unified American communication law?

Glossary

absolute privilege. Complete immunity from libel suits provided to elected officials while carrying out their official duties.

absolutist theory. Theory of First Amendment jurisprudence emphasizing the absolute prohibition ("Congress shall make *no* law") upon antispeech regulations provided in the First Amendment.

acquired distinctiveness. A characteristic attributed to a trademark that was once merely descriptive (e.g., "American" Airlines) but that has become associated in the public's mind with a specific company.

actual damages. Monies awarded to plaintiffs who prove that they have been damaged.

actual malice. The level of fault required in libel cases governed by *New York Times Co. v. Sullivan*: the defendant published defamatory material either knowing it was false or "with reckless disregard as to truth or falsity."

ad hoc balancing. Method of First Amendment adjudication that balances, on a case-by-case basis, free speech interests against whatever competing interests are involved.

administrative agency. Any of the many agencies, such as the Federal Communications Commission (FCC) and the Federal Trade Commission (FTC), created to engage in rule making consistent with established law.

administrative complaint. Document filed by a federal agency alleging specific wrongdoing to be adjudicated by an administrative law judge.

administrative law judge. A judge who hears disputes between individuals and regulatory agencies, a step usually required before proceeding to federal court.

affirmative disclosure. Specific facts that the Federal Trade Commission may require advertisers to disclose in future advertising.

Alien and Sedition Acts. Very early laws (1798) criminalizing statements critical of the government.

amicus brief. An argument filed in an appellate court by parties not directly involved in the litigation.

amicus curiae. Person or organization (literally, "friend of the court") filing an amicus brief.

ancillary powers. Powers granted to the Federal Communication Commission to regulate entities that do not themselves possess broadcast licenses but whose practices may affect such licensees.

answer. In a civil suit, the initial document filed by the defendant, which may deny the plaintiff's claims or may offer specific defenses under law.

appellant. The party who lost in a lower court and is bringing an appeal to a higher court.

appellate court. A court that hears an appeal from adjudication of a case from a lower court.

appropriation. The branch of privacy law involving the unauthorized use of someone's name or likeness for commercial purposes.

arraignment. A criminal defendant's initial appearance before a judge, at which time formal charges will be made, and a plea may be offered.

block-booking. A scheme, ended by the Supreme Court's 1938 *United States v. Paramount* decision, by which movie studios would force movie theaters to accept dozens of lesser films in a block in order to obtain the rights to exhibit a few "name" pictures.

blurring. Diminishing the value of a company's trademark by offering for sale many different kinds of wholly unrelated products or services using the same mark.

brevity. A provision of the Copyright Act's *Classroom Guidelines* that limits the length of material (e.g., a book chapter, no more than 10 percent of the book) teachers may copy for distribution to their students.

brief. An argument filed in an appellate court, arguing either for the affirmance or reversal of the decision from the lower court.

candidate-access rule. Section 312 (a) of the Federal Communications Act, which tells TV and radio stations that they must make available advertising time for purchase to legally qualified candidates for federal office.

cease and desist order. As its name implies, an order (issued by an agency such as the Federal Trade Commission) demanding that a company stop engaging in an allegedly illegal practice.

certification mark. A promise through which a company attests as to a particular quality of its product (e.g., that this frozen pizza uses *Real Cheese*).

change of venire. The importation of a jury from a location ostensibly far enough away from the crime site to be untainted by any pretrial publicity.

change of venue. Moving a trial to a new location to avoid the negative effects of pretrial publicity.

child pornography. Images of underage individuals in sexually provocative poses, as defined by statutes that need not satisfy *Miller v. California* obscenity-test requirements such as judging the work as a whole or exempting works that manifest serious value.

civil (case). Court action prompted by one private party suing another.

civil contempt citation. Finding by a judge against a party who fails to perform a particular action (e.g., a reporter refusing to reveal the identity of a source).

clearly erroneous rule. A rule of federal civil procedure that states that appellate courts may review not only legal questions but also factual ones if the appellate judges determine that the trial court made a clearly erroneous finding of fact.

closure order. A judge's ruling that all or part of a judicial proceeding shall be conducted in private, with no members of the press or public present.

collateral bar rule ("*Dickinson* rule"). Accepted in only some jurisdictions, this rule holds that contempt citations may stand even if the defendant is found by an appellate court to have had a right to engage in the behavior that resulted in the citation.

collective mark. A phrase or logo, protected under trademark law, designed to call to mind an association or organization (e.g., the NAB, National Association of Broadcasters).

collective work. A creative work eligible for copyright, consisting of many elements each which of which is also eligible for copyright (e.g., a newspaper edition and its many individual articles).

common law. Law as created by judge-made precedent, rather than enacted by a legislature.

compensatory damages. Damages designed to make a victim "whole," that is, to undo harm that has been done.

compilation. A work formed by the collection and assembly of preexisting materials or of data; it is eligible for copyright protection to the extent that the selection and arrangement of those materials is itself creative.

complaint. Document filed by the plaintiff in a civil case alleging the wrongs done by the defendant.

concurrent registration. More than one company using the same brand name for very different products or services (e.g., Life cereal, but also Life, the board game).

concurring opinion. An opinion written by an appellate judge who agrees with the outcome of the case but not all of the majority's reasoning.

consent. A defense in a tort action (including libel and invasion of privacy) claiming that the plaintiff knew of and explicitly indicated approval of, or at least acquiescence to, the defendant's conduct.

consent decree. Agreement entered into by two or more parties (e.g., a regulatory agency and a regulated company) and approved by a court.

consent order. Ruling by an agency's staff directing a company to behave in prescribed ways.

conspiracy. A combination of two or more persons planning to commit a criminal act.

constitution. A government's most basic controlling document, setting forth the structure and powers of the government.

contempt of court. An act or failure to act that either obstructs a court's functioning or otherwise adversely affects the dignity of the court.

continuance. Delaying a trial's beginning.

contributory infringement. Actions that do not directly infringe on the plaintiff's rights but that enable others to do so (e.g., creating a website that enables users to make illegal copies of copyrighted works).

convergence. In media law, the state of affairs when the differences among traditionally separate communications media become less and less identifiable.

convincing clarity. A measure, somewhere between "beyond a reasonable doubt" and "by a preponderance of the evidence," of how satisfactorily plaintiff's have established their burden of proof.

copyright. The exclusive right to profit from one's own creative works.

corrective advertising. Advertising including text designed to undo in consumers' minds false impressions created by prior advertising.

courts of equity. Courts empowered to make litigants whole, as best as possible, even in the absence of a clear body of legal precedent (common law).

criminal (case). Legal action taken by a government accusing a defendant of violating a law.

criminal contempt citation. Order issued by a judge designed to punish agents who act in ways that may interfere with government function (e.g., disrupting the courtroom or violating a judge's gag order).

criminal libel. Defamatory remarks, whether aimed at an individual or a group, prosecuted by the state on the theory that such utterances will tend to lead to violence.

cumulative effect. One of the guidelines found in the *Classroom Guidelines* under the Copyright Act, which limits teachers to copying no more than two works by the same author, no more than three from the same anthology, and no more than nine works total for classroom distribution during any single semester.

cybersquatting. Obtaining the rights to an Internet address bearing the name of a famous person or company, with the purpose of later selling it to the "logical" owner for a higher price.

decision. Court decisions tell us who wins and who loses, not necessarily why.

deep linking. Inserting a hyperlink to one's own website that sends visitors to an internal page of another individual's website.

defamation. An utterance or printed material asserting the kinds of derogatory facts about another person that may lead to that person's reputation being damaged.

defamation by implication. *See* "implied libel."

defendant. A person accused by the state of a crime or by a civil plaintiff of a wrongful act.

deposition. A part of the discovery process in which potential witnesses for the opposing side are interviewed with attorneys present and with a transcript created.

derivative works. A creative work eligible for copyright protection that is based in some way on a separate work (e.g., a movie version of a book).

descriptive mark. A trademark that merely describes the product or service (e.g., *lead* pencils or *Korean* restaurant) and is thus not ordinarily eligible for legal protection.

dicta. Portions of a court's opinion that are not essential to the disposition of the case (*see* "holding").

direct infringement. Infringement on a copyright resulting from the defendant's own actions.

discovery. The pretrial process of fact-finding performed by both sides in a civil suit, which may include deposing (formally questioning) prospective witnesses for the opposing side.

dissenting opinion. An opinion written by an appellate judge who disagrees with the outcome of the case (with the majority's decision).

distinctiveness. The main quality that makes a trademark protectable; it sets one product or service apart from competing brands.

distinguish (a precedent). Deciding that an earlier case's facts were sufficiently different from the case at hand so as not to be a useful precedent.

doctrine of incorporation. Constitutional doctrine holding that the Fourteenth Amendment's Due Process Clause implies that some of the Bill of Rights' limitations on the federal government also apply to the states.

documentary materials. Information and other items gathered by, but not created by, a reporter working on a story.

due process. Fundamental fairness; the Fifth Amendment says that life, liberty, and property may not be taken by the state without "due process."

en banc. A ruling by an entire federal appellate court (instead of just a three-judge panel).

Equal Protection Clause. Provisions in the Fifth and Fourteenth Amendments admonishing the federal government and the individual states, respectively, to treat citizens equitably.

equal-time rule. Section 315 of the Federal Communications Act, which provides that broadcast stations must provide all candidates for a particular elected office approximately equal airtime if the stations allow any such candidate to "use" their airwaves in an election cycle.

Espionage Act. A federal law from the World War I era that criminalized criticizing the government or the war effort.

Establishment Clause. Part of the First Amendment; used by the Supreme Court to establish the "separation of church and state."

executive order. A change in policy promulgated by the executive branch (e.g., the president or a governor), carrying the effect of law.

fact, question of. The kinds of "did it happen or didn't it?" questions decided by trial courts, rather than appellate courts.

fair comment. A common-law defense against libel suits in which the defendant claims that the alleged libel was an honestly held opinion based on facts reasonably believed to be true.

fairness doctrine. A body of rules, most of which were rescinded in 1987 and 2000 rulings, that required broadcast licensees to cover controversial political issues and to make such coverage balanced.

fair report. A common-law libel defense in which the defendant claims to have offered an accurate report of an utterance made by a public official conducting official duties.

fair use. A defense against a copyright-infringement suit, based on section 107 of the Copyright Act, that tells courts to consider the nature of the original work, the nature of the alleged infringement, the amount taken, and the use's effect on the value of the original copyright.

false light. One of the privacy torts, similar to libel, but under which the falsity need not be defamatory.

fault. In libel law, the element of a defamation suit constitutionalized by the Supreme Court in *New York Times Co. v. Sullivan*.

federal circuit. The jurisdiction—generally several states—covered by any of thirteen federal appellate courts.

Federal Communications Commission (FCC). Federal agency established in 1934; it overseas broadcast, cable, satellite, and telephonic communications systems.

federal district court. Federal trial court whose jurisdiction is generally one state or a portion of a state.

Federal Election Commission (FEC). Federal agency charged with enforcement of the Federal Election Campaigns Act, which includes regulations applied to political contributions and expenditures as well as some content restrictions on political advertising.

Federal Trade Commission (FTC). Federal agency regulating, among other things, deceptive advertising practices.

first impression, case of. A case presenting a novel issue, a controversy never before adjudicated in a specific jurisdiction.

Food and Drug Administration (FDA). Federal agency that regulates the marketing of and the advertising for food and drug products.

for cause (challenge of juror). Each side in a lawsuit or criminal prosecution may request that a potential juror not be impaneled, providing the trial judge with a specific reason why the potential juror would not be able to make an unbiased decision in a given case. Generally, the number of "for cause" challenges to which a party is entitled is unlimited.

framing. Surreptitiously sending an online "visitor" from one website to another (i.e., site B pops up on-screen as if a part of site A).

Freedom of Information Act (FOIA). Passed by Congress in 1967, the act provides the mechanism by which citizens can obtain information held in federal government agency files; states also have analogous laws.

Free Exercise Clause. The First Amendment's prohibition against congressional interference with citizens' right to practice (or "exercise") their religion.

Free Press Clause. The First Amendment's prohibition against congressional interference with freedom of the press.

Free Speech Clause. The First Amendment's prohibition against congressional interference with freedom of speech.

gag order (restrictive order). Judicial order requiring that the target (e.g., attorneys, witnesses, jurors, or the press) refrain from speaking about or publishing specific information associated with a trial.

Gannett card. An actual card sometimes provided by news organizations to their reporters who cover the courts, with instructions to read the card aloud anytime a judge expresses a desire to close the courtroom to the press and public. The writing on the card expresses the organization's belief that such closure is likely unconstitutional and requests time to contact an attorney to make the argument more formally.

Glomar response. Federal agency response to a Freedom of Information Act request, refusing to provide the information sought and refusing to confirm or deny the existence of the requested file.

grand jury. A jury impaneled for the purpose of determining whether sufficient cause exists to charge one or more possible defendants with a crime.

holding. The essence of a court's ruling, often in the form of a rule established by the court.

idea-expression merger doctrine. Consistent with the truism that one cannot copyright mere "ideas," when only a small number of possible expressions of an idea are imaginable, those expressions will themselves not be entitled to copyright protection, because they are too closely tied to a mere "idea." *See also* "scènes-à-faire doctrine."

identification. The element of a libel suit in which the plaintiff establishes that the offensive utterance or publication was "of or about" him.

implied libel. Situations in which utterances or writings are not themselves alleged by a libel plaintiff to be untrue, but where the inferences to be naturally drawn from the admittedly true statements are untrue.

indecency. Sexually oriented speech that, unlike obscenity, may be regulated even if it has serious value.

indictment. The document by which the government articulates a list of charges against a criminal defendant.

industry guide. Document promulgated by the Federal Trade Commission that gives general guidelines concerning acceptable ways to advertise products or services (e.g., when a product can be called "natural," "low fat," or "recyclable").

initial interest confusion. In trademark law, a "shortcut" doctrine that allows a finding of liability even if a potential customer's eventual purchasing decision is not based on confusion, just so long as the defendant unfairly added a bit of confusion to the customer's beginning thought processes (such as by leading the customer to the defendant's website with hidden, deceptive meta tags).

injunction. Judicial action demanding that the target either perform, or cease engaging in, specific conduct.

intellectual property. The conjunction of protections provided by patent, copyright, and trademark law.

intensity of suspicion test. In libel law, the notion that individual plaintiffs may bring suit to the extent that a group to which plaintiffs belong and to which a defamatory quality is attributed is small or the percentage of the group said to have the quality is large.

Internet. A worldwide systems of communication networks; or, the manner in which those networks communicate with each other.

intrusion. One of the four privacy torts; the transgression occurs when another's solitude or seclusion is intruded upon, regardless of whether any information gathered as a result of the intrusion is ever published.

joint operating agreement (JOA). Federally approved arrangement in which otherwise competing local newspapers can share the cost of core functions such as printing and distribution.

judicial review. Courts deciding on the constitutionality of legislative or executive branch actions.

jump. Continuing a newspaper story on a page other than the one where it started.

jurisdiction. Geographic area governed by a specific court; or, subject matters which that court is empowered to adjudicate.

law, question of. Questions, generally adjudicated by appellate courts, that concern whether a given factual situation fits the parameters of a legal doctrine or definition.

libel. Factual allegations about another that, if believed, would tend to lower that person's reputation in the eyes of others.

libel per quod. Statements that would damage another's reputation only if other unreported facts are known by readers.

libel per se. Statements that, if believed, would themselves damage the target's reputation.

libel-proof plaintiff. Libel plaintiff whose reputation is presumed already so low that no additional criticisms could lower it.

library building. The use of VCRs to make copies of broadcast programs, which the user keeps over time rather than erases with subsequent use.

likelihood of confusion. The mainstay of a traditional trademark-infringement suit, alleging that consumers will be confused as to the source of goods or services.

majority opinion. A judicial opinion joined by the majority of the judges on an appellate court.

memorandum order. An appellate court ruling unaccompanied by a formal opinion.

meta tags. Language, akin to "keywords" in traditional indexing, that lead a computer search engine to include a specific website among the "hits" resulting from a search.

modify (a precedent). A court modifies a precedent when it determines that the general principle espoused in that precedent is relevant to the current case but that some extrajudicial societal changes dictate that the precedent not be followed closely (e.g., to accuse someone of having a "loathsome" disease might still be libelous, but attitudes toward cancer have changed sufficiently so that this particular disease is no longer thought of as loathsome).

"must carry" rules. Federal Communications Commission rules requiring that cable systems include local broadcast signals in their most basic tier of service.

neutral reportage. Libel defense, accepted in only a few jurisdictions, positing that an otherwise punishable republication of libelous remarks can be excused if done in a fair and neutral way.

Newspaper Preservation Act. Federal law adopted in 1970 that provided for the creation of joint operating agreements as a way of preserving some degree of competition among daily newspapers.

obscenity. Sexually oriented messages, wholly unprotected by the First Amendment.

official conduct. Part of the *New York Times Co. v. Sullivan* libel rule; public officials can recover only for defamatory statements that criticize the way they perform their duties or that make allegations about personal characteristics likely to affect the performance of those duties.

opinion. A court's written discussion of its reasons for making a decision.

oral arguments. Arguments made by opposing attorneys, each typically for about half an hour, in front of the judges of an appellate court.

overturn. Ruling by which an appellate court in effect changes its mind, holding that one of its earlier precedents will no longer be honored. Appellate courts can also overturn lower court decisions, and "overturn" is often used interchangeably with "invalidate" to describe what happens when any court rules that a legislative action is improper or unconstitutional.

participant monitoring. One party to a telephone conversation taping the conversation without the other's knowledge.

per curiam opinion. An unsigned opinion (literally, "by the Court").

peremptory challenge. Motion made by a party to a lawsuit or criminal prosecution, without any reason offered, seeking to remove a potential juror from being impaneled. Unlike in the case of challenges for cause, each side typically is entitled to only a limited number of peremptory challenges.

personal jurisdiction. A doctrine whereby one state's courts may claim jurisdiction over a citizen from another state.

Petition Clause. Section of the First Amendment giving Americans the right to assemble peaceably and to petition their government for redress of grievances.

petit jury. In criminal law, the jury that actually decides the defendant's guilt or innocence.

plaintiff. The party bringing a civil suit against a civil defendant.

plea. A criminal defendant's answer to a charge or indictment, such as a plea of guilty or not guilty.

plea bargain. A criminal defendant's decision to plead guilty to a lesser offense than that for which the government was prepared to try him or her.

plurality opinion. Opinion signed by one or more appellate judges agreeing with the majority's ultimate decision, but not with all of its reasoning.

pornography. Communications that include somewhat graphic depictions of sexual conduct; might or might not meet legal definitions of indecency and/or obscenity.

precedent. A court decision made prior to the one being argued at present, which at least one litigant suggests counts as a reason for ruling in a specific way in the current case.

preferred-position balancing. Presumption in First Amendment cases that speech is more important than whatever competing interest is involved in a given case.

preliminary hearing. Any judicial hearing that occurs before the criminal trial itself.

presentencing report. Report given to the judge in a criminal trial, after a defendant has been found guilty, offering arguments for severity or lenience of sentence.

presumed damages. In libel cases, damages due the successful plaintiff even without proof of specific quantifiable harm.

Printers' Ink statutes. State laws aimed at deceptive advertising.

prior restraint. A law, executive order, or judicial decree prohibiting communicative conduct before it occurs (rather than punishing it after it occurs).

probable cause. The standard of proof required to hold a criminal defendant over for trial; also the standard used to determine if a search warrant should be granted.

product disparagement. Comments similar to libel, but directed at a company's product line, rather than at its management.

product proximity. Thematic or logical relationship between one product line and another; in trademark law, infringement is more likely to be found as proximity increases.

profanity. Language the Federal Communications Commission deems "vulgar and coarse" and so "grossly offensive" that it constitutes a "nuisance"; unlike indecency, the language need not be sexually oriented.

promissory estoppel. A common-law legal doctrine providing that even in the absence of a contract, an agreement may be enforced if failure to do so would result in gross inequity.

prosecute. For the government to bring legal action against a defendant, alleging a violation of criminal law.

publication. In libel law, dissemination of the allegedly libelous remarks to at least one third party.

public disclosure. A privacy tort in which highly private and embarrassing, but true, information about the plaintiff is disseminated.

public figure. In libel law, a plaintiff who is famous or associated with a specific political cause.

public forum. A place where either by tradition (as in the sidewalks or public parks) or by government designation (as in a public auditorium), speech on a variety of topics and from a variety of viewpoints is generally welcomed.

publicity, right to. A hybrid privacy and property right to profit from the commercial exploitation of one's own name or likeness.

public official. In libel law, a government employee perceived to have decision-making authority and who occupies a position that is a frequent topic of public discussion.

puffery. Obviously exaggerated advertising claims (e.g., "we serve the best food in town") that are protected precisely because consumers do not take them literally.

punitive damages. Damage awards, above and beyond those granted to compensate the plaintiff for harm, which are designed to punish the defendant for outrageous conduct.

recuse. To remove oneself from participation (as judges will do if they believe their hearing a case would create a conflict of interest).

reporter shield laws. State laws providing media representatives some degree of immunity from having to testify in front of judicial bodies.

republication. In libel law, publishing a "defamation once removed" (e.g., "Ms. Jones asserted that her ex-husband sexually abused their daughter.").

respondent. In an appellate hearing, the litigant who won the case at the lower court.

retraction statutes. State laws that provide some measure of protection from damages in a libel suit for media outlets that have already published an admission of error.

retransmission consent. Permission granted by a broadcaster to a cable or satellite TV company to include the broadcaster's signal among the cable (or satellite TV) company's offerings to subscribers.

right-of-reply statutes. State laws providing persons who feel they have been unfairly criticized by a media outlet a right to air their side of the issue; in 1974, the Supreme Court struck down such laws as they apply to the print media.

right to publicity. See publicity, right to.

***scènes-à-faire* doctrine.** In copyright law, the notion that some film genres by their very nature virtually demand that certain stock scenes be included (e.g., a car chase in a crime drama) so that other directors' use of such scenes is not an infringement. *See also* "idea-expression merger doctrine."

search warrant. As provided for by the Fourth Amendment, a document given by a judge to a law enforcement officer permitting the search of a property where there is reason to believe helpful evidence will be found.

secondary meaning. *See* "acquired distinctiveness."

Securities and Exchange Commission (SEC). Federal agency of relevance to media law in that it can determine eligibility to write financial newsletters.

self-publication. In libel law, the unusual situation in which the publication element is established because the defamed person himself will, predictably, have to share the libelous statements with others (e.g., if he is blind and needs someone to read the publication to him).

service mark. A word, phrase, or logo designed to conjure up in consumers' minds a specific company's services.

slander. A spoken defamation (traditionally, "libel" referred only to printed defamations).

SLAPP suit. Strategic lawsuit against public participation; a libel suit designed to silence public criticism of a powerful individual or group.

Smith Act. Federal law from the 1940s making it a criminal offense to participate in an organization whose mission includes the violent overthrow of the government.

spam. Unwanted commercial e-mail messages.

special damages. Damages awarded for very tangible, demonstrable, out-of-pocket losses.

Speech or Debate Clause. Provision of the Constitution immunizing members of Congress from libel suits flowing from their conduct of their official duties.

spontaneity. A provision in the *Classroom Guidelines* accompanying the federal Copyright Act that immunizes teachers from infringement suits for unauthorized copying for classroom use if there was no time to seek official permission (i.e., the idea to use this material was too spontaneous).

spoofing. Designing a commercial e-mail message to appear noncommercial.

standards injunction. A judicial order prohibiting not only the display of a specifically named obscene work but also the whole category of works likely to be found obscene. The case law is mixed on whether such broadly constructed injunctions are constitutional.

stare decisis. Literally "let the decision stand"; an admonition to follow precedent when possible.

statute. A law passed by a legislative body, usually at the state or local level.

statute of limitations. Time period, usually stemming from the date of an alleged transgression, during which legal action must be commenced for the plaintiff (or, in a criminal prosecution, the state) to prevail.

statutory construction. The process by which a court determines the meaning and effect of ambiguous language in a statute.

strict liability. Doctrine providing that the person whose action causes a certain result is civilly or criminally liable for such result, even if no degree of negligence can be shown.

subpoena. Judicial document demanding that the recipient appear before the court or produce requested documents.

summary contempt. A judge's power to charge, "convict," and punish a wrongdoer on the spot.

summary judgment. Judicial ruling to the effect that even if any facts in dispute are presumed in favor of the opposing party, the party seeking the order must prevail as a matter of law; such judgments avoid having to present facts to a jury, or even to have a full trial.

superior court. The name usually given to state trial courts.

Supremacy Clause. Federal constitutional provision telling the individual states that their laws may not conflict with established federal law.

tarnishment. Using another company's trademark in a way that will tend to bring that company's goods or services into disrepute.

thematic obscenity. Doctrine, long ago rejected by U.S. courts, that permitted works to be found obscene if their theme, or story line, was offensive (e.g., because an adulterer did not get punished).

third-party monitoring. Taping a conversation without the permission of any of the participants.

time shifting. Using a video recorder to tape programs only to view them at a more convenient later time (not to build a permanent library).

trade dress. Use of the overall look or feel of a product or place of business to conjure up in consumers' minds a specific company.

trade libel. *See* "product disparagement."

trademark. A word, phrase, or logo designed to conjure up in consumers' minds associations with a specific company's product line.

trade regulation rule. Federal Trade Commission guidelines governing general advertising practices (e.g., when a product can be called "natural" or "recyclable"), rather than a specific company's conduct. A trade regulation rule is very similar to an industry guide (*see* "industry guide") but carries the force of law.

trial court. The court in which the first level of a judicial proceeding (the trial) takes place and from which the losing party may seek review by an appellate court.

variable obscenity. Legal doctrine holding that the definition of obscenity can be somewhat fluid depending on the target audience (especially if children are exposed to the materials).

Vaughn index. A federal agency's response to a Freedom of Information Act request in which the agency provides a list of relevant documents in the agency's possession but claims that some or all of the documents may not be released.

voir dire. The process of selecting a jury (from the old French, "to say that which one has seen," or to bear truthful witness).

work-for-hire doctrine. In copyright law, an exception to the general rule that the artist or creator owns a copyright; if a work was created as part of an employee's job description, the rights may be enjoyed instead by the employer.

work product. Materials actually created by a reporter working on a story.

Case Index

Subject Index

Note: Page numbers in *italics* refer to illustrations.

About the Author

Paul Siegel is professor of communication at the University of Hartford. For sixteen years Siegel taught at Gallaudet University, the world's only comprehensive university designed especially for deaf and hard of hearing students. He has also taught communication law courses at American University, the Catholic University of America, George Mason University, Illinois State University, Quinnipiac University, Tulane University, the University of Missouri, Kansas City, and the University of North Carolina.

Siegel has published dozens of essays in journals of communication, sociology, and anthropology, as well as in law reviews and as book chapters. Topics have ranged from product placement in movies and the development of the Supreme Court's commercial-speech doctrine to the gays-in-the-military debate and the interaction of privacy and communication law. A longtime editor of the *Journal of Freedom of Expression* (formerly the *Free Speech Yearbook*), Siegel also edited a collection of readings on the Clarence Thomas hearings.

A graduate of Northwestern University's doctoral program in communication studies, Siegel also earned degrees from the University of Wisconsin and the University of New Mexico.

Beyond work in the academy, Siegel was the founding executive director of the Kansas and Western Missouri office of the American Civil Liberties Union and has been on the ACLU's affiliate boards in Illinois, Washington, D.C., and Connecticut.

About the Illustrator

Katie Osowiecki started drawing about the time she was old enough to hold a pencil. Throughout her younger years she had a constant fascination with the world of animation and comics (mostly newspaper comics), but it wasn't until the end of her freshman year of high school that she stumbled upon Japanese comics (*manga*) and animation (*anime*) and learned that comics could in fact be done by women. From there Osowiecki's interest in comics flourished and she spent the rest of her high school career studying how comics are made and practicing her skills.

After high school Osowiecki put herself through college, first Greenfield Community College in Massachusetts, then the Hartford Art School of the University of Hartford. There, with the help of three very talented instructors, much of what she today sees as her style of drawing really took shape.

A recipient of the Society of Illustrators Kirchoff/Wohlberg Award in Memory of Francis Means, Katie has also received silver honors for her illustrations from the Connecticut Art Directors Club.

Communication Law in America is Osowiecki's first published work, and she hopes to have many more. You can visit http://katieo.kuiki.net to see more of her work.